AF249042

Vigeland+Munch

Behind the Myths

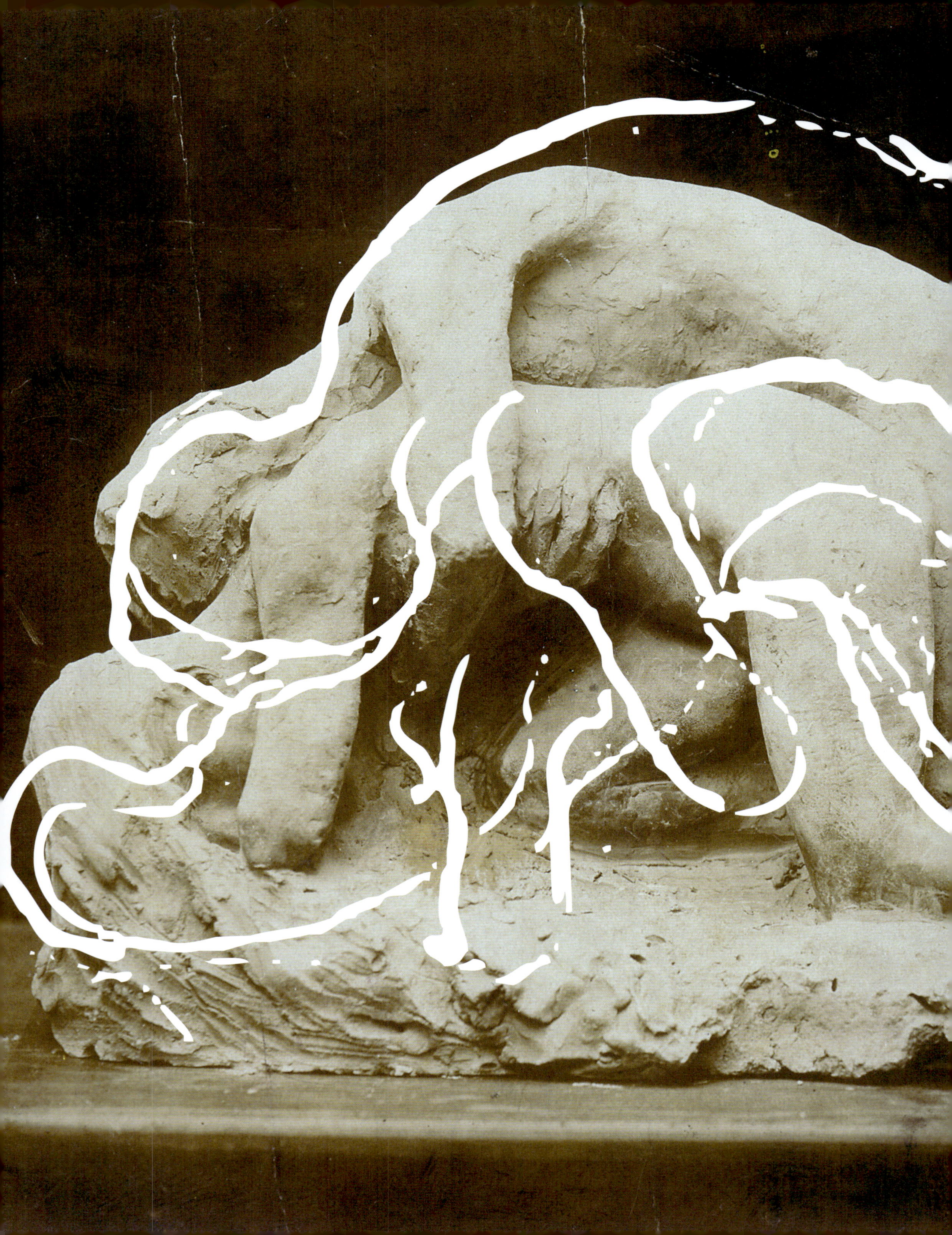

Edited by Trine Otte Bak Nielsen

Vigeland + Munch

Behind the Myths

Munch Museum

Mercatorfonds

Distributed by Yale University Press, New Haven and London

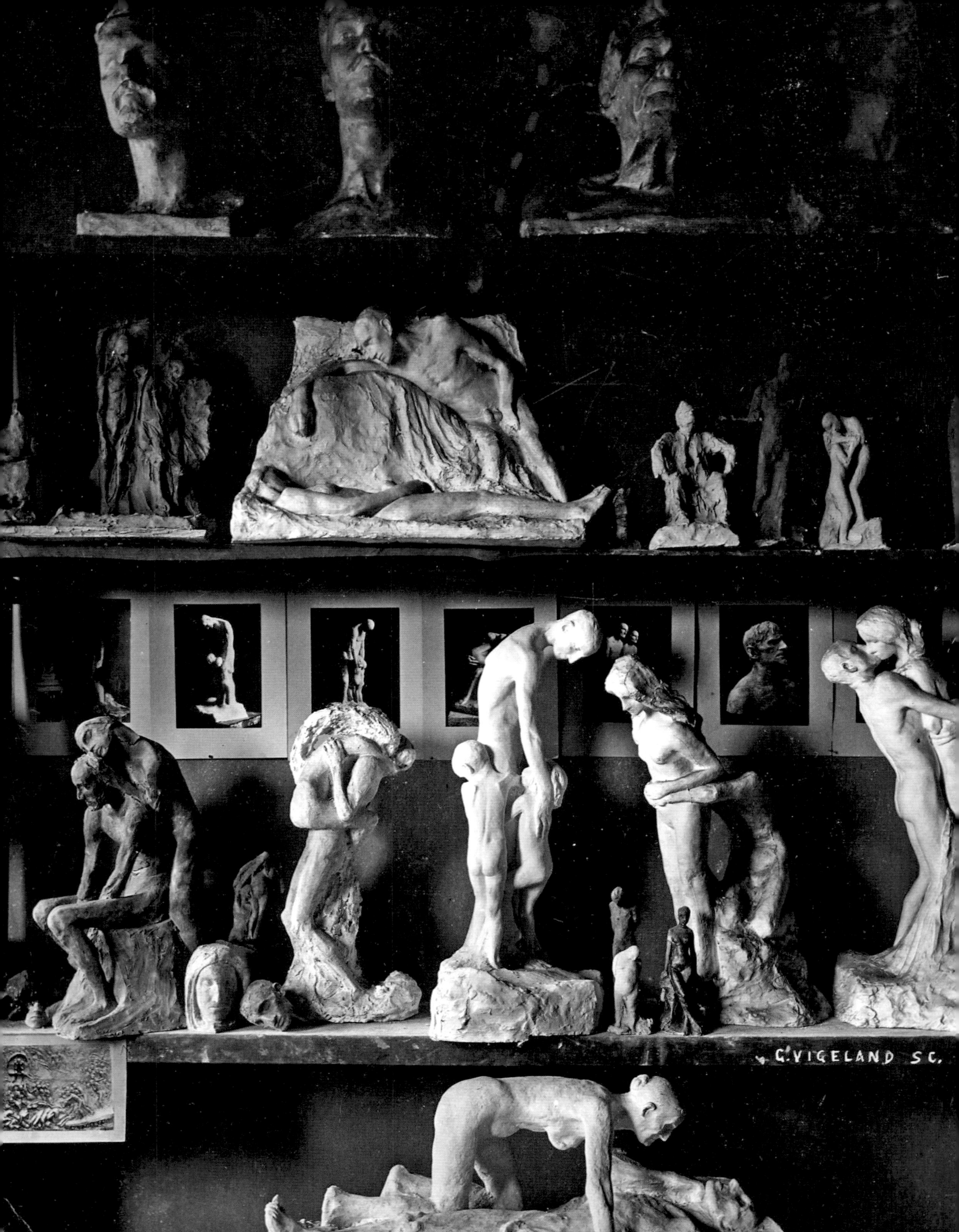

G.VIGELAND SC.

Contents

7
Foreword

9
Introduction

14
Timeline

22
Vigeland+Munch. Behind the Myths
TRINE OTTE BAK NIELSEN

56
On the Paths of the Soul. Gustav Vigeland
STANISŁAW PRZYBYSZEWSKI

81
The Work of Edvard Munch
STANISŁAW PRZYBYSZEWSKI

92
Esotericism in Modernity, and the Lure of the Occult Elite:
The Seekers of the Zum Schwarzen Ferkel Circle
PER FAXNELD

106
Images of an Era
GURI SKUGGEN

120
Observations on Two Life Friezes
PETRA PETTERSEN

134
'The Sculptor Edvard Munch. "Unknown Works" –
but is there perhaps someone who knows the history of their origins?'
ERIKA GOHDE SANDBAKKEN

146
A Brief History of Two Great Men –
the city is big enough for both of them
JARLE STRØMODDEN

156
Catalogue of Exhibited Works

280
List of Exhibited Works

292
List of Illustrations

297
About the Authors

302
Index

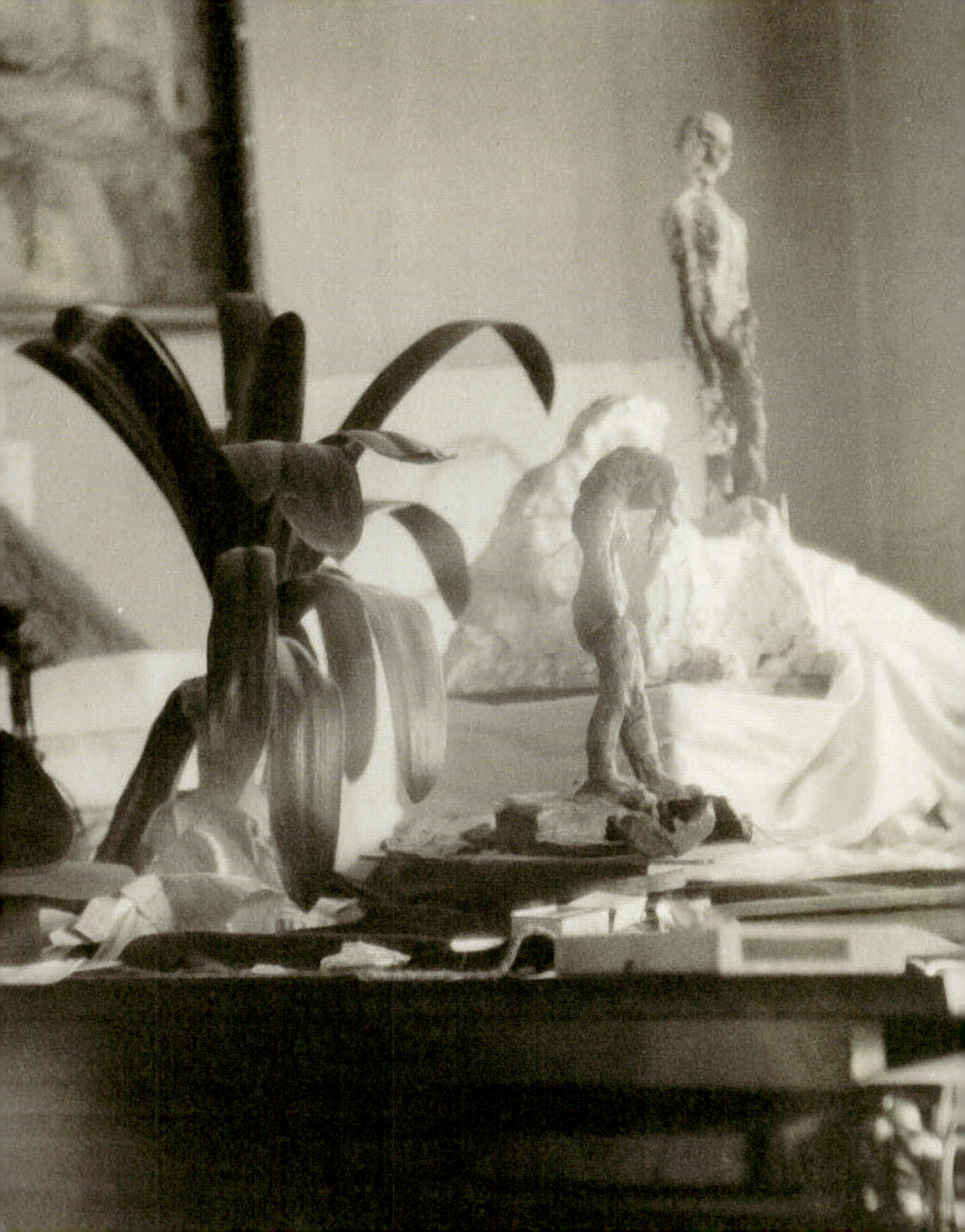

Foreword

The exhibition *Vigeland+Munch* forms part of a two-year series in which Edvard Munch's art is shown side by side with the work of six other artists. The juxta-position of Gustav Vigeland and Edvard Munch is the third in the series. The first two exhibitions were with the present-day artist Bjarne Melgaard, and with Edvard Munch's contemporary, Vincent van Gogh. Next in line after Gustav Vigeland are Robert Mapplethorpe, Jasper Johns and Asger Jorn.

There are many obvious reasons to mount a joint exhibition of works by Vigeland and Munch. They lived during the same period and worked with similar motifs and themes. They eventually became the most prominent artists of their generation, and both have left a noticeable mark on the city of Oslo, practically dividing it between them – Vigeland with the Vigeland Museum and Vigeland Park in Frogner, Munch with the monumental decorations in the University of Oslo's Aula, the Munch Room in the National Gallery, and not least, the Munch Museum with its extensive collection. Only six years apart in age, the two artists frequented the same circles and followed the same artistic trends of the time. They even lived and worked in adjoining rooms for a period in Berlin. They have a common history of development in their choice of motifs, in particular when following contemporary trends or depicting angst-ridden figures and ambiguous love motifs. Munch and Vigeland became the two giants of the Norwegian art world during the first half of the twentieth century.

Many myths have been created about Munch and Vigeland over the years, including their supposed rivalry and mutual antipathy. This exhibition sets out to delve behind the myths and provide a broader and more nuanced picture of the relationship between them and their art. Amazing as it may seem, this is also the first time the two artists are being shown together in an extensive exhibition, where their artistic careers are presented side by side.

Few are aware of the fact that Munch also worked as a sculptor. Several of his sculptures in clay, plaster and bronze will be presented for the first time in this exhibition. Among others, the sculpture *The Human Mountain* will be shown together with drafts of Vigeland's *The Monolith*.

The Polish writer Stanisław Przybyszewski's article about Munch from 1894 has been translated into Norwegian and English for the first time in the exhibition catalogue, together with his article about Vigeland from 1895. These texts were the first to be published internationally about both Munch and Vigeland, and thus have a special status when it comes to the reception of their work.

The realisation of this exhibition has only been made possible thanks to the close and productive cooperation between the Munch Museum and the Vigeland Museum. The Vigeland Museum has amongst other things loaned the majority of Vigeland's sculptures in the exhibition. On behalf of the Munch Museum I would like to extend our gratitude to museum director Jarle Strømodden and the staff of the

Vigeland Museum, in particular curator Guri Skuggen, and sculpture conservators Siri Refsum and Ingebjørg Mogstad. In addition, I would like to thank the National Museum of Art, Architecture and Design for their loan of major works. Snøhetta has created the exhibition architecture and graphic design of the exhibition and catalogue respectively. Special thanks for an inspiring and fruitful collaboration to Kjætil Trædal Thorsen and his colleagues at Snøhetta, in particular Henrik Haugan, Filippo Gazzola and Aleksandra Danielak. I also would like to thank the Freedom of Expression Foundation (Fritt Ord) for funding the catalogue and Idemitsu Petroleum Norge for providing substantial funding for the exhibition.

Our new curator Trine Otte Bak Nielsen conceived the idea and took the initiative to arrange this exhibition. Without her it would not have been realised. Special thanks are also due to the entire staff of the Munch Museum, whose customary skill and hard work have contributed to making this exhibition possible.

Stein Olav Henrichsen

Director
Munch Museum

Introduction

The relationship between Gustav Vigeland (1869–1943) and Edvard Munch (1863–1944) is surrounded by myths. Many believe they were rivals. The aim of the exhibition *Vigeland+Munch. Behind the Myths* is to refine this view by presenting new research that investigates their relations.

The connection they had with one another is often mentioned, yet never elucidated in depth. A lack of validation leads among other things to a climate where the old myths about a relationship marked by rivalry live on. Rolf Stenersen is one of many who have contributed to this. In his celebrated biography of Edvard Munch, *Close-up of a Genius*, he retells ostensibly reliable stories. However, despite their element of entertainment they are not always true to the facts, and thus assist in upholding a psychobiographical approach to Munch's life and work – something Munch researchers have tried to avoid for years. The literature on Gustav Vigeland is furthermore very limited compared to the literature on Munch, considering his importance in the Norwegian art world. Unlike Vigeland, a catalogue of Munch's graphic art and a number of monographs and extensive articles were published during his lifetime. While Gustav Vigeland basically remained a national artist, and helped elevate the status of sculpture in his native country, Edvard Munch also gained a major international position as one of Modernism's most significant artists.

Vigeland+Munch. Behind the Myths examines the connections between Vigeland's and Munch's art on several levels: biographically, thematically and with regard to their motifs. There is no previous unified overview that places the careers of these two artists in relation to each other; in this regard the exhibition and catalogue present new information. As an art historian and former curator at the Vigeland Museum I have for many years thought that such an exhibition should be made. It has thus been a great pleasure, as curator and editor of the catalogue, to have the opportunity to realise this project.

With only six years' difference in age, Munch and Vigeland belonged to the same circles and the same artistic movements of the period they lived in. Their work, artistic development and ambitions have many interesting features in common, which provide opportunities to identify as yet undiscovered connections between the two. These include reciprocal influences and common sources of inspiration, as well as thematic and formal similarities. Both artists followed contemporary trends, and depicted angst-ridden figures, ambiguous love motifs and gloomy doomsday themes. An interesting common feature that arose later on can be found in their works featuring monumental human figure groups, as in Munch's painted *The Human Mountain* and Vigeland's sculpted *The Monolith*.

In order to penetrate behind the myths, a thorough review of everything that connected Vigeland and Munch has been undertaken. The first article in the catalogue, written by the undersigned, examines their parallel artistic careers –

from their first student years until their old age as well-established artists. Here I concentrate on the periods during which they were most closely associated, for instance the infamous months in 1895 when they lived in adjoining rooms in Berlin, and where they also had a common link with the Polish writer Stanisław Przybyszewski. Other major junctures are the competition for a national monument in Kristiania (present-day Oslo), and the similar trajectories of their reception as artists.

Stanisław Przybyszewski published the first international articles on Munch and Vigeland: *The Works of Edvard Munch* (1894) and *On the Paths of the Soul* respectively (1897). Both texts are published here in their entirety. Przybyszewski perceived an artistic kinship between the two and presented them as representatives of the period's pessimistic worldview. As expressions of strong personal identification the texts seem to live a life of their own, parallel to the motifs that he describes. For example, he interprets Vigeland's sculpture *The Prostrated* (cat. 50) as: '[…] the tragedy of a young girl who has promised herself to another, or perhaps the tragedy of an adulteress. Pain has ceased to be pain: it is an apathetic downward plunge into the abyss, an apathetic abdication to the Satan of sins and devastation.' Przybyszewski's highly personal interpretations also made his writing controversial.[1]

In his article, historian of religion Per Faxneld discusses the circle associated with the Zum Schwarzen Ferkel tavern and the interest of its members in an alternative and esoteric spirituality, which took on peculiar forms during this period, and which researchers have called *occultism*. Faxneld describes how art and religion (alternative as well as more orthodox forms) began to overlap, and how this can be linked to Vigeland and Munch, most often with Przybyszewski as an important connecting link.

Vigeland Museum curator Guri Skuggen takes a closer look at a selection of portraits Vigeland and Munch made of the same people. These constitute a kind of testimony of the period they lived in and the circles to which they belonged. Skuggen sheds light on their common acquaintances and patrons, both in Norway and abroad. In her article, Munch Museum curator Petra Pettersen discusses the term 'life frieze' and its significance in Munch's art, but also questions whether it is reasonable to apply the same term to Vigeland's works, in particular those that appear in Vigeland Park. She examines the motifs that depict the life of human beings, with themes linked to the various stages of life. A common thematic point of departure will necessarily produce similarities, despite the works being executed in different media.

Munch's work with sculpture has until now been a less known aspect of his oeuvre. After 1900 he tried his hand at sculpting on a number of occasions, which has resulted in eleven remaining sculptures in clay, plaster and bronze, some of which are executed in several versions. These are presented for the first time in this exhibition, so that the public can become better acquainted with Munch's experiments in the three-dimensional form. The Munch Museum's painting conservator Erika Gohde Sandbakken presents a brief summary of Munch's references to Auguste Rodin, in addition to a dating of Munch's sculptures, his working methods and the condition of the sculptures. And finally, the director of the Vigeland Museum Jarle Strømodden examines how Vigeland and Munch lived parallel lives, yet never became close friends or colleagues. He also takes a closer look at their unique bequests to the capital, which led to their each having a museum devoted to them – in the city on which they had both definitively left their stamp.

The catalogue is copiously illustrated. All of the works in the exhibition are reproduced approximately as they appear in the rooms of the museum, thus providing a permanent record and documentation of how the oeuvres of these two artists are shown together.

Vigeland and Munch constitute part of our common cultural heritage. They created some of our most famous and popular artworks, such as Vigeland's *The Angry Boy* and *The Monolith*, and Munch's *The Scream* and *Madonna*. They have left behind public monuments of immense stature and have left their mark in every sense, not least by making Oslo an attractive destination for travellers. In a way they divided the city between them, as the great artist personalities of their time – Vigeland with his fantastic sculpture park and his museum; Munch with his magnificent paintings in the University of Oslo's Aula and his visionary bequest to the City of Oslo – which in a few years' time will embellish the newly developed area of the city called Bjørvika.

Trine Otte Bak Nielsen

1   For example, a text on Vigeland, intended for publication in the first issue of *Pan* in 1895, was rejected, and as editor of the periodical *Zycie* in Krakow he was made aware of the authorities' censorship.

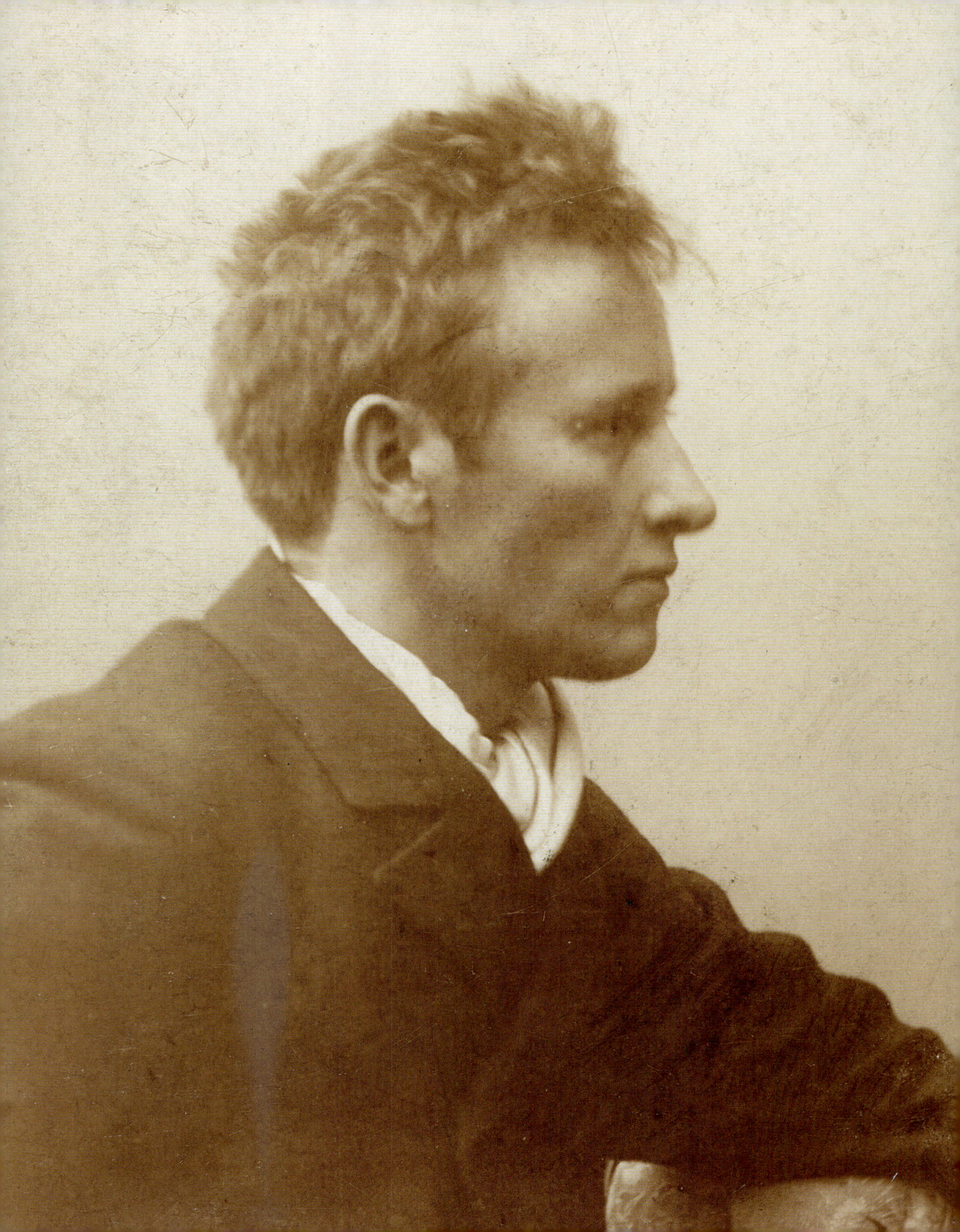

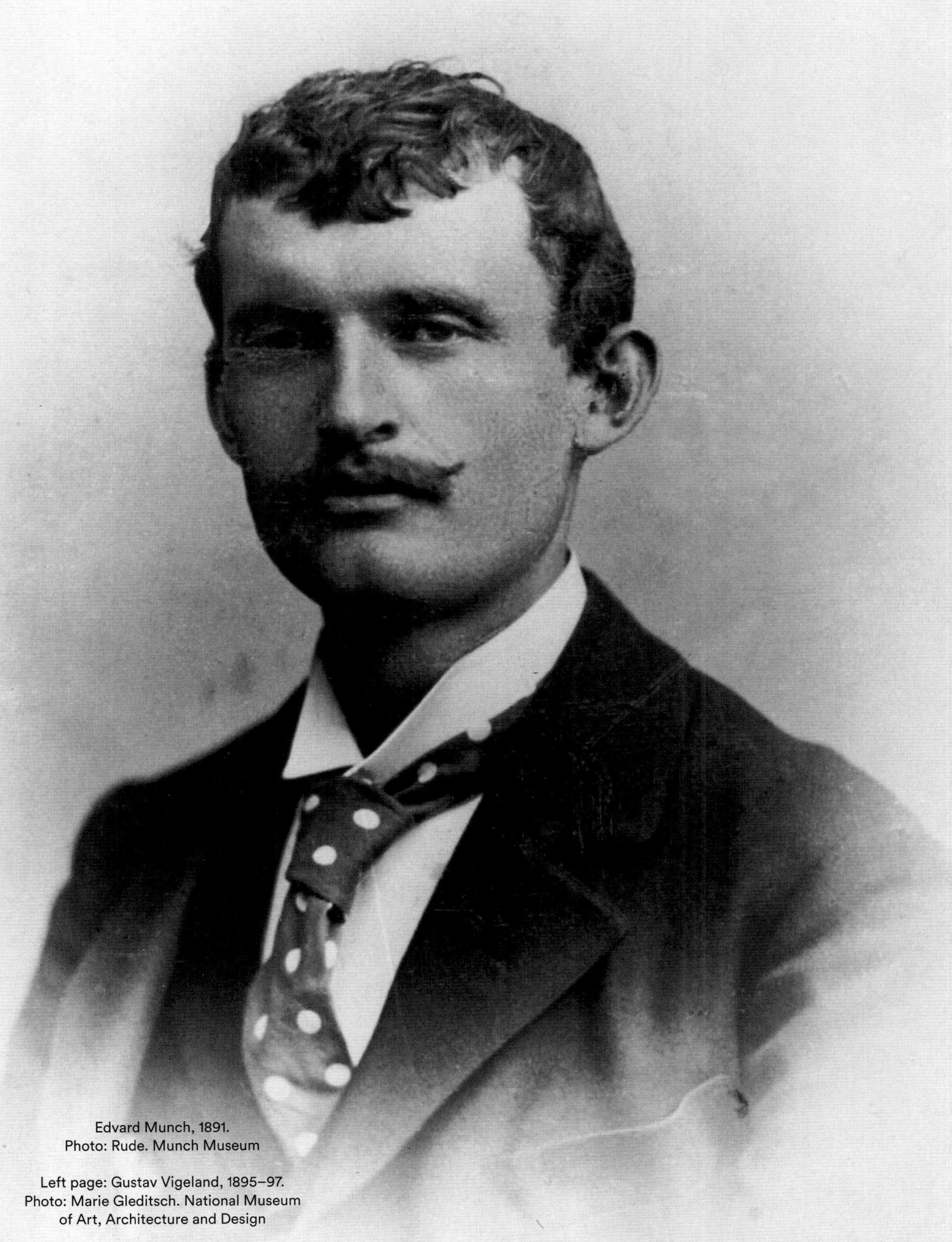

Edvard Munch, 1891.
Photo: Rude. Munch Museum

Left page: Gustav Vigeland, 1895–97.
Photo: Marie Gleditsch. National Museum
of Art, Architecture and Design

Timeline

Year	Gustav Vigeland	Edvard Munch
1863		Born on 12 December in Løten in Hedmark County, Norway, the second oldest of five siblings. His father works as a military doctor. The family moves to Kristiania (today Oslo) the following year.
1868		His mother Laura dies of tuberculosis and her sister Karen Bjølstad assumes responsibility for the household.
1869	Born on 11 April in Mandal, Norway, the second oldest of four siblings. Explores his creative talent from an early age in his father's carpentry workshop.	
1877		Loses his elder sister Sophie to tuberculosis. Memories of the deaths of his mother and sister leave an indelible mark on Munch's art for the rest of his life.
1881		Attends the Royal School of Design in Kristiania, where he follows a course run by Julius Middelthun and draws from live models.
1882		Rents a studio with six other young artists in 'Pultosten' by the Storting (Parliament), where they receive instruction from the painter Christian Krohg.
1883		Makes his debut with the painting *Study of a Head* at the Norwegian Industry and Art Exhibition. Participates for the first time in the Annual Autumn Exhibition, where *Early in the Morning* gains recognition.
1884	Comes to Kristiania at the age of fifteen to work as an apprentice under the woodcarver Torsten Kristensen Fladmoe. Remains in the capital for one and a half years.	
1885		Travels to Antwerp where he makes his international debut at the Exposition Universelle with *Inger Munch in Black*, and thereafter to Paris where he visits the Louvre and the annual Salon. Meets the writer and anarchist Hans Jæger.

Timeline

Year	Gustav Vigeland	Edvard Munch
1886	Returns home to Mandal, where his ailing father dies shortly after from tuberculosis. Studies diligently everything from illustrated exhibition catalogues to anatomy books.	
		Presents *The Sick Child* at the Annual Autumn Exhibition, where the sketch-like execution of the painting creates a great stir.
1888	After two years in Southern Norway Vigeland returns to the capital, where he finally has the opportunity to realise his ambition to become a sculptor.	
1889	Works in the studio of Brynjulf Bergslien and follows a course given by Mathias Skeibrok at the Royal School of Design. In Skeibrok's studio Vigeland models *A Revenant*, which reveals the first signs of his fascination for the doomsday aesthetic of the period.	
		Arranges his first solo exhibition in Kristiania. In the autumn he travels to Paris and studies under the painter Léon Bonnat. His father dies in November. Moves to Saint-Cloud over the New Year.
	Vigeland and Munch exhibit together for the first time at the Annual Autumn Exhibition, where Vigeland makes his debut with *Hagar and Ishmael*. Munch is a regular exhibitor by this time, and participates with two works: *Study* and *Evening*.	
1890		The two may have met for the first time via the circle associated with Ebba Dons's home in Kristiania. Its members include the art historian Jens Thiis and the writers Vilhelm Krag and Sigbjørn Obstfelder.
1891	Undertakes a one-year apprenticeship in the studio of Vilhelm Bissen in Copenhagen. Views contemporary French sculpture and models his first major work, *The Accursed*.	
		Meets Vilhelm Krag, an acquaintance of Vigeland from Southern Norway.
1892		Solo exhibition in Kristiania. Invited to exhibit at the Verein Berliner Künstler (Berlin Art Association), where the exhibition is closed down after one week. Hires a venue in the Equitable Palast, Berlin, where he re-exhibits his works, and decides to settle in the city.
1893	Travels to Paris and visits Auguste Rodin's studio, where he sees the relief *The Gates of Hell*. Back in Kristiania he begins to work on his monumental relief *Hell*.	

Year	Gustav Vigeland	Edvard Munch

Dagny Juell and Stanisław Przybyszewski meet in Berlin through the circle associated with Zum Schwarzen Ferkel and marry in August. Like the Kristiania Bohemians' passion for decadence, the Ferkel group is preoccupied with the creative and destructive forces of love.

Opens a large solo exhibition in Berlin, where six paintings are grouped in the series called *Die Liebe* [Love], which is considered to be the beginning of *The Frieze of Life*. During the course of the winter Munch and Przybyszewski's acquaintanceship develops into a close friendship.

1894

Exhibits *The Accursed* in the Sculpture Museum in Kristiania.

Przybyszewski publishes an article on Munch's work, 'Psychischer Naturalismus', and the first book on his art, *Das Werk des Edvard Munch* [The Work of Edvard Munch].

In May Przybyszewski travels to Norway for the first time. He stays for four months and becomes well acquainted with the Norwegian art world.

Obstfelder writes an impassioned article in which he compares Vigeland and Munch, claiming that their works exemplify a 'unified worldview'.

Moves to 8 Pilestredet, where he lives and works. Completes *Hell* in August and opens his first solo exhibition in October, which leads to his artistic breakthrough. He is contacted by the Przybyszewskis and the Pan Society.

Spends the summer at Filtvedt, by the Oslo Fjord, where Przybyszewski visits him and has his portrait painted.

1895

Vigeland moves into a room adjacent to Munch's at the Hotel Stadt Köln in Berlin, where they live for approximately three months. They frequent the same artist circles, which include figures such as Julius Meier-Graefe, Richard Dehmel, Count Harry Kessler and Jens Thiis. It proves a productive period for both artists, who use their hotel rooms as studios as well as lodgings.

The first issue of the periodical *Pan* – with a reproduction of Vigeland's *Hell* – is published in April.

Exhibits with Axel Gallén (Akseli Gallen-Kallela) at the Ugo Barroccio gallery in March.

Leaves Berlin on 30 April and travels to Florence, where he is inspired by the art of antiquity and the Renaissance.

Returns to Norway via Paris in the summer.

Munch visits Vigeland in his studio together with the Przybyszewskis.

Year	Gustav Vigeland	Edvard Munch
	Most likely makes his portrait of Przybyszewski, who in November completes his text about Vigeland's work, *On the Paths of the Soul*, while staying in Kongsvinger.	
1897	Przybyszewski publishes the first article on Vigeland, *On the Paths of the Soul*. Vigeland's second version of *Hell* is completed (the first version is destroyed by the artist in 1900).	
1898		The Przybyszewskis leave Berlin and move to Krakow. Przybyszewski takes over as editor of the periodical *Zycie* and continues his promotional work for Vigeland's and Munch's art by publishing texts and photographs in *Zycie* and other periodicals.
1899	Arranges his second and last solo exhibition in Kristiania, which receives glowing reviews and underscores Vigeland's position as one of Norway's leading sculptors.	
1901		Dagny Juel Przybyszewska is murdered in Tbilisi, Georgia. Her death probably contributes to the fact that neither Munch nor Vigeland maintain contact with Przybyszewski in the years to come.
1902		Exhibits 22 paintings in a series called 'The Frieze of Life' at the Berlin Secession. Max Linde publishes the booklet *Edvard Munch und die Kunst der Zukunft* [Edvard Munch and the Art of the Future], in which he compares Munch with Rodin. Munch creates etchings based on Linde's sculpture garden in Lübeck.
1902–11		Vigeland and Munch participate in several of the same group exhibitions, in Krefeld, Düsseldorf, Copenhagen, Brussels, Rome and Helsinki.
1904		Vigeland spends a few days in Åsgårdstrand during the summer, where he is invited to dinner at Munch's home. In the autumn Vigeland, as a member of the Board of the National Gallery, recommends the acquisition of Munch's painting *'Moonlight'*. The proposal is rejected.

Year	Gustav Vigeland	Edvard Munch
1907		A resolution is passed to commission Vigeland's *The Fountain* for Eidsvolls Square in front of the Storting. During the same period several competitions for ideas for a national monument are announced, in connection with the centennial celebration of the Norwegian Constitution in 1914. Both Vigeland and Munch toy with various drafts in the coming years.
1908		Has a nervous breakdown and is admitted to Dr Daniel Jacobson's clinic in Copenhagen.
1909		Moves home to Norway and settles in Kragerø by the Oslo Fjord. Begins working on a competition draft for the decoration of the University of Oslo's Aula. Vigeland and Munch are invited to participate in the *Kunstnernes Efteraarsudstilling* [Artists' Autumn Exhibition] in Charlottenborg, Copenhagen, and are presented as 'the two great' Norwegian contemporary artists.
1909–15	Hereafter he devotes most of his time to working on monuments and portraits, in addition to his life project, *The Fountain*, which will subsequently be incorporated in the Vigeland Park. The proposal to place *The Fountain* at Abelhaugen in front of the Royal Palace is made public in 1915.	Develops several ideas for sculptural monuments and starts work on his first sculptures, among them *Mother Norway*.
1910		Vigeland and Munch are referred to as 'the two masters' in the Norwegian exhibition in the Ateneum Art Museum in Helsinki. In a letter to Thiis Munch suggests an idea for the new national monument, implying a collaboration between himself and Vigeland.
1912		After 1911 Vigeland curtails his exhibiting activities. Only seven more exhibitions are known to have taken place during his lifetime. The antithesis of Vigeland, Munch participates in as many as 23 exhibitions in 1912, and among other things he is one of the main exhibitors in the Sonderbund exhibition in Cologne together with Van Gogh, Gauguin, Cézanne and Picasso.
1920s		Relations between Vigeland and Munch are minimal. Both are recognised artists living in relative seclusion, in Frogner and at Ekely respectively. Vigeland signs a contract with the Municipality of Kristiania, which assumes ownership of all of his artwork in exchange for giving him a studio that will serve as a museum after his death.

Year	Gustav Vigeland	Edvard Munch
	In 1924 the municipality approves the proposal to place *The Fountain* in Frogner and Vigeland devotes the remainder of his life to the sculpture park. He models *The Monolith* in clay in its final format in 1924–25. In 1929 the work of carving the 121 figures on the 17-metre-high column begins. It takes three stone carvers fourteen years to complete the task.	
		Munch creates his monumental painting *The Human Mountain* in the years 1927–29, and probably also the sculpture of the same name. Makes sketches for several fountains in front of the Royal Palace.
1930s		The two artists might be considered competitors based on their desire to have their works realised, but evidence of any direct hostility is hard to find. The background for Munch's irritation is his ongoing battle with the tax authorities, which demands a tax on all of his drafts and unsold paintings at Ekely. Vigeland is spared this problem thanks to his contract with the Municipality of Oslo, which owns all of his works. Vigeland and Munch are the first artists to receive the Grand Cross of the Order of St Olav: Vigeland in 1929 'for his masterpieces as a sculptor', and Munch in 1933 'for outstanding work as an artist'. Jens Thiis opens the Munch Room in the National Gallery in 1937.
1943	Vigeland contracts a heart infection in January and is admitted to Lovisenberg Hospital, where he dies on 12 March.	
1944		Munch comes down with a cold over the New Year, and dies peacefully in his home at Ekely on 23 January.
1947	Vigeland's studio in Frogner opens as a museum. The collection contains around 1,600 sculptures, 12,000 drawings and 420 woodcuts. In addition the museum manages several thousand letters, notebooks, photographs and about 5,000 books.	
1963		The Munch Museum opens in Tøyen, Oslo, 100 years after the artist's birth. The collection contains around 1,100 paintings, 18,000 graphic works and 7,500 watercolours and drawings, as well as 14 sculptures, numerous printing plates, notebooks, documents, photographs and 2,240 books.

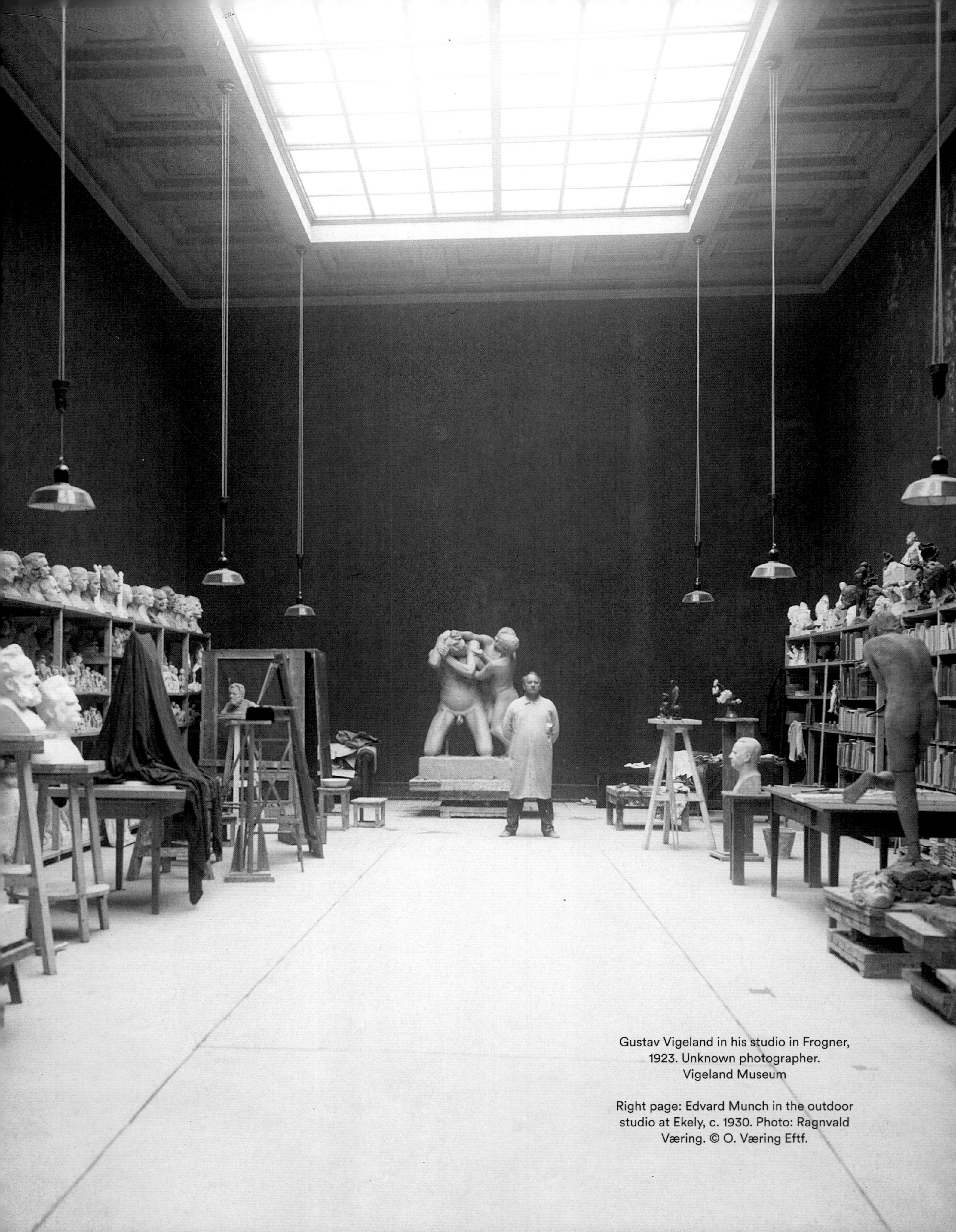

Gustav Vigeland in his studio in Frogner,
1923. Unknown photographer.
Vigeland Museum

Right page: Edvard Munch in the outdoor
studio at Ekely, c. 1930. Photo: Ragnvald
Væring. © O. Væring Eftf.

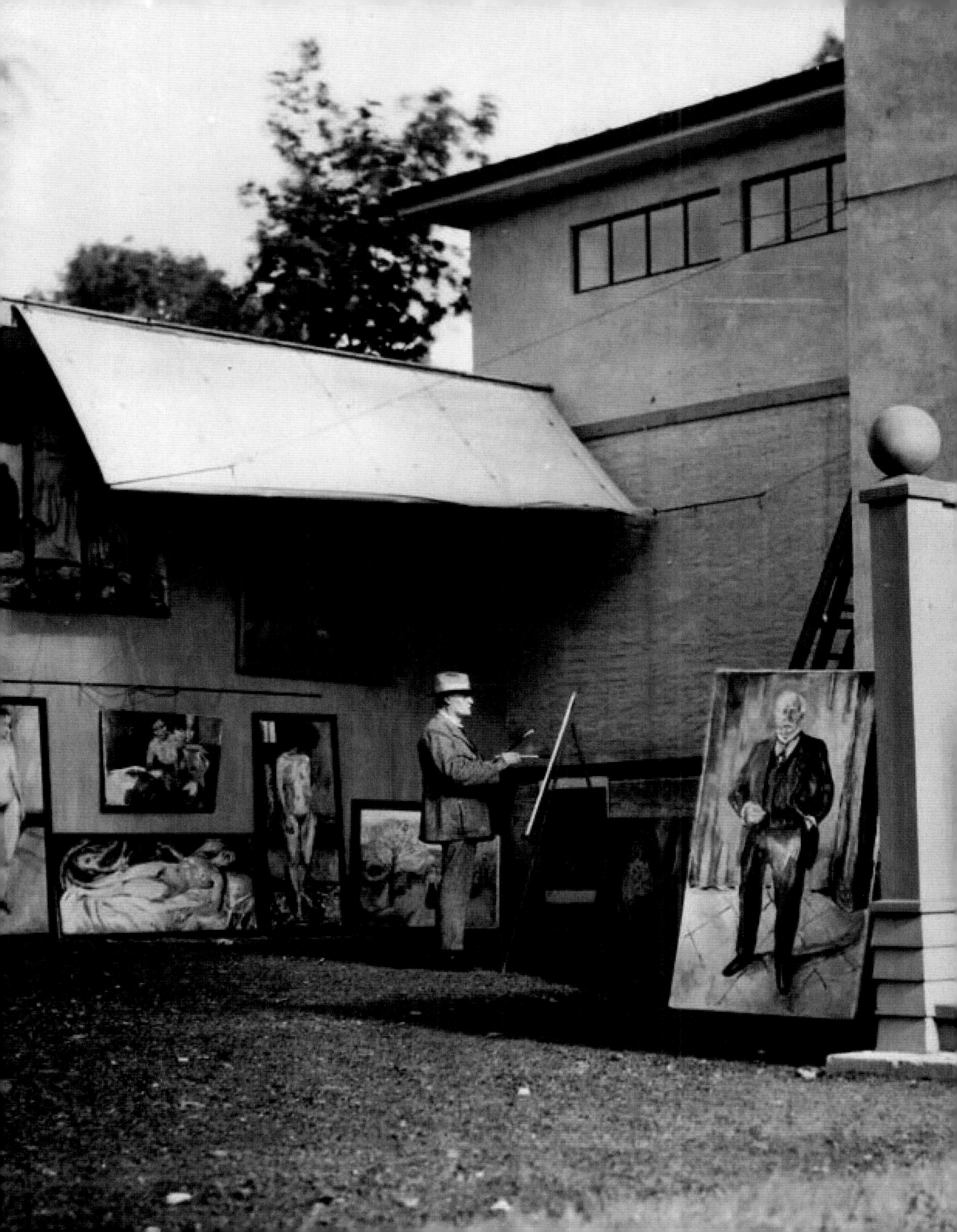

Vigeland+Munch.
Behind the Myths

Trine Otte Bak Nielsen

The relationship between Gustav Vigeland and Edvard Munch is surrounded by myths. Many have the impression that the two were rivals. It turns out, however, that they had much in common when it came to their work, their artistic development and their mutual ambitions.

Although Vigeland and Munch were contemporaries and belonged to the same artist circles, their relationship has never before been the subject of an in-depth investigation. This article will therefore examine their parallel artistic careers – both chronologically and thematically – in order to disclose similarities and possible junctures when their paths may have crossed, from their first student years until their old age as established artists.

The periods during which the two were most closely associated – and consequently those most often referred to – will be thoroughly examined to clarify the facts; for instance the infamous months when they lived in adjoining rooms in Berlin, and their mutual friendship with the Polish writer Stanisław Przybyszewski. Other major points of contact were their involvement in the competition for a national monument in Kristiania and the similar trajectories of their reception as artists.

Although there is no surviving correspondence between the two artists, and very little documentation regarding any direct contact between them, there is no doubt that they were well informed about one another's works throughout their lives.

Childhood

Both Vigeland and Munch came from families that allowed them to explore their artistic ambitions at a young age. Edvard Munch was born in 1863 in Løten, Hedmark County, north of Kristiania (today Oslo), and moved with his family to the capital when he was one year old. The second of five siblings, he lost his mother to tuberculosis when he was only five years old, at which time her sister Karen Bjølstad moved in and took over responsibility for the household. At the age of fourteen he lost his elder sister Sophie to the same disease. Memories of the deaths of his mother and sister left an indelible mark on his art for the remainder of his life. After studying drawing at Gjertsen's school and one year of engineering studies, the sixteen-year-old Edvard decided to become a painter.[1]

Gustav Vigeland was born in 1869, and grew up in Mandal on the southern coast of Norway. He was the second of four siblings and was able to test his creative talents at an early age in his father's carpentry workshop. His family belonged to the middle class and his father took an active part in the religious life of the town. Aside from woodcarving, Gustav was very fond of reading and drawing, and found inspiration among other things in the family's illustrated Bible. At the age of fifteen he left home to become a woodcarving apprentice in Kristiania.[2]

Early Careers in Kristiania

Vigeland and Munch were both young and as yet unestablished artists during the 1880s in Kristiania, where the conditions were not favourable for the coming generation of artists. The capital lacked both an art academy and a permanent venue for the National Gallery's collection.[3] To 'become a sculptor appeared to be unattainable', Vigeland recalls.[4] Since Munch was six years older, their paths rarely crossed during this early phase of their careers. We can nevertheless assume that they were aware of each other's existence, given the small size of the city's art community.

Both Munch and Vigeland followed the cultural debates of the period and were familiar with the works of the Norwegian naturalists, such as Frits Thaulow (1847–1906), Harriet Backer (1845–1932), Christian Krohg (1852–1925) and Mathias Skeibrok (1851–1896). Contact with the older generation of artists would have great significance for both of them, for instance when a letter of recommendation would decide whether or not one received a grant or an invitation to participate in exhibitions, or whether one's work was acquired by important collectors or institutions.

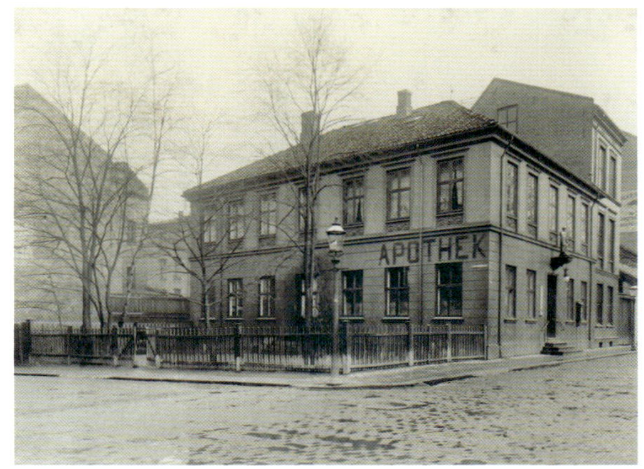

Fig. 1. The Royal School of Design on the corner of Apotekergata and Akersgata, 1897

During the 1880s both Vigeland and Munch worked in various studios and received periodic instruction at the Royal School of Design (fig. 1), but this would only be an intermediary stage for them both. The school provided the only official educational opportunity for artists in the capital. Munch enrolled there on 11 March 1881, where he took a class in drawing under the classically trained sculptor Julius Middelthun (1920–1886) and drew from live models. The studies *Reclining Male Nude with Stick* (1881, cat. 1) and *Seated Male Nude* (1881, cat. 2) reveal a serious approach down to the last detail. Middelthun apparently had a good relationship with Munch, who, according to the art historian Jens Thiis (1870–1942), was his favourite student.[5]

In the autumn of 1882 Munch rented a studio next to the Storting (Parliament) in a building known as the 'Pultosten', together with six other young artists, where they received instruction by Christian Krohg. We can see the influence of naturalism, among other things in Munch's landscape *Akerselva* (1882, fig. 2), in which the water is clear as glass and the reflections of the buildings along the river are reminiscent of Frits Thaulow's pictures from the same period.

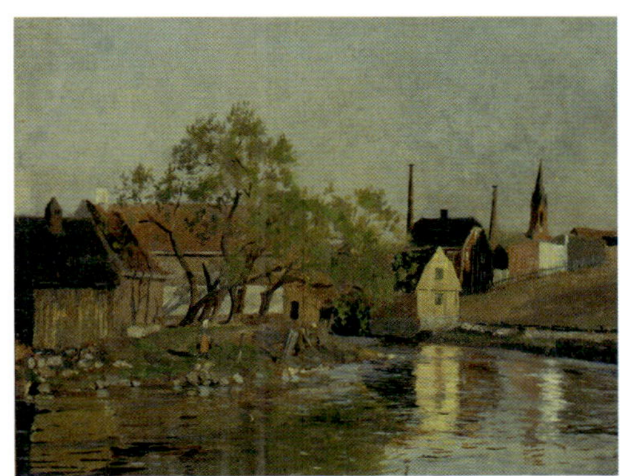

Fig. 2. Edvard Munch: *Akerselva*, 1882

The following summer, in 1883, the twenty-year-old Munch made his debut with the painting *Study of a Head* (1883, fig. 3) at the Norwegian Industry and Art Exhibition. The same autumn he participated for the first time in the Annual Autumn Exhibition, which traditionally represented an important gateway to a career as a professional artist. This was certainly the case for Munch, who experienced a swiftly accelerating success and shortly afterwards received both endowments and artist grants.[6] There were generally few exhibiting venues for art in Kristiania during the 1880s – a sad state of affairs for anyone who wished to present their art and keep abreast of the latest artistic movements in Europe.[7]

Vigeland arrived in Kristiania in 1884 to work as an apprentice under the woodcarver Torsten Kristensen Fladmoe. He remained in the capital for one and a half years, where he studied the plaster models of classical antique sculpture in the Sculpture Museum, together with works by the Danish sculptor Bertel Thorvaldsen (1770–1844), who was his great idol. While Vigeland apprenticed abroad in 1885. He travelled first to Antwerp, where he made his international debut at the Exposition Universelle with *Inger Munch in Black* (1884), and then continued to Paris where he visited the Louvre and the annual Salon, which represented the most important display of contemporary art. This demonstrates how Munch, already as a young and as yet unestablished artist, participated in exhibitions abroad and kept abreast of the latest trends in the art world.

Back in Kristiania Vigeland soon realised that he wanted to achieve more than woodcarving could offer him, but returned home to Mandal in the spring of 1886, where his ailing father died shortly after from tuberculosis. At the same time that Vigeland was at home diligently studying everything from illustrated exhibition catalogues from the Paris Salon to Paul Richer's *Anatomie artistique*,[8] Munch exhibited *The Sick Child* (1885–86) at the Annual Autumn Exhibition in 1886. The sketch-like execution of the painting provoked the indignation of conservative critics and artist colleagues. However, others found the picture 'Noble, immeasurably moving, which few or none of the other pictures are in the possession of'.[9] The leading figure of the infamous Kristiania Bohemians, the writer Hans Jæger (1854–1910), was among the painting's admirers. During this period he was an important role model for Munch, who became intrigued by Jæger's command to 'write thy life'.

After a year in Southern Norway, Vigeland returned to Kristiania in 1888 where he finally had the opportunity to realise his wish of becoming a sculptor. It is reasonable to assume that he visited the Annual Autumn Exhibition that autumn, where he would have been able to see Munch's works for the first time.[10] In February 1889 Vigeland visited the famous sculptor Brynjulf Bergslien (1830–1898), who allowed him to work in his studio, where Vigeland became influenced by classicism. His first work under Bergslien's tutelage, the relief *Patroclus Pulls the Arrow From Eurypylus's Thigh* (1889, fig. 4) is a good example of this influence, where the idealised shapes of the figures and

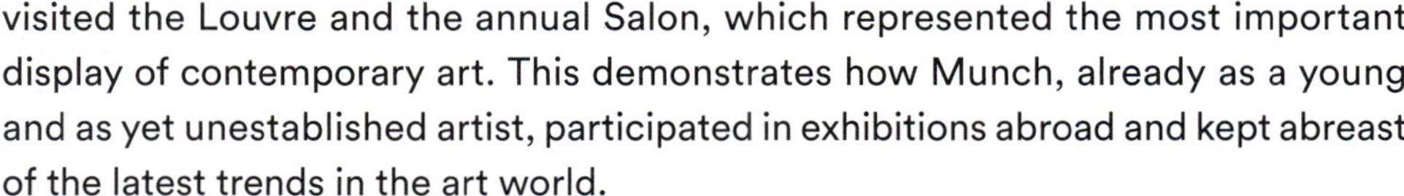

Fig. 3. Edvard Munch: *Study of a Head*, 1883

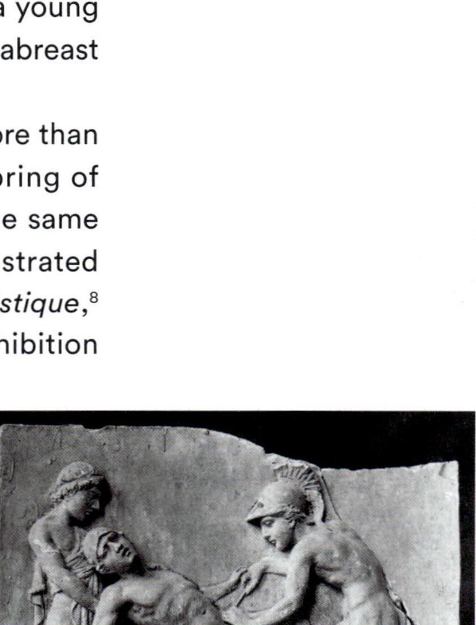

Fig. 4. Gustav Vigeland: *Patroclus Pulls the Arrow From Eurypylus's Thigh*, 1889

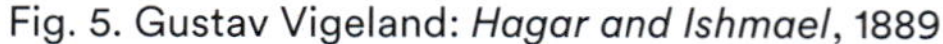

Fig. 5. Gustav Vigeland: *Hagar and Ishmael*, 1889

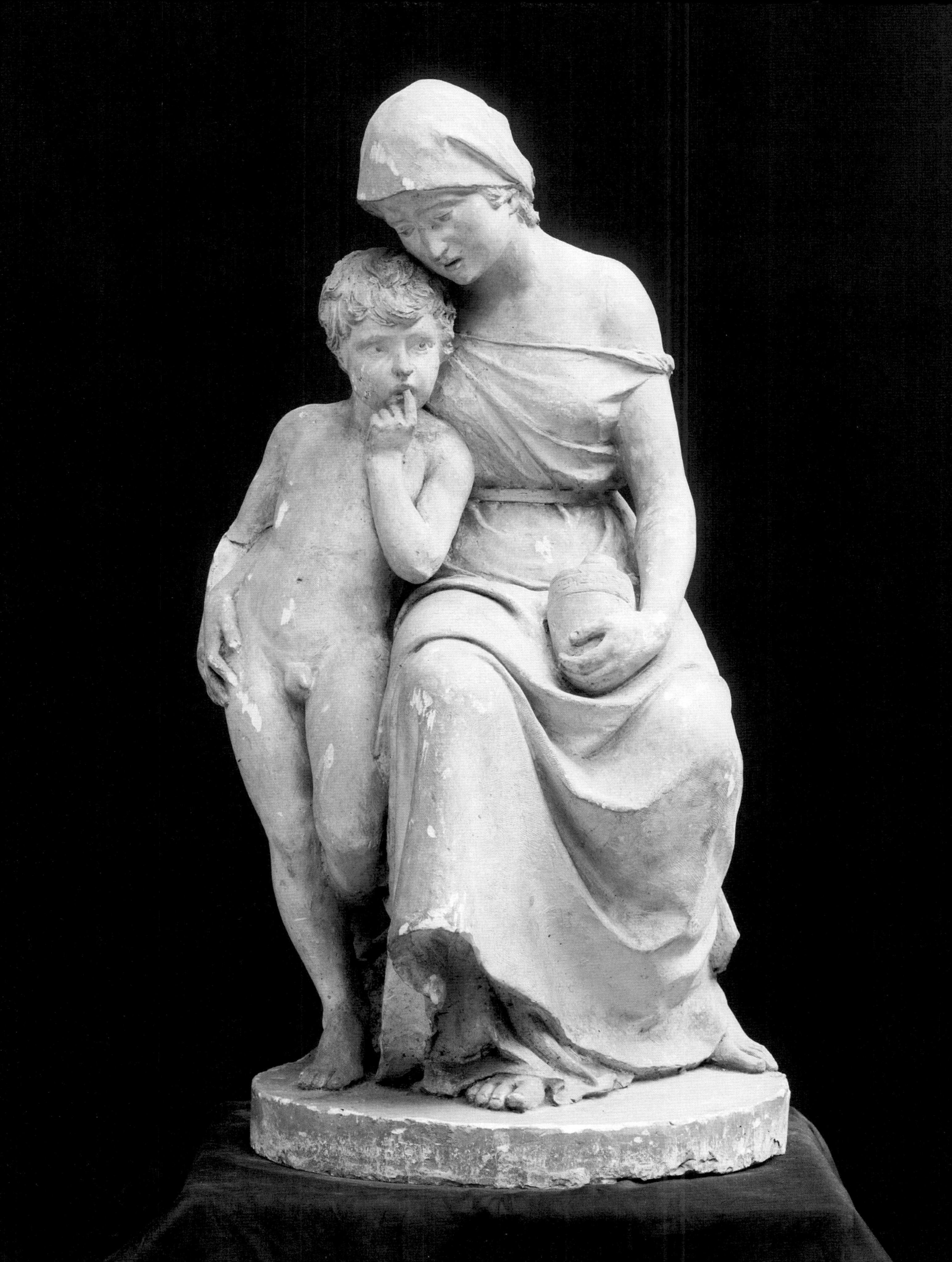

smooth surfaces are moulded against a flat background. During this period Vigeland also used the rooms at the Royal School of Design as a studio during the day, and enrolled on a course given by Mathias Skeibrok in the evenings.[11]

In the autumn of 1889 Vigeland and Munch exhibited together for the first time at the Annual Autumn Exhibition. The twenty-year-old Vigeland made his debut here with the sculpture *Hagar and Ishmael* (1889, fig. 5). Munch – who by this time had managed to become a regular exhibitor – contributed two works: *Study* and *Evening*.[12] While Munch received many reviews, Vigeland's debut piece was barely mentioned in the press. The figure group of mother and child did not distinguish itself with its execution in a late-classical style, and demonstrated that Vigeland was still experimenting within a classical idiom. Munch – with his sketch-like painterly style – was more clearly in opposition to the contemporary focus on highly realistic representations, which made him popular in artist circles. One person who devoted attention to Vigeland's sculpture was the young newspaper correspondent Vilhelm Krag (1871–1933): 'a beginner's work of distinction, I have heard experts say. There is a softness in the lines, a harmony in the overall composition, that belies an exceptional talent.'[13] This is very likely the first time Vigeland's name was mentioned publicly. Krag was an acquaintance of the sculptor from Southern Norway, and he would develop a close relationship with both Vigeland and Munch over the following years.

Munch arrived in Paris for the second time in October 1889 and remained there for about three months. During this period he studied under the French painter Léon Bonnat (1833–1922) and visited the Exposition Universelle and the Salon des Indépendants. On 2 January 1890 he moved to the suburb of Saint-Cloud, where he penned the famous lines that would later be designated as his artistic manifesto: 'One shall no longer paint interiors, people reading and women knitting. They will be people who are alive, who breathe and feel, suffer and love.'[14] During this time Vigeland was still working in Skeibrok's studio, where he created yet another relief inspired by classicism: *Tantalus is Led to the Underworld by the Eumenides* (1890, cat. 8). Yet the work also introduced a new dramatic tone to Vigeland's art, with more exaggerated movements and an expression of despair, which we will see again in several works from the 1890s.[15] Under Skeibrok's tutelage he also modelled the relief entitled *A Revenant* (1889, cat. 119), which revealed one of the first signs of Vigeland's fascination with the contemporary doomsday aesthetic related to death and Judgement Day.

As we have seen, the younger generation's interest in subjectivity rather than objectivity in art was a major factor for both Vigeland and Munch. It is possible that the two met for the first time through the group associated with the home of Ebba Dons at 2 Rosenborggaten in Kristiania during the early 1890s.[16] According to Krag it was the breeding ground for Neo-Romanticism. Among those who frequented the salon were Jens Thiis and the writers Sigbjørn Obstfelder (1866–1900), Gabriel Finne (1866–1899), Sigurd Bødtker (1866–1928) and Nils Kjær (1870–1924).[17] Vigeland and Munch may also have met the Juell sisters, Ragnhild (1871–1908) and Dagny (1867–1901), here.[18] Krag had his breakthrough as a poet in the autumn of 1890 when Jens Thiis recited his poem 'Fandango' in the Students' Union. The event is widely considered to be the beginning of Neo-Romanticism in Norwegian poetry.[19]

The following year Krag published his first collection of poems, in which a fascination for Munch's works is evident.[20]

Travels Abroad

The lack of an art academy in Norway and Vigeland's great interest in the works of Bertel Thorvaldsen most likely contributed to his leaving for Copenhagen in January 1891. During a one-year apprenticeship under the sculptor Vilhelm Bissen (1836–1913), he studied contemporary French sculpture at the Glyptotek and modelled his first major work, *The Accursed* (1891, fig. 62).[21] The sculpture revealed an expressive naturalism in which Vigeland's desire to depict the inner emotional life of humans came to light – in keeping with the Neo-Romantic trends of the period. That same autumn Munch came into contact with Krag,[22] and drew a vignette for the poet's second collection *Nat. Digte i Prosa* [Night. Poems in Prose] (1892). The literary milieu became an important part of Munch's circle of acquaintances throughout the remainder of his life – as was also the case with Vigeland, albeit to a lesser degree.

Munch's works became famous beyond Norway's borders thanks to his infamous 'succès de scandale' exhibition in Berlin, which opened on 5 November 1892 in the Verein Berliner Künstler (Berlin Art Association). The 'scandal' occurred after only five days, at which point the exhibition was closed down 'in the highest consideration for art and genuine artistic pursuits'.[23] But this was far from being a scandal for Munch, who cleverly exploited the situation by immediately sending the exhibition on tour to Düsseldorf and Cologne. Quite satisfied with events, he wrote home to say, 'all the fuss here has been very amusing. The publicity couldn't have been better'.[24] Barely a month after the exhibition closed, Munch rented a venue in the Equitable Palast in Berlin at his own expense, and showed it anew. He then made the decision to settle in the city.

All the fuss surrounding the exhibition undoubtedly reached the ears of the Polish writer Stanisław Przybyszewski (1868–1927, fig. 6), who was in Berlin at the time.[25] That autumn Munch became acquainted with August Strindberg,[26] and they most likely frequented the same tavern, Zum Schwarzen Ferkel; a gathering place for the city's Scandinavian artists and writers. It was probably here as well that Przybyszewski met his future wife Dagny Juell, and it may even have been Munch who introduced them to one another when the young piano student arrived in the city in March 1893. It did not take long for her to become a member of the circle, for which Przybyszewski became something of leader figure when Strindberg left Berlin in April. Like the Kristiania Bohemians' passion for decadence, the members of the Ferkel group were also preoccupied with the creative and destructive forces of love. Angst-ridden motifs of doom are almost customary, as we can also see in the works of Vigeland and Munch from this period, for example Vigeland's *Fear* (1892, cat. 70), which depicts a woman entangled in an indeterminate organic mass that appears to coil up the naked body towards a face that is contorted in a scream. This ambivalent,

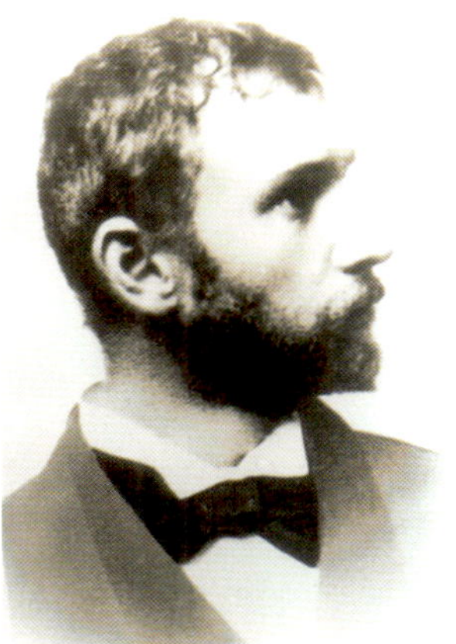

Fig. 6. Stanisław Przybyszewski, Berlin 1892

nondescript element emphasises the disturbing atmosphere. We recognise a similar emotion in Munch's *The Scream* (fig. 41), which was painted the following year. There is no direct connection between the two works, but it is nevertheless remarkable that both artists created motifs of screaming angst-ridden figures.

While Munch was in Berlin, Vigeland travelled to Paris in January 1893. For six months he studied the city's museums and galleries diligently, and visited the studio of Auguste Rodin (1840–1917), where he saw the relief *The Gates of Hell* (1880–1917, fig. 7). The Judgement Day theme, and the use of highly contrasting hollow and raised modelled segments, must have been very inspiring, even though Vigeland would later deny this. Formal elements, such as the central position of *The Thinker* (fig. 8) in the relief, can be recognised in both Vigeland's *Hell* (1894) and in several of Munch's early drawings of *The Human Mountain* (cats. 151, 194, 196). Vigeland chose to represent hell in relief as a single scene the following year, however, not in eight smaller ones as Rodin had done. When he returned from Paris in June, it is not known whether he was in touch with Dagny Juell, who was home for about a month; in love and newly engaged to Przybyszewski. Vigeland worked on several small figure groups that autumn, and made drawings and a little model of *Hell* in clay (fig. 9), which he enlarged to a monumental format in December. Shortly after the New Year he began working on the motif full-time.

Dagny and Stanisław were married in Berlin on 18 August 1893, and in December Munch opened a large solo exhibition in a venue on Unter den Linden. Here he grouped six paintings in a series he called *Die Liebe* [Love], which is considered to be the start of his famous picture cycle *The Frieze of Life*.[27] Przybyszewski used the series as the point of departure for his very first article about Munch, which he composed that winter.[28] He was enthusiastic about Munch's works, which he perceived as the best example of 'the world view of our times'.[29] Przybyszewski also had the opportunity to become acquainted with Munch's works through Dagny, who organised several of the artist's exhibitions in Berlin.[30] During the course of that winter Munch and Przybyszewski's acquaintanceship developed into a close friendship.

Przybyszewski found an outlet for his enthusiasm for Munch's work in his essay 'Psychischer Naturalismus' [Psychic Naturalism], which he published in the Berlin-based art and literature journal *Neue Deutsche Rundschau* in February 1894.[31] This was the first in-depth article about Munch's art outside Norway. Przybyszewski introduced the artist as the first who 'attempted to depict the finest and most subtle movements of the soul exactly as they appear – spontaneously and completely independently of any mental process – in the unalloyed consciousness of the individuality'.[32] The editor of the journal did not share Przybyszewski's enthusiasm and renounced Munch 'to whom we cannot attribute great significance [...] and his pictures cannot be perceived as Przybyszewski does'.[33]

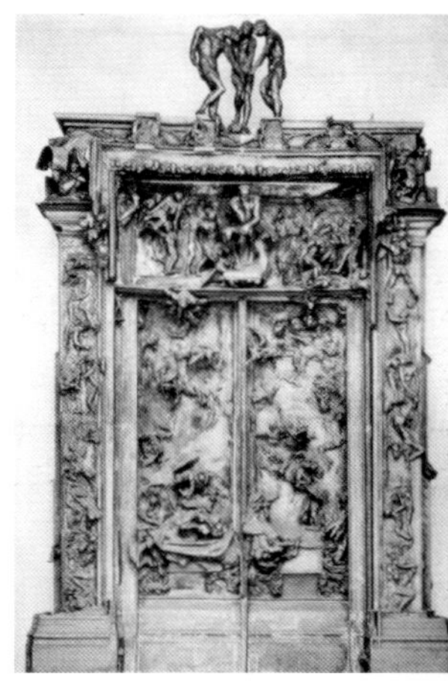

Fig. 7. Auguste Rodin: *The Gates of Hell*, 1880–1917

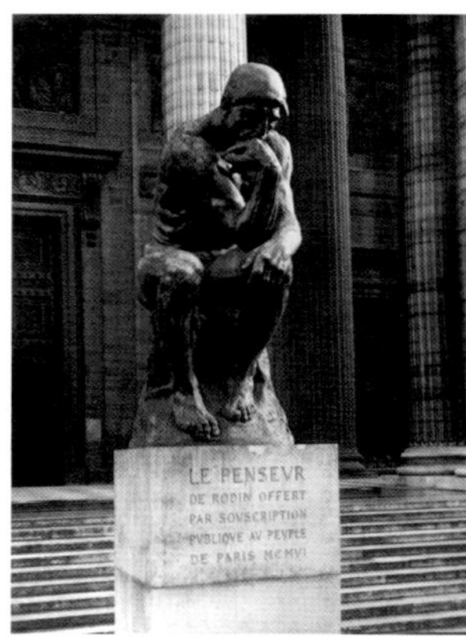

Fig. 8. Auguste Rodin: *The Thinker (Le Penseur)*, c. 1906

Przybyszewski edited a new version of the article in March,[34] and took the initiative to publish what would become the first monograph about the artist: *Das Werk des Edvard Munch* [The Work of Edvard Munch]. The intention, according to the foreword, was 'to pave the way for an appreciation of the great art of this lonely man'. Munch was presented as an artist who was preoccupied with the inner life of the soul, as opposed to the naturalists. For Przybyszewski the role of art lay in its ability to describe the various states of the soul. He believed artists should use their individual experiences in a spontaneous process that circumvented the influence of reason: '[Munch's] pictures are outright remedies for the soul painted in the instant when all grounds for reason become silent, when every activity of the imagination has ceased functioning.' In his descriptions of Munch's six paintings Przybyszewski projected a strong personal identification. In certain passages the text has a life of its own, parallel to the pictures he discusses. A personal perspective, when writing about art, was a common approach among the writers of the period. Munch and Przybyszewski spent a lot of time together during the spring of that year. Munch enjoyed living in Berlin and was enthusiastic about Przybyszewski the writer.[35]

Przybyszewski Comes to Norway

Przybyszewski arrived in Norway for the first time in May 1894, together with Munch. It is possible that Przybyszewski had his first encounter with Vigeland's work the same month, when Vigeland exhibited *The Accursed* in the Sculpture Museum, which was also written about in the press.[36] The writer's sojourn lasted about five months, and gave him ample opportunity in every respect to acquaint himself with Norway's cultural and art world. Dagny already had a strong network of friends in the capital's artistic circles, and they met Obstfelder, Finne and Thiis among others.[37]

At the beginning of July, Vigeland moved to 8 Pilestredet where he both lived and worked. On 16 August he completed *Hell* in a large-scale format, presented it to the press and received numerous reviews (fig. 10). Finne believed that Vigeland had 'managed to create an intense manifestation of a worldview, the young modern hand's profound, sorrowful worldview'.[38] It is uncertain whether Przybyszewski and Munch met Vigeland that autumn, but we can assume that they were aware of the sculptor's monumental relief.

Munch spent the summer of 1894 in Filtvedt by the Oslo Fjord, where Przybyszewski visited him and had his portrait painted (cat. 46). Utterly satisfied, he described the picture as 'fabulous with a psychological representational force'.[39] This was the first of three portraits Munch made of the author.[40] The painting from Filtvedt appears to be the most distinctly symbolist, with Przybyszewski's head floating in a misty landscape. Munch had used a thin water-based paint, which made it appear as though the motif is about to disappear into the grey tones. The bodiless head may be a reference to the biblical story of Salome who had her wish fulfilled when John the Baptist's head was brought to her on a platter. This was a popular *femme-fatale* motif[41] of the period, and a familiar theme in Przybyszewski's writing. Perhaps it was precisely for that reason Munch alluded to it in his portrait of the writer.

Vigeland opened his first solo exhibition in the Christiania Kunstforening gallery one month later, on 21 October 1894.[42] Thiis announced: 'He is young. Let us heed him, and let us not be unjust towards his talent. He has ventured more than anyone before him.' *Hell* (fig. 44) was without a doubt the highlight of the exhibition and the work that gained the most attention. Vigeland received many positive reviews, while the negative critics expressed the same objections as with Munch's works; when they regarded the sculptures as unfinished it was an attack on their execution rather than their motifs. Thiis on the other hand claimed that the sculptor's art was 'profoundly modern'.[43] Since Munch had a solo exhibition on view in Stockholm during that period,[44] it is unlikely that he saw Vigeland's exhibition, but we can assume that he was aware of the attention it attracted via mutual acquaintances.

The first tangible sign of the Przybyszewskis' enthusiasm for Vigeland's art appeared just days after his solo exhibition closed in the middle of November. In a letter from Dagny he was informed that the photographs he sent of his works were received with wild enthusiasm by the artists in Berlin, and that '"Pan" shall arrange an exhibition of Vigeland's works in Berlin next winter (1895)'.[45] She wrote further that the first issue of *Pan* would be published on 1 April the following year, and that this was very timely since Przybyszewski's article on Vigeland would thus 'be read and familiar to the public' before the exhibition opened. Finally, Dagny invited him to come and live with the couple in Berlin. A few days later Vigeland received a letter from the Pan Society, which expressed interest in his works after having seen them reproduced in photographs.[46] Due to all these enquiries, he made plans to travel to Berlin in November.[47]

Obstfelder wrote an enthusiastic article that year in which he compared Vigeland and Munch, claiming that the works of both 'express a unified worldview'. Like Przybyzsewski, Obstfelder saw them as examples of the spirit of the times, with a common desire to depict the inner emotional life of human beings. The reference to melancholy is pointed out in particular by Przybyszewski, who interprets Vigeland's art as an expression of the pessimism of the times: '[…] the young Vigeland dreamt his first works in the atmosphere of a similar hopelessness and despair, amid the hard and unrelenting "will of evil" and deep repentance.'[48]

Although both the Przybyszewskis and Munch were in Berlin that winter, they probably met less frequently than before, since Munch was fully occupied with his first graphic works. It is possible that he made his lithographic portrait of Przybyszewski, which he dated 1895 (cat. 122), over the New Year.

Adjoining Rooms in Berlin

Vigeland arrived in Berlin on 6 February 1895, and initially stayed with the Przy-byszewskis in the suburb of Pankow (fig. 11).[49] After a few days he moved to the centre of town, in a room adjoining Munch's in the Hotel Stadt Köln at 47–48

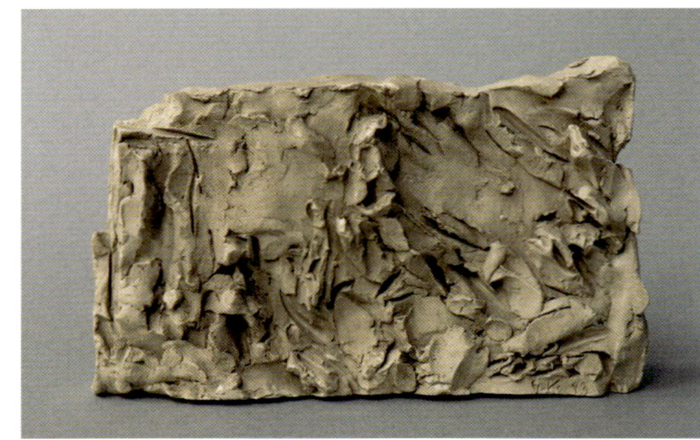

Fig. 9. Gustav Vigeland: *Hell*, 1893

Fig. 10. Gustav Vigeland standing in front of *Hell* in his studio in 8 Pilestredet, 1894

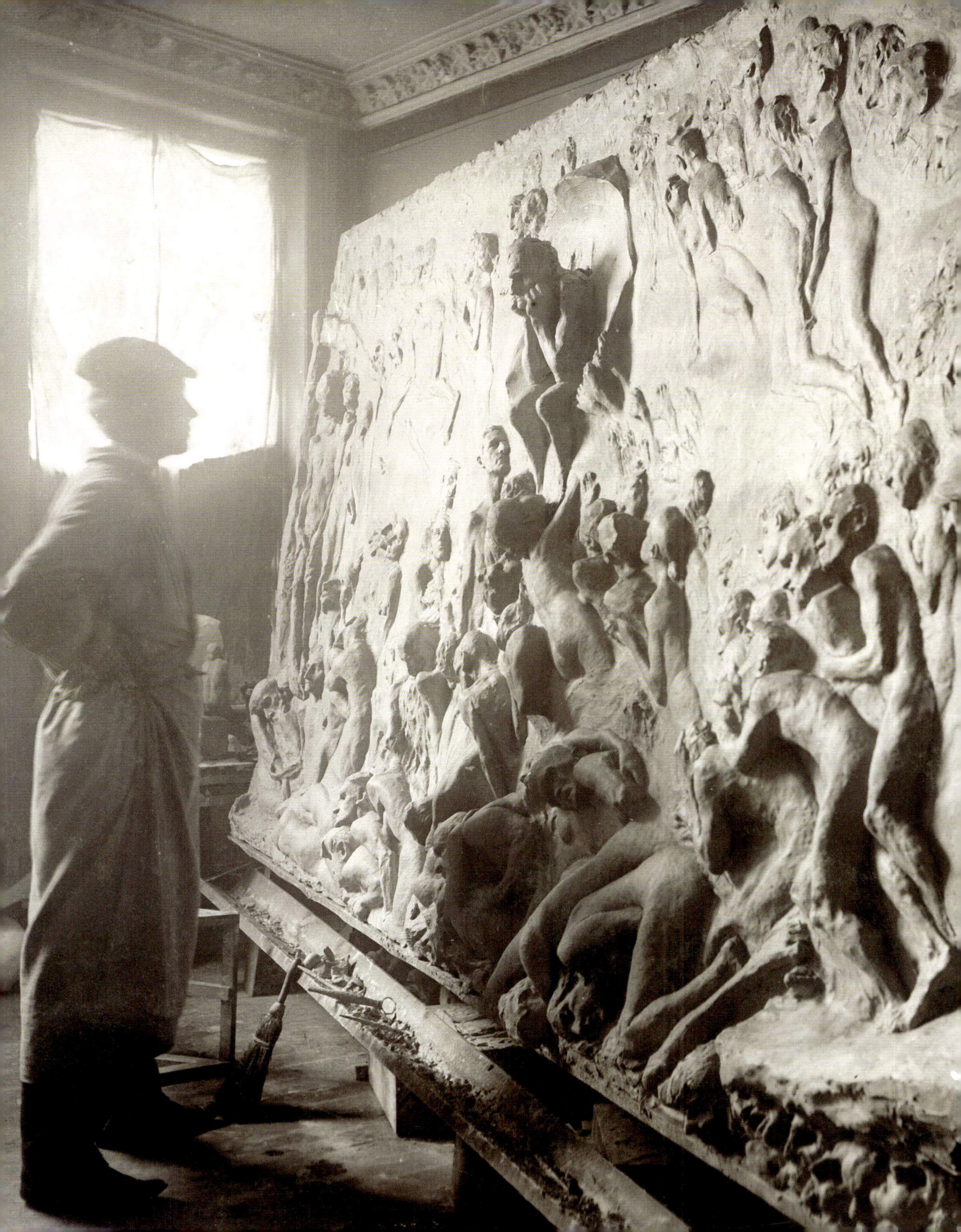

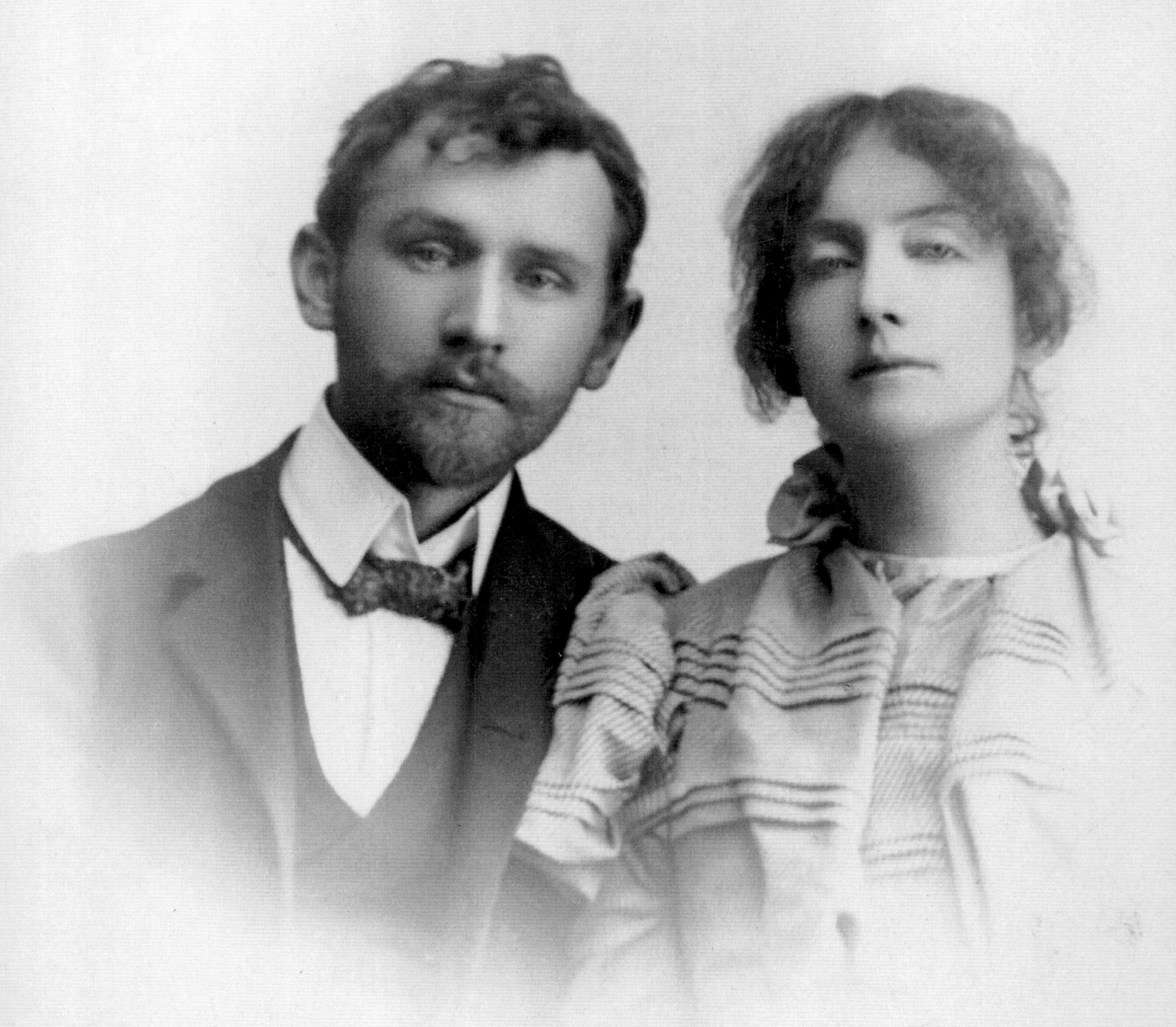

Mittelstrasse, where Obstfelder was also installed (fig. 13). Vigeland and Munch lived side by side for nearly three months, only a few blocks from Zum Schwarzen Ferkel (fig. 14). This is the most mythologised period regarding the relationship between the two artists. Rolf Stenersen's legendary biography on Munch may have played a role in this. He wrote among other things that Vigeland and Munch became arch-enemies in Berlin supposedly because of a shared girlfriend, whom Munch had gone out with the day it was Vigeland's turn to spend time with her. When they came home and Vigeland saw them together, he threw his bust of Munch at them so that it shattered.[50] Stenersen quotes Munch as supposedly saying that he 'didn't dare to stay in Berlin as long as Vigeland was on the loose. He is mad as a hatter, Vigeland is. And I don't think much of his art either.' Stenersen concludes, 'Munch and Vigeland never became friends again'.[51] This is a truth with modifications. Hans P. Lødrup, Vigeland's first biographer, gives a somewhat different version by quoting Vigeland as saying: 'I had [...] begun 2 Busts, one of Munch, the Painter and one of Mrs. Przybyszewski. But one day I had been out strolling in Thiergarten [*sic*], where it was incredibly lovely. Spring had arrived. And when I returned to my barren, gloomy Hotel room I smashed both of the Busts. Munch's was nearly finished. But it doesn't matter.'[52] There is thus no doubt that Vigeland modelled two busts in Berlin, one of Edvard Munch and one of Dagny Juel Przybyszewska. He referred to the busts as works that he 'was very preoccupied with',[53] but does not say why he destroyed them. It may just as well have been due to his straitened financial situation, and insufficient clay for new sculptures. In addition it was both difficult and expensive to ship sculptures home to Norway. In Berlin Vigeland also made a small drawing of Munch, which is the closest approximation we have today of the appearance of the bust (cat. 43).

The months spent in Berlin were a fruitful period for both artists, who used their hotel rooms as studios as well as lodgings. Vigeland recalls: 'In Berlin 1895 I was together with him [Munch] and Thiis, Munch and I lived at Mittelstrasse 45 or 47, in adjoining rooms, he would carry lithographic stones to the printing house and there was always a Silberstein Goldstein or the like [...] he would visit.'[54] According to Thiis the period was both productive and social. They visited 'museums in the morning [...] raised their glasses in the evening and worked at night',[55] and spent a great deal of time in the same artist circles associated with *Pan* (fig. 15) and Zum Schwarzen Ferkel.

In Berlin they were also both in contact with Count Harry Kessler (1868–1937), the writer and patron of the circle surrounding *Pan*. He sat as a model for a lithographic portrait (cat. 41) in Munch's hotel room.[56] He was also clearly enthusiastic about Vigeland's works and commissioned a version of *Dance* (cat. 89): 'I have hardly ever seen love's rapture rendered so powerfully.'[57] The interest Vigeland's sculptures attracted in Berlin was largely due to Przybyszewski's advocacy. Aside from *Pan*'s reproduction of *Hell* in April,[58] Vigeland had brought photographs of his works with him.[59] Przybyszewski was in contact with the artist Max Klinger (1857–1920), who

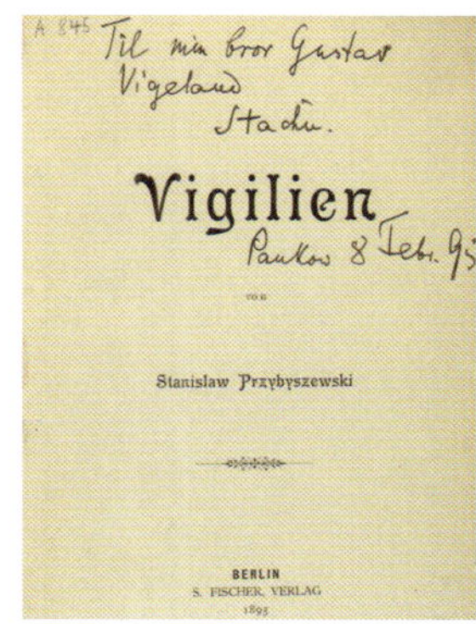

Fig. 12. Dedication in *Vigilien* from Stanisław Przybyszewski to Gustav Vigeland, Pankow, Berlin, 8.2.1895

Fig. 11. Stanisław Przybyszewski and Dagny Juel Przybyszewska at Kongsvinger, 1890s

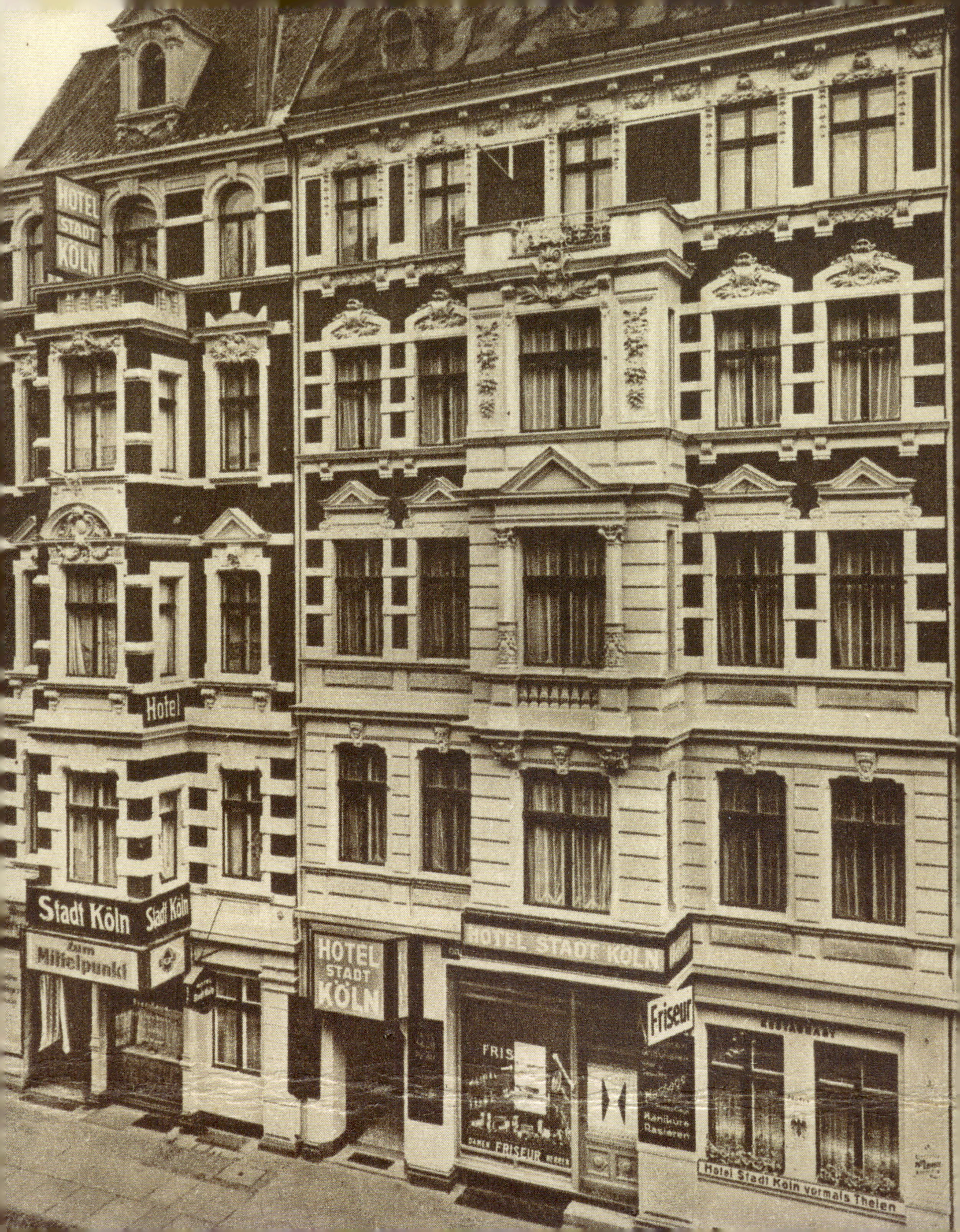
HOTEL
STADT
KÖLN
Hotel
Stadt Köln
Stadt Köln
zum
Mittelpunkt
HOTEL
STADT
KÖLN
HOTEL STADT KÖLN
Friseur
FRISEUR
DAMEN FRISEUR
Maniküre
Rasieren
Hotel Stadt Köln vormals Thelen

wished to contribute 500 German marks for the casting of *Hell*.[60] Vigeland mentioned yet another acquaintance, the writer Peter Hille (1854–1904), and proudly recounted how the author was writing lengthy articles about him in which he was described as "'Dante in Thon". – Flattering, is it not?'[61]

One of the most widely quoted stories from this period provides an impression of the animated atmosphere that characterised the Scandinavian group. It was Thiis who recounted what took place at a lively party, where 'Dehmel recited his beautiful verse [...] Obstfelder was forced to read a few of his poems [...] Vigeland presented photographs of his works, "Hell" and the first passionate figures of couples in love, which aroused the greatest interest [...] Munch spoke extemporaneously with his disjointed and stirring paradoxes. The music was provided by Staszu [Przybyszewski], who played Schumann and Chopin with the whole of his abundant temperament, and Obstfelder, who often carried his violin around with him, played Grieg, Svendsen and Bach. It was a delightful evening [...] Yes, such were our young years, full of madness, friendship and exalted artistic enthusiasm.'[62]

In addition to his modelling work, numerous drawings reveal how Vigeland concentrated on male and female motifs while in Berlin, from enamoured couples to gloomy themes related to jealousy and death. It appears that some of Vigeland's drawings, perhaps inspired by Munch, were also intended and created solely as drawings and not as preparatory sketches for sculptures, such as *A Couple in the Woods* (1895, cat. 62). Vigeland has included two trees here that vertically separate the man from the woman in the picture, a compositional device Munch had employed earlier, for example in *Woman. Sphinx* (1894).

Vigeland presumably paid a visit to the Ugo Barroccio gallery in Unter den Linden, where Munch and the Finnish painter Axel Gallén exhibited together in March 1895. He even recalled that Munch 'was keen on Gallén from the start'.[63] Among Munch's exhibited paintings was *Kiss*, a motif that may have inspired Vigeland when he modelled the first version of his sculpture *The Kiss* in Berlin.[64] The sculpture no longer exists, yet Munch reproduced its characteristic appearance in a drawing (cat. 42). Both the sculpture and the drawing represent the couple as one, joined together in a single embrace. Munch had perhaps also been inspired by his colleague when he made a new graphic version of *Kiss* in Berlin, with features that resembled Vigeland's sculpture. Unlike Munch's painting *The Kiss* (1891, cat. 51), where the couple are presented clothed and fused together in a simple dark shape, the figures in the etching are undressed and moulded by light and shade. It has previously been suggested that Munch's observation

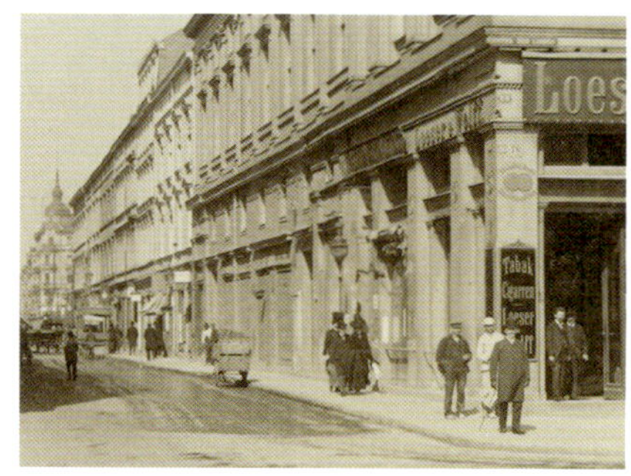

Fig. 14. View from Unter den Linden towards Neue Wilhelmstrasse, 1906. Zum Schwarzen Ferkel was situated behind the tobacconists.

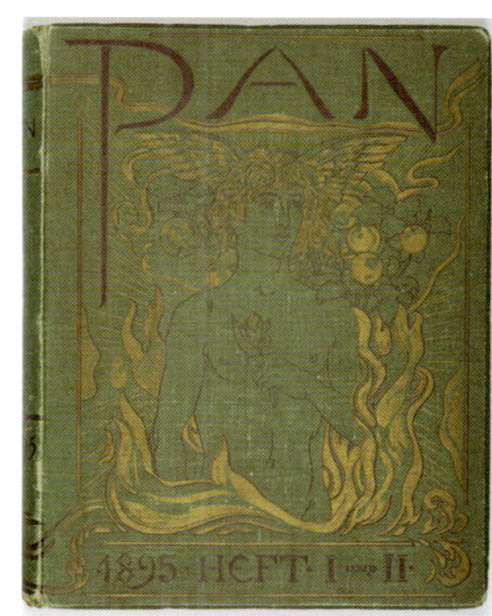

Fig. 15. *Pan* (1895)

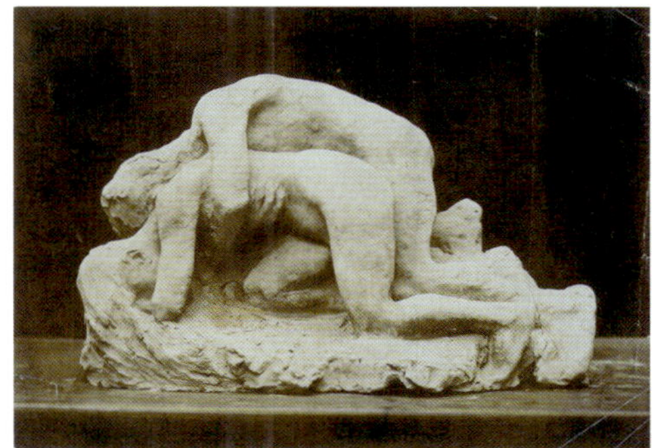

Fig. 16. Gustav Vigeland: *The Prostrated*, c. 1895

Fig. 13. Hotel Stadt Köln, 47–48 Mittelstrasse, Berlin, c. 1930 of the sculptural qualities of Vigeland's works may have caused him to undress the two figures.[65] Munch's interest in the sculptor is also demonstrated by the drawing he made of Vigeland's sculptures *The Kiss* (cat. 52) and *The Prostrated* (cat. 50) in Berlin. In the foreground of the drawing (cat. 42) one can glimpse a relaxed Vigeland reclining and smoking next to Obstfelder – probably at the hotel where all three resided.

The sculpture *The Prostrated*, which shows a crouching couple with the man bowed over the woman, is one of five sculptures Vigeland modelled in Berlin.[66] Looking back, he recalled that when Munch saw the sculpture he remarked 'that he should have included it in his "series"'. Upon hearing this Gunnar Heiberg said that Vigeland would never receive greater praise, 'for Edvard Munch does not recognise anything'.[67] That Munch thought well of *The Prostrated* was also demonstrated by the fact that he kept a photograph of the sculpture, which is probably of the original version in clay from Berlin (fig. 16).[68] According to Lødrup this is the only sculpture Vigeland kept from his stay in the city.[69] Vigeland eventually tired of Berlin and longed to make his way south to Florence. He was obviously also disappointed when he understood that nothing would come of Przybyszewski's planned article about him in the second issue of *Pan*, nor of the exhibition in Berlin the forthcoming winter, which had been promised him before his departure from Norway.[70] He left the city on 30 April 1895.

Contact with Przybyszewski Wanes

In the summer of 1895, after a stopover in Paris, Munch returned to Norway, where the married Przybyszewski couple were now staying in Kongsvinger. They visited Kristiania regularly, meeting up with Munch and Knut Hamsun among others.[71] Vigeland returned to the city at the beginning of July. The fact that Vigeland and Przybyszewski had retained their close relationship was confirmed when the couple asked Vigeland to be the godfather of their first child, Zenon.[72] Przybyszewski completed the first draft of his article about the sculptor, *On the Paths of the Soul*.[73] It was published two years later as the first monograph on Vigeland.[74]

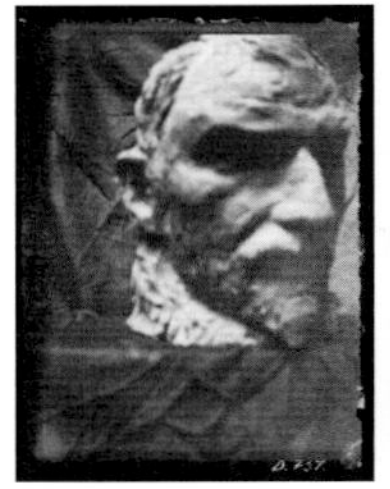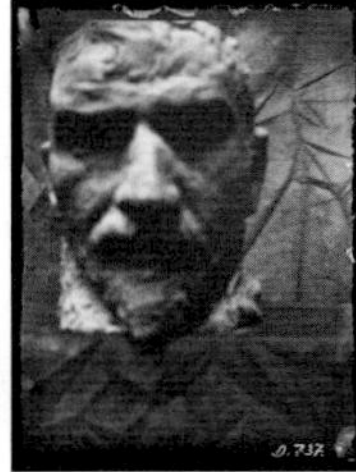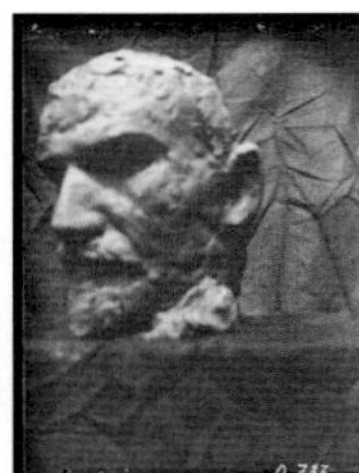

Fig. 17. Gustav Vigeland's clay portrait of Przybyszewski

It seems likely that Vigeland and Munch met repeatedly around this time, as it was probably that Christmas Vigeland was referring to when he reminisced about his various encounters with Munch during the 1890s, when they were clearly together 'at "the Grand" on Christmas Eve until 10, after which he [Munch] went home to his sister et al. and I went up to Pilestredet to lie down on the floor to sleep'.[75] In his memoirs Vigeland also remembers a jovial encounter with Munch when he came to Vigeland's studio 'together with Stanisław Przybyszewski and Mrs. Dagny and when I had given Przybyszewski a little figure group [a sculpture] E. Munch held it. And when they left E.M. sang: "Behold we are moving forward [....]"'.[76] Przybyszewski visited Vigeland several times that autumn,[77] and it was possibly during one of these visits that Vigeland made his portrait (cat. 45),[78] the first of two portraits he made of the writer.[79] Compared to the contemporaneous portraits of *Kristian Hagberg* (1894) and *Aksel Heiberg* (1895) it stands out because of its impressionistic execution. Here we see a sketchier model-ling, where the writer's characteristic Mephistophelean moustache and beard, together with his introverted gaze – as with his Obstfelder portrait, also from 1895 – may have been seen to symbolise the writer's focus on the inner emotional life. Vigeland greatly valued the portrait, 'which is executed in a unique manner'.[80]

After 1895 contact between Przybyszewski and the two artists waned, and the three were rarely to be found in the same city again. Vigeland travelled to Florence in February 1896, where he remained for six months to study the art of antiquity and the Renaissance. Munch left for Paris that same month. It did not make matters any better when Przybyszewski published his novel *Over bord* [Overboard][81] with descriptions that Munch felt offended by.[82] Nor was Vigeland satisfied with Przybyszewski's interpretations of his works, and a debate appeared in *Aftenposten* between Przybyszewski and Sophus Larpent (1838–1911)[83] in connection with the publication of Przybyszewski's article on the sculptor, 'Ein Unnbekanter' [An Unknown].[84] Larpent claimed to have support from Vigeland in his view, and referred to a letter in which the artist expressed his surprise over Przybyszewski's descriptions. After having read the article, Vigeland writes in frustration: 'Damn it all, he makes me out to be a person who walks about with an uncontrollable sex drive, unhappy and nearly on the verge of madness. And none of this is me.'[85] Despite his scepticism, two weeks later Vigeland wrote again to Larpent: 'The article has pleased me after all, it touches upon and concerns many things, and I think it is passionately done. While reading it I repeatedly exclaimed: This is the best damned discussion on art I have read. And as I sit here I believe it still.'[86] Despite diminished contact, Przybyszewski continued his promotional work for the two artists.

Munch and the Przybyszewskis probably met for the last time in Paris in the spring of 1898.[87] Thereafter the relationship mainly consisted of correspondence, also on Vigeland's part, since the couple moved to Krakow in September of that year. There Przyby-szewski took over the position of editor for the periodical *Zycie* (fig. 18), which would become an important organ for the group of artists of the coming gener-ation known as 'Young Poland' (Młoda Polska). He continued his promotional work by publishing texts and photographs of Vigeland's and Munch's art, in his own as well as other periodicals.[88] He perceived an artistic kinship between the two, as exemplified in the last sentence in an article about Munch where he mentioned Vigeland: 'For he [Munch] is an exceptional, peculiar phenomenon, as is his fellow countryman Gustav Vigeland in the sphere of sculpture, in whom every emotion is expressed in the language of form and line.'[89] In addition to publishing articles, Przybyszewski sold photographic reproductions of their works, as announced in *Zycie* in 1899 (fig. 19).[90] All of this contributed to making Vigeland and Munch known among artist circles in Poland, as well as in a number of Central European countries.[91] Dagny continued to remain an important link between Munch and Przybyszewski,

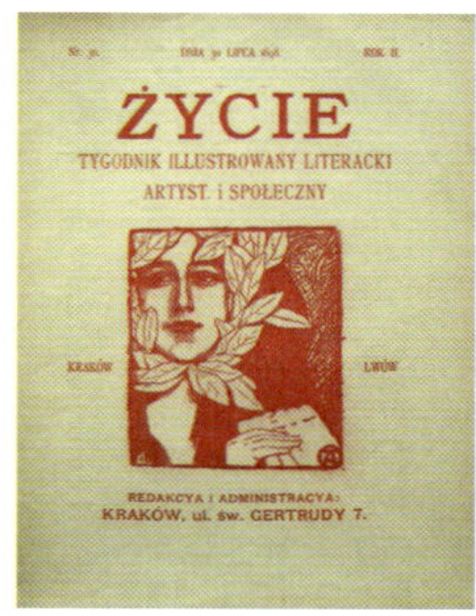

Fig. 18. *Zycie* (1898)

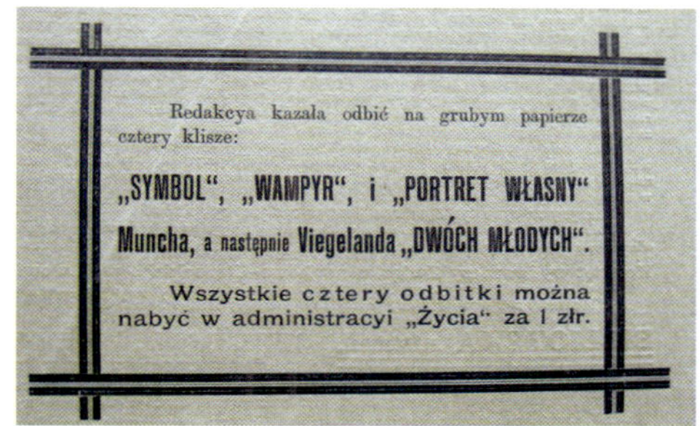

Fig. 19. Advertisement in *Zycie* (1899) urging people to buy reproductions of Edvard Munch's and Gustav Vigeland's works for one zloty each

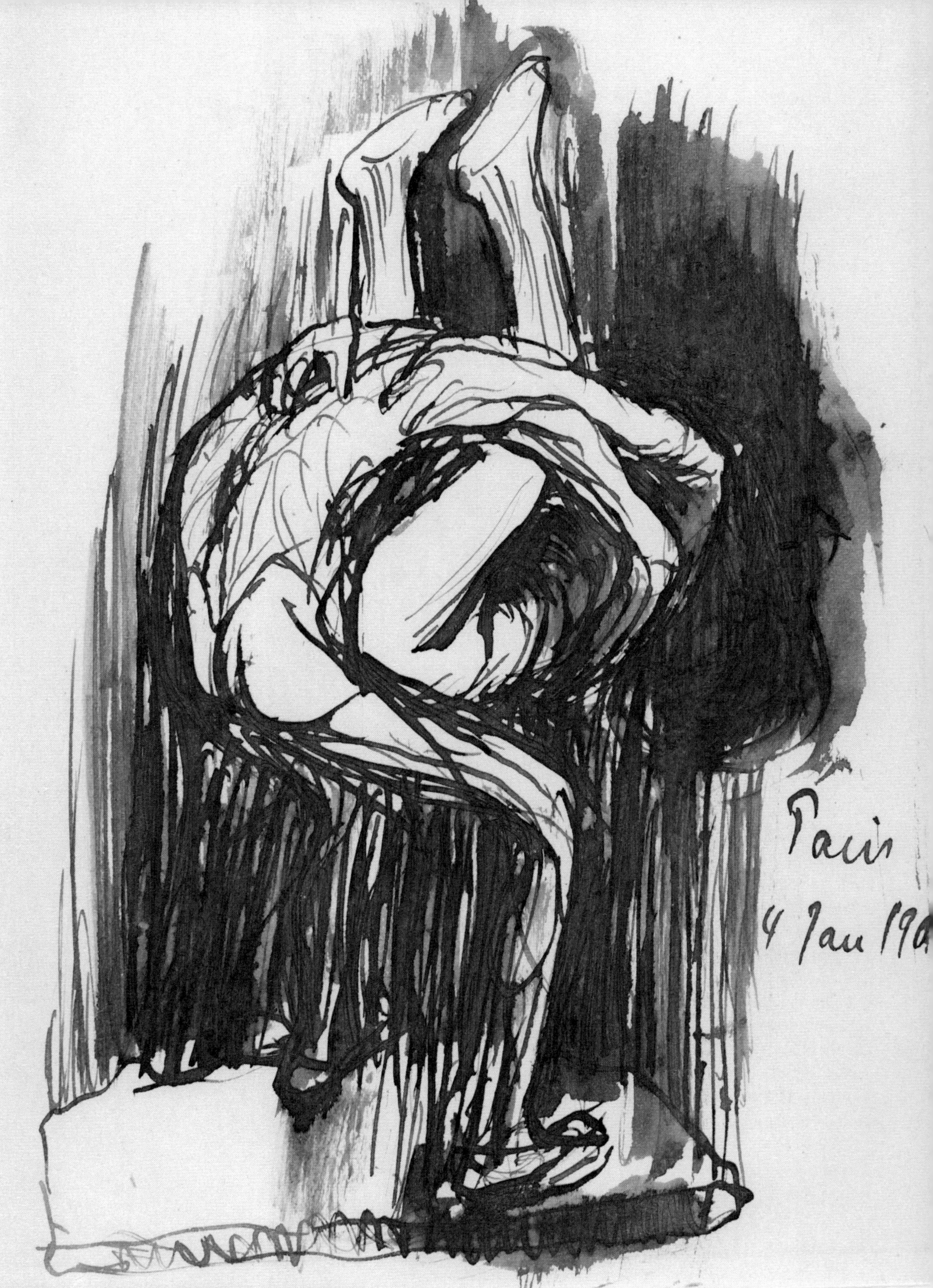
Paris
4 Jan 190

and shortly before she was killed in 1901 she had been lobbying in Warsaw on behalf of Munch.[92] Her death may have contributed to the fact that neither Munch nor Vigeland maintained contact with Przybyszewski in the years to come.

Eros

The two artists diverge most clearly from one another in their approach to erotic motifs. Whereas Vigeland depicts a number of direct and audacious representations of intercourse, Munch presents his subjects almost exclusively in a more veiled and composed manner (cats. 101, 118). *Madonna* is an interesting case in point (1894, cat. 114) being one of Munch's most famous erotic motifs. There are no direct depictions of intercourse in Munch's oeuvre, yet – based on the angle of the figure – we can imagine the presence of a male counterpart here. When the painting was exhibited at the Blomqvist Kunsthandel gallery in Kristiania in 1895 it was entitled 'A Woman Making Love'. And this is precisely how many perceive the motif; as a woman in the throes of ecstasy, reclining with eyes closed and her head slightly turned and tilted backwards. Furthermore, we recognise Munch's characteristic undulating, organic lines which encircle the female torso. He provoked many with this image, of course. The religious overtones indicated by the hint of a halo and the title of *Madonna*, did not simplify the matter.

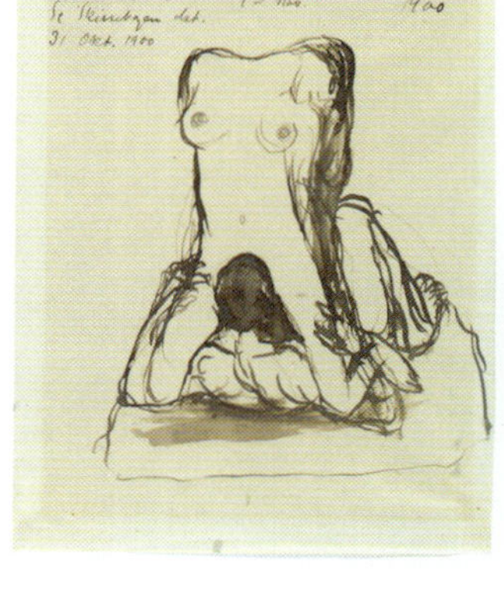

Fig. 21. Gustav Vigeland:
Erotic Drawing, 1900

In contrast to Munch, Vigeland created a motif of the act itself: *Coitus* (1897–98, cat. 16). This is the first depiction of intercourse in modern sculpture that does not hide behind a title inspired by mythology.[93] Keeping in mind the criticism that *Madonna* received, it is understandable that Vigeland never allowed *Coitus* to be exhibited. There is no doubt about what we see here. Vigeland has moved away from the characteristic *femme-fatale* representations, and he does not depict the act in a particularly dramatic or bestial manner. Nor is the woman in a dominating position. The couple appears mainly to be in a harmonious state of ecstasy, in a state of mutual sensual gratification. It is interesting to note certain similarities to Munch's *Madonna* when viewing Vigeland's sculpture from above: both of the female figures are leaning their heads backwards, slightly turned to the left, with long flowing hair spread around their faces and arms in a similar position, extended out to the side.

Vigeland's erotic fantasy was able to develop further when, in 1900, he travelled to France and England for an entire year, where he made hundreds of drawings with an even more risqué mode of expression (figs. 20, 21). Admittedly these were probably never intended for the public, but we can nevertheless observe that Vigeland added a plinth in most of the drawings, as if they were intended as sketches for later sculpture drafts. Here we see how Vigeland represented the act of intercourse more directly, compared to Munch. In Vigeland pure physical love is visualised.

Fig. 20. Gustav Vigeland:
Erotic Drawing, 1901

Around 1900

Vigeland had made a name for himself as a sculptor around the turn of the last century and he gradually sought inspiration from the art of the Renaissance and Classical Greece and Rome, rather than from his own contemporary art scene. He toned down his dramatic style and distanced himself from a melancholic atmosphere. His choice of motifs moved in the direction of more idealised male and female representations, such as *Young Man and Woman* (1906, fig. 22). This meant that both the formal elements and content that he shared with Munch during the 1890s disappeared. During this period Vigeland received many portrait and monument commissions,[94] which presumably made him certain about his change in style. In addition he met Inga Syverten (1883–1968), who would become his girlfriend, cohabitant and assistant for the following nineteen years.

Vigeland and Munch had minimal contact with each other during this period, with a few notable exceptions. Vigeland re-called a visit Munch made to his studio in 1900 'when my relief The Resurrection was cast in plaster'. Both of them had by now attained major stature in the art world, with occasionally overlapping backgrounds. As when Munch, the following year, in his obituary of Dagny writes: 'why has no one mentioned […] what she has done to introduce Norwegian art abroad, for example the sculptor Vigeland.'[95]

Munch was not in very good health during these years, largely due to excessive use of alcohol and a strained relationship with Tulla Larsen. Despite this he continued his travels and, in contrast to Vigeland, increased his exhibition activities in the following months. In spring 1902 Munch had his definitive breakthrough in Berlin when he exhibited *The Frieze of Life* at the Berlin Secession. It was also then that he met the ophthalmologist Max Linde from Lübeck, who would become his first patron.

Vigeland spent a few days in Åsgårdstrand in the summer of 1904, where he visited the author Jonas Lie of whom he modelled a portrait. As coincidence would have it, Vigeland recollected, when I 'disembarked in Aasgaardstrand Munch appeared, and he asked me if I wouldn't pay him a visit'.[96] Vigeland remembered 'a captain's cottage with a garden, a shed and a slope leading down to the fjord. In the room where we ate there was an enormous bed and a young female confirmand, who cooked and served the food. When I teased him about this, he said: I pay well.'[97] It must have been an enjoyable get-together, as they were served 'Salmon and ham (which was evidently carved with the world's dullest knife) and blueberries for dessert. In addition to beer and brandy and coffee in the garden.' Vigeland was not very excited about the paintings he saw; 'Enormous yellow and red canvases stood

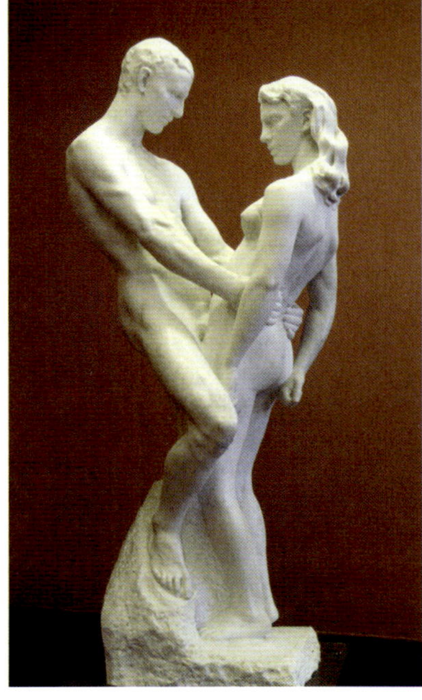

Fig. 22. Gustav Vigeland: *Young Man and Woman*, 1906

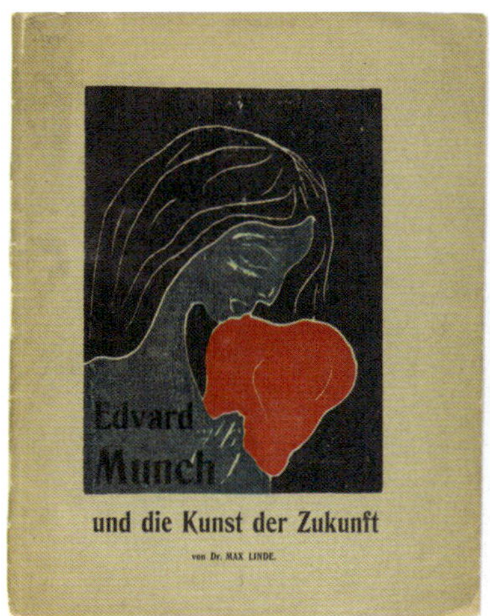

Fig. 23. Max Linde: *Edvard Munch und die Kunst der Zukunft*, 1902

Fig. 24. Edvard Munch: *Starry Night*, 1893

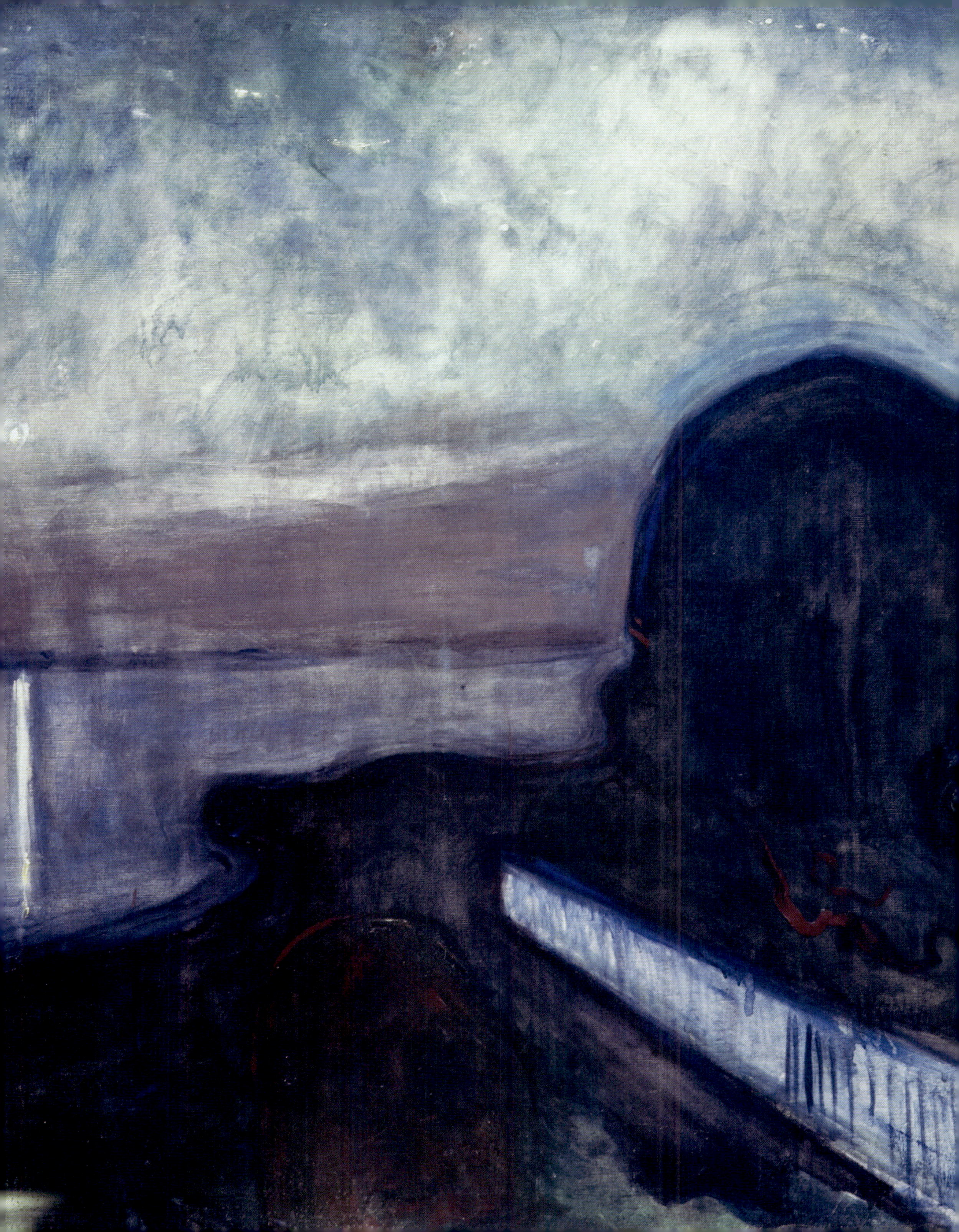

out in the yard, horrible things when it came to form', but appeared more interested in some of the lithographic caricatures of Gunnar Heiberg and Sigurd Bødtker.[98] The two men undoubtedly exchanged many anecdotes in Munch's garden, and Vigeland finally felt that he should go, because, as he wrote: 'He talked my head off.' Back in his hotel in Horten, he remembered the story of the Munch bust that he had smashed in Berlin, and contemplated aloud in a letter home to Inga: 'Perhaps I will make a mask of him; that is such an old story, that incident with the Munch bust. But then I may not be in the mood for it at all.' Only a few lines later in the same letter Vigeland comes to a decision: 'When I think about the bother with all the plaster I will postpone Munch's bust, or mask, it would, even if I were able to model him up until Saturday, be too short a time, so slow down. I do not wish to immerse myself in new pieces, we have enough to do for the time being in Hammersborg, too much, way too much.' So nothing came of the Munch bust after all.

When Munch opened a large solo exhibition that autumn in the Dioramalokalet on Karl Johan Street, as a board member of the National Gallery Vigeland suggested that they should acquire the painting *'Moonlight'*,[99] but the proposal was defeated. The exhibition – and Munch – received a glowing review in *Aftenposten*, penned by Vigeland's friend the art historian Hans Dedekam: 'Munch's superiority and significance stems from the deep roots that he has plunged into the psychological and emotional life of our times, in addition to his great talent as an artist, not least as a colourist.' He then pointed to Munch's kinship with Vigeland, by observing that they were both representatives of the artistic movements of the period: 'In Munch's and Vigeland's art one can sense the heartbeats of our time, in the future here at home one will find in it some of the most enlightening artistic documents of our time.'[100]

Joint Exhibitions

Vigeland and Munch participated in many of the same exhibitions, from Vigeland's debut at the Annual Autumn Exhibition in 1889 to the presentation of Norwegian art in Helsinki in 1911. The years 1902–11 stand out in particular, as both artists participated in exhibitions in Krefeld, Düsseldorf, Copenhagen, Brussels, Rome and Helsinki. Their reception varied yet they were repeatedly referred to as 'the two greats' from Norway.

The summer of 1902 was the first time they exhibited together since 1889, at the Nordic Art Exhibition in Krefeld.[101] The exhibition seems to have attracted little attention.[102] An important patron for Munch during this period was the German entrepreneur and art collector Albert Kollmann (1837–1915). He advised Munch to show his works together with Vigeland's in Berlin in spring 1903: '[…] it would be a guaranteed success in Berlin. But you cannot exhibit here again alone.'[103] Munch had participated in the Berlin Secession and had arranged a solo exhibition in Berlin the previous year, so a new joint show was perhaps sensible, but it is not known whether steps were taken to arrange such an exhibition. Both artists were busy; Munch was taken up with his accelerating exhibiting activities and Vigeland was

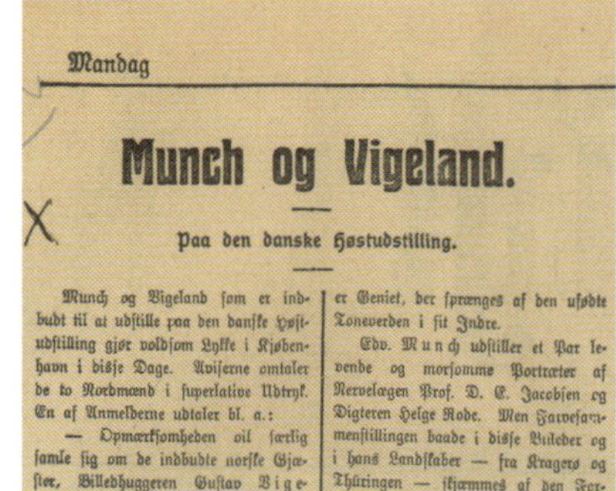

Fig. 25. 'Munch and Vigeland. At the Danish Autumn Exhibition'. *Dagens Nyt*, 8.11.1909

fully occupied that autumn, having taken over an old studio in Hammersborg that belonged to the municipality.

Munch exhibited eight paintings and Vigeland six portrait busts at the Norwegian Exhibition held in Charlottenborg, Copenhagen, in autumn 1906.[104] The exhibition received considerable press coverage, but it was primarily the older painters who are mentioned. Naturalism still held a dominant position. *Jyllandsposten* did not much like Munch's symbolist motifs *Moonlight* (1893) and *Starry Night* (fig. 24), and thought that it looked 'as though the artist had poured the contents of an enormous inkwell over a large canvas, and then come to the conclusion that it should depict "Night"'.[105] And further, that Munch had a 'complete lack of national Norwegian character'. Interestingly enough, the newspaper perceived Vigeland's works as the exact opposite: 'When one goes to the Norwegian exhibition to get a first-hand impression of the Norwegian people's distinctive character, one will actually find it most evident in Vigeland's expressive, strangely captivating portraits of men like Ibsen, Lie and others.'

'Munch and Vigeland [...] are enjoying enormous success in Copenhagen right now', *Dagens Nyt* could report three years later, in 1909.[106] Both artists had returned to Charlottenborg, especially invited to participate in the *Kunstnernes Efteraarsudstilling* [Danish Autumn Exhibition] (fig. 25),[107] where they were presented as 'the two great' living Norwegian artists. Many newspapers mentioned their participation,[108] and even claimed that they 'perform the same service as Hybenkradsere' (a strong alcoholic drink).[109] As usual some of Munch's works were criticised for being 'unfinished', but the superlatives were often waiting in the next sentence. Vigeland's 'lumpy treatment' was slightly better received this time, as when *Berlingske Tidende* called him a 'master of the sketch'.[110] Such extreme variation of opinion is difficult to understand. On the other hand, the newspaper called them both courageous; where Munch is not 'afraid of exposing his innermost being, and for whom art is far more than a pastime', and 'Vigeland is more unremitting and volatile than we are accustomed to down here, and his art is also an expression of what he has on his mind'.

Politiken wrote: 'In his best forms Gustav Vigeland has something of the power of salt, while Edvard Munch continues to have the effect of pepper.' The journalist was particularly enthusiastic about Vigeland's 'striking naturalism, and lifelike and concise style', while Munch's works were 'as always, very dissimilar'. Munch kept abreast of what was being written and remarked proudly: 'Kunstbladet thought that Alpha and Omega is the best work at the Charlottenburg [*sic*] exhibition – where Vigeland is also exhibited.'[111] The Danish periodical saw Munch's palette as his 'weakest feature' and as having 'a slightly garish tone', but admittedly also added in parentheses: 'compared to the lithographs, which are perhaps the best of what the exhibition has to offer.'[112] The same critic thought that Vigeland was superior to the other sculptors with: 'an intensive talent akin to Munch's.'

In 1910 the Exposition Universelle took place in Brussels, where both artists had a unique opportunity to show their works to an international public.[113] Twenty-six countries participated in the exhibition, which was very popular with a total of 13 million visitors. *Morgenbladet* reported that Munch had sent 'his large three-part bathing scene' and that Director Thiis had promised 'to be as helpful as possible with regard to the loan' among other works of Munch's '"Spring" and the portrait of his sister'.[114] Vigeland participated 'with some figure groups', which we can assume included *The Beggars*, *Man and Woman*, *Beethoven* and a bust in marble.[115]

The works were in all probability sent on to Rome, where the *Esposizione internazionale* opened on 27 March 1911.[116] *Ørebladet* was harshly critical of the presentation of the Norwegian section, and felt that 'a certain randomness has prevailed when it comes to the hanging, as well as the selection'.[117] Despite good pictures by Munch, the newspaper felt that his sparse representation 'is a palpable loss for our section', and blamed the contemporaneous exhibition in Finland for having robbed Norway of 'the representation it was entitled to at an international exhibition'. The reviewer had a point. There was little coverage of the Rome exhibit in the Norwegian press, and both artists were participating with a large number of works in Finland.

On 21 February 1910 the Norwegian Exhibition opened at the Ateneum Art Museum in Helsinki. Vigeland and Munch were referred to as 'the two masters' among the forty-five Norwegians participating.[118] Thiis had expedited the loan from the National Gallery in Kristiania and was responsible for the hanging of the artworks. Munch exhibited fifteen paintings, which were supplemented with a selection of lithographs after the opening.[119] Vigeland, the only participating sculptor, showed three portrait busts, as well as *The Beggars* and *The Sleepwalker* (1909). *Nya Pressen* wrote exultantly that he had 'his distinctive style and his immutable types [...] and a feel for lines and silhouettes, which places him far beyond the type of naturalism that characterises his treatment of details'.[120] Despite Vigeland's good reviews, it was Munch who received the greatest attention due to the Ateneum's acquisition of *Bathing Men* (1907, fig. 26). The critics were as usual divided into two groups: those who admired Munch's works, and those who found them grossly simplified. The acquisitions committee fortunately stuck to their decision, which they justified as follows: 'A picture can be unfinished in certain areas, and careless in details, without necessarily being a hurried sketch, and nevertheless exemplify painstaking studies, technical mastery and a powerful conception on the part of the painter.'[121]

The Helsinki exhibition was the last in which Vigeland and Munch participated together. One more attempt was actually made by Erik Werenskiold (1855–1938), in connection with the anniversary exhibition commemorating Norway's independence in 1914, when he endeavoured to have them present their work together with 'The Fourteen' in a separate art section.[122] Werenskiold wrote to Munch: 'Gustav Vigeland is with us. He says that he immediately swore to himself that he would not exhibit in a provisional building in Frogner as a showcase for the others. I think we should put the pressure on them, now that we have the opportunity; we should have the exhibition in our own building.'[123] However, both Vigeland and Munch were conspicuously absent from the exhibition in 1914.

After 1911 Vigeland slowed down his exhibiting activities. Only an additional seven exhibitions are known to have taken place during his lifetime, and most of them occurred in connection with his work on *The Fountain* and, later, the sculpture

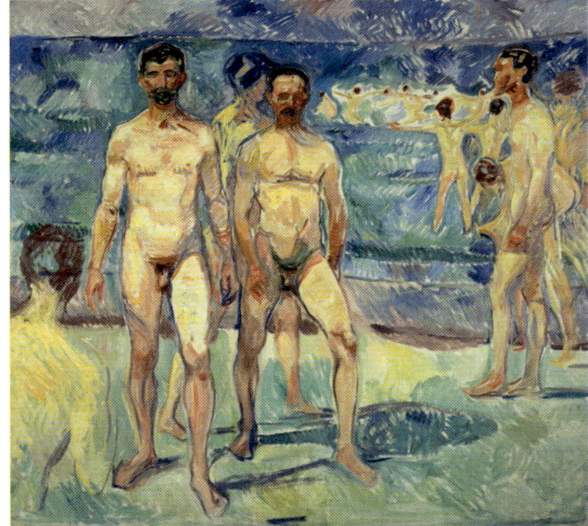

Fig. 26. Edvard Munch: *Bathing Men*, 1907

park. He no longer went to any great trouble to exhibit his works, and presumably had the same attitude as ten years previously, when he wrote to the Swedish art collector Ernest Thiel: 'Incidentally I do not like to exhibit [...] I find it distasteful to send my works on tour as though they were actors.'[124] The antithesis of Vigeland, Munch participated in a total of 23 exhibitions in the course of 1912 alone.[125]

The Struggle for a National Monument

When the union with Sweden was dissolved in 1905 the desire for an Eidsvoll monument arose to commemorate the new Kingdom of Norway in connection with the approaching centennial celebration of the Norwegian constitution in 1914. In 1906 a competition was announced for proposals for a monument to be placed in front of the Storting in Eidsvolls Square. Vigeland was already well advanced with his draft of *The Fountain* for the same location, which caused him concern, and he did not participate in the competition. However, he carried out an important tactical ploy with great success by exhibiting his model of *The Fountain* in the Museum of Applied Arts in Kristiania that same autumn.[126] A 'Fountain Committee' to support the project and collect funds was established and its prime mover, Hans Dedekam, tried to enlist the support of Munch, among others. Munch declined and asked Ludvig Ravensberg for assistance: 'Will you be so kind as to explain to Dedekam that I cannot – and why I cannot participate in the Fountain campaign – regardless of how fond I am of Vigeland's art – It is because I have been assailed by a dangerous internal ailment.'[127] Vigeland gained support from Andreas Aubert, Heiberg, Thiel and Thiis, among others, while Krohg and Gunnar Utsond stood in opposition.[128] Following a lengthy process a resolution was adopted in 1907 to commission *The Fountain* for Eidsvolls Square. At the same time a new and open competition for proposals regarding the Eidsvoll monument was announced in 1908. Vigeland was asked whether he could deliver a draft, but responded that he did not have the time.[129] He did work on several ideas for a tower-like monument in several drawings however, one of which possibly represents the first sketch to resemble a human column (fig. 27) composed of many figures that appear to swarm upward around the pillar. This may have functioned as a model when Vigeland made his first drafts for *The Monolith* in 1919 (cats. 199, 201).[130]

The first drafts for the second competition for an Eidsvoll monument were exhibited in spring 1909 at the Blomqvist Kunsthandel gallery.[131] At this time Munch was staying at Dr Jacobson's Clinic in Copenhagen, where he had received a visit the previous year from his childhood friend Olav Herman Paulsen (1862–1948),[132] who had won Second Prize in the monument competition in 1908 and 1910.[133] We can assume that Munch and Paulsen had animated discussions about the various entries. Following his return to Norway in the summer of 1909, Munch registered for the competition for the decoration of the University of Oslo's Aula (great hall). He immediately set to work on the drafts. Parallel with this work he wanted to sculpt and envisioned a sculpture of his 'large grave monument the *Funeral March*' (cat. 148),[134] possibly influenced by the current debate regarding the Eidsvoll monument. On 5 December 1909 *Aftenposten* launched a new proposal by the architect Henning Kloumann for a 20-metre-tall memorial tower in Vettakollen.

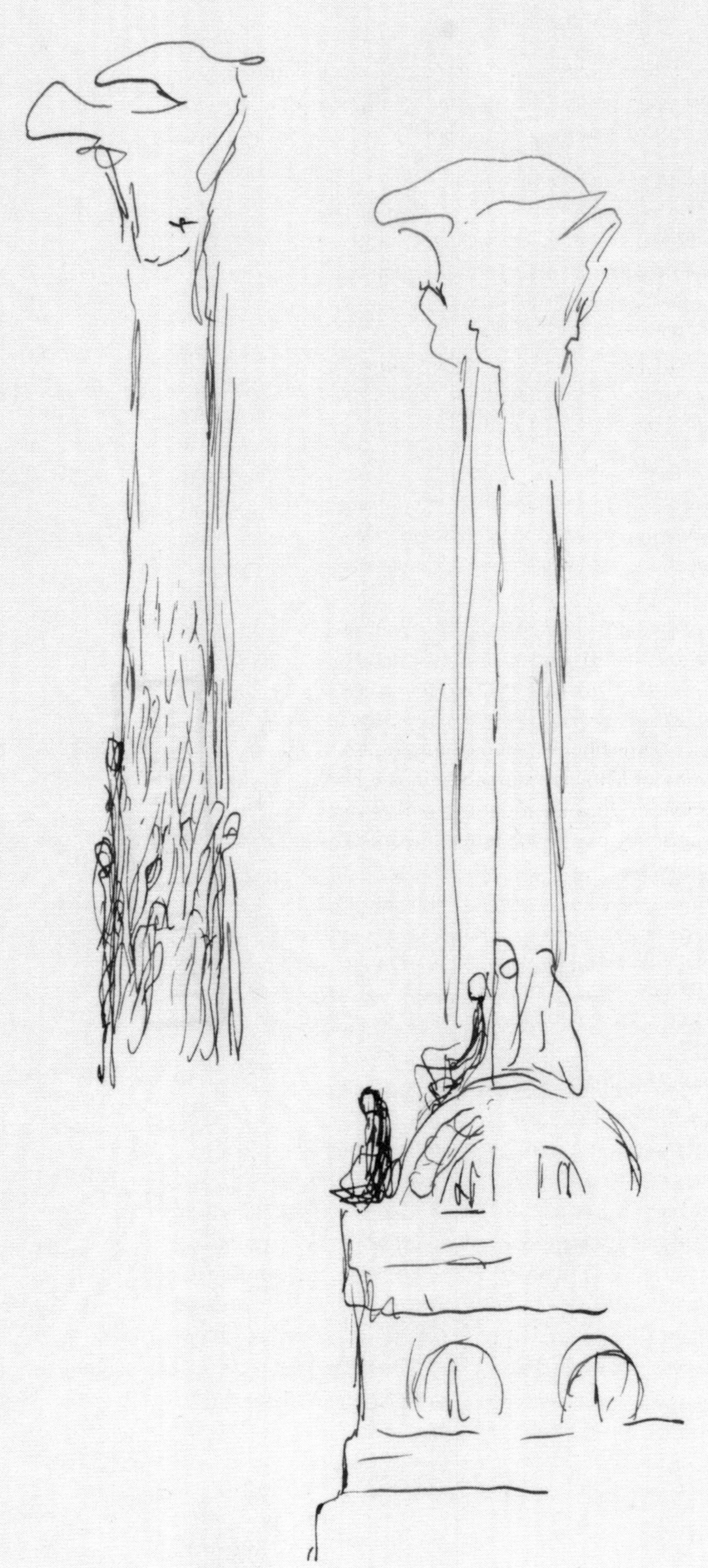

The tower's lower section was envisioned as a 'sculptural work in memory of events and people from the year of liberation'. Munch followed the debate with interest and wrote to Thiis from Kragerø:

> Incidentally! What do you think of the tower as Eidsvol [*sic*] monument? Kloumann's proposal? I myself think it is good – but I do not think Kloumann is the [right] architect – I believe a simple streamlined tower with large decorative panels and sculptures is a good idea – for example by me and sculptures by Vigeland – there would have to be a competition I suppose – I have not thought a lot about the idea for the panels – but I have thought a little about Norwegian landscapes in delightful springtime – and figures, resisting humans and chained human figures that have been liberated – In short, forces that are liberated.[135]

It was an exciting proposal coming from Munch, yet the collaboration was never realised. A joint effort by the 'two greats' might have had a good chance of winning the competition for a national monument. On the other hand, the committee never succeeded in erecting a monument to commemorate the anniversary of the Norwegian constitution in 1914. Munch did not stop creating countless sketches for sculptures and monuments in the next few years, however. There were figures that stood on columns (fig. 28) and plinths (cats. 182, 185), as well as large figure compositions (fig. 29). Nor did he put aside the idea of 'Chained human beings who are liberated'. In a large number of drawings from this period we see *Mother Norway* represented by a majestic female figure resembling *Alma Mater* sitting next to a young man in chains (cats. 177, 179). Parallel to his comprehensive Aula project, Munch also developed several ideas for monuments in the sculptural medium. Drawing did not satisfy his creative ideas, and he began to model some of his first sculptures.[136] In a letter to Gustav Schiefler of 11 May 1910, Munch enclosed a photograph of himself in front of the sculpture model for *Mother Norway*, and wrote: 'You see, I have also begun modelling – it is old Mother Norway with her young son (Norway's Independence) intended as a monument' (cat. 154).[137] As Gerd Woll has pointed out, all of the models of the *Mother Norway* motif undoubtedly had great significance for the *Alma Mater* figure that Munch was simultaneously developing for the Aula decorations, which incidentally also gained the character of a national monument.

In April 1915 the proposal to place *The Fountain* at Abelhaugen in the gardens of the Royal Palace was made public. The following year Vigeland exhibited expanded plans for the project along with models in his studio in Hammersborg. The viewing was a huge success, attracting hordes of viewers with accompanying press coverage. In this context, a few of Munch's drawings in which he sketched

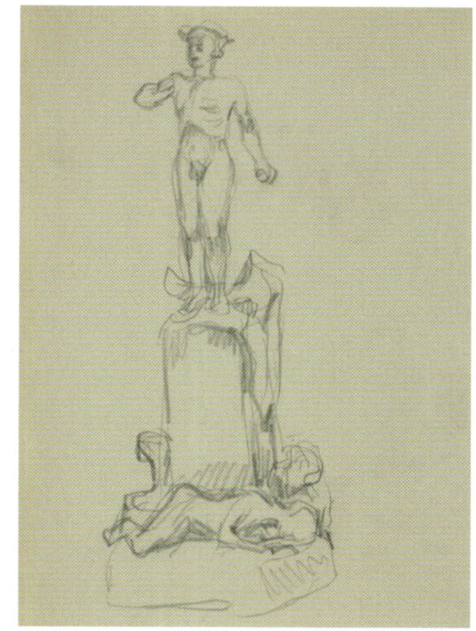

Fig. 28. Edvard Munch: *Sketch for a Monument*, 1910–20

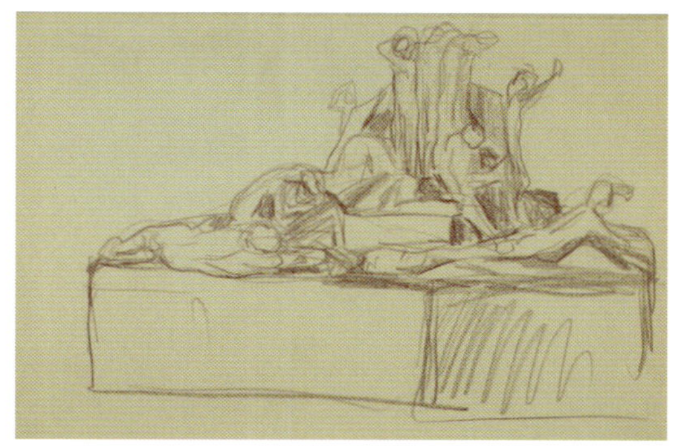

Fig. 29. Edvard Munch: *Draft for a Sculpture*, c. 1920

Fig. 27. Gustav Vigeland: *Draft for a Column Monument*, c. 1910 large-scale fountains are of particular interest (cats. 210, 211). Perhaps Munch was toying with the idea of a fountain of his own? In any case, inspiration from Vigeland appears to be likely since the fountains – like Vigeland's – are surrounded by figure groups, and in addition, appear to have the same location in mind: Abelhaugen.

After 1914 and the announcement of a competition for the Eidsvoll monument, Vigeland explored ideas for a monument, and in 1915–16 modelled a group of figures sitting tightly together, with standing male figures guarding them on either side (cat. 173). He continued to develop the group and placed it on a tall triumphal arch (cat. 172), and in 1920 offered to submit it as a proposal to the monument committee. The offer was accepted, but Vigeland did not submit his model until 1 January 1924[138] when a trial mock-up was mounted in front of the Storting in order to give an accurate impression. The proposal was rejected shortly after, on the grounds that it would lead to 'an insoluble clash in architecture styles between the monument and the buildings that comprised the Storting' (fig. 30).[139] In 1934–36 Vigeland resumed work on the sculpture, modelling it in a monumental format for placement in the sculpture park.[140]

In 1925 the subject of the Eidsvoll monument was raised for the last time, and a new competition was announced with the specific requirement for 'a column monument at least 20 metres tall, crowned with a figure that symbolised freedom, or the joy derived from freedom'.[141] Incredibly this coincided with Vigeland's completion of *The Monolith* in clay in its final format, over 17 metres tall. The sculptor Wilhelm Rasmussen (1879–1965) won the competition with an approximately 30-metre-tall column covered with reliefs and with an equestrian figure on top.[142] Interestingly enough Munch drew a standing figure on top of a tall column during the same period (fig. 31), in addition to new versions of *Mother Norway* in the same sketchbook. Here the figure was placed on a base shaped like a little mountain,[143] on a square foundation with a frieze[144] in a circular room with walls covered in decorations.[145] Munch probably modelled his sculpture *Mother Norway* during this period (cat. 174), which also has a high robust base, resembling many of the drawings. The sides of the base are flat – perhaps Munch envisioned subsequent additions of texts or a decorative frieze.

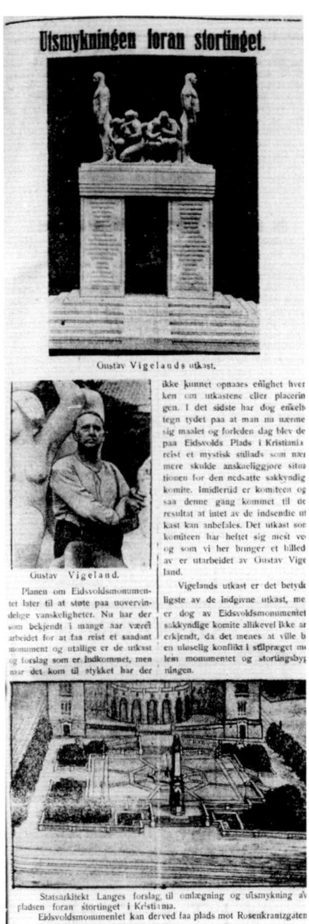

Fig. 30. 'The embellishment in front of the Parliament building'. *Nordre Bergenhus Amtstidende*, 4.2.1924

Established Artists

From the 1920s onwards there was minimal contact between Vigeland and Munch. They were both recognised artists who lived in relative isolation: Vigeland in Frogner and Munch at Ekely – both with good working conditions. Munch purchased the property Ekely in 1916, where he lived until his death. The eleven-acre estate consisted of a garden nursery, open fields and an orchard, and eventually a winter studio designed by an architect along with several large outdoor studios. In 1921

Vigeland signed a contract with the Municipality of Kristiania, which stated that the city would take over all of his works of art, and in exchange Vigeland was given a studio that would remain at his disposal for the rest of his life. It was also decided that the studio would later serve as a museum for the sculptor's works. In 1914 he moved in, and the same year the City Council approved the proposal to situate *The Fountain* in the open fields in Frogner. Vigeland devoted the remainder of his life to the sculpture park.

There is one last project that brought the two artists together: the commission to decorate the Freia Chocolate Factory's garden and premises in Rodeløkka, Kristiania, by its owner, Johan Throne Holst. Munch painted twelve pictures that were mounted in the women's cafeteria in 1922. The frieze was chiefly based on earlier motifs, with Åsgårdstrand's coastline as a unifying element. For the Freia garden Holst purchased sculptures by several artists, among them Vigeland's *Girl on a Bear* (1921) in 1926, for the pleasure of his employees.

During the 1920s and 1930s Munch uttered several bitter and rather offensive remarks about Vigeland. The utterances have most likely contributed to the mistaken perception of the two artists as arch-enemies.[146] The press – which gladly repeated rumours about the two, for instance the one about the encounter between 'the wholesaler and the travelling salesman' – also supported this misconception.[147] However, the following story, retold here by Vigeland, is not a myth:

> One day [Munch] and Jappe Nilssen came towards me in Kongensgate, it was outside Exellent and he said: 'You earn lots of money, you earn lots of money, you earn lots of money'. I patted him on the shoulder and said: Listen 'probenreuteren' [travelling salesman] He became perplexed, recoiled, took a few steps backward and said: 'Who-who-wholesaler. Wholesaler.' This encounter was incorrectly retold in the Swedish papers, but in its essence it was correct; E.M. started it. I only said the two mentioned words.[148]

They admittedly might be considered competitors during this period due to their desire for funding to realise their projects, but it would be difficult to find evidence of any direct hostility. The background for Munch's irritation was his ongoing battle with the tax authorities, which wanted to tax all of his drafts and unsold paintings at Ekely because they viewed the works as assets. Vigeland, on the other hand, avoided the problem because of his contract with the municipality, which owned all of his works. That he received considerable attention during this period, for his work on the sculpture park, may have also intensified Munch's irritation. As when he presumably read *Vor Tid*'s presentation of Vigeland's new studio and park project in 1924: 'Finally – one might say – the City Council has made its decision and Vigeland's fountain, the largest monumental work of our time, has found its spot – the spot which the artist himself had wished for.'[149] It is quite understandable that Munch felt that he was unfairly treated: 'My work can be compared with Vigeland's and everyone knows how he receives support, while I must keep my work including large works going with my own means.'[150] It was also important for Munch to point out that he was the first to develop the idea of a frieze of life, 'my decorative drafts which I have worked on for 40 years – have the same content about life as Vigeland's – but were nearly completed as large sketches many years before [Vigeland]'.[151]

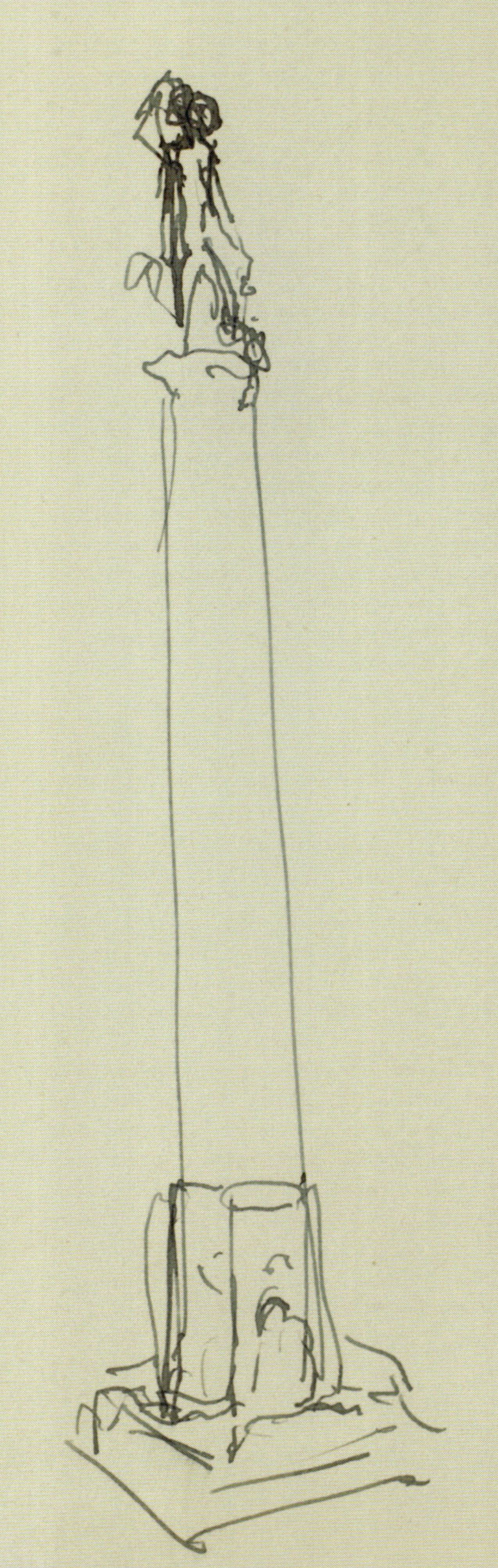

Munch continued: 'With all due respect to my friend Vigeland, but for me who has experienced how difficult it is to drum up money for one's work, it is mind-boggling to hear about their contribution of millions.' His irritation reached a climax in the notebook entitled 'My march through the Polar regions. Taxes and the Studios', in which Munch notes sarcastically: 'Look at how one fawns over Vigeland – He has only to spit and it is set in gold', and he repeats: 'the Government gives millions upon millions to Vigeland's Fountain – my idea [...] exhibited in the Berlin Secession four years before Vigeland initiated his which has the same content.'

Several of Munch's views were repeated to Vigeland: 'One day Johan Anker came by my studio in Hammersborg and told me he had met E.M. in Akersgaten. Munch stopped him and said: "Is Vigeland going to stretch himself all the way to Hamar with his work, to Trondhjem." Why does Munch say such things I asked Anker. Envious, you see, envious, you see, responded Anker.' Jens Thiis, who had had a falling out with Vigeland several years previously, supported Munch's criticism of the sculptor and reassured him by saying, 'you will never become egocentric and ruthless like him', and believed that Vigeland had changed 'from being an enchanting person in his youth' to become 'a self-appointed deity'.[152] Munch's criticism of Vigeland did not go unnoticed. As the sculptor wrote rather indifferently in 1933: 'I never think of E.M. but it seems that he never forgets me.'

Munch's biographer Atle Næss explains Munch's accusations and comparisons with Vigeland with the argument that 'Munch needed an adversary', and that 'his identity was so intimately linked to being "persecuted artist" that he had to create some of the persecutors himself'.[153] On the one hand, Munch's envy is understandable based on his taxation problems. On the other, it appears rather fruitless for the two elderly, established artists to waste their energy arguing whether one of them had conceived an idea before the other some thirty years ago. In addition, the frieze of life, or the cycle of life if you will, was a common theme popular with many artists.

Despite quarrels and critical remarks during their senior years, this article demonstrates that Vigeland and Munch were neither foes nor bitter rivals throughout their lives. They had many mutual acquaintances and interesting encounters when their paths crossed. Both of them repeatedly showed an interest in, and supported, the endeavours of the other – as when Vigeland encouraged the Executive Board of the National Gallery to purchase Munch's paintings, or when Munch envisioned plans for the two of them to create a national monument together. They met on several occasions, in addition to the period in Berlin – both in Vigeland's studio in Kristiania and for dinner at Munch's cottage in Åsgårdstrand. If critical opinions about one another eventually surfaced, it seems quite natural when one considers their position as Norway's 'two great' artists. This assessment was ultimately corroborated when the two became the first artists to receive the Grand Cross of the Royal Order of St Olav: Gustav Vigeland on 11 April 1929 'for his masterpieces as a sculptor' and Edvard Munch on 12 November 1933 'for outstanding work as an artist'.[154]

Fig. 31. Edvard Munch: *Standing Figure on a Tall Column*, 1920–30

1   For a more detailed account of Munch's early schooling, see Erik Mørstad, 'Edvard Munch's First School Years', in *Munch Becoming 'Munch': Artistic Strategies 1880–1892* (Oslo: Munch Museum/Labyrinth Press, 2008).

2   For an introduction to Vigeland's early schooling, see Guri Skuggen, 'Gustav Vigelands unge år', in *Billedhugger Gustav Vigelands Separat-Utstilling 1894* (Oslo: Vigeland Museum, 2008).

3   The building that now houses the National Gallery was at that time Kristiania Sculpture Museum, which consisted of the middle section only. The Sculpture Museum came under the jurisdiction of the Executive Board of the National Gallery in 1902.

4   Gustav Vigeland, *Erindringer* [Memoirs] (unpublished manuscript, Vigeland Museum), p. 22.

5   Jens Thiis, *Edvard Munch og hans samtid: slekten, livet og kunsten, geniet* (Oslo: Gyldendal Norsk Forlag, 1933), p. 65.

6   Munch participated in the Annual Autumn Exhibition every year between 1883 and 1891.

7   The exhibiting venues in Kristiania consisted mainly of the Sculpture Museum, the Christiania Art Association and Blomqvist Kunsthandel gallery as well as occasional use of the premises of the Dioramalokalet and the Tivoli. The National Art Exhibition (Annual Autumn Exhibition) was arranged annually but in alternate venues. In addition, bookshops had small displays in their windows, as when Olaf Væring's (1837–1906) photographs of Vigeland's *Hell* and *Judgement Day* were displayed at Grimsgaard's in Karl Johan Street, during Vigeland's solo exhibition in autumn 1894. Sophus Larpent, *Vigelandiana*, chronological records of Gustav Vigeland 1892–1903, unpublished, National Library of Norway, Oslo, Ms.fol.1821, p. 47.

8   Gustav Vigeland, *Erindringer*, p. 43.

9   Nils Messel, 'Edvard Munch and His Critics in the 1880s', in *Munch Becoming 'Munch': Artistic Strategies 1880–1892* (Oslo: Munch Museum/Labyrinth Press, 2008), pp. 168–69.

10   The Annual Autumn Exhibition was shown in the National Gallery's venues during the period 22.9.1888–31.10.1888. Munch most likely participated with the paintings *Evening* (1888) and *Karen Bjølstad* (1888).

11   Vigeland mentioned in his memoirs that he also had the landscapist Philip Barlag as a teacher at the Royal School of Design. Gustav Vigeland, *Erindringer*, p. 18.

12   According to the exhibition catalogue it was these two paintings Munch exhibited.

13   'En vestlandsk Billedhugger', *Fædrelandsvennen*, 4.11.1889. Jostein Andreassen, *Vilhelm Krag skriver... Avis- og tidsskriftartikler av Vilhelm Krag* (Brennåsen: Læremiddel-avdelingen, 1992), pp. 17–18.

14   Edvard Munch, *Livsfrisens tilblivelse* (Oslo: 1928–29).

15   Skuggen, 2008, p. 14.

16   Tone Wikborg writes that Vigeland also attended these gatherings 'on occasion'. Tone Wikborg, *Gustav Vigeland. En biografi* (Oslo: Gyldendal Norsk Forlag, 2001), p. 88.

17   They were all acquaintances of her children Vilhelm, Margrete, Kathrine and Ragna. Ragna was later married to Jens Thiis, Margrete to Nils Kjær and Kathrine to Erik Lie. Ole Mæhle, *Jens Thiis. En kunstens forkjemper* (Oslo: Gyldendal Norsk Forlag, 1970), p. 43.

18   The Juell sisters were introduced to literary circles in Kristiania by Hjalmar Christensen, who spent a lot of time with Krag. Roar Lishaugen, *Dagny Juel. Tro, håp og undergang* (Oslo: Andresen & Butenschøn, 2002), p. 54.

19   Harald and Edvard Meyer, *Norsk litteraturhistorie* (Oslo: Aschehoug, 1996), pp. 245–46.

20   The collection includes the poem 'Nat. Maleri af Edv. Munch' [Night. Painting by Edvard Munch], *Digte* (Bergen: John Grieg Forlag, 1891), pp. 34–37.

21   Vigeland attracted considerable attention with *The Accursed*, both in Charlottenborg and at the Annual Autumn Exhibition in 1892.

22   Hans-Martin Frydenberg Flaatten, *Edvard Munchs 'Skrik'* (MA thesis, Oslo: University of Oslo, 2004), p. 62.

23   Atle Næss, *Munch: En biografi* (Oslo: Gyldendal Norsk Forlag, 2004), p. 134.

24   Munch in a letter to Karen Bjølstad 17.11.1892, Munch Museum, MM N 786.

25   Przybyszewski had already travelled to Berlin in 1889 to study architecture. By the time Munch arrived in 1892 he had made a name for himself in the local art and literary circles for his essays on Chopin, Nietzsche and Ola Hansson.

26   Karen Bjølstad wrote to Munch on 11.12.1892 that she had read in *Dagbladet* that he had painted a portrait of Strindberg. Munch later donated the painting to the Nationalmuseum in Stockholm, and today it is in the Moderna Museet's collection.

27   The series called 'Love' probably included the six paintings *Summer Night's Dream*, *The Voice*, *Kiss*, *Vampire*, *Madonna*, *Melancholy* and *The Scream*.

28   In a letter to Franz Servaes dated December 1893, Przybyszewski mentions that he has begun an article on Munch. Władysława Jaworska, 'Munch-Przybyszewski', in *Totenmesse. Munch-Weiss-Przybyszewski* (Warsaw: Museum of Literature, 1995), p. 28.

29   Stanisław Przybyszewski, 'Foreword', in *Das Werk des Edvard Munch*, with contributions by Stanisław Przybyszewski, Franz Servaes, Willy Pastor and Julius Meier-Graefe (Berlin: S. Fischer Verlag, 1894), p. 4.

30   Upon the death of Dagny Juel Przybyszewska in 1901 Munch wrote, 'I recall for example, how in the last days before my exhibition in Berlin opened, she nearly took more initiative than I, and helped with the hanging and arrangement', *Kristiania Dagsavis*, 25.6.1901.

31   Stanisław Przybyszewski, 'Psychischer Naturalismus', in *Neue Deutsche Rundschau (Freie Bühne)*, vol. 5, no. 2 (Berlin: S. Fischer Verlag, 1894), pp. 150–56.

32   Translation from German by Margaret Clarke. See the article by Przybyszewski in this catalogue.

33   In a footnote to the title of the article the editor, Otto Julius Bierbaum (1865–1910), explains that the text was published on the credit of the author's esteemed reputation after the publication of *Totenmesse*, and not because of Munch's pictures. Przybyszewski, *Psychischer Naturalismus*, 1894, p. 150.

34   Among other things he deletes the title *Psychischer Naturalismus* and shortens the text.

35   Munch wrote home to his aunt Karen: 'I have good faith that there will soon be an improvement in the monetary situation [...] I have several good friends down here so I can always manage – I spend a lot of time with a promising Polish poet Przybyschewski [sic].' MM N 803, Munch Museum.

36   *The Accursed* was exhibited in the Sculpture Museum's showcase room and received extensive coverage in *Dagbladet*, 17, 20, 23.5.1894.

37   Thiis has written about one festive June day that summer, which began at the Grand Café in the company of Obstfelder, Finne and Przybyszewski, and continued at Finne's place in Nordstrand, after which they took the morning train down to the city, where they wandered together along Karl Johan with a violin-playing Obstfelder in the lead. Thiis, 1933, p. 212.

38   Gabriel Finne, 'Et stort Skulpturværk', *Norske Intelligenssedler*, 16.8.1894.

39 Przybyszewski in a letter to Eberhard von Bodenhausen, August 1894, ('etwas fabelhaftes an psychischer darstellungskraft'), Michael M. Schardt (ed.), *Stanisław Przybyszewski. Briefe 1879–1927*, vol. 8 (Oldenburg: Igel Verlag Literatur, 1999), p. 60.

40 There are two painted portraits in existence, dated 1894 (cat. 46) and 1895 (cat. 25) and a lithograph dated 1895 (cat. 122).

41 For example Munch's woodcut *Salome Paraphrase* (1898), the lithograph *Salome* (1903) and the intaglio print *Salome II* (1905).

42 The exhibition included 51 works and was shown in the period 21.10.–16.11.1894. Trine Otte Bak Nielsen, 'En uhyggelig Kunstudstilling', *Billedhugger Gustav Vigelands Separat-Udstilling 1894* (Oslo: Vigeland Museum, 2008), p. 23.

43 Jens Thiis, 'Gustav Vigeland II', *Verdens Gang*, 9.11.1894.

44 Munch presented drawings and 69 paintings in Konstföreningen in Stockholm, during the period 1–31.10.1894.

45 According to Larpent the letter was dated 16 or 18.11.1895. Larpent, 1892–1903, pp. 57–58, notes 47 and 48.

46 The letter from *Pan* was signed Julius Meier-Graefe (1867–1935), art historian and one of the periodical's founders, and according to Larpent was dated 17.11.1895. Larpent, 1892–1903, p. 61.

47 Larpent, 1892–1903, p. 63. for unknown reasons the trip was postponed for a few months.

48 Stanisław Przybyszewski, *On the Paths of the Soul*, in this catalogue.

49 Here Vigeland received Przybyszewski's latest book *Vigilien*, which he signed 'To my brother Gustav Vigeland Stachu. Pankow 8 Febr. 95' (fig. 12). The book exists in Vigeland's preserved library in the Vigeland Museum.

50 Stenersen apparently quotes Munch: 'In our poverty we shared everything, even a girlfriend. One evening I took her out, although it was really Vigeland's turn. When I came back and was on my way upstairs I saw Vigeland's burly figure at the top landing. As soon as I was in sight he ran back into the room and returned a moment later with a bust of me he had just finished. This he threw at me with great fury – barely missing. It frightened me so that I dashed out and ran all the way to the railway station and jumped onto a train.' Rolf Stenersen, *Edvard Munch: Close-up of a Genius* (Oslo: Gyldendal Norsk Forlag, 1969), p. 13.

51 Stenersen, 1969, p. 25.

52 The letter, which according to Lødrup was addressed to Larpent and dated 13.3.1895, is not included in the Vigeland Museum's Correspondence Collection and thus cannot be verified. Hans. P. Lødrup, *Gustav Vigeland* (Oslo: Nasjonalforlaget, 1945), p. 52.

53 Gustav Vigeland, notebook 1, 1935, unpaginated, Vigeland Museum.

54 Gustav Vigeland, notebook W179, 1933, upaginated, Vigeland Museum.

55 Thiis, 1933, p. 221.

56 Næss, 2004, p. 155

57 7.12.1894, Count Harry Kessler, *Tagebuch, 1892–1897*, vol. 2, trans. Elisabeth Lønnå (Stuttgart: Deutschen Schillergesellschaft, 2004), pp. 300–1.

58 The first issue of *Pan* was published on 1.4.1895 in Berlin. This was probably the first time Vigeland's works were presented to a foreign public, and with a full-page reproduction of *Hell*. Among the Nordic contributors were Axel Gallén (Akseli Gallen-Kallela; 1865–1931), Arne Garborg (1851–1924) and Theodor Kittelsen (1857–1914), in addition to more established figures such as Arnold Böcklin, Félicien Rops, Max Klinger, Stéphane Mallarmé and Richard Dehmel. Vigeland was thus accepted into the fold, when placed alongside major European writers and artists from the symbolist art movement of the 1890s. The Norwegian public also had the opportunity to see this, as *Pan* was sent to Kristiania and the Blomqvist Kunsthandel gallery, where the journal was displayed to the public.

59 These were most likely the 14 photographs that the renowned photographer Olaf Væring had recently taken of Vigeland's works: 'Pigen/The Girl – Bedende kone/ Praying Woman – Father and Daughter – Life and Death – Tvivleren/The Doubter– Dance – En syg Mand/A Sick Man – Man and Woman. Forfölgelsen 'Vold'/ Persecution 'Violence' – Barnebuste/ Bust of a Child – Helhesten/Journey to the Underworld – The Drunkards. 'The Murderer prays for the Drunkards' – Old Mother and Two Children – To Unge/ Youths – The Revenant.' Larpent, 1892–1903, p. 60.

60 The offer was probably well received by Vigeland and Larpent, who from the time of the solo exhibition in Kristiania had attempted to raise enough money to cast it in bronze. Vigeland in a letter to Sophus Larpent, 19.3.1895, no. 1138, Vigeland Museum.

61 Vigeland in a letter to Sophus Larpent, 30.4.1895, no. 1139, Vigeland Museum.

62 Thiis, 1933, p. 221.

63 '[...] they exhibited together, but then M. felt that G. received excessive praise and G. felt that M. received excessive praise and so they had a falling out', Gustav Vigeland, notebook W179, 1933, unpaginated, Vigeland Museum.

64 Vigeland made a new version in 1898 (see cat. 52).

65 Arne Eggum, *Edvard Munch. The Frieze of Life from Painting to Graphic Art* (Oslo: J.M. Stenersens Forlag AS, 2000), p. 165.

66 Aside from the portrait busts of Dagny and Munch, which he destroyed, he made 'two groups and a relief'. The relief is difficult to identify, but the groups were most likely *The Prostrated* (cat. 50) and *The Kiss*. Vigeland in a letter to Sophus Larpent from Berlin, 16.3.1895, no. 1137, Vigeland Museum.

67 Gustav Vigeland, notebook 1, 1935, unpaginated, Vigeland Museum.

68 The photograph is included among Munch's preserved possessions.

69 Lødrup, 1945, p. 52.

70 Vigeland in a letter to Sophus Larpent from Berlin, 19.3.1895, no. 1138, Vigeland Museum.

71 Knut Hamsun in a letter to Heinrich Martens, autumn 1895, Harald S. Næss (ed.), *Knut Hamsuns brev 1879–1895* (Oslo: Gyldendal Norsk Forlag, 1994), p. 484.

72 Zenon was born on 28.9.1895, but when he was christened in St Olav's Church in Kristiania on 29.5.1896, Vigeland was probably in Florence. As a non-Catholic Vigeland's name was not registered in the church records. Lishaugen, 2002, p. 107.

73 He signed the text 'Kongsvinger (Norwegen) 11.1895'.

74 The monograph was published by Kritik Verlag in 1897; see the complete text in this catalogue.

75 Gustav Vigeland, notebook W179, 1933, unpaginated, Vigeland Museum.

76 Gustav Vigeland, notebook W179, 1933, unpaginated, Vigeland Museum.

77 Vigeland also mentions a visit from the writer in a letter to Elin Danielson, 20.8.1895, no. 1720, Vigeland Museum.

78 The portrait mask's previous dating to 1894 most likely stems from Hans Dedekam's note: 'Apparently 1894.' Dedekam writes in the same note that the bust was not made in Berlin, but in Pilestredet in Kristiania. Hans Dedekam, *Dedekams dagbokopptegnelser, 1907–27*

(unpublished, Vigeland Museum), p. 50. As there is no documentation to confirm that Przybyszewski and Vigeland met in 1894, as opposed to the following year, it is more likely that the correct dating should be 1895. Lødrup has also dated the portrait mask to 1895; see Lødrup, 1945, p. 37.

79 Vigeland made a woodcut of the author around 1929 (fig. 43).

80 Vigeland in a letter to Sophus Larpent, 20.1.1901, no. 33, Vigeland Museum.

81 Stanisław Przybyszewski, *Over bord* (Copenhagen: Det Nordiske Forlag, 1896).

82 It was probably the novel's main character, a melancholy painter, that Munch believed was intended to represent himself. Dagny adamantly denied this: 'I cannot quite fathom how you for a second could believe that Stachu would write something that was disturbing to you. I hardly know anyone who he is more fond of.' Dagny Juel Przybyszewska in a letter to Munch, undated, K 1935, Munch Museum.

83 Larpent was an art collector and an important patron for Vigeland throughout the 1890s. He bequeathed his Vigeland collection, which consisted of 55 sculptures, one charcoal drawing and 46 drawings for *Hell*, to the National Gallery. Skuggen, 2008, p. 20.

84 In 1896 Przybyszewski published 'Ein unbekannter' in four parts in the German periodical *Die Kritik*; the same article was printed in the Czech *Moderní Revue*. 'En ubekendt' was published in the October issue of the Danish periodical *Tilskueren*. This version was shortened by several pages, which suggests that Przybyszewski may have edited the text after having read Larpent's critique.

85 Vigeland in a letter to Sophus Larpent, 20.6.1896, no. 1167, Vigeland Museum.

86 Vigeland in a letter to Sophus Larpent, 8.7.1896, no. 1169, Vigeland Museum.

87 On his way home from Spain Przybyszewski met Munch and several Polish artists.

88 Przybyszewski contributed articles to various periodicals including *Zycie* (Krakow), *Tilskueren* (Copenhagen), *Die Zeit* (Vienna), *Die Kritik* (Berlin), *Chimera* (Warsaw), *Moderní Revue* (Prague) and *L'art* (Paris).

89 Stanisław Przybyszewski, 'Edvard Munch', *Moderní Revue*, V (Prague: 1897). There is a typewritten translation in the Munch Museum Library.

90 In *Zycie* an advertisement announced that one could purchase photographic reproductions of a selection of Munch's works for one zloty per photo by contacting the editors.

91 Przybyszewski was a driving force in Polish cultural circles, in particular within the art movement known as 'Young Poland', whose members were influenced by Munch's works.

92 Dagny was in contact with the art salon Krywult. Contact between Munch and Krywult continued after her death, and in December 1903 Munch opened an exhibition of about 70 graphic works in Warsaw.

93 Jan Kokkin, 'Gustav Vigelands erotiske kunst i europeisk perspektiv', in *Eros i Gustav Vigelands kunst* (Oslo: Grøndahl Dreyers Forlag, 1996), p. 43.

94 Among the most important projects that consolidated Vigeland's position was his monument to the mathematician Niels Henrik Abel (1905), which was unveiled in the gardens of the Royal Palace in 1908.

95 *Kristiania Dagsavis*, 25.6.1901.

96 Vigeland in a letter to Inga Syvertsen, 27.7.1904, 1768, Vigeland Museum.

97 Gustav Vigeland, notebook W179, 1933, unpaginated, Vigeland Museum.

98 Gustav Vigeland, notebook 1, 1935, unpaginated, Vigeland Museum.

99 It is not known which painting the catalogue title refers to. In 1907 Vigeland again proposed to order a painting by Munch; 'as I think it would surely be a good thing if we also had in the museum's possession "Sick Girl" painted in the manner in which Munch paints today. Incidentally I don't think it is possible. I will with difficulty probably only get 1 vote along with mine like the last time I proposed the purchase of a Munch picture and the Chairman asked me to give my opinion.' Wikborg, 2001, p. 235.

100 Hans Dedekam, 'Kunst og folkemening', *Aftenposten*, 22.10.1904.

101 'Nordische Kunstaustellung', Krefeld, Germany (15.5– 22.9.1902). Munch exhibited one painting and Vigeland seven sculptures.

102 The next exhibition they participated in together, the international art exhibition in Düsseldorf (1.5.1904 – 23.10.1904), also attracted little attention. Catalogue in the Vigeland Museum Library.

103 Albert Kollmann in a letter to Munch, 31.10.1902, K 3940, Munch Museum.

104 The exhibition opened on 1.10.1906.

105 'Norsk Malerkunst. Udstilling paa Charlottenborg. III', *Jyllandsposten*, 15.11.1906.

106 'Munch og Vigeland. Paa den danske høstudstilling', *Dagens Nyt*, 8.11.1909.

107 Exhibition period: 6.11.1909 – 19.12.1909. Munch exhibited the paintings *Helge Rode*, *Daniel Jacobson*, *Weeping Woman*, *Spring in Kragerø* and *Snow Landscape, Thüringen*, and twelve lithographs from the series *Alpha and Omega*. Vigeland exhibited *The Beggars*, *Beethoven*, *Man and Woman (Adoration)* and *Ernest Thiel*.

108 Several newspapers drew attention to the artists in their headlines: 'Munch og Vigeland. Paa den danske høstudstilling' (*Dagens Nyt*, 8.11.1909), 'Edv. Munch og Gustav Vigeland' (*Morgenbladet*, 8.11.1909), 'Munch og Vigeland i Danmark' (*Verdens Gang*, 30.11.1909) and 'Norsk kunst paa Efteraarsudstillingen. Vigelands 'Tiggerne'. – Edv. Munchs Portræter' (*Politiken*, 28.11.1909).

109 F.B., 'Kunstnernes Efteraarsudstilling', *Berlingske Tidende*, 10.11.1909.

110 'Kunstnernes Efteraarsudstilling', 10.11.1909.

111 Munch in a letter to Jappe Nilssen, 1.2.1910, brevs. 604 (PN 733), National Library of Norway.

112 Harald Giersing, 'Kunstnernes Efteraarsudstilling II', *Kunstbladet*, December 1909, p. 319.

113 Exhibition period: 23.4 – 1.11.1910.

114 'Norsk kunst i Bruxelles og Rom', *Morgenbladet*, 15.6.1910.

115 According to the catalogue for the international exhibition in Rome the following year, where it is likely that the same works were shown.

116 With the exception of Munch's three-part bathing scenes. According to the catalogue Munch exhibited only two paintings: 'Portrait of the Artist's Sister' and 'The Patient'. The latter is probably the painting *Spring* (1889). 'Catalogo Della Mostra Di Belle Arti', *Esposizione Internationale di Roma* (Bergamo: Istituto Italiano D'arti Grafiche, 1911), Munch Museum Library.

117 'Fra Udstillingen i Rom. Kritiske bemerkninger om den norske Afdeling', *Ørebladet*, 16.4.1911.

118 A.M. Tollet, 'Den norska utställningen', *Hufvudstadsbladet*, 12.3.1911.

119 Erik Kruskopf, *Edvard Munch och Finland*, in the series Munch-museets skrifter, vol. 4 (Oslo: Munch Museum, 1968), p. 309.

120 The sculptures are described in S.F., 'Den norska utställningen', *Nya Pressen*, 8.4.1911.

121 'Munchs tafla', *Nya Pressen*, 21.4.1911.

122 The artist group 'The Fourteen' was composed of young Norwegian

painters inspired by Matisse, who broke out of the official art section due to a breach of trust in the exhibition's artistic leadership. Marit Werenskiold, *De norske Matisse-elevene. Læretid og gjennombrudd 1908–1914* (Oslo: Gyldendal Norsk Forlag, 1972), pp. 105–06.

123 Erik Werenskiold in a letter to Munch, 8.11.1910, MM K 1241, Munch Museum.

124 Vigeland in a letter to Ernest Thiel, 9.12.1899, no. 796, Vigeland Museum.

125 Practical causes – in addition to economic challenges – made it difficult for Vigeland to ship his sculptures to exhibitions. Fragile sculptures in plaster could easily be damaged, and heavy bronze sculptures demanded extra transportation requirements. In comparison, it was simpler to handle paintings and prints.

126 Around 30,000 people visited the exhibition during the period 14.10.–25.11.1906. Tone Wikborg, 2001, p. 248.

127 Munch in a letter to Ludvig Ravensberg, 1.2.1907, MM N 2849.

128 Vigeland does not seem to bear any grudge against Munch after this, as he sends a proposal in December to the National Gallery suggesting that the Board of Directors approach Munch to commission a new version of 'The Sick Girl'. Vigeland in a letter to the gallery's Board of Directors, 10.12.1907, Journal, no. 107/1907, National Gallery/NG-1000, Da-L0008.

129 Tone Wikborg, *Gustav Vigeland. Mennesket og kunstneren* (Oslo: Aschehoug, 1983), p. 126.

130 He executes *The Monolith* in its final size 1:1 in 1924–25.

131 Gerd Woll, *Edvard Munch. Monumental Projects 1909–30* (Lillehammer: Lillehammer Bys Malerisamling/Munch Museum, 1993), p. 59.

132 Paulsen thanks Munch for the time they spent together in 'Copenhagen last year' in a letter to the artist dated 23.3.1909, MM K 898, Munch Museum.

133 Glenny Alfsen, 'Olav Paulsen', *Norsk kunstnerleksikon* (20.11.2014). This information is taken from the website https://nkl.snl.no/Olav_Paulsen (accessed 15.4.2015).

134 Munch in a letter to Gustav Schiefler, 10.6.1909, no. 492, in Arne Eggum (ed.), *Edvard Munch/Gustav Schiefler. Briefwechsel*, vol. I, 1902–14 (Hamburg: Verlag Verein für Hamburgische Geschichte, 1987), p. 35b.

135 Munch in a letter to Jens Thiis, 1909–10, MM N 3092.

136 See the article by Erika Gohde Sandbakken in this catalogue.

137 Munch in a letter to Gustav Schiefler, 11.5.1910. Eggum (ed.), 1987, p. 377.

138 Wikborg, 2001, p. 386.

139 'Utsmykningen foran Stortinget', *Nordre Bergenhus Amtstidende*, 4.2.1924.

140 This was Vigeland's biggest sculpture after *The Monolith*, which was not cast and installed in the park until 1988.

141 Arne Brenna, *Eidsvolds plass Studenterlunden og Glasshuset* (Oslo: Selskabet for Oslo Byes Vel, 1985), p. 26.

142 Due to the artist's membership of the Norwegian fascist party Nasjonal Samling the work was halted after 1945.

143 MM T 00195-51, Munch Museum.

144 MM T 00195-73, Munch Museum.

145 MM T 00195-32, Munch Museum.

146 Rolf Stenersen also contributed to the mystification surrounding Munch's criticism of Vigeland in his biography on the artist: 'They never became friends' and 'It tormented Munch to see how Vigeland got hold of 10–12 million kroner, while he had to spend money on taxes'. Stenersen, 1969, p. 14.

147 The story was retold among other places in *Svenska Dagbladet* (8.6.1927), *Aftenposten* (10.6.1927) and in Stenersen, 1969, p. 81.

148 Gustav Vigeland, notebook W179, 1933, unpaginated, Vigeland Museum.

149 The periodical is included in Munch's personal library in the Munch Museum. S.K., 'Fra Vigelands atelier', *Vor Tid*, no. 51, 1924.

150 Munch in a note, 1930–40, MM N 82, Munch Museum.

151 Edvard Munch, undated annotation in a sketchbook, MM T 2703, Munch Museum.

152 Jens Thiis in a letter to Edvard Munch, 25.4.1941, MM K 1171, Munch Museum.

153 Næss, 2004, p. 462.

154 O. Delphin Amundsen, *Den kongelige norske Sankt Olavs Orden 1847–1947* (Oslo: Grøndahl & Søns Forlag, 1947), p. 23.

Stanislaw Przybyszewski.

Auf den Wegen der Seele.

On the Paths of the Soul.
Gustav Vigeland

Stanisław Przybyszewski

I.

The road to understanding life is twofold: one broad, well-trodden, safe and comfortable, the other unpaved, running over precipices, abounding in mortal dangers ... Don't the old stories tell us so?

The comfortable road is the way of the brain, of the wretched five senses, capable of grasping life solely in its fortuitousness, in its hopeless commonplaceness.

The steep, precipitous road is the way of the soul, for which life is a heavy dream and gloomy foreboding, the real existence in its essence and contents.

These ways differ, for the brain is the weekday, the day of work and heavy toil, mathematics and logic, while the soul is a rare feast-day, the lack of rules, a lightning that throws logic away on top of a rubbish heap.

The soul is an organ that comprehends what is infinite and spaceless and in which heaven and earth flow into each other, the organ through whose help Catherine Emmerich, a rather uneducated person, described – with a meticulous, almost archaeological precision – the places where Christ suffered, and depicted the torments of his Way of the Cross with a physiological knowledge of the matter. The soul is an organ of visionary ecstasies and somnambulistic *clairvoyances*, the organ of the highest morbid excitement in which Rops created his *Sataniques* and Chopin the B-minor Sonata.

For the brain two times two is four but for the soul it can be a million, because the soul knows no intervals, either in time or in space. For the brain an object can exist solely within space and time, whereas the soul can perceive the objectless, spaceless and timeless essence of things. And what is inconceivable for the brain can occur in the soul; the soul strips everything of accidentality, of all the forms in which it shows itself to the brain. The soul perceives only what is immortal, infinite and boundless, undulating between the two poles and continuing throughout all times and all generations: the *matrix* of all phenomena.

The brain stands for materialism in the field of knowledge; it is the science of the smallest forces of mass, psychophysics, psychology (which claims the right to be called *chimie de l'âme*), socialism and uncountable economical systems whose aim is to make man happy by means of collective work. The brain is also the art of the thoughtless and soulless mob – naturalism.

The soul is the fear of depth, unending inner vision, unusually rare manifestation of power and abilities, the organ endowed unlike the brain, which has at

Stanisław Przybyszewski: *On the Paths of the Soul*, 1894. Published by Kritik Verlag, Berlin, 1897 its disposal only five miserable senses. The soul is a state in which life, dispersed among millions of particles, regains its unity; millions of particles combine into a single simple form and millions of centuries blend in one second.

Artists follow twofold paths in their quest for the ultimate truth of life. Some try to render their sense impressions faithfully, the others listen to the sacred mysteries that take place in their heart of hearts, where in the abysmal mirror of the soul exterior events and experiences refract and combine into new forms, hitherto unseen by the human eye, where mysteries become revealed, never solved before.

Let us compare two artists who fanatically follow their own paths: Liebermann and Munch.

Liebermann paints the sheep as they are. He paints crippled old men with all the symptoms of their dullness, thus as the cripples usually are. He paints women who mend fishing nets as if they were real, similar to those whose thousands inhabit the shores. He also paints trees during storms, several Dutch landscapes; he has not painted flowers only because he is a genuine naturalist. In brief, Liebermann paints nature *sans phrase,* descriptively, pedantically, without any concern for 'sense'. He is a typical naturalist grown in the age of Americanisation and lack of ideology, in the epoch of photography and constant shortage of time. Consequently, he is cold and devoid of useless considerations. He never allows himself any extravagance of ecstasy and his famous motto reads: Fantasy is only a surrogate!

To the contrary, Munch paints fever and vision. He paints nature as it appears in specific states of the soul. His trees turn into huge spectres. His imagination, tormented by fear, transforms white birches immersed in a dark night into figures wrapped in white sheets. Munch paints the scene of death experienced by a boy exactly the way it has survived in his memory, not caring for an 'objective', 'true' reality. All that had sunk into the boy's soul, feverish with the atmosphere of death, found its way into the painting made by an adult: the apoplectically red face of the father, dulled with the pain of despair, the sister's face, emaciated by sleepless nights, that entire stiff atmosphere, imbued with the smell of medicines, and in the background an awkward boy, sneaking out, perturbed by the awesome mystery of death. Munch represents nature not 'as it is', namely, a fiction of nature, mechanically perceived by the eye, but the nature changing under the influence of the soul's states. The same landscape which not long ago cried out to the world a brute despair in the glaring chaos of hues, in another painting has been vested in the dark azure of the dawn marked by deep yearning.

Munch paints remembrances, visions, the instantaneous concoctions of the soul in the moods when the brain's consciousness becomes superseded by an alien – the soul's consciousness.

Munch and Liebermann represent not only the most distant poles of art but stand for something more. Their works have become the most glaring symbols of our epoch, the symbols of the most desperate fight that gives a peculiar expression to our times – the struggle between the brain and the soul.

The Middle Ages did not know this struggle as they still remained under the exclusive reign of the soul. Its revelations were proclaimed to prevent even the smallest doubt as to the existence of the soul's power, totally separate from the brain. The supernatural and suprasensuous were discernible everywhere, likewise the chaotic pressure of various forces, whose *vis agens* was hidden and inaccessible to human intellect.

The rule of the soul was, however, hard and burdensome. Its revelations were always accompanied to a greater or smaller degree by the destruction of the brain's consciousness and the psychoses of individuals among affected masses. The mind interpreted those revelations falsely, it deformed and made them shallow, and – consequently – brought unhappiness to the masses. Those unusually deep (from the psychological viewpoint) germs that constituted the basis of the devil's and witch's essence, that visionary-intuitive cognisance of the relationships between human existence and the universe became in the hands of the rabble a terrible force that sent thousands to the stake. Under the soul's rule everything was torment – the search for God, recognition of evil, painful struggles with nature's secrets and with the hidden essence of existence.

Humanity felt tired with the eternal suffering; it craved for liberation, comfortable happiness and a new religion that would slightly postpone the eternal felicity and give hope for a small portion of earthly bliss.

The promise of the other world, filled with happiness that would eventually come after the torments of the mundane life, tempting at the beginning, and sanctifying the soul's government, was gradually losing its influence. The fundamental dogma of Christianity (drawn from the ancient pessimism) that man is born to suffer, has now been called into question.

This marked the beginning of the end.

The most profound recognition and at the same time the most significant revelation that life is only a series of afflictions has been substituted with the deceitful lie of the brain: happiness is here on earth.

The human race began to free itself from the oppression and heavy duties imposed by the soul. Already Martin Luther's pronouncements were nothing else but the paving of the way for the reasoning mind, rationalism and common sense of the herd. At first, the soul managed to cope with this attack. Yet charges, growing in strength, repeated more and more often throughout the centuries. There came an age of superficial and light-hearted minds – the age of the Encyclopaedists. The mob listened with great satisfaction to the wisdom of a certain Voltaire. The young, shallow brain toughened and had the rabble on its side. New fighters were flowing in. Trivial mediocrity was spreading over vast areas. Finally, a rapid flourishing of natural science, appropriated by the materialistic brain's megalomania, confirmed the collapse of the soul's life. The brain celebrated a great triumph and the soul's hatred was reminiscent of the bull's rage at the sight of a red cape.

Indeed, the plebs had always hated the soul.

Antiquity could not yet boast didactic popular science treatises, so the mob revered all those initiated to the suprasensuous existence of the soul. The masses mainly feared their might, which could cause harm, and were, possibly, secretly terrified by the unknown mysterious powers they themselves did not possess. Even Socrates could quite seriously claim that his wisdom had come from a daemon, unafraid that he should be ridiculed by his relatively well-educated epoch.

The medieval plebs became more and more arrogant. Under the influence of the Christian teachings (best captured by Manichaeism) about the androgynous god, the God of Good and Evil, the populace divided the spiritual phenomena into the areas of black and white magic. It venerated saints, expecting benefits from them, but it killed all those who failed to give it something tangible and from whom it expected only the evil: magicians as well as the fathers of science and philosophy, who fathomed the secrets of life and – despite their rather naive language – possessed a much deeper understanding of Nature and its mysteries than all our present scholars taken together.

Yet never has the hatred of the soul felt by the mob been so strong as today, in the period of the absolute rule of natural science, money and prostitution. All spiritual phenomena are persecuted and destroyed with furious doggedness. A new slogan has appeared in science: Facts! Facts! Facts! Crookes, Zöllner, Wallace and Ulrice have been ridiculed, now passing for madmen. Politics and public life have been invaded by squalor, stupidity, money and a race for happiness. In art naturalism reigns, understood most broadly as the representation of 'reality'.

Naturalism, the terminal stage of the gradual demise of the soul, has become the highest ideal in the art of the modern mob. This term, however, is understood in a limiting way, with reference to a specific kind of technique. Yet, it should be consistently applied within the entire field of art, no matter whether the processes in nature and life are rendered in the spinach green or the most grey greyness, whether the painter's models are transposed onto the canvas in ragged workmen's clothes or in the armour of medieval knights. Naturalism is the art of merchants – and who isn't a merchant today? – and ought to represent things that can be controlled by the merchant's brain.

Naturalism is 'reality' in art, irrespective of whether it is represented by Meyerheim, Defregger or Liebermann, irrespective of whether it is seen with the naked eye or with the help of a magnifying-glass, or whether it shows a couple of lame old men or an elegant young lady.

'Fantasy is useless!' cries Liebermann. So what remains is, according to Zola's famous wording, temperament. But even temperament is only a platitude. Naturalistic art in literature requires a notebook, in the plastic arts – a good eye and sure hand. And so does a simple soldier. Thus, strangely enough, the two most symptomatic phenomena of our times – militarism and naturalism – converge in their common aspiration. They both signify the atrophy of individualism and the regimented uniformity of the barracks.

Once art used to be practised only by God's darlings, by prophets who hid themselves in caves, seeking visions of a liberated soul; by anchorites who led lonely lives in the wilderness. In the Greek times a poet, a gloomy ecstatic – like Aeschylus or Sophocles – was possessed by divine frenzy. Thinking was sanctity and Socrates felt no cold when he stood barefooted in high snow, absorbed in his ponderings.

A medieval artist prepared his soul through long prayers and fasting, and in a convulsive tension of his entire being he had implored the Holy Ghost for grace, before he started to work.

A contemporary artist, fallen to the reporter's role, needs a different sort of preparation. For the modern artist it is photography that has become the Holy Paraclete of revelation and impecuniousness – the strongest incentive for creation.

Thinking is cheaper than bread and art has turned into a light bread. Who can't be an 'artist' today? And it is not even so difficult to become a 'genius', for the utterly stupid claim that 'Diligence is genius' has become symptomatic of our contemporary views on art.

A modern artist is expected, above all, to meet one condition: he must be stupid, he must become the stupidity incarnate, if he is not stupid yet. He must not think, he must lose the habit of thinking, if he is not already an imbecile. He is not allowed to see in nature anything more than what can be brought to our attention by good photography. First of all, he is supposed to carry art to the highest ideal set by colour photography, which one day will make art redundant.

Far from this *profanum vulgus* walk the exiles, the sacred priests of Agni, who make their offerings to the soul; those few ones in whom the old tradition of the sacredness of thought and art is alive more than ever before; those few ones who create only at the moments of the most intense flight of the soul, its most painful explosion; new prophets who proclaim the soul's eternal return; mystics endowed with grace who encompass the world not only with their eye or ear, but with a sacred organ of the soul – a synthesising organ that can perceive only immortal things and grasp their essence.

The woman of Félicien Rops is a woman who stands beyond time and space, an archetypical woman – Hecate or Medea. Equally well, she can be a woman of the Apocalypse or a murderess. It is a woman who had once received holy orders and who kissed the devil's behind; the woman who has liberated masculine force in humanity and who has pushed the selfsame humanity into atrocity, grime and rottenness.

Rops's oeuvre occupies the same level as that of Schopenhauer's. His prints constitute a powerful philosophical system, deeper and more painful than the philosophy of the Frankfurt thinker, the system derived not from effect but from cause – from lust, which has given origin to 'will'. Thousands of volumes on the inferiority or superiority of woman would not be enough to balance, even partly, his sexual pessimism. Rops has analysed female psychology in great depth and with considerable courage, while Strindberg's pathological misogyny seems to be only a craving to avenge his sexual dissatisfaction.

In turn, man as seen by Goya in his *Capriccios* is no definite individual. He is not a Spaniard from the previous century, despite his attire. He is none of the numerous enemies of the artist, as implied by a certain discriminating art historian, capable of spotting obnoxious caricatures everywhere. Goya's man is Adam, ridiculous since time immemorial, who for five seconds of sexual pleasure would gladly sell his soul to the devil. He is that eternally funny peacock, dancing attendance with his tail spread in front of a hen. He is a dog that can smell a bitch from afar and chases her madly; a stupid sexually-oriented male beast led by the nose by the weak female, cheated and deluded by her, drawn to a plough on a par with an ox and pushed into the crime's embraces. Goya's man is simultaneously an ass, a pig and – above all – the most unfortunate among animals, a ram. It is man viewed as a sex-driven animal by the wide-open eyes of the Magus's soul, the Magus anxious lest his masculinity be soiled and abased by woman, the Magus who prophesised through the mouths of Janus de Villiers: *Chaques fois que tu aimes une femme, tu meurs d'autant.* But even the Magus himself could become a swine. Gilles de

Rais in his sexual madness went so far as to commit bestialities; Paracelsus ended his life in the mire of the most sordid iniquity and John Dee himself came to his undoing in the most horrid libertinism...

The portrait of Schumann by Félix Vallotton does not resemble the Schumann known to his contemporaries. Probably, he never looked like this. But such was his soul, which in its mad and painful resignation to suffering reveals itself in the overture to the Sonata in F-sharp minor, which in the *Flight* is shouted out in the sick *Cupio dissolve*, and which in the Novelette in F-sharp minor wanders aimlessly, circling astray, only to rage suddenly in the wild jumps of St Guy's tarantella. And such exactly is the powerful creation of those artists who have dissolved the human soul in themselves, who have allowed it to take on a new shape and assume a new face, who have captured the soul with its entire existence in a couple of verses.

Those artists will never be understood by the masses, for this would go against the idea of future development, against the business of procreation and reproduction.

And so they pass for 'immoral' or 'obscene'. Their works are rotting away in *l'enfer de la bibliothèques* or are condemned to slow destruction in museum store-rooms...

I want now to present one among the Chosen, to whom the soul has revealed its innermost secrets – Gustav Vigeland, a sculptor.

II.

Gustav Vigeland was born in Norway. It is a country of bright nights, the land of mountains and the sea, the land of awful seriousness and heavy, oppressive melancholy – the most tragic country in Europe. This scarce soil produced by the mountains crumbling over millions of years had been washed by glaciers down and across the sea to the fertile Frisia and the Netherlands. Another desperate attempt was made and again a tiny amount of soil appeared, soon overgrown by forests, by limitless forests – Norway's sole natural resource.

Melancholy manifests itself most strongly in autumn, when in October trees become naked and the ground is covered with rotting leaves, when – for weeks on end – rain beats against windowpanes and trickles down, sobbing; when for months you cannot see the sun, only fog, the everlasting fog. It is in this season that the forlorn seclusion becomes so hard and empty to live in. A man is, as it were, excluded from the world; he sees the same faces and the same yellow lamplight all day long. People walk silently, passing one another wordless; the closest neighbour's house is often a mile away. There, in Europe, nobody really knows what solitude and sadness really are.

And in this emptiness, among those sobs and laments of rain, under the cloak of the leaden sky, which – even in the room – can be felt as a ghostly weight over one's head, the tough soul of a sensible Norwegian slowly begins to slacken. Bad, gloomy thoughts begin to rise like bubbles from the marshes. Unknown feelings crawl fearfully out of the soul's secret recesses; the brain gradually loses control over them and the naked, hitherto unrecognised life of the soul starts to dominate, unconfined. The man has no more strength to tame those terrifying and destructive forces and no longer defends himself against the sorrow that overflows his heart. He finds the dusted Bible, immerses himself in the Divine words, perverts their meaning, then tries to find it anew. The last sparkle of reason appears, pointing out that all this is sheer madness. Too late! The man searches the deepest recesses of his heart, re-lives his whole life second after second; he wants to re-think each thought but fear and despair rise steadily. Sin is everywhere, the dreadful heinous sin present in every deed and every thought. And whatever is not sinful, it will be made so by the insane brain, sunk in meditation. For this overflowing cup of sins there is no mercy, no forgiveness. From the bottom of despair there appears a terrible, criminal face of the biblical Satan of Jehovah, this same Jahveh who punishes for sins with which he himself has infected his tribe. There is no help! Satan, the consoler of the desperate, grabs the soul into his claws. The sense of doom and eternal death penetrates the soul's pores like a wedge. It's all the same now!

Neither penance nor punishment will save the damned soul. And after the days of the most desperate pensiveness come the days of the most desperate drunkenness. For when you have once fallen into Satan's arms, it is immaterial what sins you are going to commit.

Several Germanic artists have dealt with this phenomenon. Jan Luyken, a furiously fanatical Calvinist, has shown – in a great number of copperplates – the inner terror and delirious anxiety of the soul tormented by despair. With unmatched intensity, Arne Garborg described this spiritual process in the novel *Fred*, one of the most soulful books humanity can boast. Huysmans, a through and through Germanic artist by his provenance and sensitivity, presents in *En route* the most painful and intense forms of this confusion of feelings, while the young Vigeland dreamt his first works in the atmosphere of a similar hopelessness and despair, amid the hard and unrelenting 'will for evil' and deep repentance.

Vigeland's entire oeuvre has its roots in the despondency of the soul whipped by terror. Everywhere there surfaces one feeling that dominates others and vanishes in the whirl of eternity – the foreboding of darkness, damnation, rejection and everlasting death. And so the heavy leaden skies and the revengeful anger of Jehovah overhang all that Vigeland has created. All his works perspire with a dreary, pensive vision of a pessimist who can see in life nothing but pain and violence.

Already his first creation, *The Accursed* (fig. 62), reveals his outlook upon life.

Adam with his wife and offspring is hurrying forward thoughtlessly. In utter despair, he shouts his first greetings to the Unknown that awaits them with all its horrors. Beside him walks Cain, the father of the evil, harbinger of Satan and his kingdom. Closely behind, Eve follows with a little sleeping innocence, Abel in her arms. She is leaving Paradise to *reveler l'enfer*, as Simon de Montfort says, but she is looking up to heaven, to the coming Son of Man, who will one day expiate her sins by his death on the cross.

Movement is noticeable in this group, some desperate rush. One can feel the presence of the Archangel above those people, a terrible memory that in the darkest hours of suffering will whirl inside the brain, full of enchanting visions of the happiness once lived. And one more thing by way of consolation – a whining dog is running along, the only creature that has remained faithful to the outcasts. He is their only friend, for only a dog can be a friend unfailing in misery.

This is the beginning of a thundering song of the distressed humanity, the choking *Salve Regina* of the exiled and the doomed, who in their yearning for the Paradise lost abandon themselves to the devil, sin, prostitution and crime. Here begins the history of the poor, damned progeny of Adam, defiled by the original sin, never to be redeemed by either baptism or penance; the progeny branded by the parental crime, which will revenge itself down to the millionth generation; the progeny destined for damnation by the heaviest curse of God – the compulsion to live!

One of Vigeland's low-reliefs shows some heavily drunk people (cat. 130). Reeling, they try to move forward. Maybe a precipice is awaiting them, into which they will fall in a moment, with their bodies torn to pieces in the sharp crevices of rocks. A figure of a praying woman protrudes out of the relief. She is beseeching God for his grace and care. It is no longer a prayer but a cry of man who has lost all hope and is waiting for a miracle. Some spasm of the soul has broken this figure in two, has made her cross her hands so that they could vehemently unclasp in the sick slavish resignation: Thy will be done!

In another place a man is crying for salvation, delirious and possessed by a legion of devils, gnawed by remorse. His face, twisted in suffering, is shouting out the terrible *là-bas* of humanity, consumed by the fire and pestilence descended from heaven, and surrounded by infernal flames gaping at its feet. The man seems to be a symbol of the times past when hordes of flagellants marched through towns and villages, and in an ecstatic madness wounded their backs; the hordes of wild beasts, famished peasants plundering and setting fire to manor houses, starved for murder. He symbolises the times when the age-long urge of mankind to get delirious spent itself painfully in the spasms of the Sabbath, only to die out in the helpless despair devoid of memory, future or God.

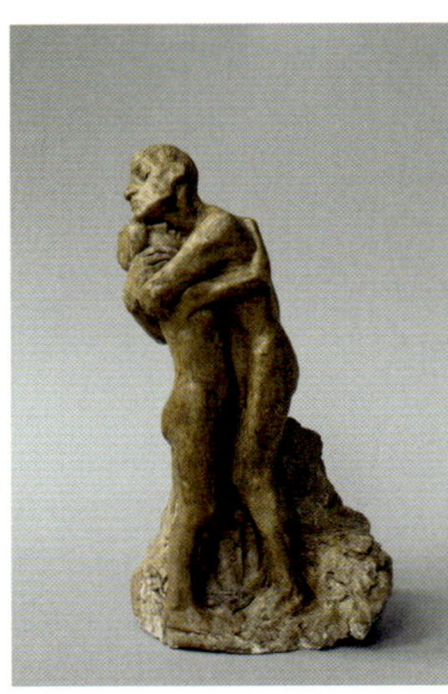

Fig. 32. Gustav Vigeland: *Man and Woman Embracing Each Other*, 1893

Man became too tired to call upon God, who had turned a deaf ear to all complaints and sufferings. The half-closed eyes and drooping facial muscles, the whole figure as if taken down from the cross – in this way exactly Vigeland depicts an old man in his daughter's embrace (fig. 32). She is tensing her muscles, as though she wanted to catch the sad ruin of his body in her arms, but her wide-open eyes show no hope, no way out. It is only an instinctive sense of duty experienced by the child who wants to support her father to the very end, to become mother to him. The daughter who mothers her own father! This uterine instinct, the strongest female instinct, has been shown here with unparalleled beauty. Both of them stand in the deaf expectation of the last merciful blow of grace, which will extract from their mouths a painful sigh: I wish the end would come soon!

And the end has arrived. Death has come, yet not the quiet one that brings liberation, but the one that marks the beginning of a new terror, of new sufferings. An old man lies dead on the ground and over him an old woman is kneeling, convulsively bent over the stiffened figure (cat. 129). She is watching the dead face, penetrating the corpse with her insane vision. She cannot understand, and never will, the most terrible secret of life ...

In the infinite area of pain, there is no expression that Vigeland would not have rendered in his art, from common fear to deadly despair that manifests itself through a beastly bellow; from an inner disquietude that tries to calm down pain by means of senseless, aimless movements to a dull narrow-mindedness; from heart-rendering prayers for salvation to insane deliria, when a man gushes out the most furious blasphemies, becomes a devil and perpetrates evil due to evil. The scale of represented emotions has seemingly no end.

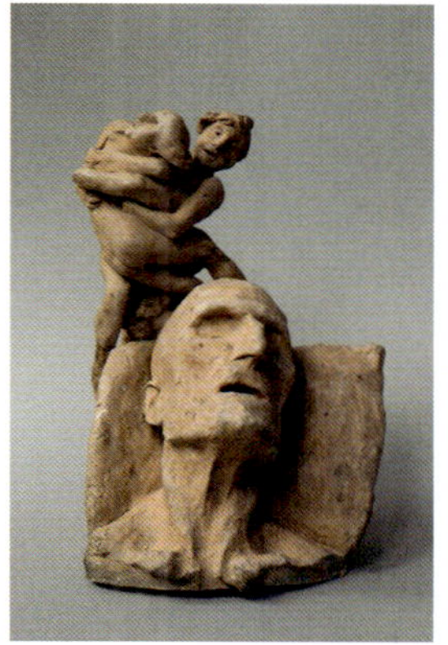

Fig. 33. Gustav Vigeland: *Death and Life*, 1893

There is here also a cancer that festers in contemporary mankind – the fear of life. Above a huge male head, life is whirling tumultuously. Three figures are spinning in a mad dance over the abyss of death (fig. 33). They throw themselves into the maelstrom of life, whose short funnel sinks into the black infinity of non-being. They are plunging head-down, blindly, with piercing shouts of joy, yet aware that everything is drawing to the inevitable end. Once again, it is solely the frenzy of despair, which seeks oblivion in the dissolute orgies; the conscious frenzy of the individual who offers his whole future to hell for one single moment of pleasure. So rages mankind when its destruction is inescapable. Such must have been the orgies celebrated by the Sodomites when sulphur was streaming down on them from heaven. Such had been Sardanapalus's frenzy, before he had himself burnt at the stake with his concubines. The king of Sion, Johann von Leyden, in the face of a terrible famine and imminent doom, turned into a beast whose lust knew no limits.

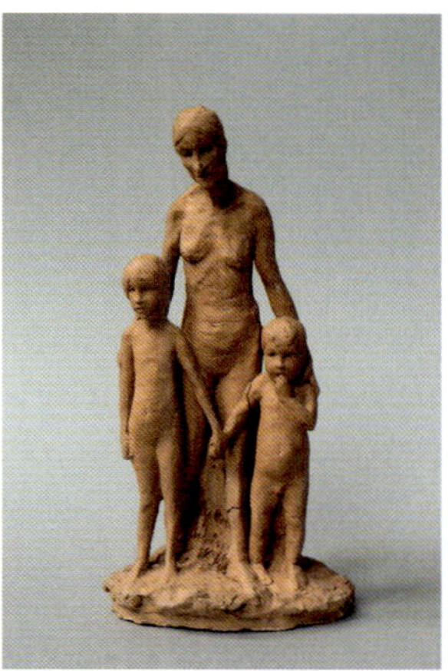

Fig. 34. Gustav Vigeland: *An Old Mother with Two Children*, 1893

And into this earthly Inferno, into this fear and dirt, into this morass of lust and torment, an old woman introduces two children and procures them to life: a boy and a girl (fig. 34). She leads into a thoughtless dance of life these poor, unaware human beings, the eternal sacrifice to be offered to the Satan-fate in the Sabbath of existence. The boy, shy and clumsy, with an insipid gaze directed towards that outer trashy sham brilliance, is a miserable stupid Adam, born to become a woman's slave, deceived and deceitful, the Magus and a swine.

The girl, apparently conscious of herself, with a trace of painful disdain in the corners of her mouth, seems to apprehend her future. Instinct has disclosed to her that her destiny is to beget children in sexual squalor, unless she wants to fulfil the Apocalyptic prophecy and destroy the world with the poison of prostitution.

There is also love shown to those children: the desperate love of Abraham, who burdens his son with the weight of the future stakes; the love of Gilles de Rais, who tenderly hugged children to his chest before slaughtering them; the love of Schumann singing his insane lullabies to the little things. And there is also a prophetical suffering of Christ, who allows children to come to himself in order to see them so pure and innocent, before they multiply their fathers' sins by a thousand times and bring to this world new crimes and new deprivation.

III.

In this manner exactly existence presents itself to a thinker who does not see with the brain, the poor brain that takes into account too many haphazard and secondary factors, too much pleasure and joy of life, too many distracting occupations, such as businesses and stock exchanges, politics and art, various ways leading to 'happiness', 'peace' and healthy rest.

Yes, the life as received by the brain is truly wonderful!

Go inside millions of homes – how much happiness in the bosom of the family, how many satiated, contented faces! Have a look into the bedrooms of respectable spouses, filled with blissful, tender satisfaction! Visit the Evangelical societies of workers – what a wonderful harmony between capital and work! Go to the universities and be convinced that we have travelled a long way on the road to absolute happiness. All that made our life difficult, namely fear and the striving after the eternal life, has found a happy solution. For God does not exist and no professor has ever seen a soul. After all, the soul is only the reverse of matter, the soul and matter can be likened to a watch-glass, which has both the convex and concave sides. It remains only to create protein and Satan's words: *Eritis sicut Deus!* will come true. Go to the theatre and feel your hearts vibrate joyfully, watching a solemn order, morality and justice of the universe. After guilt there always comes penance, after conflicts a harmonious peace, and even death shines with the aureole of eternal quietude amidst the repulsive cadaverous vermin.

And what does it matter that millions of hands stretch out for bread! *Ecrasez l'infâme!* Peace is the first civil duty, calls out a poet who associates with the mighty of this world.

And what does it matter that thousands perish in this fiendish dance of life? This only proves that mankind has been created for happiness though some, unluckily, must go astray.

And what does it matter that for a moment of bliss one has to pay with the long-lasting torment? This only proves that light-hearted people do exist, who spend their money and run after prostitutes!

Indeed, happiness does exist, on lease to respectable tax-payers. There also exists the 'art' which demonstrates that the sense of happiness still lives in its coryphaei.

Yet, the soul knows no happiness. A joyful, enraptured soul is an abnormity, a square circle, a whip made of sand. The soul remains sombre, for it is all passion and exaltation, for it has suffered the fiery contractions of lust and all kinds of tempests in the process of development, the deliria of anxiety and extreme sufferings at the time of crises.

That's why for the artists of the soul life appears as a *sale corvée*, dirty burden, constantly gyrating fear, incessant doubt and resignation, unsuccessful strife, and helpless capitulation.

For them, love – the greatest happiness of the human male, the animal satisfaction of the mature phallus – turns into the deepest and most destructive pain.

The sexual pessimism of those artists is as old as the hills since its source lies in the deep hatred felt towards woman by the masculine soul, the soul that through its contact with a female becomes miserable and squalid.

Already antiquity hated and despised woman, this everlasting stimulant of sexual urge, *dulce malum pariter favus atque venenum*. However, at that time woman did not possess as yet this destructive force, for sexual impulse was not so one-sidedly differentiated as it is today. But the Eastern nations already had their Astarte, the Indian people their terrible Maya, the mother of illusion, the Greeks – Medea, Hecate, Erinyes and Pythia, who maintained contacts with daemons. Finally, the Old Testament represents woman as the humanity's plague, the element of ignominy and evil spirit that will kill whatever is noble in man (Sirach VII, 2c).

Christ brought salvation to woman, made her evil powers spirituous; he extended his care to an adulteress and the Magdalen. His most brilliant disciple, Paul, completed the oeuvre of his master. There begins an epoch of penitent prostitutes, the most zealous servants of Christianity, to mention solely Tecla, Lydia, Chloe, Phoebe…

Woman recovered her honour. Mother of God, *virgo paritura*, holds power and influence over Divinity itself. A 'widow', this ridiculous garrulous prying old hag, whom the Talmud compares to an Egyptian plague, suddenly becomes a *kalogrie*, a 'beautiful old woman', venerated as a person consecrated to God – woman becomes ordained in the deaconship.

But the female rule did not last long. Already Manes, the inventor of the androgynous god, father-mother, the dual god of Good and Evil, claimed that woman is evil, passion, restlessness, the mother of heresy, a witch and a Sabbath, in a word, the devil incarnate!

In the bosom of the Church a conviction is born that woman is even worse than Satan. 'Among numerous snares that the crafty Satan has thrown upon the earth – says Marbodius – none is so evil and dangerous as a woman … *Femina, triste caput, mala stirps, vitiosa propago, plurima quae totum per mundum scandala gignit.*' One council after another attempts to break woman's power, to excommunicate her from the Church; the question was even posed whether woman really possesses a soul.

The centuries of the most zealous hatred towards woman follow, excepting comical erotomania of few ridiculous troubadours. Now, it is not only the Church that has rejected the female but most of all the secret society of Magi, the most powerful and wonderful people brought forth by the Middle Ages. Khunrath, Raymond Lulle, Cornelius Agrippa, Paracelsus, Janus de Villiers… *La femme a du miel dans la bouche et le sel arsenical dans la Coeur*, states Khunrath, the father of theosophy. The Magus was ashamed of his provenance from Adam, who had lost his own sacred distinction of Magus through the union with a woman. His first father is Samyâsa, who performed a heavy sacrifice of sexual intercourse in order to beget a wonderful generation of Magi. The Magus was not allowed to touch a woman since intercourse with her meant the loss of immortality, the decline of divine capacities, a downfall and infamy.

But now woman rises in her terrible revenge: a sorceress and a witch, the priestess of Satan, the source of sacrilege and blasphemy, a rabid hyena in the shape of Nekate or Magdalen Bavent, who – by the very aura that surrounded her – infested convents with sin, debauchery and Sabbath. At the close of the seventeenth century a woman possessed by the devil reigned unbridled in her infernal might. She grafted perversion, pest and venereal poison across the whole world – in Versailles and the Vatican, in monasteries and princes' courts. She destroyed the nobility and the clergy. In broad daylight she shamelessly said masses in praise of Satan in churches consecrated to God. She was a mistress of Baphomet and Louis XIV at the same time. There was no sacrilege she would not commit, no crime that would terrify her, no mire in which she would not wallow with an orgiastic satisfaction.

For the last time her power flashed during the French Revolution in the banal *culte de la raison*, deprived of all fantasy, later to hide for long in private beds.

Our epoch perceives woman in a new shape, together with a modernised cult of Satan. Satan himself has also become modern. He walks around in a dress-coat and patent-leather shoes; his goat-like face has assumed a decent appearance thanks to a beard shaven à la Henry IV; he has a bald head and manners of an oldish diplomat. The place of Nekate has been occupied in France by the Huysmanian Madame Chantelouve and the women possessed by devil of Canon Docre, in England – by Miss Diana Vaughan, editing prayers to Satan for Palladian revues, in Belgium – by a refined poisoner Joniaux, and in the sad North – by the heroine of Hans Jæger's book *Sick Love*.

The Satan of hysteria and boredom has triumphed over woman. The modern man has fallen into mental decrepitude and has been seized with a desire to lift woman up to the 'heights of his education', for in the atmosphere of philosophical cynicism and atheism there always grow and lavishly spread ill propensities. And again woman has become a 'rope on which Satan pulls man towards him', to use Bodinus's words. New satanic temples have cropped up in the shape of Moulins Rouges, Orpheum, or flowery halls, destined for 'superior' members of the famous *circles*. A modern can-can has taken place of fantastic dances of medieval witches, while the witch's poisonous *aphrodisiacum* has been transformed into a syringe of morphine. Still, the emotional foundation has remained the same – a greed for crime, blasphemy and an inhuman increase of lust that can be satiated only by perversion.

Rops, the most penetrating psychologist of sex in our century, provides a synthesis of the modern courtesan and the medieval witch. She is active and consciously destructive; she is always a half-lesbian – the way a witch was represented by Baldung Grien in the eponymous cycle – or at least a masturbant, like in the *verni mou* of Rops's *Le diner d'athées*. In any case, she always hates man because she feels an infinite disdain for him. *Et puis l'homme c'est si laid*, can be read under a picture of Foraine's, in which an elder girl is trying to seduce a younger one …

Munch and Vigeland give a synthesis of the German woman of our epoch, the woman who – admittedly – does not follow a traditional ritual of the satanic cult but in whom lurks the power of evil and attraction to the devil.

Rops's woman is swallowed by a vortex; she emits shouts of rapture, she suffers, blood overflows her brain until she has forgotten about everything and succumbed to the 'influx' of her ruler – Satan. She is a sort of satanised St Theresa. The woman of those two northern psychologists of sex, the German woman *par excellence*, is frugal. She has a narrow soul, narrow heart and dreadful amount of common sense. In this lies her satanic might. Man suffers endlessly. His soul disintegrates, his balance

Fig. 35. Gustav Vigeland: *Man Embracing a Woman*, 1893

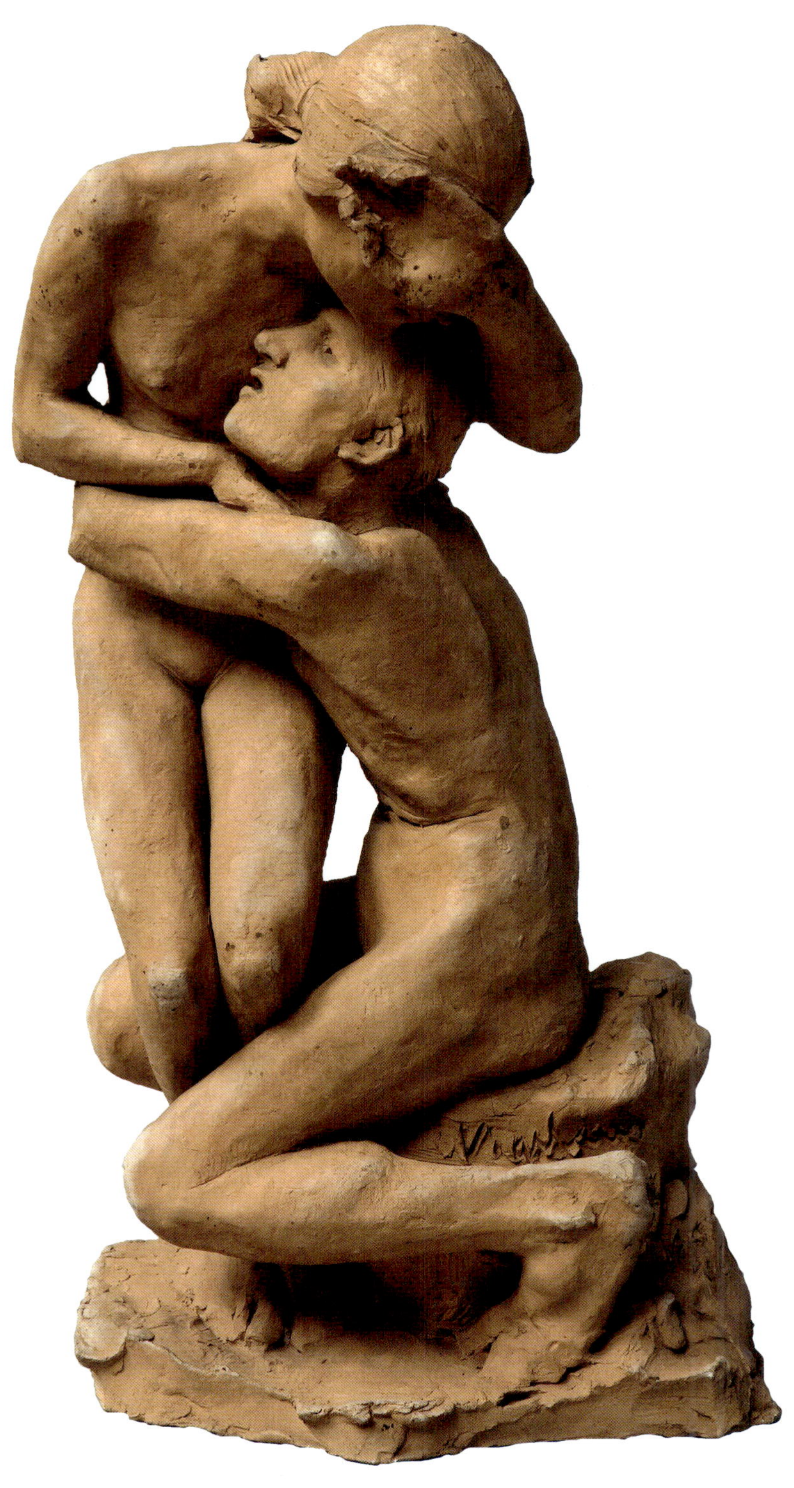

is upset, mad sorrow overwhelms his brain, the criminal attacks of frenzy flare up wildly. This is a clinical depiction of an incurable illness caused by vapours of love.

But this love is desperate, a mighty *officium desperationis*, a volcanic revolt of the tormented lust, a shout of the famished body, the black fodder that has encompassed all the past and future Ways of the Cross.

In the whole series of works, Vigeland recreates this modern Walpurgis Night of love.

One of them, dubbed *A Young Couple* (fig. 35), has been composed in this way. A man has fallen to the ground, convulsively clasping the woman's knees. His mouth is twisted by lust and its desperate hunger. One can almost hear inarticulate sounds of his oversensitive nerves; one can see that he is trembling and his teeth are chattering feverishly. She, in turn, is slumping and covering her eyes with one hand, unnaturally big, as if she wanted to conceal all her shame. Above this hand a huge skull is visible, swollen with inner fight. Yes, she will surrender to him, to satisfy his desire. They are both sinking in a speechless, brutal ecstasy of their bodies that fails to appease lust but rakes their nerves, begetting hatred and repulsion.

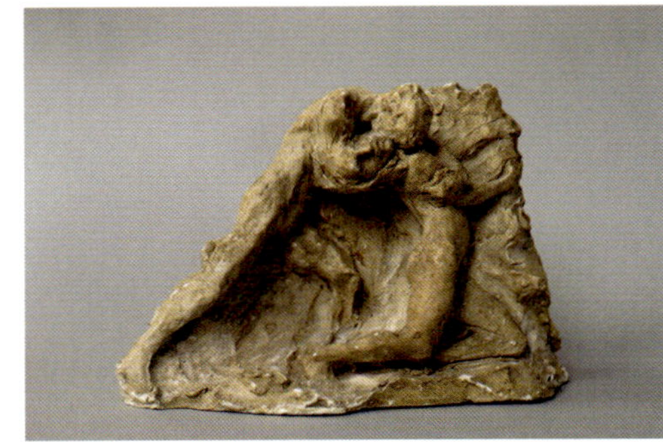

Fig. 36. Gustav Vigeland: *Woman Caught from Behind by a Man*, 1894

And her? She will rise full of disgust for the man who has defiled her and deprived of what she will never recover – her purity. She will be afraid of him, she will be running from him, while his desire will grow until blood has flushed and deluded his brain. And he will see nothing but her naked body, which he desperately wishes to tear to pieces in his bestial craving. And he will feel nothing but her body's feverish glow, until he becomes a beast and rapes the woman.

This moment is shown by Vigeland in the following bas-relief (fig. 36). The man has caught the woman flying away, then trying to defend herself. Faint, exhausted and defenceless, she has fallen to her knees, grabbing some object with her hands. He got hold of her in one jump and his brutal arm, like an iron lasso, has coiled around her body. Vehemently, he has bent her head back and buried his lips in her neck.

With the surprising exception of Rops, among the modern nations only the Japanese are able to represent such terrible pains of lust. Yet Rops is a disciple of Baudelaire, of Barbey d'Aurevilly, of contemporary students of diabolism, who all carry the tradition of black masses in their blood. Vigeland and the Japanese have had life as their teacher. The living pain of rapture has imbued and saturated their eroticism to such an extent that it has lost its primary meaning and opened the depths of the human soul instead.

This is no longer an individual sense of pleasure that endows an erotic work of art with sensuous character – here, eroticism has been stripped of any sensuality. Here is lust for its own sake – a cold cruel power of nature that mercilessly and brutally throws two people at each other, the lust that makes out of two human beings a means to its own end.

In Japanese drawings the sexual trance resembles torture. The limbs are gnarled in a kind of epileptic contraction, the fingers are cracked in pain, the nerves seem to tear away into pieces. Women are lying here as if in a painful premortal fight, in postures that can be provoked only artificially in cataleptic states. This is no longer the copulation of two beings but an inhuman symbolic coitus of entire Nature.

The same torture, transferred onto the psychic regions, is visible in Vigeland's oeuvre. I consider one of his sculptures unparalleled in its spiritual force (cat. 50). A woman is kneeling, with her head buried in the ground, wrapped in her streaming hair. A man has mounted her. With two arms he is strongly, even painfully, embracing her body, his face violently pressed in her nape.

This may be a tragedy of a young girl, possibly united to another man, or else a tragedy of an adulteress. Pain ceases to be painful and becomes a passive sliding into an abyss, the resignation to the Satan of sin and destruction. She had been fighting until the last moment but his panting sexual will overcame her. But now that he has achieved his goal, he daren't possess her. He is only pressing her into his body, his passion is dissolving and the happiness he had so much craved after is becoming a torture.

No! There is no happiness for the poor *exules, filii Hevae*, because love – the love through which they could be strong and powerful and live again the unearthly raptures of the Paradise lost – has turned into new tortures, hatred and anger.

Satan, the father of bad conscience, has captured the love of the miserable tribe of Adam – the evil Satan, who tramples the most beautiful hopes and who changes the elation of the highest tension of will into a repugnant drooping.

Already Crespet (*Deux livres de la hayne de Sathan…* 1590) provides a minute description of all the means utilised by Satan to prevent love. But none is so effective as the raising of distrust towards woman in the man's soul. This despondency dissipates and destroys his masculine will; it turns the lightest movements of lust into hatred and makes the desire to be united with woman in ecstatic love degenerate into a cesspool.

For does such a woman exist in whom man would not have to doubt? Does such a woman exist who would turn a deaf ear to Satan's whispers? The fallen woman and the man drawn mad by distress are the principal themes of all 'erotic' artworks by Vigeland. But none is so powerful in this respect as *A Doubter* (cat. 49).

A woman has buried herself into the lap of a sitting man. He, apparently, fails to notice her; he is supporting his head with his hand and looking up with an expression of unspeakable pain.

He has already understood the futility of all desperate inner struggles. He has succumbed to the daemon of man's deepest instinct that demands purity of a woman. But this woman has already rested in other arms and there have been many into whom she nestled with the same obnoxious zeal that she is demonstrating now. This thought has fallen on the fertile soul of his soul, struck roots and grown into a huge weed in the tropical heat of a suffocating fever.

At first it was only an unpleasant feeling, later it turned into a painful contraction of the heart; now he cannot touch her without thinking about his predecessors. He can't get rid of the cynical sensation of doubt in the love that has too often travelled from one man to another. He can't get rid of the feeling that in this woman's life he is only a wayside station, a consecutive number. He madly attempted to bear her again in his soul, to forget this alien now rolling in front of him. In vain! His wounded soul refuses to accept her.

Now, a sudden lightning pierces this hell of love, this doubt and will for self-destruction, this sexual insanity – a joyous triumph of lust, in which the carnal ecstasy is so strong that it smothers pain; a loud flourish of blood; a heavenly Alleluia of unity, of an absolute dissolution of two souls in a passionate kiss. The sitting man is holding a woman in his arms like a child. Clasping his neck wildly, she is violently resting her feet against his arms and their mouths have found each other in a deep kiss.

But this was only a sick yearning of the Doubtful One. He would crave to blend with his woman but he cannot – his predecessors are pulling them apart. He would crave to cuddle her, but instantly hatred is kindled in him, which makes him throw her to the ground and trample over her.

This is the most painful dream that can overwhelm the Doubtful One, the mortal combat of his bleeding soul.

Or, maybe he could beget her anew in himself, if only he got rid of his own daemons and tried to become reborn himself? Oh, yes! For there exists such a mighty luminous mood when lust becomes deaf and all animal instincts die down. There exists such a meek pain of longing that aimlessly flows above every space, like a polar seagull that yearns for no homeland.

When at close of day the autumnal sun glows with a subdued metallic light, when the sky merges into the sea and a pale merciful starlight sifts onto vast plains, when it is so quiet that you can hear a tired sight of the decaying soil, when the sound, colour and shape blend in the pulsation of nostalgia, encompassing the whole world, then a sick heart is wrapped in painless peace…

From such a mood was born Vigeland's *Dance* (cat. 89).

The Doubtful One has forgotten the female body; he forgot and buried her lust that lashed his heart with repulsion and hatred.

Now, she has become a part of his heart, and their hearts together only a tiny part of the bleeding heart of the earth. They are cuddled together like two doves during a storm that have finally found rest in each other's company … The earthly weight of their bodies has fallen away and a great melancholy of dawn is carrying them above the crushing destitution of life and its anger.

Deep below there remains a wild whirling crowd full of dreadful human pain. They have forgotten it all, dancing over the earth, wrapped in the song filled with the melancholy of the forebodings begotten from dreams. A sullen sobbing complaint for the lost life can be heard:

Dis qu'as-tu fait, toi que voilà
De ta jeunesse?

which fuses with the ineffable bliss of yearning:

Un vaste et tendre
Apaisement
Semble descendre
Du firmament
Que l'astre irise…
C'est l'heure exquise.[1]

… Happiness exists, indeed, but it is unworldly …

IV.

The bourgeois brain has attempted to invent the rules and conditions of a happy existence. Yet these laws are the laws of human stupidity, the real Saturnalia of idiocy. The bourgeois ethics, or in other words the teachings about the existence filled with happiness and harmony, is the only natural and truly authentic 'Communist Manifesto' of the modern plebs. The English, and especially Spencer, have fathered the socialist assumption that man has been created in order to be happy. Yet, this happiness demands uniform minds and the worldview established by dogmas. Happiness calls for animal, physiological functions utilised by lust. However, this childish Spinozean ideal of decrepit old men, the ideal of a man-philosopher who wants to subjugate all passions, dreams and instincts with the help of his brain, the ideal that carries on its miserable existence only in the present-day 'great aristocracy of the mind' has originated from a negative emotion – from the fear of suffering.

Nature itself knows no happiness. The progressing path of evolution is characterised by more and more intense pain and tension, the increasing predominance of suffering. Some have attempted to make cause out of effect, or at least a correlate of development, to separate sublimation and culture, and to make the latter responsible for the so-called 'degeneration'. Notwithstanding the fact that such separation is only a ridiculous by-product of an intellectual game, the term 'degeneration' is stupid in itself. Our doctors, alas, do not study history. Otherwise they would know that the phenomenon taken to be a malaise of our age existed in all previous epochs. Degeneration is a regularly returning phenomenon of every development, no less necessary than what we call normality. Nay, it is even a million times more necessary because norm is stupidity and 'degeneration' – genius. Can we point to a man suffering more strongly from neurasthenia, vexation of nerves and psychotic fevers than the prophet of Protestantism, Martin Luther? Norm is Max Nordau, a brainwashed philosopher of the crowd, degeneration is Nietzsche!

Every progress is characterised by a very special readiness to experience almost all emotional values as suffering. And it is perfectly natural that our fast intellectual evolution should be subjectively reflected as an uninterrupted chain of torment and the Way of the Cross. Our conscience has grown terribly sensitive, our memory tends to keep above all the tortures suffered and only women are capable of forgetting the pains of childbirth. The fear of suffering, magnified by the remembrance of past miseries, evolves into insanity, which grows more and more unbearable and hopeless with every knot marked on the strap of our existence.

The brain has unlearnt to believe. The excessively developed brain has lost all points of support – it doubts everything and at the same time it can explain and accept everything as possible. The essence of our entire existence lies in the fear of suffering, the fear of life (which is nothing else but a series of miseries) and the fear of death. Everything is one huge fear, unrest and torment.

The force which stands behind those spiritual tortures, behind the mad rush of evolution towards a growing intensity of suffering is Satan!

Satan existed before God, for God is good. What is primeval must be evil because suffering is primeval and, together with despair, it has begotten evil. Evil is primeval and it must have created good, only to demonstrate its frightful power. In popular consciousness Satan is more powerful than God. The common people do not dread God but Satan and his deceit. God, indeed, is only a protective measure against evil, called upon by man to free him from Satan's grip. But from the very beginning man has been possessed by the Satan of pain and desperation.

Religious rites of all primitive peoples were born out of the fear of evil, the hopeless fear of torment. It has been noticed recently that the sources of classical religions can be traced back to orgiastic follies related to the cult of phallus. The Medieval Ages knew but one religion – Satan!

Satan is the Adonai of evil. He is the god of the poor and the hungry, of the discontented and the ambitious, the god of Nature and evil instincts, the god of the damned and the inquisitive, for every quest denotes the loss of God. Satan is a cover-term for all that is punishable by the divine and human law.

Nietzsche has brilliantly sketched the type of a creative pale transgressor who has to advance stealthily in the dark. He shatters tablets, he creates, but all creation means the birth of new pains, the sowing of new crimes under the pressure of base instincts, ambition, distress and doubt, the will to negate and destroy.

And in this sense they all were criminals, even the rabbi Joshua, who – suffering on the cross – asked his Father in despair why he had forsaken him. In doubt and desperation, Jesus offended his God. One of the most perspicuous medieval psychologists, Matthias Grünewald, represented him as a 'transgressor', as a man who died in torment due to an illusion, as Christ, who – in terrible pain – despaired of his divine nature.

And those heretics, the most bourgeois among the bourgeoisie, the new Luthers of the free-thinking middle class – Strauss and Renan – aren't they criminals as well?

And isn't this nonsensical irony of history a crime? The history that allows us to juxtapose Christ with the talkative sentimental Renan, Calvin with Strauss, the father of the educated rabble, an idiotic coxcomb Vaillant with the great Henry, who has given life to modern anarchism, the banal Nana with Jeanne de Domrémy?!

They are all Satan's children: those who for some idea disturb the peace of thousands, Alexander and Napoleon, those who pervert the youth, no matter whether their name is Socrates or Schopenhauer, those who dare to look into the soul's abyss and grow fond of evil – Poe and Rops, those who love suffering for its own sake and watch the Golgotha of mankind – Chopin and Schumann, all those sons of the earth who want to see through the mystery of a double beginning, all those who walk aside, for every deviation from the path is a crime in the divine and human understanding.

The age-long [!] prototype of the criminal, the pariah, the damned one and the anarchist is Satan. Satan has been the first philosopher and anarchist. He is also the inconsolable, sombre and painful destiny of the dispossessed – the destiny that has become most painful even for itself, since Satan has been a constant sufferer. 'Why are you violating my peace?' he is asking those calling on him, because he has so secluded himself in his torment that he considers it the state of rest.

The medieval Satan was desperate and his despair begot evil. The modern Satan creates evil, because he cannot do otherwise and this has become his desperation. The modern Satan is a power propelled by some demoniacal passion that madly advances across the world, sowing despair and destruction. This dismal passion forces it to register and describe its crimes. This power can no longer feel – like in the Middle Ages – the orgiastic pleasure in perpetuating evil but ponders in grim feebleness over destiny that makes it incite others to crime.

It is in this way that Vigeland conceived of and represented Satan. His Satan rules over the hell of existence, that is, destiny and life devoid of aim or sense, in which murderous and destructive instincts become manifest.

The naive Middle Ages tried to make Satan even more terrifying and depicted him as a human and animal bastard. The medieval Satan bore the face of the goat with a huge nose of an eagle and had loosely hanging female breasts. The lower part of his body was borrowed from some animal and most frequently contained goat or horse hooves. Naturally, the Middle Ages paid a special attention to the sexual organ – a long crooked phallus, drooping but glowing red, which at the tip was bisexual.

Félicien Rops was the first to break with this tradition. Yet, his Satan is still a daemon of debauchery and sexual orgies. It is still a combination of Docre, the notorious priest of modern black masses, with a shameless and mischievous but polite jester, a mixture of a senile profligate with a pimp. Rops, actually, despises Satan and the roots of his conception of the devil are steeped in the false half-desperate half-sceptical cult of Satan spread by Baudelaire.

In turn, Wiertz conceived Satan to be the ruler of entire life, a gruesome force of Nature, destructive and imbued with despair, as represented in the imposing picture *Napoleon in Hell*. Still, Gustav Vigeland has been the first to create – with full awareness and a stroke of genius – the modern Satan, embodied Satan-*logos*, Satan-god, Satan-instinct, Satan-nature and Satan-destiny.

In the centre of an imposing low-relief sits Satan with his face pressed into convulsively clasped fists. His forehead is mighty, broad and lined with inner torment, with two huge bulging bumps. His mouth is screwed up; his eyes – reflecting an all-powerful murky soul paralysed in the smothered shouts of desperation – are looking gloomily from under strong brows, as though out of two dark caves. He is sitting voiceless – the Hercules eaten from the inside by Nessos's shirt, the Napoleon multiplied a thousand times, who among the heaps of bodies torn into pieces thinks about other thousands that he is bound to sacrifice. This is the Satan-genius, who has to destroy and invent ever new means of destruction; the Satan-god, who feels above himself the presence of the almighty mother Heimarmene, a sort of super-brain, which directs him and forces him to commit ever new crimes and multiply victims.

All ancient religions tell us about the race of upstarts who come to overthrow old dynasties of rulers and occupy their thrones. The Greeks had their Kronos and the Jews – Lucifer, hurled down by Jehovah.

And this particular Satan is beautiful with the aristocratic beauty of the soul of Lucifer, who had invented poetry and philosophy. He is beautiful with the charm of criminal courage and disinterestedness of a great malefactor, he is cruel with a fanatical cruelty of an anarchist, ready to sacrifice his brother for his ideals. Indeed, Satan is the first anarchist.

Satan, like every divinity, is unique in his trinity. He is the god of debauchery and incest, the god of thieves and murderers. His temples are brothels and *chambres separées, cafés chantants* and criminals' dens. In a triumphant procession he enters marital bedrooms and monasteries, royal courts and – most willingly – the shabby huts of all the dispossessed and desperate.

But he is also Lucifer, the spirit of distrust and revolt, of curiosity and unbridled anarchy. He is a future deity in the Kingdom of Antichrist, the god of creation and eternal return, of fight and disinterested dedication of fighters. *O, il faut aimer les demons,* says St Angela of Foligno.

Around this Satan, a frantic crowd gyrates. People are pressing towards him, some falling down, some raised upwards. The crying hands reach out towards him, spasmodically clinging to his throne. From the right side flows a wave composed of human beings that separates in the foreground. Some people interlock in a wild eddy of bodies, one huge body comprised of hundreds of arms, heads and legs, shouting in the delirious pain the hellish *de profundis*: *Libera nos Satan!* Others fall down onto a pile of repulsive bodies, intertwined and whirling. Some trample others and pull them down with a desperate energy of the drowning. This is one huge symbol of the most brutal and bestial combat – the struggle for survival.

In the same manner will crowd and trample one another the people trying to get through a narrow door out of the burning church; those who in mindless insanity are looking for an exit out of the sinking ship; those who at the time of famine are mangling one another in their fight for the offal of rotting carrion.

To the left side, the ravaging tempest begins to calm. There, people gaze blankly in front of them, depressed and aware of the futility of all efforts.

All are here, all miserable children of Satan, people of every age – adults, young-sters and old men, old women and girls, none is missing in that awesome holy mass of despair.

In one place a dull-brained streetwalker, who has grown so accustomed to dirt that she no longer feels any repulsion, is staring at Satan with her brute bulging eyes and silly impudent face. In another, an adulteress who 'had been first broken by marriage before she broke her marital faith', in Nietzsche's words. In yet another an old profligate is visible, with a woman hanging at his neck and pulling him down. Over there, a couple of incestuous siblings appear as well as a procurer who has sold her own daughter in the white-slave traffic, a poisoner and a murderess of her own husband. Yes, all are here, placing their offerings on the altar of prostitution, debauchery and crime.

An arthritic cripple who takes revenge on animals for his deformity, a minor stock-exchange gambler who makes his living on the sweat and blood of hundreds of beings whom he has ruined, a swindler and a horse thief, a martyr of sexual passion whose spine has been bitten through by poison – all rascals and world-reformers are here, Spinoza and Ravachol, a workman and a priest, a harlot and a woman pining away with love.

I would like to bring to light a few more figures, drawn from the swarm of this devilish tribe.

Deep down a woman can be seen, quiet with some tense, almost ecstatic, peace. She is a witch who knows but one god – Satan – a Palladist, who has never believed in any other god. She is a type of witch about whom one of old chronicles says that she could have been saved, if she had only given herself to an executioner's mate. Yet, she shoved him away with indignation. How on earth could she surrender to a lackey of the rich, a base flunkey of civil order and its rights, she who had kissed the bottom of Satan, the father of the poor and the unhappy! Never in her life! And in this lies the greatness and 'pathos of distance'…

Unperturbed with this swirling criminal mass, an old man watches the turmoil with a quietude full of dignity and curiosity. He is one of the fathers of learning, Cornelius Agrippa, who knows all the crimes and feels a deep liking for all those fearing daylight. Agrippa, who knows everything and who has annihilated his oeuvre by ridiculing it in a bloody satire on all human knowledge, the satire in relation to which the facetious works of Heine or Voltaire seem clownish jokes. This is a mind that refuses to accept any laws, any country, any fellow creatures. It is a mind born of Lucifer's spirit, the instigator of revolutions, the father of anarchism that gives priority to the rule of Satan on earth over the kingdom of God in heaven.

And, finally, comes a passive servant of Satan. He stands erect, in a stiff servile pose, with his glance fixed on his master's face – his master, a powerful ruler who is looking straight ahead, impassive, deaf to all servility and humility. The servant is an embodiment of the limited loyalty of a careerist, of a servile thoughtless crowd ready to slaughter its prophets at every beck and call of the ruler. He stands for the obedience devoid of dignity, the obnoxious toadying of servants and subjects grateful to their lords even for the lashes. It is a mighty symbol of 'my' people, the good people that accept all the plagues composedly and humbly because they come from God himself. He is a symbol of all those good citizens who – according to the advice of their coryphaei – value peace most. He is a symbol of rottenness, a social symbol of those who fight with rebels in defence of the existing order, with those unworthy to belong to 'my' people.

Even Satan can boast his flunkeys, whom he despises but whom he needs. His progeny are immemorial rioters and anarchists, who hate all authorities and regulations.

One day these sufferings will wear themselves out and Satan will see his rule endangered. Yet, the treacherous Judas will sow new torments and inject a new criminal poison into humanity. Then Satan will grow in strength, becoming a usurper mightier than ever before; he will overthrow the old Jehovah to ultimately rise in his new power as the only lord of heaven and earth and to fulfil the Church's prophecy as the Paraclete one in the Satanic Holy Trinity – as Antichrist.

V.

Recently, a lot has been said and written about a certain 'new art'. Every year brings us some 'new' trend and every five years critics ascertain that now finally a new spring of art has arrived.

So what is the 'new' contemporary spring in art?

In literature it is a shocking acrobatics of words that clothe some regularly returning moods. For those moods of the new art it is not at all difficult to work out a scheme easily discovered in the works by the 'new' poets.

These creators know neither sun nor night – they sit, dreamy, in a faint semi-darkness, enwrapped in nostalgia that slowly dies away and in suffering that silently burns out. They never speak but whisper, and whisper infrequently. They are only dreaming, watching the secrets of some somnolent maidenly eyes. Neither do they walk but sway or glide on blue mists over pale-green meadows. They are not interested in people as the 'softened cogs' of their fantasy do not tolerate the 'ruckling of death and triumphant shouts of life'. They despise suffering, which destroys and mars the form; to the contrary, their wish is to recreate the 'eternally beautiful and harmonious life'. For them 'life is beautiful because it is divine'.

A beautiful and harmonious life – a butcher full of self-satisfaction, who at dusk stretches out at the side of his spouse, could not glorify it more handsomely.

What dominates in painting is wallpaper, poster and – at most – tapestry. Here, the 'new' artists exhaust themselves in combinations of colours and forms, recently borrowed with great relish from the Japanese. And again the same themes – silent virgins skimming over paradisiacal meadows and subtle young men who follow the heavenly cortège in an innocent union with delicate maids.

Everything is subdued, soft, subtle and innocent.

Innocence and purity, subtle yearning and sweet hope – weren't such things already sung by Schiller?

They call it 'spiritual art'.

Well, this art is piteously poor. It shows only a tiny segment of our existence. It shows life in the convalescent room – faded and as wise as the impassiveness of the old man. Yes, terribly wise.

As a matter of fact, these artists are only sickly and asthmatic heirs of the greatest among the plebeians – Zola. But while Zola grasped the whole of life with his sweaty hands, his disciples only touch it delicately, diving into the aroma of its salons. They are fugitives from the 'stinking' camp of awful work, beginning with Bourget, who now only buries himself in women's skirts, and ending with this tired generation whose imagination exhausts itself in the sterile art of versification, stripped of any emotion. Their art is descriptive *par excellence* but where Zola gathered huge piles of stones, they laboriously carry their particles of emotions and ideas; where Zola – departing from his doctrine – built great scenes, raising the matters of his times to the rank of a powerful symbol, his epigones attempt at evoking some mood from eternally returning images. Their vocabulary can easily be composed of white swans gliding on quiet canals, black birds hovering above violet seas, white lilies swaying around glittering altars, etc.

It appears that only sculpture has not yet reached that 'new' stage. In fact, the sculptor – with minor exceptions – has long since distinguished himself by a particular lack of imagination. He has always been rather accommodating. He has been satisfied with the nude, whose limbs he twisted in accordance with various trends and into whose hands he inserted some objects. Sometimes, he joined two nudes, in order to obtain a harmonious 'whole', to which he then added an appropriate label.

With such 'spiritual art' Vigeland's oeuvre has nothing in common. It is neither old nor new; it is mere life, an all-powerful passion, vigour and depth; it is a revelation of the soul.

The soul has never been delicate, pure and languorous for it is an eruption of volcanic forces, an age-long fight between Jacob and the Angel. The soul is a clenched fist stretched out against heaven and bursting its gates; a shout that furrows the entirety of Nature, a thunderous torment of a dying giant that has wanted to pull down the sun but is perishing under its weight.

Rough and difficult is the way of the soul and those ready to travel along it will grow more and more scarce in this confined century of electricity and stock-exchange, of usury and the teachings about a happy and harmonious existence. And yet such people are a flight and Ascension of mankind. For our times they are what Magi once were for the Middle Ages.

The medieval artist enjoyed respect and understanding, while the Magus, never understood, met with contempt; he was a prosecuted pariah.

But it is a Magus exactly, a great philosopher and exuberant visionary, a meditating scholar and powerful poet in one person, such as Raymond Lulle, John Dee or Paracelsus, who is a genuine ancestor of those advancing along the soul's trails in our times.

The Magus was a cosmopolitan of the spirit, an arrogant anarchist who knew neither 'nation' nor 'humanity'. He fearfully defended his sacred knowledge. Thus, even the most severe tortures could not bend Alexander Sethon to give away the secret of the philosophers' stone to Christian II, Elector of Saxony. The Magus revealed his arcana to truly few ones.

So isn't the contemporary Magus like his medieval brethren?

He is equally homeless and surrounded by incomprehension and his holy mysteries are uncovered only to a few chosen people.

In the epoch that calls for national poets and national art, in which capital more and more strongly divides the nations, while socialism wants to flatten them out into an imaginary homogeneous mankind, the Magus is the Only One who stands above all, who venerates as his forefather not Adam, the father of the herd, but 'Samyâsa', the father of the Only One.

And his art is not a creation of the mediocre mind directed to the 'people', it is not the art of the sickly blasé nerves for the puny frequenters of perfumed consulting rooms, but the eternally old and eternally new art of the Only One for the Only One.

Kongsvinger (Norway)
November 1895

1   Verlaine.

2   For God's sake, we do not mean
     the funny clown of mysticism Sar
     Mérodack Joséphin Péladan. Anyway,
     it is him who wrote a very humble
     motto for the 'new' Parnassians:
     '*Lorsque ta main écrit une ligne
     parfait, les cherubim eux-mêmes
     descendent s'y complaire comme dans
     un miroir.*' Une ligne parfaite – isn't it
     enough for this amazing Ecce poeta!
     To attract an admiring herd? Ha!
     Ha! … One should read the words of
     the holy Magus Zarathustra about
     the 'last' men to be able to fully
     appreciate this statement in its noble-
     minded modesty.

Stanisław Przybyszewski:
The Work of Edvard Munch, 1894.
Published by S. Fischer Verlag, Berlin

DAS WERK

DES

Edvard Munchs

HERAUSGEGEBEN

VON

Stanislaw Przybyszewski

The Work of Edvard Munch

Stanisław Przybyszewski

Preface

The culturally advanced countries have a well-known habit of neglecting an artist during his lifetime and making amends to him for this posthumously by erecting monuments to his memory. I fear this is how it may go with Munch. For he belongs to that elite group of artists who wander uncomprehended and alone through life; he is of the tribe of those to whom we awake only late, very late.

There is no doubt that appreciation of Munch is particularly difficult for us. Our ideal of art, which rests upon on a very long tradition, is so immeasurably different from that of Munch, and the most recent stage in the development of art – naturalism – has so alienated us from the psychological and the imaginary, and has so dulled our perception of the deep and fathomless, that it is now virtually impossible suddenly to try to think our way into a new artistic ideal – one that eschews all use of realist technique and consists solely in the psychological, in the subtlest and finest movements of the soul.

To pave the way for a proper appreciation of the masterly art of this solitudinarian, to open up this richly complex and original artistic personage to the public is the purpose of the present book.

All the embryonic ideas that find expression in Munch's works are present in almost every complex human personality. The worldview and philosophy of life from which they spring are the worldview and philosophy of life of our age: all that is needed is a little guidance to render comprehensible that which might otherwise remain unintelligible or might be seen as a fanciful obsession of the artist's.

And this is precisely what is so impressive and so full of promise about Munch – that everything deep and dark, everything for which language as yet possesses no sound and which expresses itself only as a dark, foreboding compulsion, clothes itself in colour in his work and so steps into consciousness.

I was well aware that a personality as richly complex as this must not be considered from one point of view only and I therefore turned to the handful of critics who, in the reviews they have already published, have demonstrated a thorough-going appreciation of Munch. As a result, I am now in a position to present to the public a work containing as accurate and multi-faceted a portrait of this artist as it is possible to furnish.

In producing the book, I have certainly not adopted a blinkered approach. I did not intend that the work should be a piece of puffery in favour of the artist, or a means of trumpeting his praise to the world at large. Hence, taking its place alongside my own critique, which is unreservedly supportive of Munch, we have that of Franz Servaes,[1] which expresses only qualified approval; and alongside the calm, objective exposition offered by Willy Pastor[2] we find Meier-Graefe's[3] ecstatic fantasy. This latter is perhaps the most vivid testament to the power of Munch's creative action to fructify a fertile spirit.

The usual insinuations will, I know, inevitably be made. Naturally, we are happy to concede to each and every person the pleasure of questioning the artistic integrity of our enterprise; but all the doubts in the world could not have prevented me from publishing a work such as this.

As an artist, Munch is an absolutely mature, fully rounded personage; there is no possibility whatever that he will deviate, be it by an inch, from his chosen path. Hence, from this point of view also, our book cannot be deemed to be precipitate.

Of Munch's life there is little to relate. He was born on 12 December 1863 in Löiten[4] in Hedmark County, Norway. He was brought up in Christiania,[5] studied for a short time in Paris, and moved to Berlin a few years ago. He is a scion of an old established family that has produced many of Norway's leading menfolk, including, for example: B.P.A. Munch, who was the first to chronicle Norway's history; also Andreas Munch, an extremely erudite and exceptionally talented writer; and, in addition to these, a celebrated painter and sea-captain named Munch, whose daughter was the mother of the renowned painter Thaulow.[6]

Munch is still young and, one hopes, will have sufficient energy to accomplish the mammoth task of painting a cycle of pictures that encompasses the whole of life – a cycle of which the first section, 'Love', is almost complete.

Berlin, March 1894
The Editor

—

I once had a dream which literally came true. But when the event prefigured in the dream came to pass, I was seized by a strange feeling, a peculiar mixture of fear, dread and horror, a feeling of deep disquiet. A sudden jolt went through my brain as it registered the fact that the principle of least mental effort[7] had just taken a drubbing.

And so I began to try to make sense of the episode. There could be no other explanation but that my brain had seen and heard things in its surroundings which 'I' had not seen or heard but which formed the causal continuum that had eventually culminated in the event in question. These impressions of sight and sound lay somewhere deep in another consciousness; they lay there catching hold of other, related impressions, ordering them and combining them into logical sequences until they suddenly appeared in my personality's consciousness.[8]

This manifestation of my individuality, with its ability to see and hear that which my personality cannot perceive, this revelation of a Something within me that is living a life other than the one of which I am aware and that has finer senses than those at my command, this Other within me – it was this that filled me with disquiet.

The very same feelings came over me when I stood before Edvard Munch's works. I again found myself confronted with manifestations of a naked individuality, products of a somnambulic, transcendental consciousness commonly dubbed 'the unconscious'. One may give it whatever name one chooses. I call it 'individuality' and when I do so, I intend this not as a categorising concept, according to which it would denote only the lowest, 'scarcely perceptible', rung of consciousness, but as an individualising concept, conceived of as a counterpole to the consciousness of the personality. To me, individuality is that which is immortal, inalienable. It is the root-stock onto which, through heredity, new traits are continually grafted; it is the bearer of that which is passed on; it endlessly propagates itself and has been in existence since primeval times, from the first glimmerings of life inside the organic spore right up to the highest stage of development – the human being. It is like an ever-swelling wave, a seed that propagates itself ad infinitum through repeated metempsychosis. It thus gathers together in each human being all the traits that characterised the distinct sections of their entire developmental course – a pangenesis in the sense that Darwin conceived it, with each germ-cell carrying within itself the complete individual and all their distinguishing features.

Individuality endows sense impressions with intensity and quality; within it lies the point of convergence where all impressions flow together, where the most disparate things are perceived as the same because individuality reacts to all of them with identical emotion; colour becomes line, scent becomes sound: 'Les parfums, les couleurs et les sons se répondent.'[9]

Individuality is the immortal part of a human being; and because it is so immeasurably older than the youthful brain, and because it is so immeasurably more receptive than the brain, and because it possesses so immeasurably finer a set of sense organs than the brain, it is the primal ground in which the psychological life is rooted; it saturates the sense impressions, endows them with life, pours itself into them via the mighty bloodstream of feelings and passions. It is thus the mighty force that shakes foundations, the furious energy that heaps Pelion on Ossa,[10] the power that captivates us, the great flow of warmth, life and the beating heart.

Two people see a landscape. One sees it with the pitiful faculties of the brain: impressions of light, colours, shapes, lines – a nicely ordered conglomerate, lack-lustre, soulless, hackneyed and boring. In the consciousness of the individuality this landscape takes on a different appearance. The colours glow and burn and have heightened intensity; lines that a child might have scrawled onto its slate acquire a powerful pulsating energy; they establish a rapport with the innermost life of the soul; they merge with forms in the soul and the onlooker becomes one with the landscape, lives in and through it.

This is the secret that drives that most intimate of all feelings – love of one's homeland, of the fatherland. It is also the secret that inspires the sensibilities of an artist of power and stature.

Let us just consider one random theme – a woman's revenge – as handled respectively by 'personal' and 'individual' artists.

The artist who is capable only of working in a personal way, who is familiar only with forms he has accumulated from his experience, who is unable to move beyond certain traditional ways of thinking – this artist will no doubt produce a painting of a *vitrioleuse*,[11] lying in wait behind a wall for the approaching couple.

Now compare this with an etching by Félicien Rops.[12] Rops's *Vengeance d'une femme*[13] is composed as follows: a woman stands in corset and petticoat inside a burial vault. She is lifting the petticoat and pointing towards her private parts in a gesture of wanton, savage, cynical grandiosity. At her feet lies a coffin and through holes in the wall on either side of the doorway in which she stands we see men's arms protrude, bearing lamps that light up the scene. This is the horrific tragedy of man destroyed by woman, by the Whore of Babylon;[14] this is Mylitta[15] and the Great Whore of the Apocalypse; this is Georges Sand[16] and Nana[17] rolled into one. This is a gigantic symbol of the eternal and ferocious battle of the sexes.

The creative process is a synthetic one. Rops has here captured an impression that all at once lights up the innermost depths of the soul, as in the momentary flash of a magnesium lamp.[18] It is an impression of the intense hatred that can suddenly flare up in the eyes of even the most loving woman. But this impression has evolved, expanded, matured, sought out personal forms that enter the brain through the eye, and here clothed itself in the imagined figure of a woman standing before the coffin of her dead husband.

The original impression that made its way into the deepest levels of the soul, took root there, and once again grew up into the brain, is rendered as symbol, made visible, endowed with a new form, clothed in a narrative scene. But it is not captured as it is, not presented naked to the eye.

Edvard Munch is the first to have attempted to depict the finest and most subtle movements of the soul exactly as they appear – spontaneously and completely independently of any mental process – in the unalloyed consciousness of the individuality. His pictures are tantamount to painted specimens of the soul, fixed at the moment when all the voices of rationality have fallen silent, when all mental activity has ceased. They are specimens of the soul-as-animal, the reasonless soul captured as it writhes, as it swirls up tempestuously, as it sinks into states of gloomy semi-existence, as it screams in paroxysms of pain, as it howls with hunger.

—

Of the works which Munch exhibited in December last year, I here select only the cycle entitled *Love*, because this series of paintings fully conveys the essence of the artist. In all, there are six paintings: *Spring Mood*,[19] *The Kiss*, *Vampire*, *Jealousy*, *Despair*[20] and *Madonna*.

The first painting (fig. 37) shows a young girl in the foreground, her figure largely blurred in a mystical half-light. Between trees of an intense green we see a stretch of sea merging into the sky, a moon and its test-tube-shaped reflection in the water, and, far away in the background, half floating in the sky, a boat.

Clearly, the representational content is in itself utterly inconsequential, but when it comes to evoking the mood, it plays a very powerful role. That mood is the yearning that comes with puberty. It appears suddenly, burgeons, swells, churning shapeless to and fro; it flows hither and thither, masses itself together and cries out for form and shape. And at that moment it can happen that heaven and earth merge and the trees turn into green telegraph-poles and everything spins round you in a whirlwind and such a fire takes you that your tears boil over. This is the yearning of becoming and beginning, the whole agonising yearning that comes with transformation, the trepidation born of anxious expectation – the rapt attention to the inner voice, half dread, half desire, rooted in the dark sensuous depths of sexual arousal. This is Venus Anadyomene, as symbolised so wonderfully by Richard Dehmel.[21]

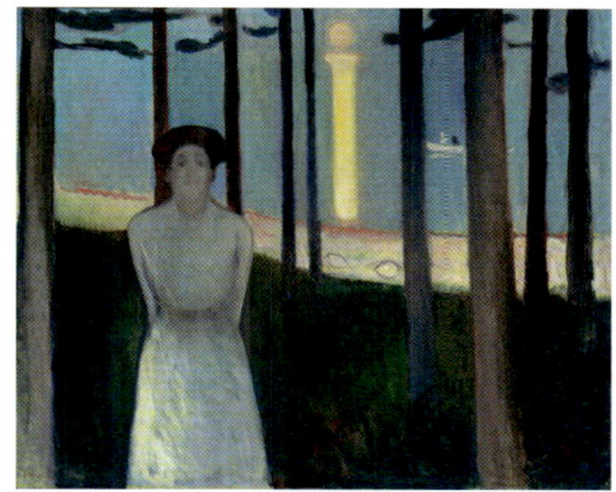

Fig. 37. Edvard Munch: *Summer Night's Dream. The Voice*, 1893

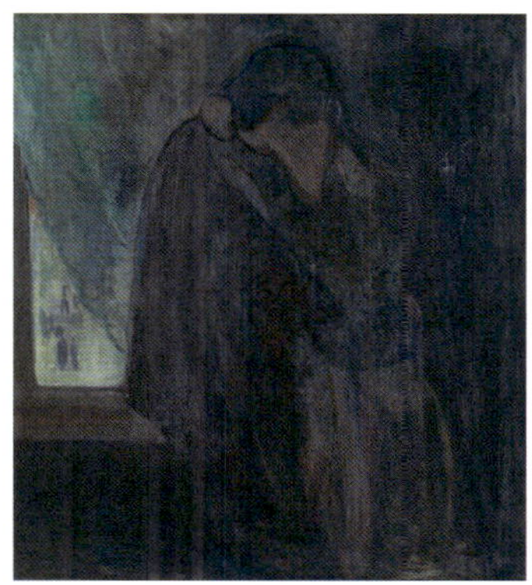

Fig. 38. Edvard Munch: *The Kiss*, 1892/97

The subject of the second painting is *The Kiss* (fig. 38). We see two figures with their faces merged into one other. Not a single feature is distinguishable. All we see is the locus of fusion, looking like a huge ear and rendered utterly deaf to the world as the blood scales the heights of ecstasy; it has the appearance of a small pool of liquefied flesh – there is something repulsive about it. The symbolism is certainly odd, but the whole voracious fervour of the kiss, the terrible power of that erotic, achingly tongue-lolling desire, the disappearance of the consciousness belonging to personality, the melding of two naked individualities, is visualised in so honest a fashion that we manage to move beyond the combined sensation of repulsiveness and oddity.

The third painting presents us with a madonna. This is a woman clad in a shift and caught in that characteristic motion of utter abandonment in which the sensations of every organ in the body are transformed into erethisms of intense pleasure; a madonna in déshabillé recumbent on crumpled sheets and bearing the halo of the martyrial travails to come; a madonna captured at the moment when the unfathomable mystery of that age-old procreative frenzy floods the woman's face with the glow of beauty, when sensation attains to its greatest depths as the civilised human being, with its metaphysical urge to eternity, encounters the wild beast with its frenzied lust for destruction.

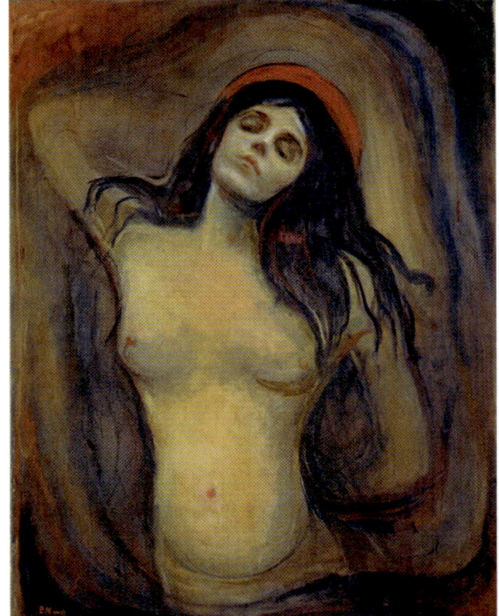

Fig. 39. Edvard Munch: *Madonna*, 1894–95

In the next painting Munch gives us a depiction of love and pain (fig. 40): a broken-spirited man is pictured with a vampire sucking at the nape of his neck. The background is a curious motley of blue, purple, green and yellow, each mixed into the other, blending with one another, juxtaposed or dovetailed with one other crystal-fashion. There is something terrifyingly calm, terrifyingly devoid of passion about this picture; an immeasurable sense of fatality that comes with resignation. The man is tumbling forever downward into fathomless depths, without will or strength, and he is glad that he can roll away so unresistingly, like a stone. But he will not be free of the vampire; and he will not be free of the pain; and the woman will always be seated there, will always be biting him with a thousand adder's tongues, with a thousand poisonous fangs.

This painting is perhaps the most individual in its conception. In a peripheral sense, love may well be a blessing: in the consciousness of the personality it offers gratification, it enhances the mental powers so wonderfully, it saturates sense impressions so gloriously, and it bewitches the mind so splendidly that it rolls like a roulette ball around the few pathetic boundary markers of bliss. But the age-old soul that resides in the pit of the stomach and has lived through all the upheavals of evolution, all the convulsions of natural selection – this soul experiences love differently. In the depths of that soul, love becomes a piercing pain, a gnawing vampire, a terrible torment of never being able to shake off the woman, never being able to satisfy the ravenous demon of the senses. And into the very midst of the wonderful sense of bliss erupts the torrent of fiery lava spewed out by the primeval volcano. And now comes the moment when we realise that this whole happiness is, in reality, a worm-riddled euphoria hatched in the filth by the heat of the sun.

Another picture from the same cycle, entitled *Jealousy*, depicts a landscape traced in finger-thick lines and cast in a crass, stultified chiaroscuro. In the foreground – as in Chinese paintings – we see a man's head looking out from the picture-frame. One eye resembles a triangle – a symbol of the neverendingness of this most commonplace and agonising of emotions. Contained in this picture is the whole mindless, obdurate brooding of a passion that has tipped over into the most insane kind of desperation-induced idiocy. The picture is essentially the embodiment, in paint, of the physiological experience of light and dark associated with the *cicisbeo*;[22] it is essentially a representation, in paint, of the philosophy of natural selection and its torments. This is the kind of landscape that forms in the mind of a male member of the species when a female to whom he is drawn by the most intimate urges of natural selection is claimed by another: the savage prehistoric battle for the female of the species turns into the civilised man's dismal, pusillanimous, stultifying sulk.

And so we come to the last painting: *Despair* (fig. 41). On a bridge or similar structure – exactly what it represents is immaterial – stands a grotesque creature with jaws agape. Love's man of courage is clearly defunct: his sexual urge has slunk out of him and is now wandering through the countryside howling for a new incarnation in which it might once again experience the same torment, the same struggle. There is something terrifyingly macrocosmic about this painting; it is the concluding scene in a horrendous battle that has pitted the rational against the sexual and seen the latter emerge victorious. There is only one other painter who has depicted this struggle on the same grandiose scale – albeit with other means – and that is the French[23] artist Delville. [In Delville's portrayal,] a man

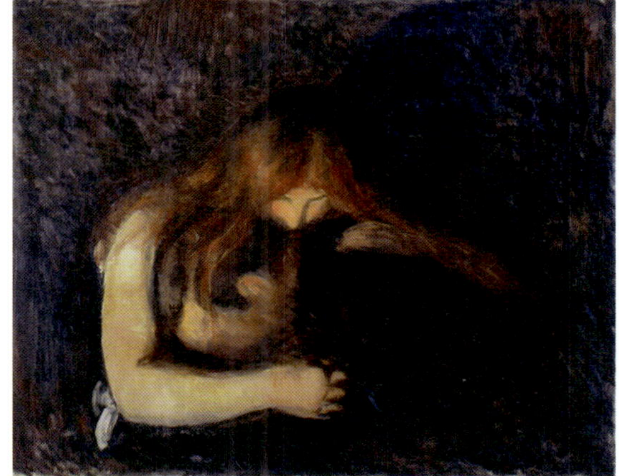

Fig. 40. Edvard Munch: *Vampire*, 1893

with a mighty torso struggles for release; every muscle is a hellish ordeal of pain-ridden striving for deliverance; every sinew an extension of the spinal cord labouring in agony to break free of the torment. But wrapped around the man's waist is a demonic female figure with a body that extends down into a huge, fully individualised genitalia. The woman is essentially nothing but one huge sex-organ. Around the two figures extends a network of thorny stems and blood-vessels; the whole giant plexus of uterine blood-vessels has wound itself around them and the woman-sex-organ is convulsed with laughter at the man-mind's glorious ascension into heaven. The next stage in the struggle is shown to us by Munch. The mind has attained deliverance through destruction, and the sexual urge, that primordial and timeless force, howls for new victims.

Of especial interest in this picture are the topographical features. What we have is a landscape of emotions, as is the case in all Munch's works. Such landscapes are merely emotional correlates, just as the raw, unmusical music of a savage's interjections are absolute correlates of the latter's feelings. There is a mystical emotional process at work here, of the kind noted, for example, by Baudelaire when describing an autumn landscape (in his 'Artist's Confession'): 'Toutes ces choses pensent par moi ou je pense par elles, car dans la grandeur de la rêverie, le moi se perd vite; elles pensent, dis-je, mais musicalement, et pittoresquement, sans arguties, sans syllogismes, sans déductions.'[24]

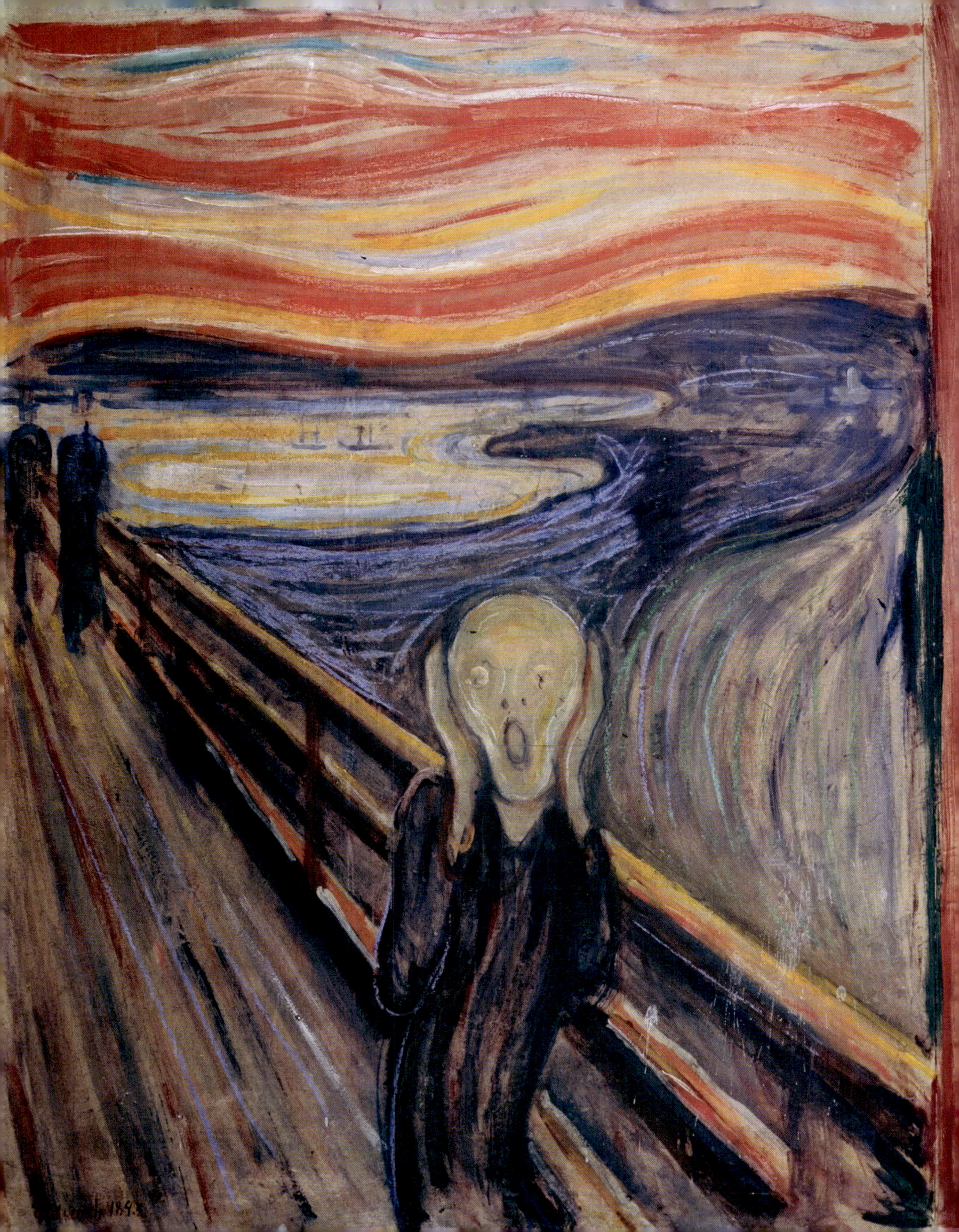

From this same mood, Gautier[25] also conjured up a landscape – one of metallic, marmoreal aspect, in which everything is rigid and highly polished. But where this sensuous chiseller of words offers us a process of pure intellectual refinement, which merely enacts a structured idea, Munch offers us the pure, naked emotions of the individuality. His landscape is the absolute correlate of naked feeling; every quiver of the nerves exposed as the ecstasy of pain reaches its climax is translated into a corresponding colour-sensation. Every stab of pain is a blood-red smear of paint, every lingering howl of agony is a girdle of blue, green and yellow strokes laid down furiously alongside one another without thought of harmony or balance – like the seething elements of inchoate worlds in the wild throes of genesis.

—

Despite the huge number of favourable and unfavourable reviews of Munch that have appeared over the last few years, scarcely a single critic has grasped the essence of Munch's art. He has simply been measured against the template of a conventional artist – an artist who, primed by age-old tradition, has a multitude of forms, lines and colours to draw on. An attempt was made to lump him in with the symbolists. In the end, no one had any idea how to approach him. We can't blame the critics: finding one's way around Munch is a rather difficult task. All painters to date have been painters of the external world. Whenever they wanted to depict a feeling, they clothed it in some kind of external scenario; whenever there was a mood to evoke, they expressed it indirectly, through the external surroundings. The effect was always generated indirectly, through the agency of the world of external phenomena. Expression of psychological phenomena through external scenarios, of *états d'âmes* through *états de choses*,[26] has so far been the unshakeable tradition that no painter has dared to flout. Munch has broken utterly with this tradition. He seeks to depict psychological phenomena directly through colour. He paints things as only a naked individuality can see them whose gaze has turned from the world of external phenomena to the life within. His landscapes are visualised in the soul, perhaps as Platonic recollections of a past existence; his forms are conceived musically, rhythmically; his rocky crags stand before us like the grimacing devils that inhabit fever-induced nightmares; his clouds are like spectroscopic conglomerates of colour; the boundary set by the horizon is absent and boats seem to travel across the sky – Munch's paintings are, quite simply, exact correlates of particular groups of emotions. What we have here is thus an entirely new realm of art which Munch has entered for the first time. And he must indeed be viewed as the first-comer: he has no forerunners, he has no tradition – or if he does, he will, one hopes, throw it overboard forthwith, lock, stock and barrel.

What Munch aims to do, in short, is to render a psychological, naked event, not in a mythological way – that is to say, by means of metaphors perceptible to the senses – but directly, in its colour-equivalents. From this point of view, Munch is the

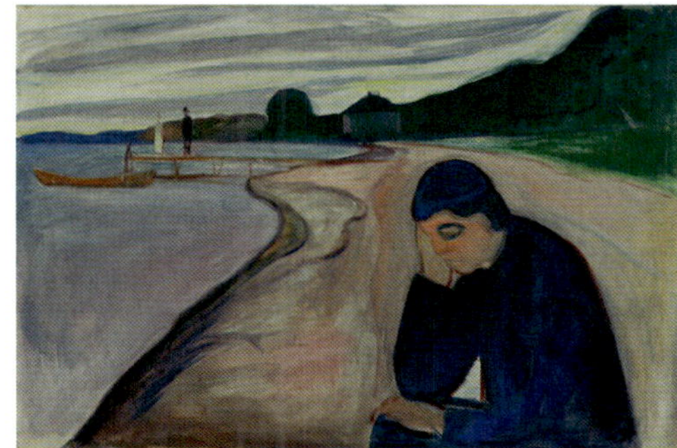

Fig. 42. Edvard Munch: *Melancholy*, 1893

Fig. 41. Edvard Munch: *The Scream*, 1893

premier naturalist interpreter of psychological phenomena, just as Liebermann,[27] say, is the most uncompromisingly naturalist interpreter of the external world.

Munch paints hauntedness and existential angst; he paints the chaos of the fevered mind and the presentient dread of the abyss; he paints a theory that cannot be elaborated logically and can only be sensed in a muted, ill-defined way – in the same way that we sense what death is and yet cannot picture it.

In this realm, there are no forms created by the operation of artistic preference or tradition. The laws of aesthetics, based as they are solely on externalities, have no sway here. There is only an urge to exteriorise inchoate ideas through raw symbols, impulsively snatched together, and through ill-defined, anthropomorphic forms half-melting from view. There is only the frenzied energy of impulses crying out to be given form – an energy such as I have only ever seen once before, in a work by the *artiste-prêtre* Wagner (Théo): a woman is pictured legs agape, with the wildly contorted face of one possessed and with the frightening pent-up energy of someone ready to fend off attack. In order to express this fearful energy and the whole frantic welter of incipient motor-impulses paralysed by an unnameable, nightmarish terror, the artist gives the figure four or five legs and as many arms, pictured in diverse defensive positions.

To my mind, therefore, Munch is the painter who portrays the psychological drive of emotional impulses to embodiment, the painter who portrays the frenzied psychological energy through which an emotion expresses itself at its point of greatest intensity. Hence the rawness, exaggeratedness, grotesqueness of his manner of painting. Munch – so my friend Peter Hille[28] shrewdly remarks – has the audacity of the grotesque.

These things are all the products of a brain in a highly precarious state of consciousness, where the conscious and the unconscious flow into one another. These are all creations of a consciousness that has witnessed everything and has a different tradition from that of the newcomer-mind of the personality, with scarcely more than a human lifetime's experience to draw on. These are phenomena which, in psychological terms, rank alongside manifestations of pure individual life – vision, clairvoyance, dreams and so on.

Munch does have a tradition, albeit one of which he will scarcely be aware – a literary tradition.

In Brussels and Paris there are some (naturally!) 'completely insane' people who have stumbled upon the (naturally!) 'completely crack-brained' idea of transposing into words the finest, subtlest psychological associations, the faintest, innermost expressions of emotion that flit like shadows through the soul.

[For these individuals], their soul, their inner life, is the only reality, an entire cosmos, and they have taken it upon themselves to convey, to capture in words, to express through the music of words how the processes of this world unfold, how the most deeply buried substructures and roots of this world momentarily reveal themselves, how impressions work their way up from the depths, through the mist and fog, into the consciousness, only to disappear again immediately, how the scarcely perceptible agitation of the birthing process, the faint glimmering of becoming, shivers through the soul, how a whirlwind whips up in fury.[29]

In this kind of art, there are no longer any narrative scenes: impressions are presented in their never-ending comings and goings, without the logical connections that arise through reflection. Consciousness as controller is rejected because, by constructing logical sequences that are not there originally, it deflects the image generated by the soul.

This kind of art operates only through the sound of words, which convey a mood, or through a series of images that evoke this mood through allusion and suggestion.

'Nommer un objet', says Stéphane Mallarmé, 'c'est supprimer les trois quarts de la jouissance du poème qui est faite du bonheur de deviner peu à peu; le suggérer, voilà le rêve.'[30]

I must forgo any deeper examination of this subject here, or any consideration of the significance it might have for the future course of art. For the present, this kind of art exists only for those few souls in whom the very subtlest of feelings can arouse the same intense aesthetic pleasure as that which others experience as they revel in pleasingly constructed, rhythmical processes of thought, for those few souls who derive greater pleasure from the glimmering of some nameless mood deep within themselves than from clearly defined objects and their assemblage into narrative scenes.

The exponents of this art are the creators of value, the re-fashioners, the true aristocrats of the spirit – and Edvard Munch is just such an aristocrat, every last inch of him. That is truly how I see him, with his proud, quietly wrathful defiance of unconscionably vicious attacks which Nietzsche would have described as exceeding human measure and bordering on the bestial; that is how I see him, with his preference for the close-lipped solitude of those who tread their own path and with the onerous fate of those who, as Barbey d'Aurevilly[31] has put it, have only one proof of their genius during their lifetime: hunger and misery.

1   German critic and writer (1862–1947).

2   German art historian, critic and writer (1867–1933).

3   Julius Meier-Graefe (1867–1935), German art historian, critic and writer.

4   Now spelled Løten.

5   Present-day Oslo.

6   Frits Thaulow (1847–1906), Norwegian painter.

7   'L'Inertie mentale et la loi du moindre effort' was published by the French philosopher Guillaume Ferrero at about this time (*Revue philosophique de la France et de l'étranger*, vol. 37, pp. 169–82).

8   'Persönlichkeitsbewusstsein'. Przybyszewski distinguishes between what seems to be an unconscious inner self and a conscious, 'public' self, which he terms, respectively, 'Individualität' (individuality) and 'Persönlichkeit' (personality). It is in these senses that the terms have been retained in their English forms throughout the text.

9   'Perfumes, colours and sounds resonate with one another' – a quotation from Charles Baudelaire's 'Correspondances'.

10 From Greek mythology: two mountains in northern Greece which the giant brothers Otus and Ephialtes are said to have tried to pile on top of each other in order to attack the gods in heaven (Homer, *Odyssey*, 11: 305).

11 A woman who seeks revenge by throwing acid. Possibly an allusion to the contemporary engraving *La Vitrioleuse* by the Swiss engraver and decorative artist Eugène Grasset.

12 Belgian graphic artist (1833–1898).

13 'A Woman's Revenge'.

14 Whore of Babylon, Great Whore of the Apocalypse: as depicted in the Bible (Revelations/Apocalypse 17).

15 Babylonian goddess of love at whose temple Babylonian women are said to have been required once in their life to offer themselves to a stranger, hence the connection with harlotry.

16 Pseudonym for the French feminist and writer Amantine-Lucile-Aurore Dupin (1804–1876).

17 Emile Zola's eponymous novel recounts Nana's rise from common prostitute to courtesan.

18 A photographic allusion: the use of magnesium lighting was a relatively recent introduction in photography.

19 Later titled *Summer Night's Dream. The Voice*.

20 Later titled *The Scream*.

21 The poem 'Venus Anadyomene' [Venus Rising from the Sea] appeared in a collection published by the German poet Richard Dehmel (1863–1920) in 1893.

22 It was accepted practice in eighteenth-century Italy for married women of high birth to have an officially recognised gentleman escort. Such a person was often referred to as a *cicisbeo*.

23 In fact, the symbolist painter Jean Delville (1867–1953) was Belgian.

24 'All these things think through me, or I think through them – because the "me"

is quickly lost in the hugeness of reverie. When I say they think, I mean musically, and pictorially, with no quibbles, no "if thens", no "therefores"': Charles Baudelaire, 'Le Confiteor de l'artiste', from the collection *Le Spleen de Paris*.

25 Théophile Gautier (1811–1872), French writer and critic.

26 'States of mind through states of affairs or physical situations.'

27 Max Liebermann (1847–1935), German painter and graphic artist.

28 German poet and writer (1854–1904) who led an impoverished, vagabond existence, and was known to many in the intellectual circles of the time.

29 [Original footnote] Readers with an interest in this area are referred to Maeterlinck's *Serres Chaudes* (Brussels: Paul Lacombiez, 1891, new edn). [*Serres Chaudes* – 'Hothouses' – is a collection of poetry published in 1889 by the Belgian symbolist writer Maurice Maeterlinck.]

30 'Naming a thing robs us of most of the enjoyment we derive from a poem, which consists in gradual discernment. To suggest the thing – that's the dream.' Mallarmé in an interview on the literary trends of his day. Jules Huret, *Enquête sur l'évolution littéraire* (Paris: Bibliothèque-Charpentier, 1891), pp. 55–65.

31 Barbey d'Aurevilly (1808–1889), French writer.

Esotericism in Modernity, and the Lure of the Occult Elite: The Seekers of the Zum Schwarzen Ferkel Circle

Per Faxneld

Our story begins in Berlin, at a small establishment nicknamed Zum Schwarzen Ferkel (The Black Piglet). In the mid-1890s, a group of artists regularly gathered at this tavern to drink, argue, exchange ideas, forge intense bonds and, as it would turn out, change the history of European art and literature. The subsequently legendary Ferkel circle included among its many on-and-off-again members the Pole Stanisław Przybyszewski and several Scandinavians, for instance August Strindberg, Edvard Munch, Axel Gallén (Akseli Gallen-Kallela) and Gustav Vigeland. Among the things they shared was an interest in alternative, heterodox spirituality – or more precisely, esotericism. In this period, esotericism had come to assume a specific shape, which scholarship has designated *occultism*.

Let us now take a step back, to clarify the context of the artists' interest. First of all, what does the term occultism signify? During the stage in modernity that we are dealing with here, esoteric currents had to find a way to deal with the advances of natural science. How was a ritual magician, for example, to handle the discovery of X-rays (1895) and microorganisms (awareness of germs as the cause of disease in the 1850s, and wide acceptance of cell theory in the 1860s)? Both seemed to indicate the existence of hidden dimensions of the world around us, albeit in a manner quite different from classic esoteric understandings. Was this an affirmation of the esoteric worldview, or something that would topple it? Needless to say, such developments caused considerable anxiety.

The esotericism specialist Wouter Hanegraaff has suggested the term occultism as a label for the various coping strategies. As an etic term (a scholarly classification, rather than an 'insider' or contemporary understanding), this would designate 'attempts by esotericists to come to terms with a disenchanted world or, alternatively, by people in general to make sense of esotericism from the perspective of a secular disenchanted world'.[1] Occultism, then, is the phase in which esotericism, and views of it, were to an unprecedented extent affected by the complex processes of secularisation, which were so intense in the nineteenth century. A practical example might be how esotericists try to make their teachings somehow conform to the findings of natural science, or when a vocabulary is borrowed from such contexts to strengthen one's legitimacy and, so to speak, 'keep up with the times'. Here, we can commonly observe a rhetoric claiming that the supposed opposition between esotericism and science is false and will be, or already has been, conquered.[2] Przybyszewski, for instance, would in a late stage of his career argue that while astral bodies and similar phenomena defied the science of his time, and thus appeared 'supernatural', a more advanced science would surely eventually be able to comprehend them.[3] A typical organisational example of occultism, in Hanegraaff's sense, would be the modern version of Theosophy (more on which presently), where ambiguous appeals to the legitimacy of science are a prominent theme.[4]

Commonly, occultist attempts to achieve legitimacy simultaneously entailed a *delegitimation* of established, orthodox religion. It was plain to all that Christianity was under attack during the late nineteenth century. The aggressors were everything from evolutionists in the natural sciences, to atheist socialists. Last but not least, it was also challenged by the upsurge of alternative new religions, such as the Theosophical Society, founded in 1875. The latter, based around the idea of a secret common core to all spiritual teachings across the world, had quickly become a successful semi-mass movement. By 1889, the Theosophical Society had 227 sections all over the world. Moreover, many of the era's foremost intellectuals and artists were strongly influenced by this new religion, which drew on a plethora of concepts from older esoteric traditions. Avant-garde painters, in particular, took the teaching to heart, and, aside from the Ferkel circle, it marked the work of pioneers of abstraction like Piet Mondrian, Wassily Kandinsky, Paul Klee and Hilma af Klint. Literary figures, such as the poet and Nobel Prize laureate William Butler Yeats, also became members, and incorporated Theosophical motifs into their writings.[5]

Unlike the obscure lore presented earlier by Eliphas Lévi and similar authors, which mostly ended up attracting a small portion of freethinkers, Theosophy was a phenomenon that appealed to a broad upper- and middle-class audience. Far from everyone who took an interest became a member of the society. Instead, people commonly read Theosophical literature independently, contemplating its ideas and then accepting some and rejecting others. This was the case with several artists and authors. Strindberg, for example, was quite critical of Theosophy, but nevertheless incorporated some of its ideas into his own thinking and writing.[6] Though it was probably the most prominent esoteric current of its time, Theosophy was far from the only one. Many of the other varieties also appealed to artists. The esoterically influenced works the artists subsequently produced in turn spread awareness of the ideas in question to a wider audience. An important thing to bear in mind is that it was not only the avant-garde of high culture producing art that conveyed esoteric themes, and was embedded in such discourse. 'Low' or popular culture in the nineteenth century was just as much a part of this, with authors like the notorious hack Edward Bulwer-Lytton (fig. 49)

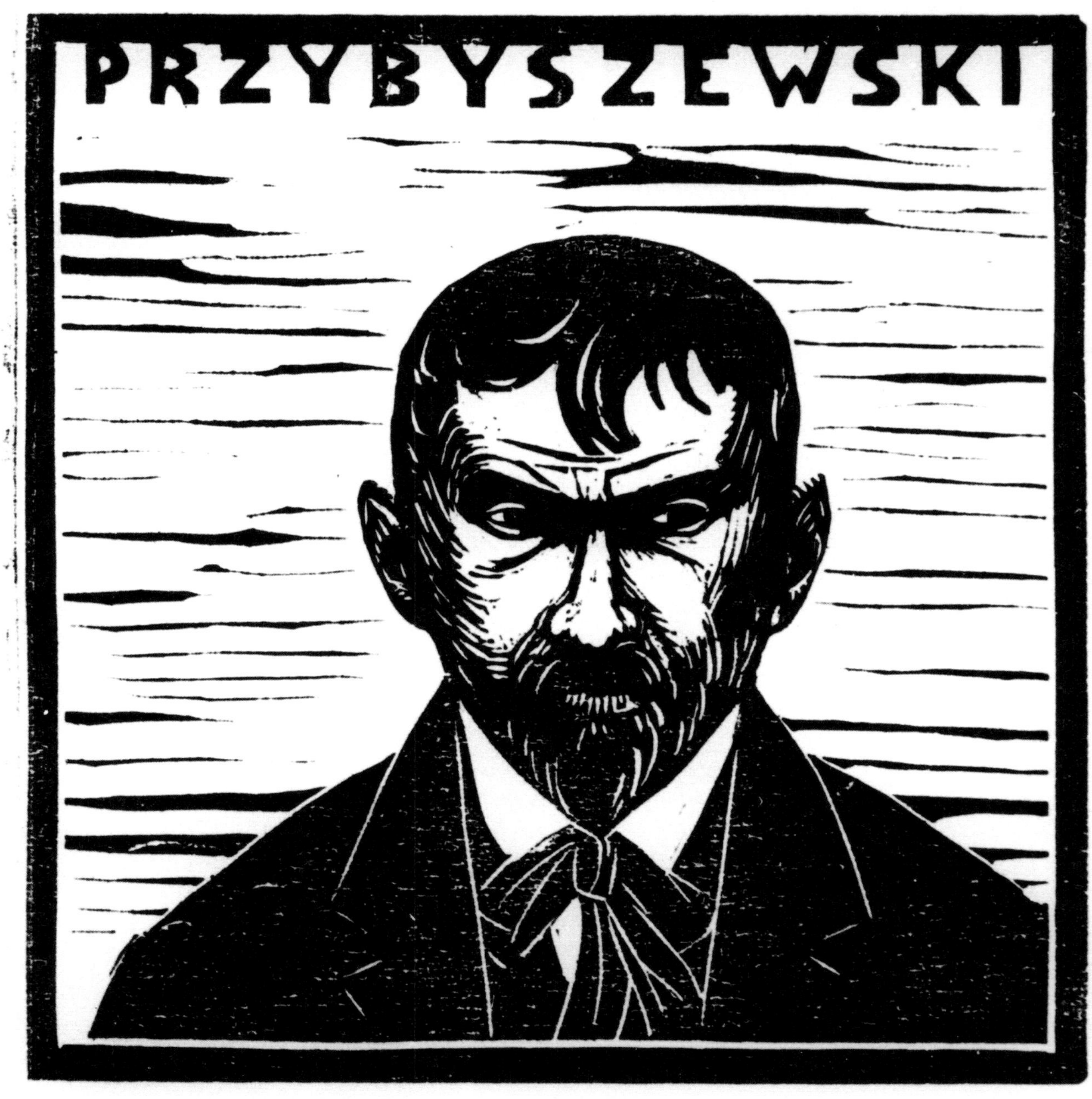
PRZYBYSZEWSKI

selling huge numbers of his poorly written but entertaining novels about strange energy fields, secret societies and transcendental initiatory knowledge.[7]

The totality of the cross-fertilisation of esotericism and art (high and low) is perhaps best understood through the lens of religious studies scholar Christopher Partridge's analytical concept *occulture*. This term signifies a reservoir of heterodox, alternative worldviews, which both feed into and are fed by popular culture.[8] Partridge originally intended it to be applied primarily to the period from the end of the Second World War onwards, but the Finnish art historian Nina Kokkinen has convincingly argued that it has relevance for nineteenth-century material as well.[9] Another argument for why this may be the case can be found if we consider how the founding father of esotericism studies, Antoine Faivre, views occultism. He perceives it either as 'a group of practices or a form of action that would derive its legitimacy from esotericism' (in other words, esotericism is the abstract theory, occultism its practical application), or, more interestingly for our purposes, as a form of esotericism appearing with Eliphas Lévi during the second half of the nineteenth century.[10] The latter meaning might seem to be close to Hanegraaff's stance, yet Faivre does not specify what is unique about this later development. However, he remarks that the appearance of the new term occultism, popularised by Lévi (as an -ism) in the 1850s, 'coincided precisely with the appearance of a trivial esotericism'. In other words, he seems to evaluate occultism as a vulgar form of neo-esotericism, which can be contrasted with a more noble and elevated predecessor.[11]

This latter understanding is compelling in the present context because it can be seen as connecting quite closely with Partridge's occulture theory. Even if Partridge does not pass judgement on occulture as being trivial, what he describes may be considered a process whereby esoteric motifs migrate from more lofty and secretive contexts to become commonplace and non-exclusive. This, then, might be an important second aspect of the phase of esotericism that Hanegraaff describes as occultism: its integration into a broader occulture, made possible by modernity's advances in mass media (primarily through increased literacy, and the rise of mass-market fiction, newspapers and special interest journals) and the weakening of Christianity's hegemony. In fact, the uneasy overlap of high and low occultish art may, just like the clash of esotericism and science, be seen as part of occultism and occulture's characteristic hybridity.

That being said, and even if Partridge tends to focus on popular expressions, the merging of high art with esotericism in itself fits well with the occulture model. Art and (alternative as well as more orthodox forms of) religion had begun to blend in more and more idiosyncratic and individualistic ways towards the end of the nineteenth century. Such dissolution of boundaries – where religion increasingly became a concept one could reshape into the form one found pleasing, or appropriate for irreverent artistic projects – was part of the process of secularisation. Rather than eradicating religion, this process often instead pushed it back from the public sphere to the private realm. Under these circumstances, established churches were unable to exert control to the extent that had earlier been

Fig. 43. Gustav Vigeland: *Stanisław Przybyszewski*, c. 1929 the case, and heterodox hybridisations, for example between art and religion, flourished. Paradoxically, these new alternative (and 'private') spiritualities could then re-enter the public sphere, reconfigured as artistic products.

In a later piece where he develops the concept of occulture further, Partridge has specified it as 'a democratised occult, an open esotericism' which is, in a sense, everyday, popular and accessible.[12] Yet, while esoteric texts were no doubt widely available at this time, much of the allure still lay in its 'elite' nature, or, at least, its rhetoric of elitism. It is easy to see why this was an important point for avant-garde artists, who often saw themselves as standing above the vulgar mass of men. Quite pertinently for such elitism, the religious studies scholar Kocku von Stuckrad conceptualises esotericism as a discourse where a central position is occupied by rhetoric of secrecy pertaining to higher knowledge and the means by which it can be reached.[13] Hanegraaff and Faivre have both argued against *actual* secrecy as a requisite for something to be considered esoteric, as much of the material has long-since intentionally been widely disseminated (see for example Partridge's view of an 'open esotericism').[14] While this is true, Stuckrad has a point that a *rhetoric* of secrecy – which may pertain less to the physical accessibility of the material than to what Stuckrad designates 'the dialectic of the hidden and revealed' – is nonetheless almost always present in the discourses most scho-lars see as esoteric (in whatever sense they employ the word), even if the actual mode of circulation is anything but secretive.[15] The dimension of secrecy is directly related to the status esotericism enjoyed with the avant-garde, as the self-understanding of esoteric thinkers tends to be that the 'masses' are unable both to understand and appreciate their teachings, wherefore this wisdom is best kept to the enlightened elite – very much in keeping with the inflated self-image and superciliousness of many of the modernist artistic schools.

As Nina Kokkinen has explained, members of this artistic elite tended to think of themselves as 'seekers', which can be related to sociologist Colin Campbell's influential 1972 delineation of a heterogeneous 'cultic milieu'.[16] Such a milieu func-tions as a repository of the various forms of 'rejected knowledge' underpinning an eclectic multitude of new religious movements ('cults', in Campbell's terminology).[17] Campbell highlights an ideology of 'seekership' as central to the milieu, and this fits well with the biographies of esoterically inclined nineteenth-century cultural figures like Strindberg, Munch and Przybyszewski.[18] The latter's term 'wanderers of the paths of the soul' (see below) could to an extent be seen as indicative of this exploratory mindset, which strives to reach beyond orthodox religious con-ceptions of the world, but is reluctant to make firm commitments to any single new alternative.

Notions of the figure of the artist as an explorer of the occult realm – in a sense that here, however, tended towards the metaphorical – were also widespread in non-esotericist critical discourse on art. Walter Pater's chapter on Leonardo da Vinci in *The Renaissance: Studies in Art and Poetry* (1873), for instance, promi-nently featured an 'esoterisation' of its subject, portraying Leonardo as a sort of magician.[19] In addition to art critics outside of the esoteric circles, writers who were occultists themselves also contributed to this discourse. A notable later example of this was the flamboyant Parisian Joséphin Péladan (1858–1918), who founded an esoteric fraternity, L'Ordre du Temple de la Rose + Croix, and was a central figure in the esoteric milieu of turn-of-the-century Europe. Moreover, he was a successful novelist (at least in terms of sales figures), and played a pivotal role in the development of symbolist art. Among those who were inspired by him was Strindberg. During his esotericist phase, the famous playwright appears to have been impressed by Péladan's novels, and was even persuaded to write the preface to a German translation of one of the Frenchman's books.[20] Péladan's fame reached far beyond the avant-garde intelligentsia, however. Between 1892 and 1897, he organised exhibitions of idealist, 'spiritual' art that were massively popular. Through these endeavours, which can be described as triumphs of advertising as much as anything else, esoteric concepts in direct connection to visual art were brought to the attention of mainstream society.[21]

For the first Rosicrucian exhibition in Paris, two thousand invitations were sent out and more than 22,600 calling cards were left by people who came to view it. 'Everyone' attended, from the painters Puvis de Chavannes and Gustave Moreau, to authors like Emile Zola and Paul Verlaine. In the catalogue for the exhibition, Péladan famously declared that the artist is to be considered a priest and a magus.[22] The subsequent Rosicrucian salons were successes, too. In 1893, Péladan was allowed to use parts of the prestigious Palais du Champ de Mars, where the official art salon was also held. This Rosicrucian group was clearly no longer a peripheral and obscure phenomenon.[23] The Ferkel circle certainly included others than Strindberg who were familiar with Péladan. Axel Gallén, for example, had visited the first Rosicrucian salon, although he was not very impressed.[24] This is not to say he rejected the notion of the artist as a mage and mystic, which constituted a distinct leitmotif at Péladan's salon. Many symbolist artists all over Europe took this idea to heart.[25] One of them was Jean Delville (1867–1953), a collaborator of Péladan's who was later to become the secretary of the Belgian section of the Theosophical Society, and author of the esoterically tinged book *La mission de l'art: Etude d'esthétique idéaliste* [The Mission of Art: A Study of Idealist Aesthetics] (1900).[26]

A partly comparable view of art is to be found in the writings of Przybyszewski. Being a self-professed Satanist, and very much occupied with magic, in his mid-1890s art criticism he managed to find pro-Luciferian themes and sorcery of some sort in works that often had a fairly limited explicit amount of such content.[27] His interpretations had a decisive effect on the reception of many influential artists, especially Vigeland and Munch. In his study of Munch in this catalogue, Przybyszewski designates the Norwegian's works 'the creations of a somnambulistic, transcendent consciousness', and connects his art to 'vision, clairvoyance, dream'.[28] In Przybyszewski's view, Munch belongs to the same tradition as certain authors who are able to reach 'the most secretive foundations and roots of this world'. He further likens Munch to the composer Richard Wagner, whom he describes as an *artiste-prêtre*, and holds his friend up as 'a true aristocrat of the spirit'. In other words, Munch is portrayed as an explorer of hidden, 'esoteric' dimensions, and a member of a spiritual elite with the power to access

Following pages: Fig. 44. Gustav Vigeland's first version of *Hell*, 1894. Destroyed by the artist in 1900

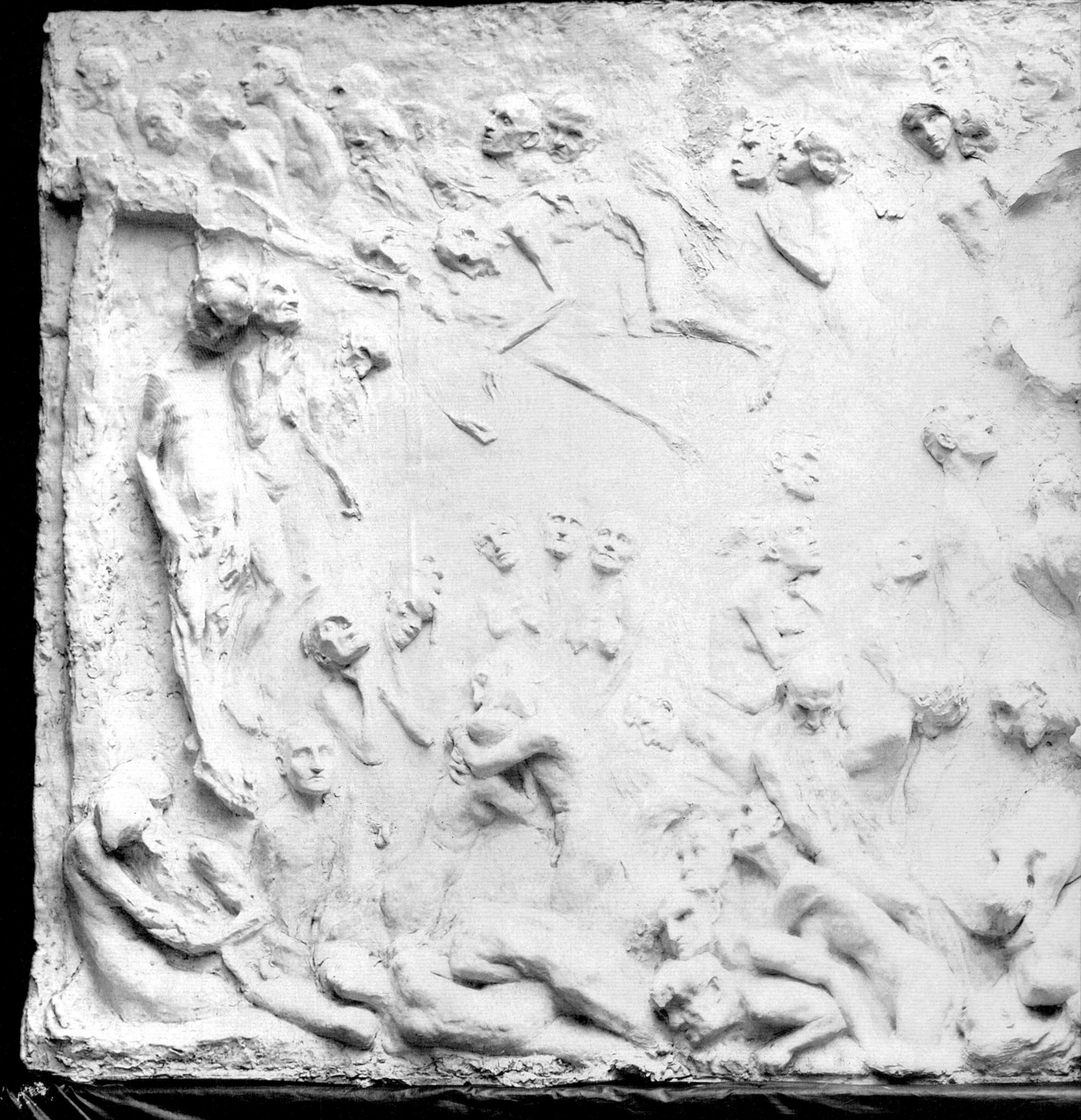

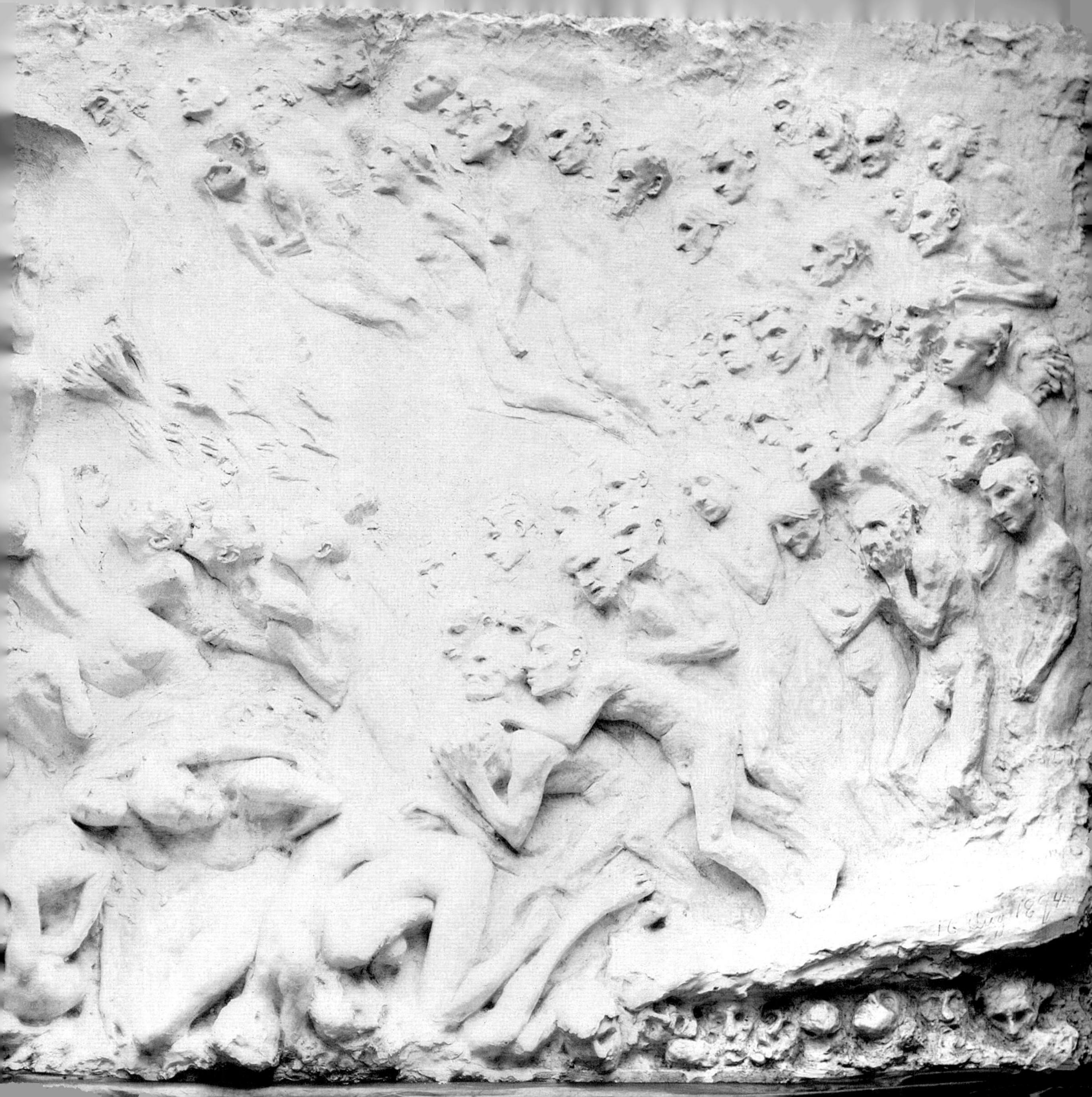

this secretive domain. The imagery of esotericism is combined in this text with notions from the nascent discipline of psychiatry, making it quite characteristic of occultist discourse.

Famously, it was Przybyszewski who came up with a new title for Munch's *Liebe und Schmerz* [Love and Pain], instead calling it *Vampire* which then became its established title. He thus radically changed the way the public viewed an image that, according to the artist, originally had nothing to do with the supernatural and demonic.[29] This is not to say that similar themes are necessarily absent in Munch's oeuvre. When Przybyszewski gave him a copy of Alexander Aksakow's *Spritismus und Animismus* (1895), he was supposedly so captivated that he read it all the way through in a single evening.[30] Hence, such sources may be an explanation for the strange, pulsating energy fields that are recurrent in Munch'sworks from this period (according to many esotericists, all living creatures are surrounded by an aura, or invisible waves of energy).[31] This might also reflect the complex interplay of the sciences (for example discussions about X-rays) and traditional esotericism in the characteristically modern hybrid occultism. Be that as it may, we at least know that there were in-fluential contemporaries aside from Przybyszewski who felt the images conveyed esoteric notions. When Munch exhibited in Paris in 1896, Strindberg celebrated him as an 'esoteric' painter in his review for *La Revue blanche*.[32]

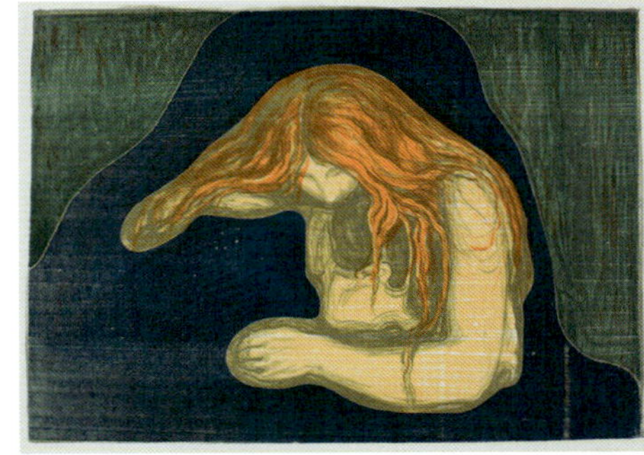

Fig. 45. Edvard Munch: *Vampire*, 1895

In his art critical writings on Vigeland, Przybyszewski's 'eso-terisation' of the artist was at least as prominent, and not unlike what Pater had done with Leonardo da Vinci (see above). According to Przyby-szewski, Vigeland and the other contemporary artists who are, in his phrasing, 'wanderers on the paths of the soul', ought to be seen as the latter-day successors to the magicians of old.[33] Esotericists like John Dee and Paracelsus are their true precursors. Their art is not for the masses, but for the elect few (a category paralleling typical esotericist elitism and exclusivity) that are able to comprehend its greatness.[34] These phrasings hover between the metaphorical and the literal, and few Ferkel artists would probably have concurred in full with Przybyszewski's hyperbole. Clearly, however, the Ferkel circle was generally quite knowledgeable about esotericism, and fascinated by it in some manner. This did not necessarily entail outright acceptance of such worldviews. Even Przybyszewski, who was highly preoccupied with esotericism, was severely critical of the great names in its nineteenth-century manifestations. In a letter to a friend of March 1897 he wrote: 'Are you familiar with the mystifier Eliphas Lévi, that blockhead, who always employs worn-out formulas? Further, I swear to you that he knows nothing more than we all do. [...] Libera me Satan!'[35] Przybyszewski did not hold Theosophy, Rosicrucians or Freemasons in high esteem either.[36] His favoured period was the Middle Ages, and he preferred romanticised visions of medieval black magic. Nevertheless, his writings on esotericism are inescapably *fin-de-siècle*, and fit perfectly with Hanegraaff's delineation of occultism.

In one of his essays on Vigeland, Przybyszewski contemplates how his subject has sculpted Satan in the relief *Hell* (1894) and writes of 'a Lucifer who invented poetry and philosophy'.[37] The struggling human figures surrounding Satan are interpreted by the Pole as a picture of the 'battle for existence'; perhaps indicating that he perceives the work as a vast panorama of social Darwinist Satanism.[38] Evolutionism was a central theme in Przybyszewski's thinking, clearly indicating the merging of science and esotericism that is typical of occultism (the specific blend of a form of evolutionism with esoteric ideas is also prominent in Theosophy). His view of Satan as the originator of the arts, integrated with the elitist notion of the survival of the fittest, is furthermore reflected in his opinions about the nature of true art. The essay 'Confiteor' ('I avow', published in the Polish avant-garde art journal *Zycie*, January 1899) is a good example. Here, Przybyszewski first attacks didactic art, and then continues: 'The Democratic art, the art for the masses, stands even lower. The art for the masses is a loathsome and shallow banalisation of the means the artist employs.'[39] For Przybyszewski, the artist is a figure 'beyond Good and Evil', to use Nietzsche's term: 'The artist stands above life, above the world, he is the lord of lords, no law binds him, no human power restricts him.'[40] The artist is, we could say, close to the Nietzschean superman Przybyszewski depicts the magician or Satanist as, conflating the figures into one. Effectively, this also conflates art and esotericism.

Ideas like these, then, were among the topics of conversation at Zum Schwarzen Ferkel. This did not always result in clear expressions of such themes in the works of art. Vigeland is a case in point. The time he spent in Berlin was a formative period, which appears to have contributed to his embrace of a symbolist approach to art, as opposed to realism. His Polish friend, who wrote such forceful prose about art, would – at the very least – seem a plausible partial catalyst in this development.[41] It is difficult, however, to discern any clearly esoteric motifs in Vigeland's art, which in the years before and after his time in Berlin rather tends to be mythological and biblical (*Hell*, 1894; *Hell II*, 1897; *Judgement Day*, 1894; *The Accursed*, 1891), or Gothic and nightmarish (*The Apparition*, 1889). Possibly, some sculptures might be read as referencing esoteric iconography. For example, *Girl (Genius) Floating Between Branches* (1907) reminds one of imagery of the astral body roaming around, but such an analysis remains on the level of conjecture. All the same, Vigeland's preserved library shows that he decidedly had an interest in esotericism, at least a few years after he was in Berlin. It includes, for example, editions like Edouard Schuré's *Les Grands initiés* [The Great Initiates] (Paris 1911, originally 1889), Anton Christian Bang's *Norske hexeformularer og magiske opskrifter* [Norwegian Witches' Formulas and Magical Recipes] (1901–02), Emanuel Swedenborg's *Himmel och helvete* [Heaven and Hell] (Stockholm 1906, originally 1758), and the unattributed *Frimureriets hemmelighet* [The Secret of Freemasonry] (n.d.).[42] Incidentally, a 1907 German translation of Schuré's book, which was one of the period's esoteric bestsellers, can also be found in Munch's library.

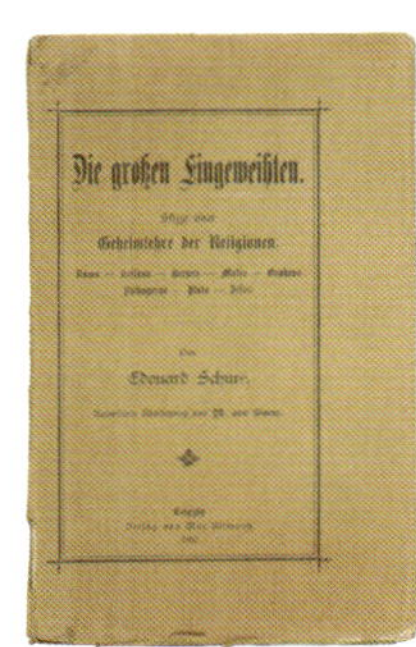

Fig. 46. Edouard Schuré: *Die grossen Eingeweihten. Skizze einer Geheimlehre der Religionen*, 1907 German translation of Schuré's esoteric bestseller

A fascination with the esoteric is more conspicuous in some other cases. For example, when Gallén arrived in Berlin in January 1895, he had read several Theosophical works and wrote in letters to friends that he was employing his 'sixth sense' to observe the world around him, and that he had successfully opened his 'inner eye'. Similar Theosophical notions may have inspired such comments. Recently, Nina Kokkinen has shown how there are probable references to esotericism in several works by Gallén.[43] Strindberg's esoteric interests are even better known, and have been the subject of a number of studies. During the 1890s, he explicitly set out to write esoteric novels. In an 1896 letter to his Theosophist friend Torsten Hedlund, Strindberg proclaimed that he wanted to become 'the Zola of occultism'.[44] He corresponded with and met representatives of a staggering array of esoteric movements, but being too much of an individualist and, perhaps, too much of a megalomaniac, never committed himself to any of them.[45] Famously, he attempted (and claimed to have succeeded in) producing gold through alchemical experiments. The Swede also wrote in esoteric journals such as *L'Initiation*, which made him a figure of admiration among French occultists, who praised him as a new Swedenborg.[46]

Taking esoteric beliefs to heart could, unsurprisingly, have certain troublesome consequences when paired with the volatile, highly-strung dispositions of the Ferkel men. In a letter dated January 1897, Przybyszewski described how Strindberg had developed paranoid fantasies that his Polish friend was conspiring with Munch to murder him by telepathic means.[47] In a fit of rage, Strindberg therefore moved from his apartment, which was close to Munch's, and wrote to the latter: 'Everybody knows that it is physically possible to extinguish a light through a thick wall. I am sure that you want to kill me. But I'll prevent it. You are not to become my murderer.'

It is a fact that many occultists – for example Péladan – were keen to integrate the world of art into their own shadowy astral realm. The French scholar Pierre A. Riffard has even identified a tendency to view works of art as depositories of hidden spiritual knowledge as typical of esotericist discourse.[48] This tendency, as we have seen, was also prominent in non-esotericist critical discourse on art during the late nineteenth century, indicating a broader 'esoterisation' of art criticism, and hence art itself, than has usually been acknowledged. It was not only artists who were influenced by esoteric traditions and motifs, but critics as well. This, in turn, even led to works of art that were created without knowledge of esotericism being absorbed into an 'esotericising' discourse. Przybyszewski can be seen as an important figure in this regard, and others such as Strindberg – with his above-mentioned review of Munch as an esoteric painter – also played a part. The Ferkel circle as whole can, in fact, be considered an excellent illustration of how the artistic avant-garde was – not always willingly or intentionally – very much part of a broader, and distinctly modern, occulture.

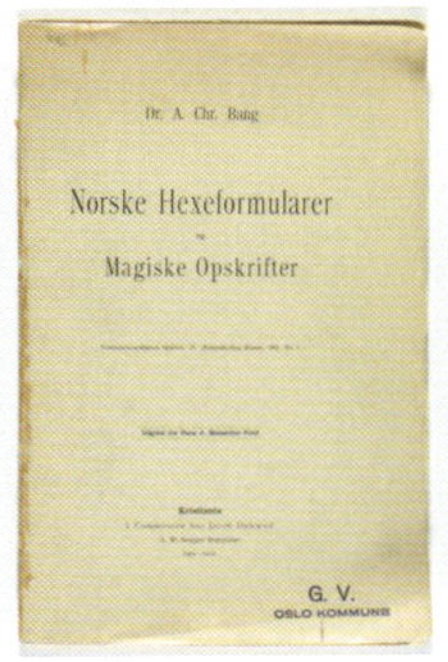

Fig. 47. Anton Christian Bang: *Norske Hexeformularer og magiske Opskrifter*, 1901–02

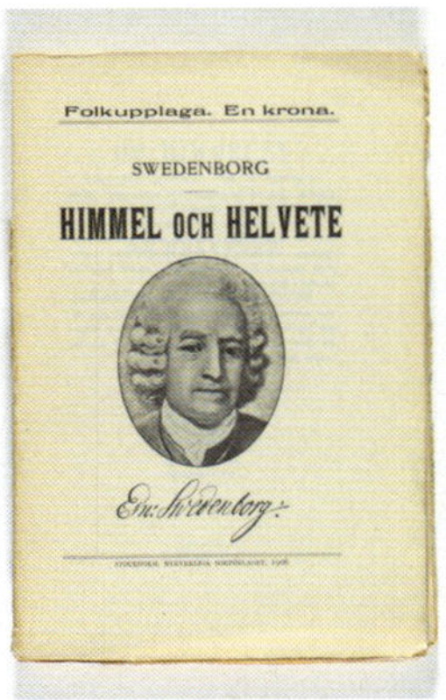

Fig. 48. Emanuel Swedenborg: *Himmel och Helvete*, 1906

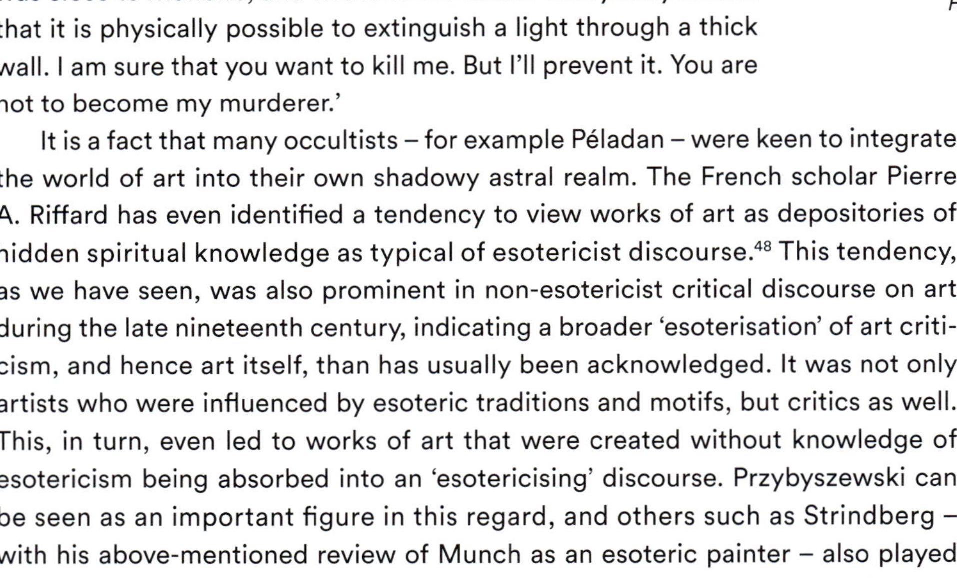

Fig. 49. Henry William Pickersgill: *Edward Bulwer-Lytton*, c. 1831

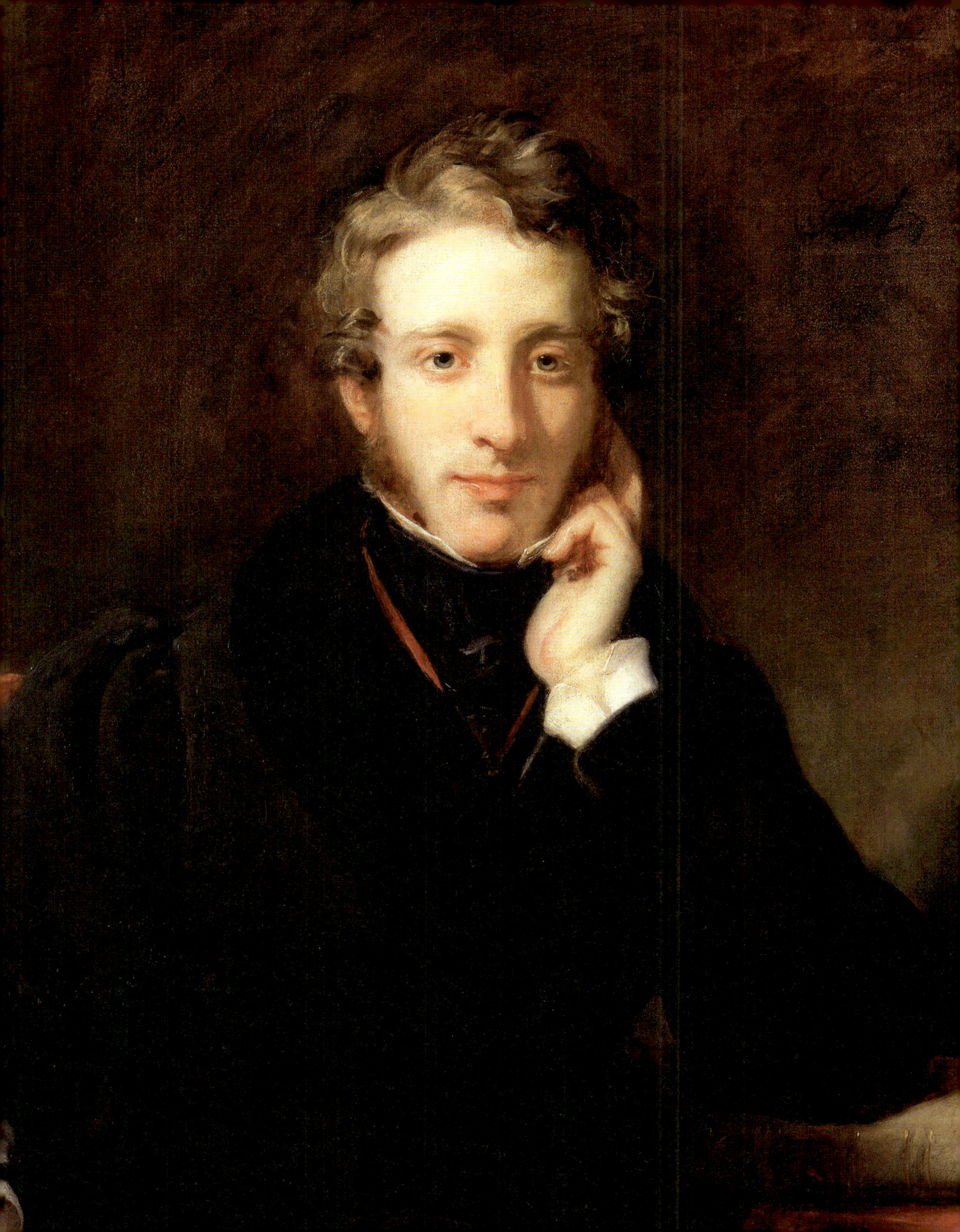

1   Wouter J. Hanegraaff, *New Age Religion and Western Culture: Esotericism in the Mirror of Secular Thought* (Leiden: Brill, 1996), p. 422. Italics removed.

2   Olav Hammer, *Claiming Knowledge: Strategies of Epistemology from Theosophy to the New Age* (Leiden: Brill, 2004), pp. 204–25.

3   Stanisław Przybyszewski, *Werke, Aufzeichnungen und ausgewählte Briefe*, 9 vols (Paderborn: Igel Verlag, 1990–2003), vol. 6, pp. 131–48.

4   Hammer, 2004.

5   Håkan Lejon, *Historien om den antroposofiska humanismen: Den antroposofiska bildningsidén i idéhistoriskt perspektiv 1880–1980* (Stockholm: Almqvist & Wiksell, 1997), p. 43; Eszter Szalczer, *Strindberg's Cosmic Theatre: Theosophical Impact and the Theatrical Metaphor* (diss., Ann Arbor: City University of New York, 1997), pp. 48–56; Emily B. Sellon & Renée Weber, 'Theosophy and the Theosophical Society', in *Modern Esoteric Spirituality*, ed. Antoine Faivre & Jacob Needleman (New York: Crossroad, 1992), pp. 326–27.

6   Szalczer, 1997.

7   On Bulwer-Lytton, see Fredrik Gregorius, 'Edward Bulwer-Lytton och myten om vril-kraften', in *Förborgade tecken: Esoterism i västerländsk litteratur*, ed. Per Faxneld & Mattias Fyhr (Umeå: H:Ström, 2010), pp. 124–42.

8   Christopher Partridge, *The Re-Enchantment of the West: Alternative Spiritualities, Sacralization, Popular Culture, and Occulture*, 2 vols (London: T & T Clark, 2004–05).

9   Nina Kokkinen, 'Occulture as an Analytical Tool in the Study of Art', *Aries*, vol. 13, no. 1 (2013), pp. 8–9, 11, 22–23.

10   Antoine Faivre, *Access to Western Esotericism* (Albany: State University of New York Press, 1994), p. 35.

11   Faivre, 1994, p. 34.

12   Christopher Partridge, 'Occulture is Ordinary', in *Contemporary Esotericism*, ed. Egil Asprem & Kennet Granholm (Sheffield: Equinox, 2013), p. 119.

13   Kocku von Stuckrad, 'Western Esotericism: Towards an Integrative Model of Interpretation', *Religion*, vol. 35, no. 2 (2005), pp. 88–91.

14   Hanegraaff, 1996, p. 485; Faivre, 1994, p. 5.

15   Kocku von Stuckrad, *Western Esotericism: A Brief History of Secret Knowledge* (London: Equinox, 2005), p. 10. Italics removed.

16   Kokkinen, 2013; Colin Campbell, 'The Cult, the Cultic Milieu and Secularization', in *Sociological Yearbook of Religion in Britain*, vol. 5 (London: SCM Press, 1972).

17   Campbell analyses the post-Second World War period, but see also Kokkinen's (2013, pp. 29–30) comments on Campbell's usefulness for the study of older periods.

18   Campbell, 1972, p. 123.

19   Per Faxneld, 'Mona Lisa's Mysterious Smile: The Artist Initiate in Esoteric New Religions', *Nova Religio: The Journal of Alternative and Emergent Religions*, forthcoming.

20   Strindberg started reading Péladan in May 1897 (*Ockulta dagboken*, 1.5.1897, p. 24). Later, Strindberg praised Péladan in a letter written to his friend Richard Bergh on 14.2.1901 (letter 4478, vol. XIV, p. 25), and designated him 'a seer and a prophet' in a letter to Emil Schering on 12.9.1904 (letter 5051, vol. XV, p. 66). Moreover, Strindberg exchanged several letters with Péladan in 1905 and 1906 (letter S584, vol. XXII, p. 172; letter 5362, vol. XV, p. 267).

21   A thorough recent study of Péladan in relation to esotericism is Sasha Chaitow, *Redemption through the Arts: Joséphin Péladan's Platonic Legendarium* (diss., University of Essex, Department of Literature, Film and Theatre Studies, 2014). It is likely to become the standard work on Péladan's thinking.

22   Robert Pincus-Witten, *Occult Symbolism in France: Joséphin Péladan and the Salons de la Rose-Croix* (New York: Garland, 1976), pp. 104–09.

23   Pincus-Witten, 1976, p. 148.

24   Salme Sarajas-Kortes, *Vid symbolismens källor: Den tidiga symbolismen i Finland 1890–1895* (Jakobstad: Jakobstads tryckeri och tidnings AB:s förlag, 1981), p. 86.

25   Pincus-Witten, 1976, p. 171.

26   Jean Delville, *The New Mission of Art: A Study of Idealism in Art* (London: Francis Griffiths, 1910).

27   For an introduction to Przybyszewski's ideas, see Per Faxneld, 'Witches, Anarchism and Evolutionism: Stanisław Przybyszewski's Fin-de-siècle Satanism and the Demonic Feminine', in *The Devil's Party: Satanism in Modernity*, ed. Per Faxneld & Jesper Aa. Petersen (Oxford: Oxford University Press, 2013).

28   See the article by Stanisław Przybyszewski in this catalogue.

29   In a letter draft from the early 1930s, Munch explained that the image does not depict a vampire at all: 'in fact it is just a woman kissing a man on the neck'. Quoted in Ragna Stang, *Edvard Munch: The Man and his Art* (New York: Abbeville Press, 1979), p. 107. Whether we are to accept the artist's own words (from a later period, when the occult and Gothic were no longer fashionable) at face value is not completely clear. For a discussion, see Per Faxneld, 'Blood, Sperm and Astral Energy-suckers: Edvard Munch's *Vampire*', in *eMunch.no. Text and Image*, ed. Mai Britt Guleng (Oslo: Munch Museum, 2011), pp. 187–89.

30   Przybyszewski, 1990–2003, vol. 7, p. 164.

31   Arne Eggum, *Munch and Photography* (New Haven & London: Yale University Press, 1989), pp. 60–62. See also Faxneld, 2011.

32   Werner Timm, *The Graphic Art of Edvard Munch* (New York: New York Graphic Society, 1969/73), p. 40.

33   Przybyszewski, 1990–2003, vol. 6, p. 45.

34   Przybyszewski, 1990–2003, vol. 6, p. 45.

35   George Klim, *Stanisław Przybyszewski: Leben, Werk und Weltanschauung im Rahmen der deutschen Literatur der Jahrhundertwende* (Paderborn: Igel, 1992), p. 98.

36   Klim, 1992, pp. 272–73.

37   Przybyszewski, 1990–2003, vol. 6, p. 40.

38   Przybyszewski, 1990–2003, vol. 6,
      p. 41.

39   Przybyszewski, 1990–2003, vol. 6,
      p. 207.

40   Przybyszewski, 1990–2003, vol. 6,
      p. 208.

41   Trine Otte Bak Nielsen, 'Gustav
      Vigeland and Stanisław
      Przybyszewski', *On the Paths of
      the Soul: Gustav Vigeland and
      Polish Sculpture around 1900* (Oslo:
      Vigeland Museum, 2010), p. 243.

42   Vigeland Library, visited June 2010.

43   Nina Kokkinen, 'The Artist as
      Initiated Master: Themes of Fin-
      de-siècle Occulture in the Art of
      Akseli Gallen-Kallela', in *Fill Your
      Soul! Paths of Research into the Art
      of Akseli Gallen-Kallela* (Espoo: The
      Gallen-Kallela Museum, 2011), pp.
      51–52, 57–58.

44   Letter to Torsten Hedlund,
      23.8.1896 (letter 3359, vol. X, p.
      307).

45   Gallen-Kallela similarly expressed
      critical opinions of Blavatsky, at
      least at a later date. Kokkinen, 2011,
      pp. 55, 59.

46   Henrik Johnsson, 'Livet som dikt:
      Strindbergs esoteriska biografi', in
      Förborgade tecken, ed. Faxneld &
      Fyhr, 2010, p. 65. The most recent
      study is Johnsson, *Strindberg
      och den ockulta vetenskapen*
      (Stockholm: Malört, 2015).

47   Quoted in Andrzej Nils Uggla,
      *Strindberg och den polska teatern
      1890–1970: En studie i reception*
      (diss., Uppsala: AB Lundequistska
      bokhandeln, 1977), p. 25. Strindberg
      famously worked these fantasies
      (which may to an extent have been
      part of an 'intentional' madness to
      create material for his writing) into
      literary texts, such as *Inferno* (1898).

48   Pierre A. Riffard, 'The Esoteric
      Method', in *Western Esotericism
      and the Science of Religion*,
      ed. Antoine Faivre & Wouter J.
      Hanegraaff (Leuven: Peeters, 1998),
      pp. 70–71.

Images of an Era

Guri Skuggen

Gustav Vigeland and Edvard Munch belonged to the same generation and, consequently, made portraits of many of the same people. The portraits are a visual record of the times they lived in and the circles to which they belonged. These two Norwegian artists never became close friends, but in time they acquired many mutual acquaintances and patrons, both in Norway and abroad. There is a similar temperament in their art, causing them to appeal to the same people. In Norway it was the art historian Jens Thiis in particular who became passionately involved in their art. In Sweden, the banker Ernest Thiel was an important patron, and the art collector Klas Fåhraeus acquired works by both artists. German admirers included the art historian Julius Meier-Graefe and the museum director Count Harry Kessler. Ernest Thiel had his portrait made by both Munch and Vigeland (fig. 50 and cat. 39), whereas only Munch painted portraits of Meier-Graefe and Count Kessler (cat. 41).

Edvard Munch and Gustav Vigeland as Portraitists

For Munch and Vigeland portraits were an essential part of their production, both in their quality and quantity. Vigeland executed more than one hundred busts, while Munch painted over two hundred portraits, as well as producing a significant number of sketches and lithographs. Neither artist staged exhibitions consisting exclusively of portraits, yet the portraits had a prominent position, and were often singled out by the critics as the highlights of their displays.

In most cases when a portrait was to be made, it was the artists themselves who took the initiative, the underlying reason typically being that they found the person intriguing. The possibility of selling the work might also have played a role, especially early on in their careers when their income was otherwise limited. Vigeland in particular could be very strategic in his choice of models. He used his portrait activity quite deliberately to gain contacts, and thereby exercise influence on significant figures over issues of importance. For instance in 1903 he offered to make a portrait of the Minister of Ecclesiastical Affairs, Vilhelm Andreas Wexelsen, who was chairman of the Abel Committee at the time – an acquaintanceship from which he would later benefit. For Munch it was important to develop a personal relationship with the people he painted. He did not necessarily need to know them first, yet for the portrait to be successful it was desirable that he and the model connected in some way. It is therefore understandable that painting portraits on commission could be problematic. According to Munch's own estimation he hardly painted more than twelve formally commissioned works over the course of his life. When he was in need of the money he did not receive any commissions, and when the commissions began to arrive, he did not require them any longer and often turned them down.[1]

Vigeland and Munch have a reputation as superb portraitists. Both had a unique ability to perceive and to accentuate a model's characteristic traits. This talent presumably stemmed from their interest in the human psyche, as well as from their sensitive natures. Photographic likeness was never the aim of their portraits. Not even during the 1880s, when Munch was under the influence of Christian Krohg and naturalism, did he paint portraits that showed a likeness in the traditional sense. Nevertheless, his earliest portraits of family members can be said to fit into this style of painting, due to the choice of motif; he painted his father reading and his aunt knitting, everyday motifs typical of naturalism. Some of Vigeland's earliest portraits can also be said to be naturalistic in style, for example three busts from 1892: *Sleeping Woman* (cat. 13), *Trine Louen* and *Lorentz Dietrichson* (cat. 6), all of which are straightforward representations based on studies of the models. It became clear for them both, however, that naturalism's strict demands for a true representation of reality, where nothing should be added or detracted, did not suit their rich imaginations. There is an almost conspicuous similarity in the way they emphasise the importance of personal interpretation in art. Vigeland wrote the following lines in a letter to his friend and patron Sophus Larpent in 1901:

> For the Whole impression shall likewise be perceived personally! Details and Foreshortenings shall likewise be perceived Personally! [...] If we were to see real Photographs of the Models of all of the old, the best, Portraits, we would probably say: And we who believed that there was a likeness. There is hardly any likeness at all! – Everyone sees differently. Not merely each Epoch; but each Human being! Yes, a Human being sees differently, a thousand times a day we see things differently. A thing is not unchanged from one day to the other. One adds, one discards, what one previously believed etc.[2]

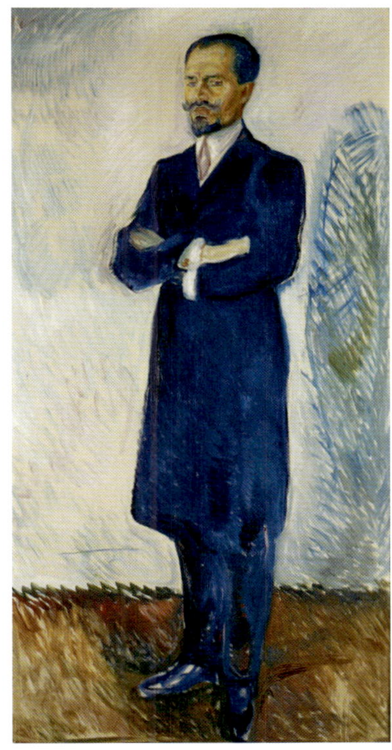

Fig. 50. Edvard Munch: *Ernest Thiel*, 1907

Munch writes practically the same thing in one of his sketchbooks towards the end of the 1880s:

> The fact is one sees with different eyes at different times. One sees differently in the morning than in the evening. The way one sees is also dependent upon one's state of mind and how one otherwise feels. This is why a motif can be seen in so many ways.[3]

The lack of photographic likeness sometimes led to dissatisfaction among both clients and models. For example, Ludvig Meyer refused to pay Munch for the portrait that he had commissioned of his children in 1894.[4] With the help of the solicitor Harald Nørregaard, who was also one of Vigeland's acquaintances, Munch filed a civil lawsuit, and Meyer was sentenced to pay for the portrait.[5] Another cause of dissatisfied 'portrait victims' was the harsh honesty with which they were portrayed. Munch discloses both vanity and arrogance in his portraits, while Vigeland often emphasises the physical defects of his models. For example, many found his portraits of Henrik Ibsen (1902 and 1903, cat. 32) offensive, precisely because he depicts the physical decline the playwright had suffered. Nevertheless it was rare that a model was unhappy with the result. With a certain degree of self-awareness one could appreciate that the portrait was good.

Friends and Enemies

Munch and Vigeland were of the same generation, but there were nevertheless a few significant years between them. Vigeland was too young to be a part of the artist group frequented by Edvard Munch during the 1880s. Munch's encounter with the circle around Hans Jæger (1854–1910), the leader of the Kristiania Bohemians, would be decisive for his development. It was in particular Jæger's uncompromising demand that one should 'write thy life' (Bohemian Commandment No. 1), in other words that one should base one's art on one's own experiences, which is often mentioned in this context.

Hans Jæger had moved to Paris the year Vigeland made his debut at the National Art Exhibition (1889) in Kristiania. He did not return to Norway until 1898, and there is no evidence that indicates that they ever met. Vigeland read Jæger's books with great interest, however. In a photograph from February 1903, he sits bowed over one of them (fig. 51),[6] either *Bekjendelser* [Confessions] (1902) or *Fængsel og fortvilelse* [Prison and Despair] (1903), volumes two and three of Jæger's autobiographical trilogy. Both are included in Vigeland's library, in addition to *Anarkiets bibel* [The Bible of Anarchism] (1906) and *Min forsvarstale i høyesterett* [My Defence Speech in the Supreme Court] (1886). Vigeland also attempted to get hold of *Fra Kristiania-Bohêmen* [From the Kristiania Bohemians] (1885) and *Syk kjærlihet* [Twisted Love] (1893) – which, like *Bekjendelser* and *Fængsel og fortvilelse*, had been banned in all of the Nordic countries – but these proved impossible to obtain.[7] In other words Jæger's influence on Vigeland was merely of a literary nature. Yet other members of the Bohemian circle would come to have significance for Vigeland at a later date, in particular the author and playwright Gunnar Heiberg (1857–1929). They met in Paris in 1901 when Vigeland was modelling a bust of the author. The portrait bust came into being at Vigeland's initiative, supposedly because he found Heiberg's physiognomy rather interesting. Vigeland wrote to Larpent from Paris: 'I am working on a bust of Gunnar Heiberg [...] His face is like a knot, truly an uncommon shape.'[8] Heiberg sat for eight consecutive days in Vigeland's hotel room, and described these sessions as being among the most interesting hours of his life:

> He was modelling me. He assaulted my face with his gaze and from there turned it away to the wet clay. He nailed me with his gaze, and when I did not collapse every time he looked away, it was because I feared the next

Fig. 51. Gustav Vigeland reading Hans Jæger, February 1903

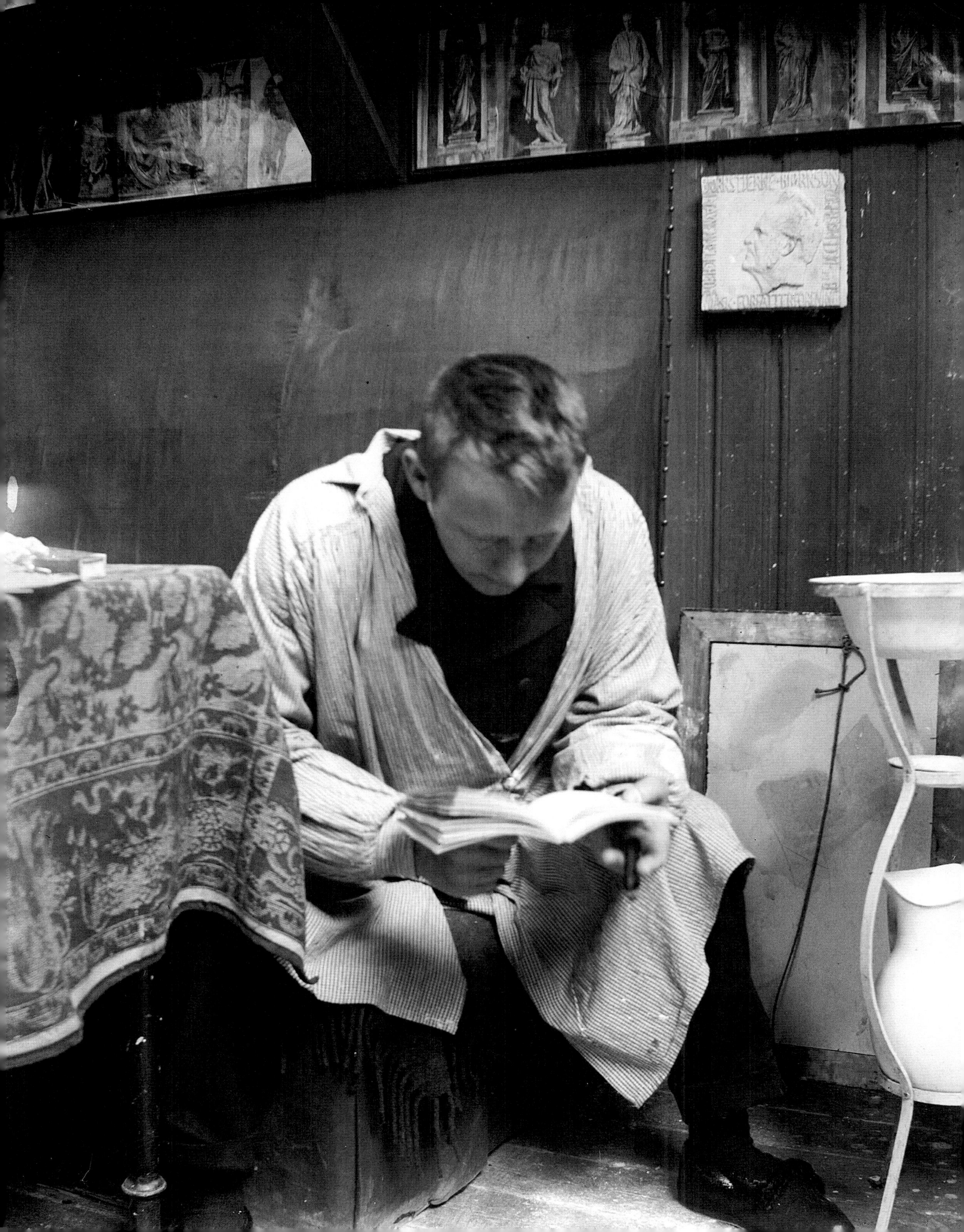

second when I would once again have that dreadful gaze aimed straight in my face. I neither dozed nor itched over my entire body as I did every other time I sat as a model. I felt like a wretched corpse and he a hyena with a hunched back and ceaselessly agitated, all-consuming and forever insatiable eyes.[9]

Further on Heiberg writes that in the end he resembled a fearsome Roman emperor. This description may seem exaggerated, but the portrait from 1901 definitely has something reserved about it. Heiberg is portrayed with a massive head supported by a muscular neck and shoulders. Vigeland was evidently not satisfied with the result, because in 1905 he made a new portrait (cat. 37), this time with an irregular cut-off point deep within the shoulders. The surface is not as smooth as in the bust from 1901, and the portrait is more vivid and imparts a milder and more sympathetic impression.

The sessions in Vigeland's hotel room in 1901 heralded the beginning of an enduring friendship. Heiberg became a great admirer of Vigeland's art and an important advocate. Among other things he wrote laudatory articles about his *Fountain* and his sketch for a monument to the Norwegian mathematician Niels Henrik Abel (1802–1829).[10] On 8 May 1901 Heiberg's article 'Staden med Fontænen' [The City with the Fountain] was published in *Verdens Gang*, and following a direct appeal from Vigeland he wrote a panegyric review of the *Abel Monument* in the same newspaper on 2 January 1903. The article was based on photographs that Vigeland had sent to Heiberg in Paris: 'What beauty! What grace in its lines! What solemnity and what bliss! How straightforward and how natural! How profound and how flawless! [...] Is it possible that there is one single reason why Vigeland's Abel should not be erected?'[11] Vigeland, in turn, set great store by Heiberg, and in a letter to his friend Gabriel Kielland in 1904 he wrote: 'How often I miss Gunnar Heiberg, that warm, warm human being.'[12]

Not everyone was as enthusiastic about Vigeland's projects. Christian Krohg openly ridiculed his Abel sketch in *Verdens Gang* in March 1903. According to Krohg, it looked like a 'Jockey at a Circus, astride two horses'.[13] Nor did Vigeland's *Fountain* draft, which was exhibited at the Museum of Applied Arts in Kristiania in 1906, appeal to him. It resembled 'a centrepiece with a punchbowl in the middle and a whole array of long-stemmed glasses around it'.[14] Krohg's attack on Vigeland may have been instigated by a number of circumstances. To begin with he may have been provoked by Heiberg's accolades. The two old Bohemians Krohg and Heiberg had had a falling out a few years earlier. Krohg's outburst may also have been a form of revenge after Vigeland, in 1901, had opposed his proposal to place Auguste Rodin's sculpture *The Burghers of Calais* at Egertorget Square in the capital.[15] Regardless of what lay behind Krohg's criticism, Vigeland was infuriated by it. From then on Krohg became his arch-enemy, and he used every opportunity

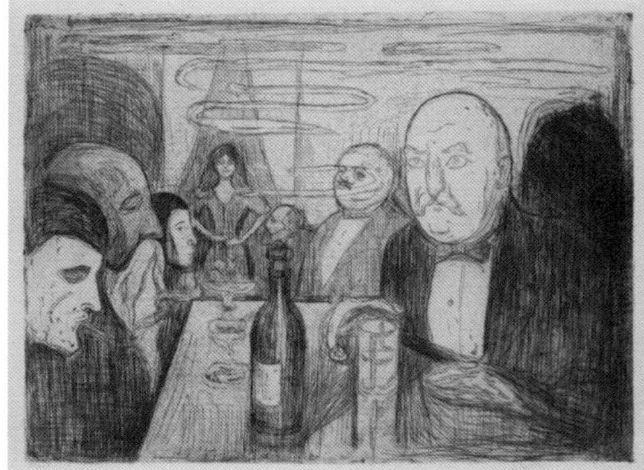

Fig. 52. Edvard Munch: *Kristiania Bohemians II*, 1895

to express his anger. Among other things he included a portrait with the aim of mocking Krohg in the wrought-iron fence surrounding his Rikard Nordraak monument (1911) in Nordraaks Square in Kristiania. According to Vigeland, one of the chained dragons is a portrait of Krohg.[16]

Another mutual acquaintance of Vigeland and Munch was the theatre critic Sigurd Bødtker (1866–1928). Bødtker, like his brother-in-law Gunnar Heiberg, was a member of the Kristiania Bohemians in the 1880s, and Munch knew them from that time. Vigeland probably met Bødtker in the early 1890s when they both frequented the circle of young Neo-Romantics in the capital. This friendship also resulted in a portrait bust, dated 24 February 1904. It is completely dominated by the pointed moustache, which appears to grow like tusks from Bødtker's face.

Heiberg appears in several of Munch's Bohemian pictures, including *Kristiania Bohemians II* from 1895 (fig. 52). There is also a pastel portrait from 1890, as well as a lithograph of Heiberg from 1896 (cat. 36). The portrait of 1890 has a soft expression and is painted in subdued colours – the only accentuated lines appear in the seams of the suit. It was included in several of Munch's exhibitions during the 1890s, among them one in Bergen, where it was commented on by a critic in *Bergens Tidende*:

> Strangely enough, I have not yet heard a single protest against this picture, that Mr Heiberg is not lemon yellow in the face, that he most probably does not wear green attire with violet seams. The picture's brilliance is striking. With all its colours, this is Gunnar Heiberg.[17]

In connection with his dramatic break-up with Tulla Larsen in 1902, Munch also fell out with both Bødtker and Heiberg. The break-up marked the beginning of a difficult period in Munch's life. Many of his old friends became foes, and were treated with great suspicion. Bødtker and Heiberg were caricatured in Munch's series *Alpha and Omega* from 1908–09, but earlier caricatures of these two also exist. Interestingly enough, they are described by Vigeland. In letters to his companion Inga Syvertsen from that period, and in a notebook from 1933, he writes about a meeting with Munch in Åsgårdstrand in the summer of 1904. During the visit Munch showed Vigeland several caricature lithographs, in which Heiberg is depicted 'fat and in a Buddha posture, and S.B. as a coiffed poodle standing on two legs serving G.H.'. Vigeland recounts further: '"Why do you bother doing this", I said. Well, they "deserve it, actually they should be flogged. They tried to thrust a girl on me, Tulla Larsen, she was ill with consumption and she used my mouth as a spittoon for a long time."'[18]

Although Vigeland was critical of Munch's caricatures, they may nevertheless have inspired him to create his own Heiberg caricature several years later. In a woodcut from 1918 (fig. 53) a naked Heiberg poses in a standing position, with a protruding abdomen and hands placed effeminately on his hips. He wears a lorgnette on his right eye, and this – together with the position of his hands – is reminiscent of Munch's full-length portrait of the Bohemian Karl Jensen-Hjell from 1885 (fig. 54).

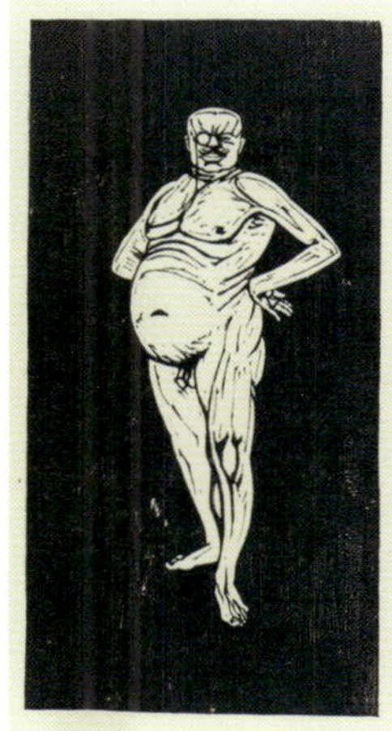

Fig. 53. Gustav Vigeland: *Gunnar Heiberg*, 1918

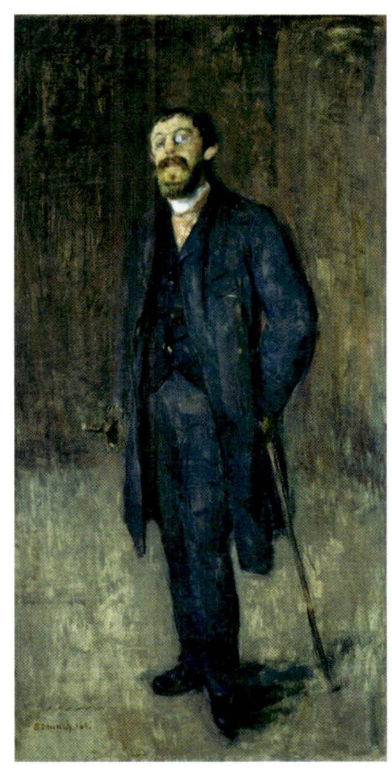

Fig. 54. Edvard Munch: *Karl Jensen-Hjell*, 1885

Neo-Romanticism as a Public Arena

In his article of 1890, 'From the Subconscious Life of the Mind', Knut Hamsun (1859–1952) presented something close to a manifesto: 'What if literature on the whole began to concern itself a little more with the state of the mind, rather than with engagements and balls and excursions to the country and tragic events as such?'[19] Hamsun sought a type of literature that deals with individuals rather than types or characters. In his famous Saint-Cloud manifesto Munch wrote: 'One shall no longer paint interiors / people reading and women knitting / They will be people who are alive / who breath and feel, suffer and love.'[20] Vigeland sought to do the same with sculpture. In a letter to Sophus Larpent he describes the Glyptotek in Copenhagen as a place where there are 'Figures with wild hair and flowing robes. <u>But no human beings!</u> Not one among all of these modern figures moved me deeply!'[21]

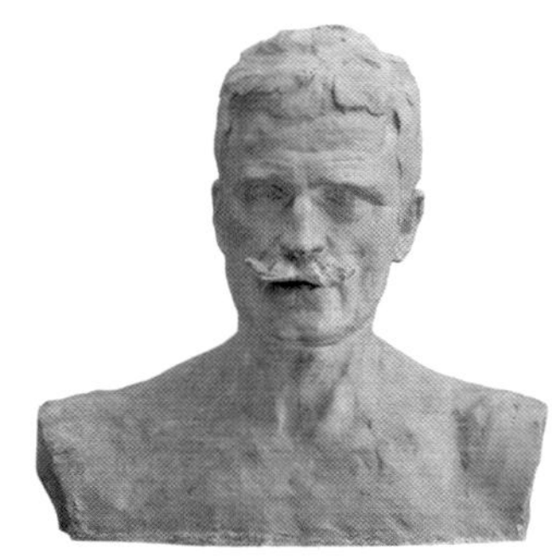

Fig. 55. Gustav Vigeland: *Knut Hamsun*, 1903

Vigeland and Munch, along with Hamsun, wanted art to probe the depths of the human mind. Hamsun was one of the people both Vigeland and Munch developed an acquaintanceship with at the beginning of the 1890s, and with whom they felt an artistic kinship.

In 1903 Vigeland made a portrait of Hamsun in his studio in Hammersborg in Kristiania (fig. 55). According to Inga Syvertsen the first preparations were made on 30 March 1903 and Hamsun sat for Vigeland for a total of nineteen and a half hours during the period 31 March to 16 April that year. He came to the studio fourteen times and sat for one or two hours on each visit. Vigeland's bust of the author is not considered to be among his best. A letter from Hamsun to Vigeland suggests that he was thinking of doing it again. Hamsun writes: 'You must not speak of making another bust, it is absolutely brilliant of course, it carries your stamp.'[22] Hamsun continues in a jesting tone, 'But you are perhaps envious of me because Vigeland has modelled me and not you, poor chap'. Despite repeated mutual invitations it is unclear whether Hamsun and Vigeland met again after 1903. Munch also executed a portrait of Hamsun. In 1896 he made an etching on commission from the literary journal *Pan* (fig. 56). Hamsun was unhappy with the portrait, which was based on photographs, and offered to buy it for the same amount the editors of *Pan* were to pay: 300 German marks. Nevertheless, it ended up being printed as a heliograph in the magazine, against his wishes.

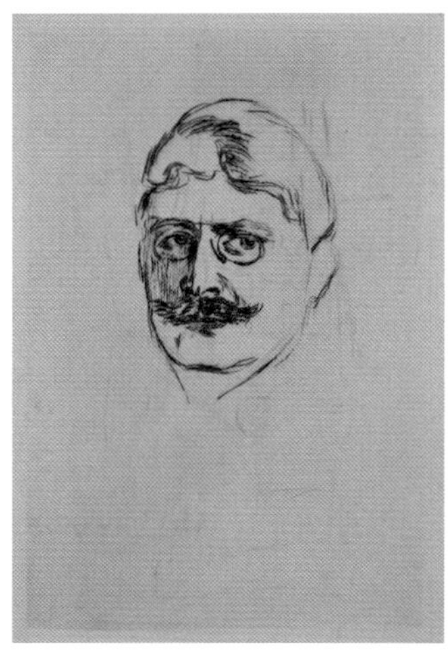

Fig. 56. Edvard Munch: *Knut Hamsun*, 1896

At the beginning of the 1890s Hamsun was among the creators of a new type of literature, Neo-Romanticism, in which subjective experiences, emotions and the imagination were emphasised. In addition to Hamsun, Sigbjørn Obstfelder (1866–1900) and Vilhelm Krag (1871–1933) were important representatives of this style of writing. The art historian Jens Thiis (1870–1942), who was a good friend of Obstfelder and Krag, is often given credit for having started the movement, when in 1890 he performed Krag's poem 'Fandango' for the first time in the Students' Union. Munch became acquainted with the three friends during his student days, while Vigeland probably met them at the Kristiania home of the Dons sisters, Margrete and Ragna Vilhelmine.[23] This was a gathering place for intellectuals and a breeding ground for Neo-Romanticism. Obstfelder, Krag, Gabriel Finne, Nils Collett Vogt, Carl Nærup and Bødtker frequented the salon, while Vigeland was an occasional participant.[24] He also made portraits of nearly all of them: Thiis in 1894 (cat. 28), Obstfelder in 1895 (cat. 27), Krag (cat. 30) and Hamsun in 1903, and Nærup and Bødtker in 1904. Krag had evidently already had his portrait modelled in 1892, but the bust has been destroyed.[25] The portrait of 1903 can be considered as part of Vigeland's nation-building project, where he appears to have had ambitions of creating a portrait gallery of the great Norwegian writers. The bust seems somewhat uninspired. It is styled in the spare idiom of the 1890s, but lacks the sensitivity that is characteristic of the period.

Vigeland made a portrait of Thiis at the end of 1893 or beginning of 1894. Thiis had recently returned home after spending several years abroad, primarily in Italy. Arne Brenna has quite aptly written that the bust came into being 'during a dream about the Renaissance'.[26] In its swan-like extended neck he sees the Gothic lines of Botticelli. Vigeland himself described the form of the bust as 'veiled'.[27] The hair and beard are not deeply delineated, but moulded smoothly, in striking contrast to the hollowed-out pupils of the eyes. After Thiis sat for Vigeland he travelled to Berlin, where Vigeland met him again during his stay there in 1895. Later the same year Thiis was appointed director of the Museum of Applied Arts in Trondheim. During the last half of the 1890s Vigeland also spent long periods in Trondheim, where he worked on the restoration of Nidaros Cathedral. He spent his leisure time there with Thiis and Gabriel Kielland. In 1908 Thiis was appointed as the first director of the National Gallery in Kristiania, but for Vigeland, who had supported this appointment, the result was not quite as he had planned. In the period that followed he was critical of many of Thiis's undertakings, and around 1911 it resulted in a falling out between them.[28]

As for Munch and Thiis, their friendship lasted for the remainder of their lives. In 1909 Munch began a full-length portrait of Thiis, but it was never completed (fig. 57). Munch's relative and assistant of many years, Ludvig Ravensberg, wrote an account of a visit to Munch that Christmas:

> This evening M[unch], Høst and I are sitting together having a pleasant conversation. M fetches all of the large portraits he had made recently. […] We die of laughter when M brings in Director Thiis's portrait, the man who fled from Skrubben in order not to be painted. I do not wish to stand like some fool, he said, and I must go home and M – and H[øst] and I laughed at the parvenu's self-importance and fright.[29]

While Vigeland's portrait of Thiis shows a young, dreaming Neo-Romantic, Munch's unfinished portrait depicts a self-important director in his prime. It is included in a series of life-size portraits of his friends, which he painted during the period after his return from Dr Jacobson's Clinic in Copenhagen. 'The lifeguards of my art', he called these pictures. A few years later Munch also made a lithograph of Thiis (1913, cat. 29). Like the portrait of Hamsun, it seems to be based on a simple line drawing.

The portraits of Obstfelder by the painter and the sculptor respectively have much in common. This may be connected to the fact that they were made almost simultaneously: Vigeland's relief portrait was modelled in 1895, whereas Munch's lithographs are from 1896. Both have created sensitive portraits, in which the author is depicted with large, wide-open eyes. He appears at once alert, introverted and alienated. Perhaps the similarity in the way Obstfelder is depicted can be explained by the mutual temperament between the three. Heiberg has described the kinship between them as follows:

> In Norwegian art Obstfelder stands together with Munch and Vigeland. They are an island unto themselves. Melancholic, full of vitality, but mostly of life's sorrow[,] the three of them stand. [...] That essence of their beings is not something they could learn from others. For it is not the outer nature, but the inner life of things that interests them. Their art and their lives are one. They are not artists on the one hand and human beings on the other. They cannot separate themselves. Their art is derived from drops of blood that are squeezed forth by their lives.[30]

Obstfelder died of tuberculosis in 1900, only 33 years of age. A collection to pay for his monument was begun immediately, and both his wife and brother expressed a wish that Vigeland should be its author. Vigeland began by developing the relief portrait from 1895, but this remained an unfinished work in soapstone.[31] He finally completed the monument in 1917. Once again, the end result lacked the sensitivity of works from the 1890s.

The Old Radicals

It might appear as though the young Neo-Romantics had a somewhat ambivalent relationship with the preceding generation. On the one hand, they sought a break with the established artistic standards. In his famous lecture series of 1891, Hamsun committed patricide on the four giants of Norwegian literature: Ibsen, Bjørnson, Kielland and Lie.[32] They were criticised for creating a literature of types, and for lacking the insight to penetrate the depths of the complex, modern human being. On the other hand, these writers were radical intellectuals who were greatly respected by society as a whole. Their significance became evident in Munch's first plans for decorating the University of Oslo's Aula. According to Ravensberg Munch intended to fill the enormous panels in the great hall with decorative images of Ibsen, Bjørnson and Lie.[33] He carried out these plans in so far as he executed three paintings in the same technique[34] and format: *Bjørnson Speaking to the People*, *Henrik Ibsen at the Grand Café* and *Jonas Lie and His Family*. All three were most likely painted in 1908, and the two latter paintings were repetitions of previous motifs.[35]

Henrik Ibsen (1828–1906)

In 1894 Ibsen visited Vigeland's first solo exhibition at the Christiania Art Society. Larpent encountered him there while he was studying the large relief *Hell*, which constituted the centrepiece of the exhibition.[36] Larpent recorded the following exchange of remarks: 'I: A very peculiar work. Ibsen: Yes, very peculiar. There was

Fig. 57. Edvard Munch: *Jens Thiis*, 1909

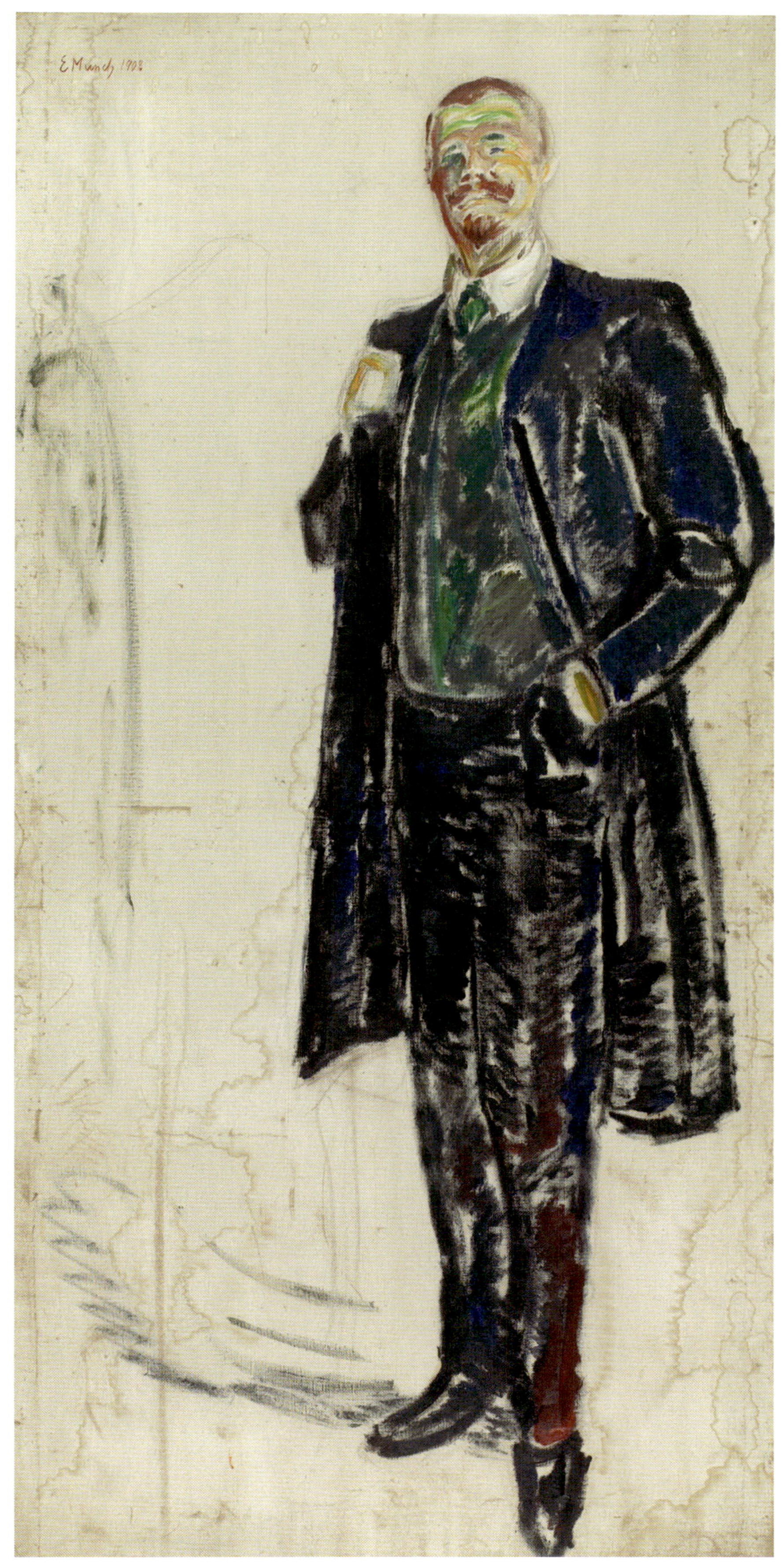

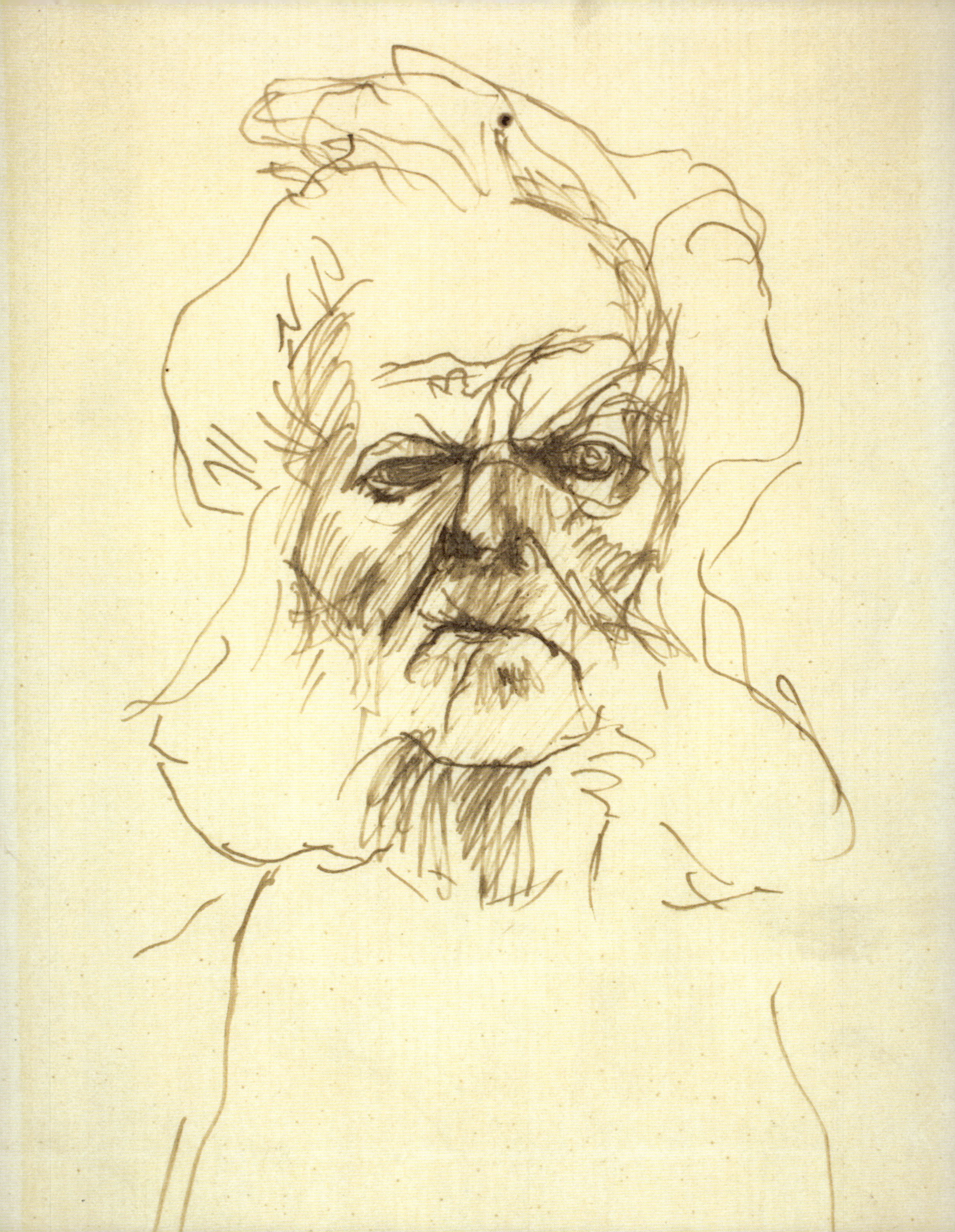

nothing more forthcoming from that taciturn man.'[37] Ibsen also visited an exhibition of Munch's works the following year, where he was given a tour by the artist himself: 'The pictures interested Ibsen greatly at my exhibition at Blomquist [*sic*] 1895 – He insisted that I show him every picture – He was greatly interested in the melancholic young man by the shore – and the three women which I called the nun, the whore and the woman with flowers.'[38] Munch points out that the same tripartite occurs in Ibsen's *When We Dead Awaken* (1899), and that his motif 'very likely prompted Ibsen's symbol'. Munch also mentions an earlier encounter with Ibsen. During his stay in Berlin in 1892 he had become well acquainted with the German art historian and Ibsen translator Julius Elias. Upon his return to Norway Munch went to Ibsen's home in Arbiens Street with a greeting from Elias. Since Ibsen was not at home, he left the card with the greeting. A few days later he was sitting at the Grand Café with his friends when Ibsen strolled by. To his astonishment Ibsen entered the café and sat down at their table. He greeted Munch and thanked him for his visit. After having uttered a few courteous remarks, he stood up and left. The brief return visit made an impression: 'Ibsen at our table! [...] We could barely speak for the emotion.'[39]

At this time Munch already had plans to paint a portrait of Ibsen[40] but nothing came of it. He probably painted *Henrik Ibsen at the Grand Café* in 1898, while the lithograph with the same motif is from 1902. In addition he painted several stage sets for *Ghosts* and *Hedda Gabler*, which were commissioned by Max Reinhardt at the Deutsches Theater in Berlin. Munch also made graphic works for *The Pretenders*, *Ghosts* and *John Gabriel Borkman*.

Like Munch, Vigeland had plans to make a portrait of Ibsen during the 1890s. He had agreed to sit for Vigeland, but for some unknown reason nothing came of it. When Vigeland returned from his long trip in 1901 he contacted Ibsen again, but by this point the playwright was reluctant. He was now 72 years of age and his health was failing. Vigeland got his way in the end, but he was granted only three sittings and they could last no longer than ten minutes. Vigeland was not quite satisfied with the first version of the bust and developed it further using photographs. In 1902, with the assistance of Ibsen's son Sigurd, he was allowed to make another visit, this time equipped with a sketchbook. The drawings from this meeting focused in particular on Ibsen's eyes (fig. 58), and it is the rendition of the eyes in particular that gives the bust from 1903 (cat. 32) its distinctive character. Ibsen is depicted as an old man, but has an alert, if reproachful, gaze.

Vigeland attended Ibsen's funeral on 1 June 1906 wearing a tuxedo, a top hat and his Order of St Olav medal. As someone who normally avoided public events, Vigeland's participation underlines how much he respected Ibsen.

Bjørnstjerne Bjørnson (1832–1910)

Munch was sceptical of Bjørnson from the outset. He was not considered as modern as Ibsen. With stories like *Synnøve Solbakken* (1857), *Arne* (1859) and *En glad Gut* [A Happy Boy] (1860), he became famous in the minds of the people as a country poet. Munch once remarked: 'As an orator Bjørnson has made an impression on me – not

Fig. 58. Gustav Vigeland: *Henrik Ibsen*, c. 1902

so much as a writer.[41] And as we have seen in the drafts of the Aula decorations, it was precisely as an orator that Munch chose to represent him. The same idea can also be found in a drawing from 1909 (cat. 34) where Vigeland also depicts Bjørnson as a man of the people. In several sketches for a monument to Bjørnson, he shows the writer carried aloft by the Norwegian population (cat. 35). Vigeland also made an outstanding portrait bust of him in Paris in 1901. Bjørnson is depicted with naked shoulders, a strong neck, high forehead and erect posture, which impart a majestic demeanour. In this case as well, the conversations that took place during the sittings marked the start of a friendship. And like Heiberg, Bjørnson would become an important supporter. Back in Kristiania he visited Vigeland's studio in Hammersborg several times, and it was the *Abel Monument* he was especially interested in. The respect Vigeland felt for Bjørnson is expressed in the following remark to Arne Brenna in 1942: 'You cannot imagine the impression it made on me when I opened the door of my studio and found <u>him</u> standing outside with snow on his shoulders, the man that I had heard about from the time I was a child.'[42]

Jonas Lie (1833–1908)

Lie lived almost uninterruptedly in Paris during the period 1882–1906. His home at 7 Avenue de la Grande Armée, was a gathering place for Scandinavian artists at the time, and Munch was among those who were invited to dinner and coffee gatherings.[43] Vigeland, on the other hand, chose not to visit Lie's home during the months that he was in Paris in 1893. He later explained that it was due to a youthful compulsion to rebel. He met Lie for the first time in Åsgårdstrand where he made Lie's portrait in the summer of 1904. Vigeland wrote to Inga Syvertsen that Lie is 'As charming as can be',[44] but his wife Thomasine was described as nagging: 'Like a little white mouse Madame Lie sits watching over everything. Now you must sit still Jonas. – Yes, but V. says that I need not sit so still. – Yes, but surely you understand that you must sit still; Your head is constantly moving. – But only when I do not have to – Now take off your skullcap Jonas, there, now I will help you to take off your glasses Jonas.' While Lie had a rich imagination and the ability to daydream, she was the critic who held him back. Yet it is not the imaginative poet that Vigeland has chosen to depict, but the ageing man. Lie's asymmetrical face is emaciated, and his eyes are set deep in the skull. The slanted, narrow lips help emphasise his age: once again Vigeland is mercilessly honest in his characterisation.

Isolation

Although the majority of the works discussed in this article are from the 1890s and the first decade of the twentieth century, the portrait activity of Munch and Vigeland was not limited to this period. Both of them made portraits throughout their lives, with a particularly active period in the beginning of the twentieth century. After 1910, however, we no longer find the same overlap in their choice of models. Vigeland and Munch no longer shared the same circle of acquaintances. With the passing of time the two artists began to isolate themselves more and more: Vigeland in his studio in Frogner, and Munch at Ekely. Vigeland's later portraits are mostly of friends and others who throughout the years had helped him in connection with the sculpture park in Frogner. After 1930 Munch also primarily made portraits of old friends and their acquaintances.

1   'When You speak of portrait requests or commissions I have hardly had more then 12 commissions throughout my entire life – I am no Zorn – When I needed commissions I received none and when I did not need them I did not make them.' Letter draft from Munch to Pola Gauguin, 1933–36, Munch Museum, Correspondence Collection, MM N 1696. Quoted in Arne Eggum, *Edvard Munch. Portretter* (Oslo: Munch Museum/ Labyrinth Press, 1994), p. 8.

2   Letter from Vigeland to Sophus Larpent, 5.3.1901, Vigeland Museum, Correspondence Collection, no. 51.

3   Edvard Munch, sketchbook, MM T2761, 1889–1990, Munch Museum, p. 44v.

4   Edvard Munch, *Ludvig Meyer's Children*, 1894, Stiftung Gemäldesammlung Emil Bretschger/ Kunstmuseum Bern.

5   The case is referred to among other places in Eggum, 1994, p. 62.

6   On the reverse of the photograph Inga Syvertsen writes: 'Gustav Vigeland reading Hans Jæger's book. February 1903.' Vigeland Museum, Photograph Collection, V02.0094.001.

7   Letter from Hans Jæger to Inga Syvertsen, 5.2.1903, Vigeland Museum, Correspondence Collection.

8   Letter from Vigeland to Sophus Larpent, 12.4.1901, Vigeland Museum, Correspondence Collection, no. 68.

9   Gunnar Heiberg, 'Vigelands Geni', *Verdens Gang*, 3.7.1903.

10   The competition for the *Abel Monument* was announced in 1902. Vigeland participated with a symbolic presentation, but was not nominated since his draft fell outside the statutes of the competition. He did not give up however, and in 1908 his monument was unveiled in the gardens of the Royal Palace.

11   Gunnar Heiberg, 'Vigeland – Abel', *Verdens Gang*, 2.1.1903.

12   Copy of a letter from Vigeland to Gabriel Kielland, 1.2.1904, Vigeland Museum, Correspondence Collection, no. 2094.

13   Christian Krohg, 'Et trekantet Spørsmaal', *Verdens Gang*, 26.3.1903.

14   Krohg criticised Vigeland's *Fountain* in three articles published in *Verdens Gang*: 'Eidsvolds Plads I' (22.12.1906), 'Eidsvolds Plads II' (5.1.1907), and 'Eidsvolds Plads III' (13.1.1907).

15   The sculpture was bestowed as a gift to the city by Frits Thaulow, and Krohg had strong opinions about its location.

16   Hans Dedekam, *Dedekams dagbok- opptegnelser* [Dedekam's Journal Entries] (unpublished manuscript, Vigeland Museum Library, 1907–27), p. 224.

17   Eggum, 1994, p. 50. According to Eggum, the article appeared in *Bergens Tidende* on 5.12.1895.

18   Gustav Vigeland, notebook W179, 1933, Vigeland Museum.

19   Knut Hamsun, 'Fra det ubevidste sjæleliv', *Knut Hamsun, Artikler*, ed. Francis Bull (Oslo: Gyldendal Norsk Forlag, 1939), p. 60.

20   Edvard Munch, note, MM UT 13, 1928?, Munch Museum, p. 7. Copy of a note written in 1889.

21   Letter from Vigeland to Sophus Larpent, February 1895, Vigeland Museum, Correspondence Collection, no. 1132.

22   Letter from Knut Hamsun to Vigeland, possibly 27.8.1903, Vigeland Museum, Correspondence Collection, KH-4.

23   Margrete Dons was married to the author Nils Kjær, and Ragna Vilhelmine Dons was married to Jens Thiis.

24   Tone Wikborg, *Gustav Vigeland. En biografi* (Oslo: Gyldendal Norsk Forlag, 2001), p. 88.

25   Dedekam, 1907–27, p. 48.

26   Arne Brenna, *Gustav Vigelands portrettbyster* (MA thesis, Oslo: University of Oslo, 1951). Manuscript in the Vigeland Museum, p. 25.

27   Dedekam 1907–27, p. 191.

28   The rift in their relationship may possibly have been prompted by an episode that occurred the same year. Thiis was supposed to give a lecture on Vigeland in Mandal, the artist's native town, but failed to show up. Vigeland perceived this as a personal betrayal. Wikborg, 2001, p. 281.

29   Ravensberg's Journal, 27.12.1909, quoted in Eggum, 1994, p. 160.

30   Gunnar Heiberg, *Set og hørt* (Kristiania: Aschehoug, 1917), p. 145.

31   Gustav Vigeland, *Dikteren Sigbjørn Obstfelder*, possibly 1900–10, Vigeland Museum.

32   The series consisted of 36 lectures given at 12 locations in Norway in 1891.

33   'Munch speaks of how he would envision the large decorations in the University's great hall, he would fill the enormous panels with monumental decorative images of Ibsen, Bjørnson and Jonas Lie.' Ravensberg's Journal, 11.5.1909, in Eggum, 1994, p. 163. These plans are also mentioned in a letter draft from Munch to Ernest Thiel, 1907–08, Munch Museum, Corre- spondence Collection, MM N 2523.

34   The pictures were painted with diluted paint on an absorbent canvas in order to reproduce the effect of al fresco painting. Eggum, 1994, p. 163.

35   See the preparatory work for *Bjørnson Speaking to the People* (cat. 34) and the lithograph version of *Henrik Ibsen at the Grand Café* (cat. 33).

36   The first version of *Hell* (1894) was shown at Vigeland's first solo exhibition in 1894. Upon returning home from Florence in 1896 he decided to create another version of the relief. This was finished on 9.6.1897 (cat. 134).

37   Sophus Larpent, *Vigelandiana*. Chronological records regarding Gustav Vigeland, 1892–1903, National Library of Norway, Oslo, Ms.fol.1821, 13.11.1894.

38   Edvard Munch, note, MM N 68, 1918, Munch Museum.

39   Edvard Munch, note, MM N 314 (undated) and note, MM N 415 (undated), Munch Museum.

40   'I will most likely paint his portrait quite soon.' Letter from Edvard Munch to Julius Elias, 1893, National Library of Norway, Oslo, brevs. 166 (PN 203).

41   Letter draft from Munch to Ernest Thiel, 1907–08, Munch Museum, Corre- spondence Collection, MM N 2523.

42   Brenna, 1951, p. 57.

43   There are two invitations from Jonas Lie to Edvard Munch preserved in the Munch Museum; MM K 666 (18.11.1896) and MM K 667 (20.1.1897)

44   Letter from Vigeland to Inga Syvertsen, 23.7.1904, Vigeland Museum, Correspondence Collection, quoted in Wikborg, 2001, p. 188.

Observations on Two Life Friezes

Petra Pettersen

The similarities between the art of Edvard Munch and that of Gustav Vigeland are pointed out from time to time, and questions frequently arise about who was first to come up with certain ideas, works or motifs. Were they inspired by one another's work, or was it contemporary art movements and motifs in general that were decisive for them? And what exactly is a 'life frieze'? A large number of the motifs created by the two artists depict the human condition, with themes relating to the different aspects and phases of life, and a common thematic subject matter will inevitably result in similarities, regardless of whether the works are executed in different visual forms or with diverging content. This article will mainly deal with the term 'life frieze' and its significance in Munch's art. It will also discuss whether it is reasonable to use this term when speaking of Vigeland's work, in particular his sculpture park in Frogner – the Vigeland Park. The article will also consider some similarities and differences in the artists' oeuvres, as seen through a selection of works and episodes, along with exhibitions and their reception.

Frieze of Life: Origins of the Term and the Formation of Munch's Series

Both Munch and Vigeland began their artistic careers while naturalism was still at its zenith in Norway, and when the art world was in a period of upheaval. It was a favourable time for two young and original artists. Munch's art developed out of naturalism, via a strong Impressionist influence, to a new style of painting. A milestone work in this respect was undoubtedly his initial version of the painting *The Sick Child* (1885–86, fig. 59). Munch's first picture with a distinctly emotional content, it was based on his own recollections of his sister's death. *The Sick Child* expresses recognisable emotions in the life of a human being and can thus be perceived as the first picture to belong to *The Frieze of Life*.

Munch first used the title *The Frieze of Life* in connection with a solo exhibition held at the Blomqvist Kunsthandel gallery in Kristiania in October 1918.[1] *The Frieze of Life* contains Munch's most famous works, which in their time both impressed and shocked the public and critics. The series consists primarily of paintings and prints, the earliest of which were mostly created during the 1890s, and includes a number

Fig. 59. Edvard Munch: *The Sick Child*, 1885–86

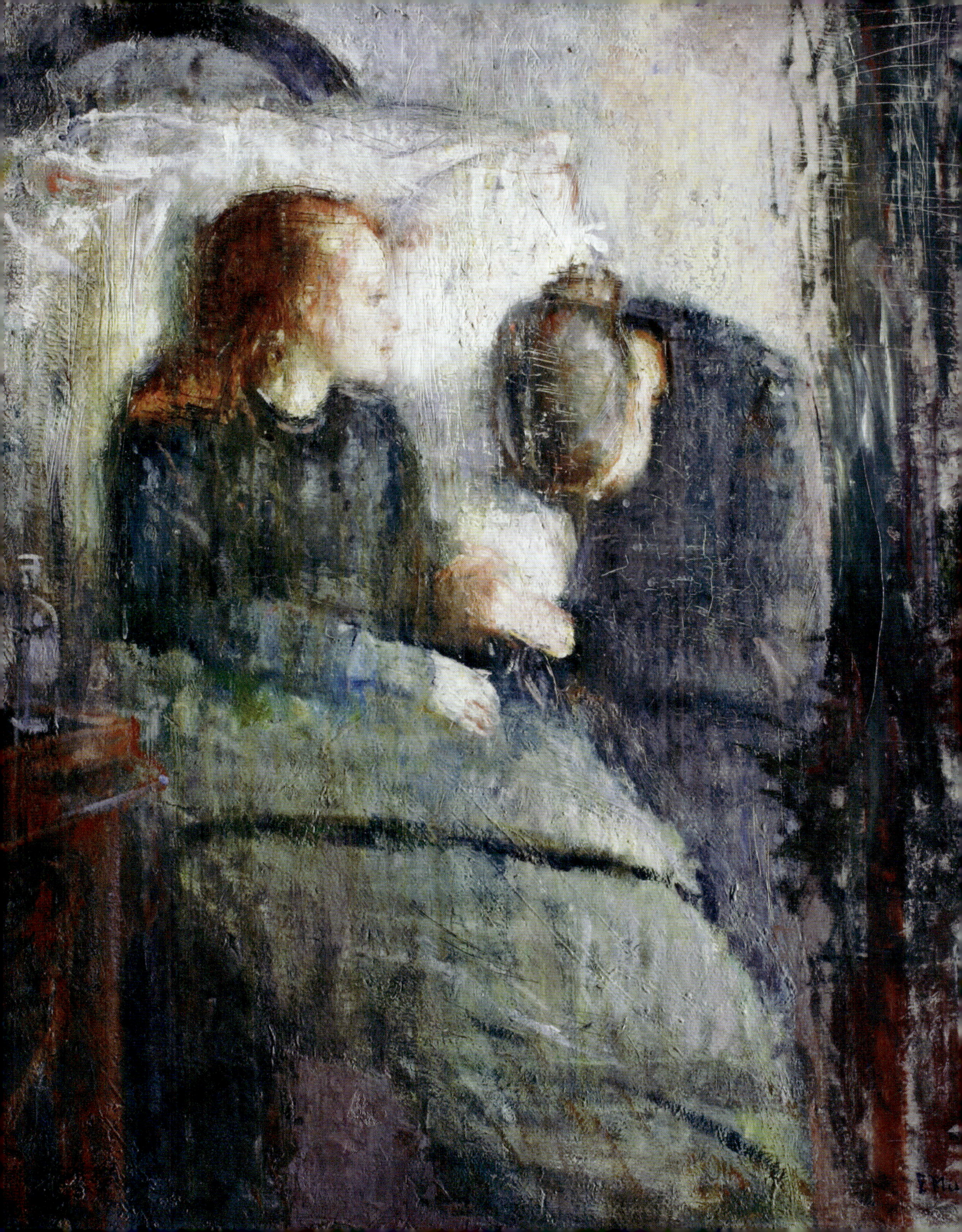

of pictures depicting the relationship between man and woman, exemplifying the different phases of love, as well as dealing with angst, illness and death as aspects of the human condition. Munch accentuated the emotional aspects of his subjects in these pictures. He worked on the series more or less throughout his entire artistic career, often painting several versions of its various motifs. These vary to a greater or lesser degree in their mode of expression, capturing a broad spectrum of emotions that the artist was interested in conveying. It is difficult to limit *The Frieze of Life* to a specific group of pictures, since Munch himself varied the selection when showing the series. This was not an entirely deliberate scheme, but rather a question of which pictures were available: some were sold consecutively, while others were detained in other exhibitions here and there.[2]

It took many years before Munch's artistic aspirations crystallised into a unified concept for a picture cycle based on the different stages of life. The idea of using his own experiences as inspiration undoubtedly arose under the influence of the Kristiania Bohemians, a group of radical writers headed by Hans Jæger (1854–1910), whom Munch met in 1884. One of the group's nine commandments was: 'Thou shalt write thy life.' Literature was viewed as a means of conveying one's own personal thoughts, emotions and experiences, as well as to advocate the practice of free love. Influenced by such ideas Munch began to write short texts relating to incidents, experiences and impressions from his life. His first romance, with a married woman in the summer of 1885, resulted in copious notes, as did his memories of illness and death in the family, but he also wrote down his observations on the art world and life in general. Munch's ambitions of publishing some of his notes in literary form never materialised.[3] Instead the autobiographical notes from 1885 to 1890 became the basis for *The Frieze of Life*. His involvement with the Bohemian circle and its radical programme would have great significance for the young Munch, and conceivably represented the most important influence on his artistic development. French symbolism from the 1890s, with its close ties to literature, would also become an important source of inspiration, and Munch's works were often described as literary. Contemporary literature, with Henrik Ibsen, August Strindberg and Knut Hamsun as its most prominent Scandinavian exponents, was preoccupied with current issues, focusing in particular on relations between the sexes, a pertinent theme in this period of nascent female emancipation. *The Frieze of Life* is a narrative in pictures of human life, and the fact that Munch collected his works in a series is rather revealing of the connection between visual art and literature in his oeuvre. The series of works about love, angst, illness and death is considered to be his most important achievement, and it includes his most famous painting *The Scream* (1893). The concept of the frieze itself is not new in art – the Parthenon Frieze, a relief sculpture on the Pallas Athena temple in Athens from around 440 BC is one of the oldest preserved picture series in Europe.

Munch's notes from a study tour of Paris in 1889–90 are today considered to be a form of manifesto linked to *The Frieze of Life*. Many of the texts were written shortly after he received news of his father's death in December 1889, a period in which his thinking was wrought with existential questions. The essence of *The Frieze of Life* is embedded in several of the texts, including one in which Munch recounts his impressions and ideas after a visit to a nightclub:

The music and the colours captivated my thoughts [...] I was going to do something – begin [working on] something. It would grip others as I was gripped now[.] I would depict two [people] in the most hallowed seconds of their lives [.] How they are gripped by that force that compels one more strongly than all else – [...] And the public will sense the sanctity of it – and they will take off their hats as in a church.[4]

The genesis of *The Frieze of Life* and its consolidation as a unified series can be traced in the catalogues for many of Munch's solo exhibitions during the 1890s, up until the Berlin Secession in 1902. The first catalogue to group the pictures thematically with respect to *The Frieze of Life* is from an exhibition in Berlin, which opened on 2 December 1893 at 19 Unter den Linden, where Munch had rented two rooms on the second floor. Six of the paintings were listed in the catalogue under the overall title 'Studies for a Series "Love"', and an unknown number were called 'Series "A Human Life"'.[5] Barely a year later, on 1 October 1894, a Munch exhibition opened at the Galerie Blanche in Stockholm, and according to the catalogue 69 paintings were displayed. The selection was divided into four groups, among them 'Emotive Pictures' and 'Studies for an Emotive Series "Love"'. *The Sick Child*, *Spring*, several works about death and the painting *Fever* were grouped under the heading 'Emotive Pictures', while *Kiss*, *Madonna*, *Vampire*, *Jealousy* and *The Scream* along with several others were listed as 'Studies for an Emotive Series "Love"'. Six months later Munch exhibited paintings at the Ugo Barroccio gallery in Berlin – together with the Finnish painter Axel Gallén (Akseli Gallen-Kallela).[6] Half of the 28 exhibited paintings were listed in the catalogue under the heading 'Love', while several other life-frieze motifs such as *Fever*, *Death* and *Puberty* were not grouped under any common title.

In 1902, Munch's *Frieze of Life* was exhibited for the first time as a completely integrated series at the fifth exhibition of the Berlin Secession.[7] A total of 22 paintings were listed in the catalogue under the common heading 'Presentation of a Series of Pictures about Life', with the subtitles 'The Seeds of Love', 'Love's Blossoming and Demise', 'Angst' and 'Death'. The pictures were arranged like a frieze, mounted with an uninterrupted white frame high up on the four walls of the room. The motifs of the frieze were also shown in a selection of prints mounted below the paintings. Munch's German colleague, the painter Walter Leistikow (1865–1908), a specialist in modern interior decoration and applied arts, helped design the exhibition. Under Munch's instructions the pictures were divided into groups that corresponded with the subtitles in the catalogue. Under 'The Seeds of Love' hung *Red and White*, *Eye to Eye*, *Kiss* (cat. 51) and *Madonna* (cat. 114); under 'Love's Blossoming and Demise' hung *The Dance of Life*, *Ashes*, *Jealousy*, *Vampire* (cat. 93) and *Melancholy*.[8] 'Angst' was represented with the pictures *Red Virginia Creeper*, *Angst* (cat. 72) and *The Scream*, and in the last group were shown *Death in the Sick Room*, *Death Struggle*, *The Mother and her Child* and others. The exhibition is today considered to be Munch's international breakthrough. The same exhibition opened at the P.H. Beyer & Sohn gallery in Leipzig at the end of February 1903, where it was fully documented with photographs of all the walls in each room (fig. 60).

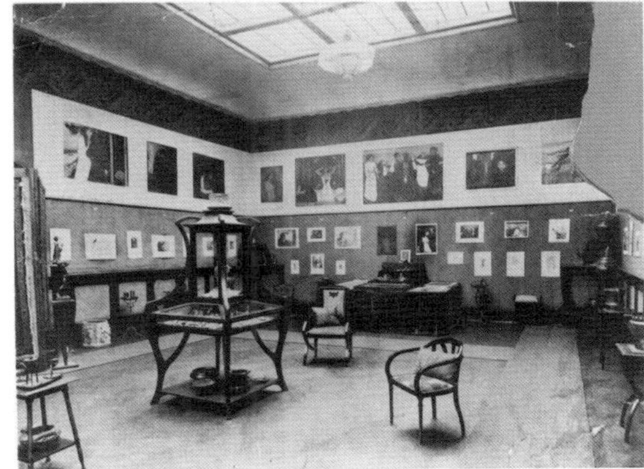

Fig. 60. Edvard Munch's exhibition of *The Frieze of Life* at P.H. Beyer & Sohn in Leipzig, 1903

From this point onwards *The Frieze of Life*, in varying sizes and combinations, became a regular component of Munch's art, with paintings executed both on commission and in anticipation of potential future assignments. The first commission came from one of Munch's German patrons, the ophthalmologist Max Linde in Lübeck. In 1902 Linde published the monograph *Edvard Munch und die Kunst der Zukunft* [Edvard Munch and the Art of the Future] (fig. 23), in which he compared Munch with Auguste Rodin in particular, rating him as the sculptor's equal. In August 1903 Linde commissioned a frieze of child-appropriate motifs for his sons' nursery.[9] But when the work was completed in 1904 Linde refused to accept it since several of the pictures were direct derivations of Munch's love motifs from the life-frieze series of the 1890s, complete with overtly erotic overtones, albeit transformed into a decorative format.[10] The central picture, *Dance on the Beach* (fig. 61), is based on a motif from his masterpiece *The Dance of Life* of 1899–1900. As was the case with many of Munch's early life-frieze pictures, all of the motifs in the *Linde Frieze* were set in nature.[11]

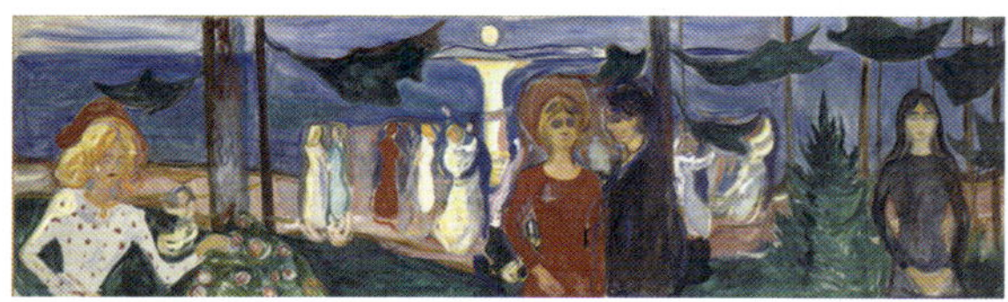

Fig. 61. Edvard Munch: *Dance on the Beach*, 1904

The *Reinhardt Frieze* was created in 1906–07. Stage and theatre director Max Reinhardt (1873–1943) commissioned the decorations for the Kammerspiele (studio space) in his new Deutsches Theater in Berlin. Munch returned to some of the motifs he had previously prepared for Linde in Lübeck, and the completed panels were also the same height, about 90 cm. The frieze consisted of twelve paintings.[12]

The exhibition at the Blomqvist Kunsthandel gallery in 1918, when Munch used the official title *The Frieze of Life* for the first time in the catalogue, was an attempt to promote the frieze and identify an opportunity to have it executed in a complete and coherent decoration. There are several theories as to why Munch arranged this exhibition at such short notice.[13] He had completed the decorations for the University of Oslo's great hall (Aula) in 1916 and was naturally interested in using his experience from this work to execute new commissions. Yet Gustav Vigeland's *Fountain* project must have been at least as compelling an incentive for Munch to promote his *Frieze of Life* with respect to potential public commissions. In April 1918 Vigeland opened his studio to the public to present his models for *The Fountain*, and it is conceivable that Munch perceived the project as a rival to his *Frieze of Life*. *The Fountain* was also presented in a collection of articles published in 1917.[14] Following the Blomqvist exhibition Munch had published a small booklet incorporating his own statement of defence for *The Frieze of Life*, together with remarks directed at its critics.[15] The booklet also contained several earlier, more favourable, reviews of his art.[16]

In January 1921 Munch received a commission from the Freia Chocolate Factory in Rodeløkka, Kristiania, to create wall decorations for the female workers' cafeteria. The paintings were executed over the course of 1922, and once again Munch based his works on the central motifs of *The Frieze of Life*, with scenic natural surroundings as the background. The frieze in the Freia factory was the last – and in Norway the only – public commission where Munch's *Frieze of Life* was incorporated into an architectural framework.

Fig. 62. Gustav Vigeland: *The Accursed*, 1891

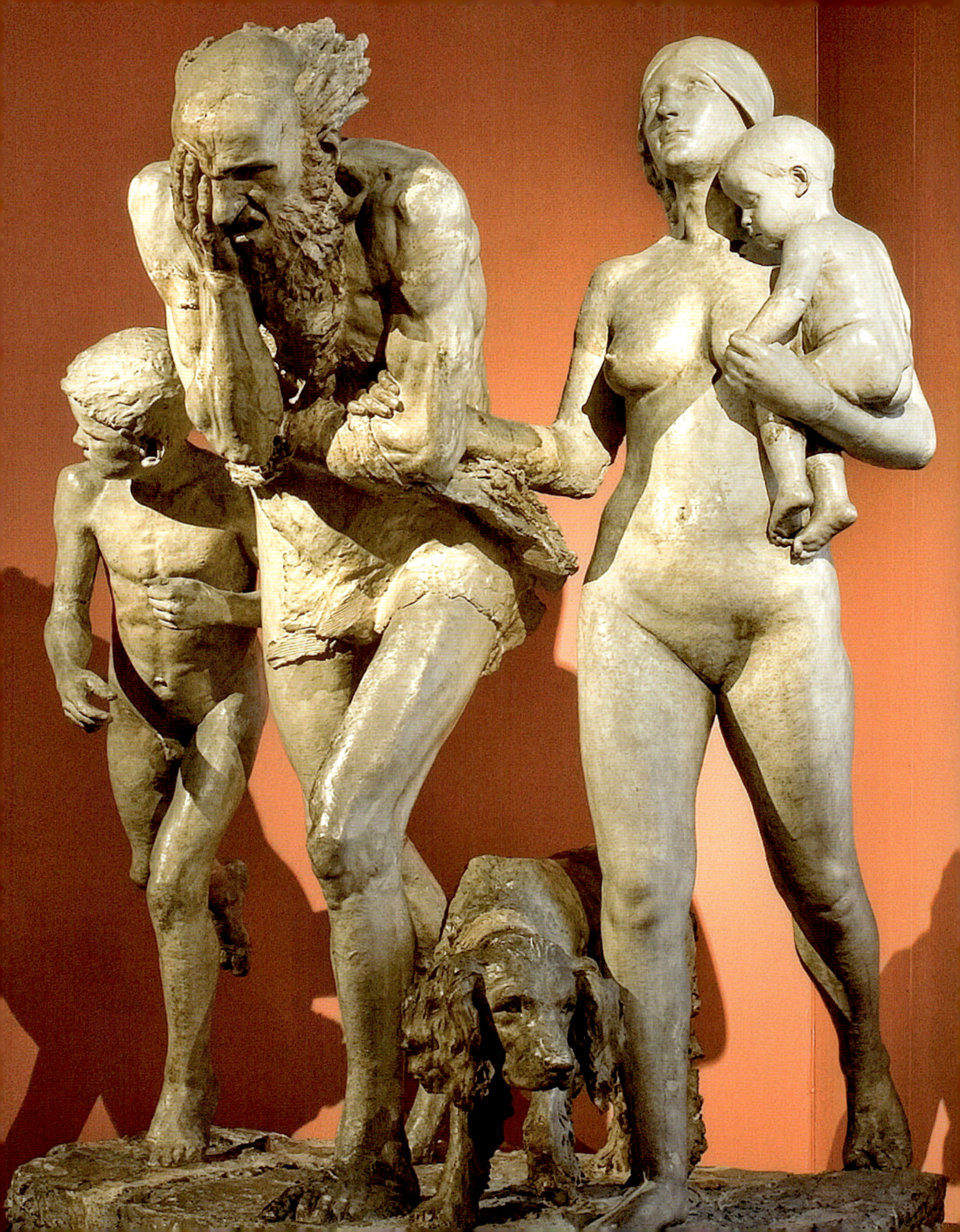

Gustav Vigeland's 'Life Frieze' seen from Munch's Perspective

Gustav Vigeland, who was six years younger than Munch, depicted many of the same motifs as the older artist during the first half of the 1890s. His mode of expression during that time was to a large degree influenced by the motif's emotional content. During the 1890s, Vigeland undertook a thorough exploration of the relationship between man and woman, both in his sculptures and in countless drawings. Many of his works on the subject were overtly erotic. He also explored other motifs relating to the human condition in works such as *Woman Praying for the Drunkards* (1893, cat. 130) and *Old Woman Watching Her Husband Die* (1898, cat. 129). Vigeland was considered an exceptional talent as early as 1892, when his work *The Accursed* (1891, fig. 62) attracted considerable attention at the National Art Exhibition.[17]

Vigeland's sculptures became more streamlined towards the end of the 1890s, and the heightened emotional content was gradually toned down. Like Munch, Vigeland focused on motifs about life throughout his entire career. After 1900, he became increasingly preoccupied by the cycle of life, a theme that he was to develop further in works for his sculpture park in Frogner. Vigeland was responsible for the design of the entire installation and all of its sculptures, a process that lasted several decades, and which began with the planning of a single fountain in the city centre around the turn of the century. The axis formed by the sculptures leading from the entrance gate via *The Bridge*, *The Fountain* and *The Monolith* plateau to *The Wheel of Life*, is also referred to as the Vigeland Park. The park was completed around 1950, after the sculptor's death.

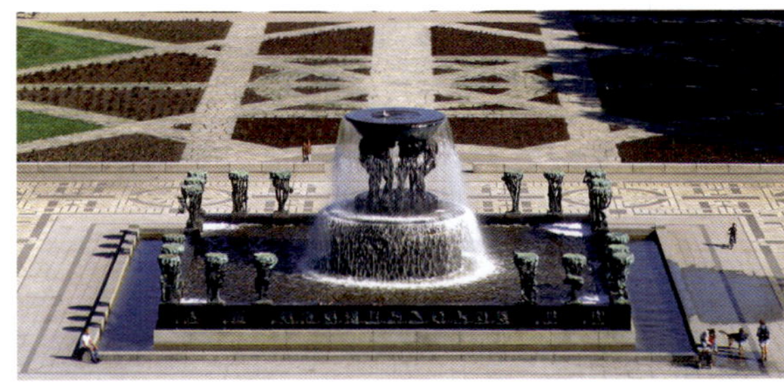

Fig. 63. Gustav Vigeland: *The Fountain*, 1909

The idea for Vigeland's own 'frieze of life' began with *The Fountain* (fig. 63), for which he had begun making sketches in 1899. The earliest draft design for the sculpture was made in 1900. The first plaster model comprises six monumental figures supporting an enormous basin with three further groups (fig. 64) arranged around the edge of a pool, decorated with relief sculptures on its outer sides. The draft designs were further modified and evolved in both composition and size over the course of several years, before an amended version was modelled in clay in 1906–14. Several proposals regarding the fountain's placement in the city centre were considered, including Eidsvolls Square, Jernbanetorget (Railway Square), the City Hall and the gardens of the Royal Palace. In the meantime the project grew in scope. In 1919 the Municipality of Kristiania came up with a proposal to build a studio for Vigeland

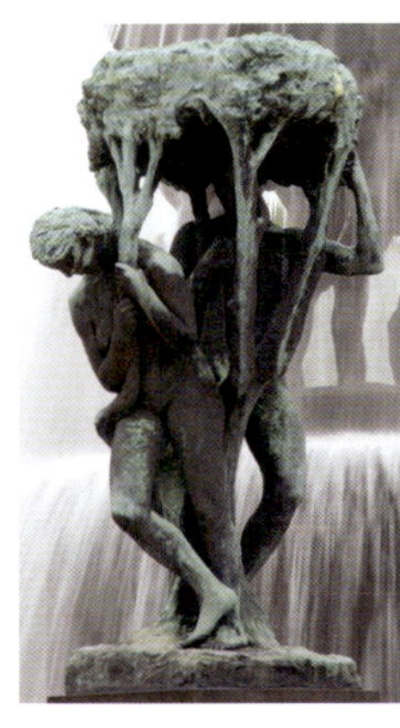

Fig. 64. Gustav Vigeland: *Man Standing Behind a Woman*. One of the tree groups around *The Fountain*, 1906–14

in Frogner, and in 1922 the idea of having a sculpture park constructed in Frogner was presented to Vigeland. The area had lain fallow since the buildings from the 1914 Jubilee Exhibition were been dismantled. The sculptures for *The Fountain*, *The Monolith*, *The Bridge* and *The Wheel of Life* in the park all depict the lives of human beings from childhood to old age. Although Vigeland never used the term 'life frieze' in relation to his work, some of his contemporaries commented that his chosen motifs were closely tied to the stages of human life.[18] Not least Munch who, many years later, described the sculptures and reliefs in Vigeland's *Fountain* as a 'life frieze', and claimed in a number of notes and letter drafts that the idea was his own.

A close kinship between Vigeland's and Munch's choice of motifs is obvious, and many of their titles are similar: *Kiss*, *Consolation*, *The Tree of Life*, *The Beggar* and *The Worker* for instance are used by both artists, and Vigeland's sculptures such as *Young Girl* (1892, cat. 18), *Fear* (1892, cat. 70), *Death* (1892), *The Kiss* (1898, cat. 52) and *Death and Life* (1893) could easily be compared to Munch's works from *The Frieze of Life*. Parallels have been drawn between Vigeland's *Young Girl* and Munch's *Puberty* (1894, cat. 17), a motif that the latter executed for the first time in 1886.[19] Vigeland's small sculpture *Fear*, which depicts a screaming female figure entangled in an organic plant-like shape, is frequently compared with Munch's *The Scream* (fig. 65), and was created before the iconic painting. Both works depict angst. In *Fear* it is triggered by the unknown, which is represented by the indeterminate form that coils around the woman. The woman's anxiety appears to be caused by the threatening shape representing the unknown, stressing the symbolic nature of the figure's scream. In *The Scream* the feeling of angst is related to an existential sense of human vulnerability, through the figure's placement in a bold perspective before a cloud-laden landscape. The representations of angst in these works are formed in two very different art media, which in themselves define the premises for interpretation.

Some years later both artists created their own treatments of the two motifs *The Urn* and *The Tree of Life*. Vigeland created water vessels for his *Fountain* in the shape of urns around 1901, and the idea of incorporating in the same work the groups of figures in trees, where life – from birth to death – evolves under the treetops, appeared around 1905. Munch's many drafts for *The Tree of Life* were created both in connection with the Aula decorations in 1909, and in the motifs *Life* (1910, fig. 66) and *Harvesting Women*. Rodin's figure of *The Thinker* (1880, cat. 135), which appears in the upper panel of *The Gates of Hell*, is very likely to have inspired Vigeland's seated man in the relief *Hell II* (1897, cat. 134). Munch also developed the seated thinker in several of his sketches for the Aula, and ended by immortalising him as a youth in several versions of *The Researchers* (1910–11), here depicted in profile (fig. 67).

Up until 1918 there is little evidence to show that the two artists viewed one another as rivals, yet it does not appear that a close friendship ever developed between them, not even during the period spent in Berlin, where they lived next door for a few months in the spring of 1895. They do not appear to have had any particular interest in each other. Furthermore, it seems that Vigeland was less preoccupied with Munch than the painter eventually became with the successful sculptor. Vigeland, who was a member of the Board of the National Gallery, occasionally supported the gallery's acquisition of a picture

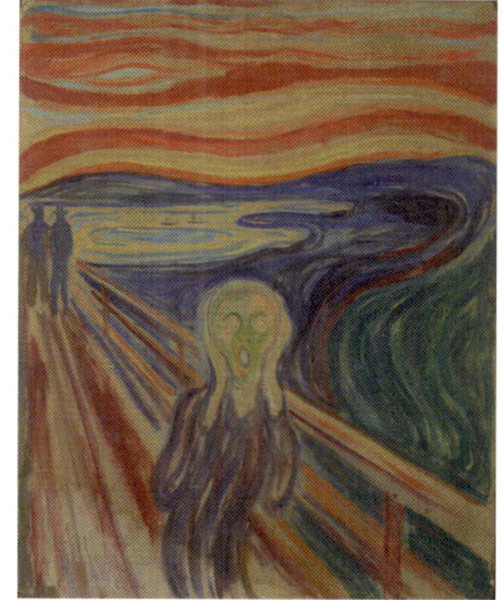

Fig. 65. Edvard Munch: *The Scream*, 1910?

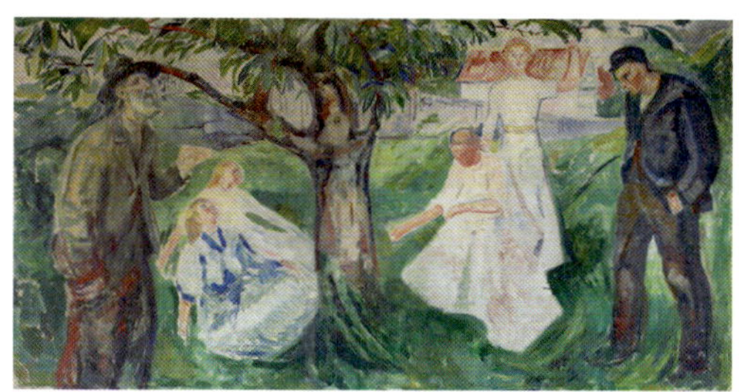

Fig. 66. Edvard Munch: *Life*, 1910

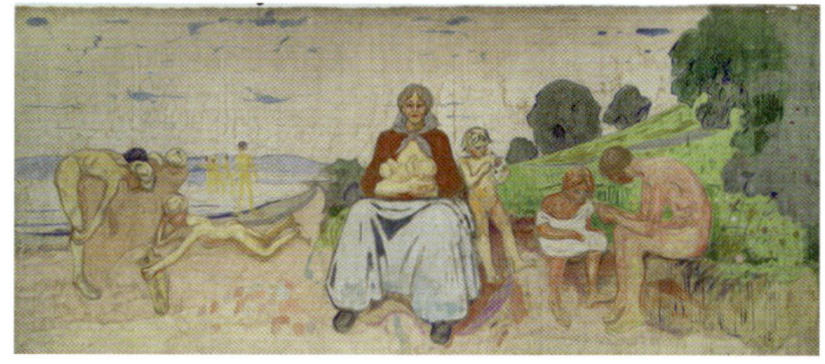

Fig. 67. Edvard Munch:
The Researchers, 1910–11

by Munch,[20] but he was evidently not entirely enthusiastic about everything that Munch made, and among other things wrote:

> Love is foreign to him; He is too barren by nature for that. But the thing he paints with intimacy, illness, that he knows. All this intrigue with jealousy, green faces of men etc. is pure nonsense. The sick and his portraits stand out [...] In his pictures of illness the distance between emotion and hand is almost brilliantly short.[21]

It is impossible to find critical descriptions of Vigeland's work in Munch's posthumous writings. On the contrary, in around 1910 he was considering a collaboration with Vigeland, which he wrote about in several letters to Jens Thiis.[22]

Eventually, however, after Vigeland was able to complete his large-scale projects, Munch expressed his bitterness in numerous notes during the 1930s in connection with what he felt was unfair treatment on the part of the public authorities. What made it even worse was that Munch was convinced that Vigeland had stolen his frieze of life idea and used it in *The Fountain*, and that the motif *The Human Mountain/Towards the Light* was the inspiration behind Vigeland's *Monolith*. Munch initially supported *The Fountain*, before the project grew to take on its final design, dimensions and position. In one of his sketchbooks he devotes more than half of the pages to issues concerning the financial support that Vigeland received from the state, and the large commission he had been assigned, while Munch had to fund his own work and in addition was required to pay taxes on his unsold pictures:

> I signed the petition for Vigeland to have his fountain without bitterness – despite it having the same content regarding life as mine – Vigeland's was at its conception, mine was completed.[23] Yet when I see the millions that are spent on Vigeland's fountain I cannot deny that I feel bitter because my friezes *The Frieze of Life* and *Towards the Light* have not received any understanding or support – and not been given the opportunity to be executed in due time.[24]

Munch wrote repeatedly that the idea was his – completed and exhibited many years before Vigeland began work on his 'life frieze':

> In 1905 Vigeland began work on his *Fountain* – It was the same idea as mine, the cycle of life – The whole idea in the later large-scale Frogner grouping with 'towards the light' as the conclusion has the same idea as my life frieze, and *Towards the Light* was submitted by me to the Aula in 1912 – My work was strangulated to smithereens [while] Vigeland sat high and mighty – I had executed the idea ten years before he began his *Fountain*.[25]

The Human Mountain/Towards the Light and *The Human Column/The Monolith*[26]

Munch's interest in the motif *The Human Mountain/Towards the Light* manifested itself in his art at several stages. Two drawings executed in 1897 (cats. 151, 194) were based on his lithographs entitled *The Crystal Kingdom* and *Funeral March* from the same year (cat. 148).[27] *The Human Mountain* motif was represented in a number of

Fig. 68. Edvard Munch: *The Human Mountain*, 1916–17

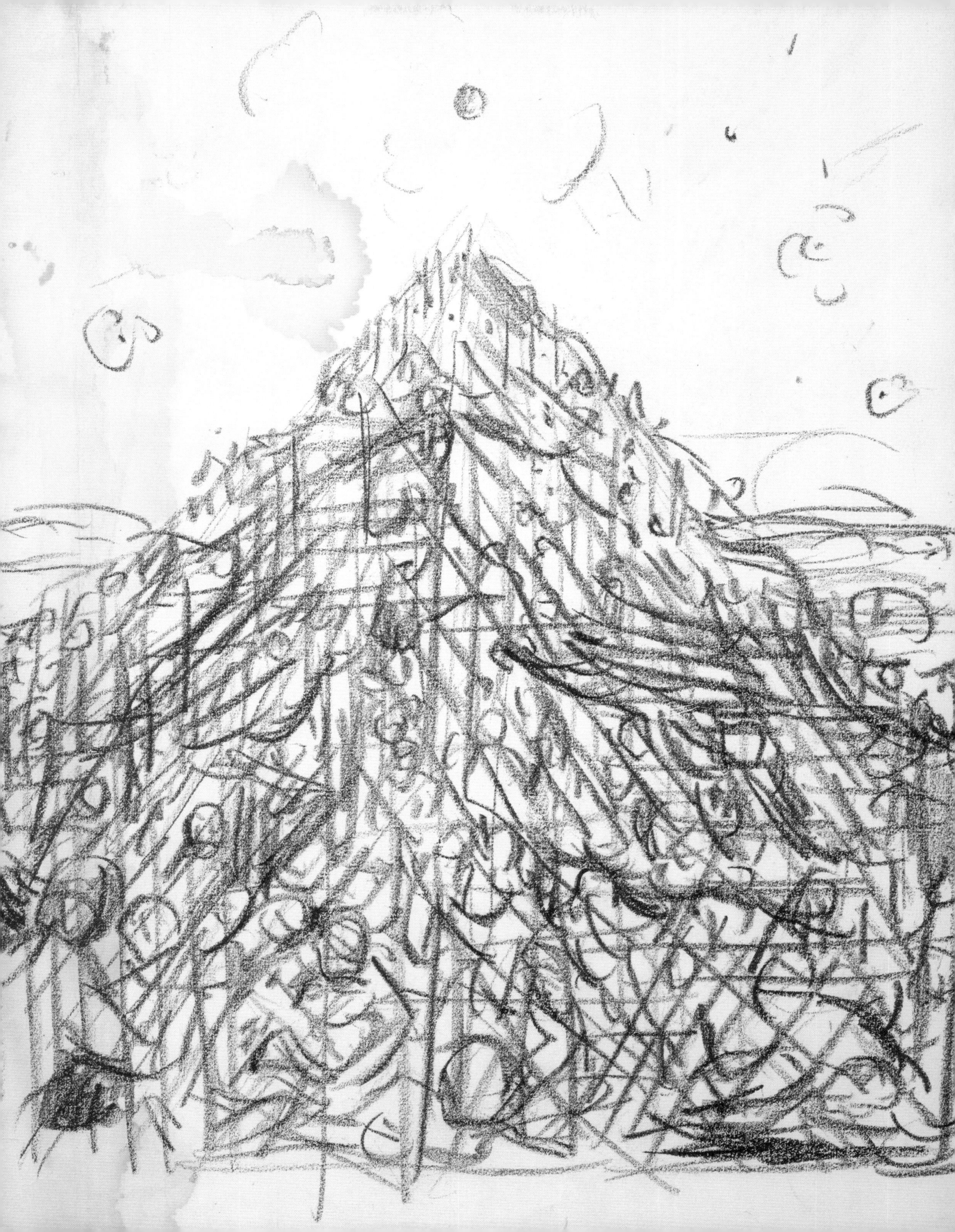

sketches when in the summer of 1909 he created his first drafts for the competition to decorate the Aula (cats. 152, 153, 193). A draft of the symbolic motif, with human figures straining towards the light, was submitted to the competition for the first time in March 1910, together with *History*, and refused. By 1916 Munch's decorations for the Aula were in place, and he returned to *The Human Mountain* motif in several drawings (fig. 68) together with two new motifs, which were probably influenced by the First World War: *War/The Storm* and *Peace/The Rainbow*.

During the second half of the 1920s Munch began working on all three motifs once again. A photograph from 1926 shows how he constructed a monumental *Human Mountain* composition, consisting of several smaller pictures, in his outdoor studio at Ekely (fig. 69). Based on this composition, which was expanded with additional pictures over the next three years, the painting *The Human Mountain* came into being between 1927 and 1929 (fig. 70), and probably also the sculpture of the same title (cat. 189).[28] The painting was planned as the central panel of a triptych, with two panels on either side symbolising human beings struggling and at rest.[29] The triptych was never realised.[30]

Vigeland began work on his *Human Column* and figures immediately after the Second World War and the first three-dimensional model was executed in the spring of 1919.[31] He originally wanted to locate the work in Railway Square, which at the time was a prominent site for public commissioned work. The proposal was denied and Vigeland decided to incorporate the column in the plan for his expanded *Fountain* project.[32] In November 1924 the municipality passed a final resolution regarding Vigeland's *Fountain* and the adjacent park's location.[33] In September 1926, a colossal granite block earmarked for *The Human Column* – a monolith – was transported from Iddefjorden to Oslo. The stone was raised in 1928, and the carving commenced in 1929. *The Monolith*, with its 121 figures, was executed as part of the sculpture park in Frogner, and the work became known under this title (which Vigeland himself had begun to use). While the main theme of *The Fountain* is the perpetual cycle of life, the column can be seen as a symbol of human yearning and the struggle en route to the afterlife.

In 1928–29 Munch arranged for the publication of a booklet containing a selection of his notes, titled *The Origins of the Frieze of Life*. It comprises a number of texts of varying length: 'The Origins of The Frieze of Life' (1890), 'Art and Nature' (1907–08), his 'manifesto' from Saint-Cloud (1889) and 'Towards the Light', the only text in the book written specially for the new publication.[34] In 'Towards the Light' Munch explains the idea behind his triptych, which was in progress at Ekely, and the circumstances in which it was originally meant to be implemented:[35]

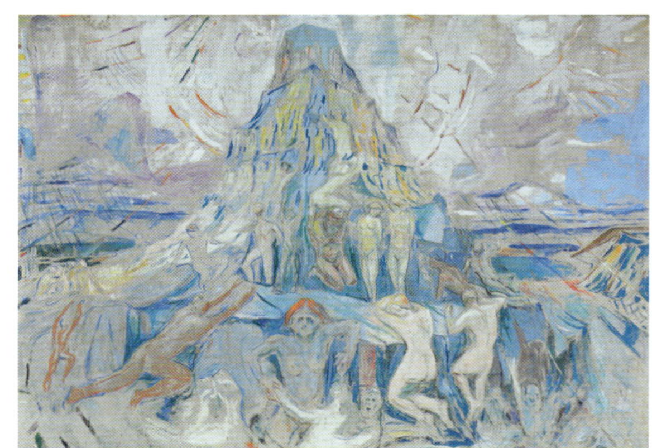

Fig. 69. Edvard Munch's *Human Mountain* composition in his outdoor studio at Ekely, 1926

Fig. 70. Edvard Munch: *The Human Mountain/Towards the Light*, 1927–29

> Towards the light – the Human Mountain or the human column – A crowd
> of naked human beings that strains towards the light – and who pile up
> like a column towards the sun. – This was intended as the rear wall image

– the other panels along the hall's lateral walls would be human beings besieged and in motion – On one of them the storm – humans that are forced to flee by the natural catastrophe – and on the other side the rainbow – human beings in repose and anticipating peace and the sun.

The creation of the monumental *The Human Mountain/Towards the Light* triptych at Ekely and the publication of *The Origins of the Frieze of Life* coincided with two important events in Vigeland's career. The transportation of the granite block from Iddefjorden was amply covered in the press in 1926, the same year that Munch began his work on the composition of *The Human Mountain*. In 1928–29 *The Monolith* was raised, and the work of carving it began at the same time that Munch's booklet *The Origins of the Frieze of Life* was published. It might seem that this was his way of making public his conviction that both *The Frieze of Life* and *The Human Mountain/Towards the Light* were originally his ideas, and that they were the inspiration behind Gustav Vigeland's *Fountain* and eventually his *Monolith*. In an undated letter draft Munch writes: 'My sister has actually created a poem in photographs about Akerselven – Is it the same urge that brings me to paint in series? Is it this family drive that Vigeland has snatched – He did not work in series until I had my life frieze nearly completed and exhibited in Berlin. It was then he threw together a line-up for the fountain and then [continued] on to my idea towards the light.'[36]

The Frieze of Life in Vogue

Creating friezes became a common practice among many Norwegian artists after the First World War. Some executed large public commissions using the fresco technique, which led to its exponents being dubbed the 'Fresco Brothers'. Among these were Henrik Sørensen, Per Krohg, Axel Revold and Alf Rolfsen. There was an abundance of large-scale public commissions in the new Norway – for instance, the Bergen Stock Exchange, Oslo City Hall and other public buildings as well as numerous churches. The subject matter was expanded to encompass human pastimes and types of employment. Axel Revold (1887–1962) was given the assignment to decorate the Bergen Exchange in 1918. His work *Commodity Exchange*, completed in 1923, depicts the city as the hub of worldwide trade, and is divided into three parts, all of which represent the bustling activity in Bergen harbour. Several other commissions carried out by the Fresco Brothers can be more directly linked to the 'life friezes' of Munch and Vigeland. Alf Rolfsen's (1895–1979) fresco paintings in Vestre Crematorium were executed in 1932–37. These too take human life as their theme. In the side aisle the journey through life from birth to death is depicted, while its liberation up through the foliage of the tree of life is the main theme of the rear wall. The tree of life motif was, as previously mentioned, used by both Vigeland and Munch. Munch commented on Rolfsen's work in Vestre Crematorium:

It is not to copy Vigeland when I wish to find a location for my life frieze – It was already completed in 1894 on a small scale and in 1902 it was exhibited in Berlin in a very large edition[.] I have worked on it all these years – After that Vigeland has made his life frieze (It has become large enough) and now Rolfsen has located his Life Frieze (It is apparently an excellent work in the Crematorium).[37]

One more 'life frieze' should be mentioned in this context. Gustav Vigeland's younger brother, the artist Emanuel Vigeland (1875–1948), had also entered a competition for the decoration of the Aula. He was influenced by symbolist trends and cultivated a mannerist style of painting, with dismal and dramatic undertones. The choice of motifs partly consisted of themes that were similar to his brother's, such as Judgement Day and relations between the sexes. This eventually led to a rather distant relationship between the two brothers, which lasted for the remainder of their lives. In 1926 Emanuel Vigeland began erecting a monumental church-like brick building at his residential property in the neighbourhood of Slemdal in Oslo, planned as a studio and museum for his own works. The vaulted main room is today a mausoleum where his urn is preserved. The walls and the ceiling are completely covered with fresco decorations of hundreds of naked figures. The large painting *Vita* recounts the human life cycle from conception to death, with considerable emphasis on eroticism. The human figures are depicted against the threatening and dark eternity represented by the cosmos, and an attempt is made to combine Christian ideas with the more modern natural sciences. Groups of figures in bronze replicate the representations of procreation on the walls. Work on the *Tomba Emanuele* was to occupy him for the remainder of his life. The Emanuel Vigeland Museum opened in 1959, and its interior stands today as one of the most striking late symbolist works of art in all of the Nordic countries.

Epilogue

Munch's *Frieze of Life* was begun during the 1890s, a deliberate concept that was created over many years and which the artist developed throughout his entire career. He was working on new versions of *The Frieze of Life* paintings in a monumental format at Ekely as late as 1935.

In addition to *The Frieze of Life*, initiated with *The Sick Child* in 1885, Munch's Aula decorations can also be seen as distinct frieze, which deals with the basic conditions of man and his intellectual development. In his published tract *The Origins of the Frieze of Life* Munch writes that *The Frieze of Life* should also be viewed in connection with the Aula decorations: *The Frieze of Life* depicts the individual human being's sorrows and joys at close range, whereas the decorations represent the great enduring forces.[38] The unfinished *Human Mountain* triptych can in this sense also be considered a frieze, with a symbolic representation of human struggles and strivings towards universal spiritual enlightenment.

According to Munch, Vigeland appropriated his life frieze and executed it first in *The Fountain*'s reliefs and groups of trees, and later in *The Monolith*. While Munch had an overtly conscious relationship to the series early in the process, Vigeland's 'life frieze' might be interpreted as beginning with *The Fountain*, which later developed into a larger 'life frieze' when a comprehensive plan was designed for the extensive sculpture park in Frogner.

It is not difficult to see that the 'life friezes' of the two artists are quite different. This is not only due to the fact that they were executed in very different mediums and time frames. Another significant factor is their point of departure: Munch's *Frieze of Life* was entirely based on profoundly personal experiences, while Vigeland's life cycle in the sculpture park in Frogner was based on a more objective perspective. Munch referred to the pictures in his *Frieze of Life* as 'Motifs from the modern life of the soul', a phrase that is used to describe his art to this day.[39] In an undated note he wrote:

> Time's religion – that is the life of its soul must be reflected – There must not only be ornamental art. This word has destroyed a lot – Art began as ornamental art they say – That is a lie – One told one's story – one conveyed one's divine belief in stone and on the surface of walls –[40]

1   Edvard Munch, *Livsfrisen* (Kristiania: Blomqvist Kunsthandel, 1918).

2   It is an established fact that Munch had little desire to sell his paintings during the second half of his career and several of the pictures from the *Frieze* that were sold in the course of the 1890s he created in new versions. See for example Gunnar Sørensen's foreword in *Edvard Munchs Livsfrise. En rekonstruksjon av utstillingen hos Blomqvist 1918* (Oslo: Munch Museum/Labyrinth Press, 2002), p. 10.

3   Munch published two small booklets, *Livs-frisen* [The Frieze of Life] (Kristiania: 1919), and *Livsfrisens tilblivelse* [The Origins of the Frieze of Life] (Oslo: 1928–29). These contained only a fraction of his notes.

4   Edvard Munch, note 1889–90, MM N 289.

5   The information in the catalogue appears to be somewhat inaccurate. Under no. 4, 'Study for a Series "Love"' six paintings are listed with individual titles in sequence under the letters 'a, b, c, d, e, f'. 'Watercolours' are listed as no. 20 and 'Drawings' as no. 21. 'Series "A Human Life"' is listed as nos. 22–50, the last entry. According to a review in *Morgenbladet* (7.12.1893), the exhibition consisted of 20 paintings and a number of drawings.

6   Ugo Barroccio, 19 Unter den Linden, Berlin, 3–24.3.1895. According to the catalogue, Gallén exhibited 31 works, while Munch showed 28 paintings and 17 works on paper: drawings, intaglio prints and lithographs.

7   *Fünfte Kunstausstellung der Berliner Secession*, April–May 1902.

8   Different versions of the motifs to those referred to in the catalogue were shown.

9   Letter from Max Linde to Edvard Munch, 8.8.1903.

10 The *Frieze* consisted of eight pictures, around 90 cm in height and of varying width (with the exception of *Girls Watering Flowers* which measured 99.5 cm in height). *Dance on the Beach* was the widest painting in the frieze, measuring 316 cm.

11 Munch's love motifs in particular unfold in Åsgårdstrand's scenic landscape. The shoreline forms the background in *Separation*, *Melancholy* and *Red and White* among others.

12 Peter Krieger, *Edvard Munch: Der Lebensfries für Max Reinhardts Kammerspiele* (Berlin: Nationalgalerie, Staatliche Museen Preussischer Kulturbesitz, 1978).

13 Gerd Woll, 'Munchs utstillingsstrategi "for å få sagt noe" med sine bilder', in *Edvard Munchs Livsfrise*, 2002, p. 37.

14 Carl Wille Schnitler (ed.), *Vigelands fontene* (Kristiania: Grøndahl Forlag, 1917).

15 Munch, 1919.

16 Lasse Jacobsen, 'Livs-frisen og Livsfrisens tilblivelse – maleren griper til sverdet og pennen', in *Edvard Munchs Livsfrise*, 2002, p. 62.

17 Tone Wikborg, *Gustav Vigeland. En biografi* (Oslo: Gyldendal Norsk Forlag, 2001), pp. 66–67.

18 Gabriel Finne, *Norske Intelligenssedler*, 16.8.1894; Jens Thiis, *Verdens Gang*, 29.10.and 9.11.1894.

19 There is no documentation regarding the appearance of the first version of the painting, which was probably quite similar to the surviving versions (from 1894–95). The painting belonged to Axel Thoresen, and was presumed lost in a fire at an unknown date.

20 Wikborg, 2001, p. 234.

21 Wikborg, 2001, p. 235, ref. p. 544: Various undated letter drafts possibly from 1904, to G. Kielland (in GV: 170–77).

22 See the article by Trine Otte Bak Nielsen in this catalogue.

23 Edvard Munch, sketchbook, MM T 2703, p. 30. Based on its content and context the book can be dated to the beginning of the 1930s.

24 Edvard Munch, sketchbook, MM T 2703, p. 48.

25 Edvard Munch, undated note, MM N 331.

26 In this article the title *The Human Mountain/Towards the Light* is used in reference to the motif, as Munch was inconsistent in his use of both titles with respect to the different versions of the work. The title *The Monolith* originated from the granite block from which the figures were carved, but Vigeland had initially referred to the work as *The Human Column*.

27 Gerd Woll, *Edvard Munch: The Complete Graphic Works* (Oslo/London: Orfeus Publishing/Philip Wilson Publishers, 2012), p. 132.

28 See the article by Erika Sandbakken in this catalogue.

29 Petra Pettersen, 'Menneskeberget. Et kunstverk blir til', *Kunst og Kultur*, no. 1/2010, vol. 93, pp. 14–23.

30 In April 1930 Munch contracted an eye disease, which curtailed his artistic activities for several months.

31 Tone Wikborg, *Gustav Vigeland. Mennesket og kunstneren* (Oslo: Aschehoug, 1983), p. 190.

32 Wikborg, 1983, p. 190.

33 *Aftenposten* (morning edition), 28.11.1924.

34 Munch, 1928–29, p. 18.

35 *The Human Mountain/Towards the Light* was submitted to the Aula competition in.3.1910 (together with *History*, which was accepted by the jury).

36 Edvard Munch, letter draft to an unidentified person, MM N 709. The draft was written after the publication of Inger Munch, *Akerselven* (Oslo: N.W. Damm & Søn, 1932).

37 Edvard Munch, undated letter draft to Jens Thiis, MM N 2074.

38 See note 35.

39 Edvard Munch exhibition, Dioramalokalet, Kristiania, 16.10.–13.11.1904.

40 Edvard Munch, undated note, MM N 315.

'The Sculptor Edvard Munch. "Unknown Works" – but is there perhaps someone who knows the history of their origins?'

Erika Gohde Sandbakken

This headline was printed in *Aftenposten* following a visit to Ekely a few weeks after Edvard Munch's death on 23 January 1944.[1] The question could equally well be posed today, as most people are unfamiliar with Munch's sculptural works. The artist himself had remarked to a journalist from *Arbeiderbladet* in 1929: 'Yes, I also do a bit of sculpting.'[2] This was true, since he had made a modest number of sculptures. Today there are eleven sculptures in the Munch Museum's collection; in addition, three of the eleven motifs are executed in two versions.[3] In total there are two in bronze, seven in plaster of Paris, four in clay, and one in Plasticine (see table on p. 145).[4] There is also a further sculpture outside the museum's collection: *Workers in Snow*. Munch made two bronze versions of this motif, and sold one of them to the Freia Chocolate Factory in 1943. In this article I will present a short account of Munch's references to Auguste Rodin (1840–1917), followed by an examination of the dates, methods and circumstances of Munch's sculptures.[5]

References to Auguste Rodin

Munch's personal library includes many art books and catalogues about sculpture.[6] The earliest of these is a small catalogue from the large-scale Rodin exhibition held in Prague in 1902. It is commonly understood that Munch was inspired by Rodin's subject matter and idiom,[7] in particular by the sculptures *The Thinker* (1880), *Kiss* (1888) and *The Age of Bronze* (1876). Munch may have seen the latter as early as in 1885 during his first visit to Paris, when it was on view in the Musée du Luxembourg. The German businessman and art collector Albert Kollmann (1837–1915) declared that he considered the root of Munch's art to be in ancient art (fig. 71). He wrote

Fig. 71. *Dying Niobid* (450–440 BC). Postcard from Albert Kollmann to Edvard Munch, 1910

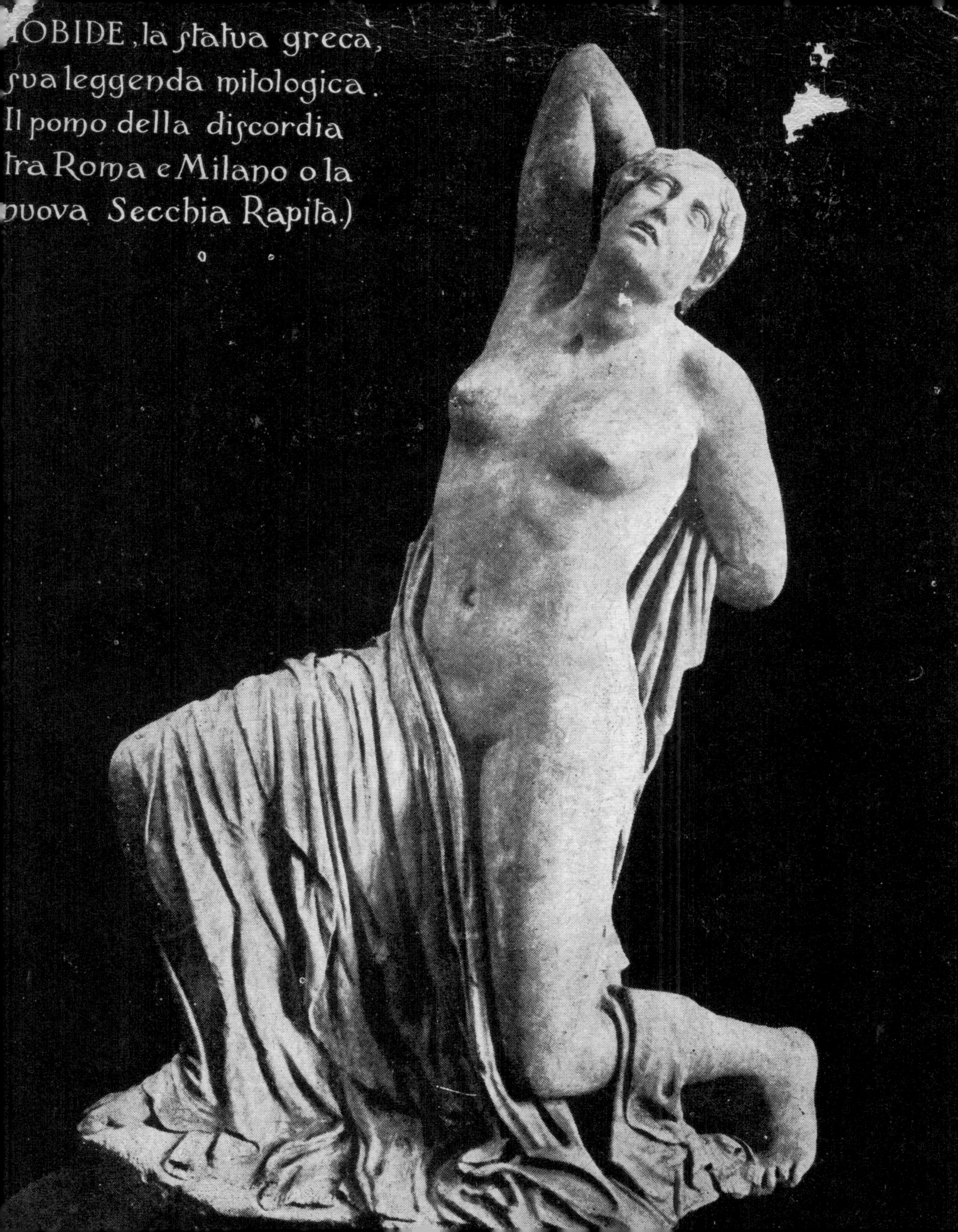
IOBIDE, la statua greca,
sua leggenda mitologica.
Il pomo della discordia
tra Roma e Milano o la
nuova Secchia Rapita.)

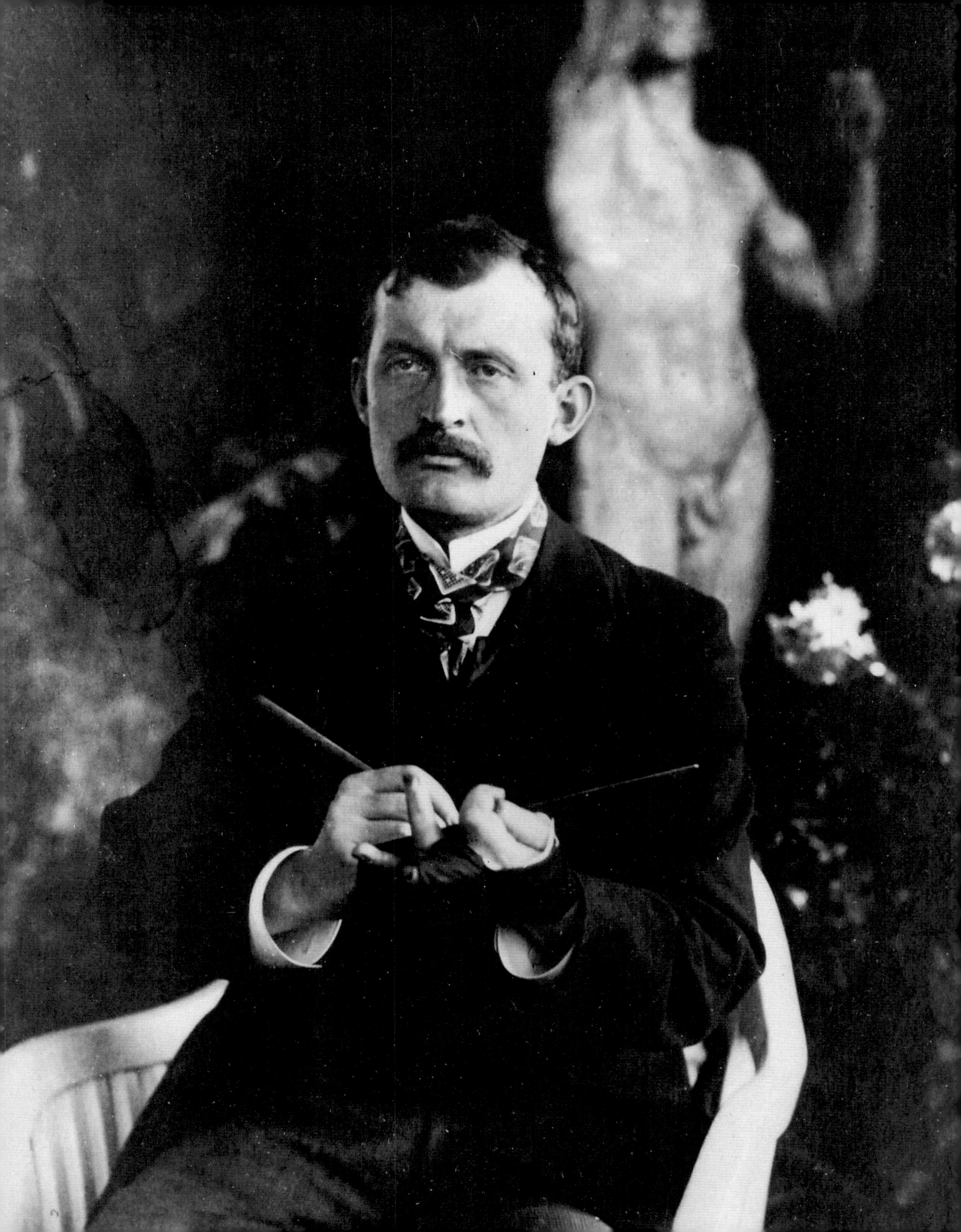

this statement on a postcard [8] depicting the classical Greek sculpture of the *Dying Niobid* (450–440 BC), which he sent to Munch in 1910. Rodin was also interested in ancient and Gothic sculpture.

After 1902 Munch had access to several of Rodin's sculptures through his patron Max Linde (1862–1949), as he lived for a period at Linde's home in Lübeck during autumn of that year.[9] Linde owned Europe's largest private collection of Rodin's work,[10] among them one of the *Age of Bronze* sculptures, in front of which Munch was photographed (fig. 72). Linde ordered sixteen intaglio prints by Munch, often referred to as the *Linde Portfolio*, of which two took Rodin's sculptures *La Faunesse* and *Danaïde* as their motifs. That same year Linde published a monograph on Munch in which he compares him with Rodin. Among other similarities he perceived a common fascination for grotesque subjects, referring to Rodin's *The Old Courtesan* (1887) and Munch's lithograph *Women in the Hospital* (1896).[11] In 1903 Linde sent his book to Rodin, and in an accompanying letter he linked Munch to Rodin's famous work *The Thinker*.[12] Linde acquired Rodin's bronze version of *The Thinker* in 1903 and it was placed in his garden in 1905.[13] Munch may have seen this sculpture when he visited the large exhibition of French art in Copenhagen in 1888, and the motif can be traced for instance in some of his versions of the work *Melancholy* (1891 and 1894–96).

Materials and Methods

Munch's sculptural methods have not previously been studied to any great extent. On the other hand, those of Gustav Vigeland and Rodin are well documented. Both of them produced large quantities of clay and plaster sculptures, which they used as the starting point for their works in bronze and stone.

Sketched Drawings and Clay Models

The process often begins with drawings, which are then modelled in clay. Munch made several clay sculptures, four of which have been preserved. Two are in a poor state of repair, almost completely fragmented, while the sculpture *Man and Woman* (cat. 157) is in reasonably good condition. This may indicate that it was modelled without a wooden or steel armature, or that it has been stored in a relatively stable environment. In one of the fragmented sculptures, 'Defective Group', the clay is built up around wooden sticks and wire, which have been exposed where the clay has fallen off. This occurred when the clay dried out, which caused it to shrink and crack and detach from the armature in pieces. In the clay sculpture *Man's Head* the armature is made from wood shavings[14] and branches that still retain their bark, suggesting that Munch used whatever materials he had to hand (fig. 73). The sculpture conservator at the Vigeland Museum believes that Vigeland used more traditional materials for his armatures, such as

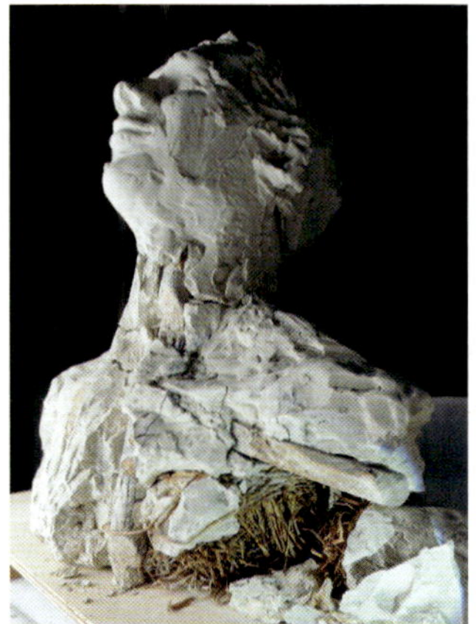

Fig. 73. Reinforcement materials exposed at the lower right of Edvard Munch's clay sculpture *Man's Head*

Fig. 72. Edvard Munch in front of Rodin's *Age of Bronze* in Max Linde's garden in Lübeck, 1902 wire. He also modelled in pipeclay, which was commonly used for sculpture.[15] It is probable that Munch used the same type of clay.

Plaster Casts

Unfired clay is fragile whether or not it is reinforced with an armature, which is why sculptures were often cast in plaster as the next stage in the process. This has to be done while the clay is still moist, and therefore relatively soon after the completion of a new draft.

Munch's plaster casts were executed using a method called 'waste mould', since the clay draft used in the process was generally destroyed.[16] Munch's draft *Man's Head* was nevertheless preserved after the casting process, since busts are often cast in a two-part mould, which is easier to separate, thus retaining the clay sculpture. The plaster casts were often equipped with armatures of iron, and the plaster itself could be reinforced with jute fibre or hemp. Munch also made another plaster sculpture, *The Human Mountain*, this time modelled directly in plaster.[17]

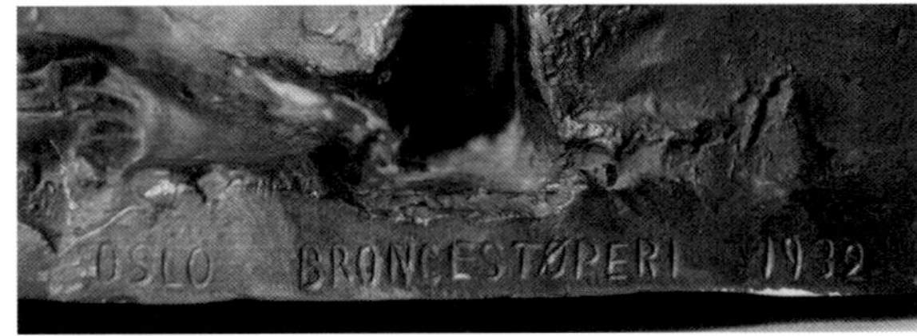

Fig. 74. Detail of Edvard Munch's *Weeping Nude*

Bronze Casts

Munch cast his bronze sculptures at Oslo Broncestøperi (fig. 74) while Vigeland employed Kristiania Kunst & Metalstöberi for many of his works. The latter was established in 1894 as Norway's first foundry devoted exclusively to art, in premises situated by the city's main river Akerselva. Munch may on the other hand have chosen a more affordable alternative, since Oslo Broncestøperi was one of several foundries that probably did not specialise in art. Sand casting was a commonly used method in Norway during this period, and traces of sticky sand are visible underneath the Munch Museum's two bronze casts from 1932, *Weeping Nude* (cat. 171) and *Workers in Snow* (cat. 180).[18]

Rodin, like many sculptors, exhibited his plaster sculptures on an equal footing with those in bronze. He also experimented with them; some had such a thin layer of plaster that even the large sculptures were very lightweight, but which also made them fragile.[19] Vigeland had a distinct preference for plaster sculpture. He wrote: '[...] a plaster bust or a work in plaster should be more costly than one in bronze. The bronze one can never be as precise as plaster.'[20]

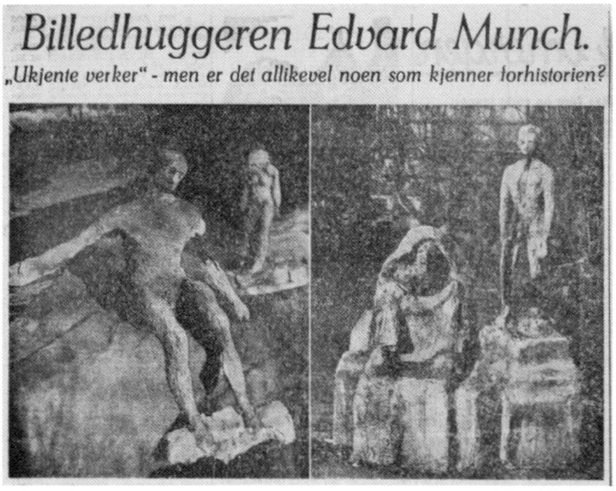

Fig. 75. Edvard Munch's *Seated Man*, *Weeping Nude* and *Mother Norway* outdoors at Ekely. *Aftenposten*, 4.4.1944

Munch's Dissimilar Sculptures – Two Periods?

After Munch's death in 1944 many spectators and journalists wanted to gain access to Ekely to get an impression of how he had lived. During the first few weeks *Aftenposten* visited the premises on 3 February and 4 March, but were granted access only to the grounds, not the buildings. After the second visit, the newspaper printed the headlines that are used as the title of this article (fig. 75): 'The Sculptor Edvard Munch. "Unknown works" – but is there perhaps someone who knows the history of their origins?' Six of Munch's sculptures were reproduced, and the caption below two of the photographs reads:

> These figures were photographed outside the porch at Ekely a few days ago. Can anyone explain the history of their origins? The figure of the girl in plaster next to the seated male is the same as the one shown elsewhere cast in bronze. What should one call the two other figures? 'Seated old woman' and 'standing young man'?

Aftenposten also printed photographs of *Workers in Snow* and *The Human Mountain*.[21]

First Steps as a Sculptor

The *Aftenposten* article also mentions Munch's early years, when he studied under the sculptor Julius Middelthun (1820–1886), before stating:

> It has been suggested that he once thought of devoting his main attention to sculpture, but his fingers could not withstand the strain of working with clay. Even in later years Munch was thought to have remarked that one finger in particular gave him trouble as soon as he began fiddling with clay.[22]

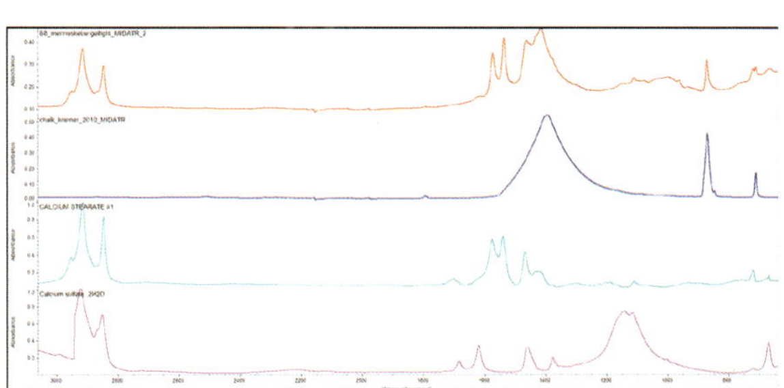

Fig. 76. FTIR spectrograph of the sample taken from Edvard Munch's *Woman's Head*. At the top is the sample from Munch's sculpture, the graphs below indicate the presence of chalk, calcium stearate (a softener) and calcium sulphate (gypsum) respectively

The first part of the quote is perhaps not quite consistent with reality, since it is unlikely that Munch had any experience with sculpture during his early education, as *Aftenposten* implied.[23] He may have been inspired by Linde's sculpture collection to make his own sculptures, after his stay in Lübeck in autumn 1902 and for periods during the spring of 1903. Munch may also have been inspired to try his hand as a sculptor in the summer of 1903, when Linde sent two packages of Plasticine,[24] or 'Plastolin' as he called it, to Munch in Åsgårdstrand.[25] Munch supposedly received 'modelling wax' from Linde in 1905 as well.[26] The little sculpture *Woman's Head* is undated, and the only one that is executed in an unidentifiable yellow-brown substance (cat. 156).[27] Micro-samples from the base of the sculpture were therefore recently taken for analysis, with the results indicating that the material is Plasticine,[28] based on the presence of kaolin,[29] chalk, some plaster and a tentative indication of a type of drying oil (fig. 76).[30] It is tempting to assume that the sculpture is composed of the Plasticine that Munch received from Linde. In that case *Woman's Head* can be dated to 1903–05, and hence be considered Munch's oldest known surviving sculpture.

1909–14

One week after *Aftenposten* encouraged the public to contact them regarding Munch's sculptures, a person by the name of F. Hagen approached the newspaper. He stated that he had worked for Munch for about a year when the artist was living at Grimsrød Manor on the island of Jeløya, on the outskirts of Moss, and he reported the following about *Workers in Snow* and *Weeping Nude*:

Two of the things Aftenposten printed pictures of last Saturday were cast in plaster some time during the summer of 1914. Two fellows from the Art Academy arrived and did it. I heard later that the figures would be cast in bronze, – it was the group of figures 'Workers' and the 'Girl' you wrote about on Saturday.[31]

It has previously been maintained that the sculpture *Weeping Nude* was cast in plaster in 1907, when Munch was living in Warnemünde,[32] possibly based on the fact that he made drawings and painted several versions of the subject that year.[33] However, there is no evidence that he made a sculpture based on the same theme while in Germany.

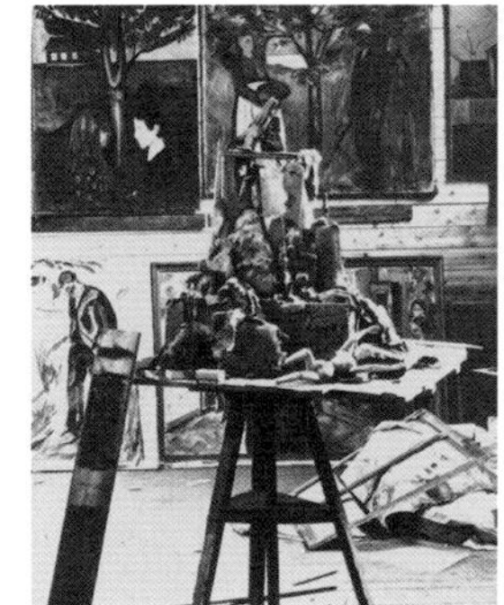

Fig. 77. Draft for Edvard Munch's *Human Mountain* at Ekely, 1929, detail

The plaster casts from 1914 mentioned by Hagen are probably those that are in the Munch Museum's collection, but it is difficult to determine when Munch made the drafts for *Weeping Nude* as there are no photographs or other preserved documentation. It is nevertheless possible that he made the drafts in the period 1909–10 while he was living at Skrubben in Kragerø. We know that Munch began working with sculpture at that time. In 1909 he wrote that he was thinking of making a sculpture of *The Funeral March*,[34] and in May the following year he wrote to Gustav Schiefler (1857–1935): 'You see, I have also begun to model – it is old Mother Norway with her young son (Norway's Independence) intended as a monument.'[35] Munch was referring to a photograph he had enclosed in the letter, of himself posing in front of the piece (cat. 154). The sculpture, which no longer exists, may have been a clay draft for the larger original plaster entitled *Mother Norway*, now in the Munch Museum.

In September 1914 Ludvig Ravensberg (1871–1958) mentions the plaster cast of *Workers in Snow* he saw while visiting Munch at Grimsrød: 'We walked again today through Grimsruds [*sic*] secret locked rooms, in the cellar is the group of workers in plaster, which the Erdmann brothers cast for him.'[36] The information Hagen gave *Aftenposten* in 1944 increases the possibility that 1914 was the year the sculpture was cast in plaster. It is likely that Munch made the models a few years prior to that, perhaps as early as 1909–10, while he was working on the draft for *Mother Norway* and possibly also *Weeping Nude*. He made sketch drawings of *Workers in Snow* in 1909, and painted the first version in 1910.

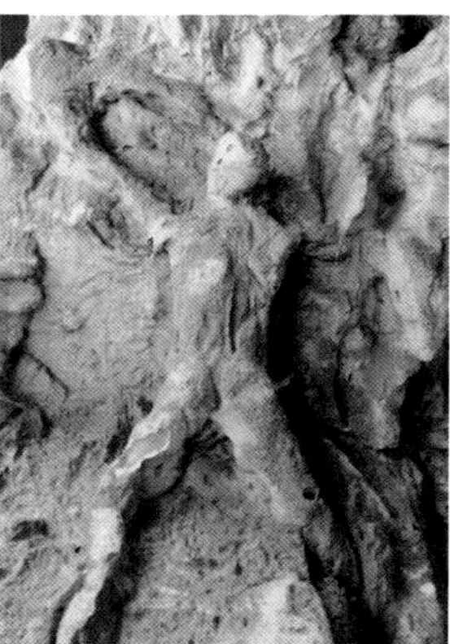

Fig. 78. Detail of Edvard Munch's *Human Mountain*

1925–32

Munch's sister, Inger Munch (1868–1952), gave the journalist from *Morgenposten* a tour of Ekely in July 1944.[37] She also showed him some of Munch's sculptures, among them *Seated Man* and *The Human Mountain,* and told him that when her brother's eyes were ailing he began to model in clay.[38] When Munch had stated, 'Yes, I also do a bit of sculpting' in 1929, it was because the journalist had observed a group of sculptures in the entrance hall of the villa at Ekely. A photograph from 1929 taken in one of Munch's studios constructed in wood[39] shows a small, modelled version of *The Human Mountain*, possibly a draft, which no longer exists (fig. 77). This suggests that Munch began modelling again before 1929.

The plaster sculpture *The Human Mountain* is possibly Edvard Munch's only attempt at making a three-dimensional monumental version of the motif (cat. 189), and dates from 1925 to 1929.[40] When *Aftenposten* photographed the sculpture in 1944, they captioned it 'Life. – Draft for Monolith',[41] which brings to mind Gustav Vigeland's famous work *The Monolith* (1924–25). The sources of inspiration that may have prompted Munch to develop this motif are many,[42] among them Rodin's *The Prodigal Son* (1886–89) which has traits in common with one of the central figures reaching towards the light in Munch's motif (fig. 78).[43] It is quite likely that Munch saw the sculpture photographed in a catalogue of Rodin's works from 1902 (fig. 79).[44]

The final version of *The Human Mountain* has a sketch-like appearance and is built up around a wooden base consisting of eight wooden sticks and planks, making the sculpture hollow. During the modelling process Munch worked in sections, applying the plaster in stages. In several areas he first dipped the jute fibre in the wet plaster, but he probably also threw the plaster, since drip marks can been seen in some areas. He then carved the work and continued to model it while the plaster was still damp. A fingerprint has been found on the surface, which is probably Munch's, as well as marks from the tools that were used. Although the plaster surface is worn and soiled after being stored outdoors for many years, the sculpture is nevertheless one of his most intricate.

In 1930, when Munch was 67 years old, he contracted an eye disease,[45] which he struggled with for about a year. During this period of illness he had to put aside demanding work and concentrate on other projects,[46] perhaps also sculpture. It has been established that Munch modelled several works during the period leading up to 1932, and photographs taken during the various seasons show several sculptures.

Among the works that no longer exist was a seated figure, possibly made from clay, in which the chair itself was incorporated in the work. Munch documented the sculpture in a photograph in c. 1930–32 (cat. 167).

In a photograph from the same year Munch is shown standing in front of the plaster original of *Mother Norway* (cat. 166). Here the sculpture looks complete, the figure of the boy stands erect and seems to be intact. This may indicate that it was made before 1932, and that it was relatively new when the picture was taken. In the photograph from *Aftenposten* in 1944 the figure of the boy is still upright, but fragmented in many places (fig. 75).[47]

In other photographs taken in the garden at Ekely in 1932 Munch poses between what seems to be a plaster version of *Workers in Snow* and a reclining sculpture, probably also in plaster. The latter is most likely *Seated Man*, which was also

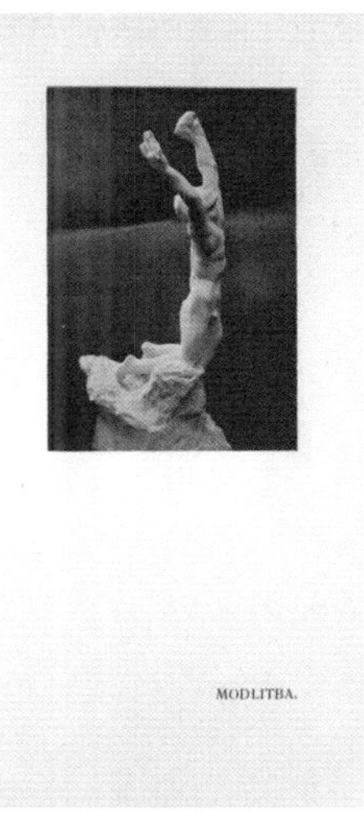

Fig. 79. Auguste Rodin: *The Prodigal Son*, 1886–89. Catalogue from the Rodin exhibition at the Manes Artists' Association, Prague, 1902

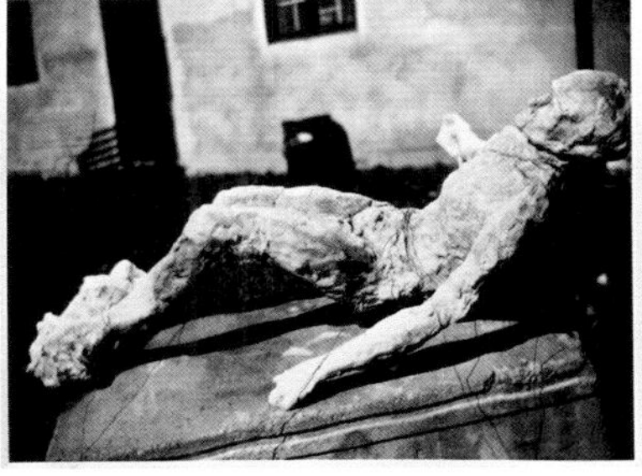

Fig. 80. Edvard Munch: *Seated Man*, c. 1930–32

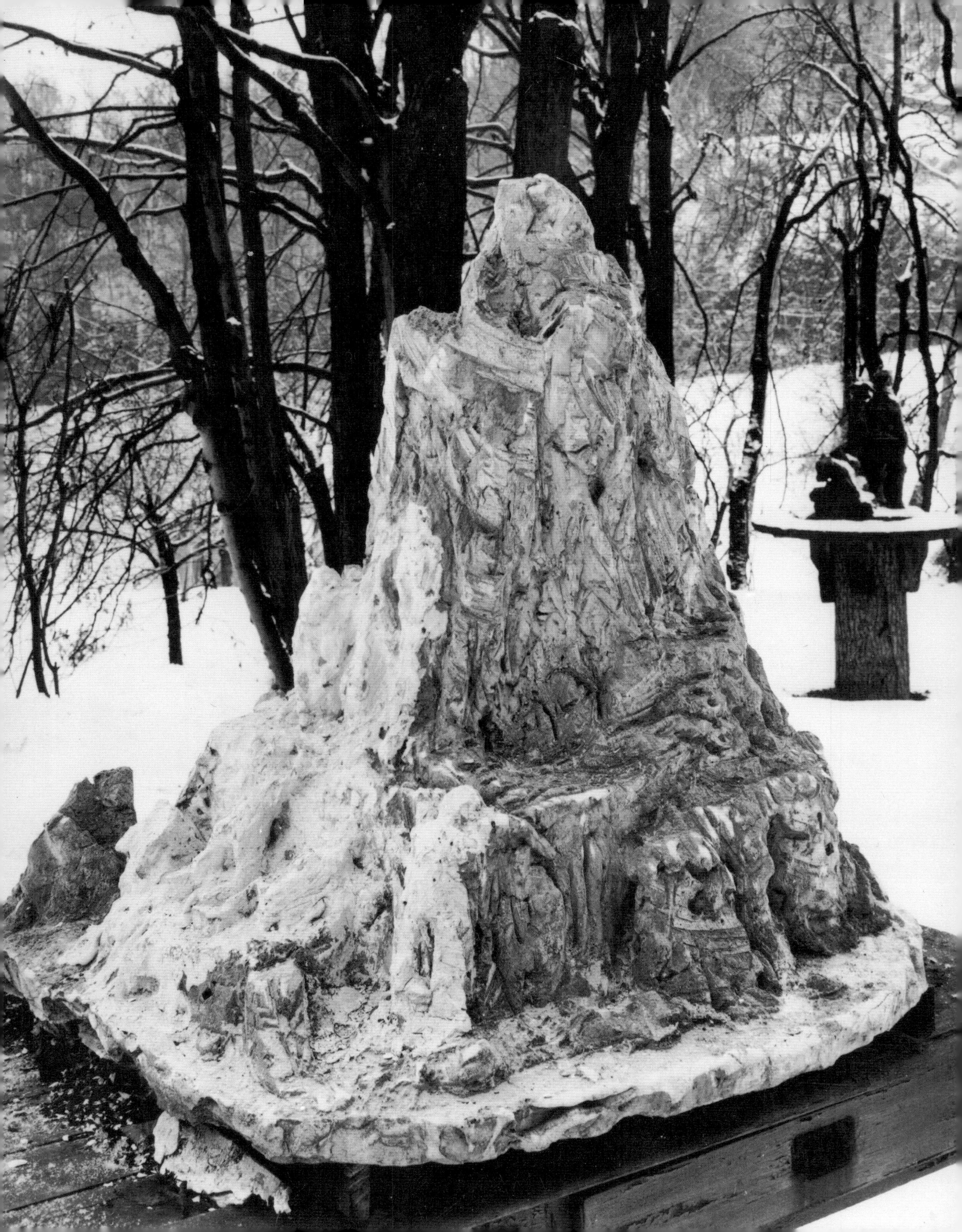

published in *Aftenposten* in March 1944 (fig. 75).[48] Arne Eggum writes that Munch portrayed himself in this sculpture; a half-scale self-portrait.[49] Eggum makes this claim based on similar drawings where Munch depicts himself occupied with literary pastimes. He worked among other things on a publication of his writings during his convalescence after his eye disease in 1930. Several close-ups of this sculpture were also taken in 1932 (fig. 80) in which it appeared intact, whereas the photos in the *Aftenposten* article reveal that it was damaged in 1944, with the large loss to the upper right arm. The condition has become significantly worse over the course of the 71 years since Munch's death, in particular with regard to the loss of plaster.[50]

The two plaster casts of *Weeping Nude* and *Workers in Snow* were cast in bronze at Oslo Broncestøperi in 1932. The Freia Chocolate Factory's *Workers in Snow* was possibly cast at the same time. In a photograph from that summer, also from the garden at Ekely, *Workers in Snow* does not appear particularly soiled. Since this is most likely the plaster cast from 1914, it may indicate that the sculpture had been stored indoors. However, it must have also been left outside for a period of time, since surface damage caused by rain has been transferred to the bronze cast.[51] The condition today indicates that it was also stored outdoors after being cast. According to the *Aftenposten* journalists who visited Ekely, they also saw sculptures inside Munch's house: 'Other figures are visible through the porch windows together with paintings.'[52] As previously mentioned, some of the sculptures were stored indoors, while others were kept outdoors over long periods, and this explains why the plaster casts of *Weeping Nude* and *Man's Head* are in better condition and less soiled than *Workers in Snow* and *Seated Man*.[53]

In a photograph taken outdoors at Ekely on a winter's day, the plaster cast of *The Human Mountain* is pictured, and in the background one of the bronze versions of *Workers in Snow* can be glimpsed. This confirms that the photograph was taken in 1932 or later, and a dating of *The Human Mountain* to before 1932 (fig. 81). The latter sculpture was probably located outdoors for at least twelve years.

Conclusion

The Munch Museum has a unique collection of Edvard Munch's sculptures. The dating of several of the sculptures is difficult. Since the design of *Woman's Head* is different, and the only one executed in Plasticine, it is probably an early work and possibly the first sculpture that Munch made in 1903–05. He subsequently modelled during two periods; from 1909–10 to 1914 and from about 1925 to 1932. Munch modelled several motifs that he had previously sketched and then developed in both paintings and works on paper. Several of the sculptures can nevertheless be perceived as drafts, or tests, as part of the process of working towards a three-dimensional rendition of a motif or a suitable technique. Hence they are not to be considered among Munch's major works, but should be included in order to make his oeuvre complete.

Fig. 81. Edvard Munch's *Human Mountain* in the
garden at Ekely, after 1932

1 *Aftenposten*, 4.3.1944.

2 B. Jullum, *Arbeiderbladet*, 7.12.1929.

3 One of the eleven sculptures is totally fragmented and has no recognisable motif.

4 In the settlement of Munch's estate only six sculptures were declared (Munch Museum Archives [unpublished], 1944), p. 65.

5 Special thanks are due to sculpture conservator Siri Refsum (Vigeland Museum) for providing information about sculpture in general, and on specific methods and materials. Thanks are also due to sculpture conservators Ingebjørg Mogstad (Vigeland Museum) and Lily Vikki (Art in Oslo), and stone and sculpture conservator Ann Meeks (Arkeologisk Museum in Stavanger).

6 The collection is not complete, however, and does not provide a complete overview of the books that Munch may have owned.

7 Arne Eggum, 'Speilinger fra Auguste Rodin i Edvard Munchs kunst', in *Rodin og Norge*, ed. Arne Eggum & Jan Kokkin et al., (Oslo: Henie Onstad Kunstsenter/Orfeus Forlag AS, 1998), pp. 111–19; Gerd Woll, *Edvard Munch – Monumental Projects 1909–1930* (Lillehammer: Lillehammer Bys Malerisamling, 1993); Gen Eisenwerth, 'Munch und Rodin', in *Edvard Munch – Probleme-Forschungen-Thesen* (Munich: Prestel Verlag, 1973), pp. 99–132.

8 See further a letter from Albert Kollmann to Munch, MM K 2669. The postcard has recently been dated and attributed to Kollmann.

9 Jens Thiis, *Edvard Munch og hans samtid: slekten, livet og kunsten, geniet* (Oslo: Gyldendal Norsk Forlag, 1933), p. 268.

10 Birgitte Heise (ed.), *Edvard Munch und Lübeck* (Lübeck: Museum für Kunst und Kulturgeschichte der Hansestadt Lübeck, 2003), p. 122.

11 Max Linde, *Edvard Munch und die Kunst der Zukunft* (Berlin: Friedrich Gottheimer Verlag, 1902), pp. 11, 12.

12 Claudie Judrin, 'The Musée Rodin's acquisition of a painting by Munch', *Revue de Louvre et des Musées de France*, vol. XXX, no. 5–6 (Paris, 1981).

13 Judrin, 1981.

14 The malleability of wood shavings makes them suitable as a stuffing or filler material.

15 Siri Refsum, 23.2.2015, personal communication.

16 In the waste mould method the sculpture was divided by pressing thin metal plates (shims) into the still moist clay before being covered with additional layers of plaster. Some of the plaster layers could also be reinforced with iron bars. Both the clay sculpture and the plaster form were normally dug out in sections and thus destroyed, hence the name waste mould. Antoinette Le Normand-Romain, 'Rodin og hans medarbeidere', in Eggum & Kokkin, 1998, p. 16; http://www.vigeland.museum.no/en/research/conservation/plaster-casting.

17 The sculpture may have been cast and covered with more plaster, which Munch then modelled. It is difficult to examine the sculpture from below, which would provide additional information about the method of its creation.

18 The casting process itself was complicated. In brief, an impression of the plaster sculpture was made using a special sticky type of French sand. A core composed of sand was also inserted before the molten bronze was poured so that the finished bronze sculpture was hollow. (Siri Refsum, 23.2.2015, personal communication.) Munch's bronze cast is bolted to the plinth. Today they would have been welded together, but the welding technique was not in use in Norway until after the Second World War.

19 Normand-Romain, 1998, p. 16.

20 Gustav Vigeland, notebooks 1912, 1913 and 1934.

21 *Aftenposten* calls *The Human Mountain*: 'Life. – Draft for Monolith.'

22 *Aftenposten*, 4.3.1944.

23 The last part of the quote is possibly a reference to the finger that Munch wounded in a shooting accident in Åsgårdstrand in 1902. It is probable that it bothered him for a long time.

24 Plasticine is composed of traditional clay (kaolin), chalk, pigments, wax and oils (http://en.wikipedia.org/wiki/Modelling_clay#Oil-based_clay).

25 Letter from Max Linde to Munch, 20.6.1903, MM K 2773/MM K 2773-02.

26 Letter from Max Linde to Munch, 23.11.1905, MM K 2815/MM K 2815-01. It is not known whether Linde consciously differentiated between modelling wax (Modelleirwachs) and Plastilin (Plasticine), or whether he meant the same thing, but unintentionally used different names for it.

27 Vigeland also used Plasticine for small sketches. The author has examined three of them, which are modelled in dark, nearly black Plasticine. These are sketches from the 1910s–20s, among them *The Angry Boy*.

28 Samples were analysed with Fourier transform infrared spectroscopy (FTIR) in ATR mode by Alyssa Hull in the Conservation Department at the Munch Museum. The samples can also contain other organic materials, such as wax, but it has not been possible to identify this using the above-mentioned method.

29 Kaolin is a white malleable clay that mainly consists of kaolinite (aluminium silicate).

30 The components of Plasticine may have varied and changed since Munch's time.

31 *Aftenposten*, 11.3.1944.

32 Arne Eggum, 'Edvard Munch – Skulpturale Arbeiten und Ideen', in *Die Maler und ihre Skulpturen. Von Edgar Degas bis Gerhard Richter* (Essen: Museum Folkwang, 1998), pp. 98–102, especially p. 101.

33 In 1907 Ernest Thiel commissioned a copy of *Weeping Nude* from Munch, a motif Munch had previously painted several times, first in 1896 (Arne Eggum, 'The woman, he must weep', in *Edvard Munch – The Modern Eye*, ed. Angela Lampe & Clémont Chéroux (London: Tate Publishing, 2012), pp. 129–51, especially p. 131.

34 Woll, 1993, p. 60.

35 Edvard Munch in a letter to Gustav Schiefler, 11.5.1910. Privately owned correspondence, PN 543.

36 Ravensberg's Journal, 30.9.1914, LR 197.

37 She had come down with a bad cold and moved from her apartment in town to live at Ekely that summer.

38 *Morgenposten*, 7.7.1944.

39 Munch had two wooden structures at Ekely, which he referred to as the southern and northern studios. In between the two he built an outdoor studio where, among other things, he created his collage of *The Human Mountain*. The timber-built studios did not have good lighting and were poorly insulated, so it is more likely that Munch used them for storage rather than as working studios. Petra Pettersen, 12.3.2015, personal communication.

40 Petra Pettersen, 14.1.2015, personal communication.

41 *Aftenposten*, 4.3.1944.

42 See, among other sources, the article by Petra Pettersen in this catalogue.

43 The figure originally belonged to the upper right section of Rodin's *Gates of Hell* (1880–1917). Rodin made several versions of the figures from *The Gates of Hell*, which he exhibited independently of the great work, such as *The Prodigal Son*, *The Thinker* and *Kiss*.

44 Munch had ordered the catalogue from Galerie Manes in advance of his own exhibition in Prague in 1905, and it is included in Munch's preserved library. See further an undated letter

from J. Heuc/St. Sucharda to Munch, MM K 04317.

45 Arne Eggum, 'Ekelyperioden i Edvard Munchs kunst 1916–1944', in *Munch og Ekely*, ed. Sissel Biørnstad (Oslo: Munch Museum/Labyrinth Press, 1998), p. 23.

46 Munch allegedly worked on his photographic self-portraits and his literary notes (Eggum, in *Munch og Ekely*, 1998, p. 23).

47 Today this section is broken and separated from *Mother Norway*. The firm O. Væring photographed the works for *Aftenposten*, and copies are preserved in the Munch Museum's archives. These formed the basis for evaluating the condition of the sculptures in 1944.

48 The sculpture has a flat seat and is designed as a seated sculpture.

49 Arne Eggum, *Munch and Photography* (New Haven & London: Yale University Press, 1989), p. 189.

50 Today the entire right arm is broken into several pieces, which are no longer attached to the sculpture. Large parts of the left arm and the upper right leg are also missing.

51 The damage is visible as characteristic small pockmarks on the surface, which give the sculpture a coarse appearance. This implies that Munch had placed it outdoors for a time prior to 1932, and that it was exposed to rain before being transported to the foundry. The photograph was definitely taken before it was cast in bronze, since the sculpture is whole (it was separated into several parts when it was cast). Lily Vikki, 11.3.2015, personal communication.

52 *Aftenposten*, 4.3.1944.

53 The plaster cast of *Weeping Nude* is in relatively good condition, but it is clear that the sculpture has been exposed to high levels of relative humidity, since the iron armature has rusted and caused discolouration in areas of the sculpture's surface. Iron starts to corrode when the relative humidity is over 70% (Lily Vikki, 11.3.2015, personal communication).

Edvard Munch's sculptures

	Title	Date, Location	Medium	Condition	Inventory Number
1.	*Woman's Head*	1903–05 (Åsgårdstrand)	Plasticine	Intact, but details in the face are worn away	MM S 8
2.	*Weeping Nude*	1914 (Grimsrød, Jeløy)	Plaster	Intact, dismantled: main figure and plinth; relatively clean but discoloured by corroded iron	MM S 2B
3.	*Workers in Snow*	1914 (Grimsrød, Jeløy)	Plaster	Divided into 1 main part with 3 figures and 7 small parts, partially broken; all have accumulated grime	MM S 1B
4.	*The Human Mountain*	prob. 1925–29 (Ekely)	Plaster	Intact, but with some loss of material and loose parts; extreme accumulation of grime	MM S 5
5.	*Mother Norway*	Before 1932 (Ekely)	Plaster	*Mother Norway* is intact, the figure of the boy is broken into several parts; the figures are separated and have accumulated grime	MM S 4A og B
6.	*Seated Man*	Before 1932 (Ekely)	Plaster	Partially broken, 1 main part and 10 fragments; accumulation of grime	MM S 6
7.	*Workers in Snow*	1932 (Oslo Broncestøperi)	Bronze	Intact	MM S 1A
8.	*Weeping Nude*	1932 (Oslo Broncestøperi)	Bronze	Intact	MM S 2A
9.	*Man's Head*	Undated	Clay	Intact, but with some defects and unstable, cracks	MM S 3A
10.	*Man's Head*	Undated	Plaster	Intact	MM S 3B
11.	*Man and Woman*	Undated	Clay	Intact, some cracks	MM S 11
12.	'Defective Relief'	Undated	Clay	20 small parts	MM S 9
13.	'Defective Group'	Undated	Clay	4 erect figures with defects plus many small parts	MM S 10
14.	'Unidentified'	Undated	Plaster	17 parts	MM S 12

A Brief History of Two Great Men – the city is big enough for both of them

Jarle Strømodden

Gustav Vigeland and Edvard Munch are unquestionably Norway's two greatest artists. They lived parallel lives, yet – with the exception of a few months in Berlin in 1895 – they never became close friends or colleagues. Hailing from modest circumstances, both succeeded in working their way up and forwards to leave their mark on the city of Oslo, on Norway, and on art.

Kristiania[1]

Gustav Vigeland and Edvard Munch grew up at a time when becoming an artist was not something one could take for granted, let alone – when seen in retrospect – one of the calibre that each in their own way represents. Educational opportunities were limited and for most it was a struggle to survive. One needed either a wealthy father or a benefactor, or perhaps one might hope for a grant.

Vigeland was born in Mandal and came to Kristiania (today Oslo) for the first time in 1884, at the age of fifteen. He worked for almost two years as an apprentice for Torsten Kristensen Fladmoe. After Fladmoe's retirement in 1886, the young Vigeland was forced to return home to Mandal. When he arrived he discovered that his father's carpentry workshop had ceased to exist and the basement of his childhood home had been turned into a disreputable tavern. Things had gone downhill fast; in March 1886 his father had been declared incompetent and was disempowered of his estate, and in June he passed away. By then, Gustav and the rest of the family had already moved to his maternal grandfather's home in Vigeland.

Munch came to Kristiania in 1864, a year after he was born. Although the family kept in touch with relatives and friends in Løten, one could reasonably argue that Munch was a Kristiania boy. What is certain is that both Munch and Vigeland were exceptionally gifted, and both were fortunate enough to be noticed by the right people in the right places. For Vigeland a pivotal moment for his future was when he summoned up the courage to show his drawings to Brynjulf Bergslien (1830–1898) during his stay in Kristiania. Upon seeing them the sculptor supposedly exclaimed: 'This is the best damned stuff I've seen.'[2] Bergslien took Vigeland under his wing, and allowed him to work in his studio for a few hours a day. Another key figure, the art history professor Lorentz Dietrichson (1834–1917), was also shown the drawings and was equally convinced. Thanks to encounters of this kind Vigeland eventually received financial support from individuals as well as state grants, which enabled him to travel abroad to study art, and other artists, in cities across the Continent.

The Museums

The city of Oslo contains two museums that are dedicated to Gustav Vigeland and Edvard Munch respectively.

Vigeland signed a contract with the Municipality of Kristiania in 1921[3] regarding the construction of a studio in Frogner. This was not a bequest to the city, but an agreement between two parties. Vigeland was offered the use of the building, including an apartment, on condition that it was to be 'employed for works, etc. which Vigeland in accordance with this agreement transfers or will later transfer to the municipality'.[4] The contract encompassed everything, large to small, as it states: 'The transferral applies to clay, plaster of Paris, wax, wood, bronze, marble and other works in stone, as well as plaster models, drawings and paintings, regardless of where the said works are located at the time.'[5] In addition, it was also agreed that the municipality should receive as part of this transfer 'the entire library and all of my photographs and visual reproductions of artworks by other artists'.[6]

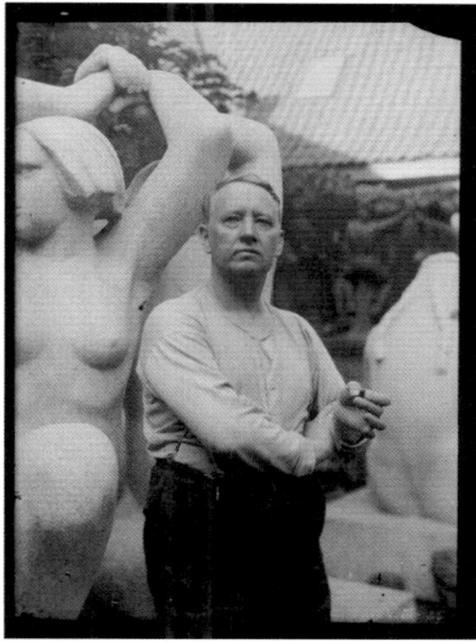

Fig. 82. Gustav Vigeland in his garden studio in Hammersborg, 28.5.1917

Vigeland began working in the completed part of the building in 1923, and moved into the apartment in 1924.[7] His studio and residence would, after his death, become a public museum of his life and work. There is no doubt that Vigeland had an advantage in being able to work in the rooms that would later house his art. The galleries that we know today as the Fountain Hall and the Monolith Hall were planned by Vigeland around 1925. It was also his intention to set aside a couple of rooms for his marble sculptures, but this was never realised. Following Vigeland's death on 12 March 1943, the municipal 'Vigeland Committee' convened to prepare the transformation of the building from studio to museum. The committee was immediately discharged by the Nazis, and was therefore inactive until liberation in May 1945, at which point it recommenced its work, and on 22 July 1947 the Vigeland Museum opened its doors to the public.[8]

Today the Vigeland Museum's collection contains approximately 12,000 drawings, 1,600 sculptures and 400 woodcuts. In addition there are around 5,000 books from Vigeland's private library and some 5,000 glass-plate negatives, which, among other things, provide extensive documentation of his working methods.

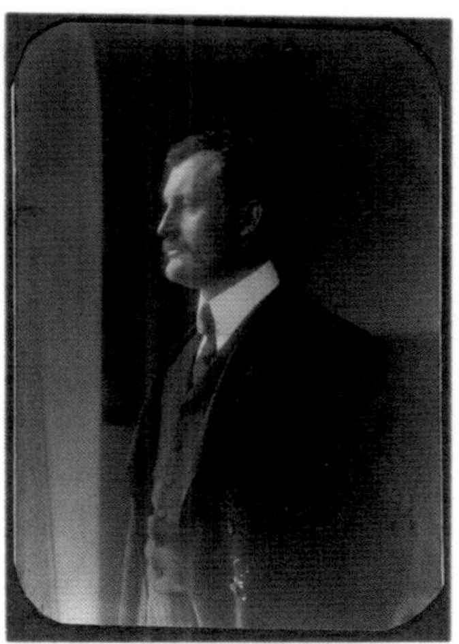

Fig. 83. Edvard Munch in Chemnitz, 1905

The Munch Museum opened in Tøyen in May 1963, almost twenty years after the artist's death. The opening naturally led to an increased interest in Munch. Young artists such as Bjørn Ransve, Frans Widerberg and Odd Nerdrum were able to see his work more or less unhindered, and this – at least for a period – had an influence on their own practice.

Munch's bequest to the city comprised around 1,100 paintings, 18,000 graphic works, and 7,500 watercolours and drawings, together with 14 sculptures, printing blocks and plates, notebooks, documents, his own collection of photographs and 2,240 books.

It was by no means predetermined that the museum should be located in Tøyen. Other alternatives such as Grünerløkka and the city centre near the Royal Palace had also been discussed. At one point a site on Halvdan Svartes Street in Frogner, directly opposite the Vigeland Museum, had been mooted, an option that was recorded in *Morgenbladet*. Captain of the Cavalry Thrap-Jensen submitted a proposal to the Executive Committee of Oslo City Council in December 1947, to locate the Munch Museum in Frogner (fig. 88). Munch had reportedly expressed interest in the idea, if one is to believe the rumours.[9]

What is certain is that the discussion went on interminably, as did the process of coming to a decision. Munch himself seems to have been at best ambivalent about the idea of a museum. His good friend and patron Jens Thiis, who had been director of the National Gallery since 1908, wrote in a letter to Munch of 9 May 1937 that he should not plan to construct a museum outside the city centre. It was only Gustav Vigeland who could think of doing such a thing. A potential Munch Museum had to be located in the centre of town, near the university and the existing museum buildings. Thiis wrote that the Frogner district contained nothing 'but a few sailors and stevedores, and [...] assassins seeking a quiet place to hide'.[10]

A few months later Munch wrote to Thiis that he was not so positive about the idea of a museum after all: 'I have thus given up the idea of a museum and have gradually come to the conclusion that a separate museum is not so beneficial for me.'[11] This remark to some extent contradicts the message Captain Thrap-Jensen would later convey to the Executive Committee of Oslo.

Despite a degree of uncertainty and vacillation, we cannot disregard the possibility that Munch may have wished to have a museum that could exhibit and preserve his entire artistic oeuvre under one roof. In his final will, written in April 1940, Munch bequeathed the artworks that he would leave behind to the Municipality of Oslo,[12] without any specified conditions or expressed wish for a museum. It was not until 1946, two years after the artist's death, that the municipality adopted a resolution to build a Munch Museum. A discussion about its location immediately arose, and it continued – including every aspect both large and small – for roughly ten years. In the mid-1950s a resolution was passed to locate the museum in Tøyen. The rest is history.

Vigeland was in a more fortunate position than Munch. He was largely able to participate in designing his own studio,

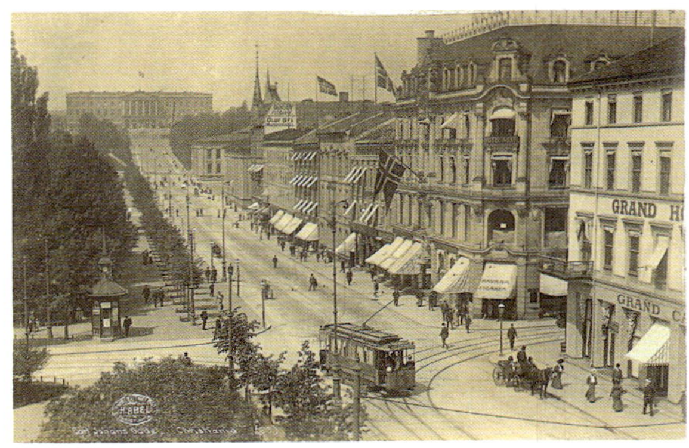

Fig. 84. Karl Johan Street, Kristiania (Oslo), 1900

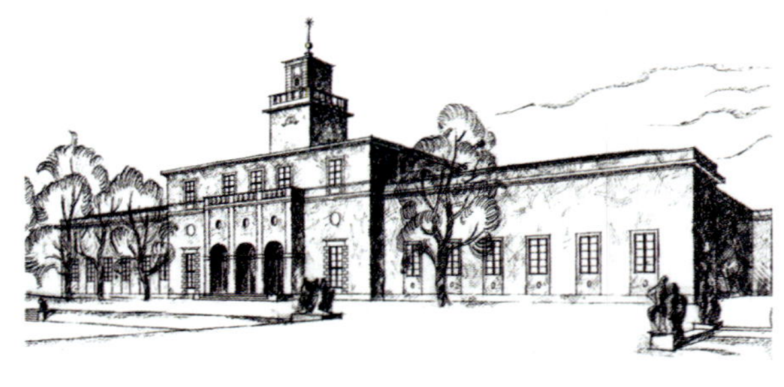

Fig. 85. Drawing from the early 1920s by architect Lorentz Harboe Ree, who was commissioned to design a new studio building for Gustav Vigeland in Frogner

Fig. 86. People queuing outside Gustav Vigeland's studio in Frogner for an exhibition, 12.6.1930

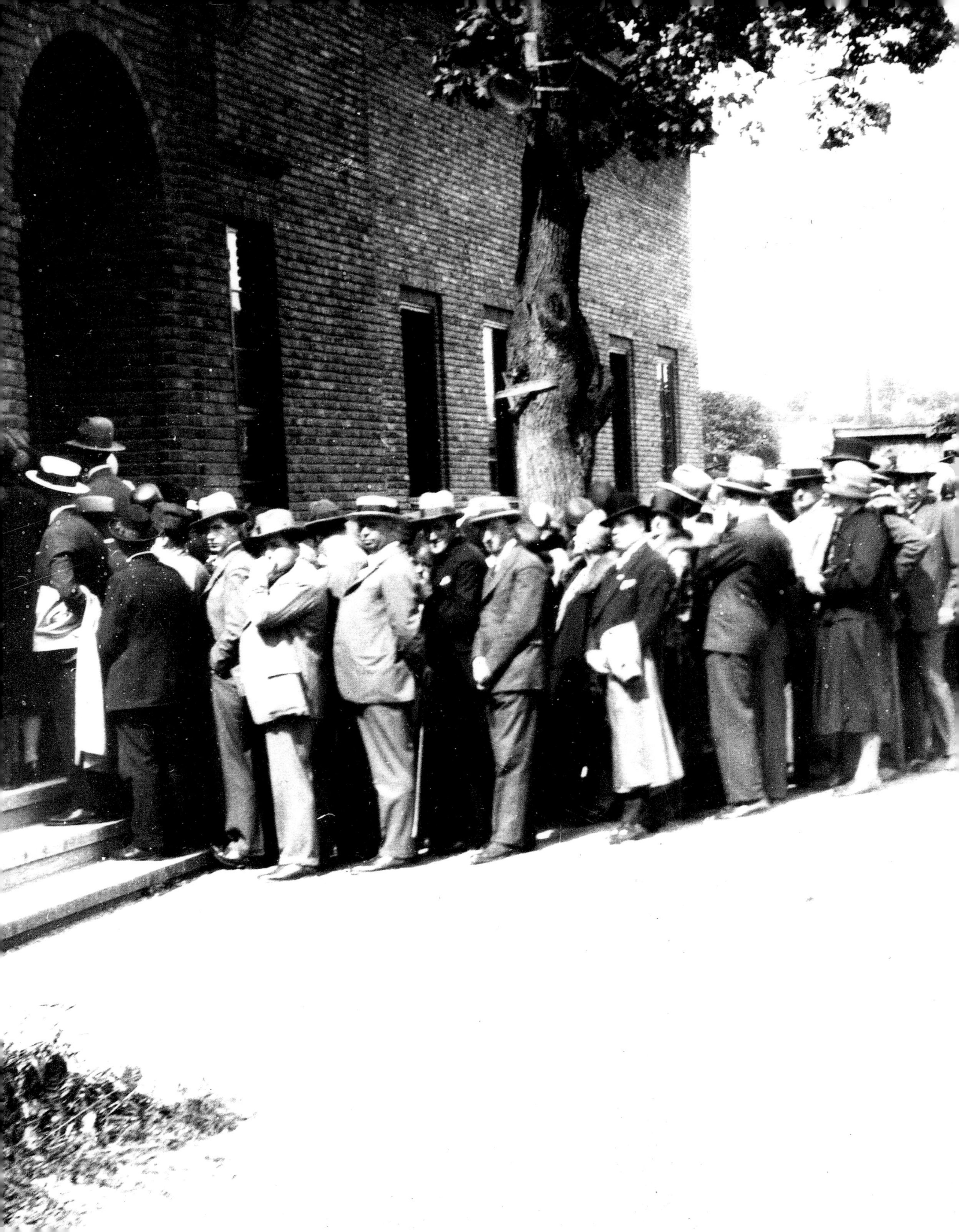

which would one day become a museum, and in that sense it constitutes a visible monument to the artist himself.

A Friend and an Enemy

Jens Thiis (1870–1942) was an important patron and friend of both Vigeland and Munch. Nevertheless, it was only Munch who would maintain a friendship with him for the rest of his life. Vigeland and Thiis parted ways around 1908, and their estrangement was to continue until the death of Thiis in 1942. When Vigeland gave his unconditional support to Thiis's nomination as director of the National Gallery, he probably hoped to be substantially represented in the collection. This did not occur, however. Once a frequent visitor to Vigeland's studio, such visits now ceased. Thiis met with closed doors, both in Hammersborg and later in Frogner. Despite his attempts at writing conciliatory letters, nothing helped. Vigeland was – as so often before – unwavering. Unsurprisingly Thiis eventually had enough of Vigeland's unyielding and irreconcilable attitude, and in a letter to Munch Thiis does not mince his words. He explains that Vigeland had been enchanting in his youth, but had now become 'a self-appointed deity [...] I for example have been refused entry to his studio. Yet I for my part have also refused to see his monstrosities, which I know merely through photographs [...] I have never seen the Vigeland Bridge, because I am loath to degrade my perception of the young Gustav Vigeland who was a great and creative artist.'[13]

The Chicken or the Egg?

Was it Vigeland or Munch who first conceived the idea of a 'life frieze'? Munch believed that it was his own invention, and in a couple of notebook pages we find a few interesting curiosities. Among other things he writes that he had begun his concept (for *The Frieze of Life*) ten years before Vigeland came up with his work *The Fountain*.[14] Elsewhere he writes that he regretted having given his support and signature to Vigeland for his work on *The Fountain*: 'It was equivalent to signing my own death sentence.'[15]

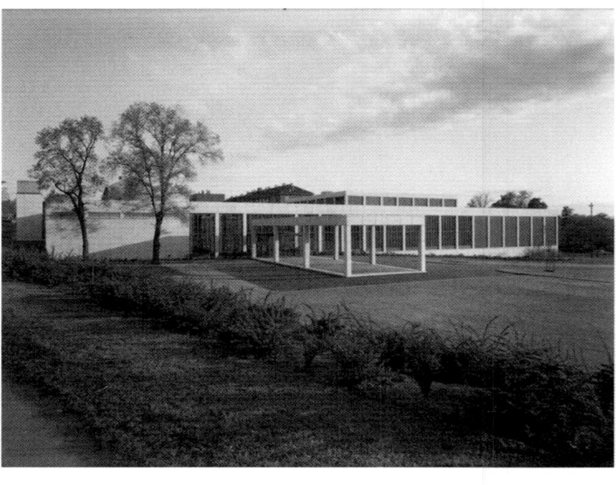

Fig. 87. Munch Museum, 1963

The remark must have been an exaggeration on Munch's part. His *Frieze of Life* is alive and well to this day, both as a work of art and as a widely recognised concept among art enthusiasts. I do not believe there are many who interpret the reliefs that surround Vigeland's *Fountain* as a 'life frieze' à la Munch, but rather as reliefs that constitute part of a greater whole. If one considers the tree groups that form part of *The Fountain*, they also have a 'frieze format'. In the group with infants ('genii') one can follow human development through the stages of childhood, adolescence, adulthood and old age, ending with death, which appears in the form of a skeleton.

The cyclical character of the frieze is more clearly evident in Vigeland's *Fountain* than in Munch's *Frieze of Life*. Having said that, it can also be claimed that Munch's *Frieze of Life* and Vigeland's *Fountain* – not to mention *The Bridge* and *The Monolith* – are still relevant to this day. The artists have succeeded in treating a number of universal themes. Interpersonal relationships, melancholy and jealousy affect all our lives in various ways, regardless of race, religion, gender or nationality.

Reception

There is a striking difference between Vigeland and Munch. Simply put, one can be described as local, the other international. The point of such a definition lies in how their art is perceived, and how they each in their own way influenced their respective art fields. On a purely practical level, it is far easier to transport ten paintings than ten bronze sculptures, whether it is from one Norwegian city to another, or from Oslo to Paris. Munch was more active on the exhibiting front during his lifetime than Vigeland, who left it at only two solo exhibitions in Oslo, aside from his regular participation in the National Art Exhibition (Annual Autumn Exhibition). He made his debut there in 1889 with *Hagar and Ishmael* (1889). In 1892 he participated again, this time with *The Accursed* (1891). *Verdens Gang* had the following to say about Vigeland: '… in time this artist will not stop short of the greatest undertakings.'[16] *Aftenposten* also wrote positively about the sculpture and, aside from certain objections, concluded by saying that 'it cannot be denied, that it testifies to a significant and original talent and contains great promise regarding the artist's future'.[17] Little did they know how accurate these claims would turn out to be.

Vigeland was reticent in other ways as well. He had an aversion to exhibiting his works. In 1909, after he had finally experienced his breakthrough with the monument to the mathematician Niels Henrik Abel (unveiled in 1908), he wrote to the Swedish banker and art collector Ernest Thiel (1859–1947): 'I don't like exhibiting by the way […] I find it distasteful to send works on tour as though they were actors.'[18]

Munch was more extrovert and consciously sought to promote himself and his art. Nevertheless, it might be considered a stroke of luck that the rather sedate marine and landscape painter Adelsteen Normann (1848–1918) happened to be in Kristiania during the autumn of 1892. Normann was a member of the exhibition committee for the Verein Berliner Künstler (Berlin Art Association). What he saw of Munch's exhibition in Kristiania was in any case convincing enough that he, together with his colleagues on the exhibition committee, invited Munch to show his works in Berlin. The exhibition opened on 5 November 1892, and it ended in a 'succès de scandale'. The show was supposed to run for two weeks, but was closed down after one. A hastily summoned meeting of the art association ended with the expulsion of the incumbent exhibition committee. Things became quite heated at times, but Munch did not suffer any great loss. Shortly afterwards he was invited by the art dealer Eduard Schulte to exhibit in both Cologne and Düsseldorf, and on top of that, a new exhibition of his works was arranged in Berlin to run over New Year's Eve.

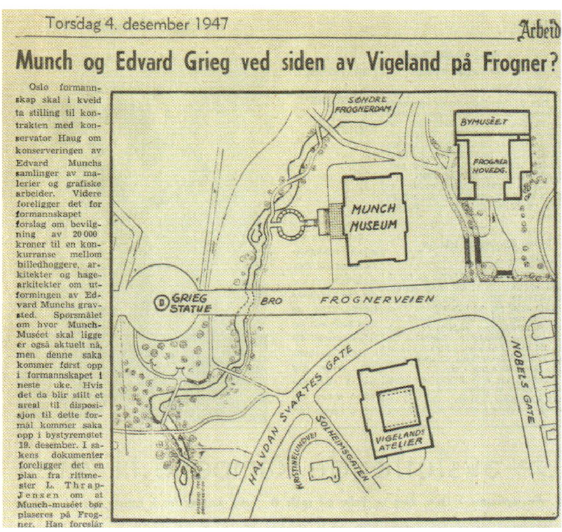

Fig. 88. Captain L. Thrap-Jensen's design for a proposed location of the Munch Museum in Frogner. *Arbeiderbladet*, 4.12.1947

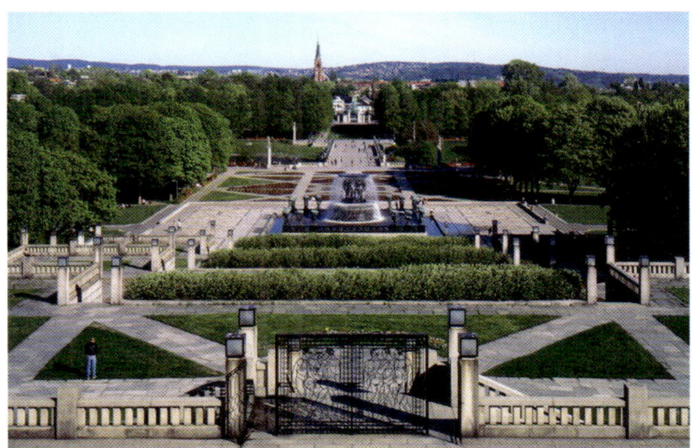

Fig. 89. Vigeland Park seen from the *Monolith* plateau

Munch, Vigeland, and their Significance

In summary, one can say that Munch contributed to a new artistic movement, whereas Vigeland helped maintain one that already existed. Munch was more receptive to the new trends in European painting during the second half of the nineteenth century, while Vigeland was relatively consistent in his excesses with respect to form. When he studied at the Royal School of Design he was the only sculptor there, surrounded by painters who were focusing on naturalism.[19] For Vigeland that was a meaningless mode of expression, for it entailed creating exacting studies from nature and to depict reality as truthfully as possible.

If one were to risk making a comparison between Vigeland and Munch, then it is Munch who has most clearly influenced visual art and artists. Over the course of his many travels, as well as time spent in cities like Berlin and Paris, he had garnered new ideas that contributed to the development of his own characteristic idiom. It would be an exaggeration to suggest that he was the one who discovered Expressionism, yet he exerted a great influence on its development. One can safely say – in retrospect, and that is the appropriate perspective – that Munch belonged to the avant-garde. Gustav Vigeland operated within quite different parameters and did not expand the idiom of sculpture as Auguste Rodin and Aristide Maillol did, for instance. One might say – somewhat mischievously – that Vigeland belonged to the 'l'arrière-garde', or in plain English, the rearguard.

Oslo

Gustav Vigeland and Edvard Munch are the most prominent artists that Norway has fostered in their respective artistic mediums, so it is fortunate for the city of Oslo that it has both of them under its wing. Munch's art has been accessible to the public at the museum in Tøyen for more than 50 years, and will benefit from improved exhibition spaces when the new museum building opens in the harbour area of Bjørvika. This will contribute to an increased focus on Munch, from which both the artist and the public will benefit. For nearly 70 years the public has been able to appreciate Vigeland's oeuvre, in the museum as well as in Vigeland Park, which is today one of Oslo's most popular recreational areas and tourist attractions. Because the park is open to the public at all hours of the day and night, it is difficult to determine an exact number, but one can safely say that more than a million people – both tourists and residents – pay a visit every year. The park has more than 200 sculptures, from large to small, and is, without doubt, the most visible manifestation of Vigeland's work. It is also the world's largest sculpture park planned and executed by a single artist.

The two artists have also left their mark on other public buildings and spaces in Oslo. As well as Vigeland Park, the monuments and memorials executed by Vigeland can be found throughout the city centre. The *Abel Monument* and *Camilla Collett* (1906) are located in the vicinity of the Royal Palace, and a stone's throw away – near the old National Academy of Art – is a monument to the composer

Fig. 65. Edvard Munch: *The Scream*, 1910?

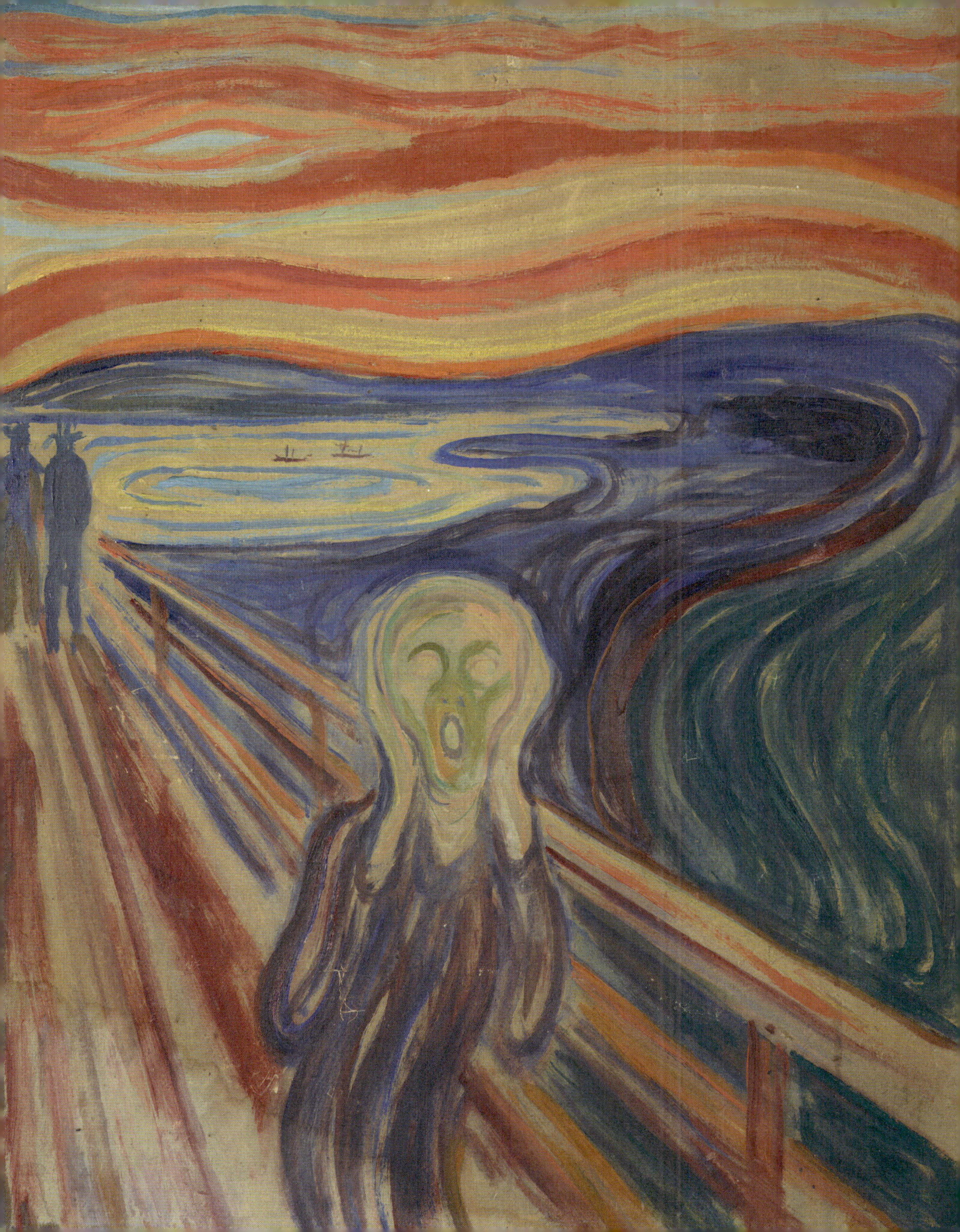

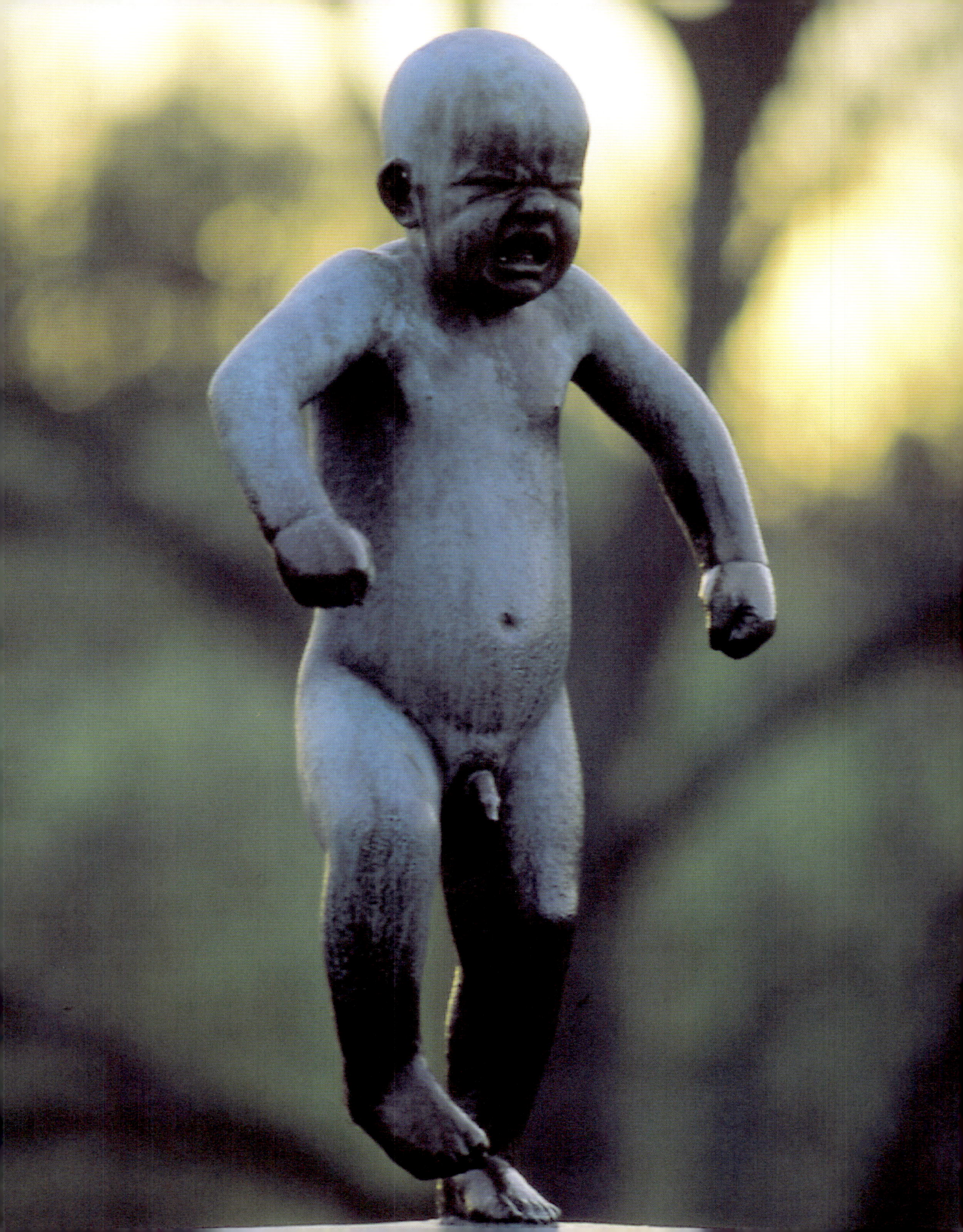

Rikard Nordraak (executed 1905, unveiled 1911). Munch created the monumental decorations for the Aula (great hall) in the central building of the University of Oslo on Karl Johan Street (1910–16). In addition, he created wall paintings in the cafeteria for the female staff of the Freia Chocolate Factory (1922), which were commissioned by the factory's owner Johan Throne-Holst. In nearby Freia Park – which was also designed for the employees – we find Vigeland's sculpture *Girl on a Bear* (1921).

It is interesting to consider how two such prominent artists, with such an enormous oeuvre behind them, conducted their work and made their mark in Oslo. It is also curious to note that their most sought-after and popular works are relatively modest in character. Munch's *The Scream* is by no means a monumental painting. One might even say that it is not strictly speaking a painting.[20] Vigeland's *Angry Boy* is his most famous sculpture and yet it is among the most inconspicuous in the park, standing as it does behind one of the lamps on *The Bridge*. These two rather unassuming works of art, which constitute a small part of a greater whole, can be seen as the respective artists' equivalent of Leonardo's *Mona Lisa* – the work of art that everyone must see. Two very different works which, each in their own way, illustrate two sides of everyone's lives.

1   From 1624 until the end of 1924 Oslo was called Christiania (from 1877 also spelled Kristiania). Since 1925 the city has been called Oslo.

2   Gustav Vigeland, *Erindringer*, 1918, p. 210. Transcribed unpublished texts from Vigeland's memoirs, hardbound, Vigeland Museum Library.

3   Document, 'Overenskomst mellem Kristiania kommune og Gustav Vigeland' [Agreement between the Municipality of Kristiania and Gustav Vigeland], dated February 1921.

4   Agreement §3.

5   Agreement §4.

6   Agreement §5. Notice the wording 'all of my photographs'. The agreement was penned by Vigeland, and then approved by the Municipality of Kristiania.

7   The entire building was completed in 1930.

8   It was hailed in the media as a significant event. In the press of 21.7.1947, *Norges Handels- og Sjøfartstidende* announced: 'Tomorrow "The Vigeland Museum" opens its doors to the public – A rare cultural event'; *Aftenposten* declared: 'The Vigeland Museum finally opens'; and in *Arbeiderbladet* Johan H. Langaard, director of the City of Oslo Art Collections, wrote an article under the headline: 'The Vigeland Museum will open

tomorrow. A milestone in Norwegian art, culture and museums.' In spring the following year the museum opened two additional departments, for the display of Vigeland's woodcuts and clay sketches. Interestingly, the museum had been closed over the winter due to heating problems. With regard to the woodcuts, *Aftenposten*'s journalist writes (3.5.1948) that Vigeland 'could have been an excellent illustrator of Snorri'. See also *Dagbladet* (3.5.1948), 'Vigeland's sketches and woodcuts'; *Nationen* (3.5.1948), 'The Vigeland Museum opens again. Two new departments showing woodcuts and clay sketches will be opened'. *Arbeiderbladet* (4.5.1948) notes that, in connection with the new opening, the museum has more reasonable opening hours: '[The Curator, Ragna Thiis Stang] deserves an extra compliment since she has arranged the opening hours from 1pm to 7pm so that everyone can find a time to go there. It is open every day but Monday.'

9   *Morgenbladet*, 3.12.1947, 'Munch said yes to the museum'. The author of the article, H. Nobel Roede, was referring to Munch's statement, 'Yes, to a museum building next to the Vigeland Museum', in a letter to Captain Thrap-Jensen, postmarked and dated Tuengen, Vinderen, 28.11.1947.

10   eMunch.no, MM K 1173.

11   eMunch.no, MM K, 25.8.1937.

12   eMunch.no: the will is dated 18.4.1940. At this point Munch was living at Ekely, which was at the time in the Aker Municipality. In 1948 Aker was incorporated into the Municipality of Oslo. Despite this it was to the Municipality of Oslo that Munch left his bequest in 1940. Regional State Archives, Oslo, Bomapper [Files regarding his Estate], Dept. III – Aker, no. 4 (PN 1253).

13   eMunch.no, MM K 1177, 25.4.1941.

14   eMunch.no, MM N 331.

15   eMunch.no, MM N 225, letter draft from Munch to Jens Thiis 1935–40.

16   *Verdens Gang*, 17.10.1892.

17   *Aftenposten*, 25.10.1892.

18   Letter from Vigeland to Ernest Thiel, 9.12.1909 (copy in the Vigeland Museum, Correspondence Collection, no. 796).

19   Guri Skuggen, 'Gustav Vigelands unge år', in *Billedhugger Gustav Vigelands Separat-Udstilling 1894* (Oslo: Vigeland Museum, 2008), p. 13.

20   There are several versions of *The Scream* and they are executed in various media: crayon on unprimed cardboard, tempera and oil on unprimed cardboard, tempera and crayon on unprimed cardboard, pastel on cardboard, and lithograph.

Fig. 90. Gustav Vigeland: *The Angry Boy*, c. 1928

Catalogue of
Exhibited Works

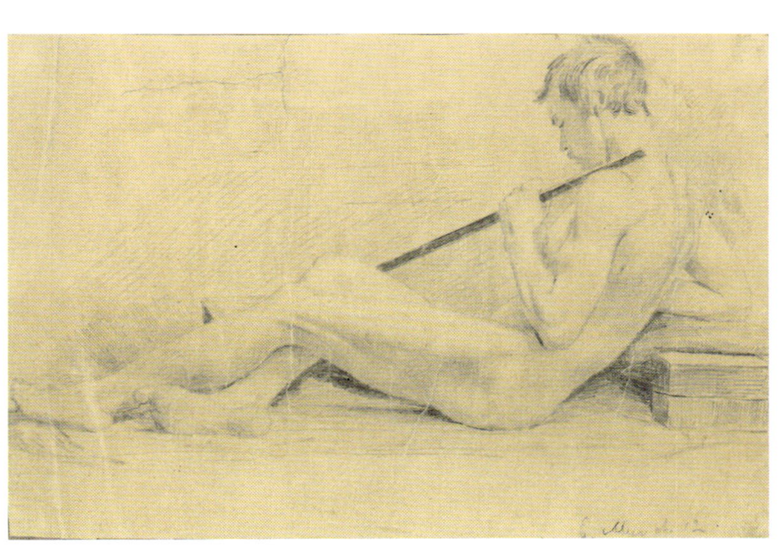

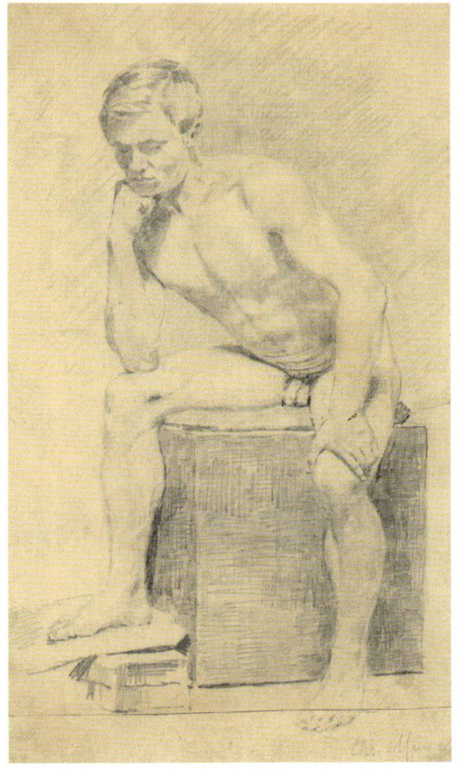

Cat. 1
Edvard Munch
*Reclining Male Nude
with Stick*, 1881

Cat. 2
Edvard Munch
Seated Male Nude, 1881

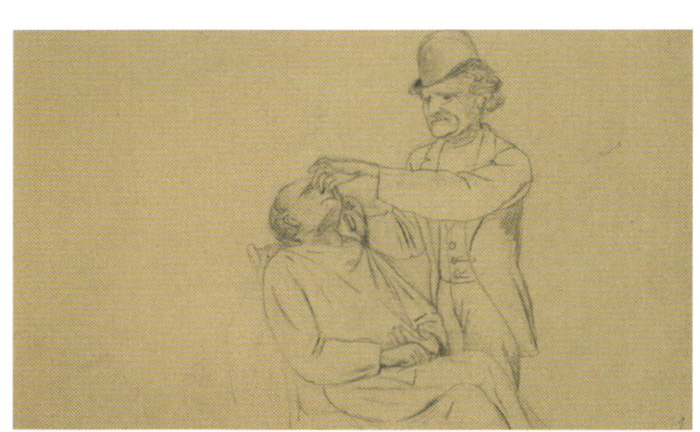

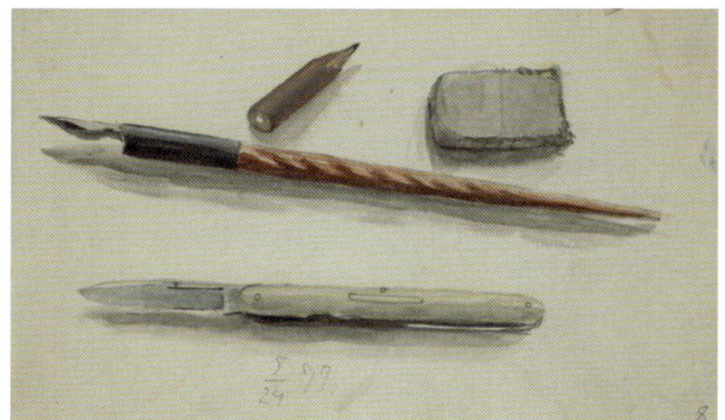

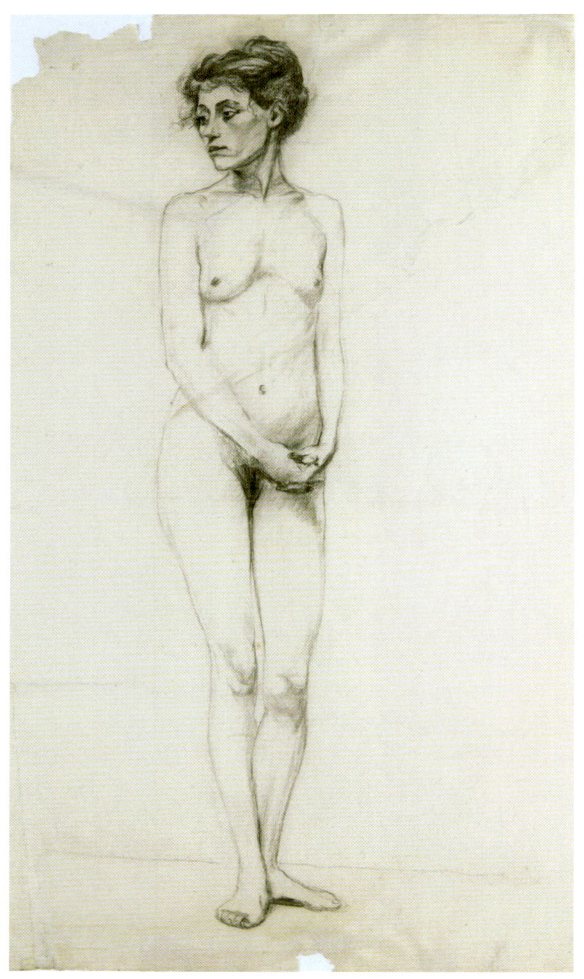

Cat. 3
Edvard Munch
At the Barber's, 1880

Cat. 4
Edvard Munch
Drawing Tools, 1877

Cat. 5
Edvard Munch
Standing Nude, 1889

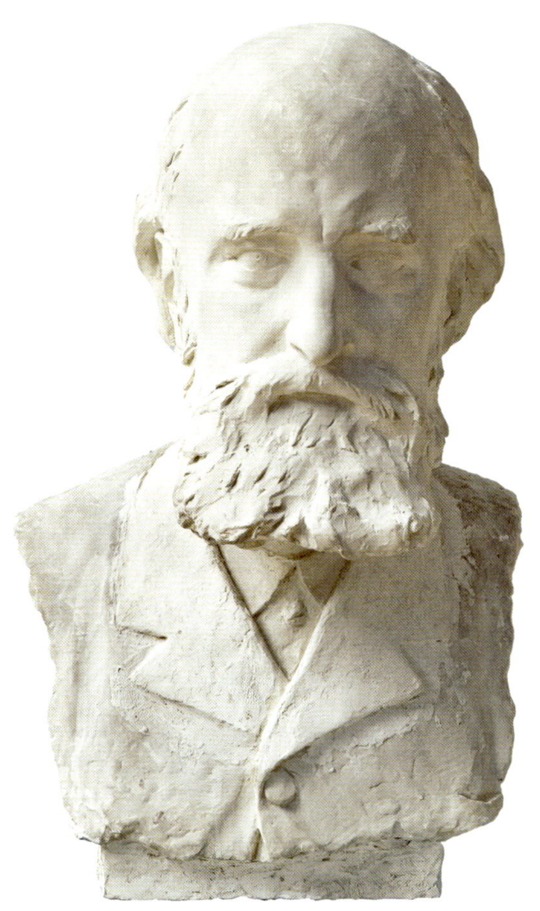

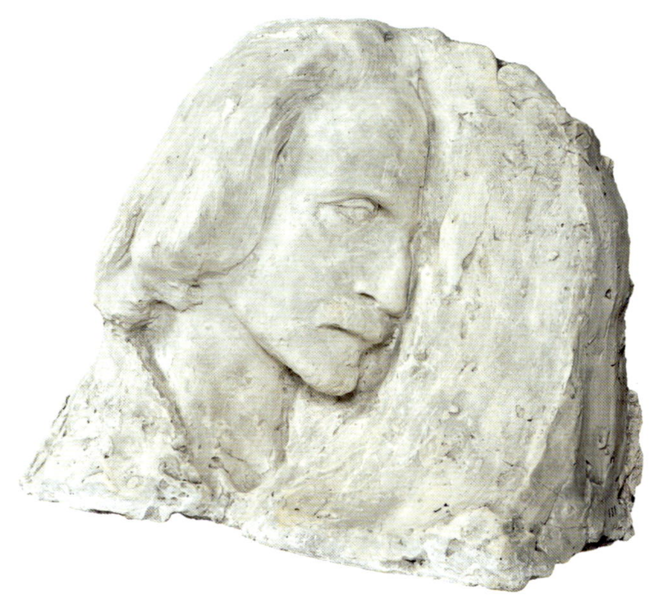

Cat. 6
Gustav Vigeland
Lorentz Dietrichson, 1892

Cat. 7
Gustav Vigeland
Julius Middelthun, before 1889

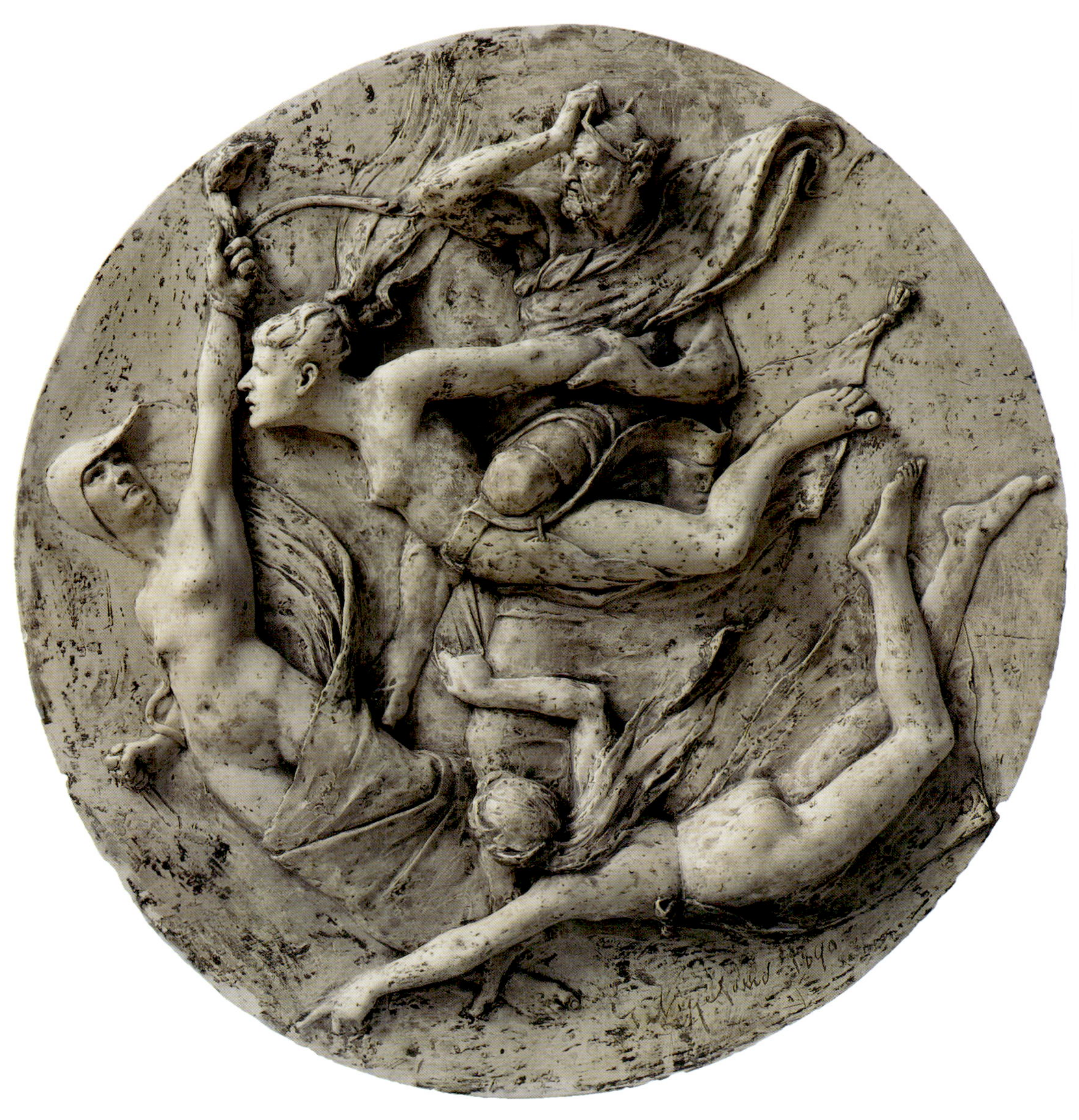

Cat. 8
Gustav Vigeland
*Tantalus is Led to the Underworld
by the Eumenides*, 1890

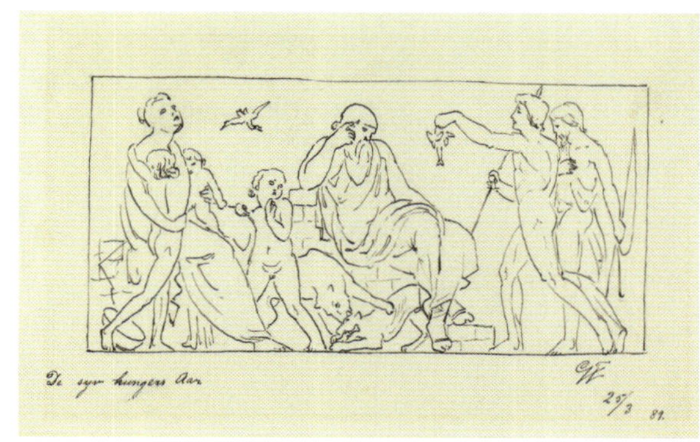

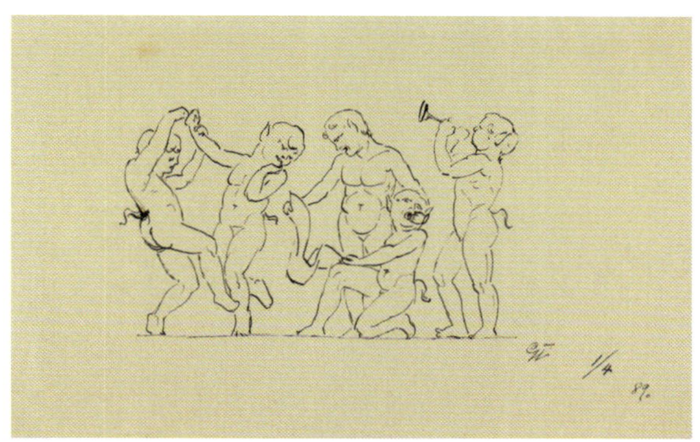

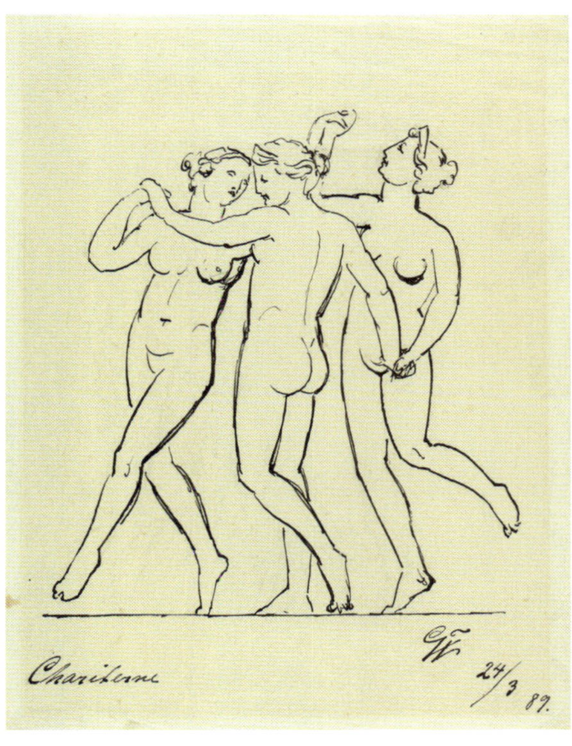

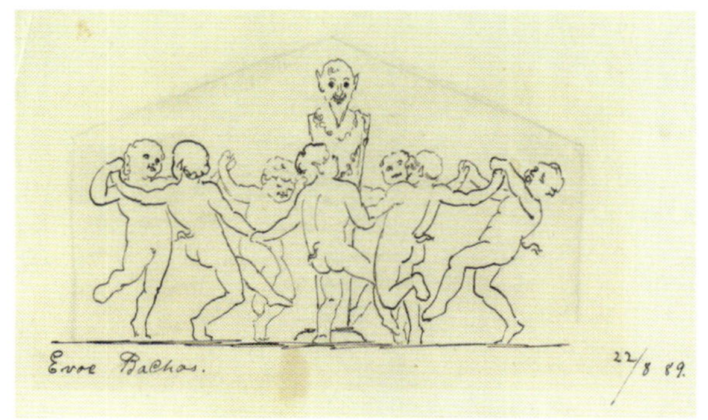

Cat. 10
Gustav Vigeland
The Seven Years of Hunger, 1889

Cat. 11
Gustav Vigeland
Little Devils Making Music, 1889

Cat. 9
Gustav Vigeland
The Charites, 1889

Cat. 12
Gustav Vigeland
Bacchus, 1889

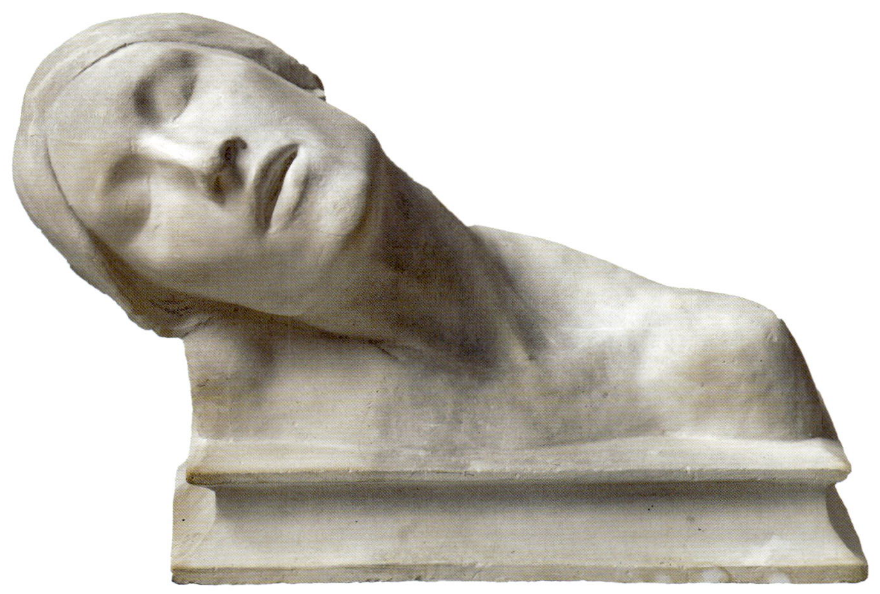

Cat. 13
Gustav Vigeland
Sleeping Woman, 1892

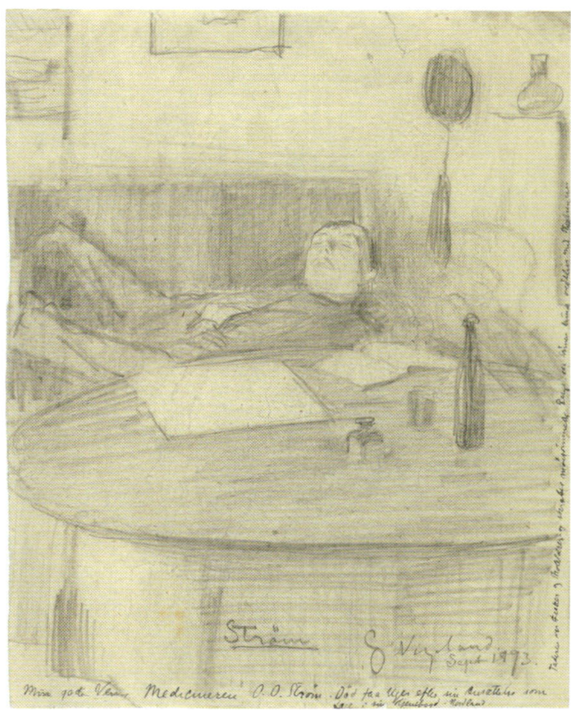

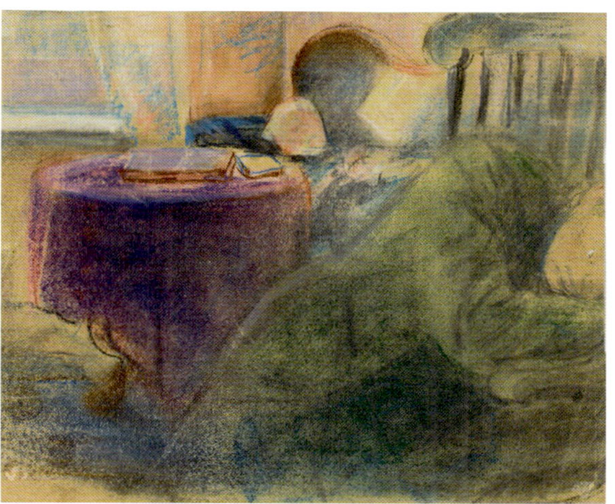

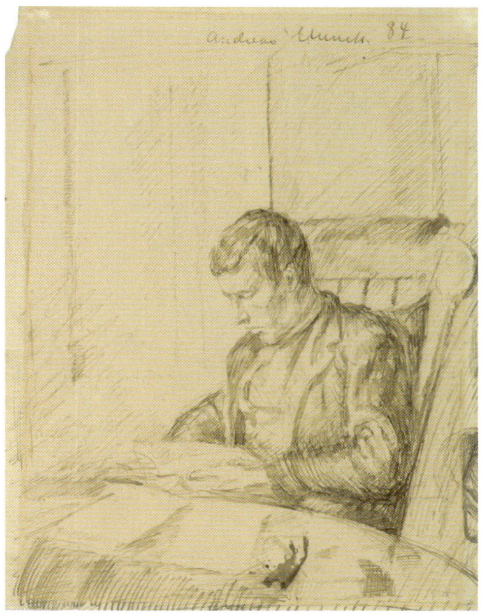

Cat. 15
Edvard Munch
Interior with Sleeping People, 1885

Cat. 14
Gustav Vigeland
O. Ström, 1893

Cat. 16
Edvard Munch
Andreas Munch, 1884

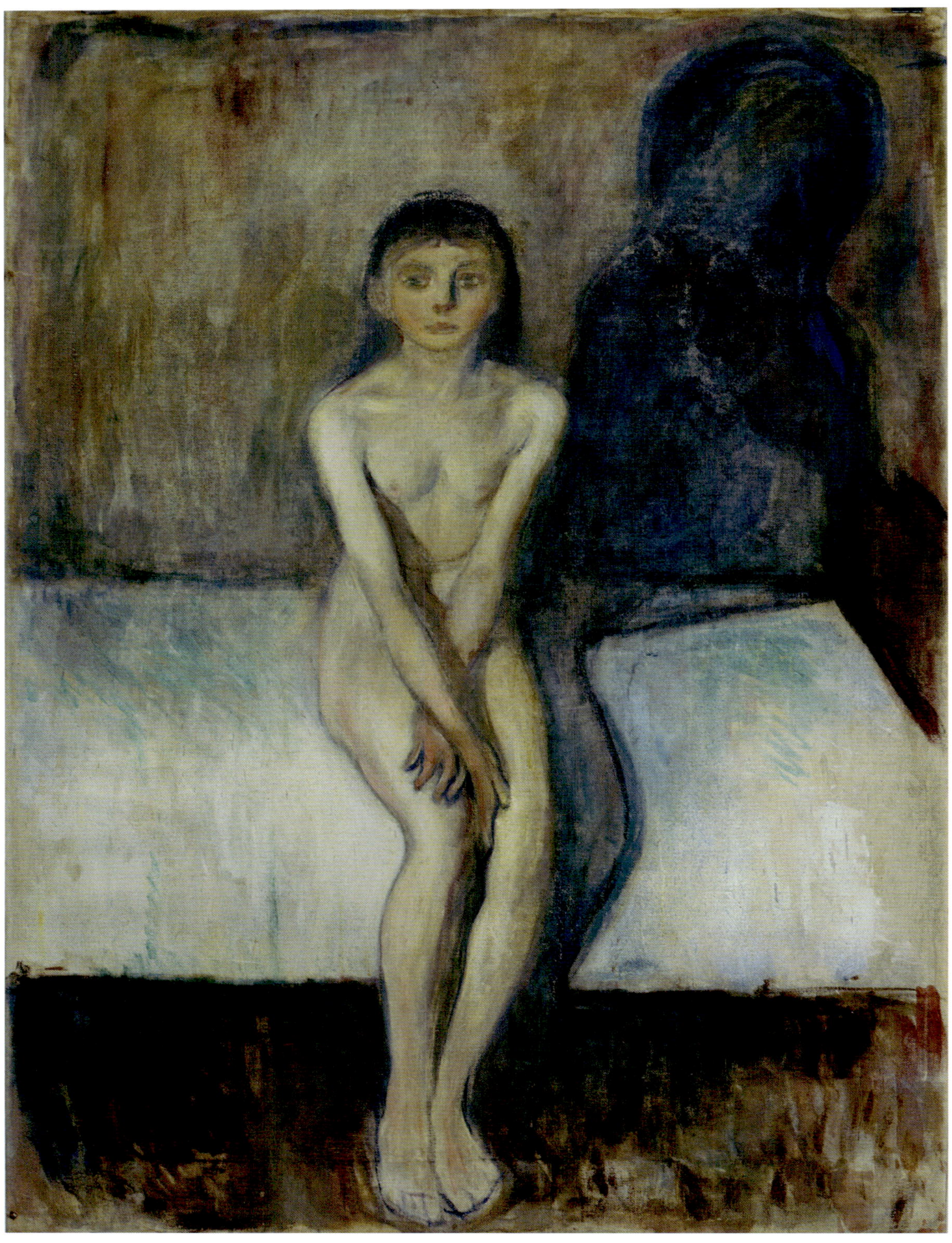

Cat. 17
Edvard Munch
Puberty, 1894

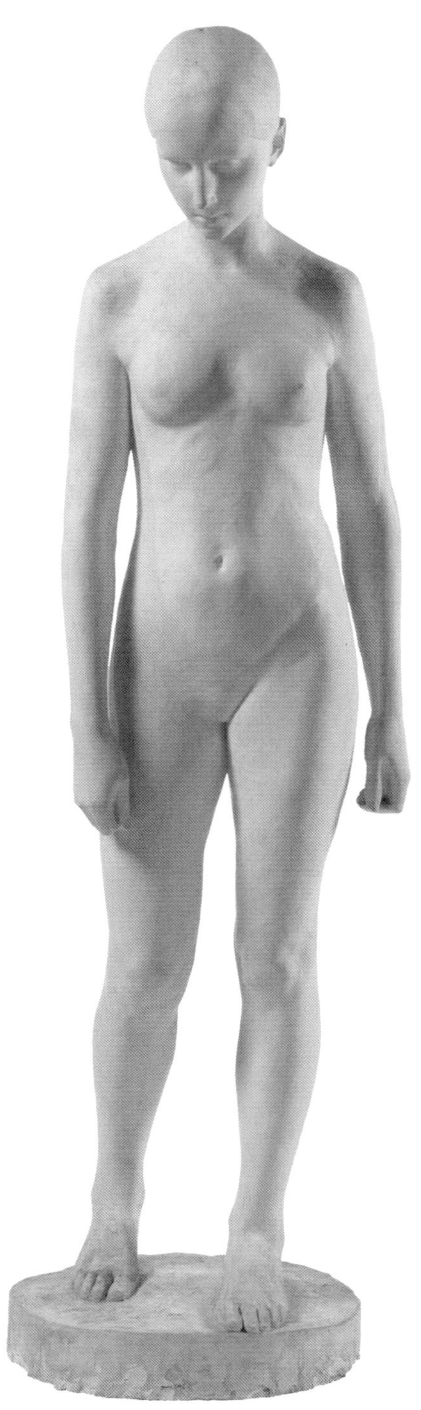

Cat. 18
Gustav Vigeland
Young Girl, 1892

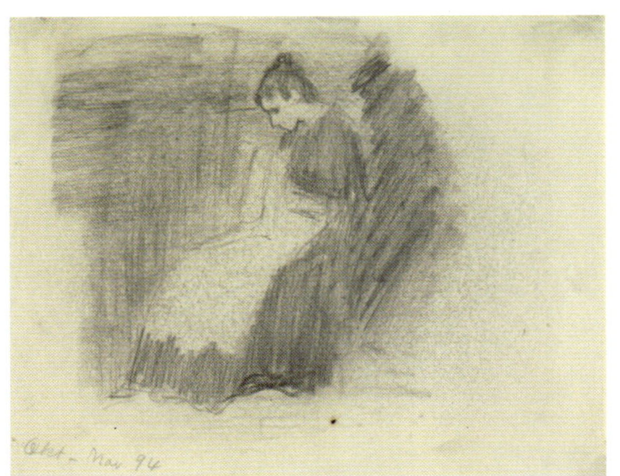

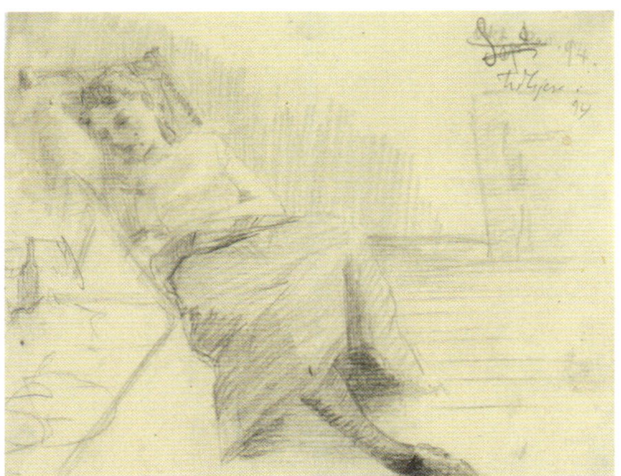

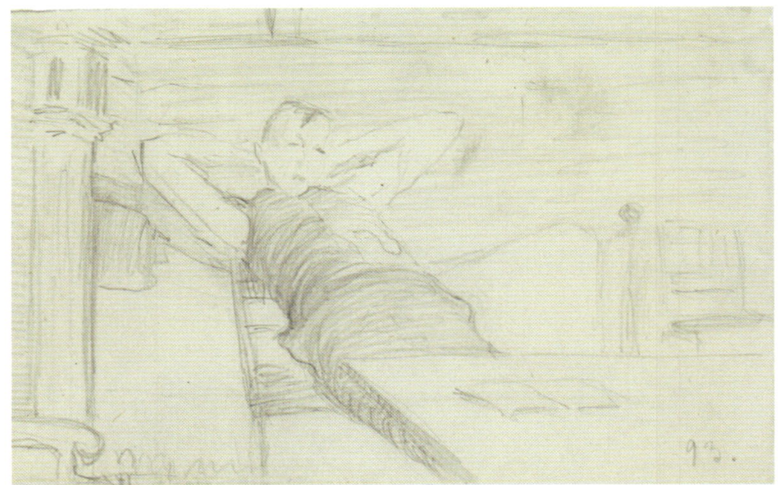

Cat. 19
Gustav Vigeland
Woman Sewing, 1894

Cat. 20
Gustav Vigeland
Sleeping Woman, 1894

Cat. 21
Gustav Vigeland
Young Man in Interior, 1893

Cat. 22
Edvard Munch
Karen Bjølstad with Shadow, 1886–89

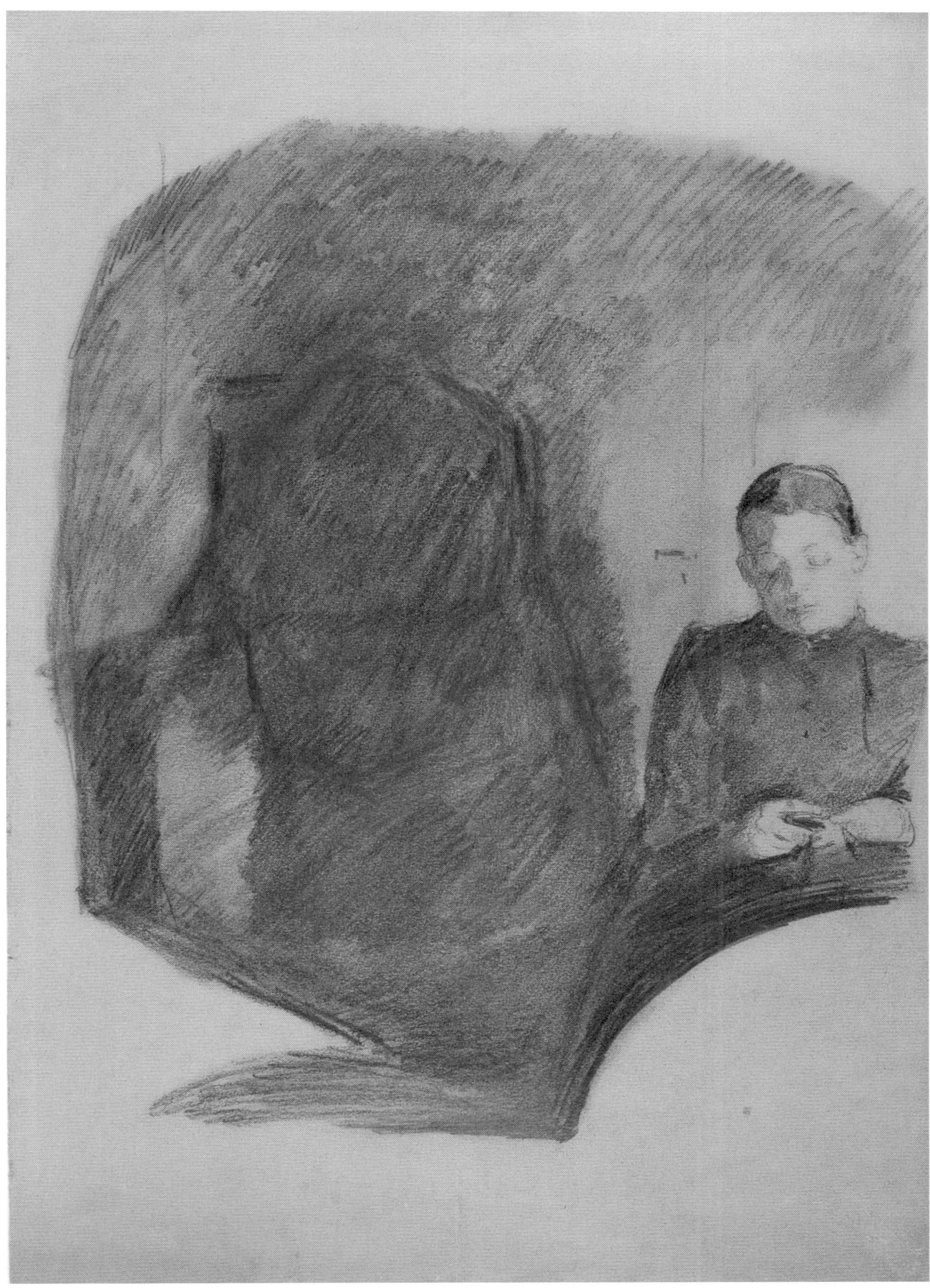

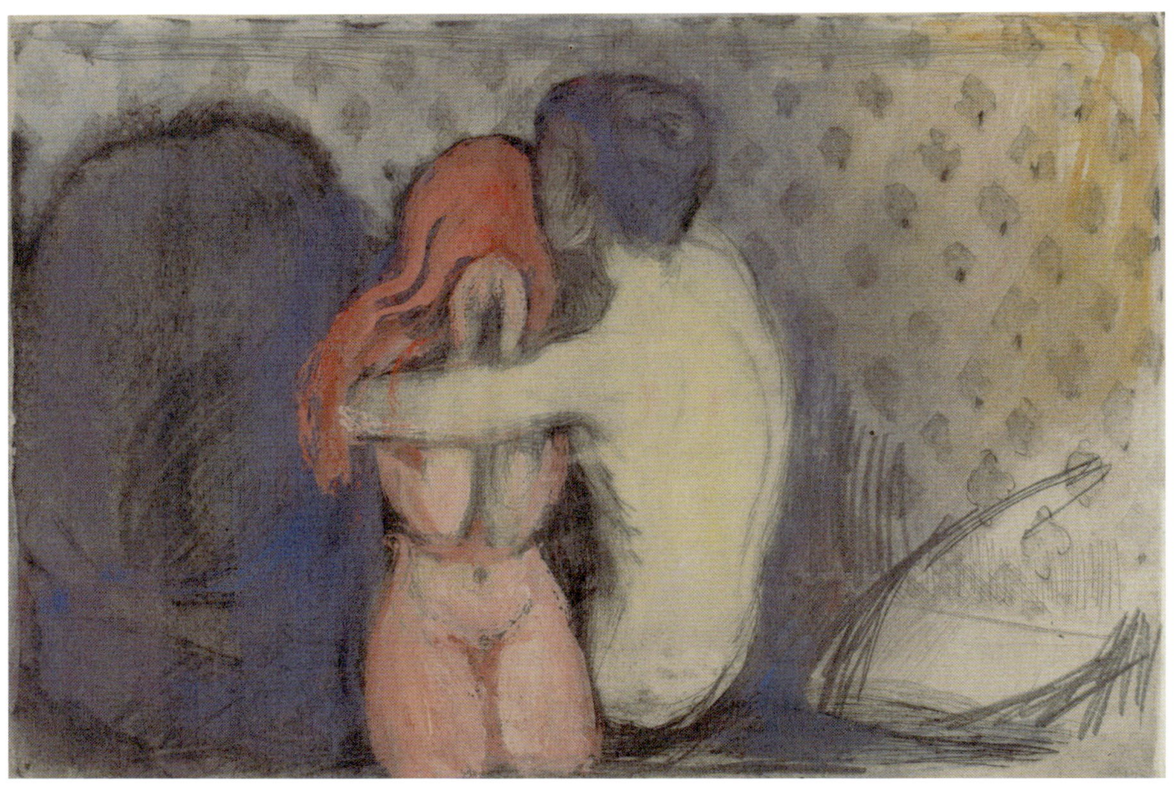

Cat. 23
Edvard Munch
Consolation, 1894

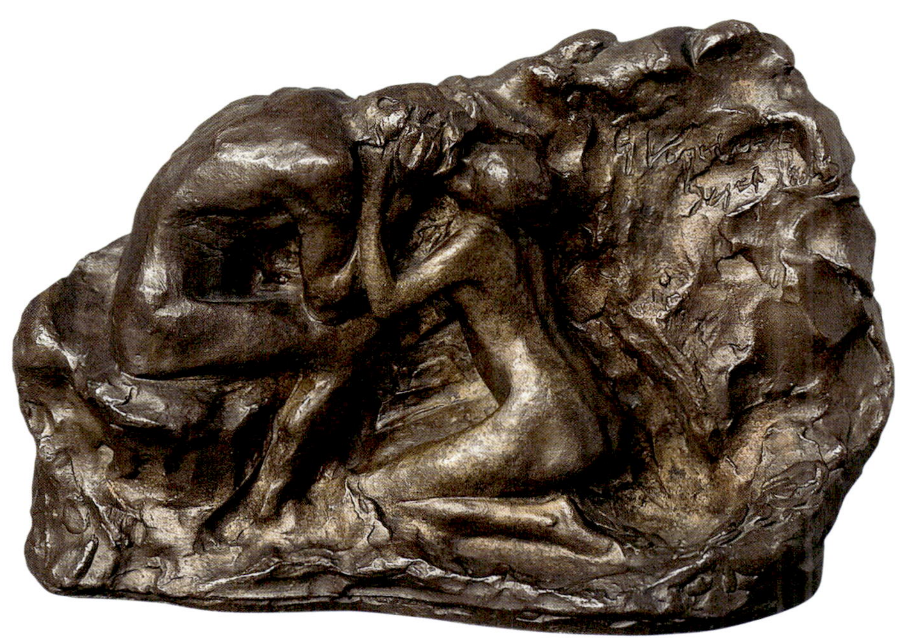

Cat. 24
Gustav Vigeland
Consolation, 1893

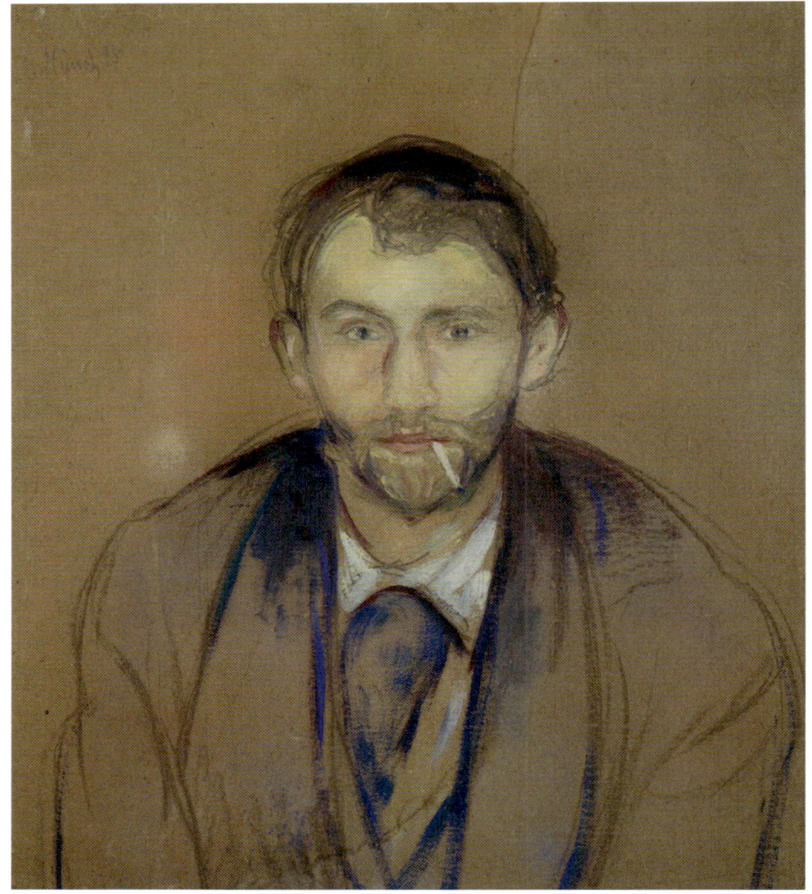

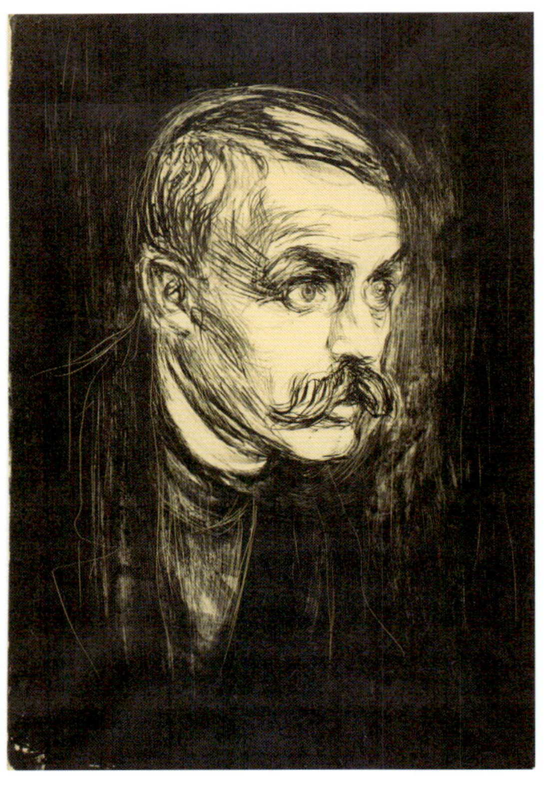

Cat. 25
Edvard Munch
Stanisław Przybyszewski, 1895

Cat. 26
Edvard Munch
Sigbjørn Obstfelder II, 1896

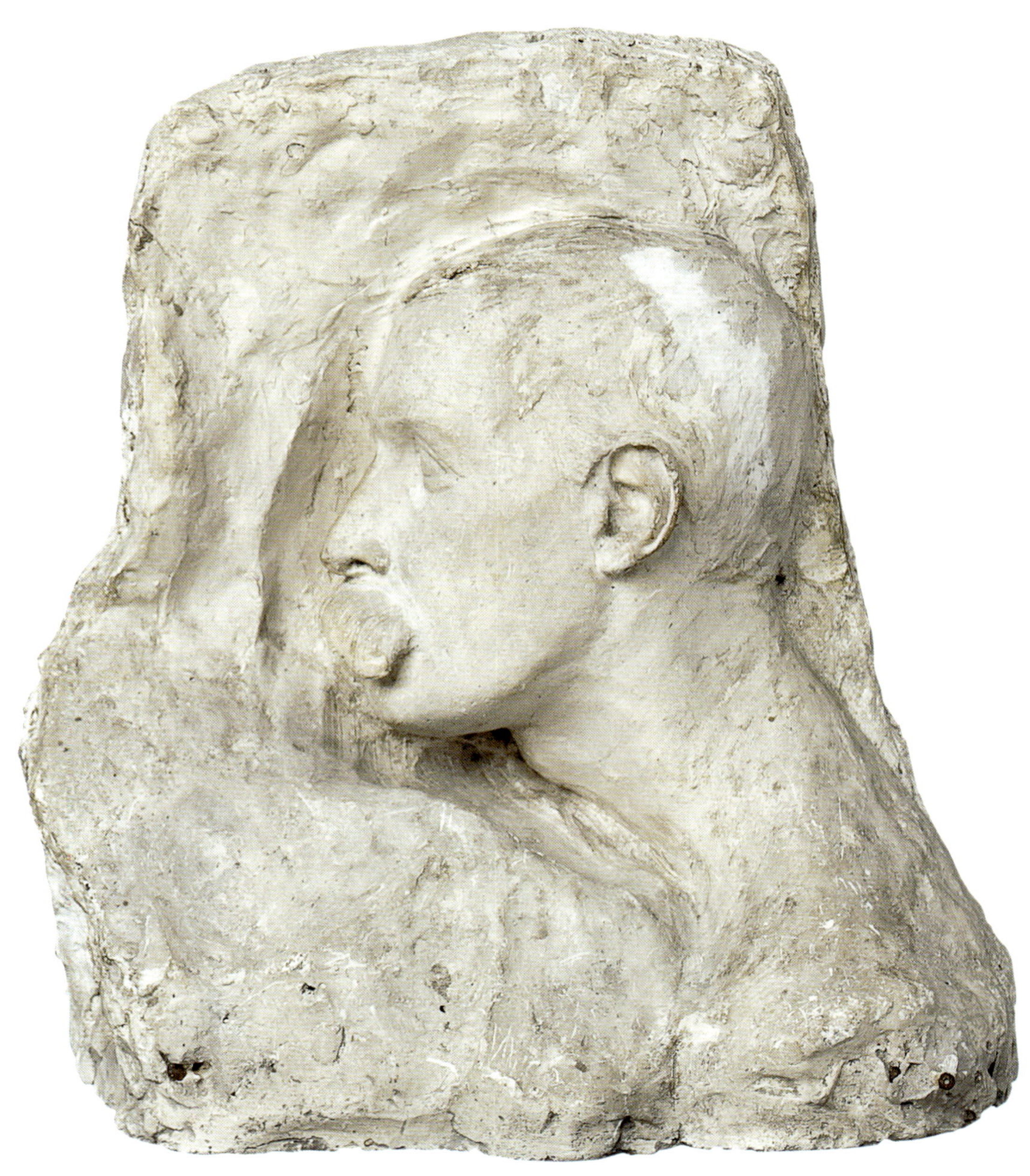

Cat. 27
Gustav Vigeland
Sigbjørn Obstfelder, 1895

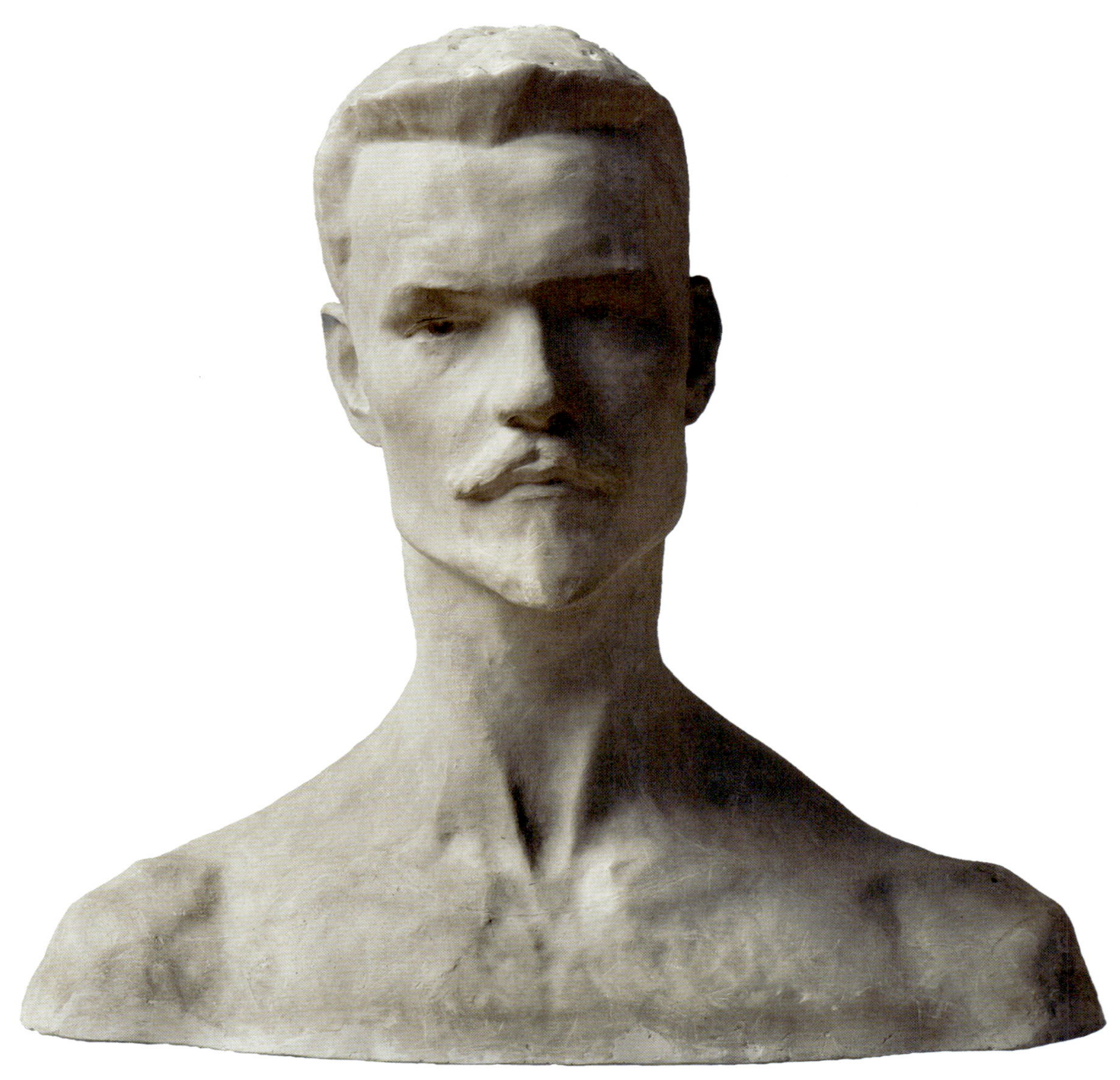

Cat. 28
Gustav Vigeland
Jens Thiis, 1894

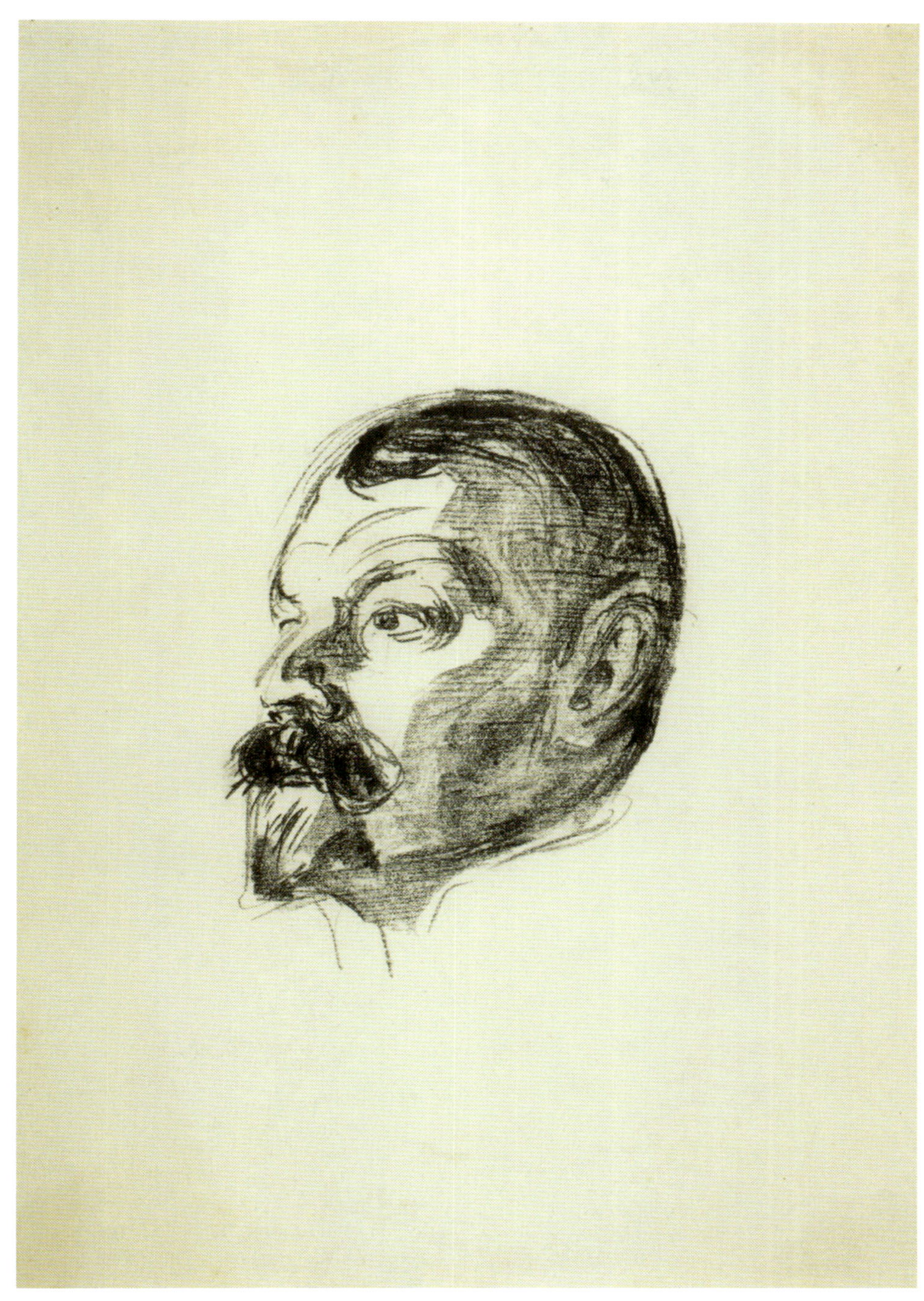

Cat. 29
Edvard Munch
Jens Thiis, 1913

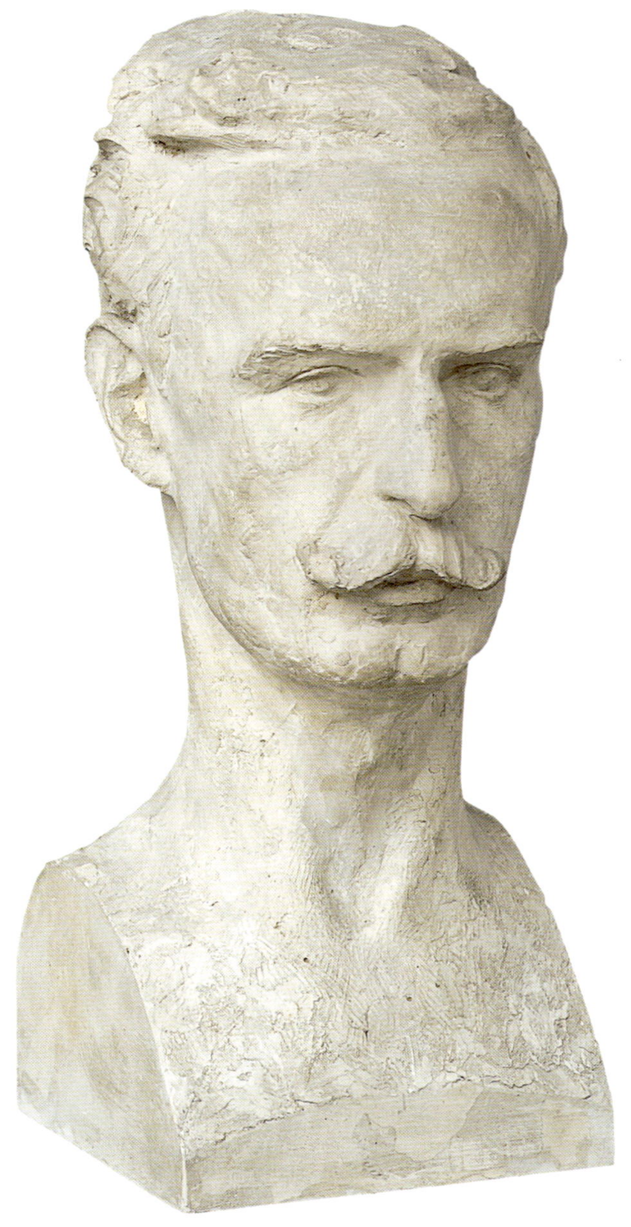

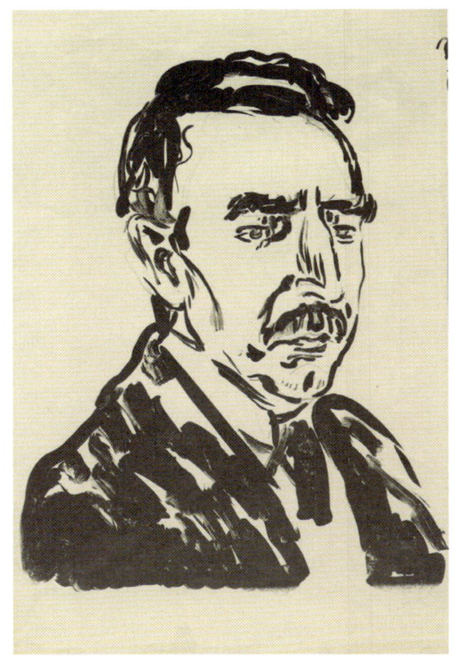

Cat. 30
Gustav Vigeland
Vilhelm Krag, 1903

Cat. 31
Edvard Munch
Vilhelm Krag, 1919–20

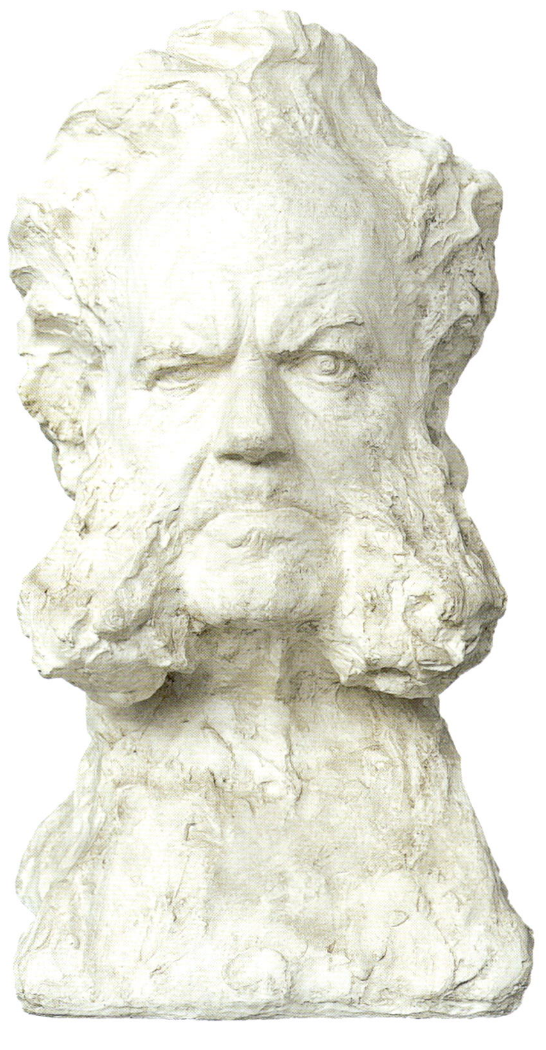

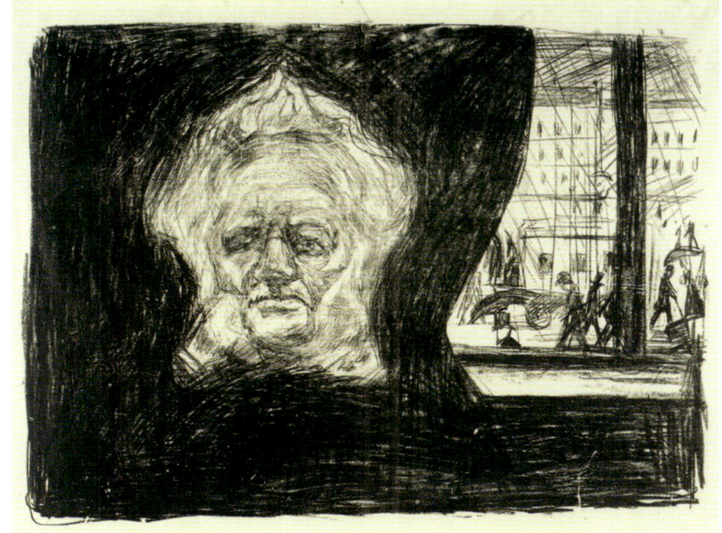

Cat. 32
Gustav Vigeland
Henrik Ibsen, 1903

Cat. 33
Edvard Munch
Henrik Ibsen at the Grand Café, 1902

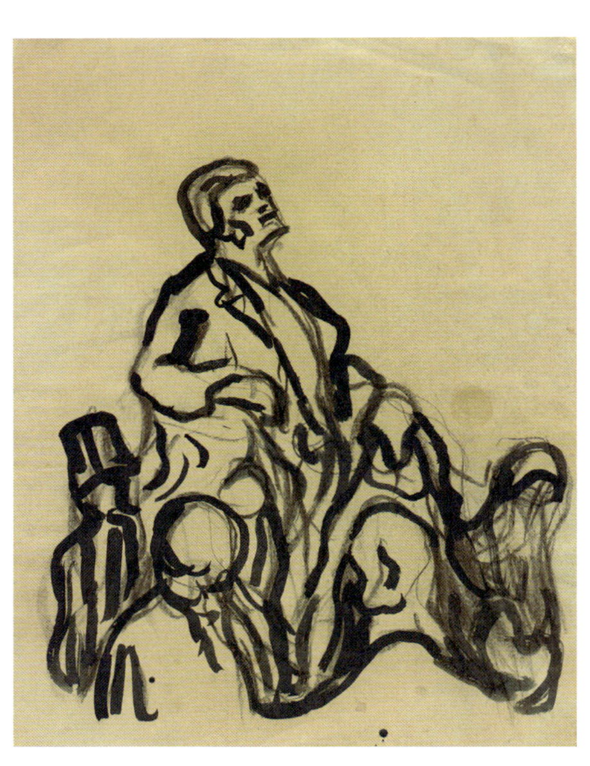

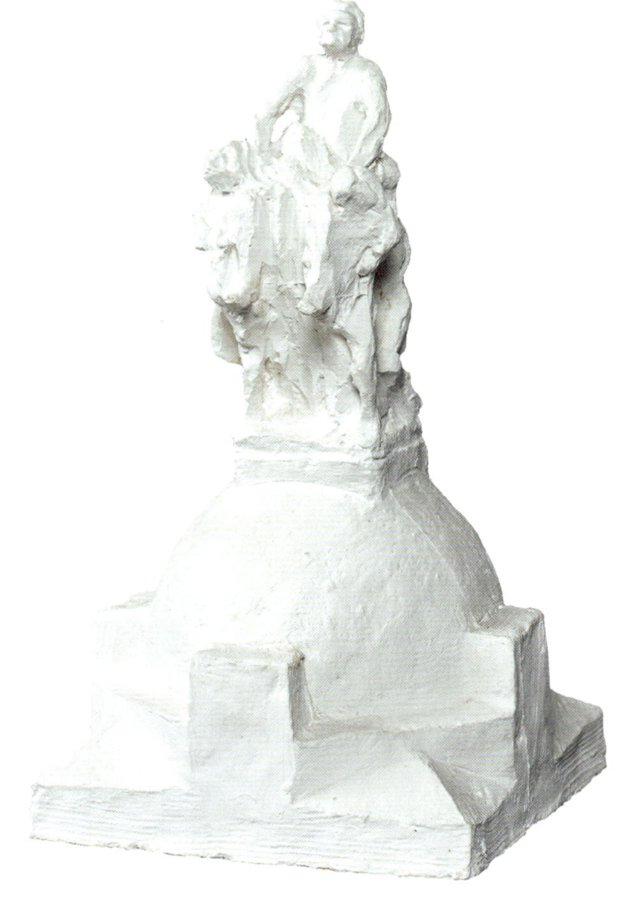

Cat. 34
Edvard Munch
Bjørnson Speaking to the People, 1909

Cat. 35
Gustav Vigeland
Bjørnstjerne Bjørnson, prob. 1914

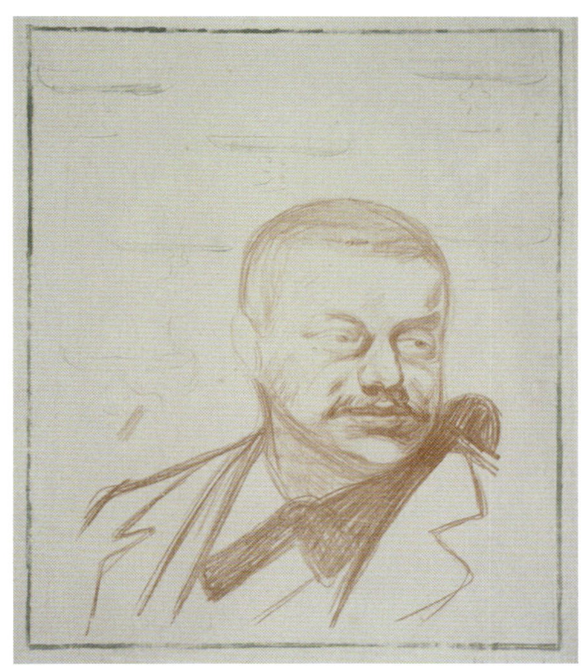

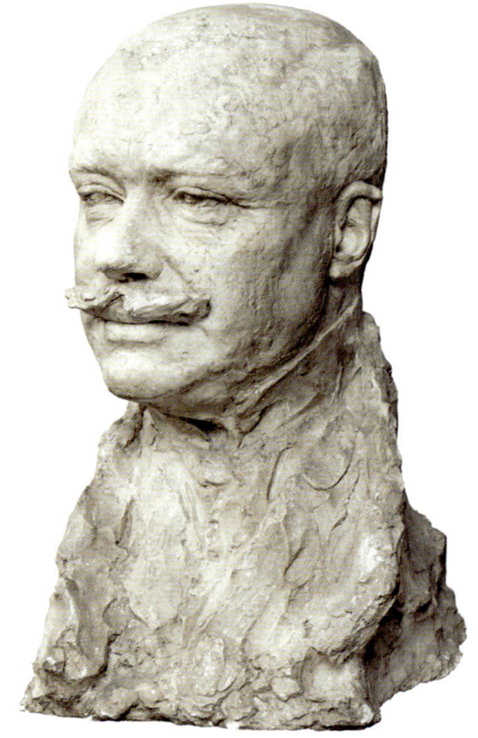

Cat. 36
Edvard Munch
Gunnar Heiberg, 1896

Cat. 37
Gustav Vigeland
Gunnar Heiberg, 1905

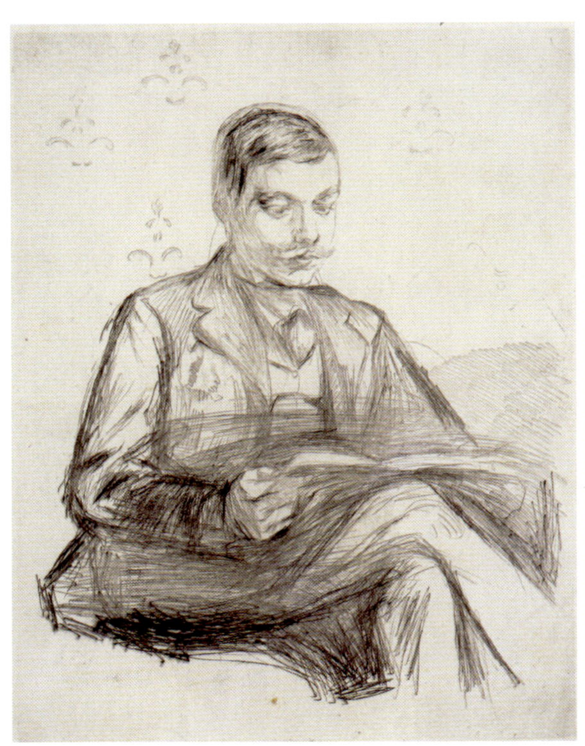

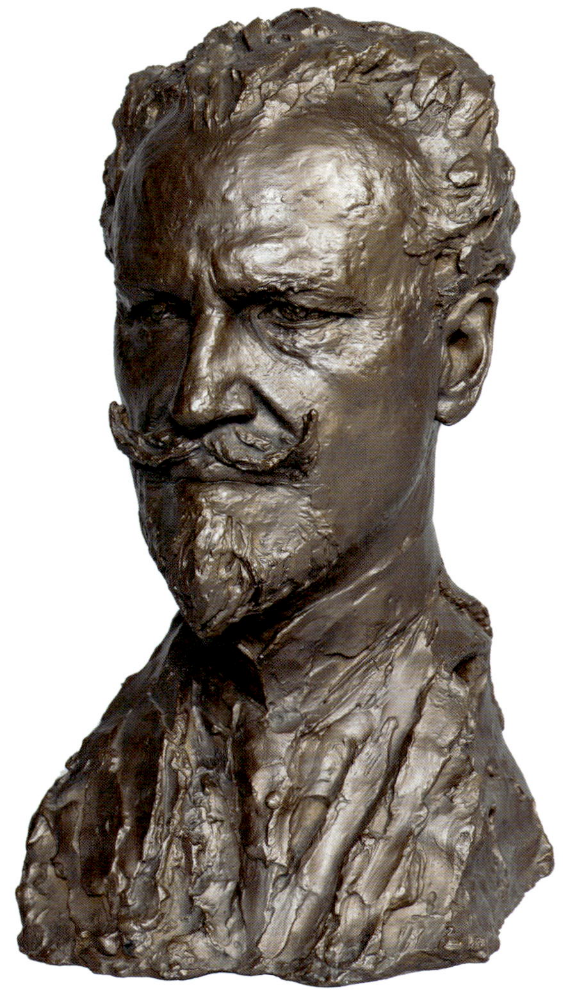

Cat. 38
Edvard Munch
Eberhard von Bodenhausen, 1895

Cat. 39
Gustav Vigeland
Ernest Thiel, 1907

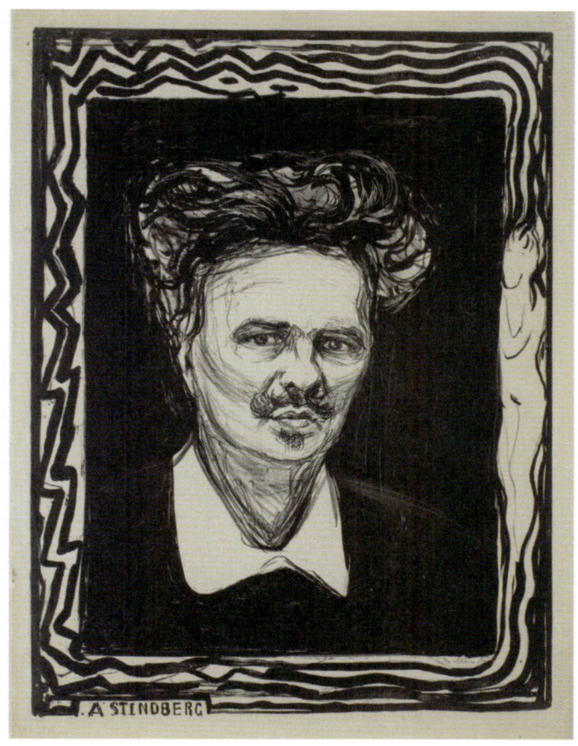

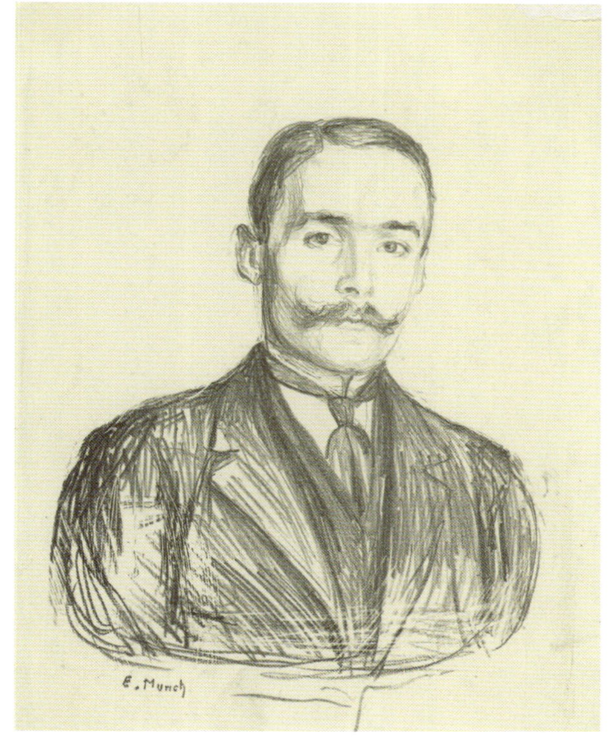

Cat. 40
Edvard Munch
August Strindberg, 1896

Cat. 41
Edvard Munch
Count Harry Kessler I, 1895

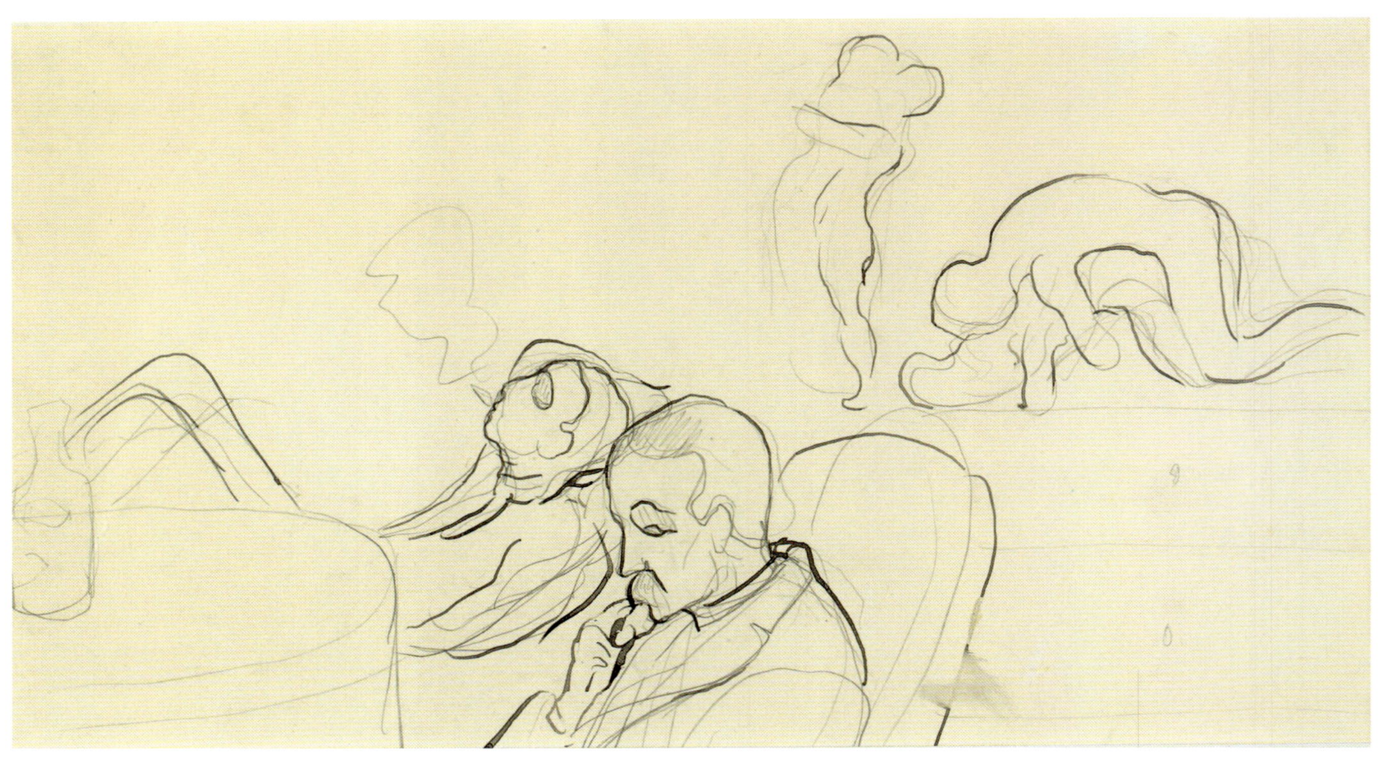

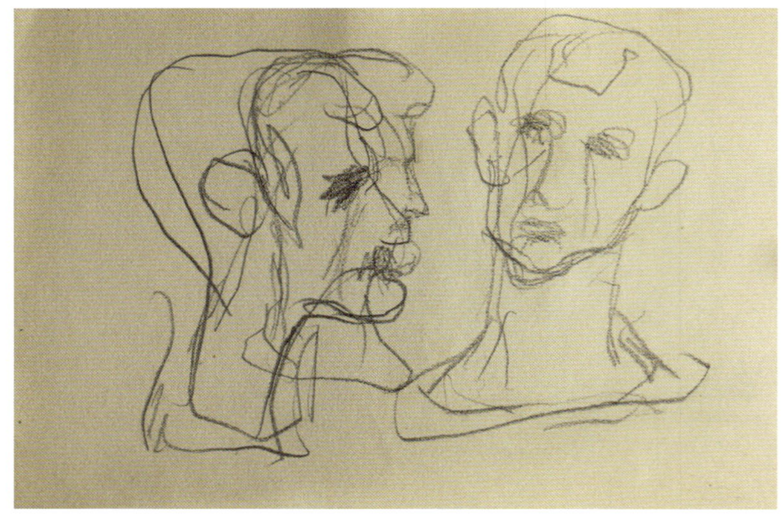

Cat. 42
Edvard Munch
Vigeland, Obstfelder and Two Sculptures, 1895

Cat. 43
Gustav Vigeland
Double Portrait, 1895

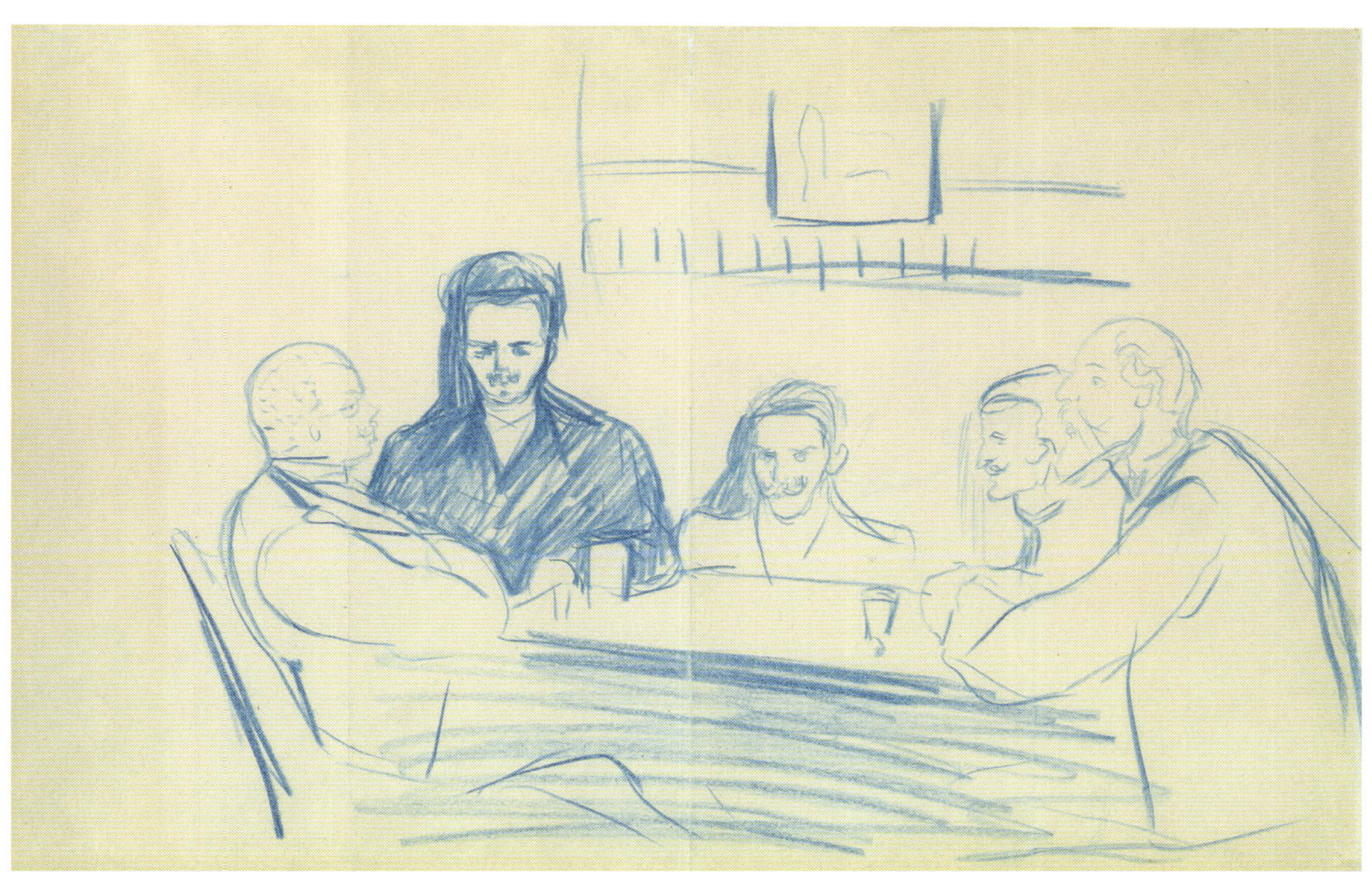

Cat. 44
Edvard Munch
The Ferkel Circle, 1893

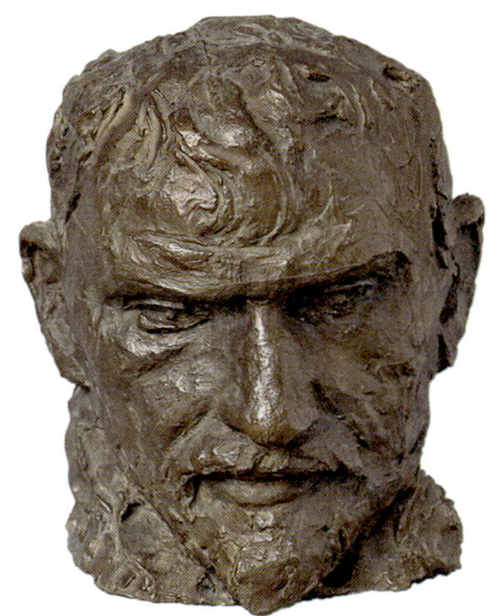

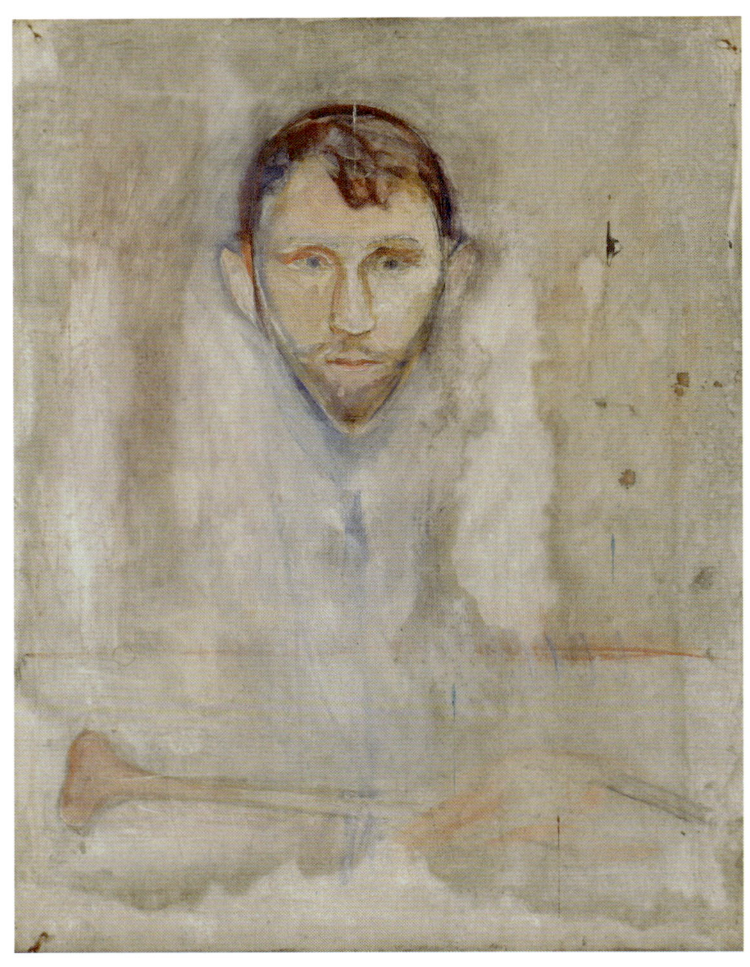

Cat. 45
Gustav Vigeland
Stanisław Przybyszewski, 1895

Cat. 46
Edvard Munch
Stanisław Przybyszewski, 1894

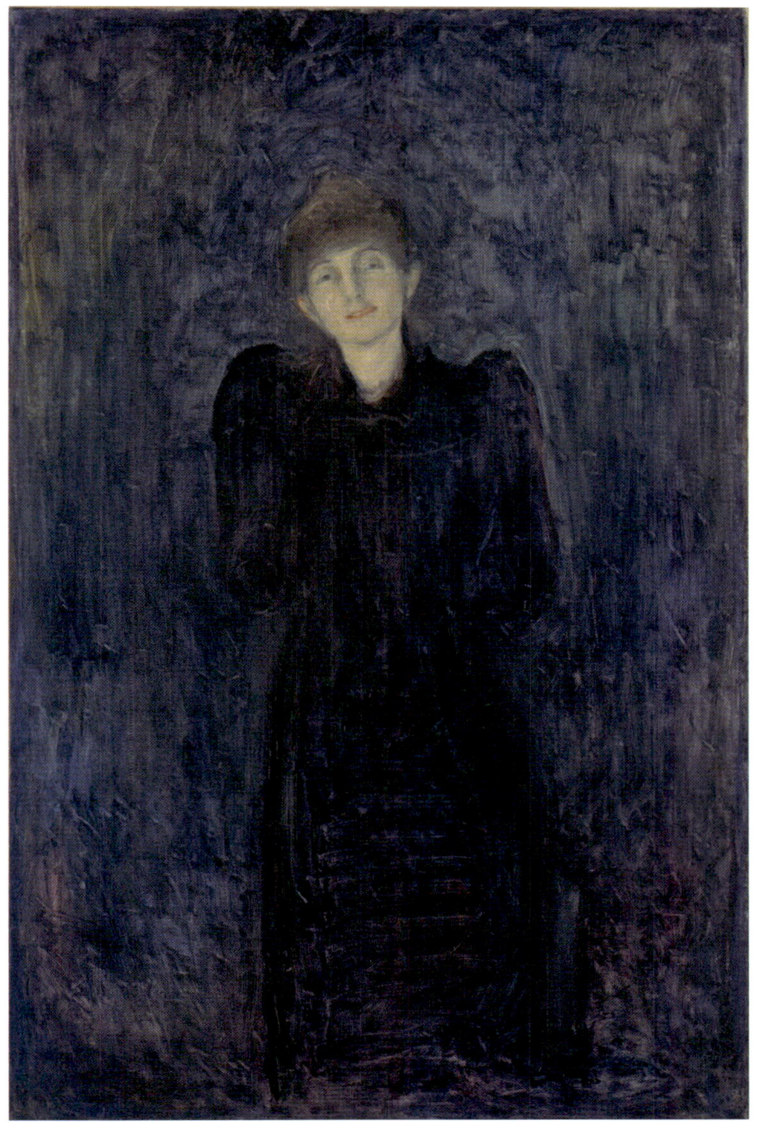

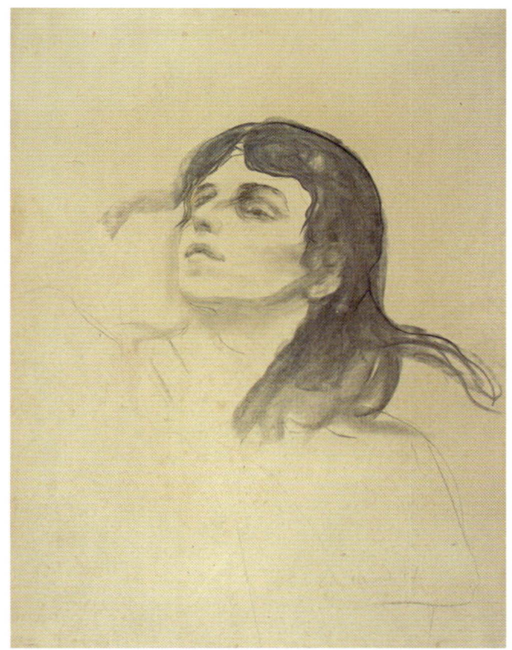

Cat. 47
Edvard Munch
Dagny Juel Przybyszewska, 1893

Cat. 48
Edvard Munch
Madonna's Head, 1894

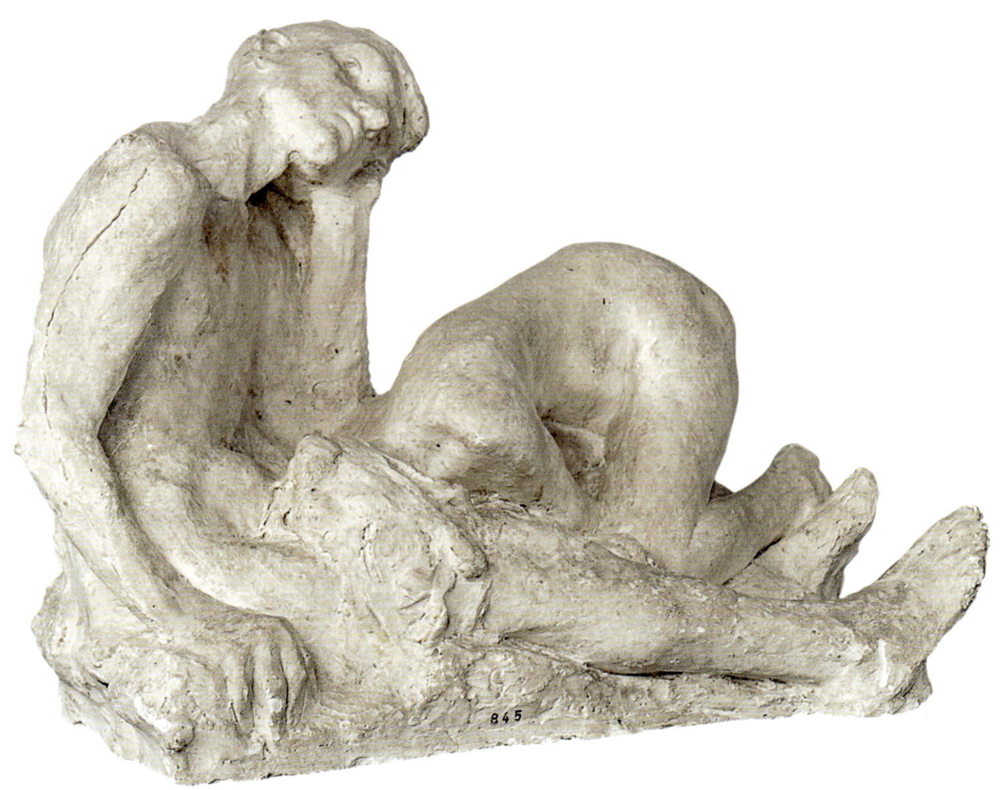

Cat. 49
Gustav Vigeland
A Doubter, 1894

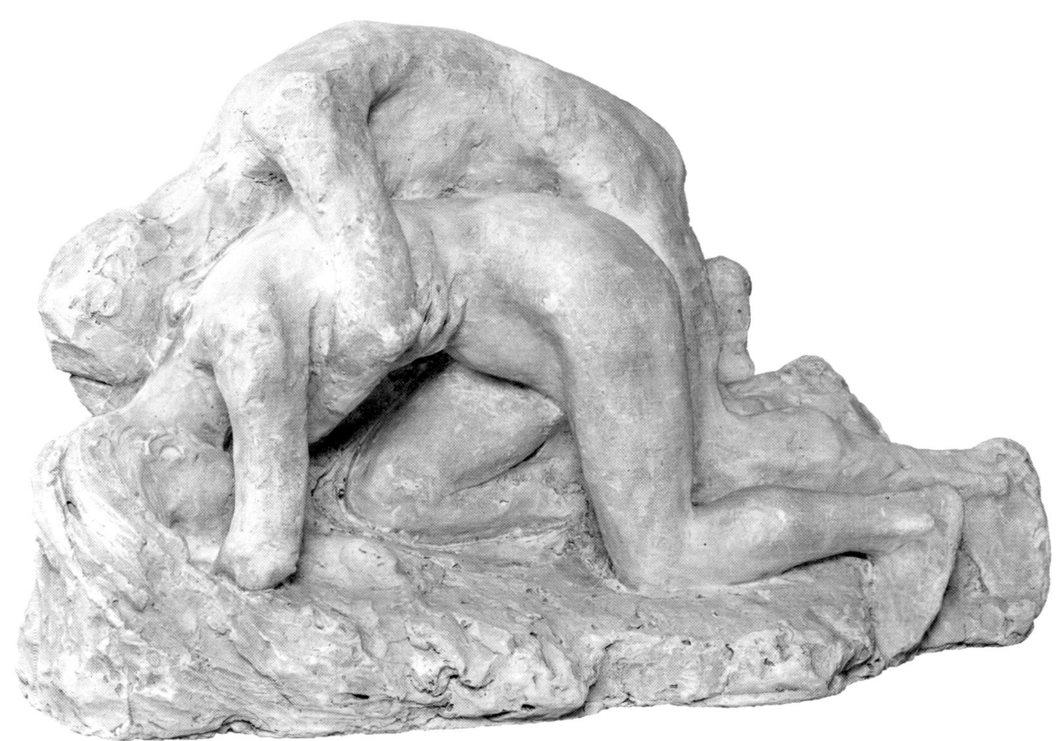

Cat. 50
Gustav Vigeland
The Prostrated, 1895

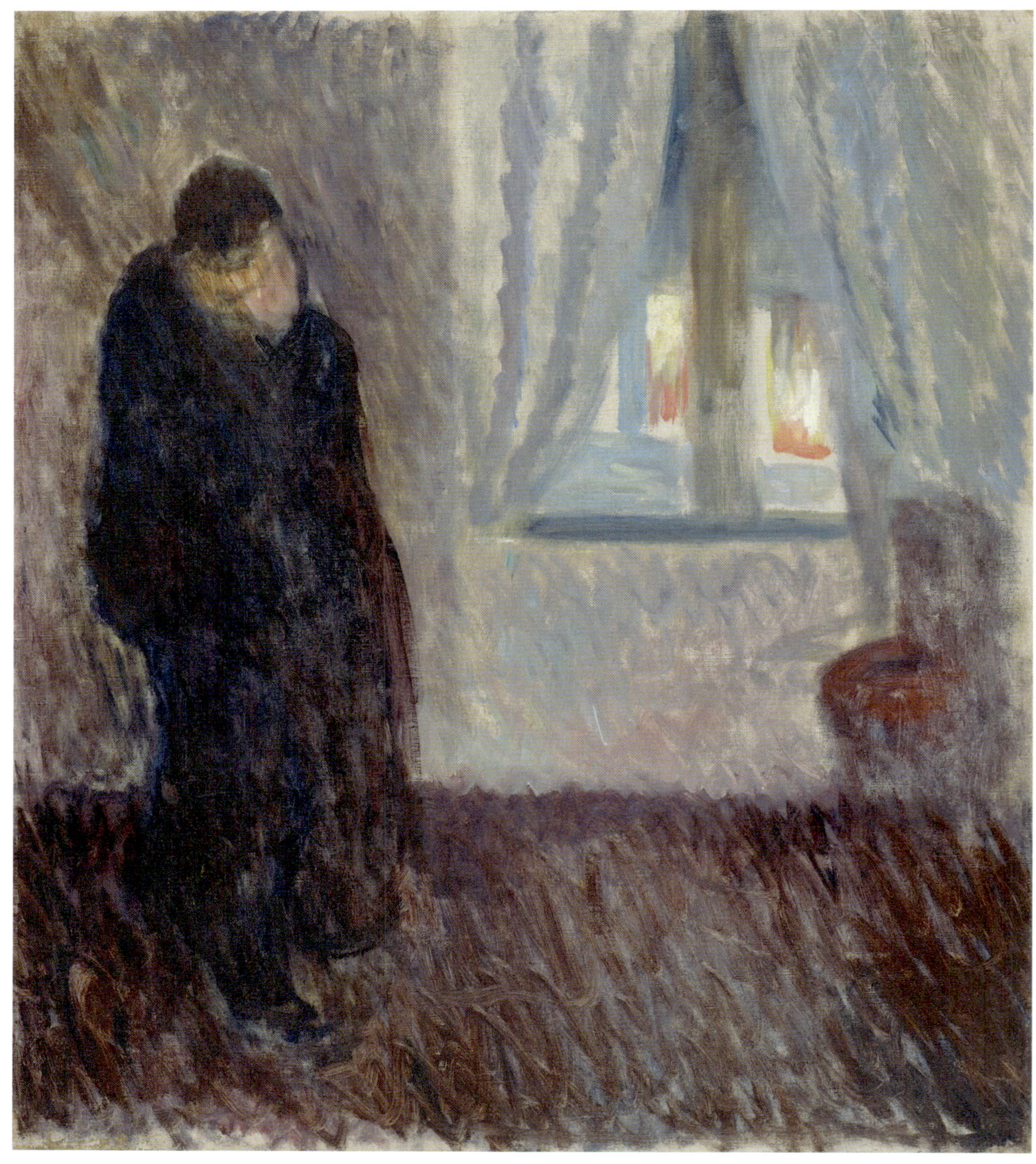

Cat. 51
Edvard Munch
The Kiss, 1891

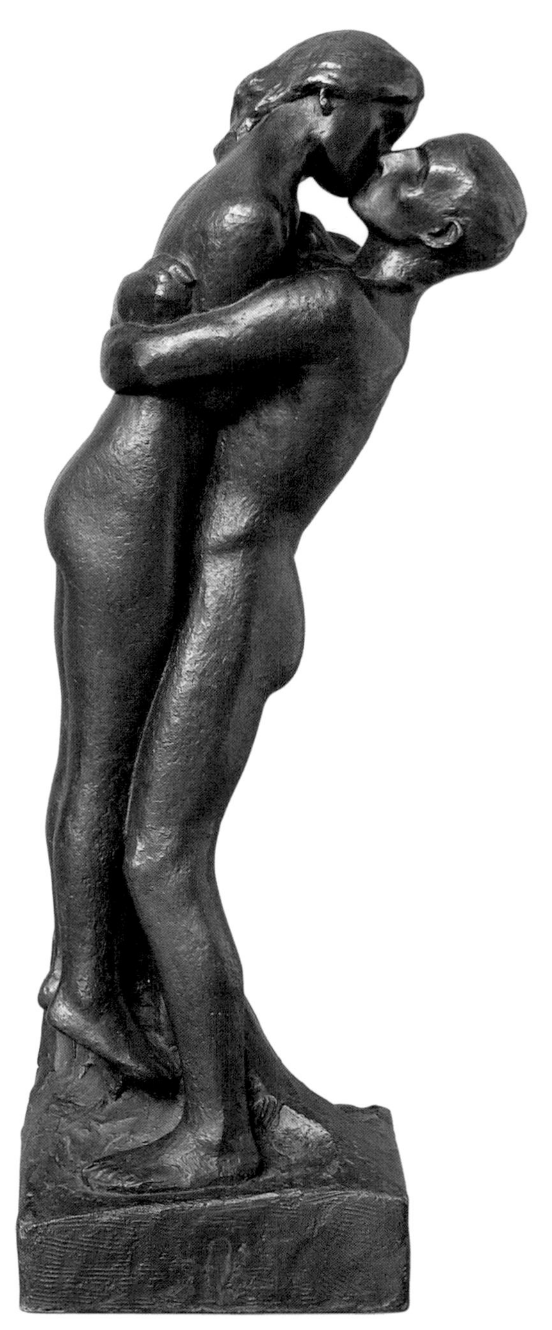

Cat. 52
Gustav Vigeland
The Kiss, 1898

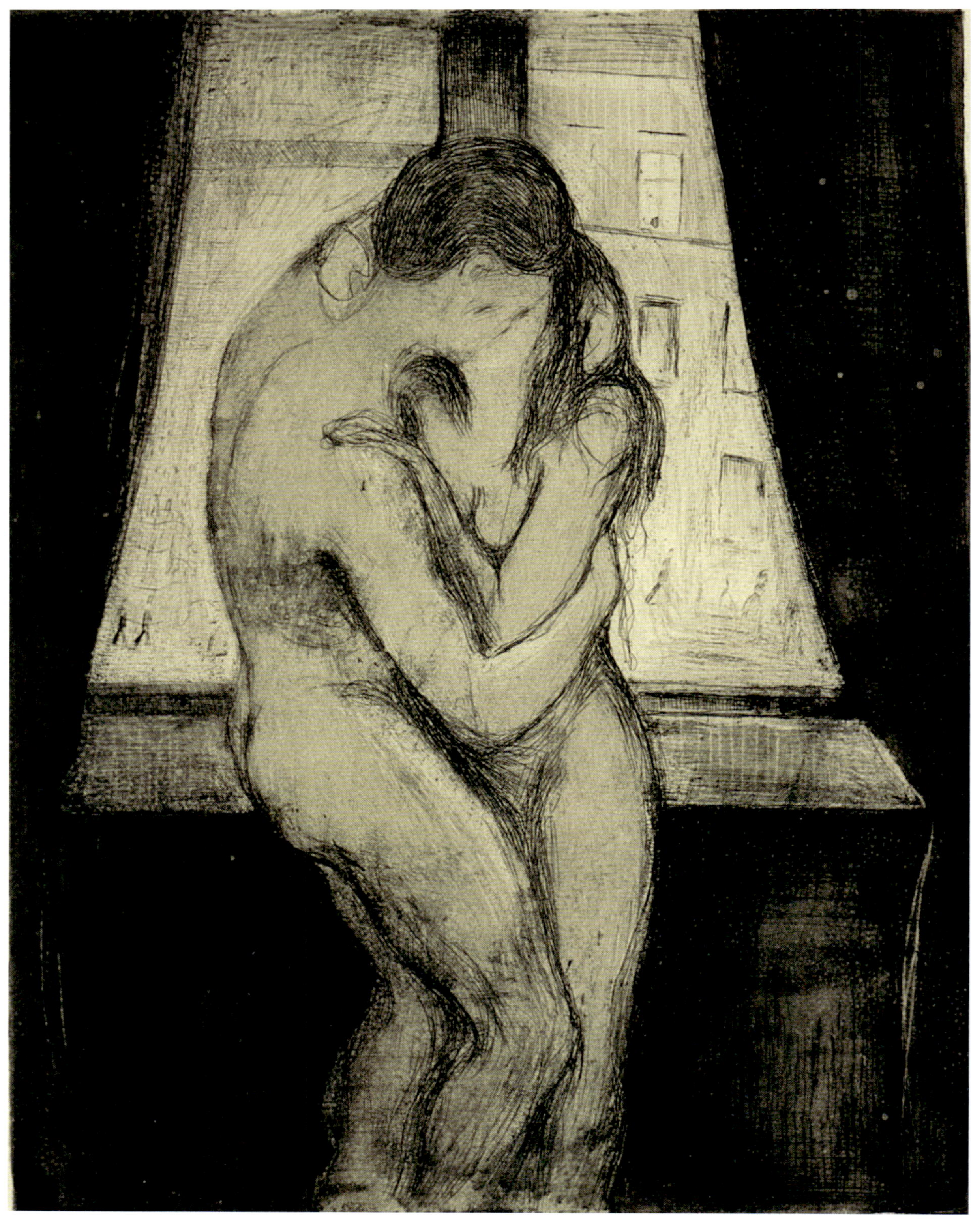

Cat. 53
Edvard Munch
The Kiss, 1895

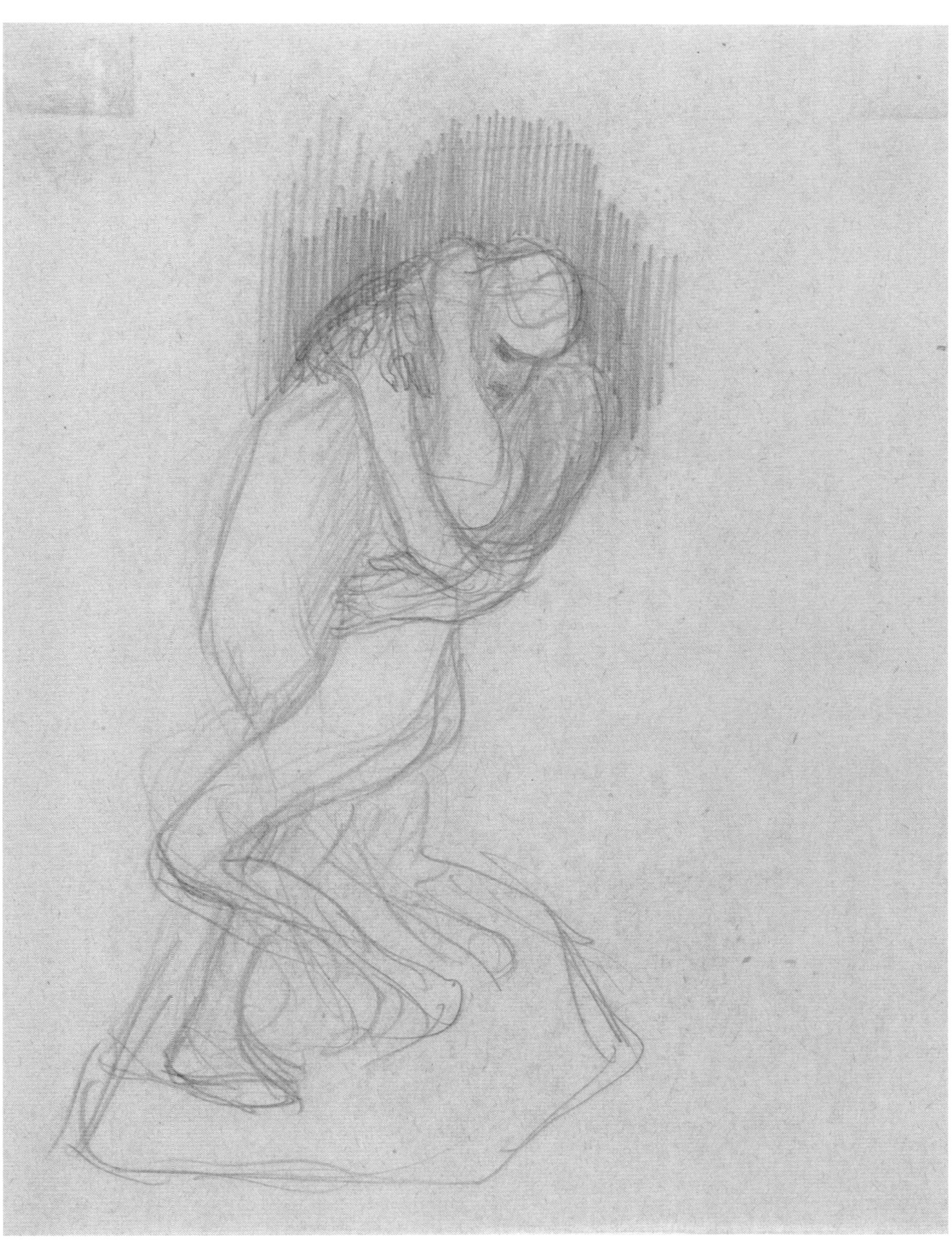

Cat. 54
Gustav Vigeland
Embrace, prob. 1890s

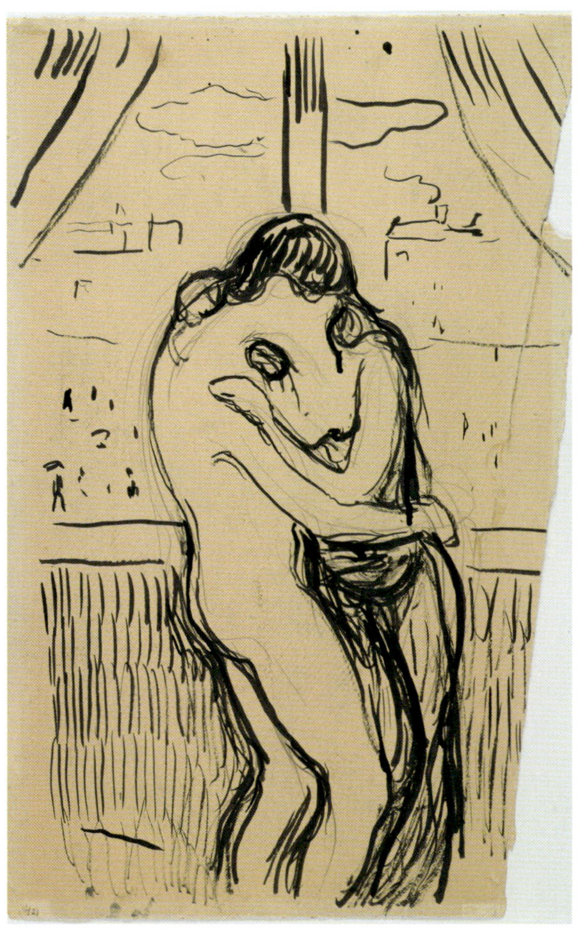

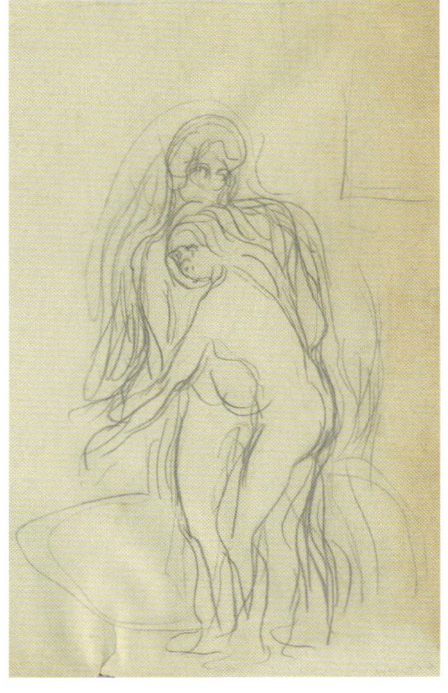

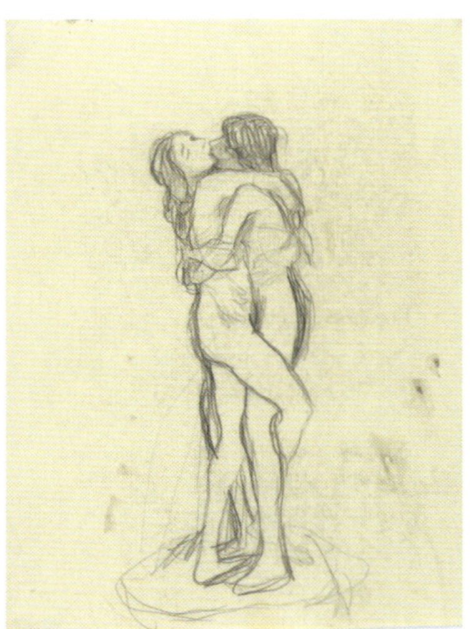

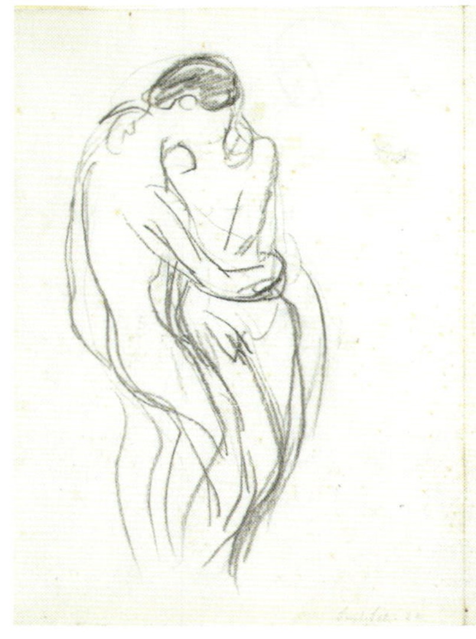

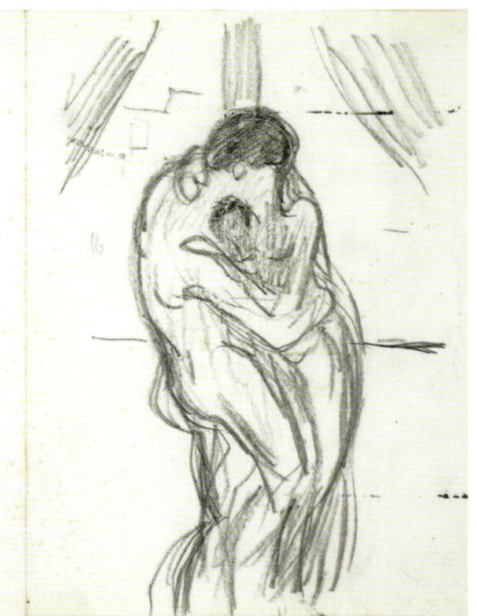

Cat. 56
Edvard Munch
Man and Woman, 1894–97

Cat. 58
Gustav Vigeland
Kiss (undated)

Cat. 55
Edvard Munch
The Kiss, c. 1895

Cat. 57
Edvard Munch
The Kiss, c. 1895

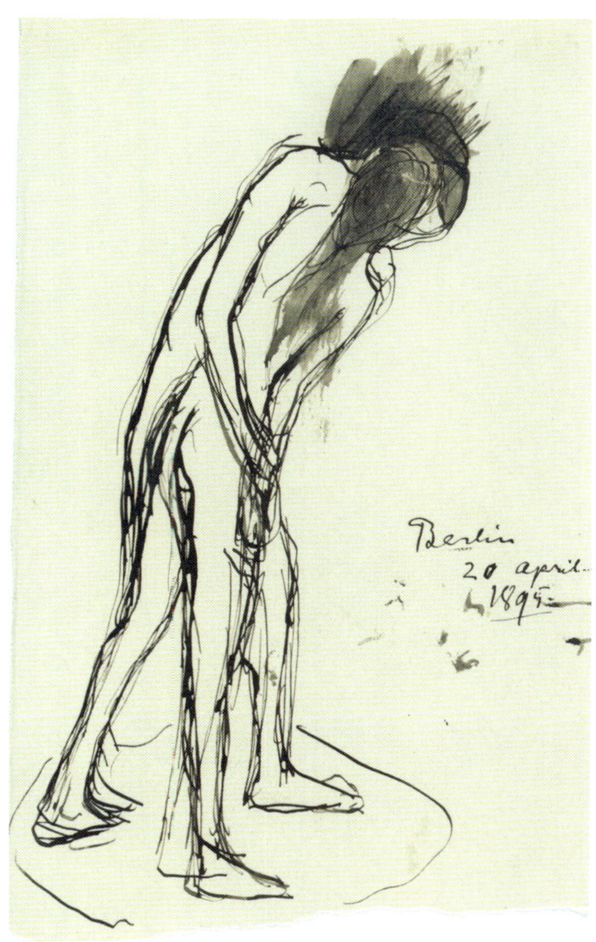

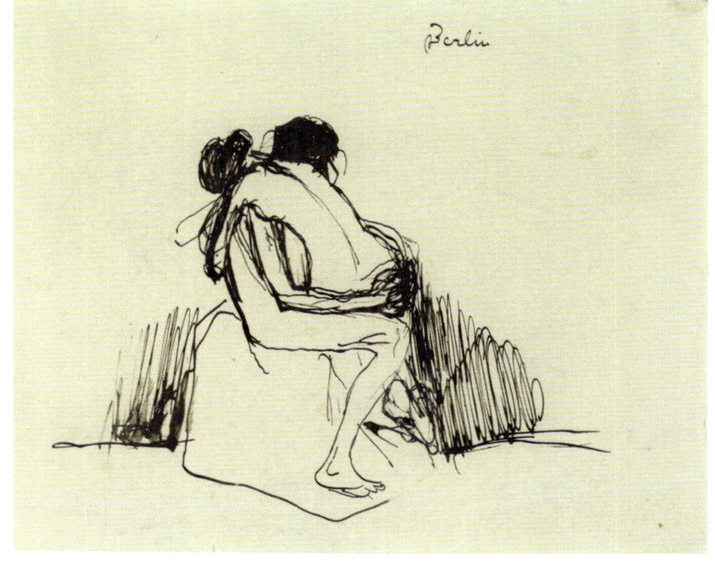

Cat. 59
Gustav Vigeland
Man and Woman, 1895

Cat. 60
Gustav Vigeland
Man with a Woman on His Lap,
prob. 1895

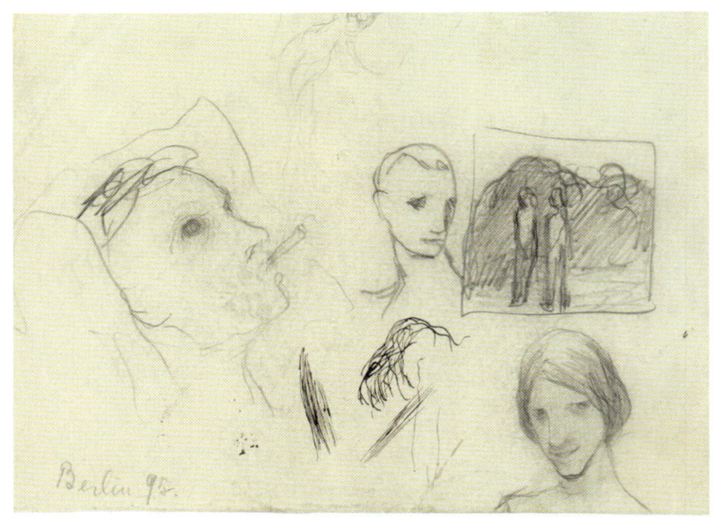

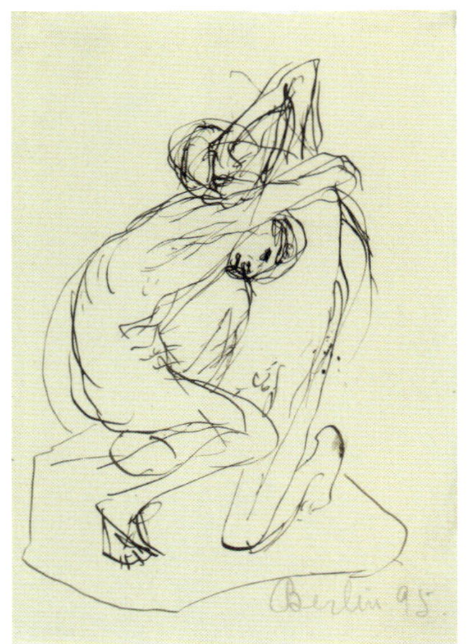

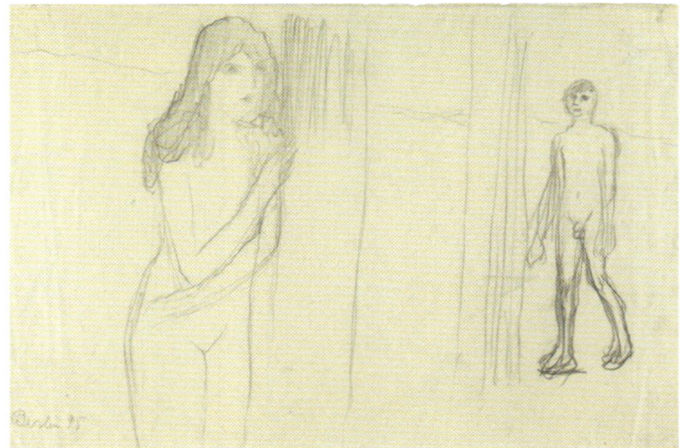

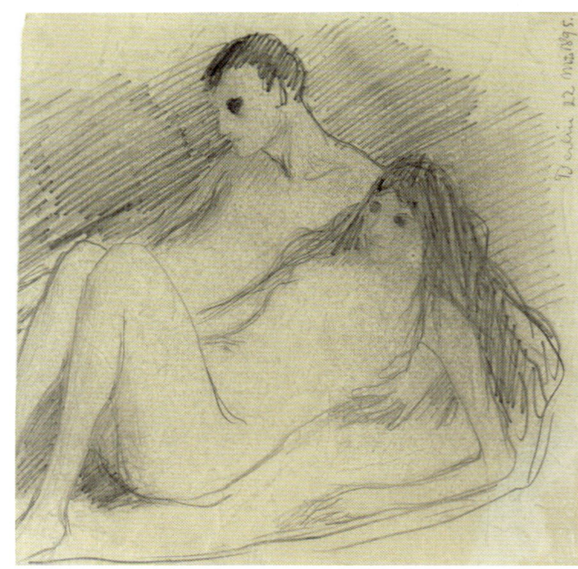

Cat. 61
Gustav Vigeland
Man with Cigarette, 1895

Cat. 62
Gustav Vigeland
A Couple in the Woods, 1895

Cat. 63
Gustav Vigeland
Fight, 1895

Cat. 64
Gustav Vigeland
Reclining Man and Woman, 1895

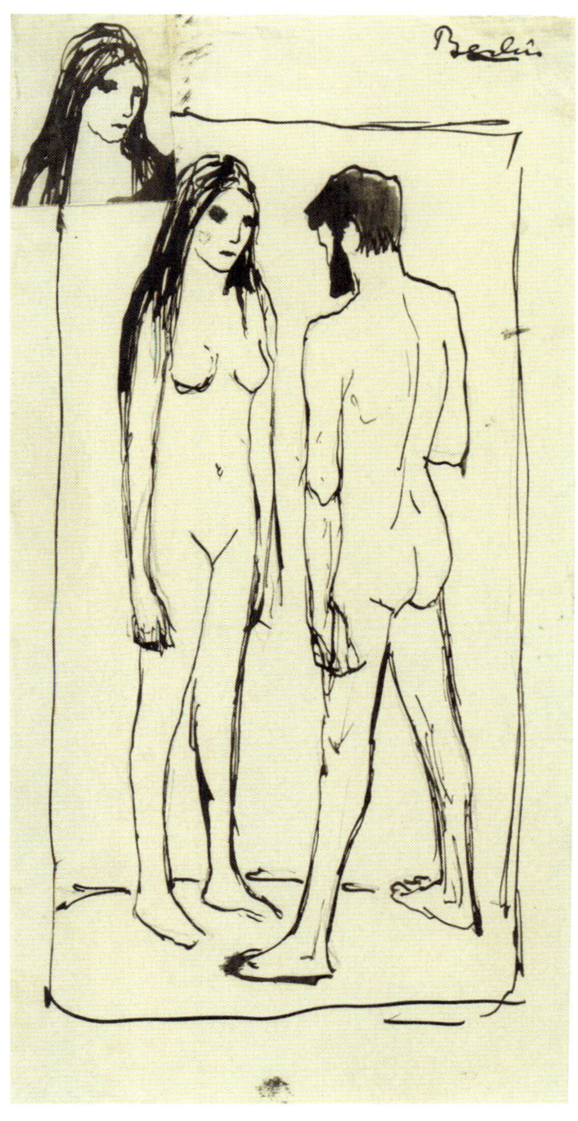

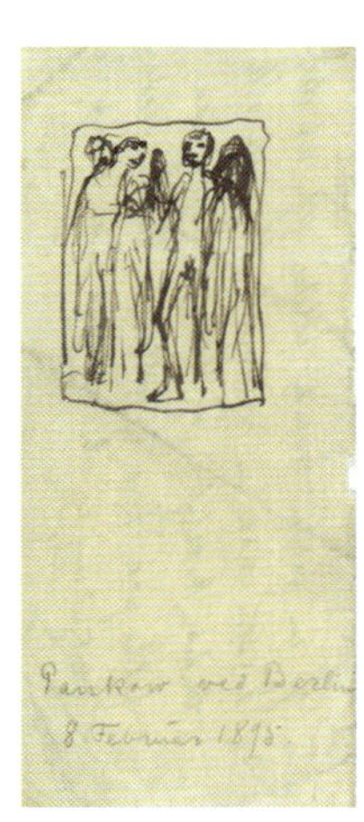

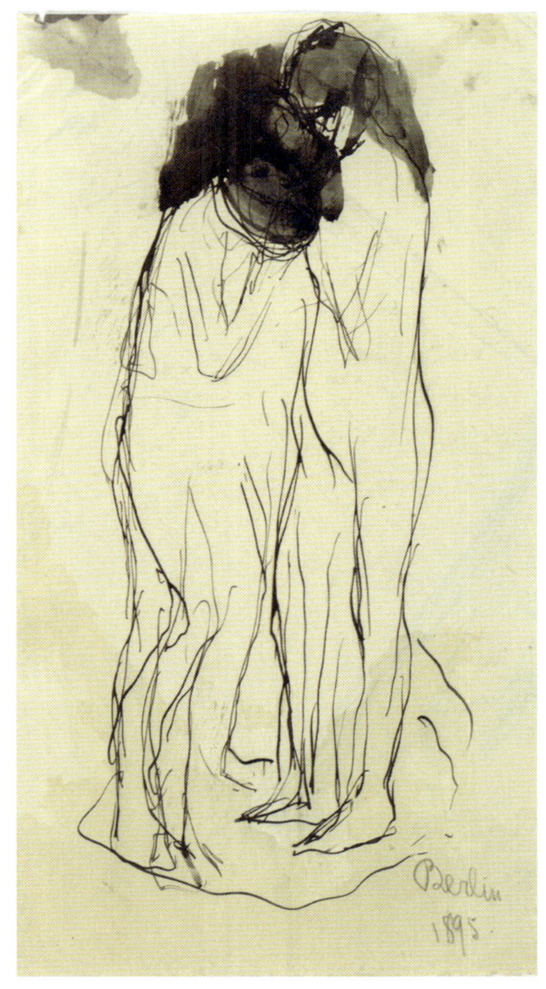

Cat. 65
Gustav Vigeland
Man and Woman, 1895

Cat. 66
Gustav Vigeland
People Standing, 1895

Cat. 67
Gustav Vigeland
Man and Woman, 1895

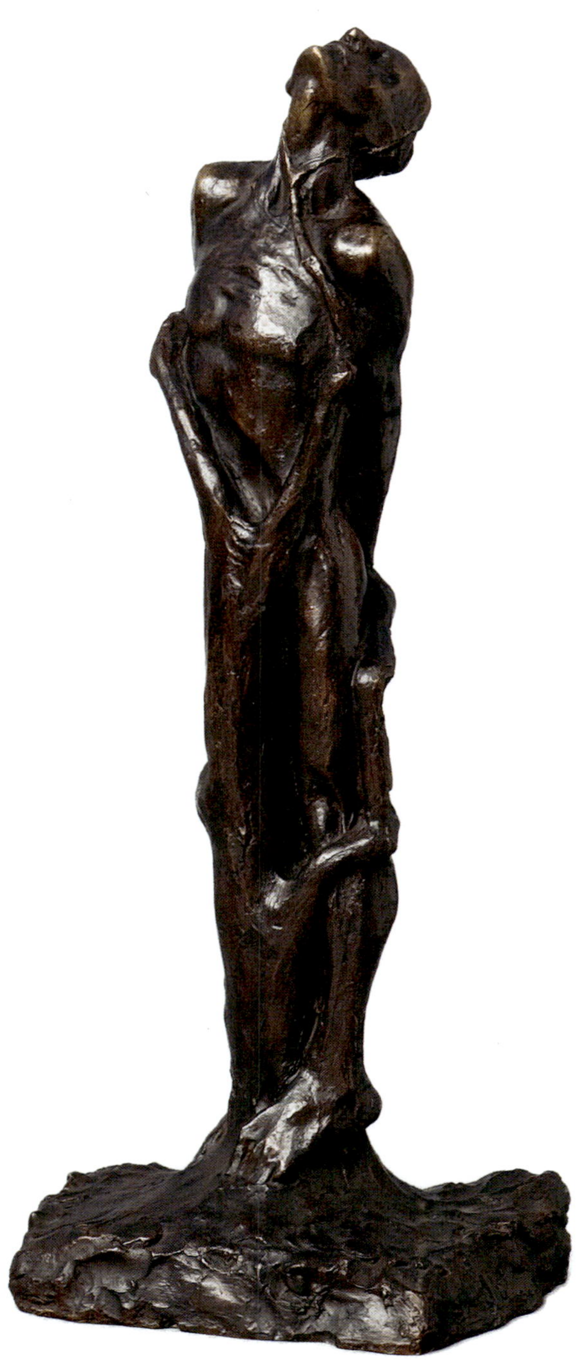

Cat. 68
Gustav Vigeland
Man Embraced by a Tree, 1900

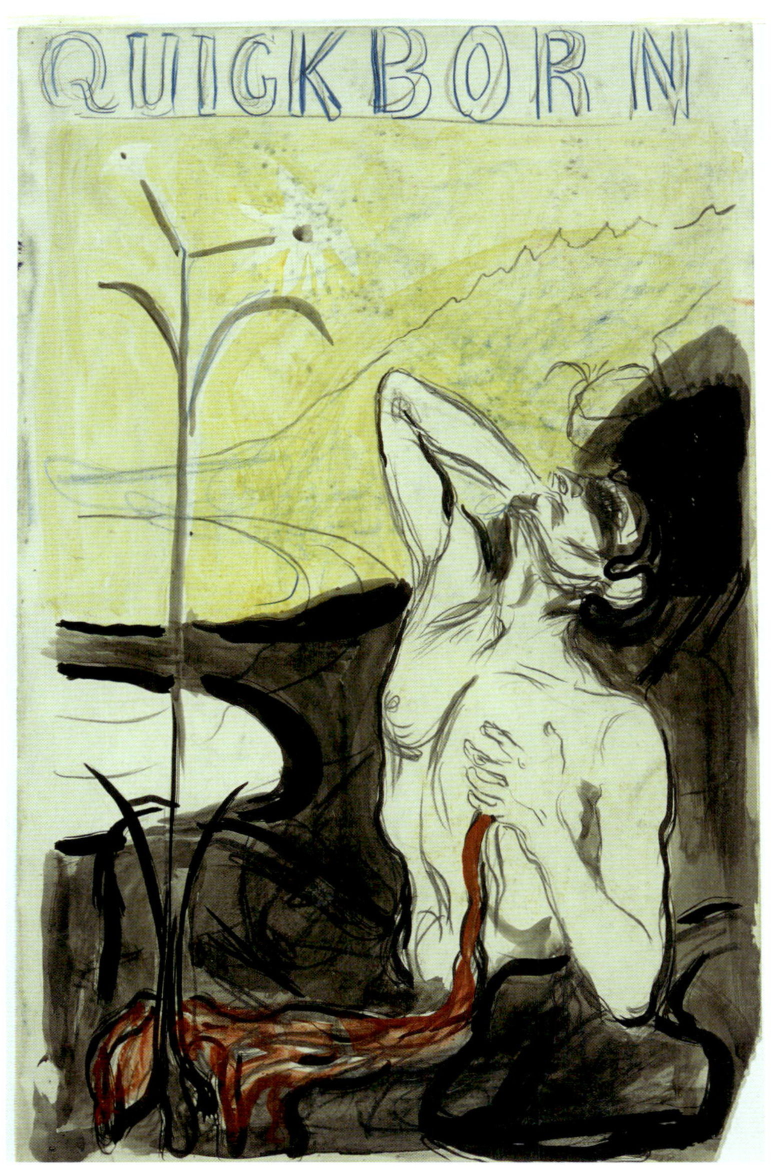

Cat. 69
Edvard Munch
Blossom of Pain. 'Quickborn', 1898

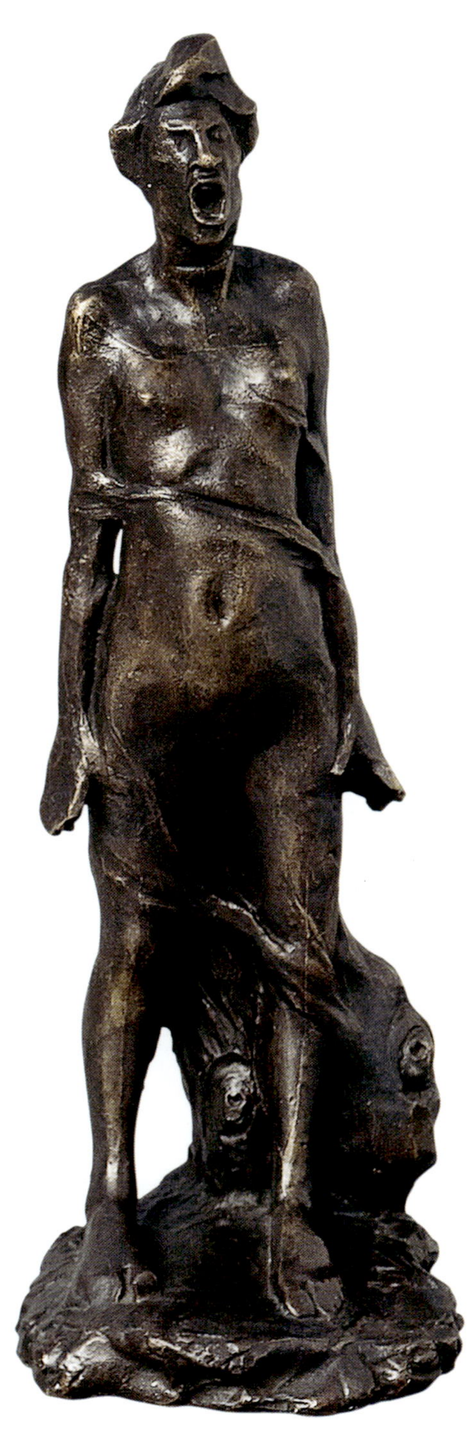

Cat. 70
Gustav Vigeland
Fear, 1892

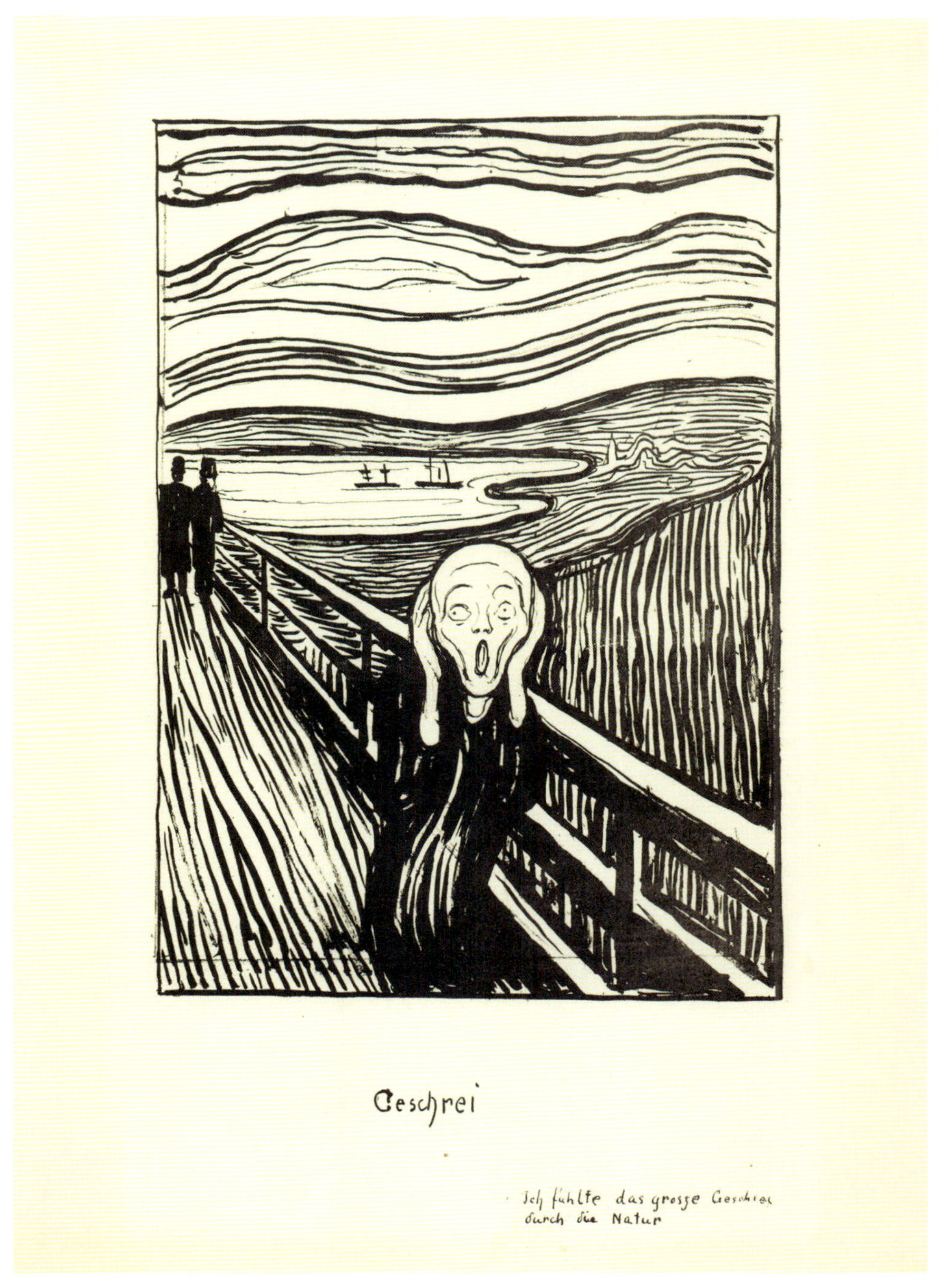

Cat. 71
Edvard Munch
The Scream, 1895

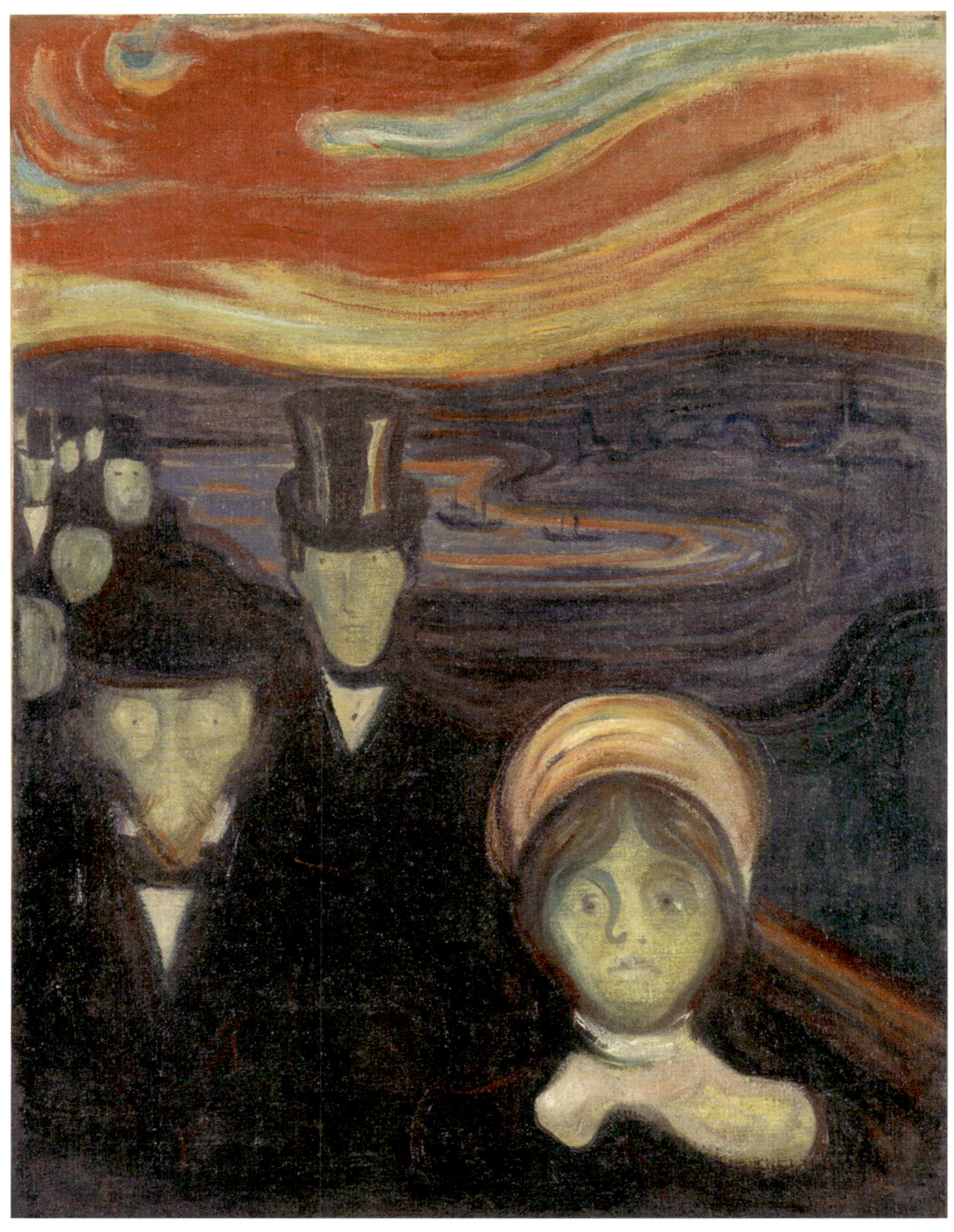

Cat. 72
Edvard Munch
Angst, 1894

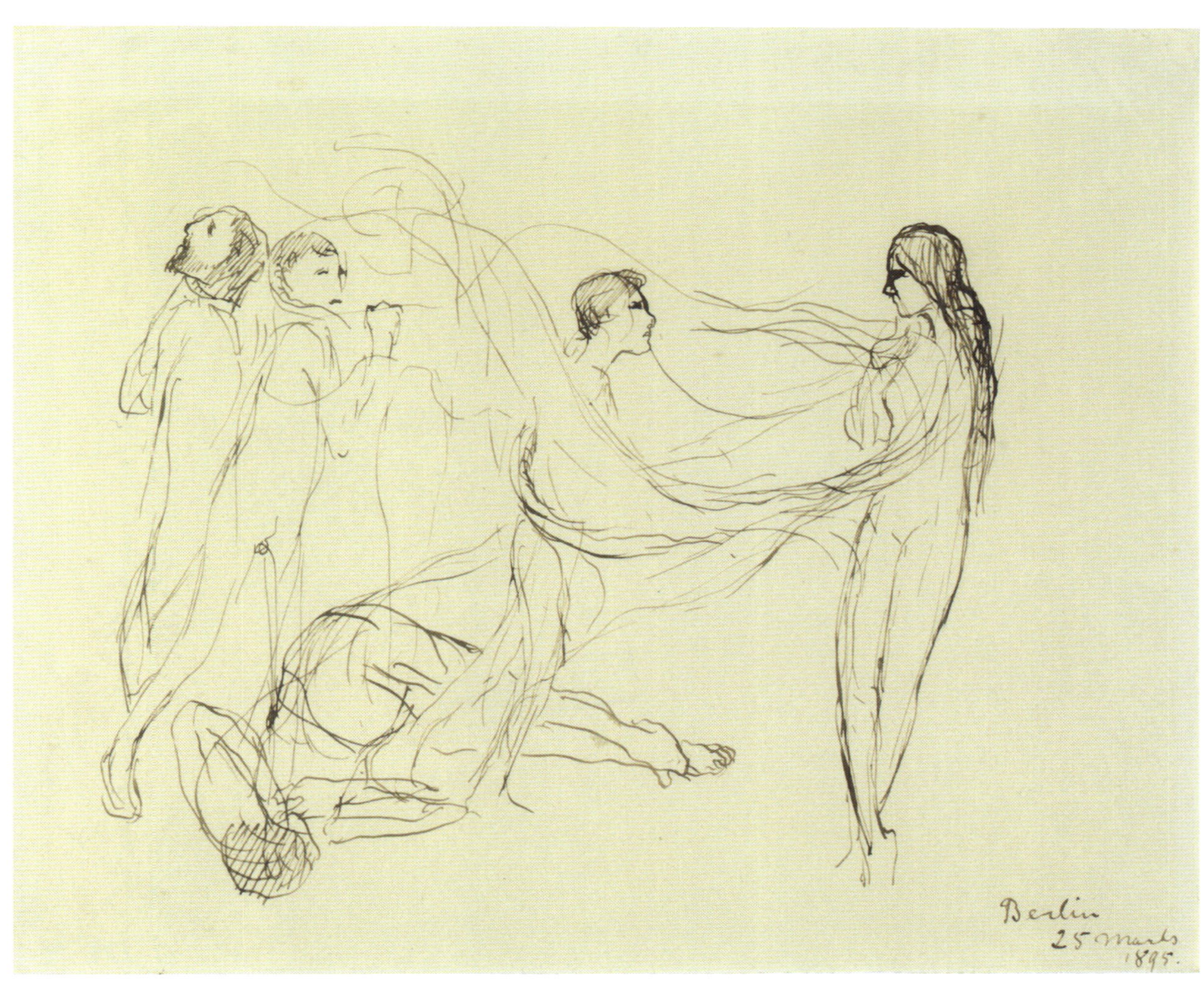

Cat. 73
Gustav Vigeland
Attraction, 1895

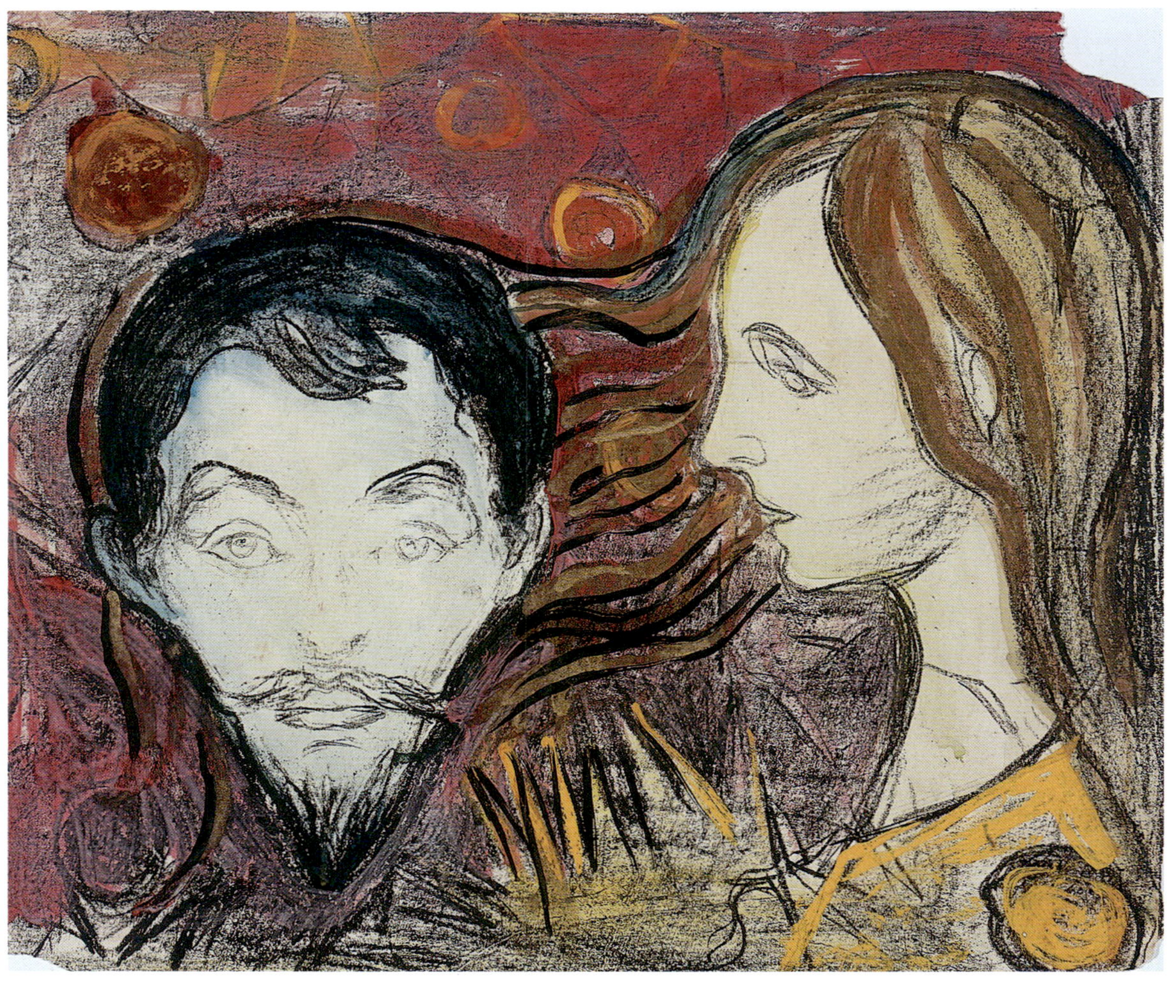

Cat. 74
Edvard Munch
Man's Head in Woman's Hair, 1896–97

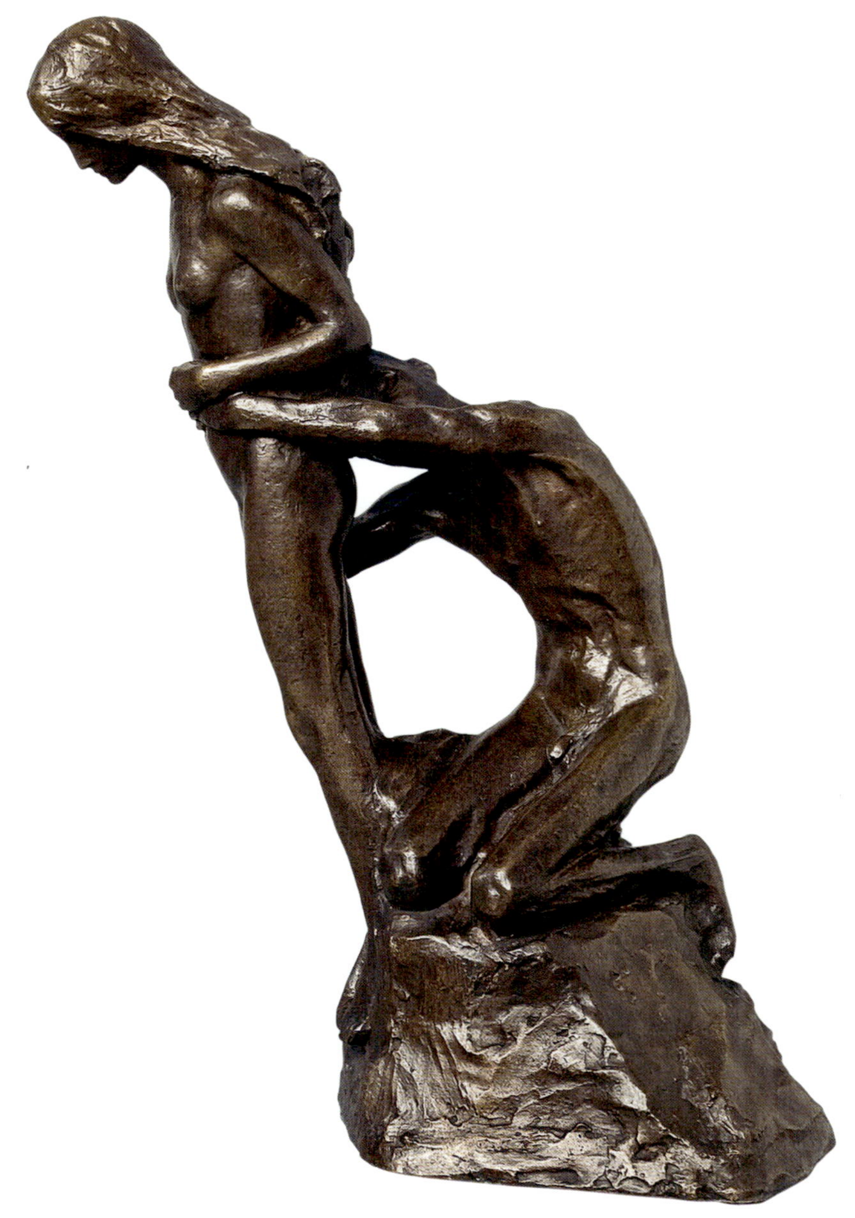

Cat. 75
Gustav Vigeland
Orpheus and Eurydice II, 1899

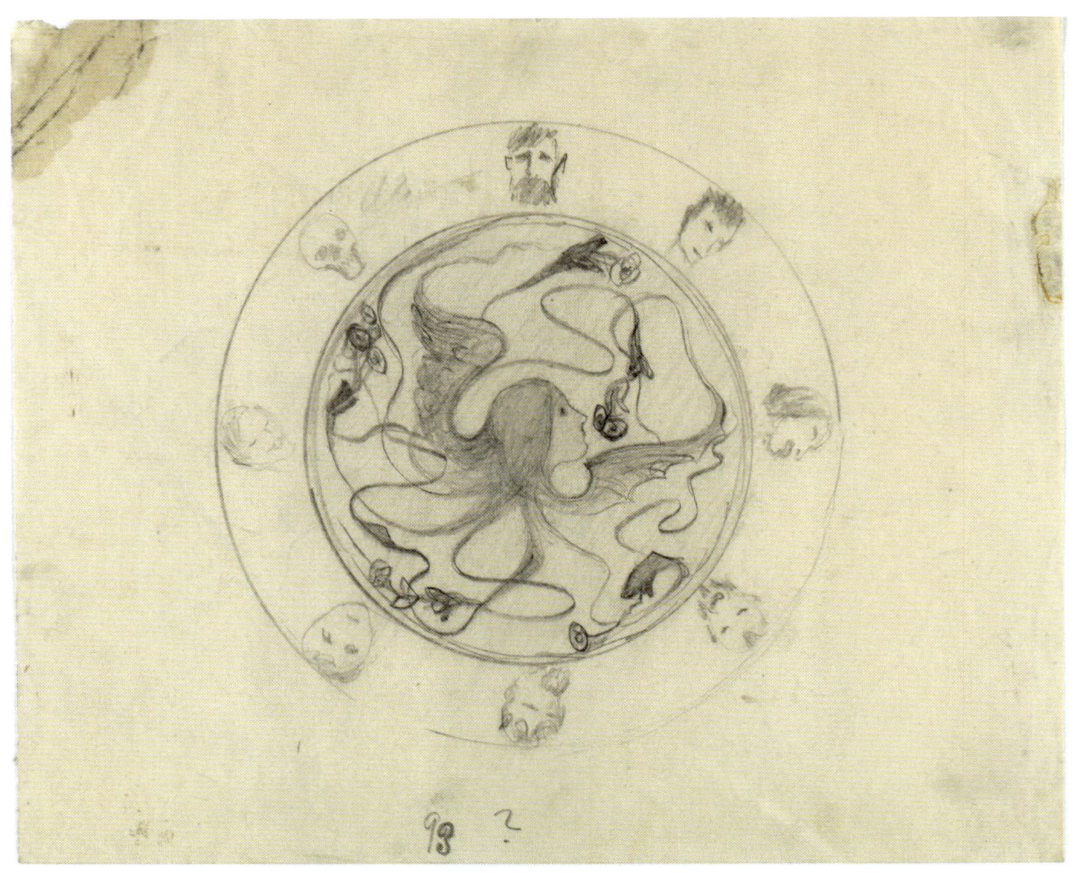

Cat. 76
Gustav Vigeland
Medusa, prob. 1893

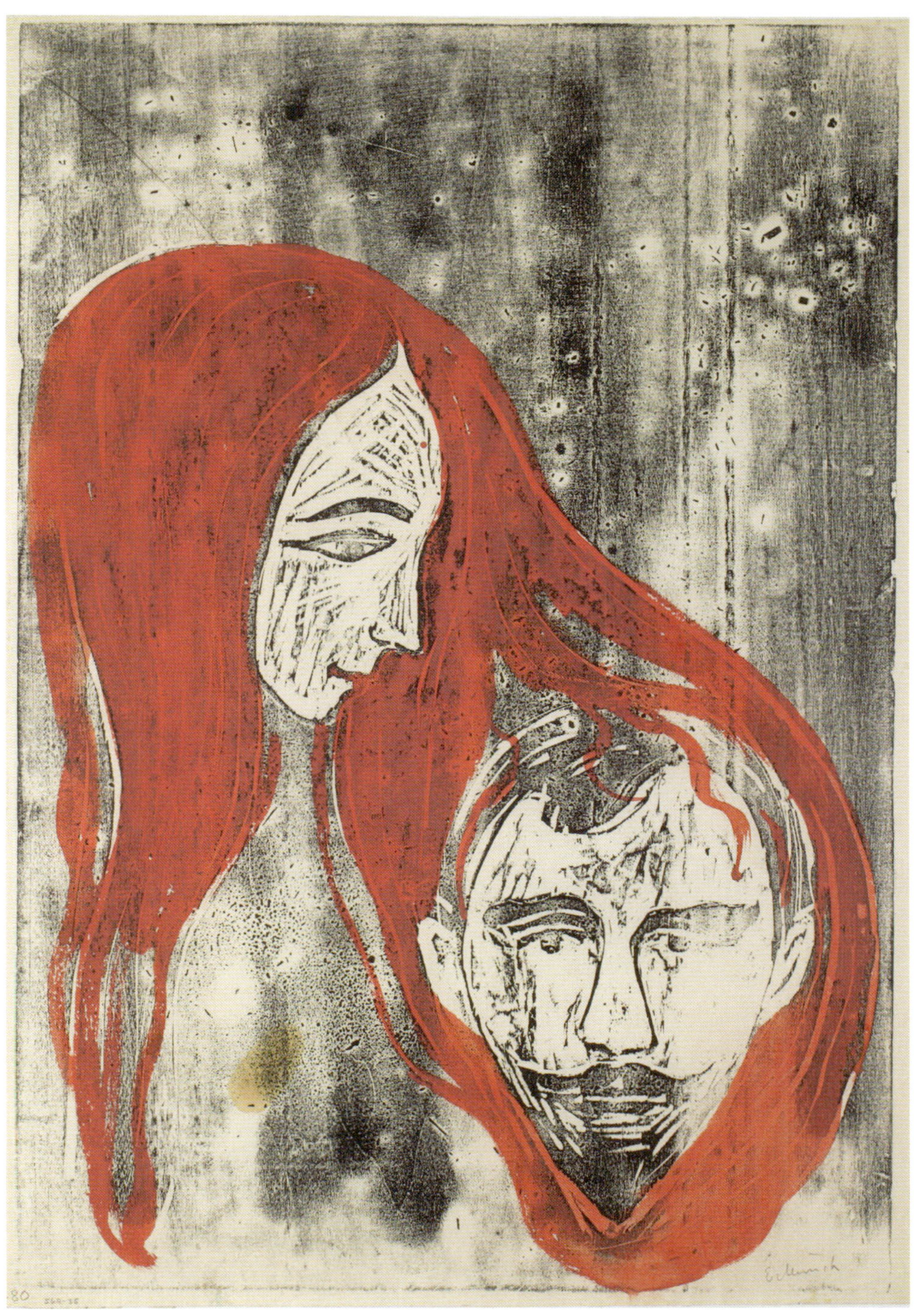

Cat. 77
Edvard Munch
Man's Head in Woman's Hair, 1896

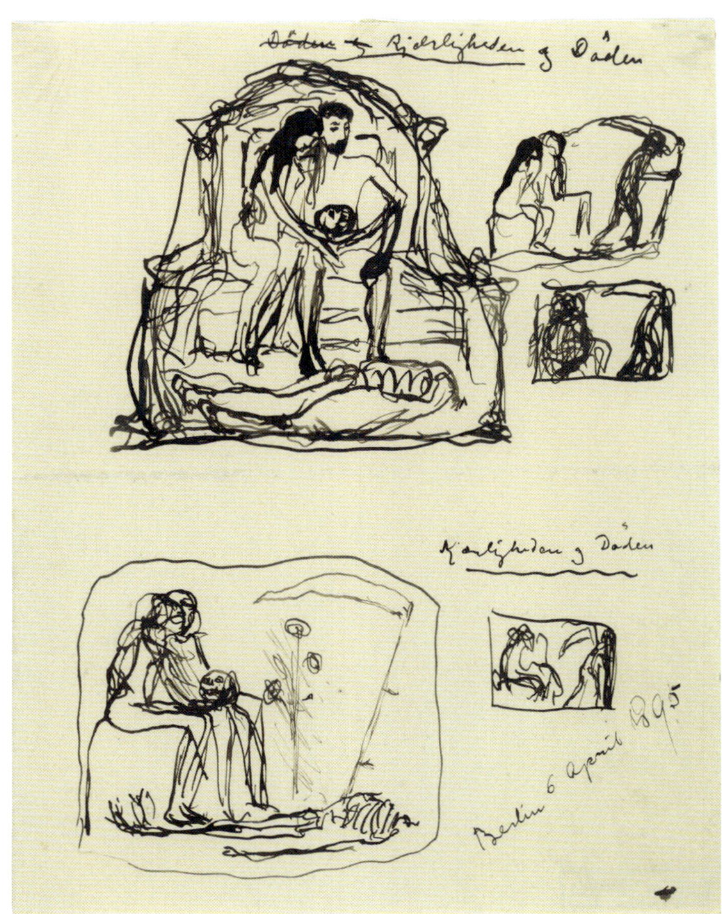

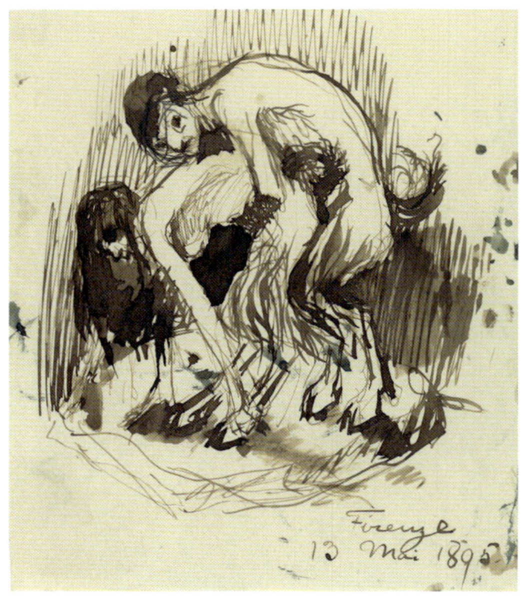

Cat. 78
Gustav Vigeland
Love and Death, 1895

Cat. 79
Gustav Vigeland
Copulating Fauns, 1895

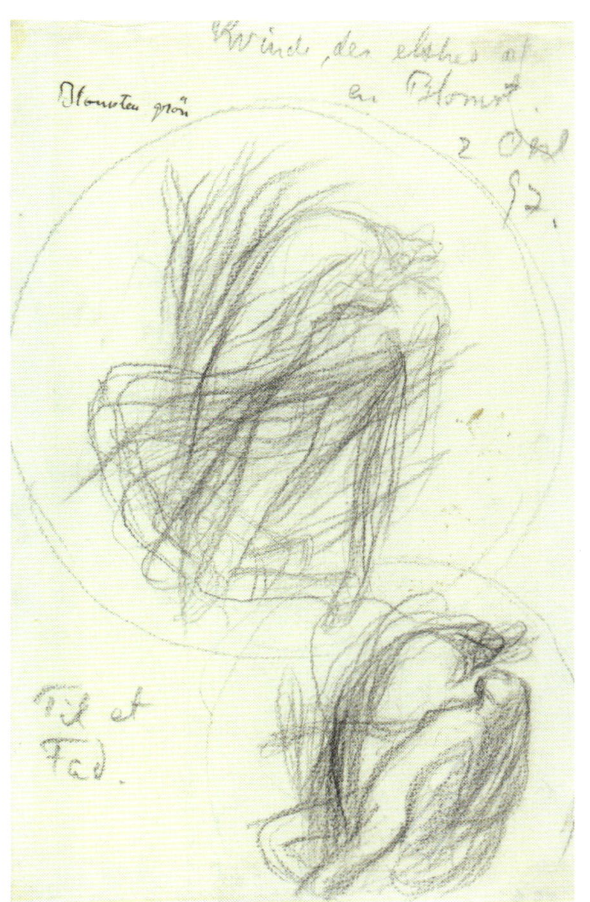

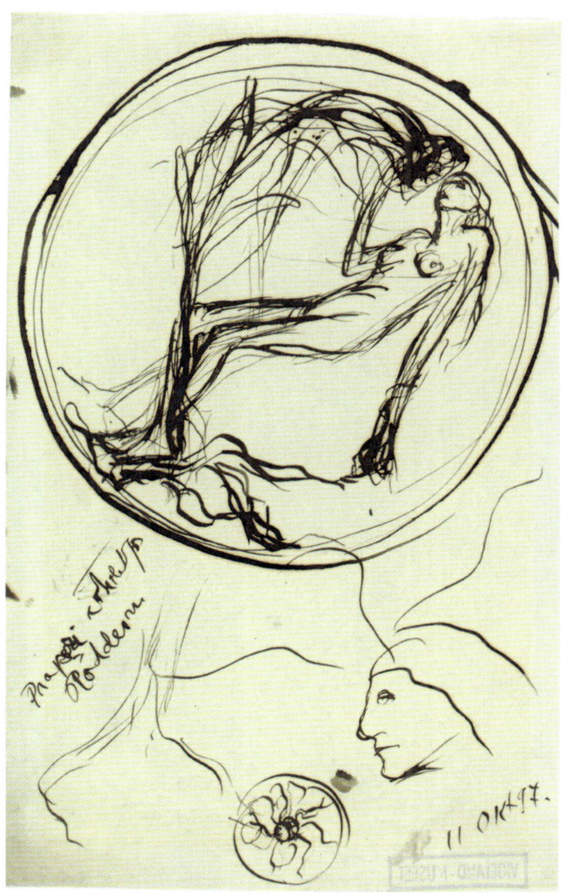

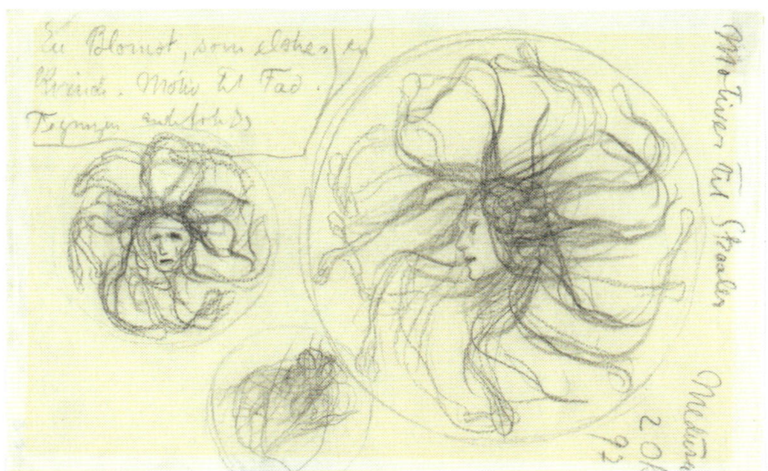

Cat. 80
Gustav Vigeland
*Woman Being Made Love to
by a Flower*, 1897

Cat. 81
Gustav Vigeland
Woman and Flower, 1897

Cat. 82
Gustav Vigeland
Medusa, 1897

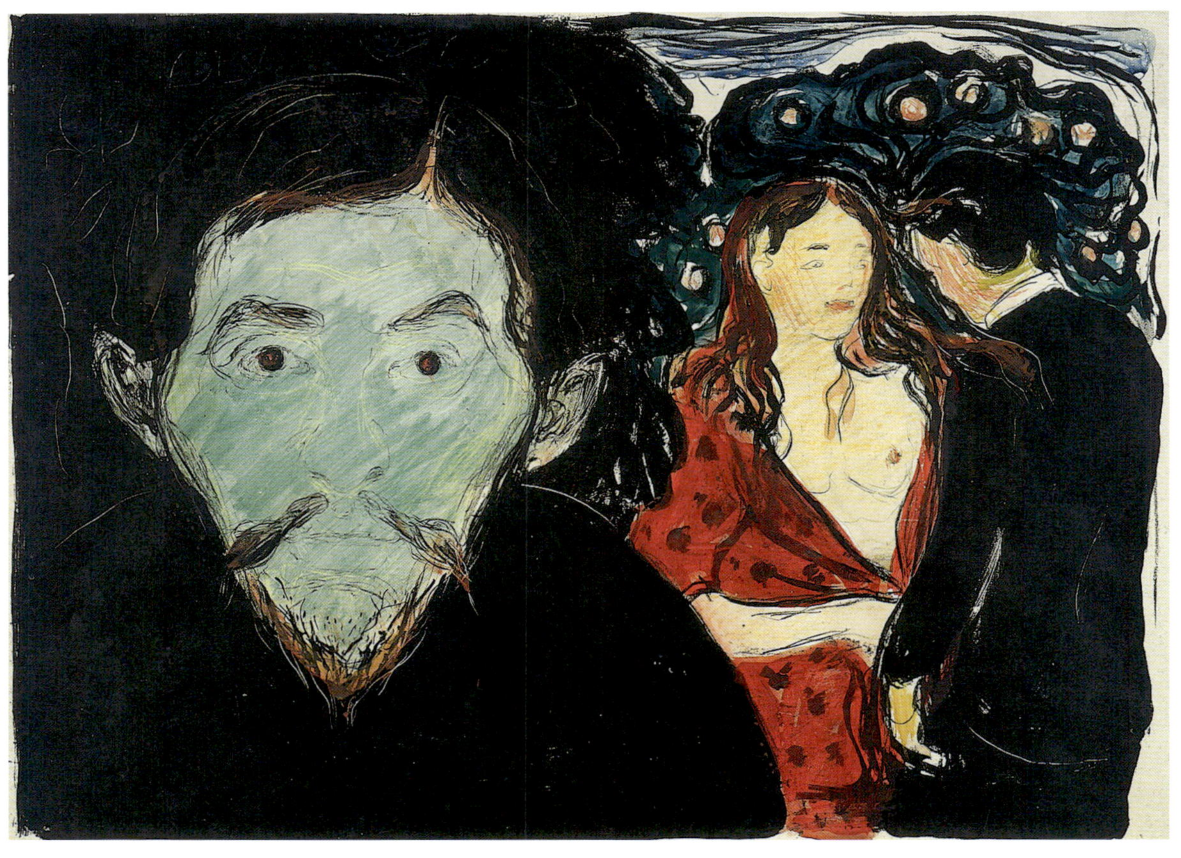

Cat. 83
Edvard Munch
Jealousy I, 1896

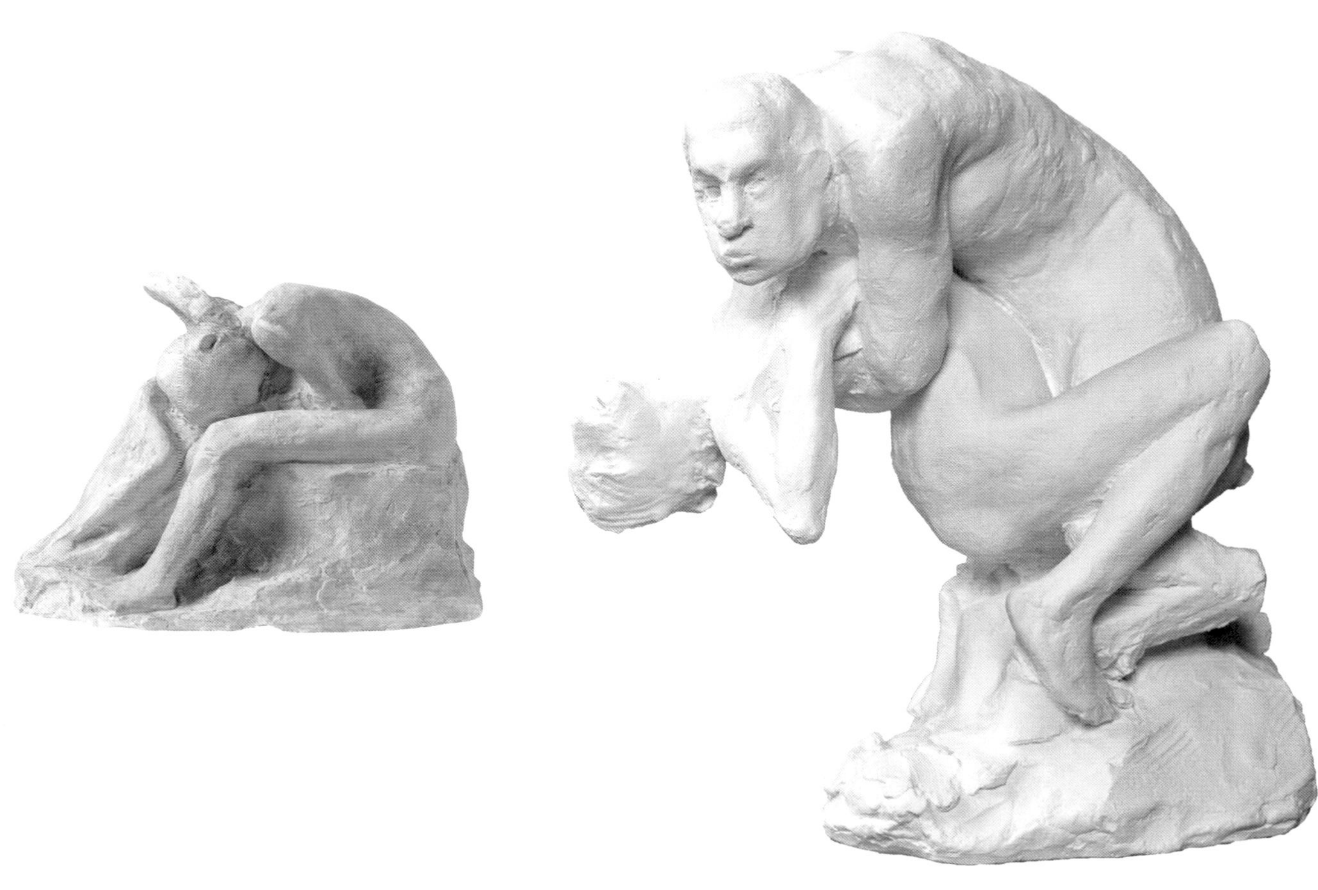

Cat. 84
Gustav Vigeland
Leda and the Swan, 1900

Cat. 85
Gustav Vigeland
Woman and Faun, prob. 1893

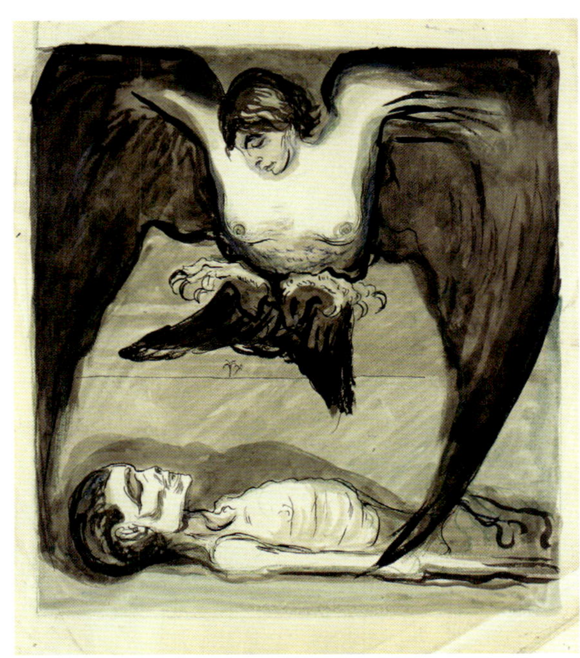

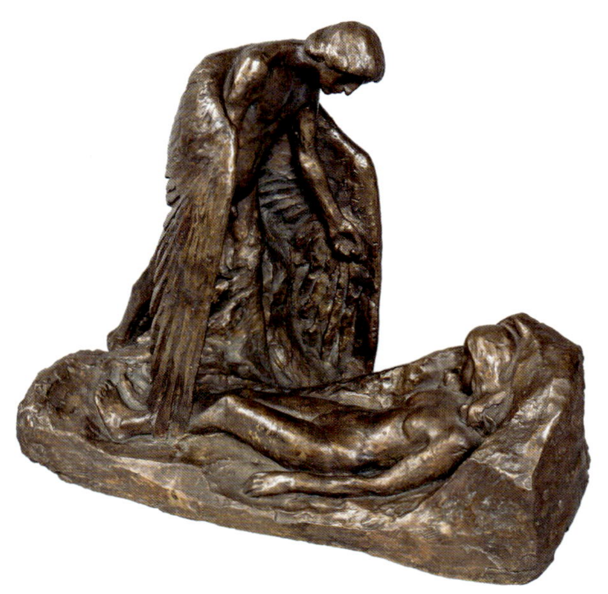

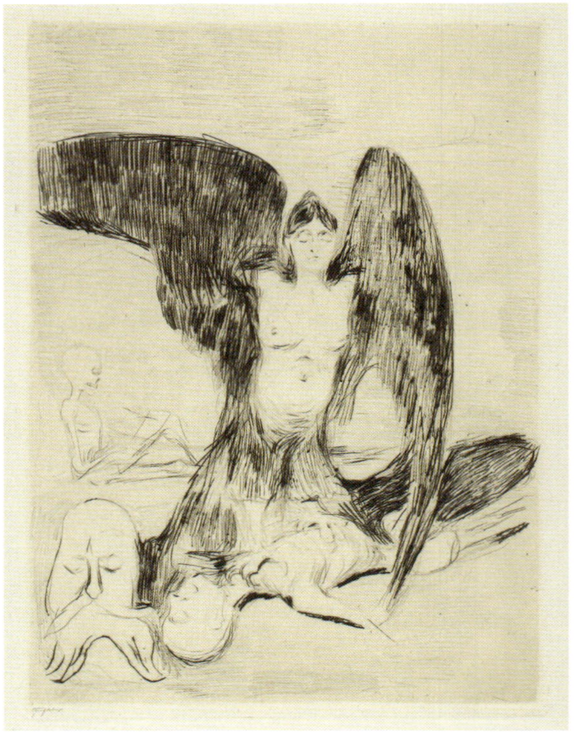

Cat. 86
Gustav Vigeland
Cupid and Psyche, 1898

Cat. 87
Edvard Munch
Harpy, 1898

Cat. 88
Edvard Munch
Harpy, 1894

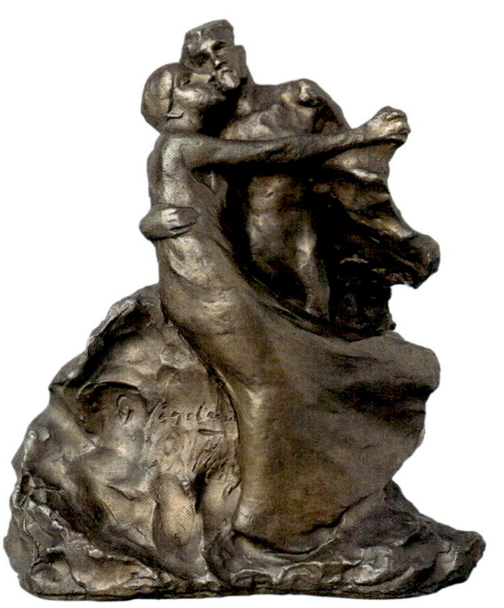

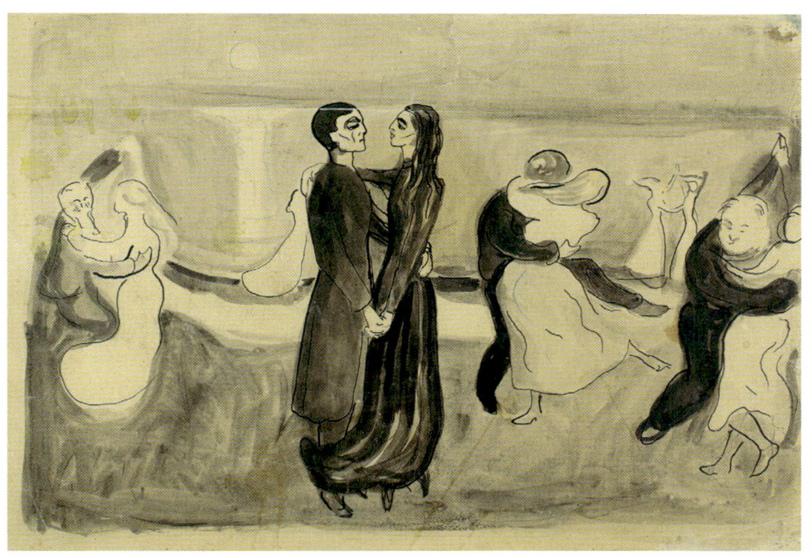

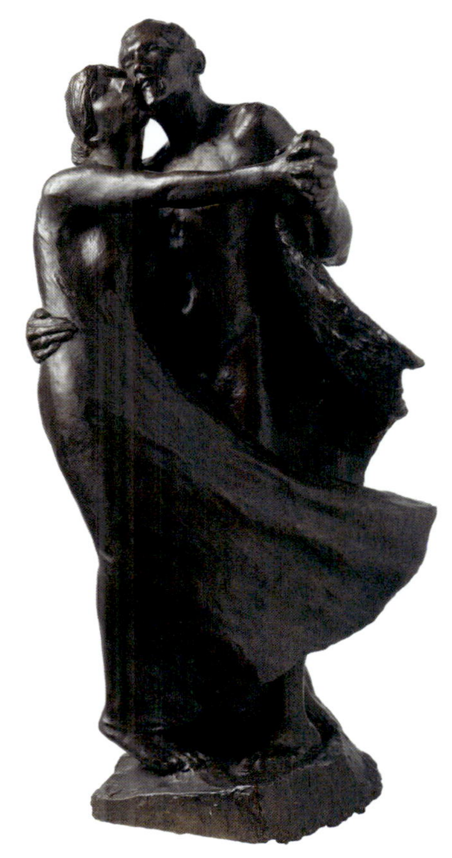

Cat. 89
Gustav Vigeland
Dance I, 1893

Cat. 90
Edvard Munch
The Dance of Life, 1899

Cat. 91
Gustav Vigeland
The Waltz, 1896

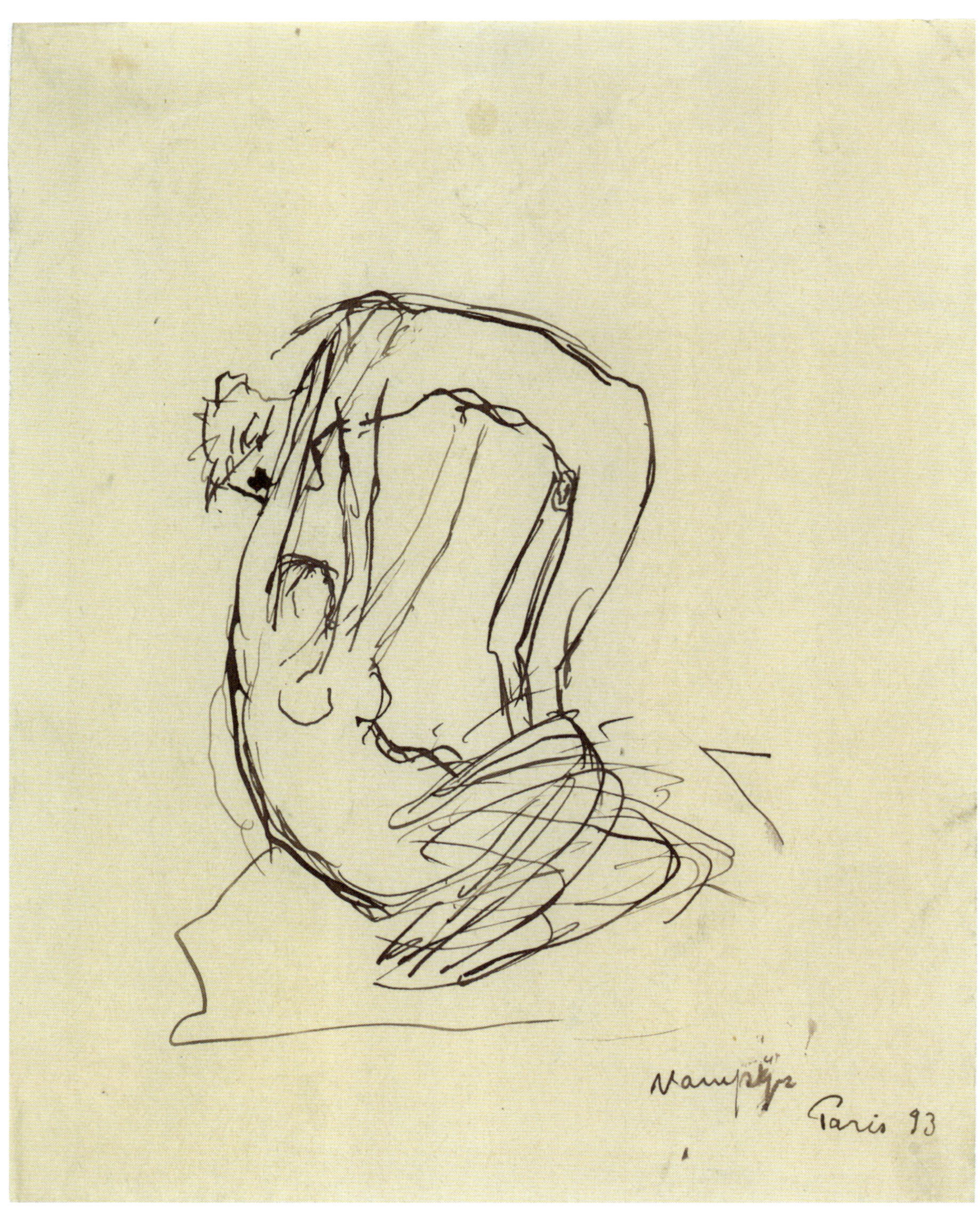

Cat. 92
Gustav Vigeland
Vampire, 1893

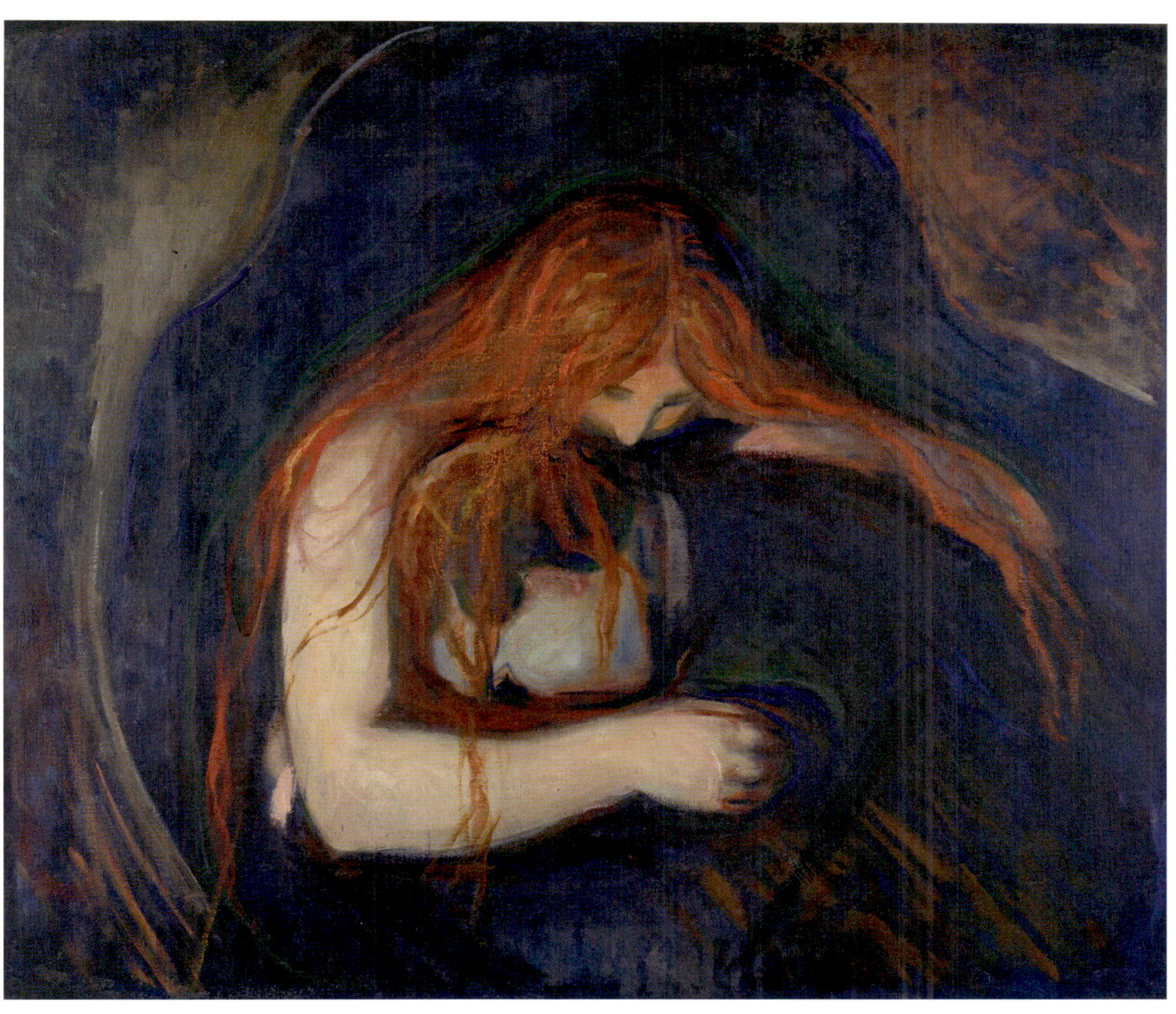

Cat. 93
Edvard Munch
Vampire, 1893–94

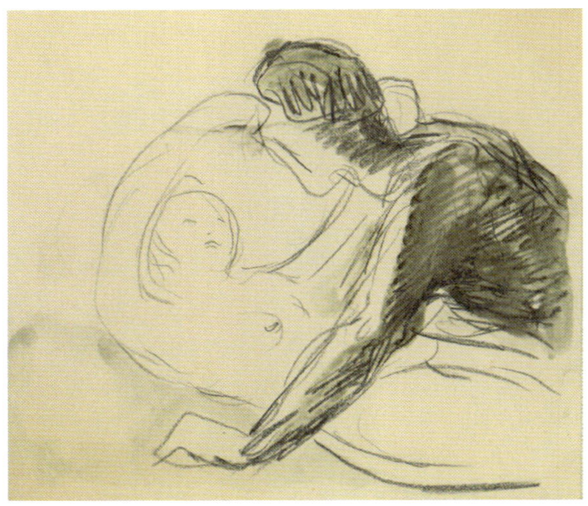

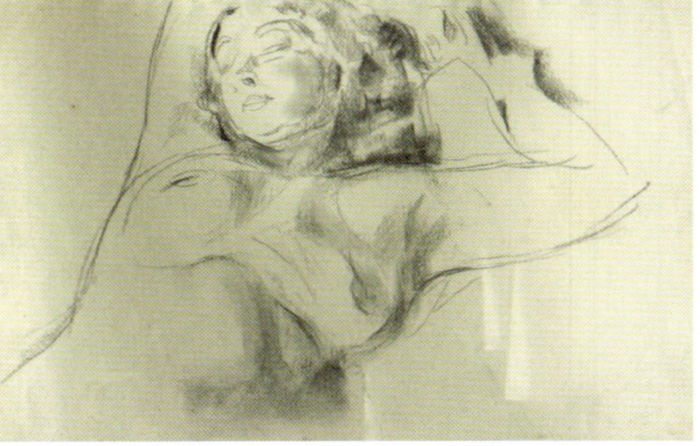

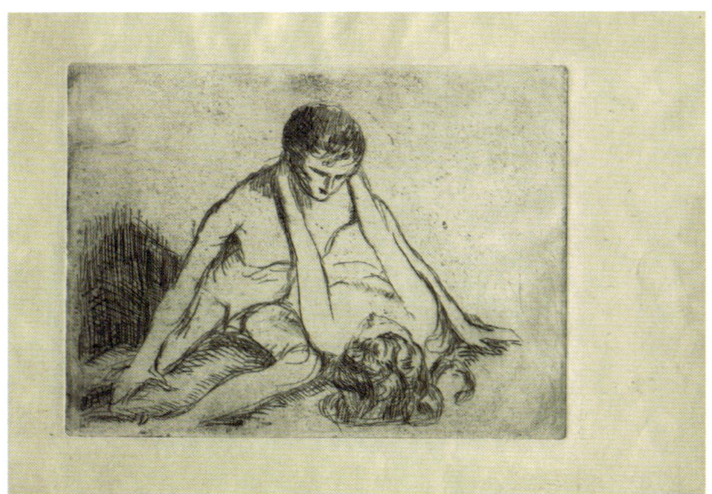

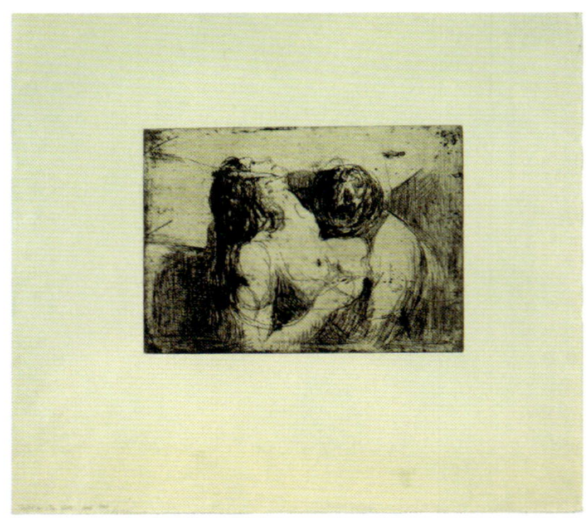

Cat. 94
Edvard Munch
Man and Woman, 1907

Cat. 95
Edvard Munch
The Cat, 1914

Cat. 96
Edvard Munch
Reclining Nude with Closed Eyes, 1911–15

Cat. 97
Edvard Munch
The Bite, 1914

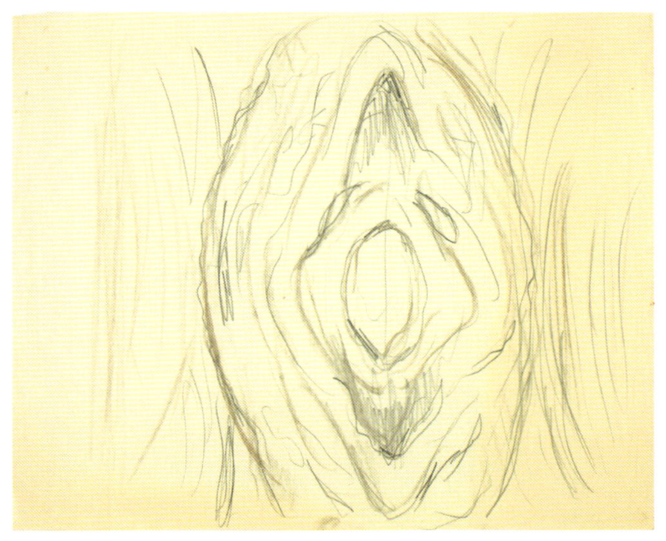

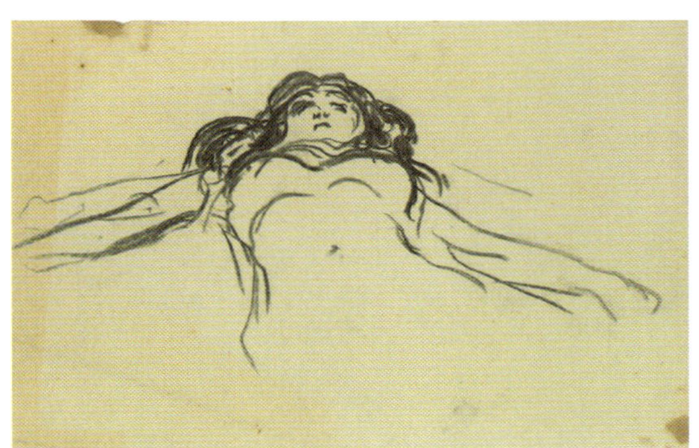

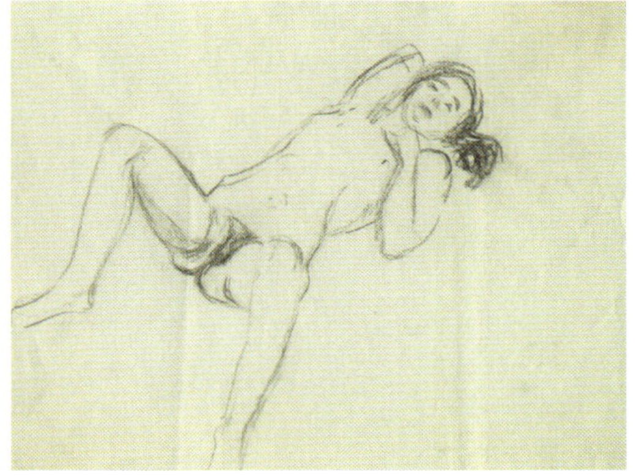

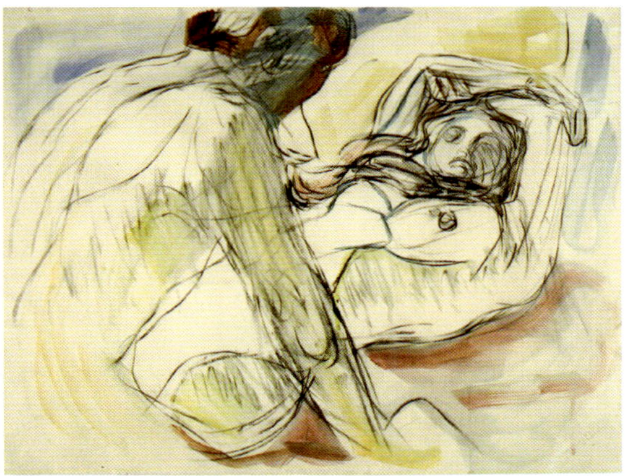

Cat. 98
Edvard Munch
Sketch of a Vulva, 1915–30

Cat. 99
Edvard Munch
Reclining Nude, 1912–15

Cat. 100
Edvard Munch
Reclining Nude, 1911–15

Cat. 101
Edvard Munch
Man and Woman, 1912–15

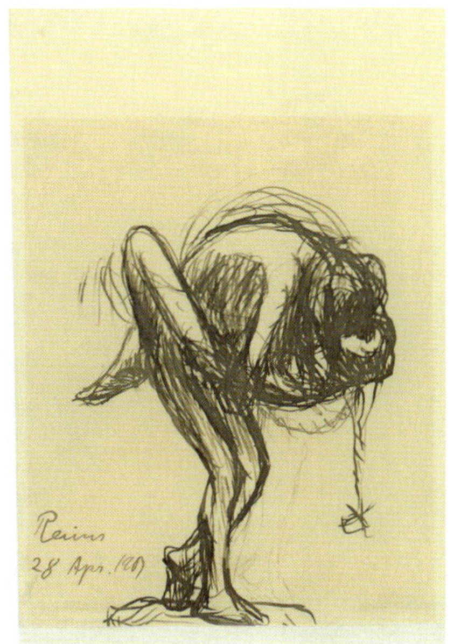

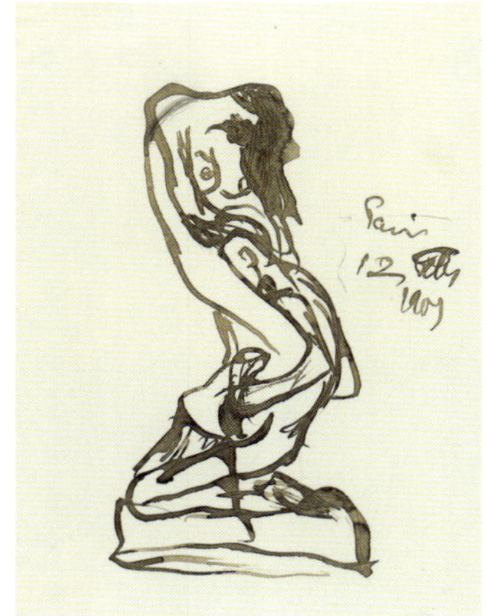

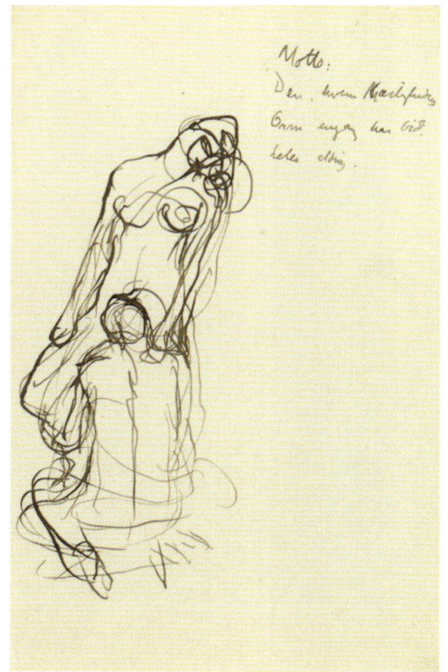

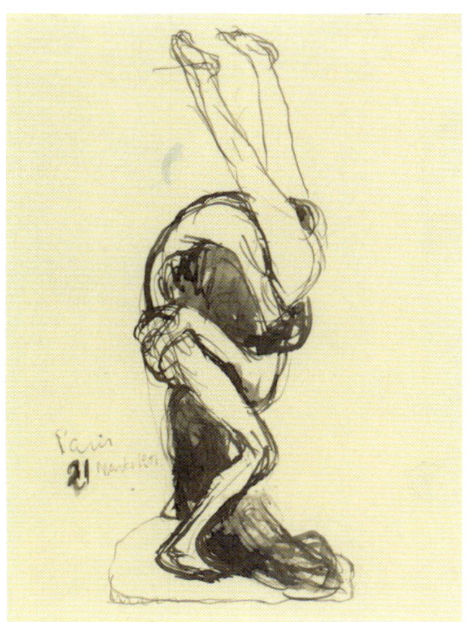

Cat. 102
Gustav Vigeland
Man and Woman, 1901

Cat. 103
Gustav Vigeland
The Serpent of Love (undated)

Cat. 104
Gustav Vigeland:
Man and Woman, 1901

Cat. 105
Gustav Vigeland
Man and Woman, 1901

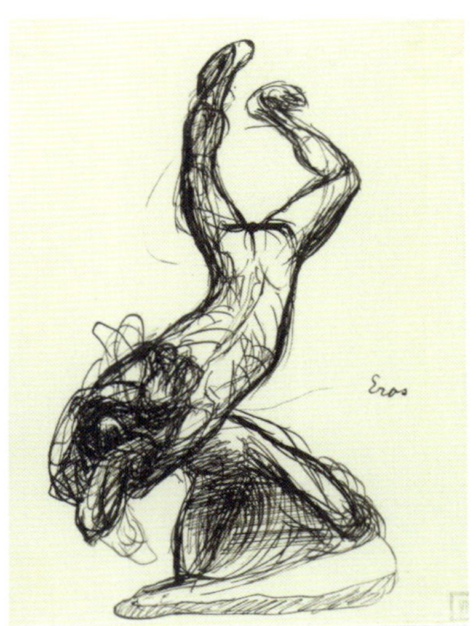

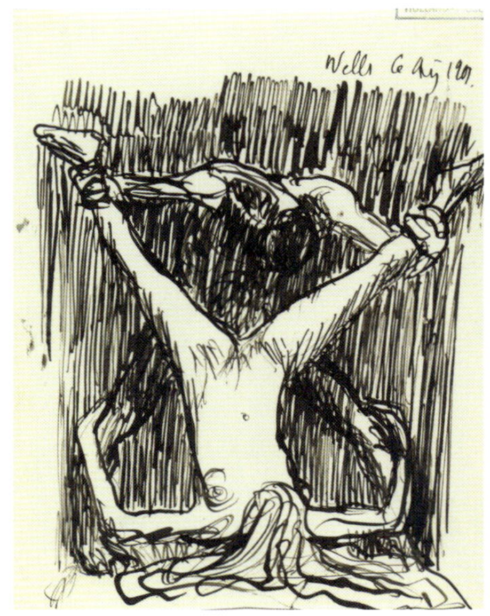

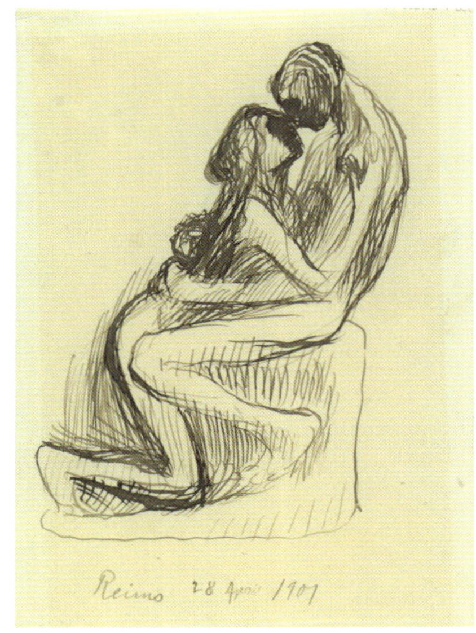

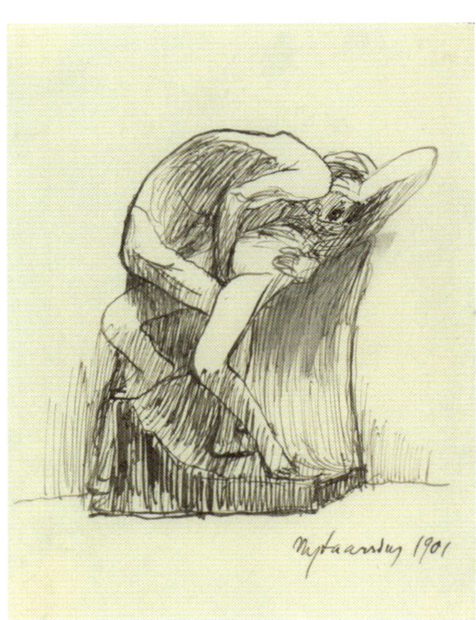

Cat. 106
Gustav Vigeland
Man and Woman, 1901

Cat. 107
Gustav Vigeland
Man and Woman, 1901

Cat. 108
Gustav Vigeland
Eros (undated)

Cat. 109
Gustav Vigeland
Man and Woman, 1901

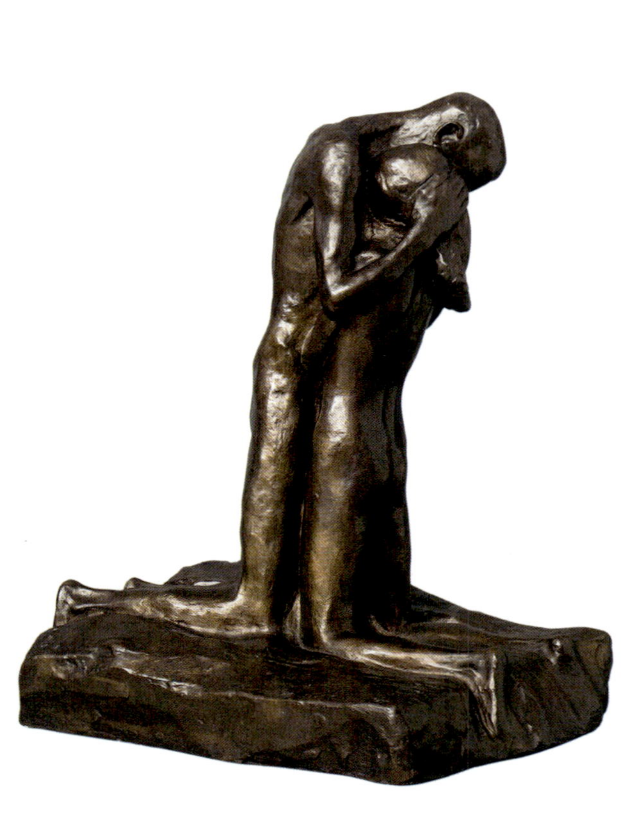

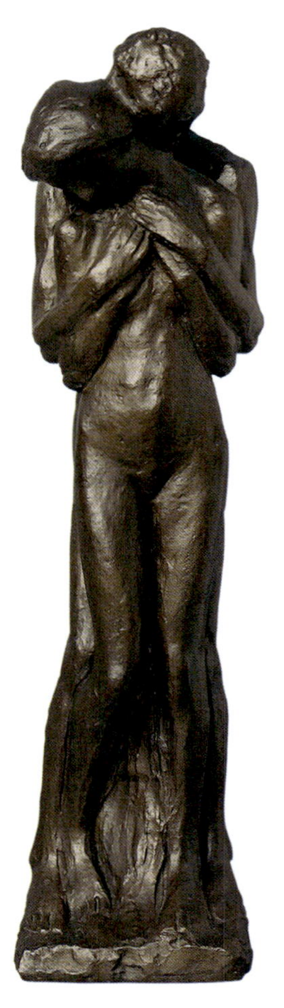

Cat. 110
Gustav Vigeland
Man and Woman, 1899

Cat. 111
Gustav Vigeland
Man and Woman, 1899

Cat. 112
Gustav Vigeland
Man and Woman, 1903

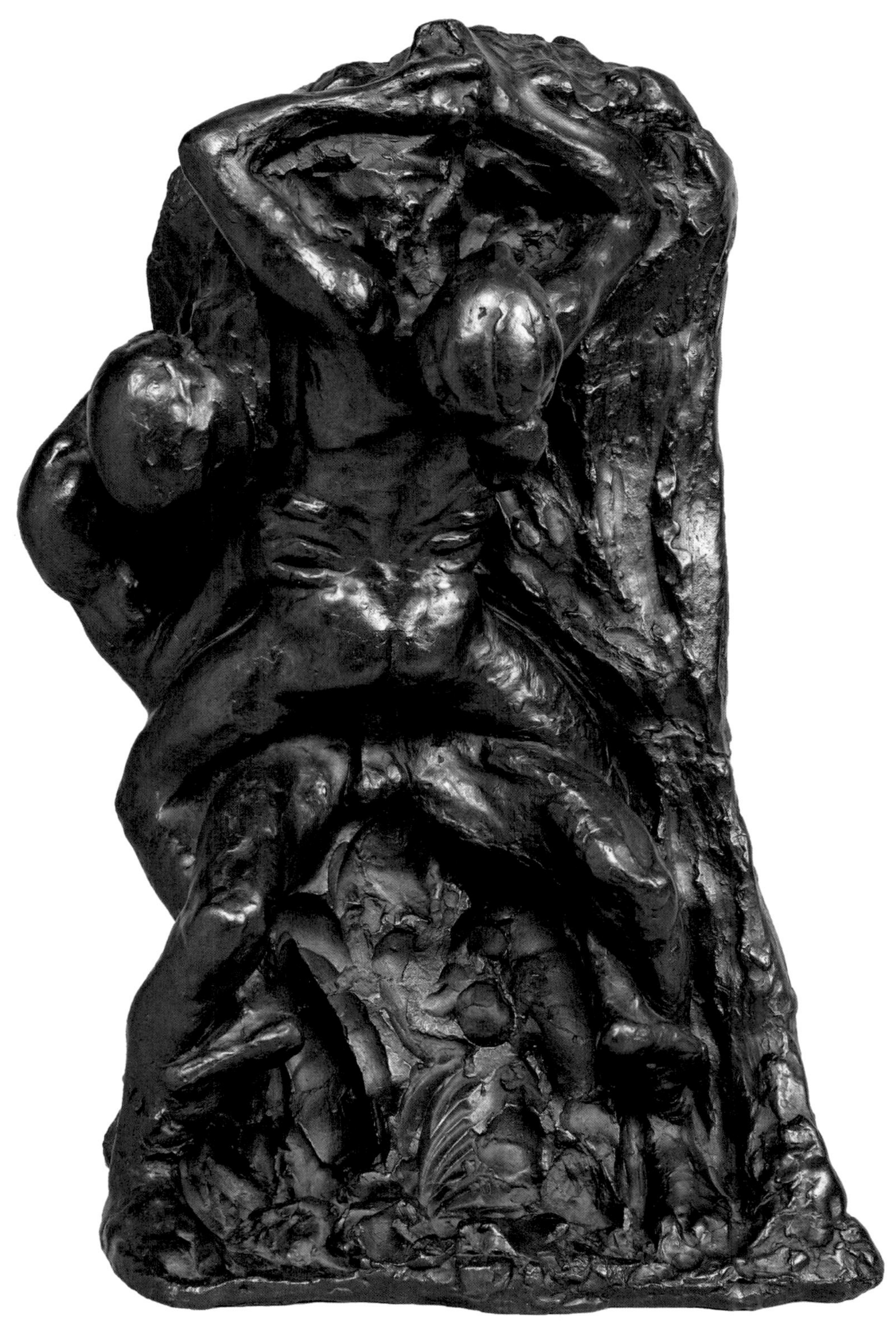

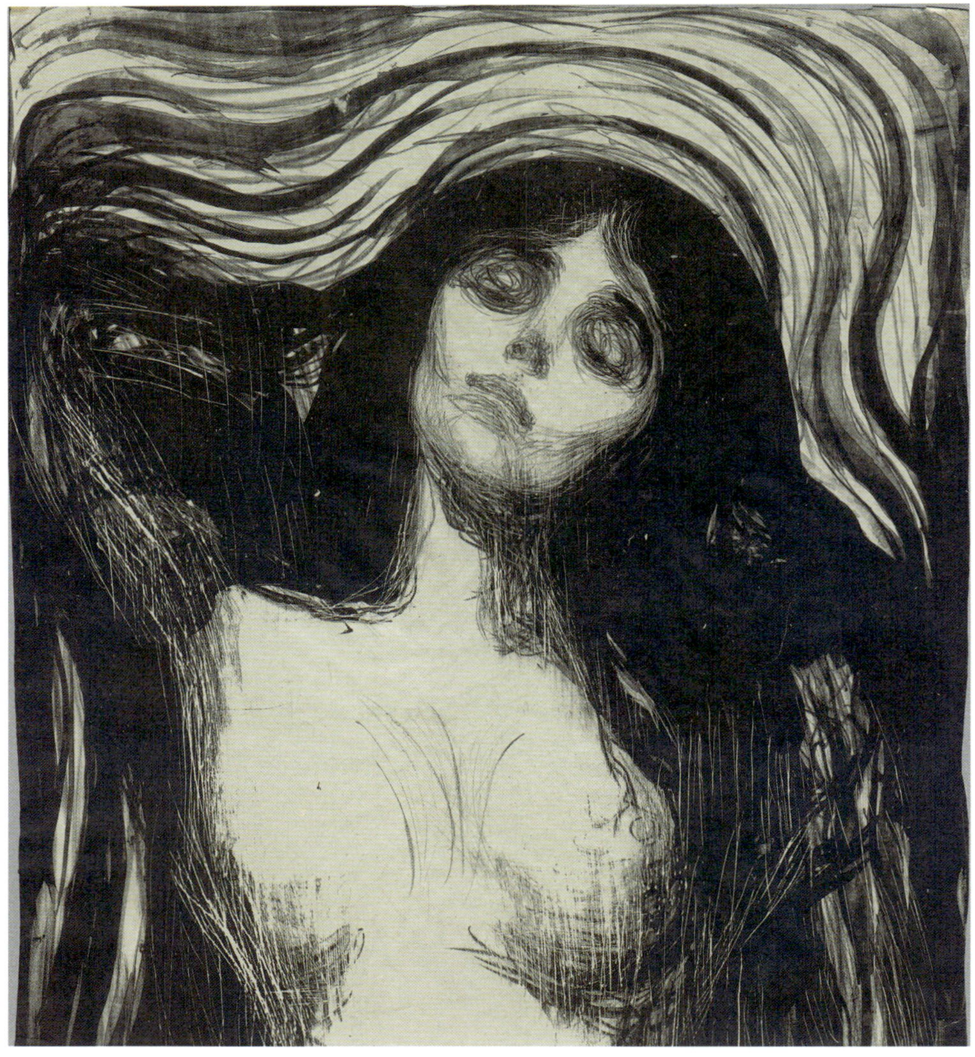

Cat. 113
Edvard Munch
Madonna, 1895/1902

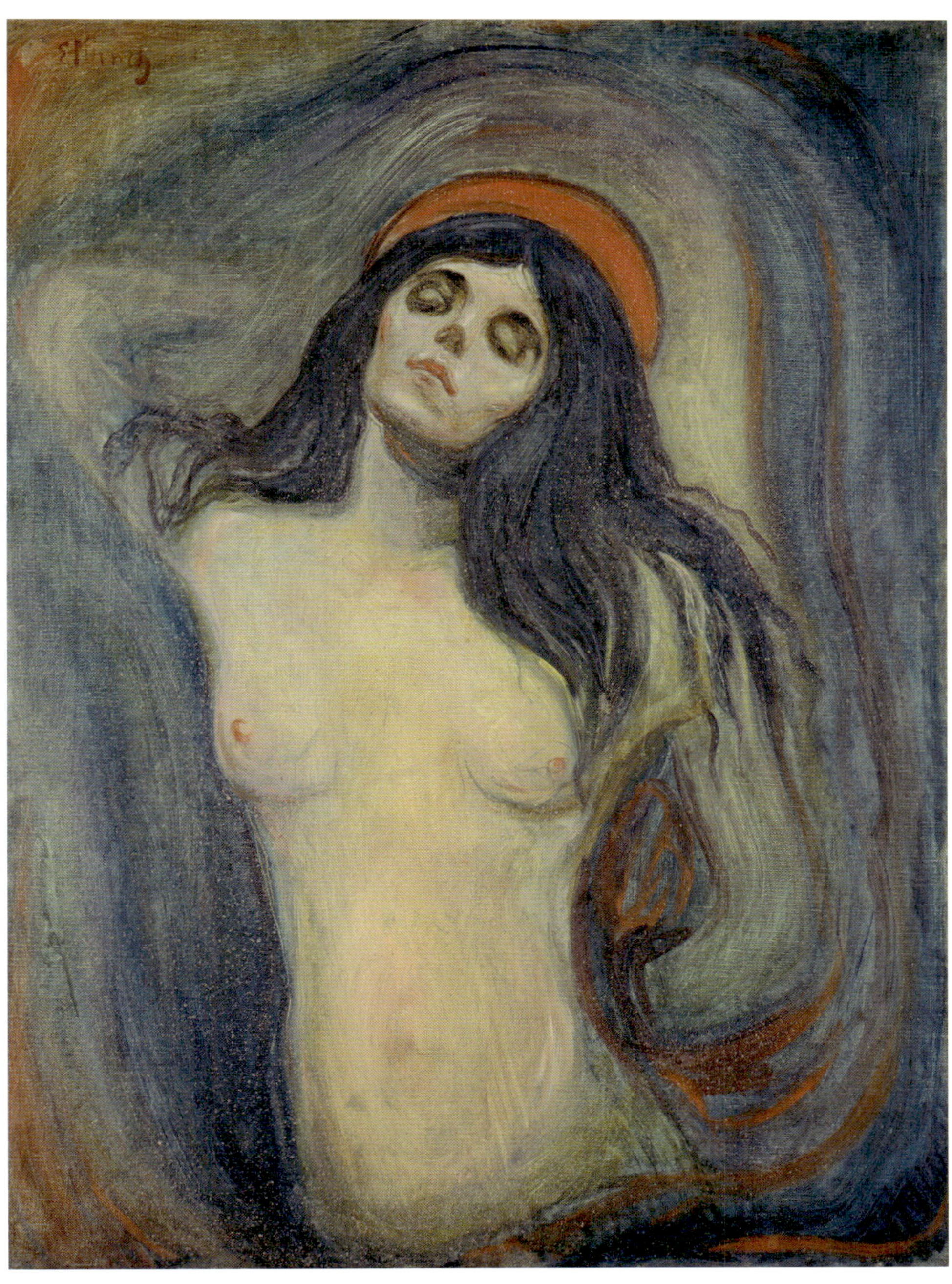

Cat. 114
Edvard Munch
Madonna, 1894

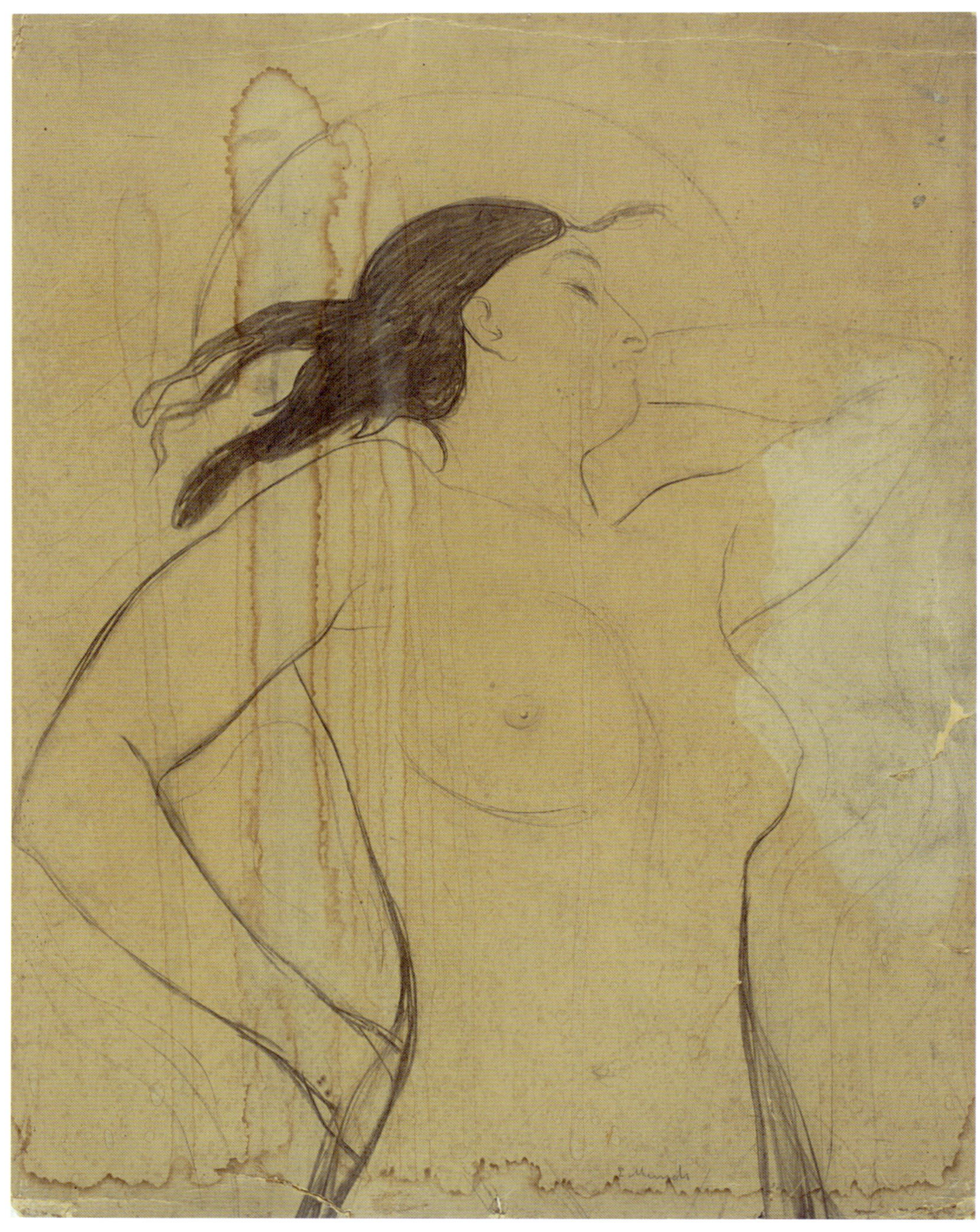

Cat. 115
Edvard Munch
Study for Madonna, 1893–94

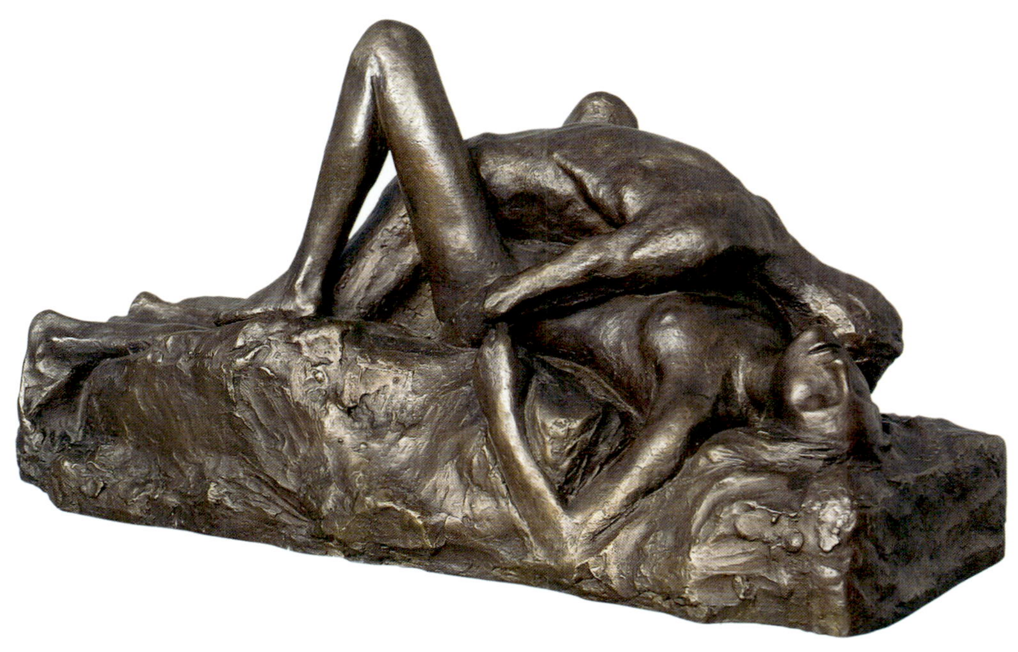

Cat. 116
Gustav Vigeland
Coitus, 1897–98

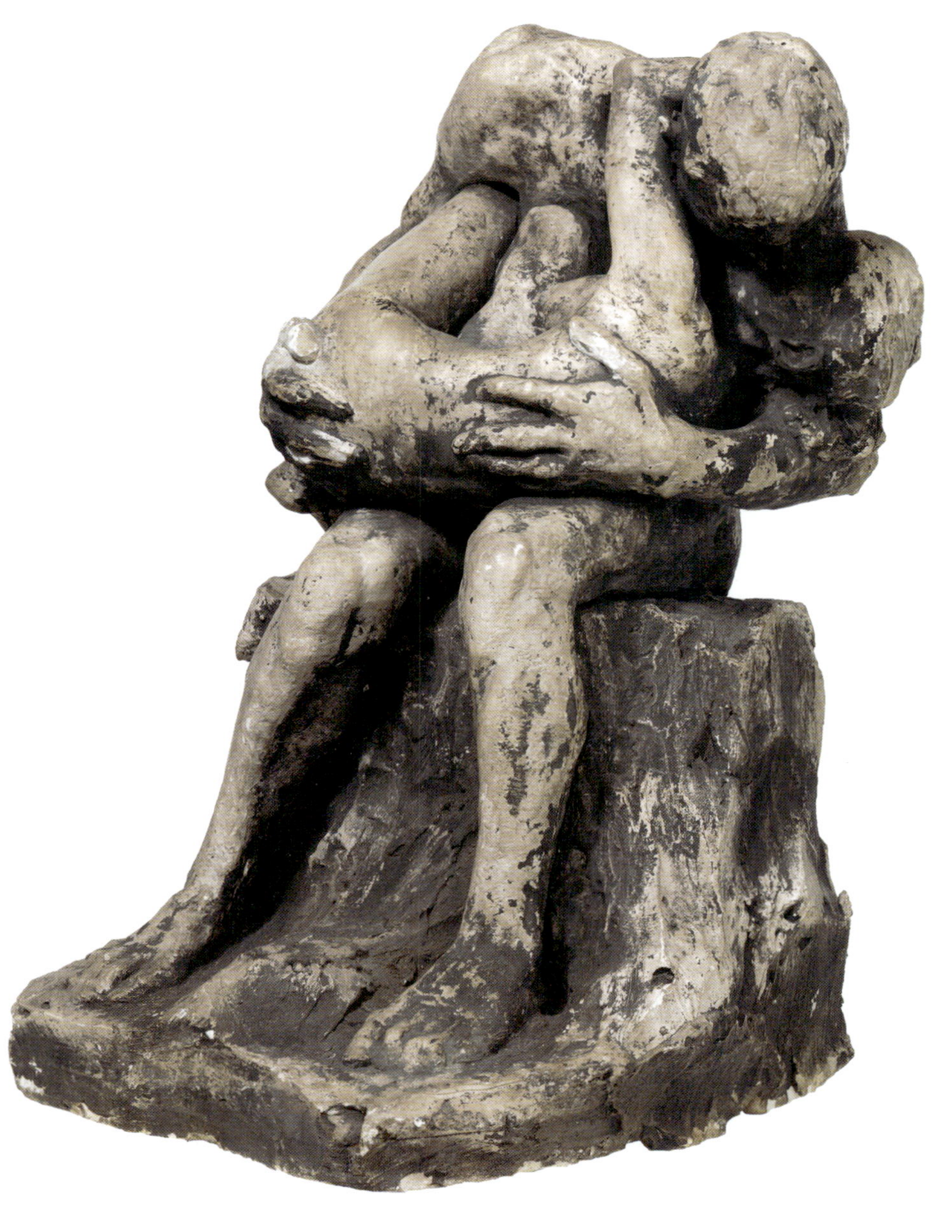

Cat. 117
Gustav Vigeland
Man with a Woman on His Lap I, 1895

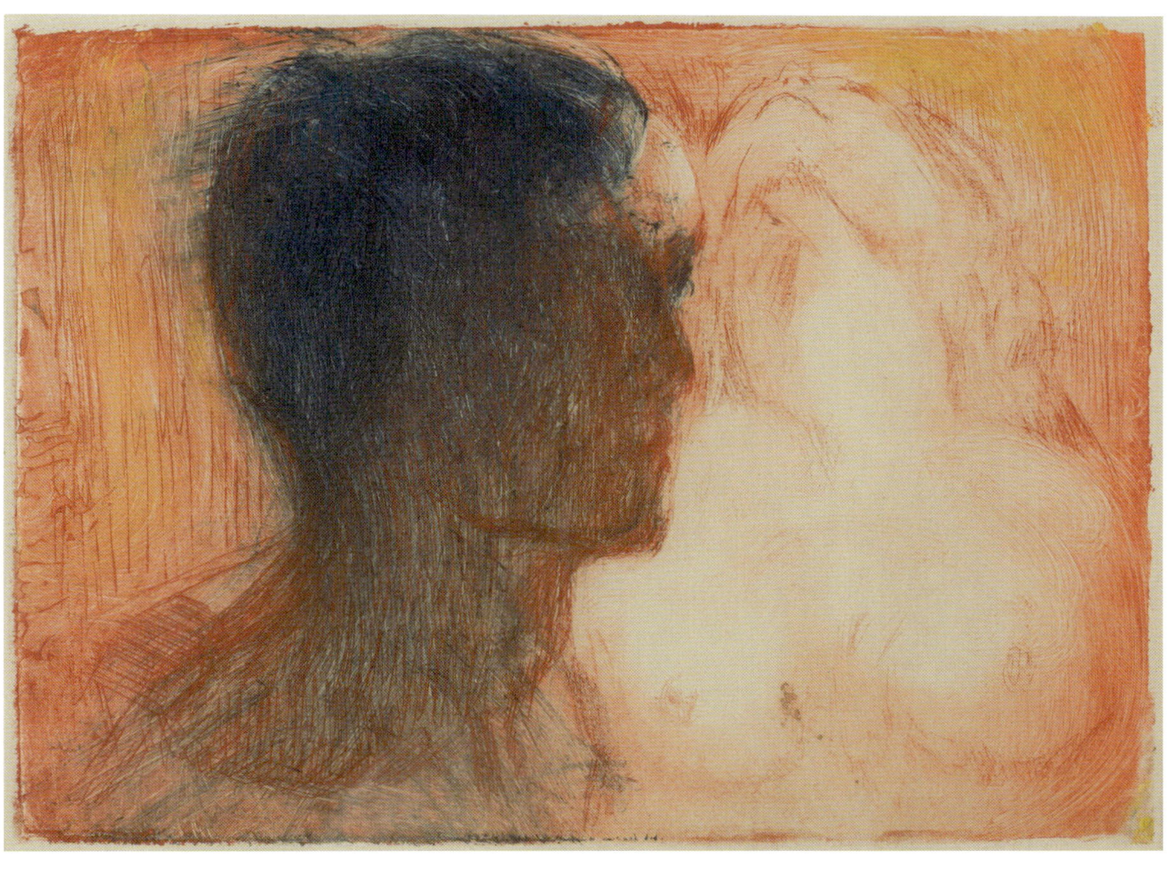

Cat. 118
Edvard Munch
Lovers, 1913

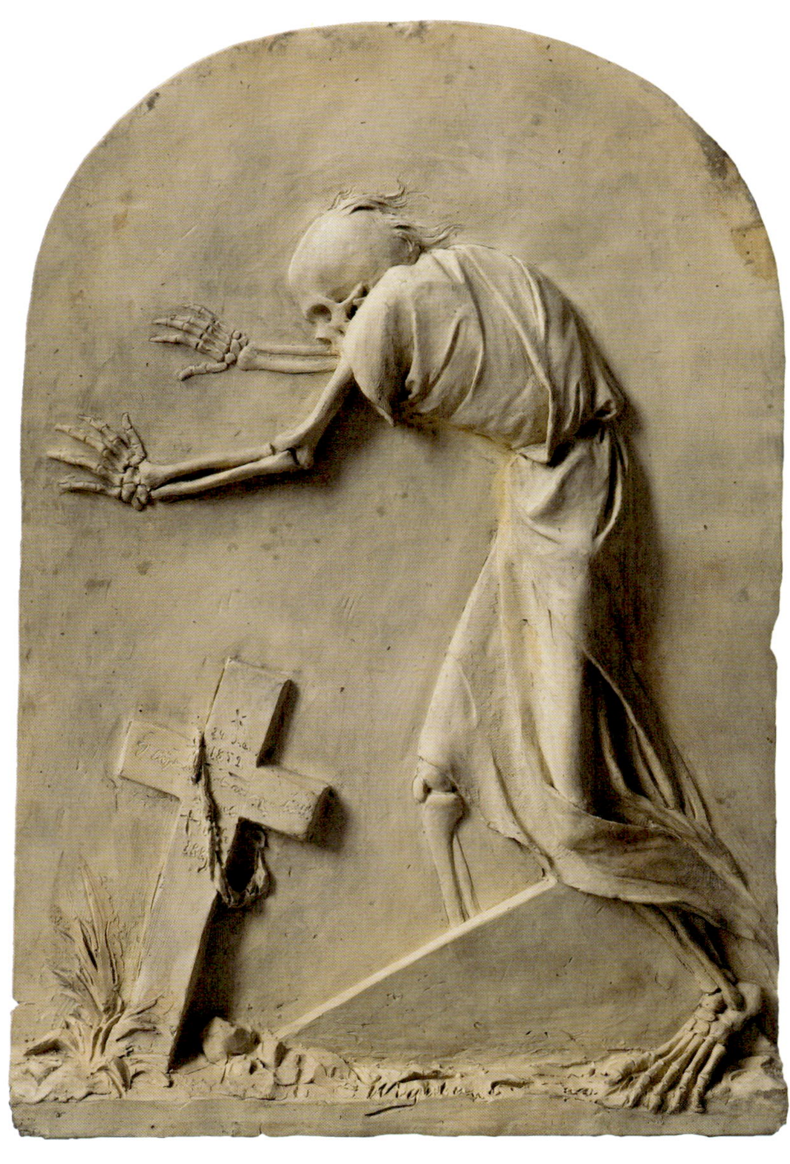

Cat. 119
Gustav Vigeland
A Revenant, 1889

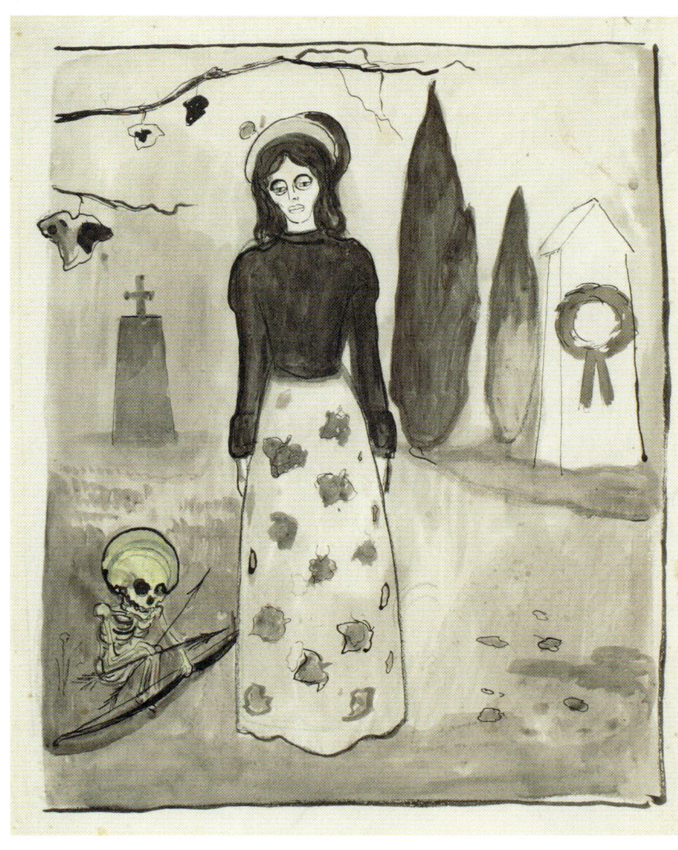

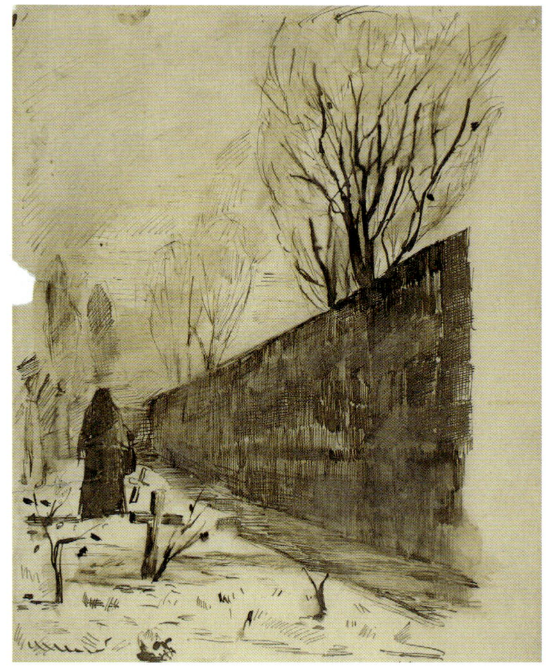

Cat. 120
Edvard Munch
Madonna at the Cemetery, 1896

Cat. 121
Edvard Munch
At the Cemetery, c. 1885

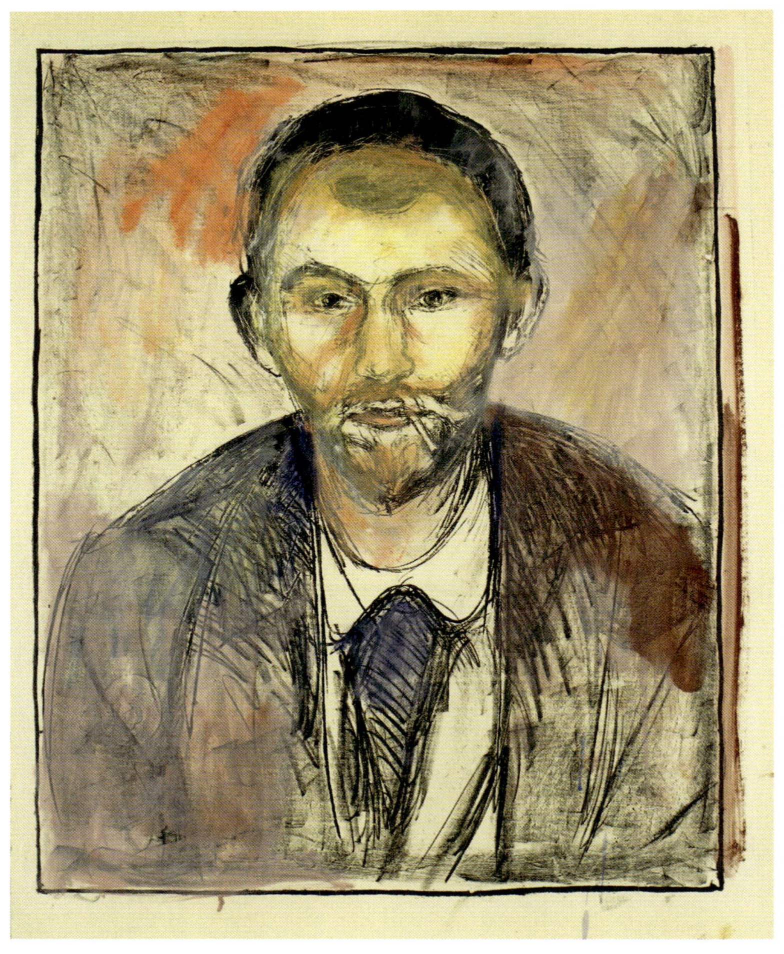

Cat. 122
Edvard Munch
Stanisław Przybyszewski, 1895 (?)

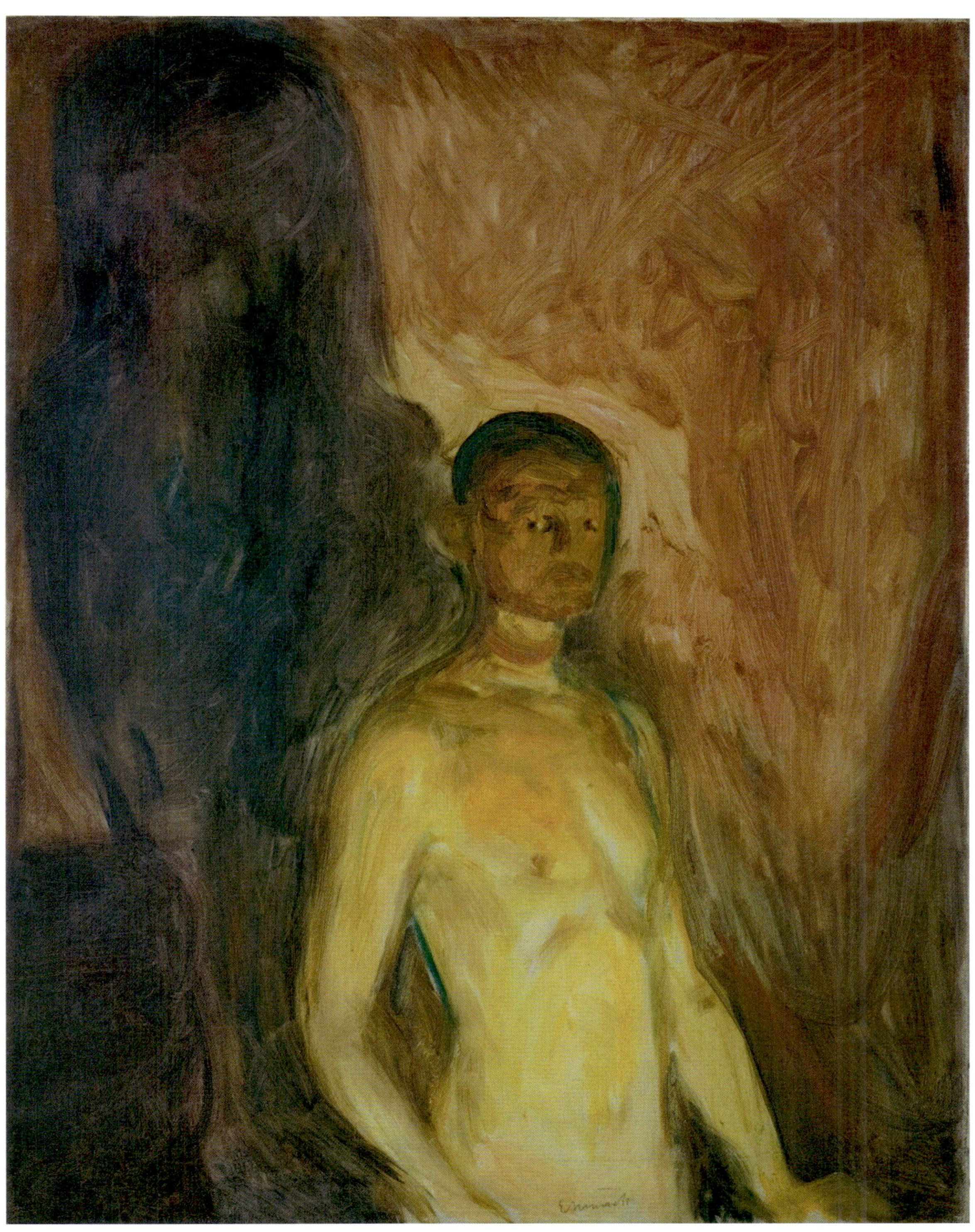

Cat. 123
Edvard Munch
Self-portrait in Hell, 1903

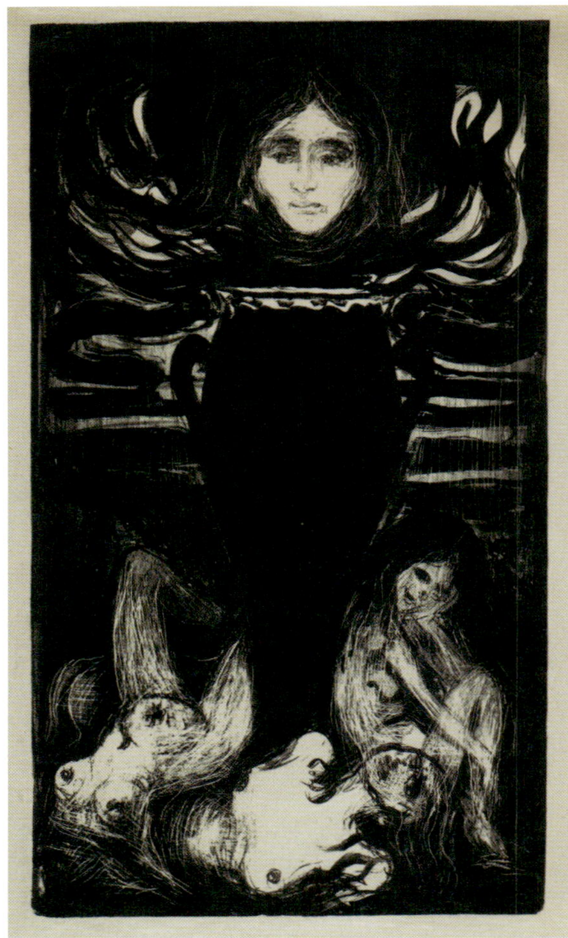

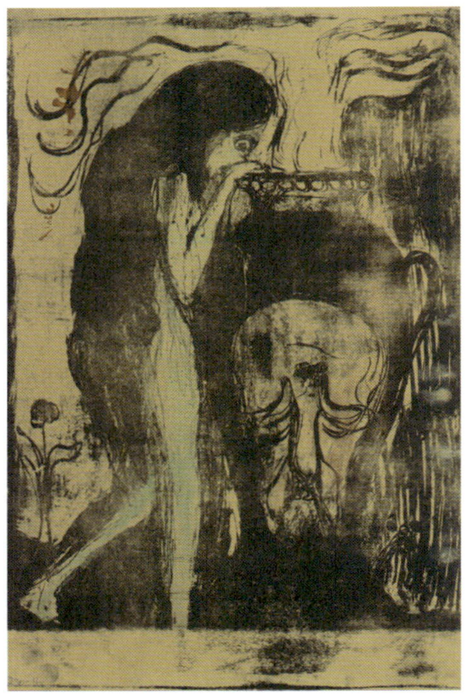

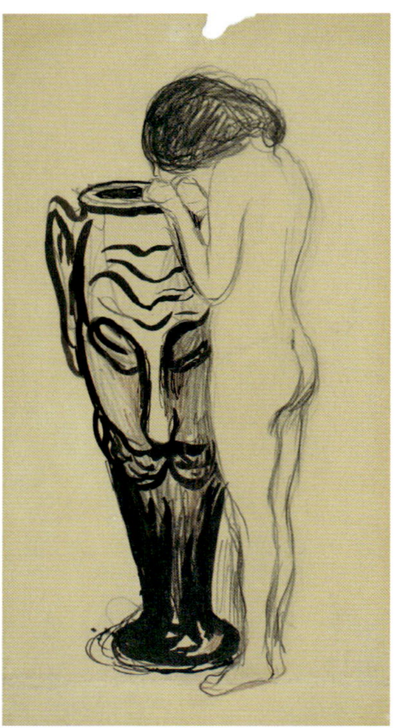

Cat. 125
Edvard Munch
The Woman at the Urn, 1898

Cat. 124
Edvard Munch
The Urn, 1896

Cat. 126
Edvard Munch
The Urn, 1896–98

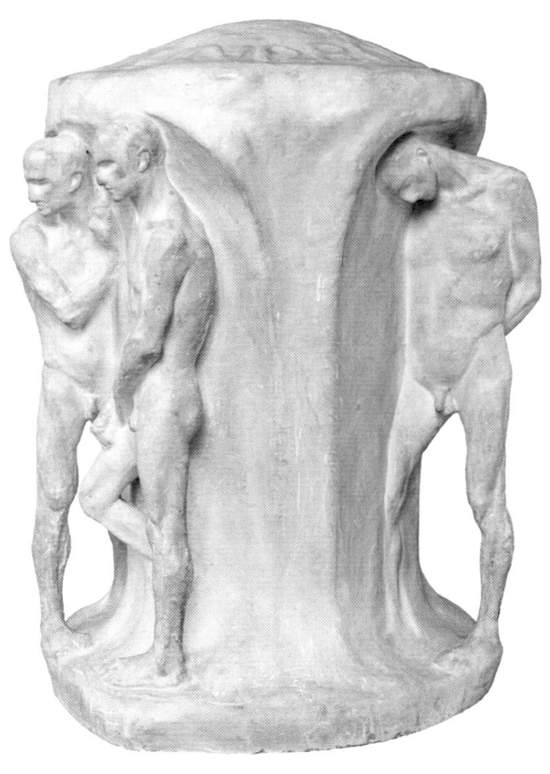

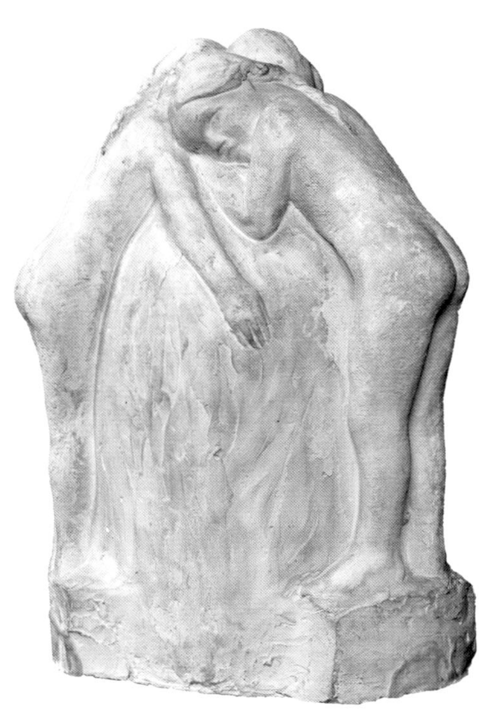

Cat. 127
Gustav Vigeland
Urn for Jacob Lindboe, c. 1902

Cat. 128
Gustav Vigeland
Ruth Syvertsen's Urn I, 1917

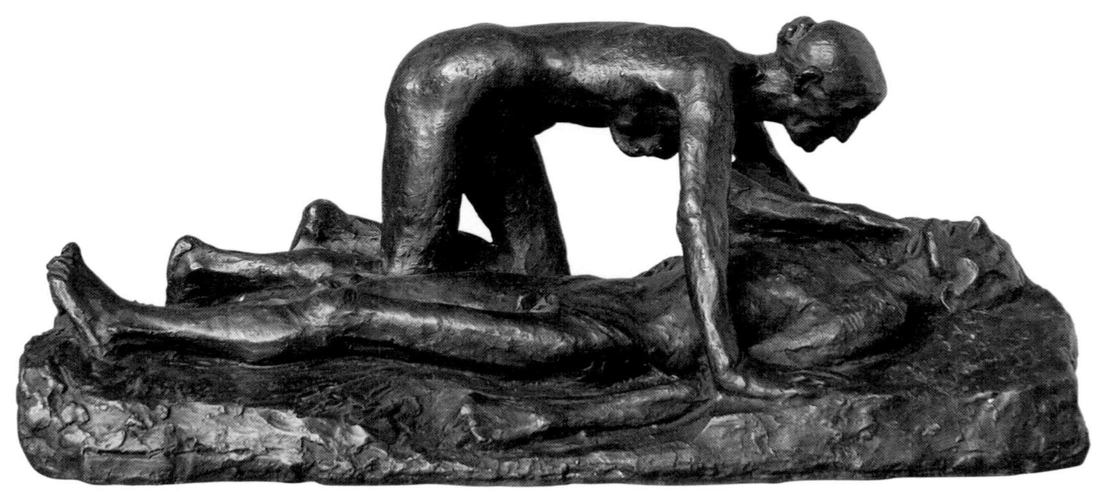

Cat. 129
Gustav Vigeland
*Old Woman Watching Her
Husband Die*, 1898

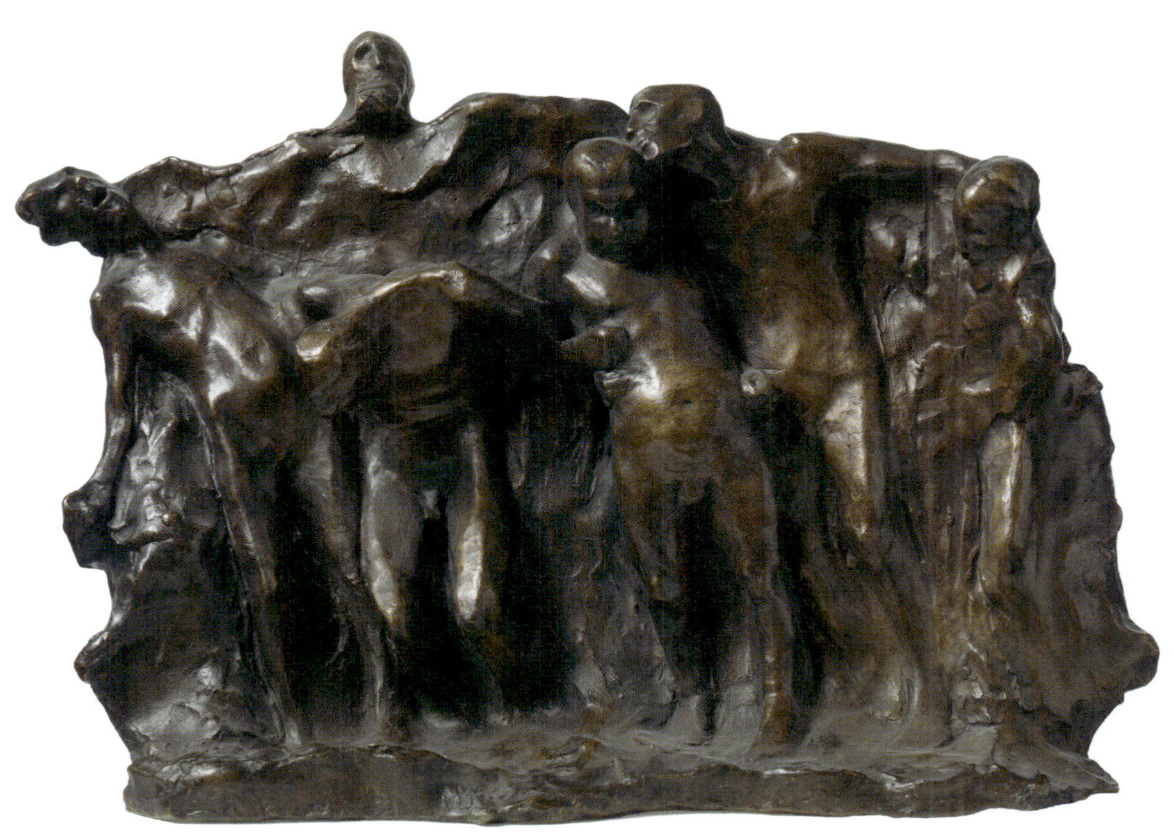

Cat. 130
Gustav Vigeland
*Woman Praying for
the Drunkards*, 1893

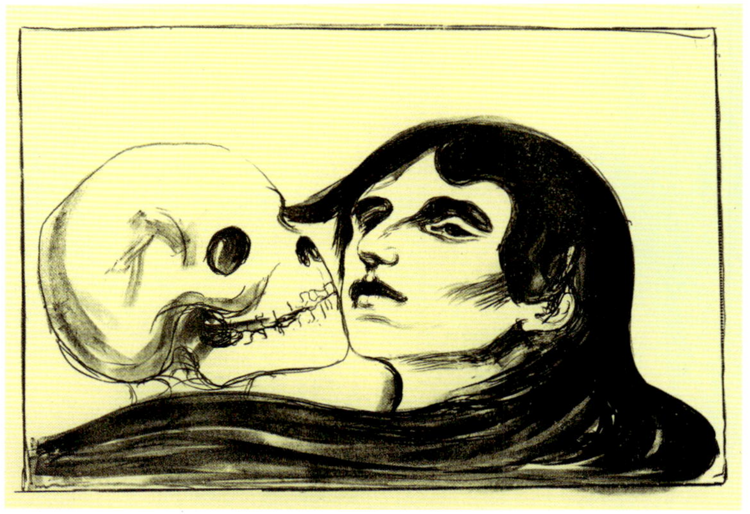

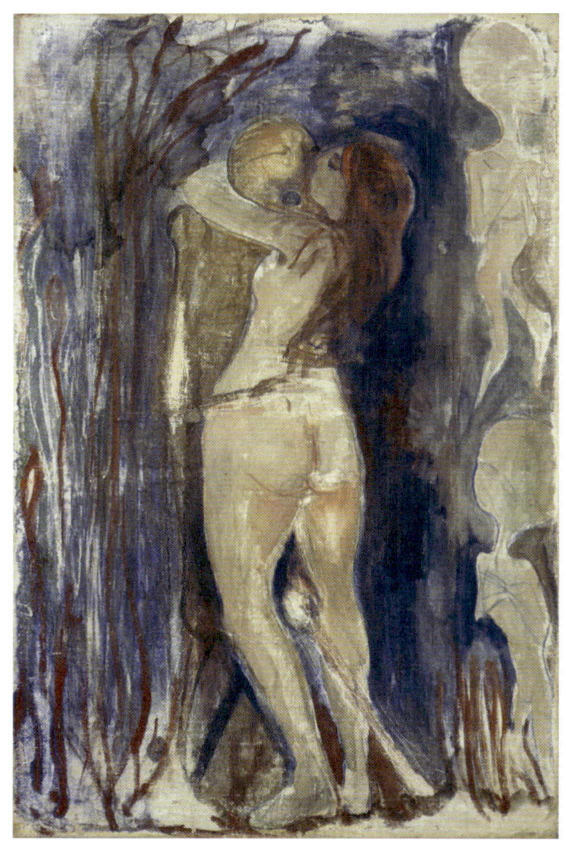

Cat. 131
Edvard Munch
The Kiss of Death, 1899

Cat. 132
Edvard Munch
Death and Life, 1894

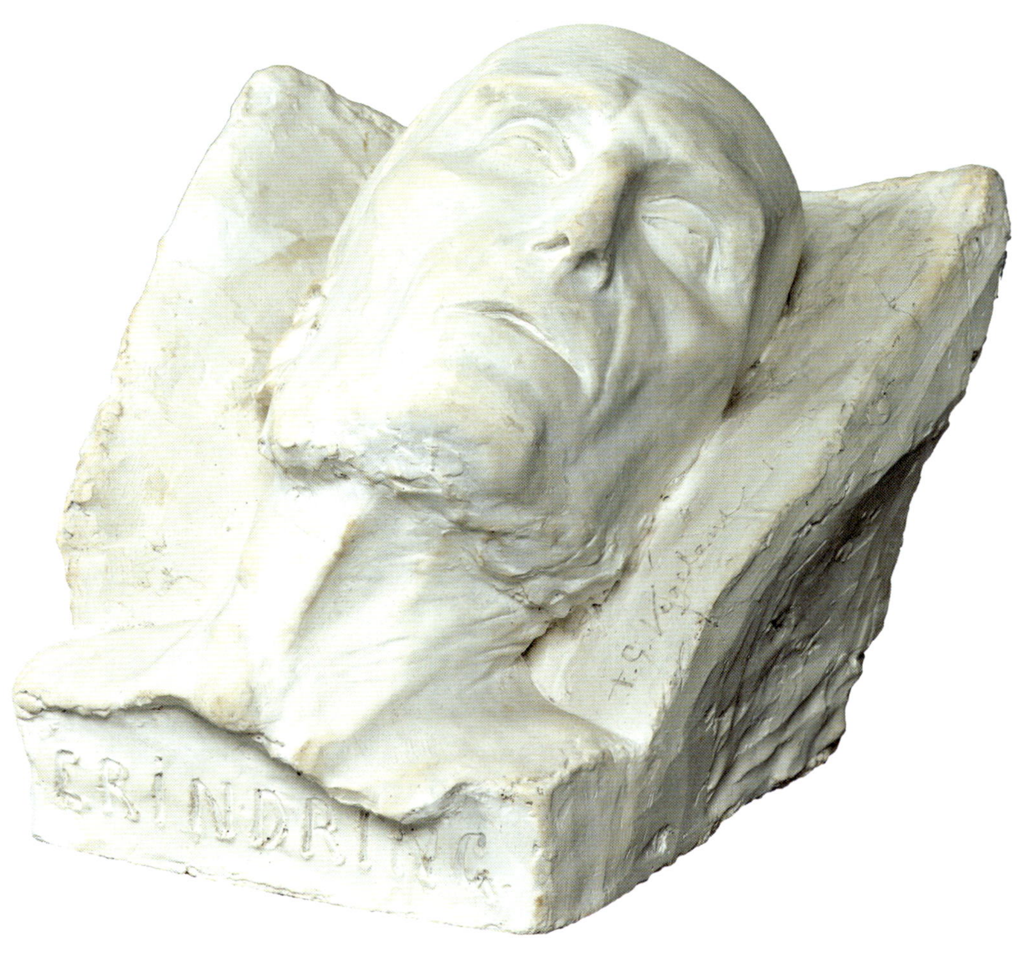

Cat. 133
Gustav Vigeland
Remembrance, 1892

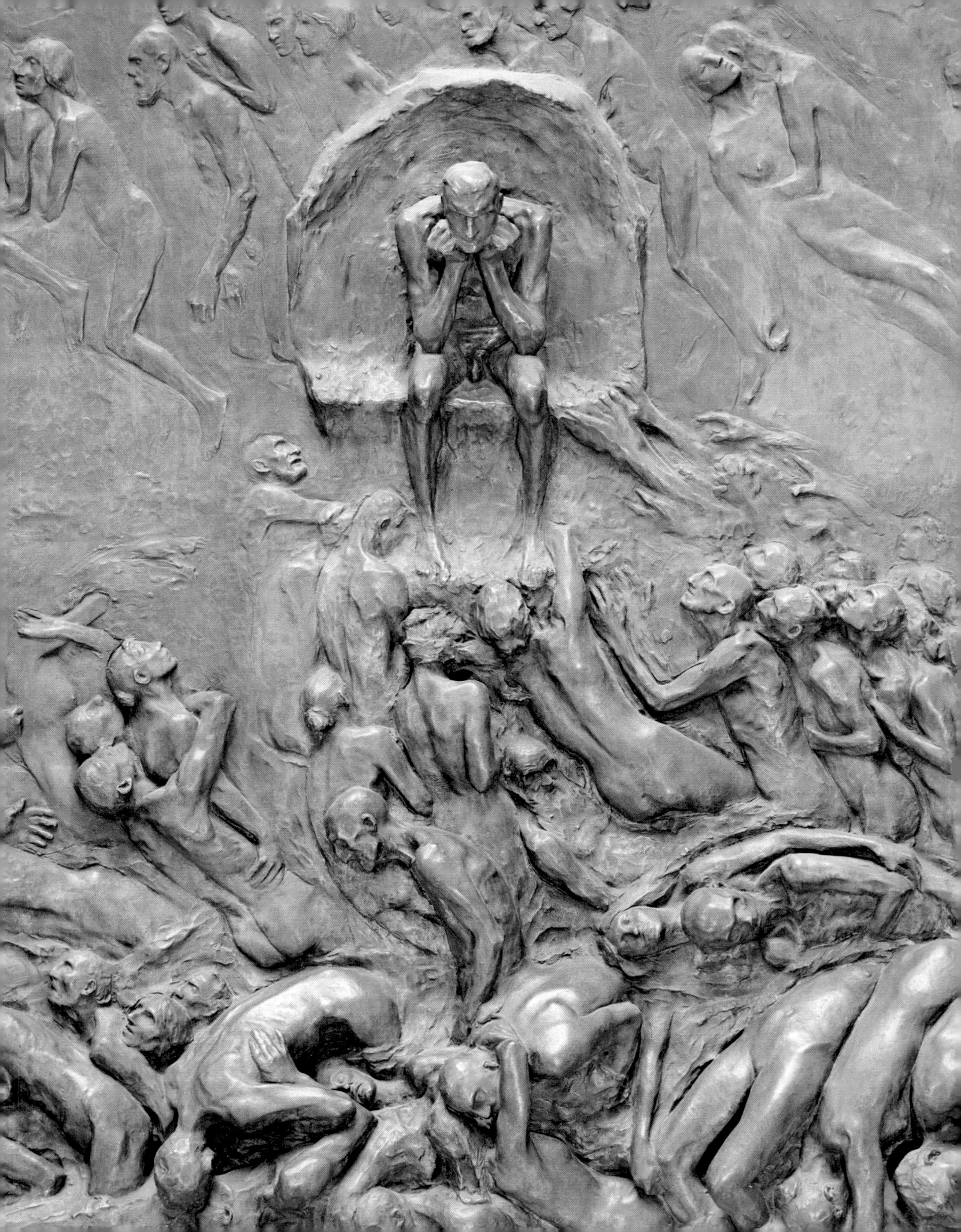

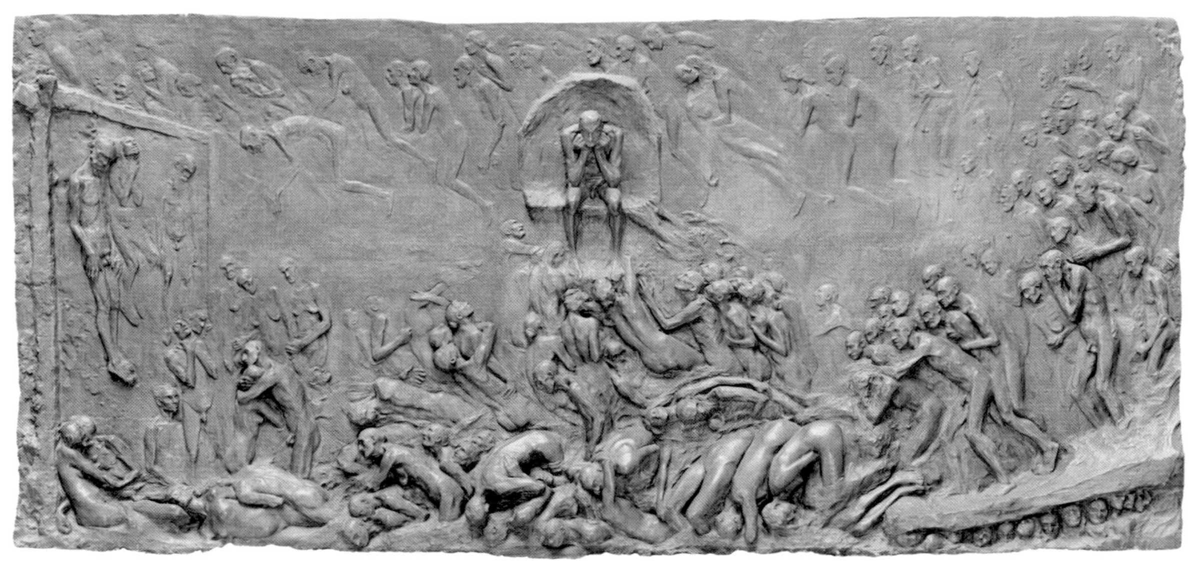

Cat. 134
Gustav Vigeland
Hell II, 1897

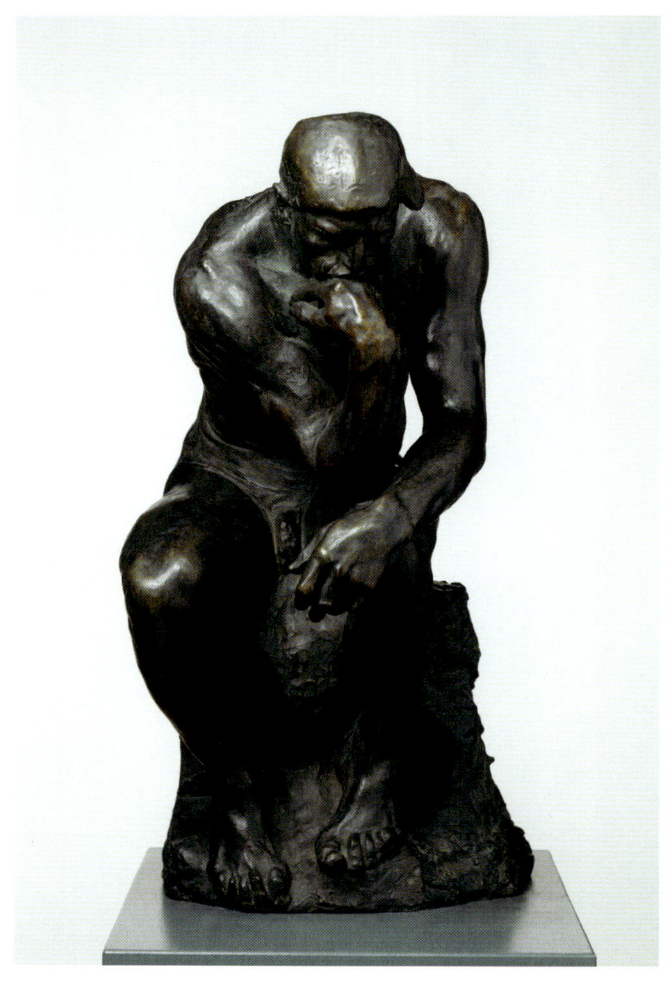

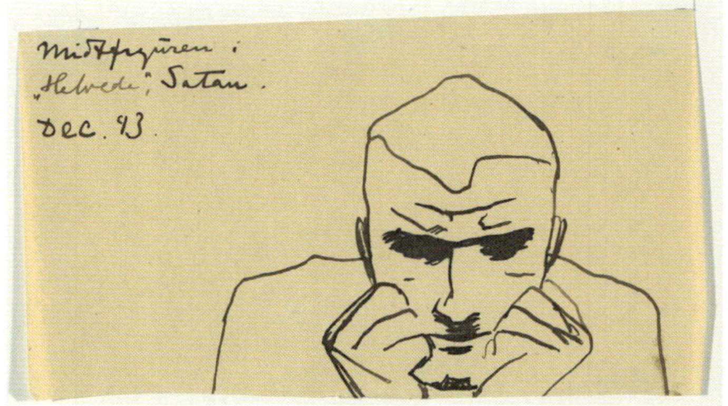

Cat. 135
Auguste Rodin
The Thinker, 1880

Cat. 136
Gustav Vigeland
The Central Figure of 'Hell', Satan,
1893

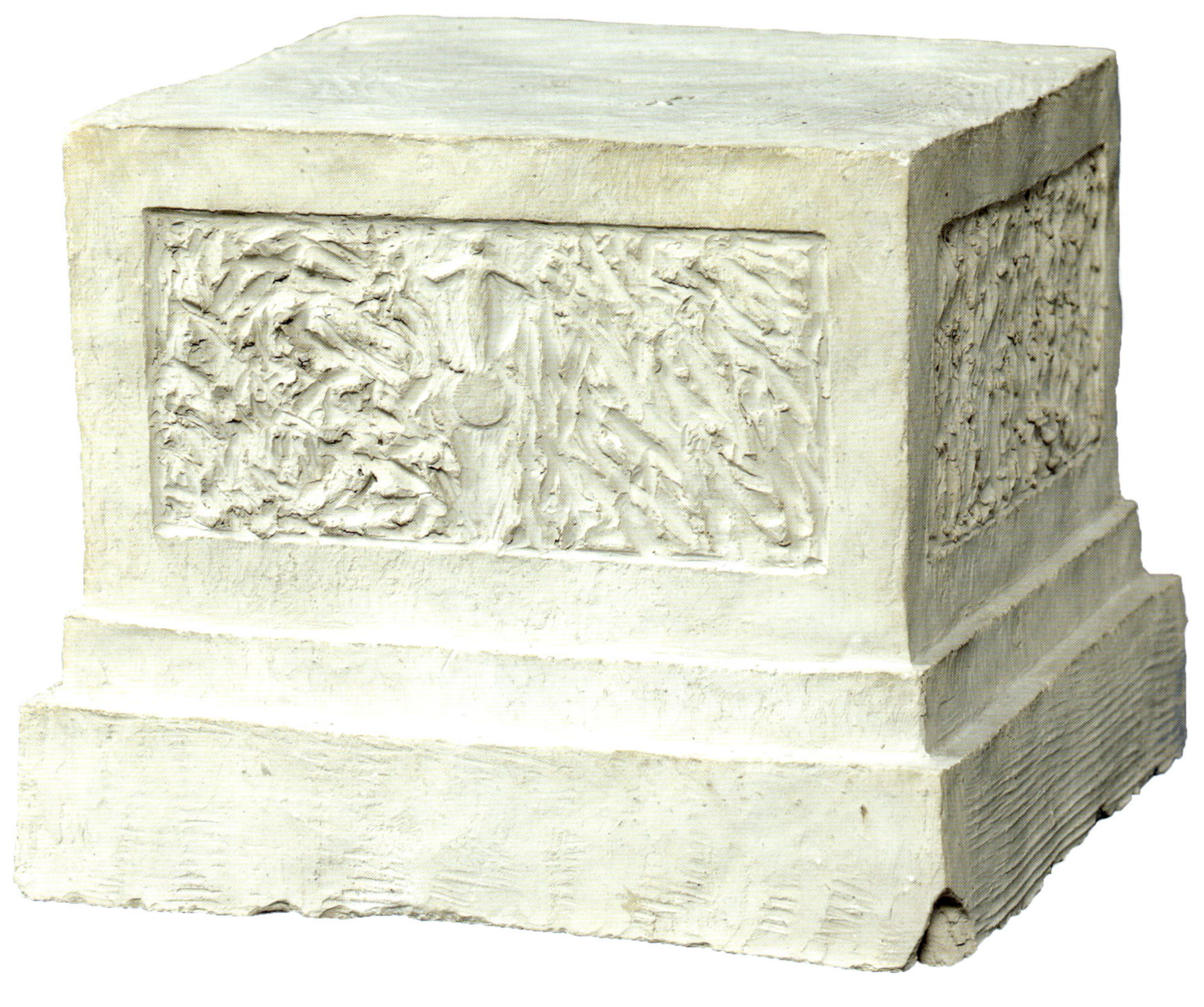

Cat. 137
Gustav Vigeland
Altar, 1923

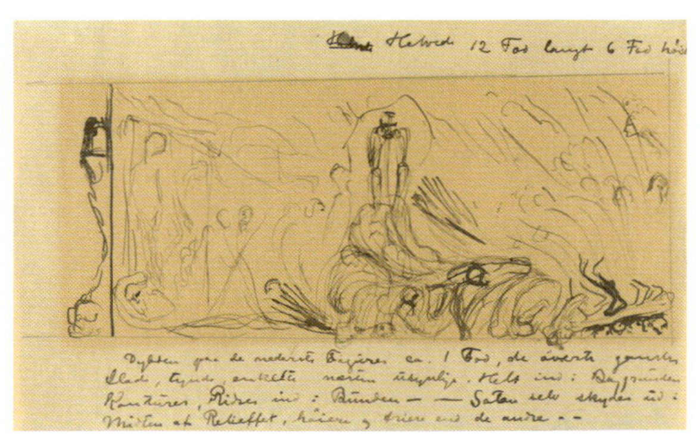

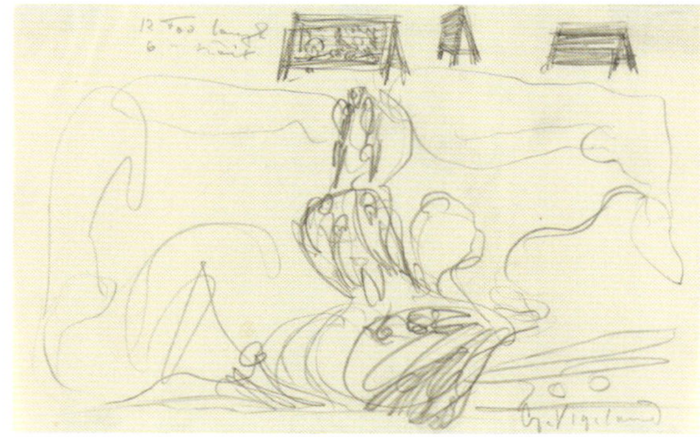

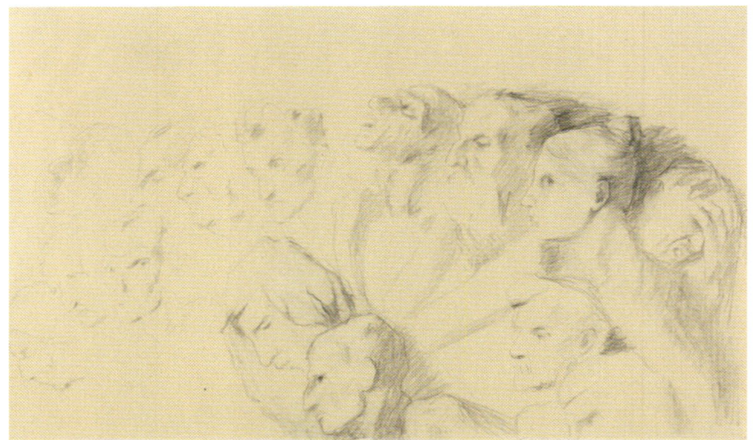

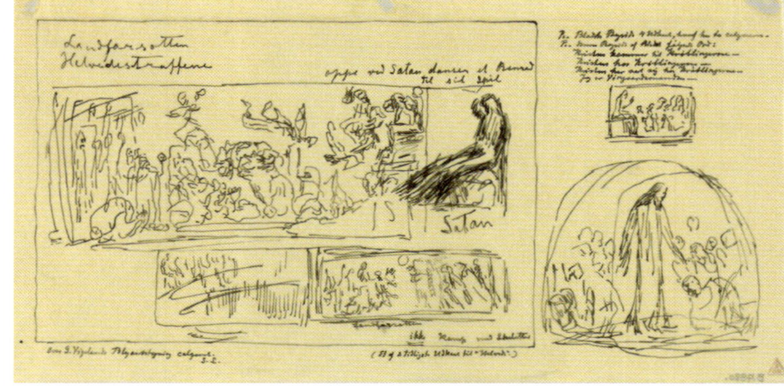

Cat. 138
Gustav Vigeland
Hell 12 Feet Long 6 Feet High,
1893–94

Cat. 139
Gustav Vigeland
Ascending Human Beings, 1893–94

Cat. 140
Gustav Vigeland
Fifteen Human Heads, 1893–94

Cat. 141
Sophus Larpent
*Copy of Gustav Vigeland's Sketches
for Hell*, 1893

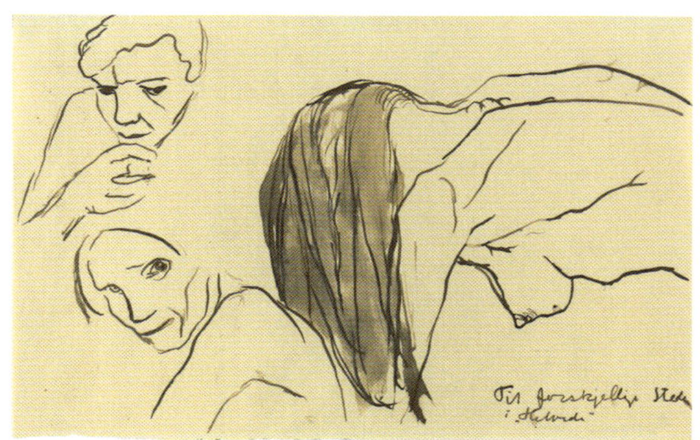

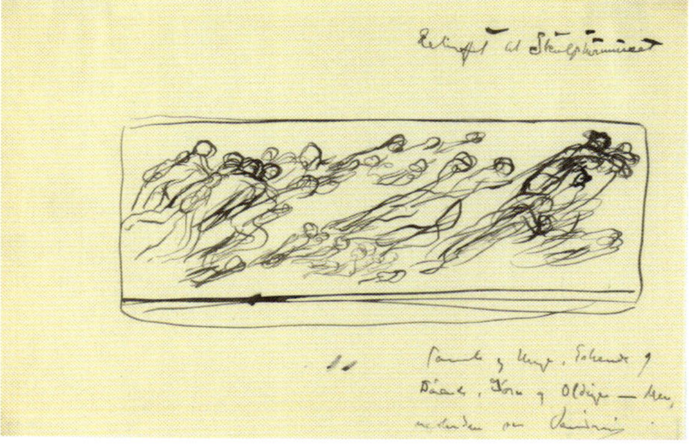

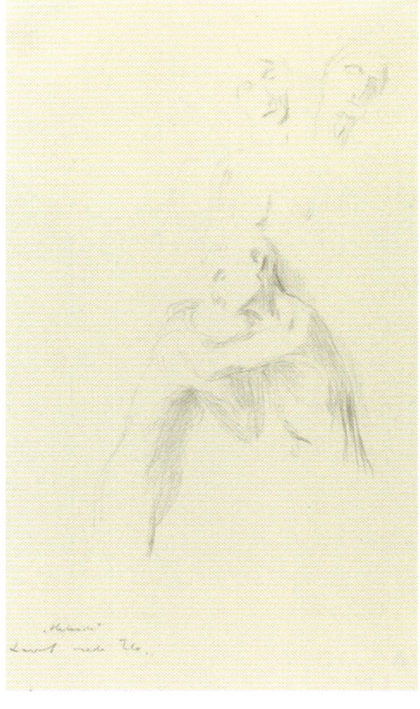

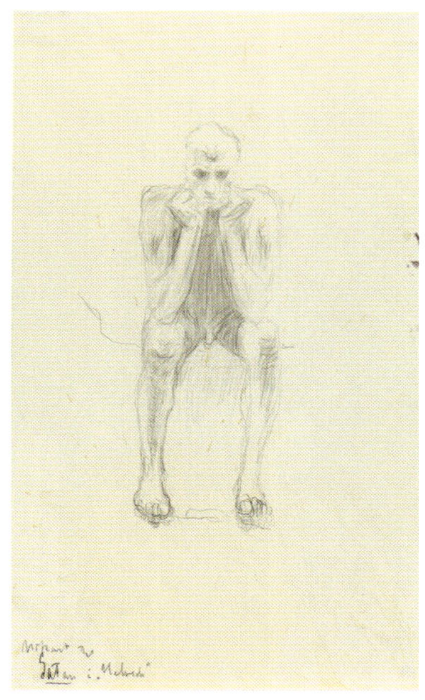

Cat. 142
Gustav Vigeland
Sketches for 'Hell', 1893–94

Cat. 143
Gustav Vigeland
Man and Woman Holding Each Other,
1893–94

Cat. 144
Gustav Vigeland
Relief for the Sculpture Museum,
prob. 1890s

Cat. 145
Gustav Vigeland
The Central Figure of 'Hell', Satan,
1893–94

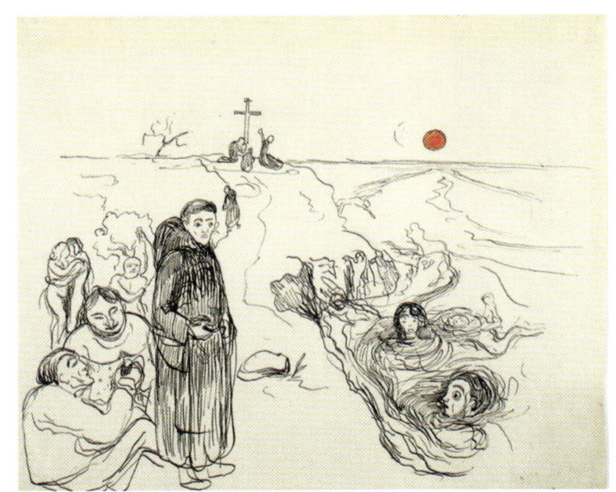

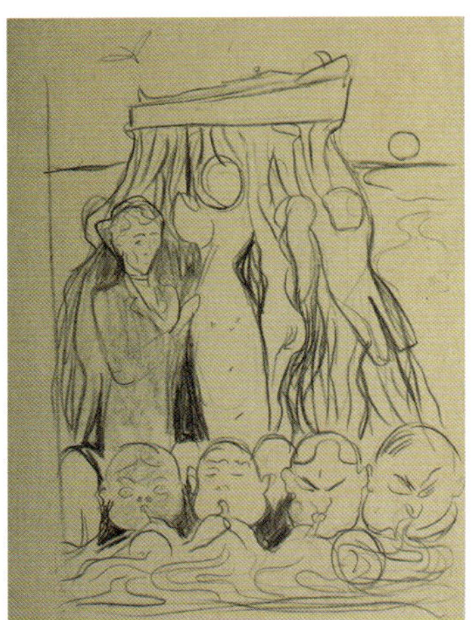

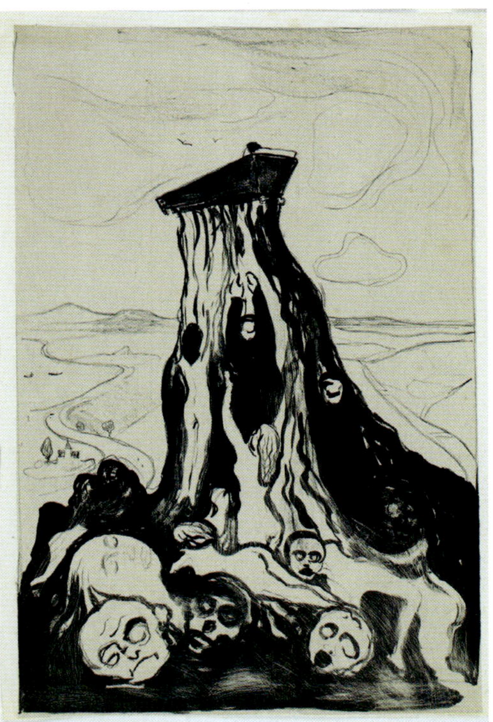

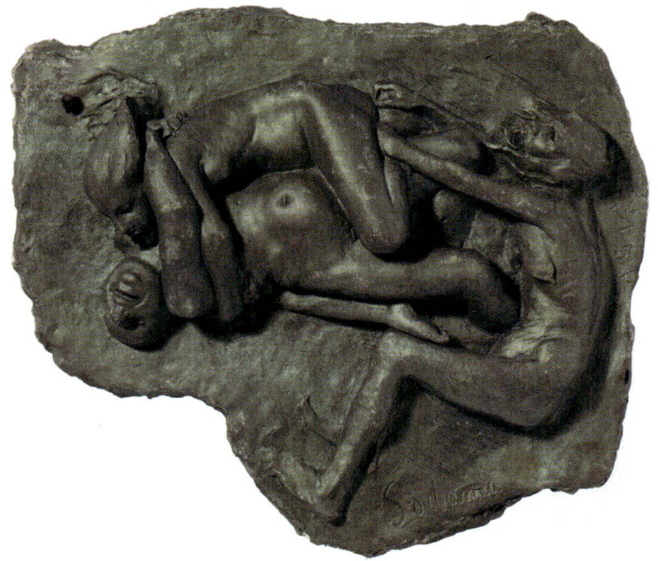

Cat. 146
Edvard Munch
The Empty Cross, 1899–1901

Cat. 147
Edvard Munch
Funeral March, 1897

Cat. 148
Edvard Munch
Funeral March, 1897

Cat. 149
Gustav Vigeland
Sodom, 1892

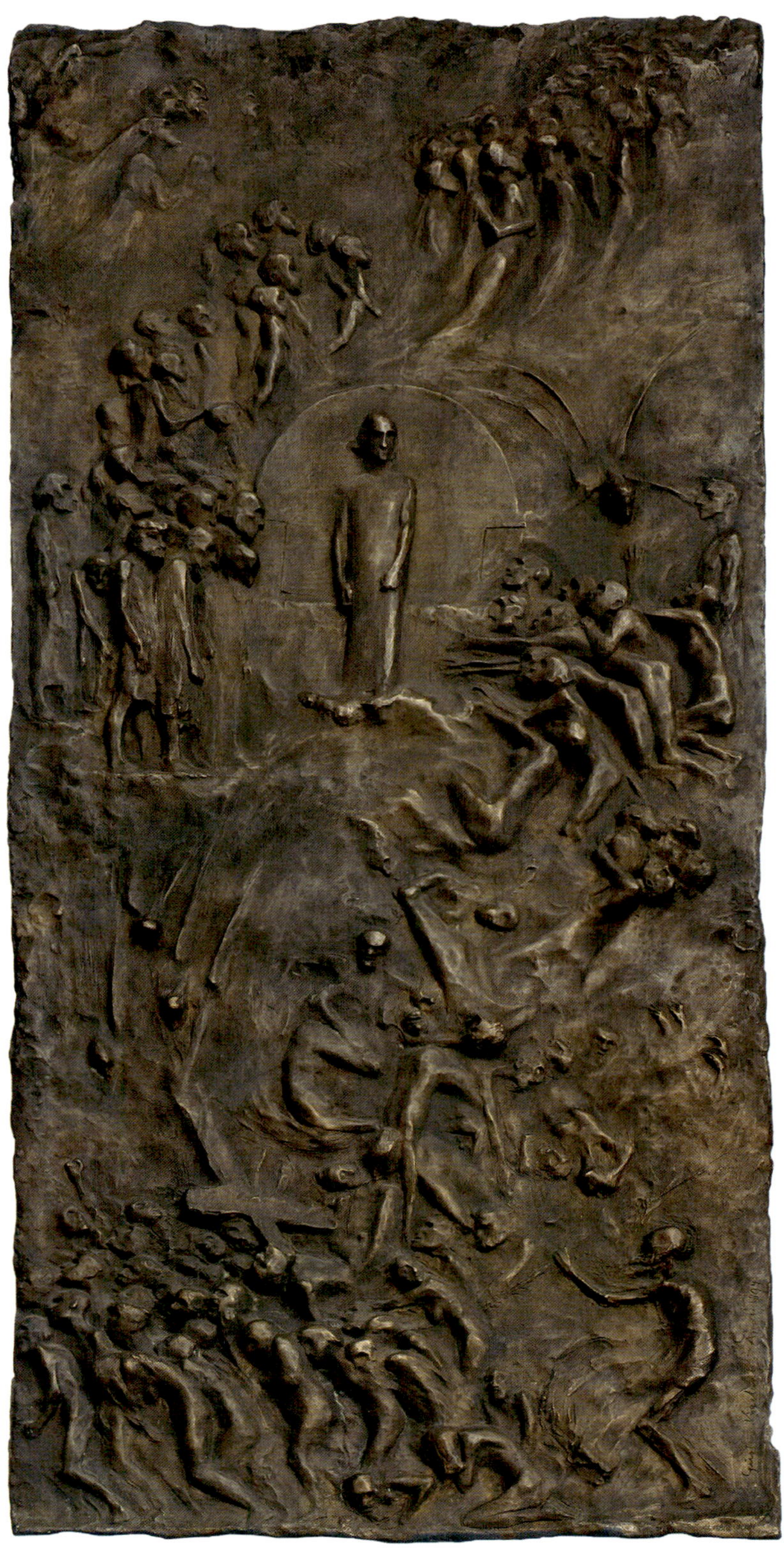

Cat. 150
Gustav Vigeland
Judgement Day, 1894

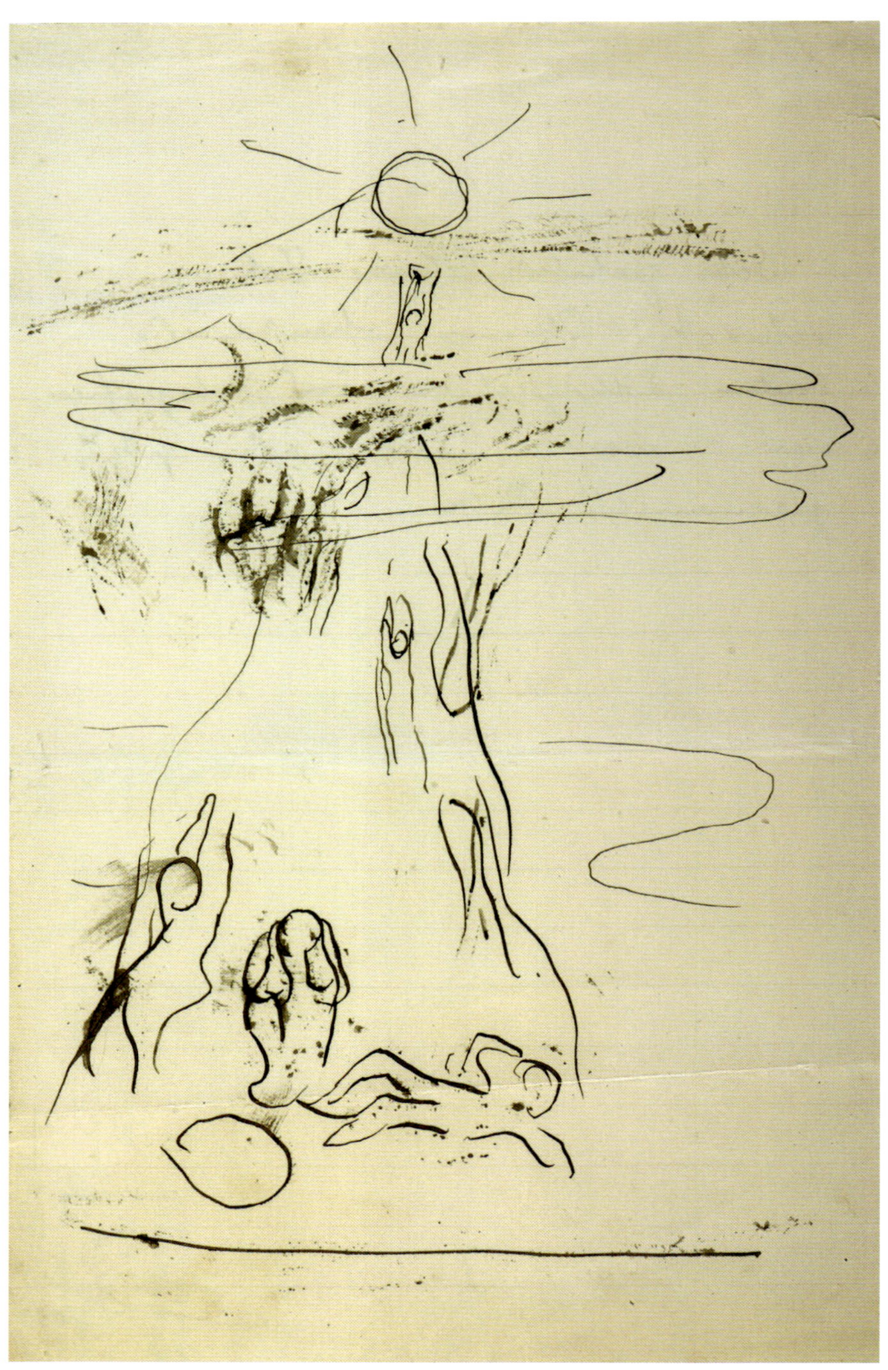

Cat. 151
Edvard Munch
The Human Mountain, 1897

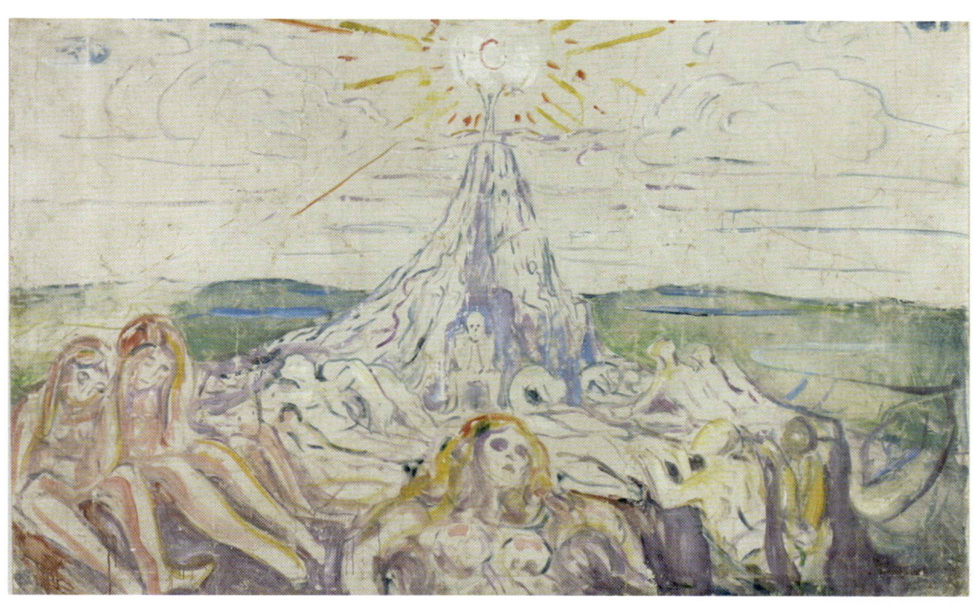

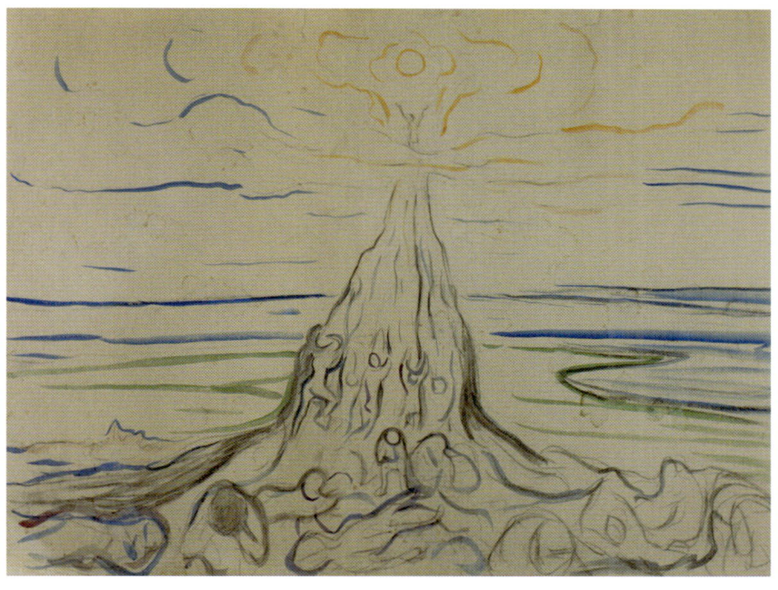

Cat. 152
Edvard Munch
The Human Mountain, 1909–10

Cat. 153
Edvard Munch
The Human Mountain, 1909–10

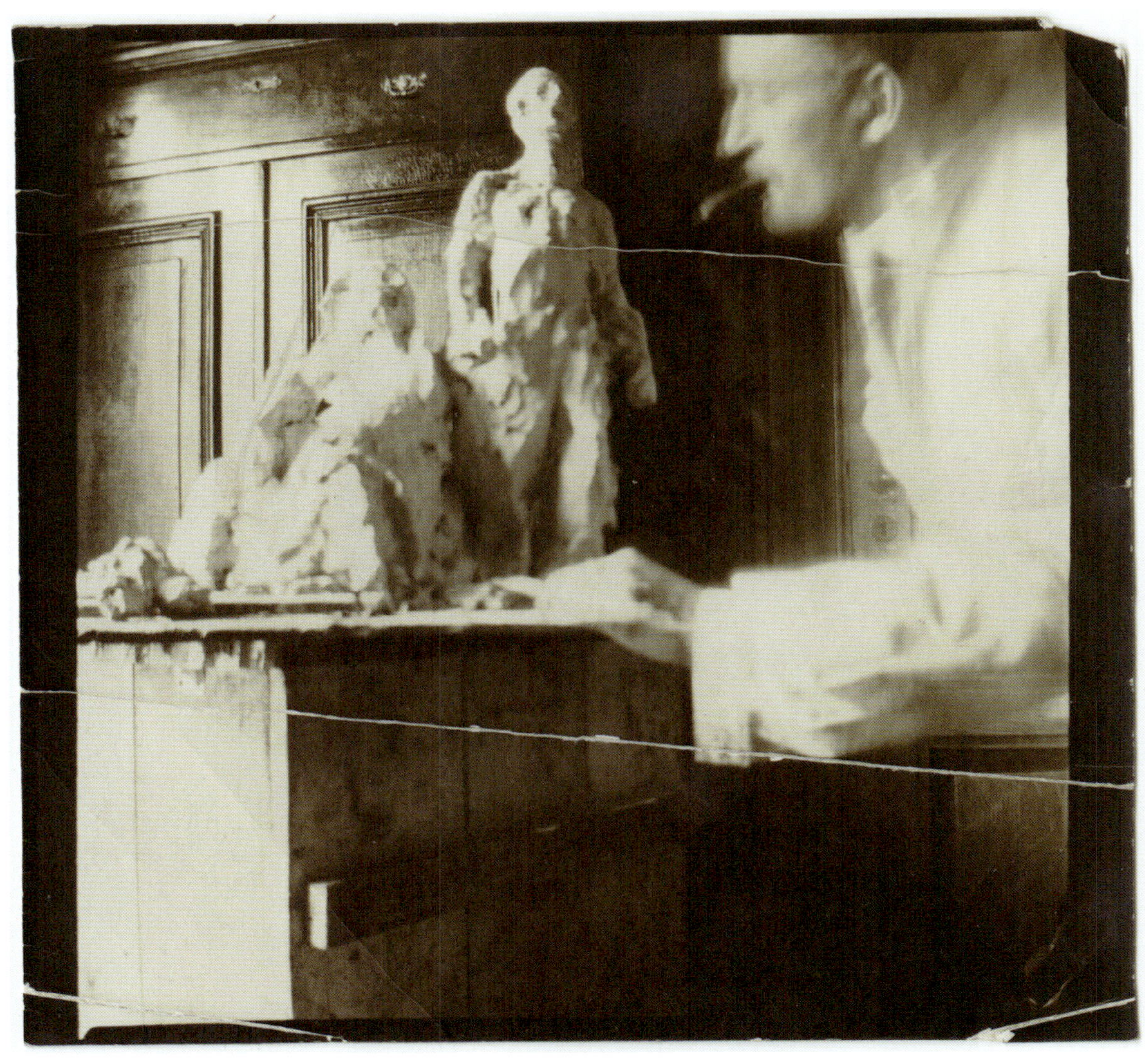

Cat. 154
Edvard Munch with *Mother Norway*,
draft for a national monument,
1909–10

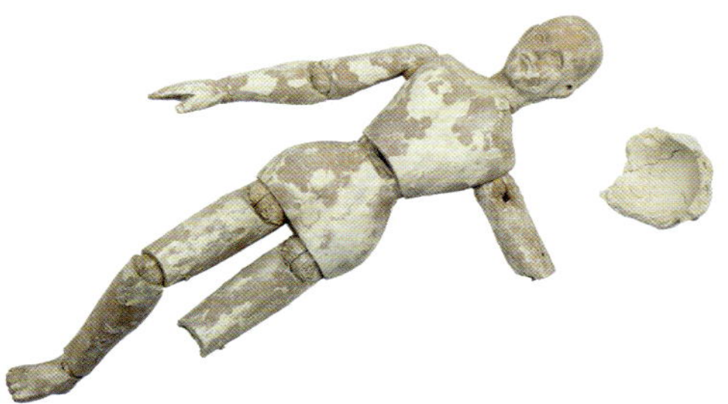

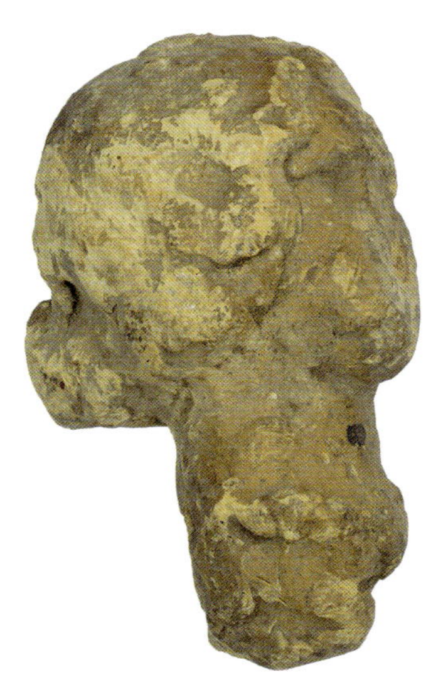

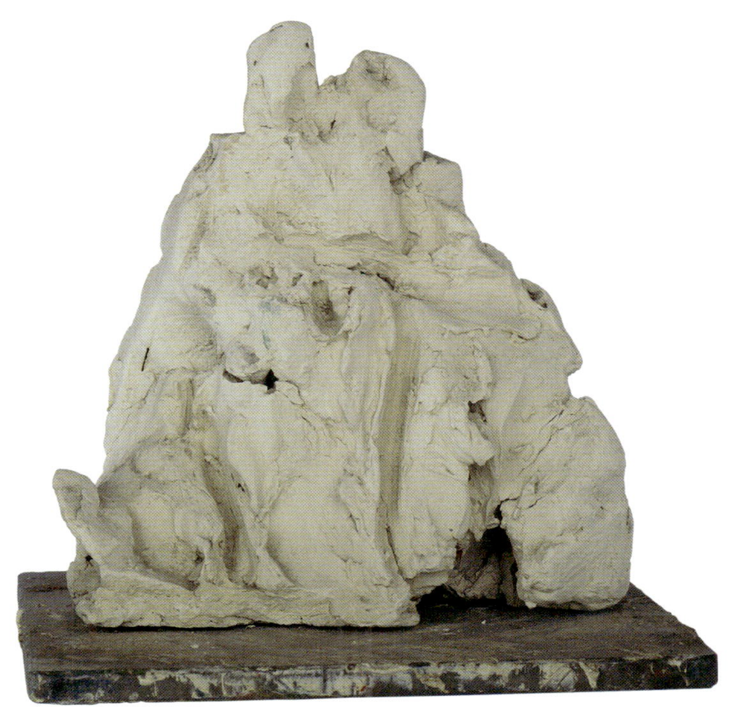

Cat. 155
Edvard Munch's jointed doll

Cat. 156
Edvard Munch
Woman's Head, 1903–05

Cat. 157
Edvard Munch
Man and Woman (undated)

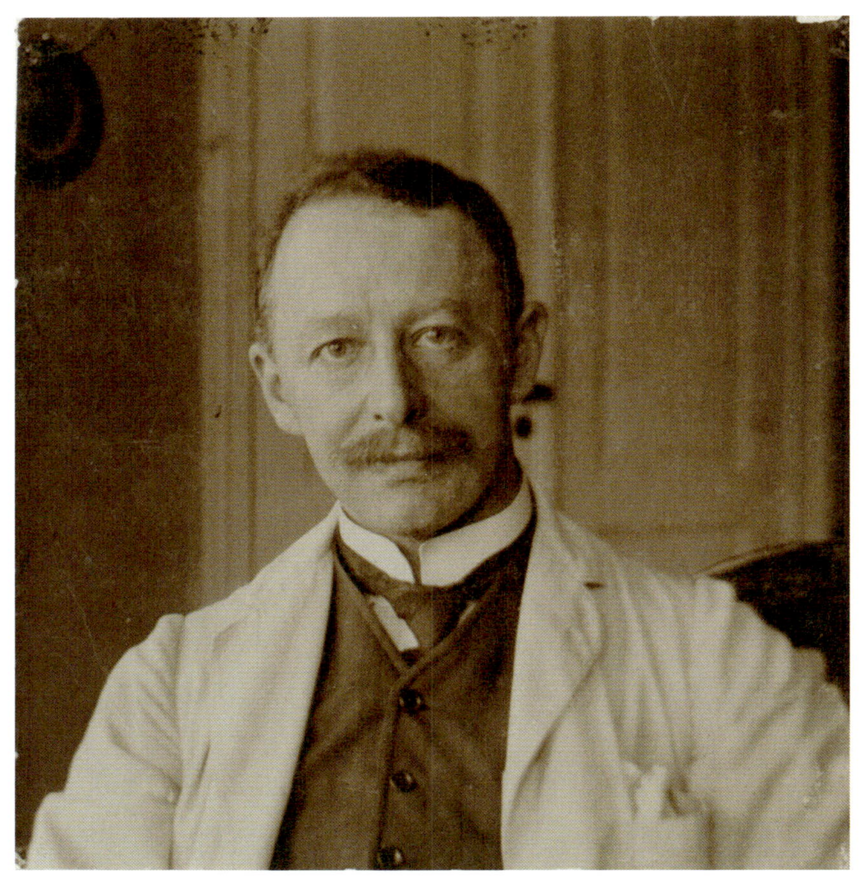

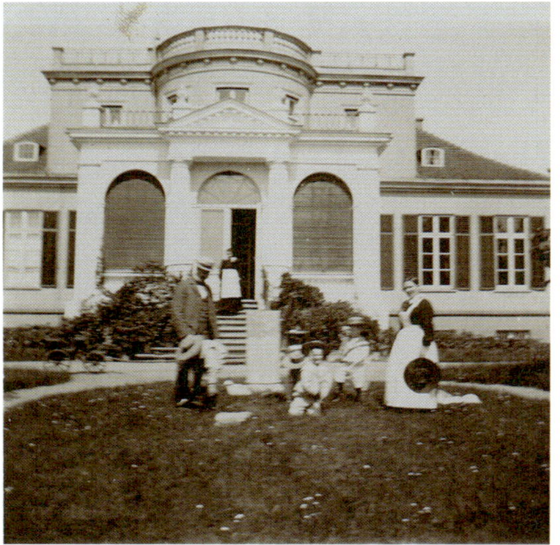

Cat. 158
Edvard Munch
Max Linde, c. 1903

Cat. 159
Edvard Munch
Max Linde's villa in Lübeck, 1903

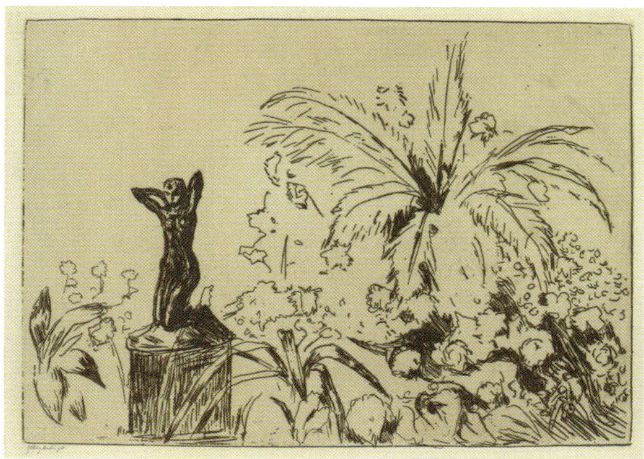

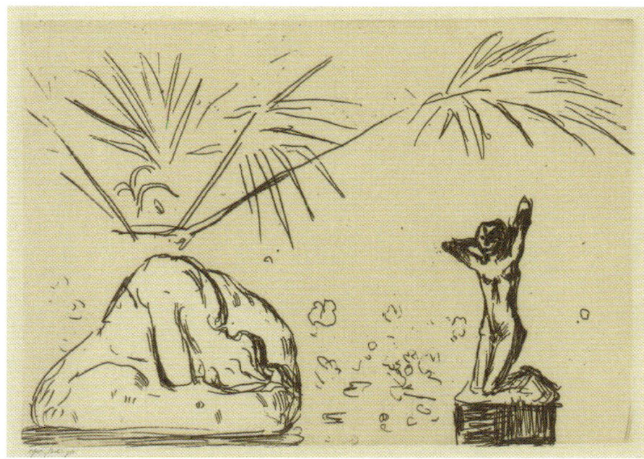

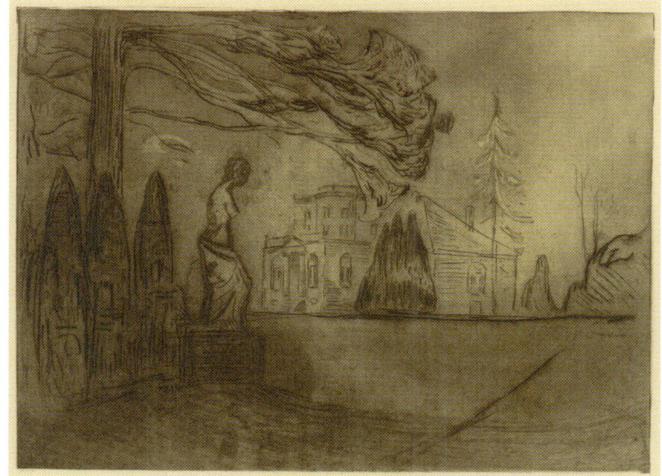

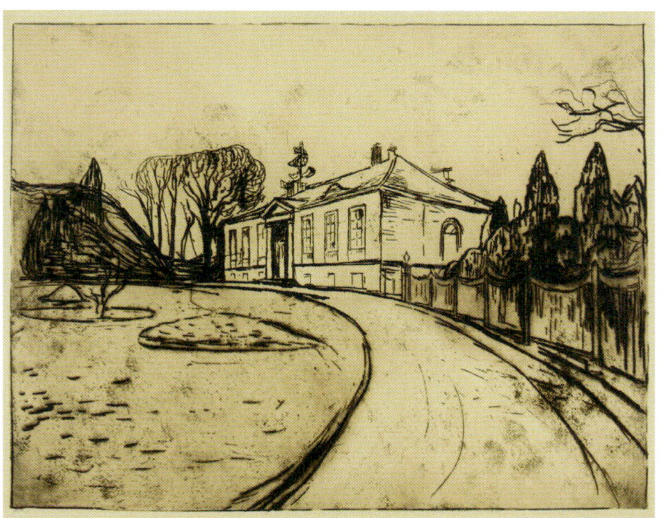

Cat. 160
Edvard Munch
Veranda (Linde Portfolio), 1902

Cat. 161
Edvard Munch
*Interior with Sculptures
(Linde Portfolio)*, 1902

Cat. 162
Edvard Munch
The Garden at Night (Linde Portfolio),
1902

Cat. 163
Edvard Munch
The Villa (Linde Portfolio), 1902

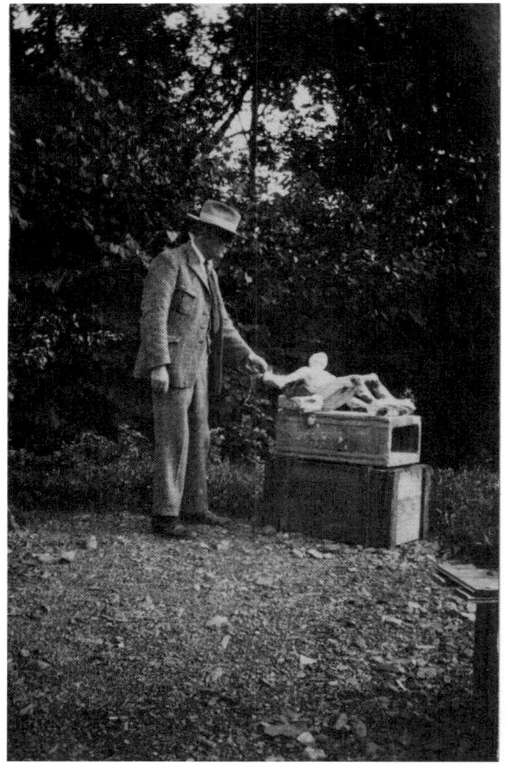

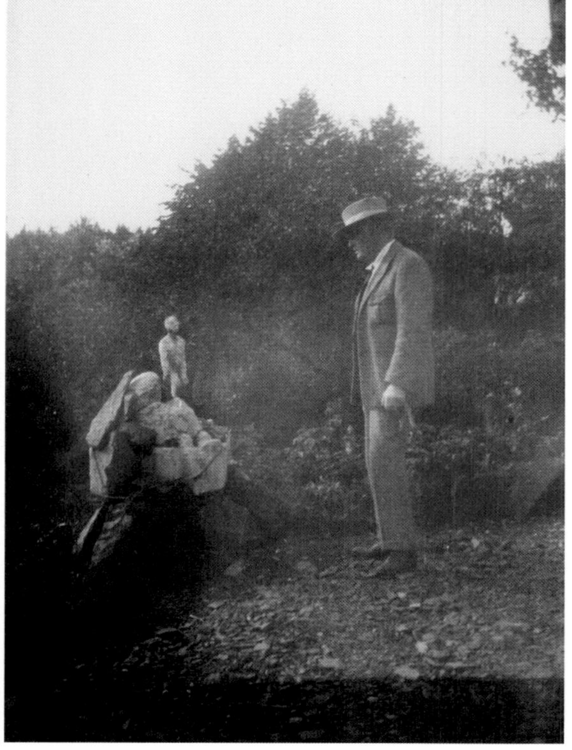

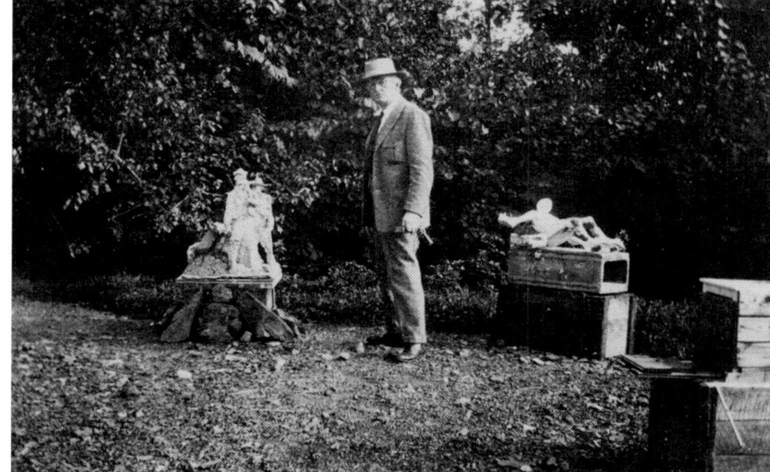

Cat. 164
Edvard Munch with the sculpture
Seated Man in the garden at Ekely,
1932

Cat. 165
Edvard Munch between the
sculptures *Workers in Snow* and
Seated Man in the garden at Ekely,
1932

Cat. 166
Edvard Munch with the sculpture
Mother Norway, 1932

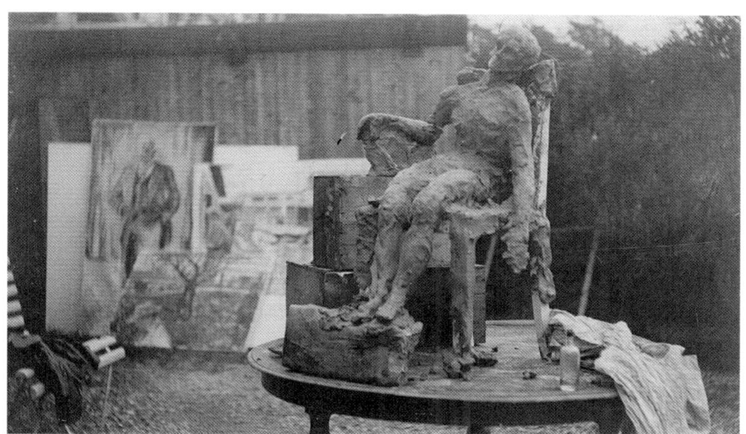

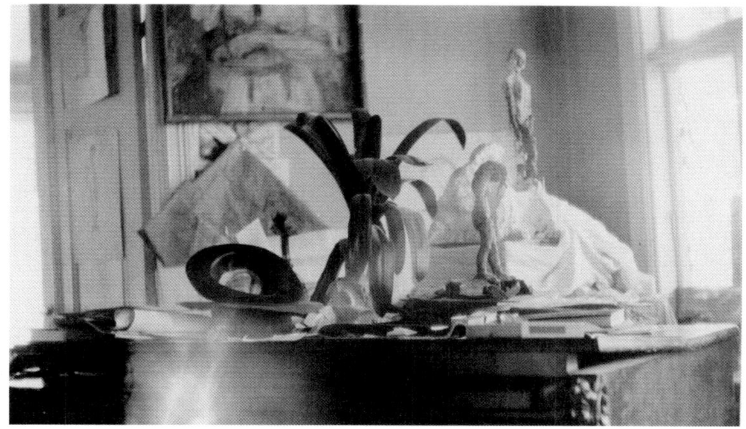

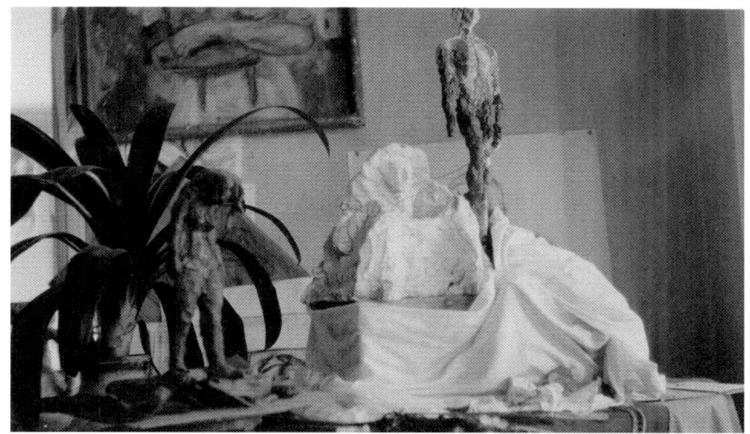

Cat. 167
Edvard Munch
Seated sculpture, 1931–32

Cat. 168
Edvard Munch
Interior with sculptures, 1931–32

Cat. 169
Edvard Munch
Interior with sculptures, 1931–32

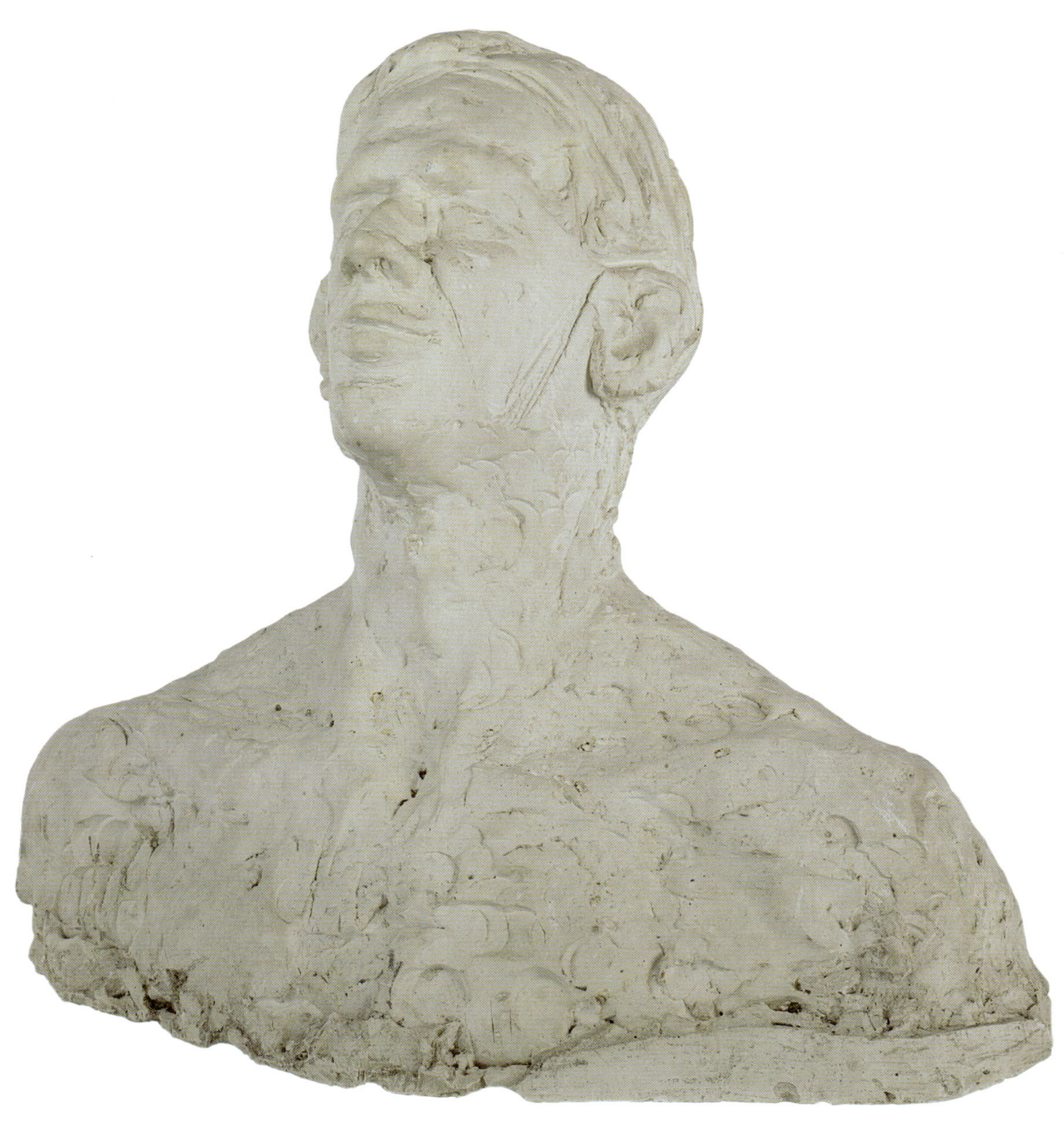

Cat. 170
Edvard Munch
Male Bust (undated)

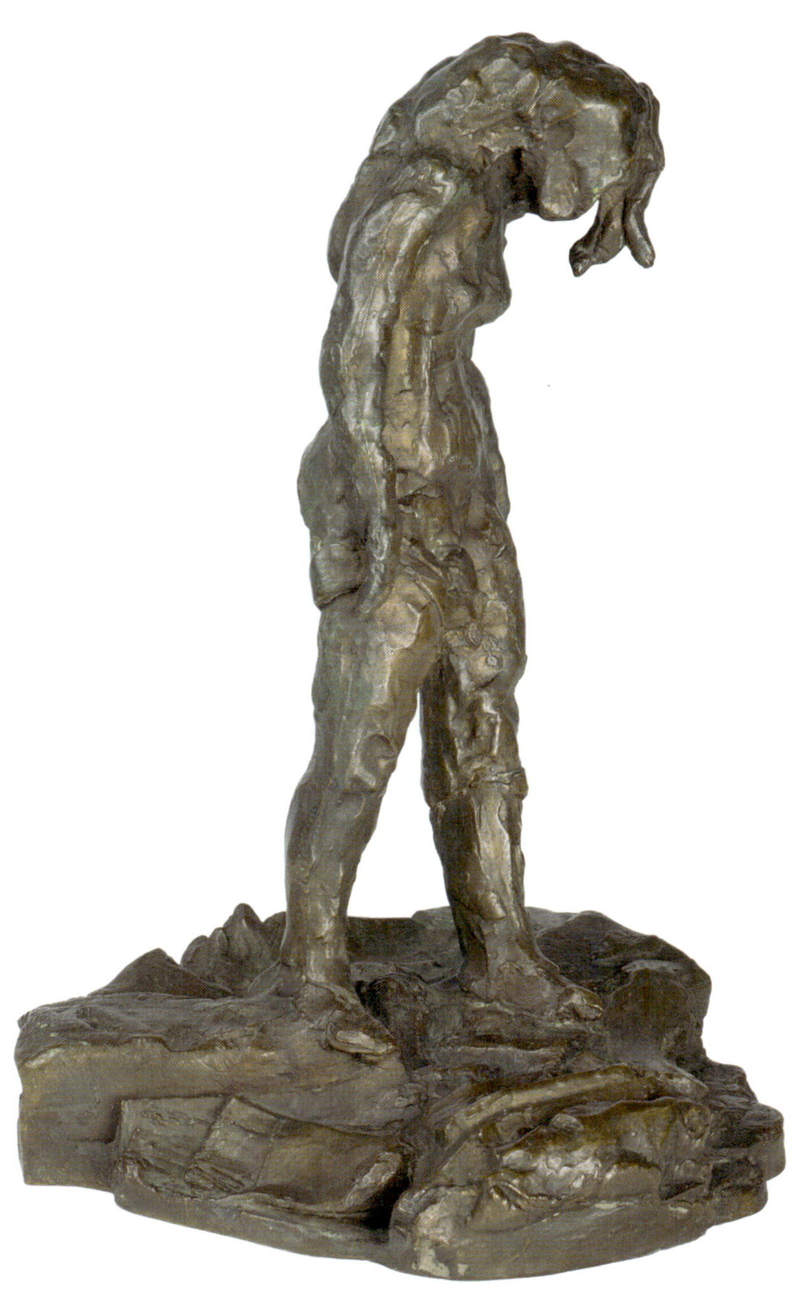

Cat. 171
Edvard Munch
Weeping Nude, 1914

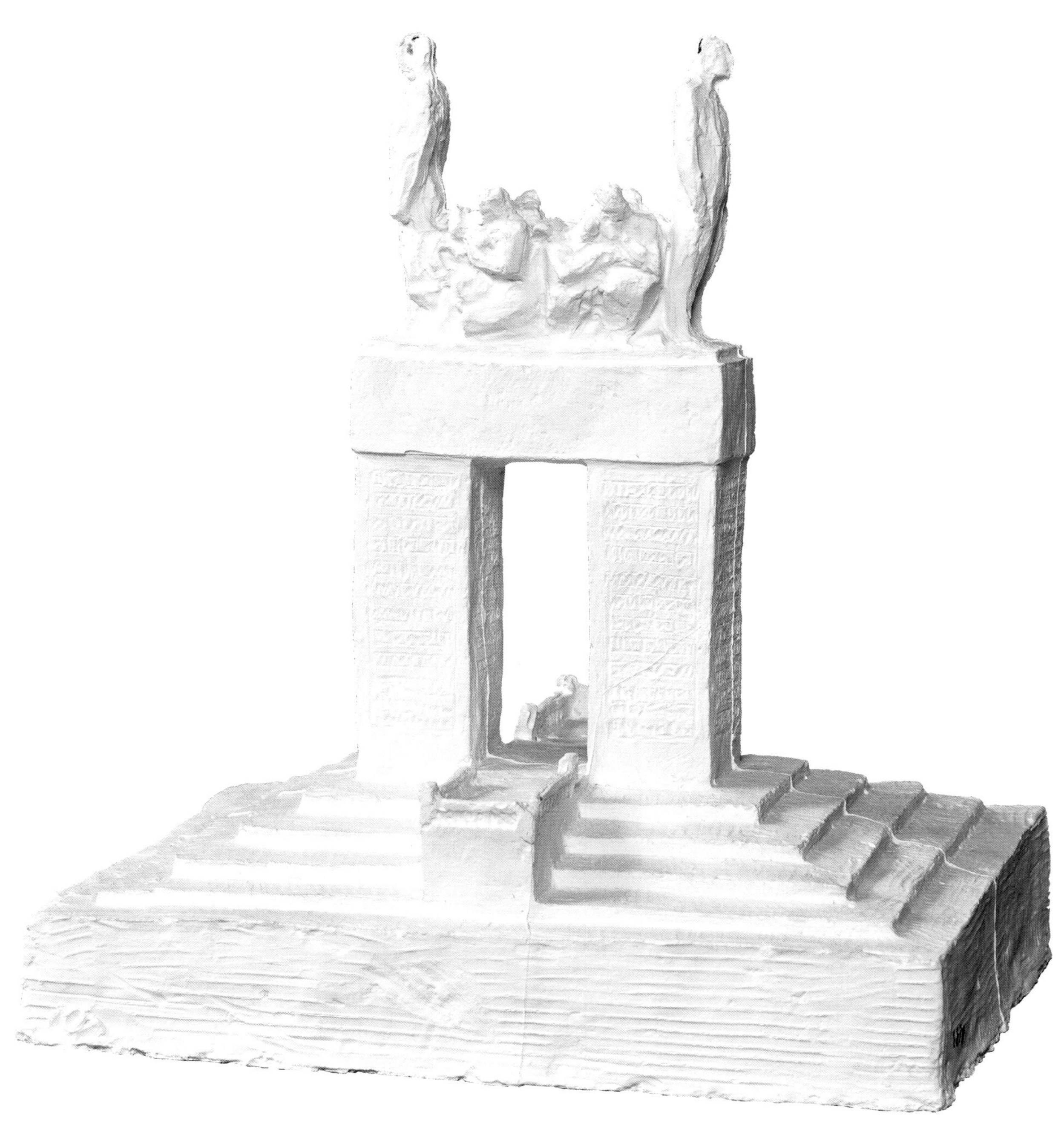

Cat. 172
Gustav Vigeland
Draft for the Eidsvoll Monument,
prob. 1919

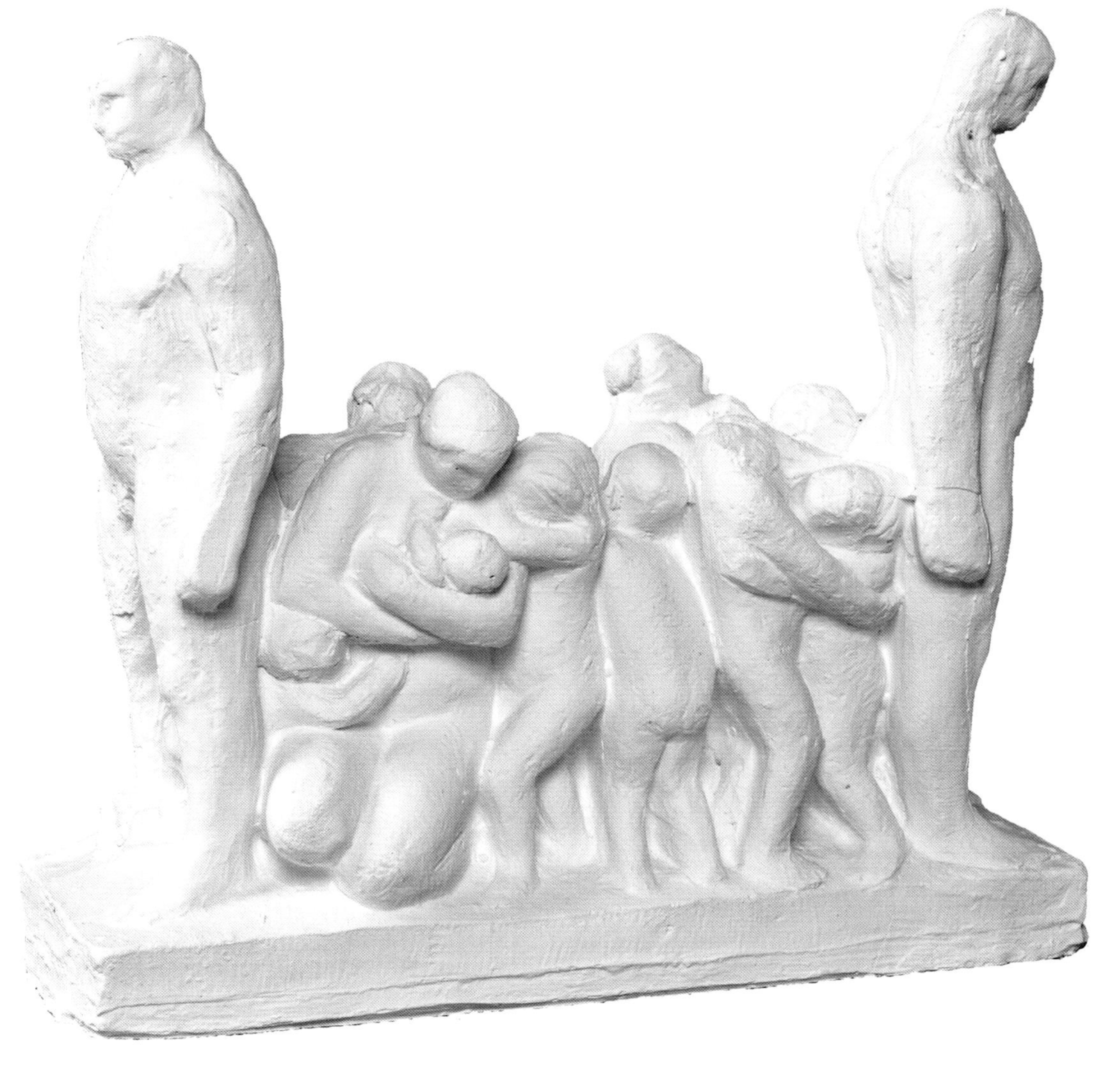

Cat. 173
Gustav Vigeland
The Clan, prob. 1915

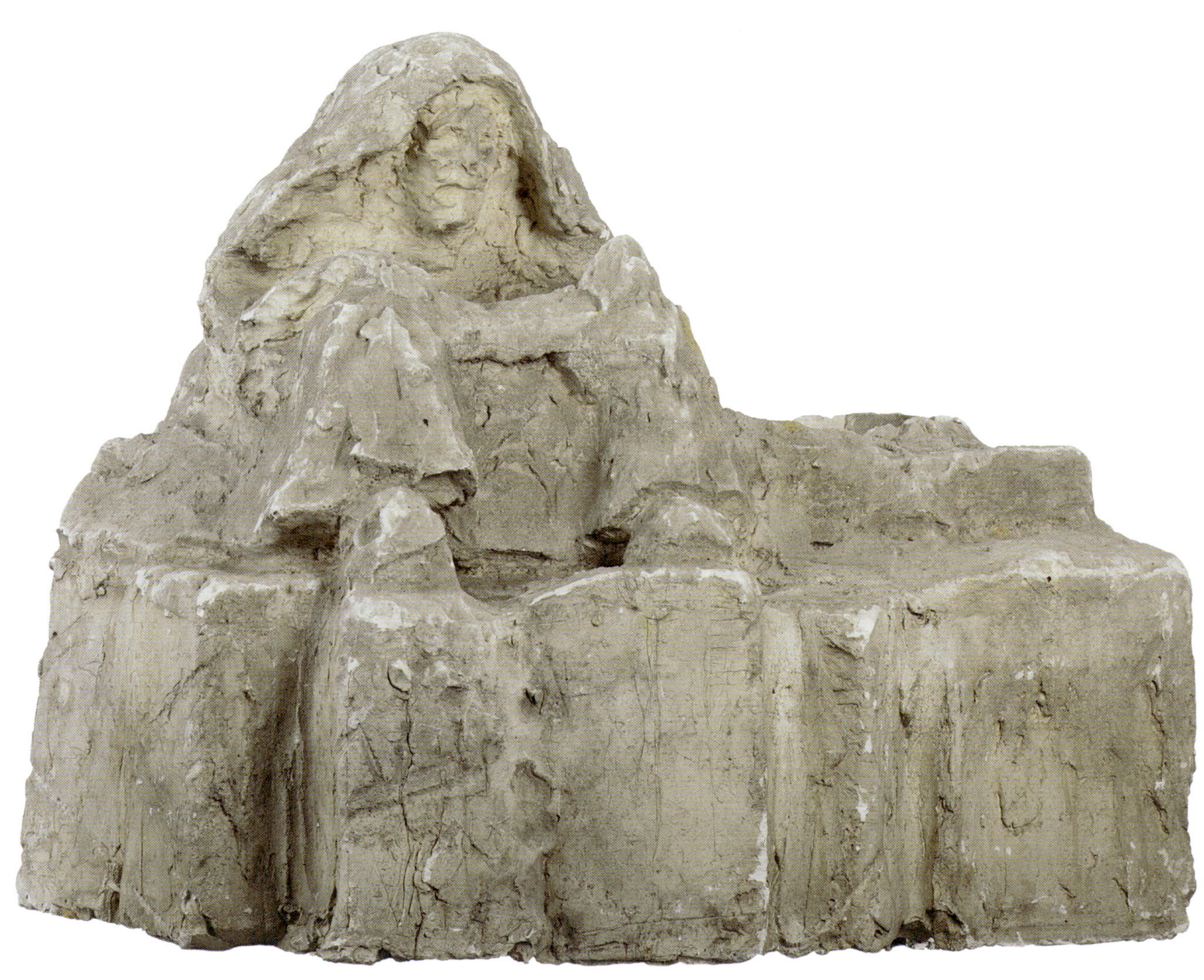

Cat. 174
Edvard Munch
Mother Norway, before 1932

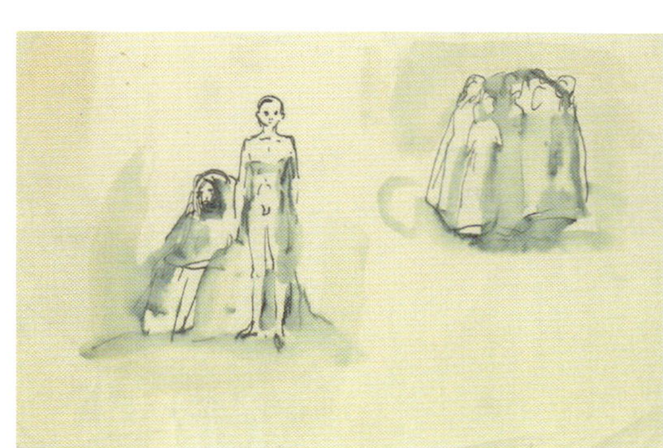

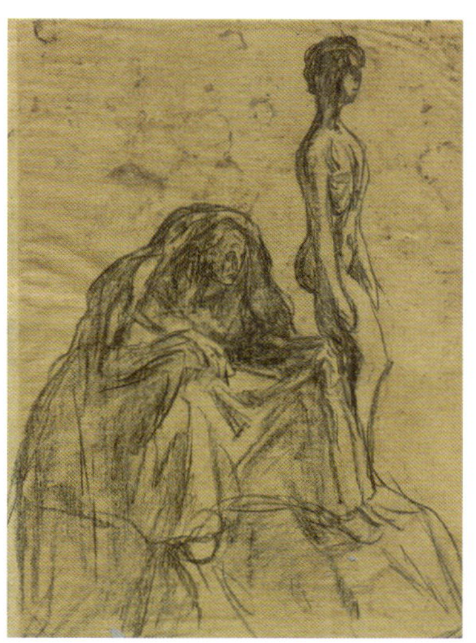

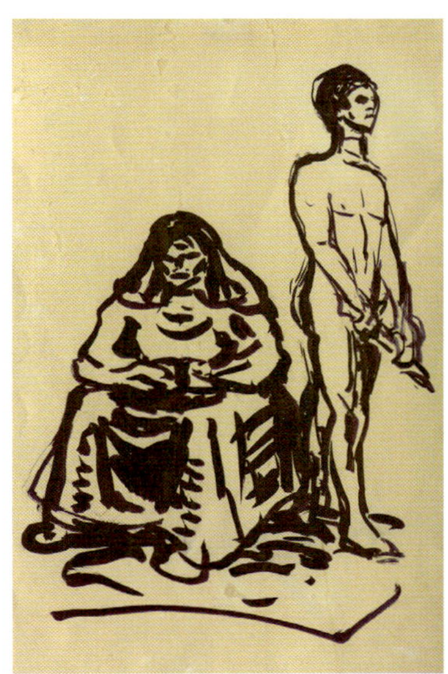

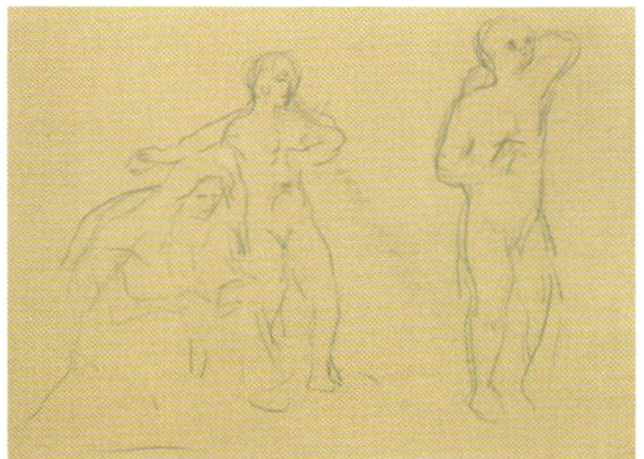

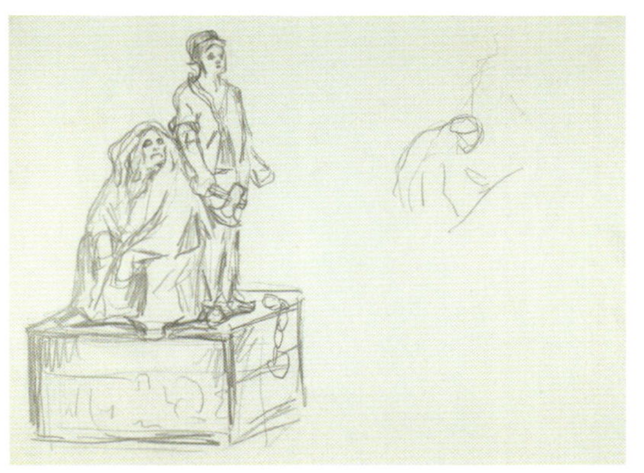

Cat. 177
Edvard Munch
Mother Norway, 1909–10

Cat. 175
Edvard Munch
Mother Norway and Group of People,
1920–30

Cat. 178
Edvard Munch
Mother Norway, 1909–10

Cat. 176
Edvard Munch
Mother Norway, 1909–10

Cat. 179
Edvard Munch
Mother Norway, 1909–12

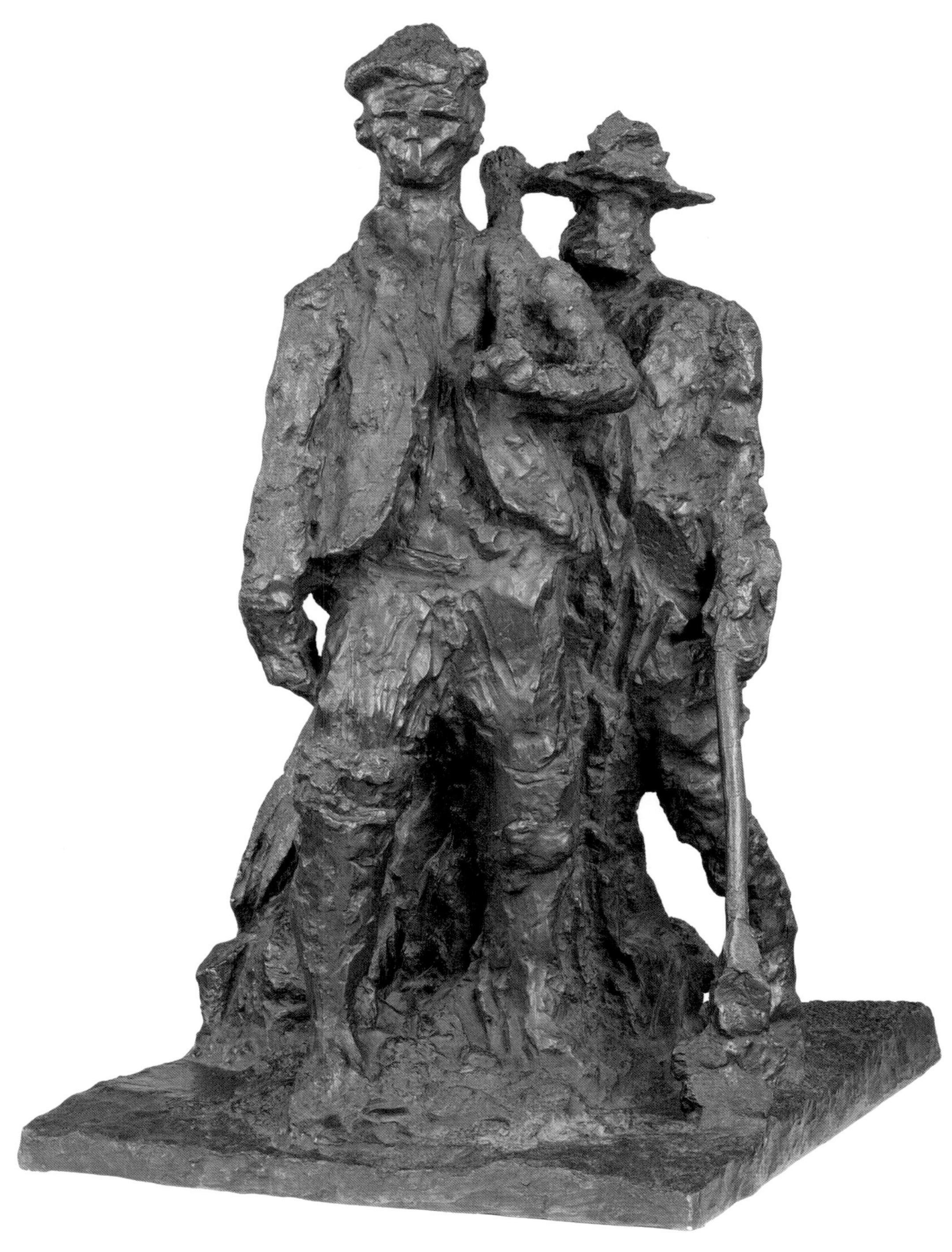

Cat. 180
Edvard Munch
Workers in Snow, 1910

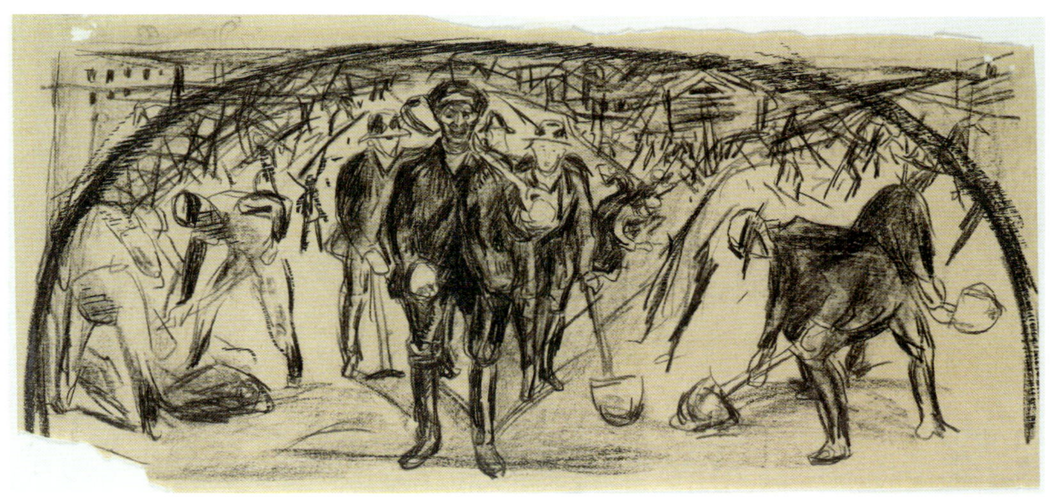

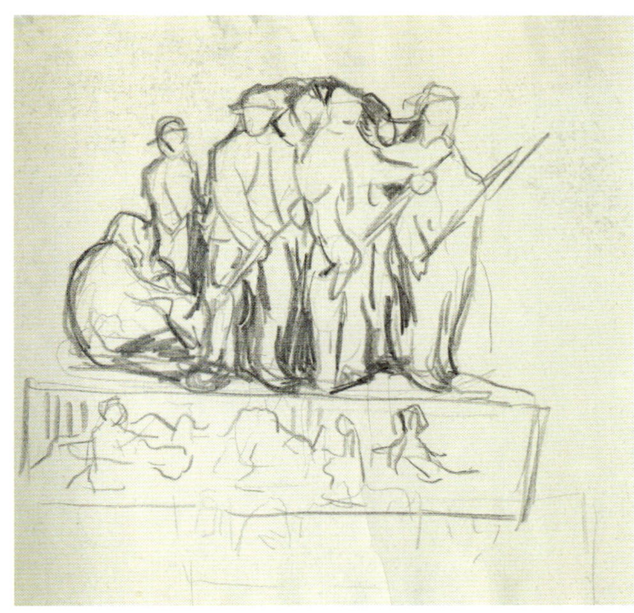

Cat. 181
Edvard Munch
Workers at Construction Site, 1931–33

Cat. 182
Edvard Munch
Draft for a Sculpture of Workers,
1915–25

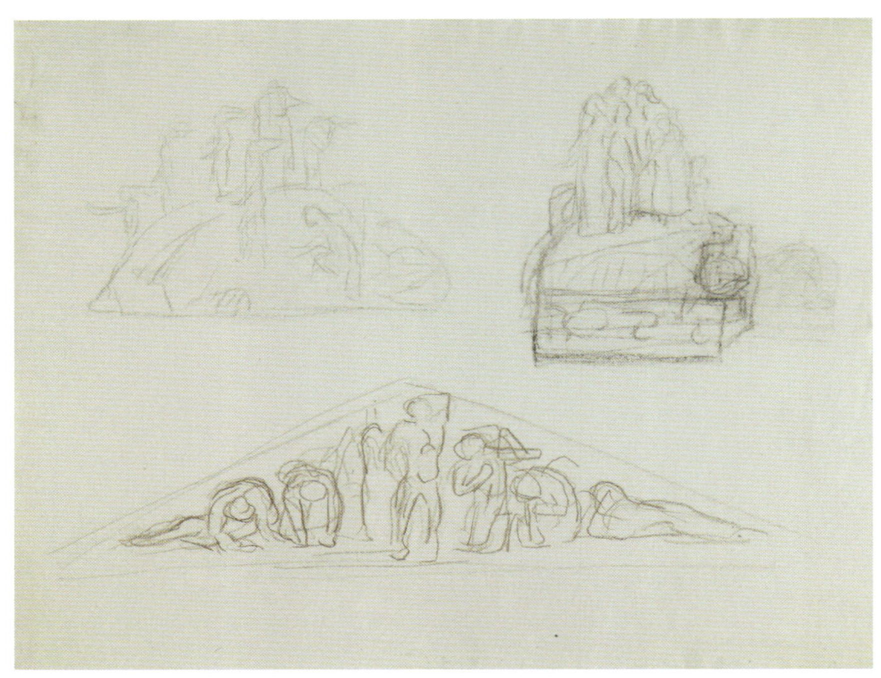

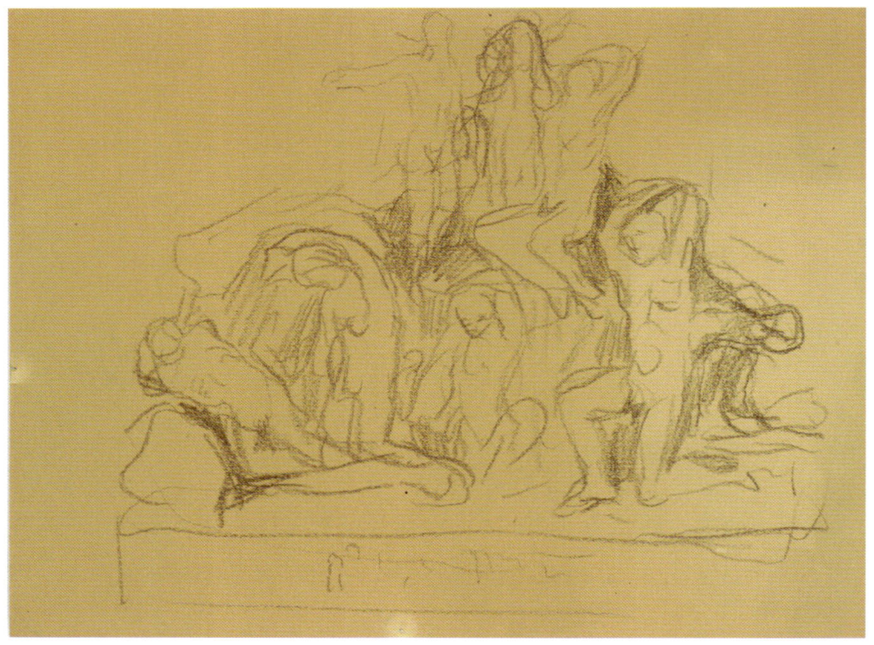

Cat. 183
Edvard Munch
Sketches for Sculpture Drafts, 1913–20

Cat. 184
Edvard Munch
Sketch for a Monument, 1924–25

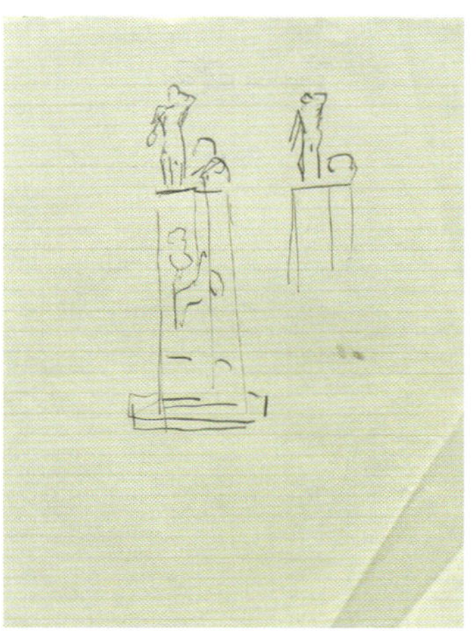

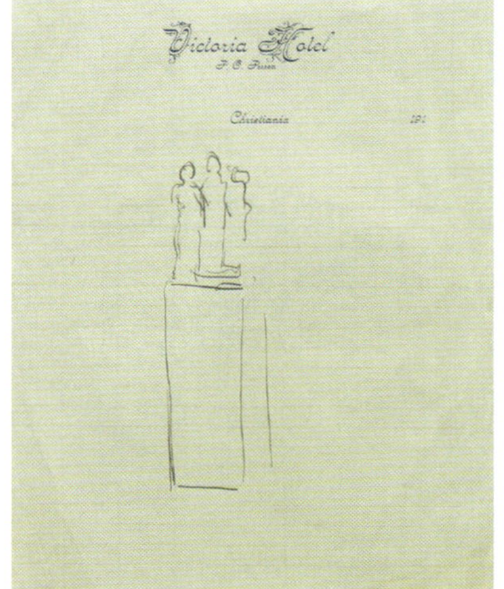

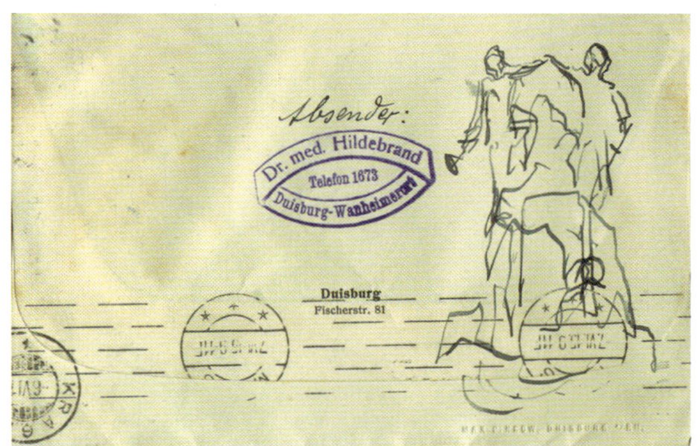

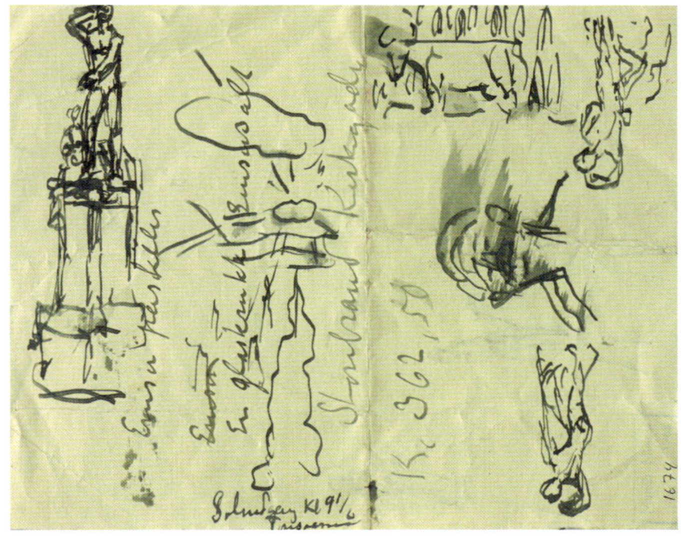

Cat. 185
Edvard Munch
Sketch for a Monument, 1910–19

Cat. 186
Edvard Munch
Sketch for a Monument, 1915

Cat. 187
Edvard Munch
Sketch for a Monument, 1910–19

Cat. 188
Edvard Munch
Sketch for a Monument, 1909–10

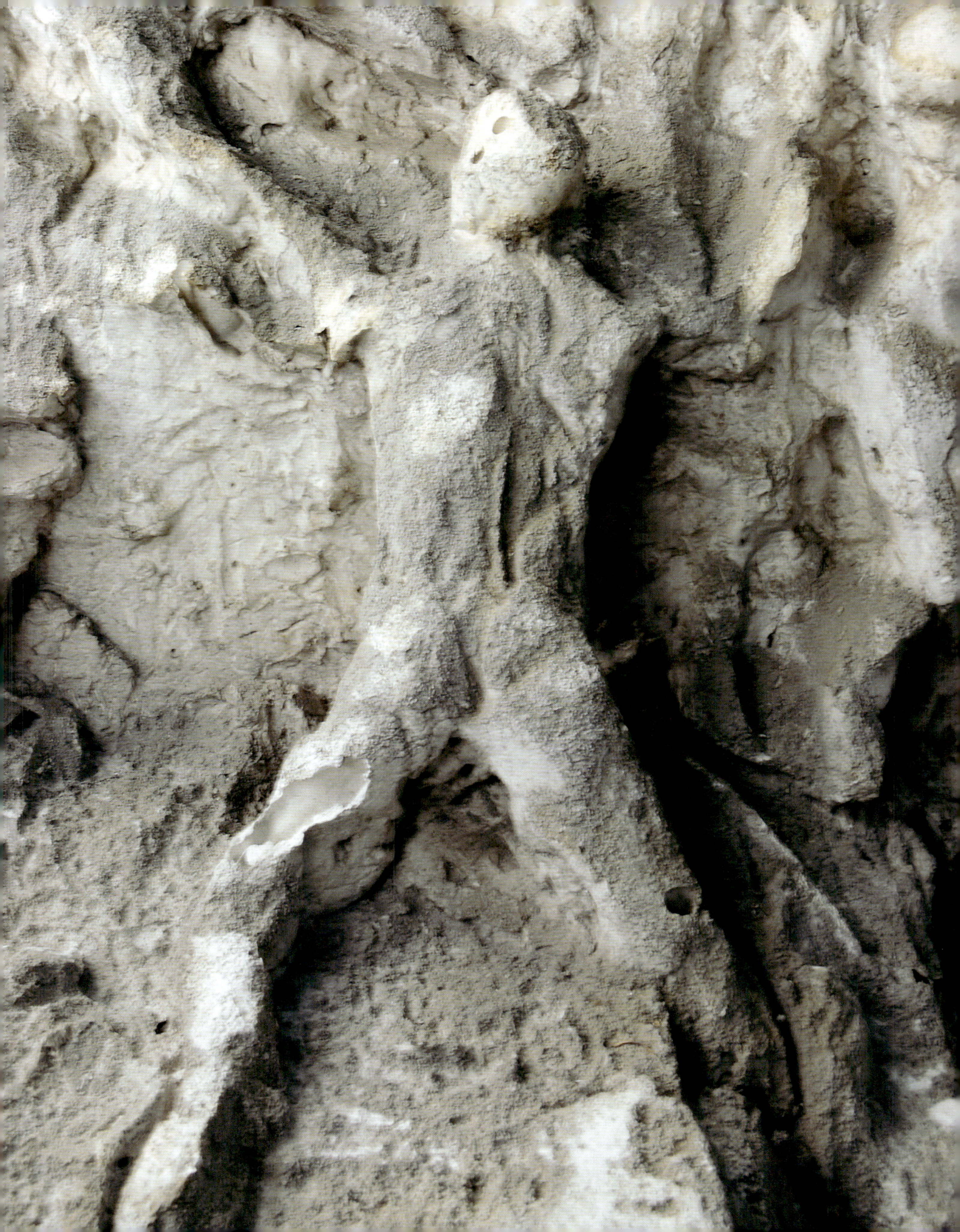

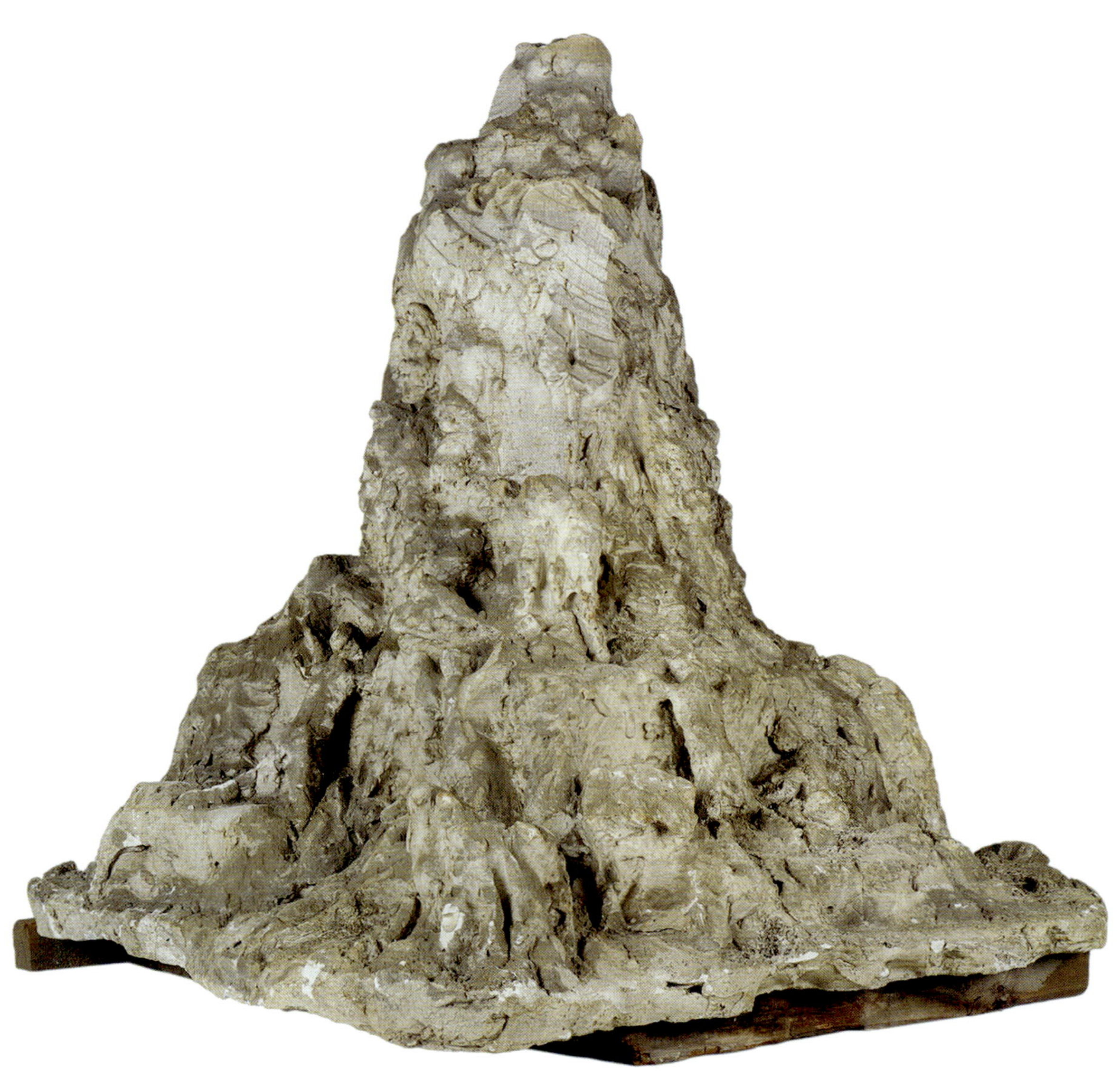

Cat. 189
Edvard Munch
The Human Mountain, prob. 1925–29

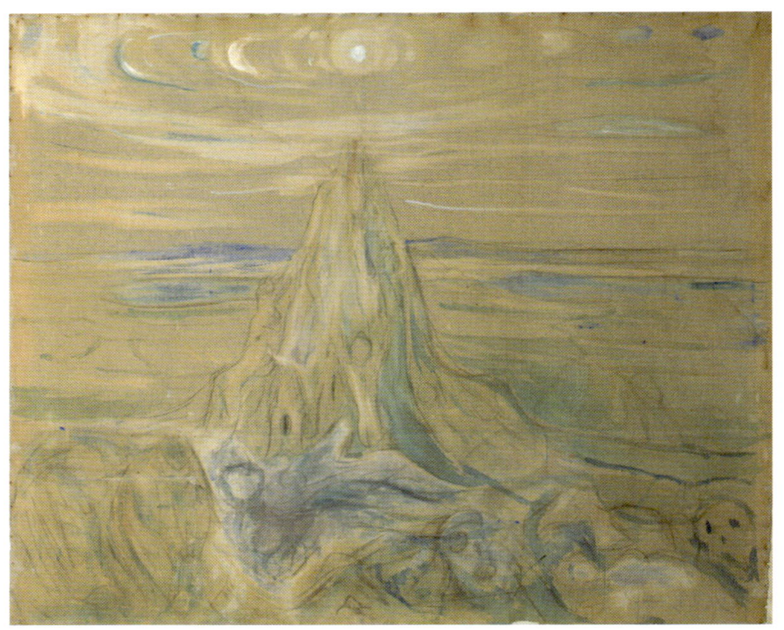

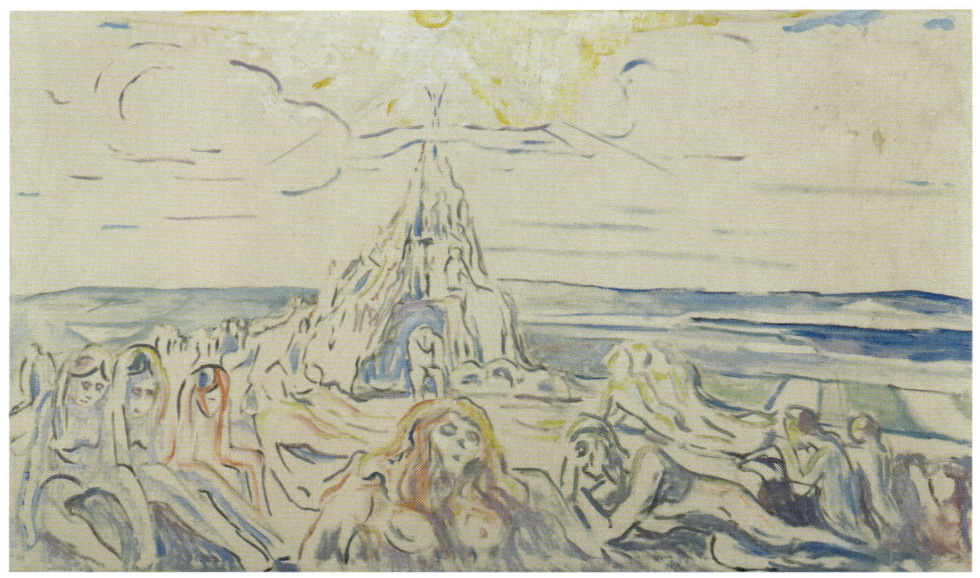

Cat. 190
Edvard Munch
The Human Mountain, 1909

Cat. 191
Edvard Munch
The Human Mountain, 1909–10

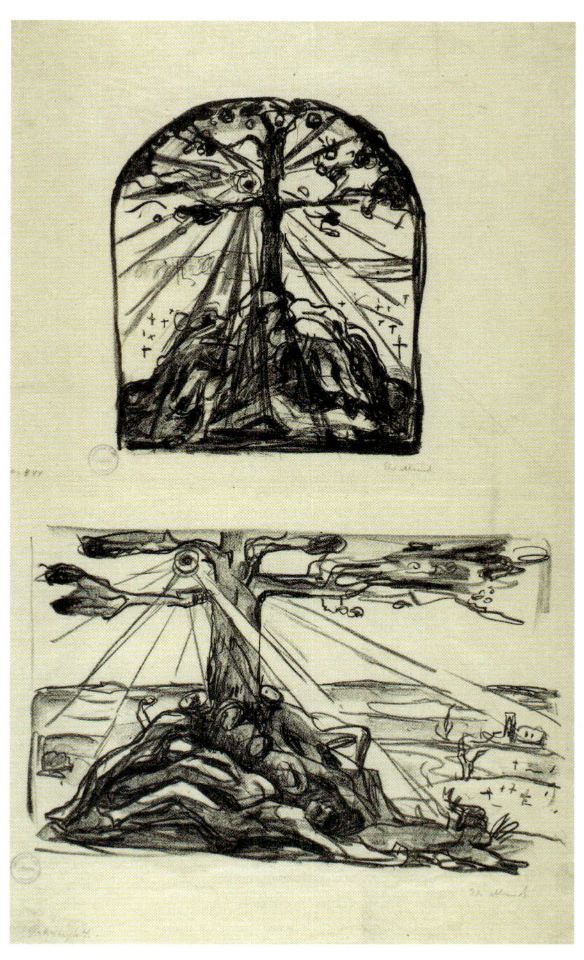

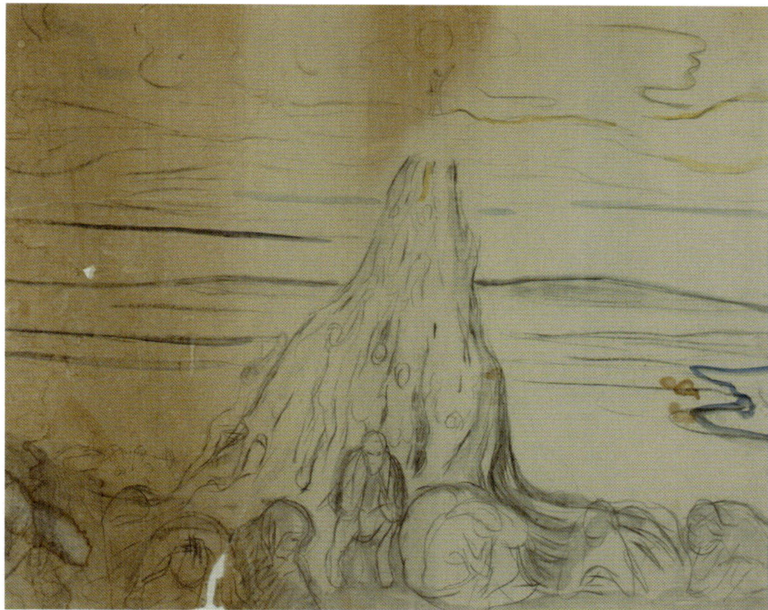

Cat. 192
Edvard Munch
The Tree III and *The Tree II*, 1916

Cat. 193
Edvard Munch
The Human Mountain, 1909–10

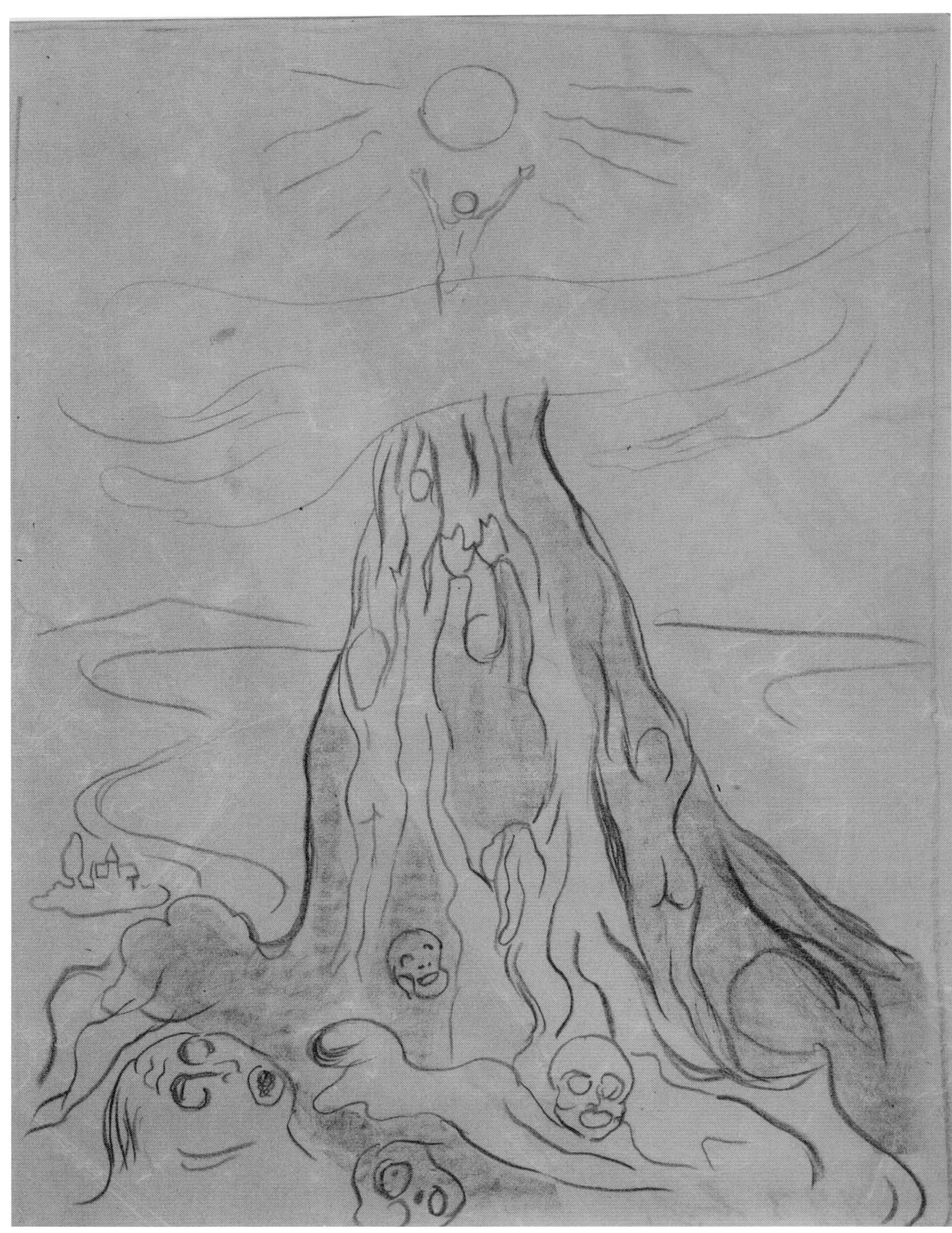

Cat. 194
Edvard Munch
The Human Mountain, 1897–98

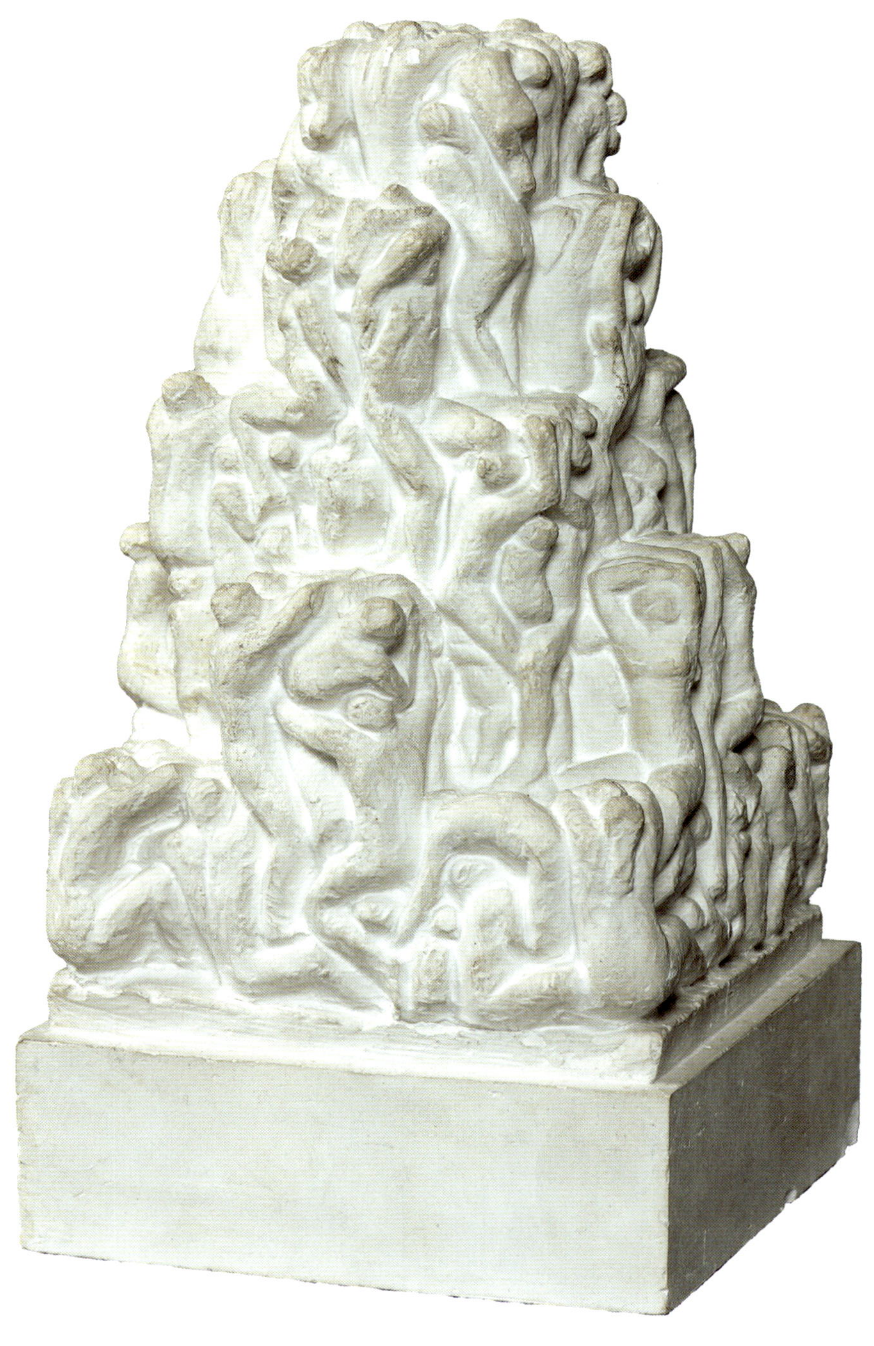

Cat. 195
Gustav Vigeland
Human Mountain, 1919

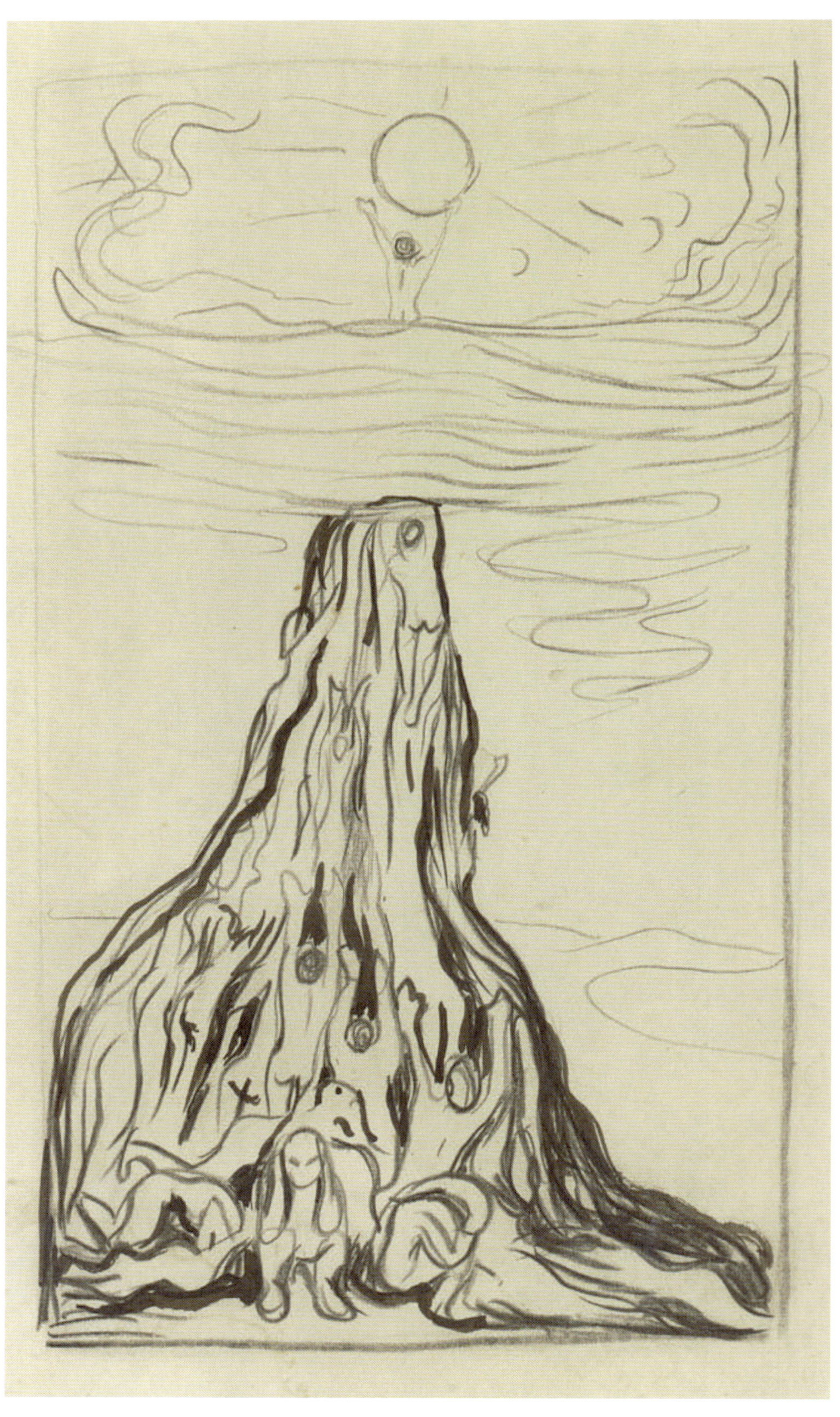

Cat. 196
Edvard Munch
The Human Mountain, 1897

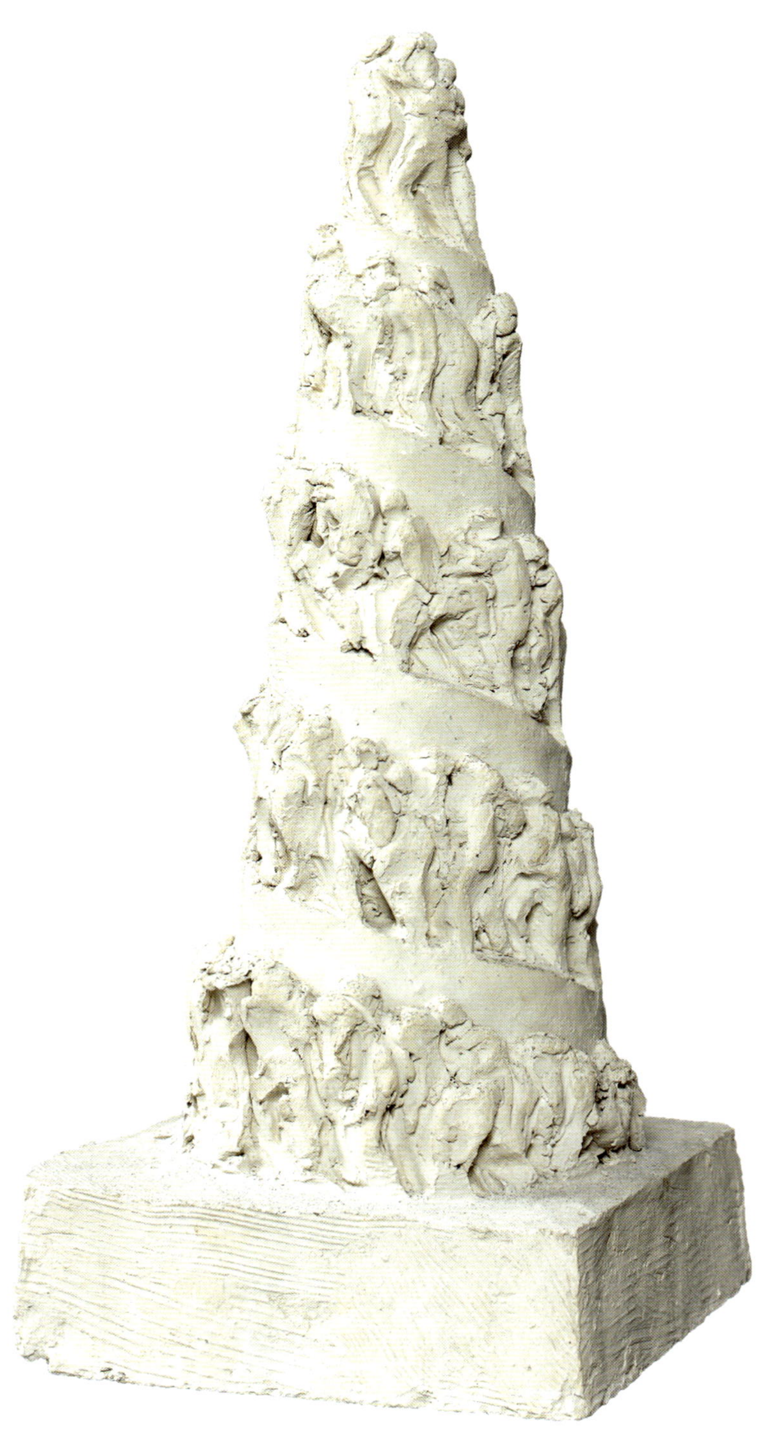

Cat. 197
Gustav Vigeland
Cone-shaped Column, 1923

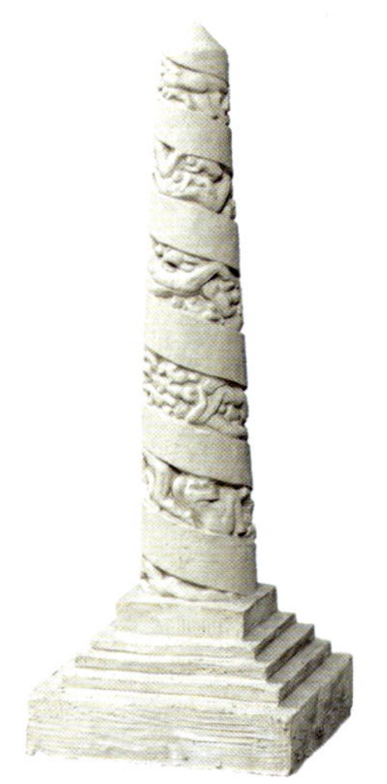
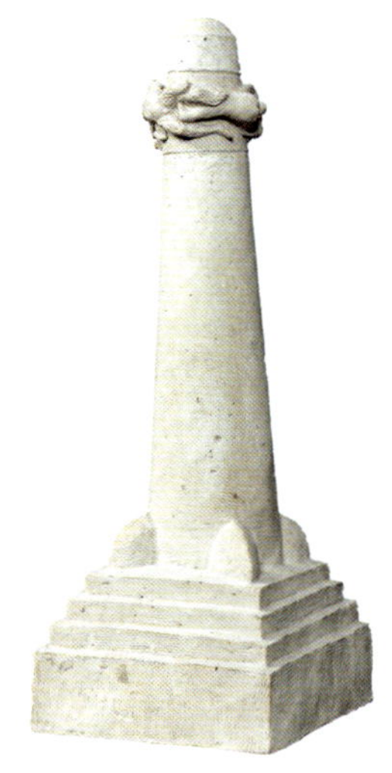
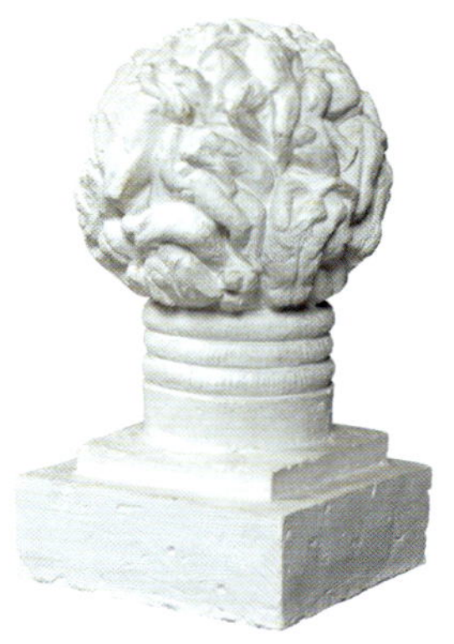
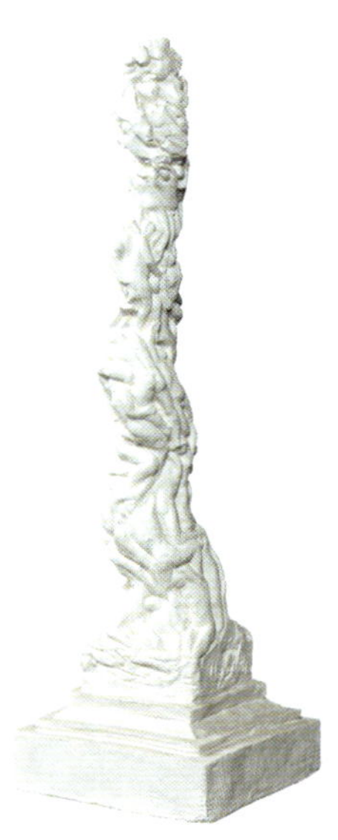
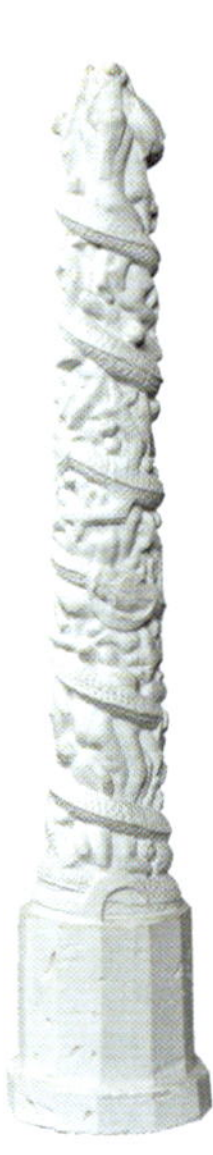

Cat. 198
Gustav Vigeland
Column with a Spiral Frieze, 1922

Cat. 199
Gustav Vigeland
Column, 1919

Cat. 200
Gustav Vigeland
*Column with a Garland
of Figures*, 1922

Cat. 201
Gustav Vigeland
Column, 1919

Cat. 202
Gustav Vigeland
Human Orb, 1922

Cat. 203
Gustav Vigeland
The Monolith, 1922

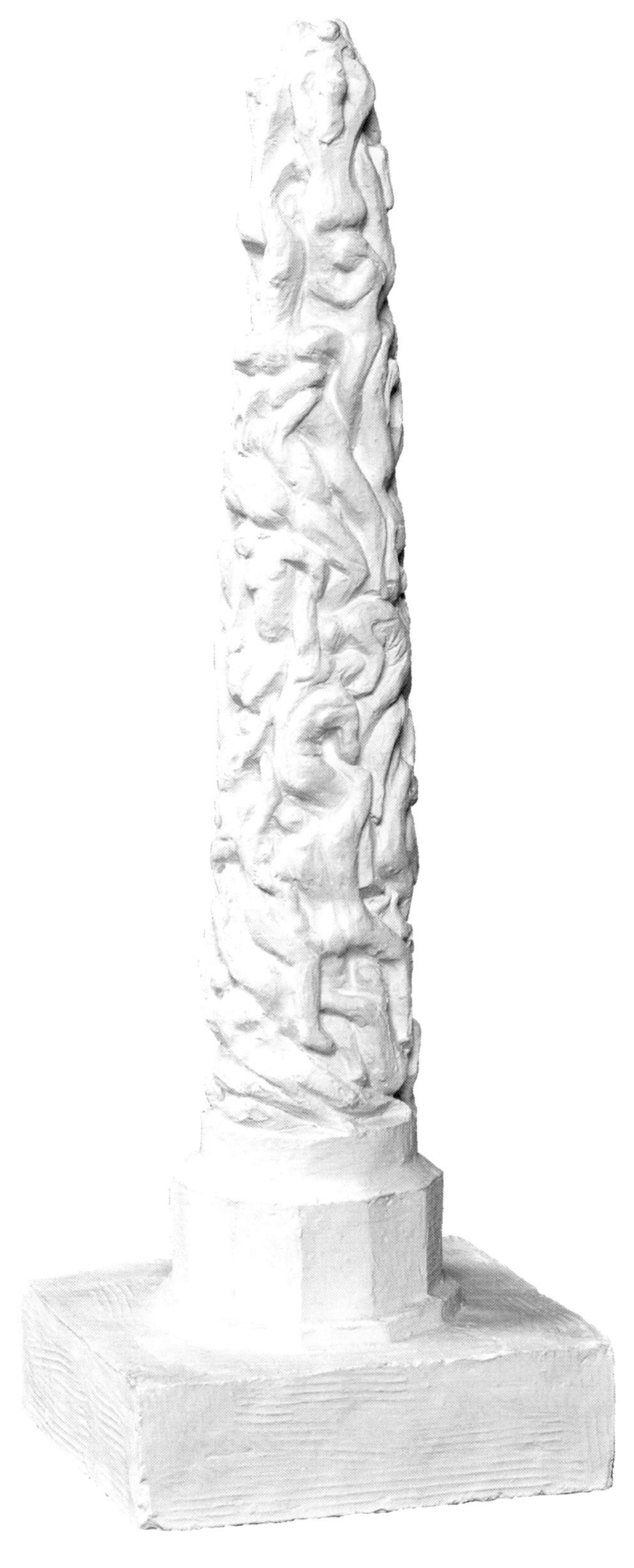

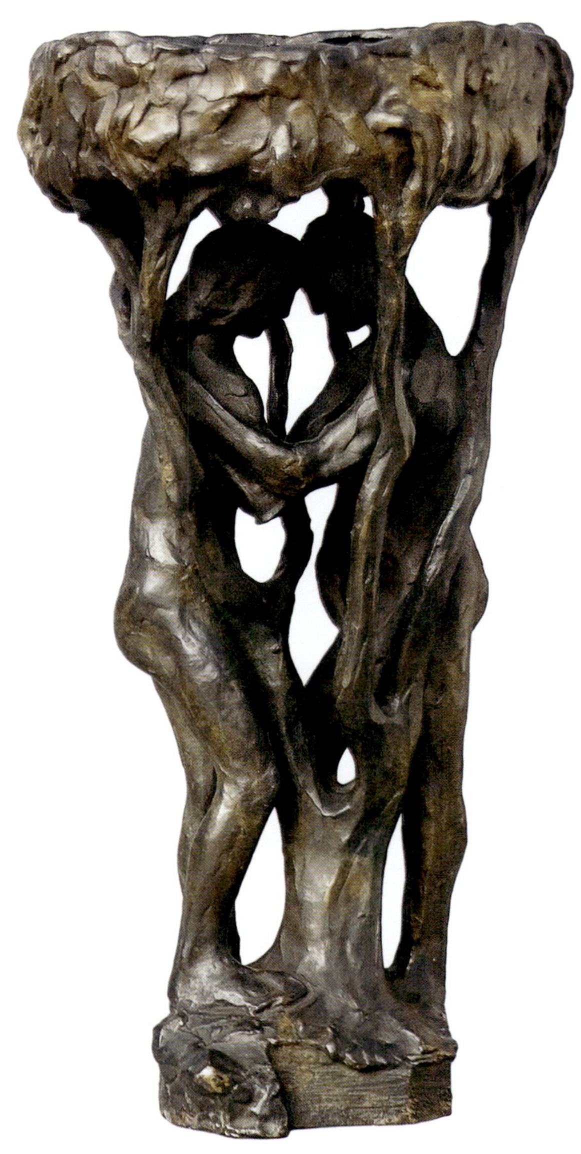

Cat. 204
Gustav Vigeland
Boy and Girl Touching Foreheads,
1905

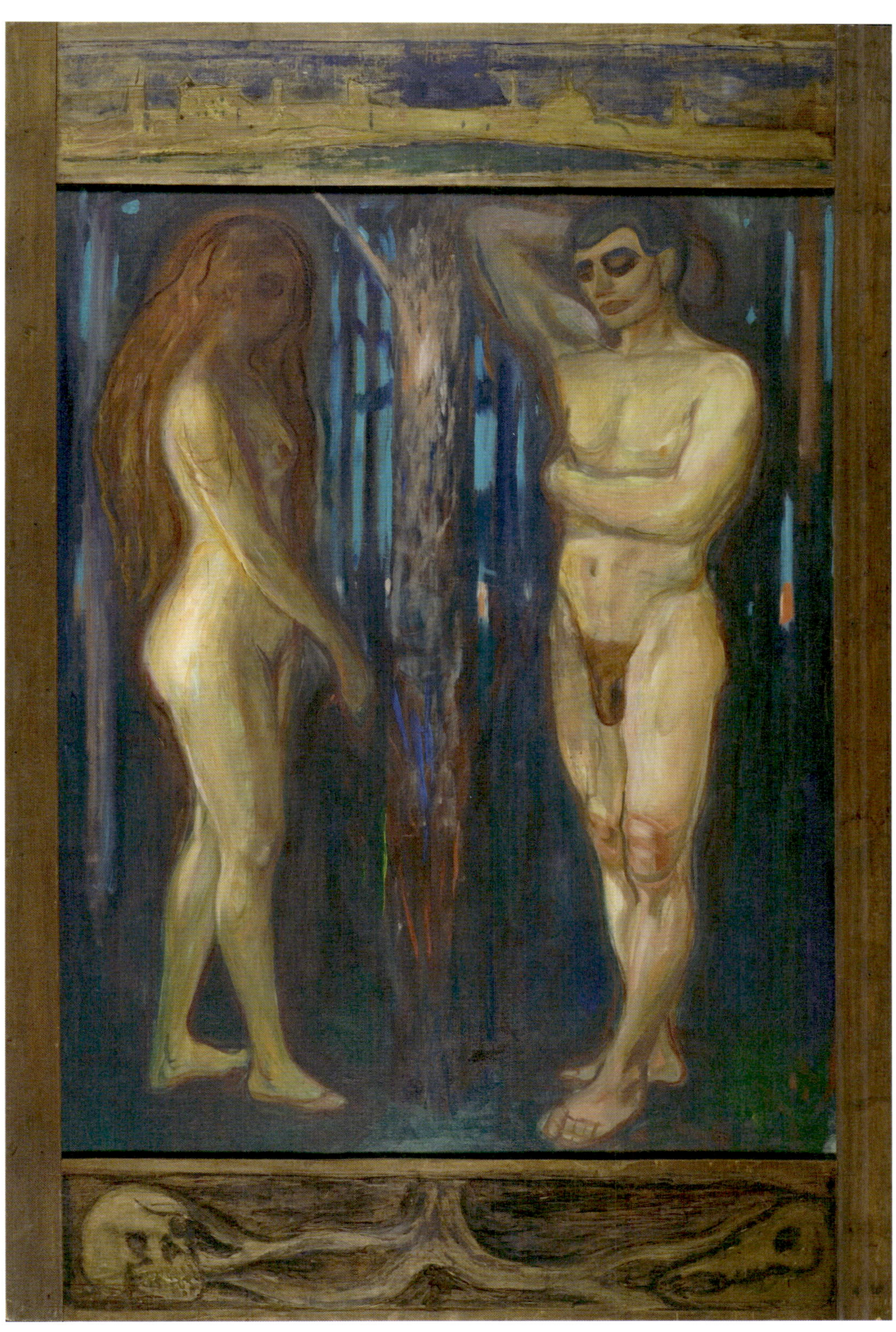

Cat. 205
Edvard Munch
Metabolism, 1898–99

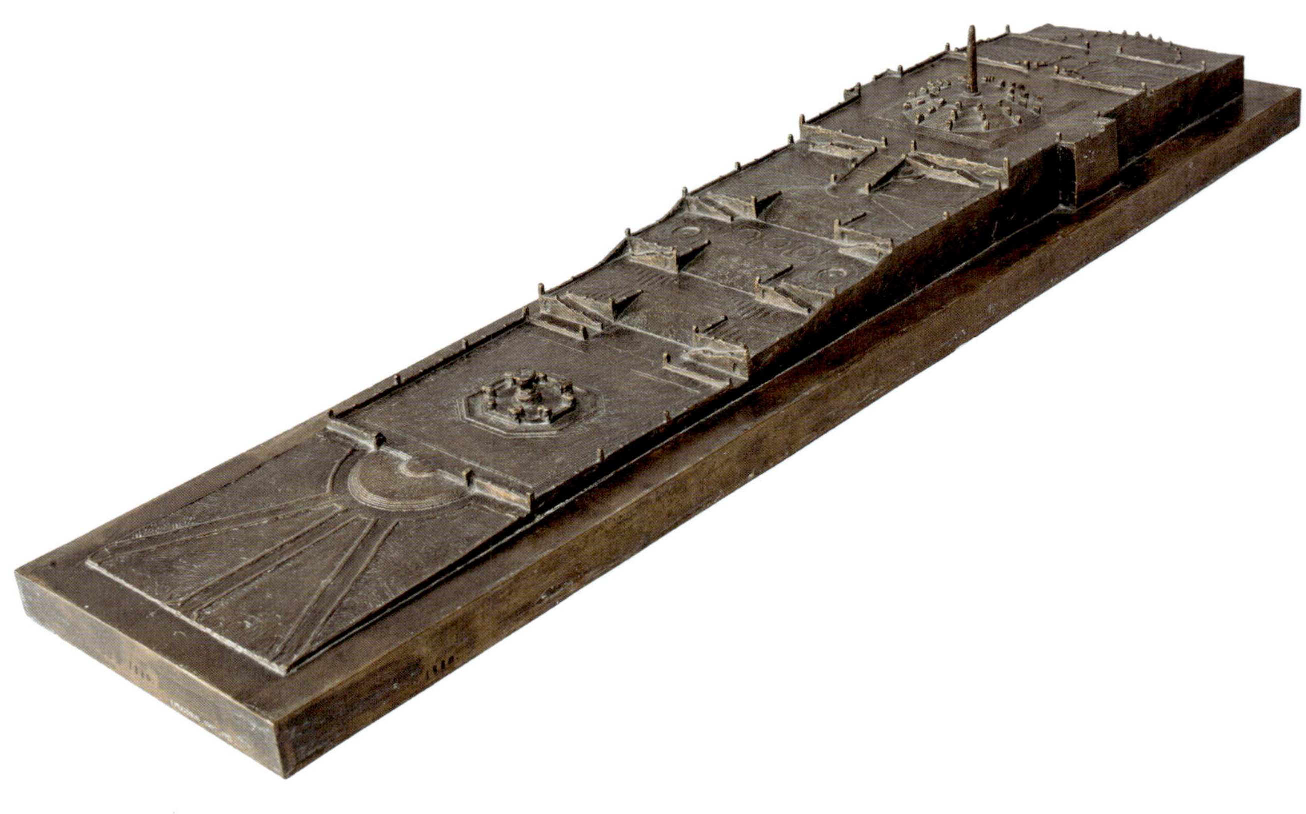

Cat. 206
Gustav Vigeland
*Model of the Park with Monolith and
Fountain*, 1922

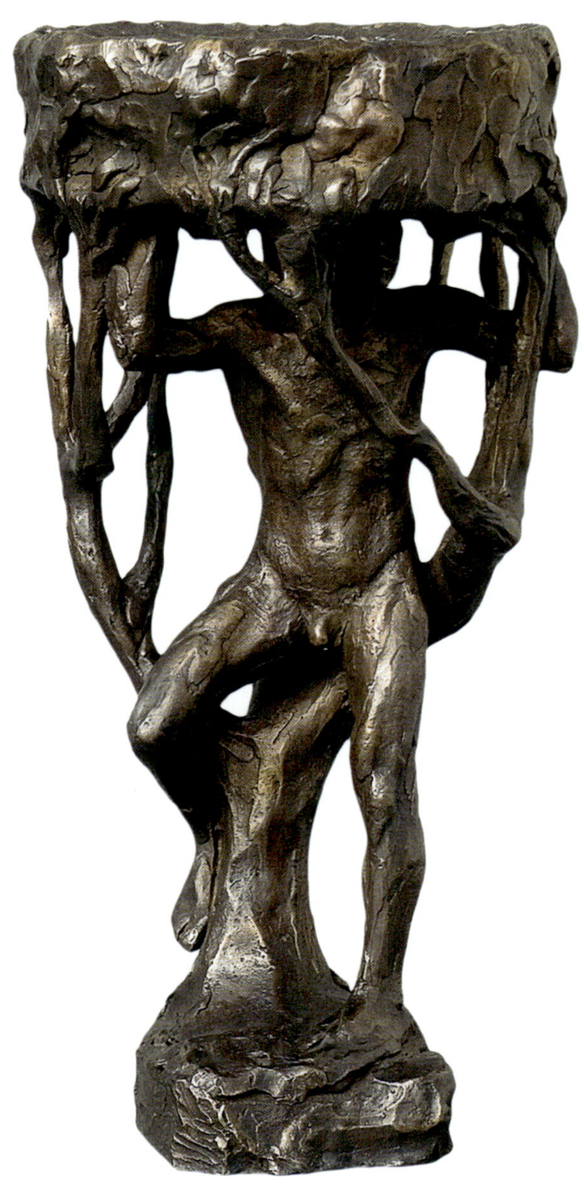

Cat. 207
Gustav Vigeland
*Man with His Head Against the Crown
of a Tree*, 1905

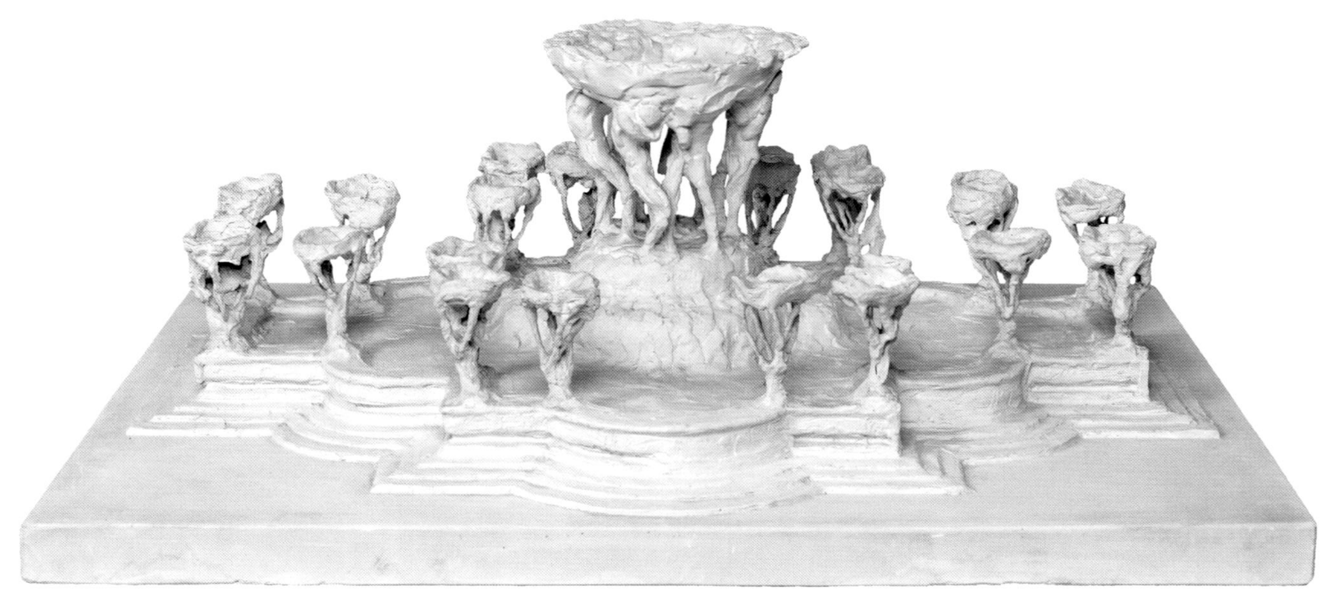

Cat. 208
Gustav Vigeland
Model of the Fountain, 1905–06

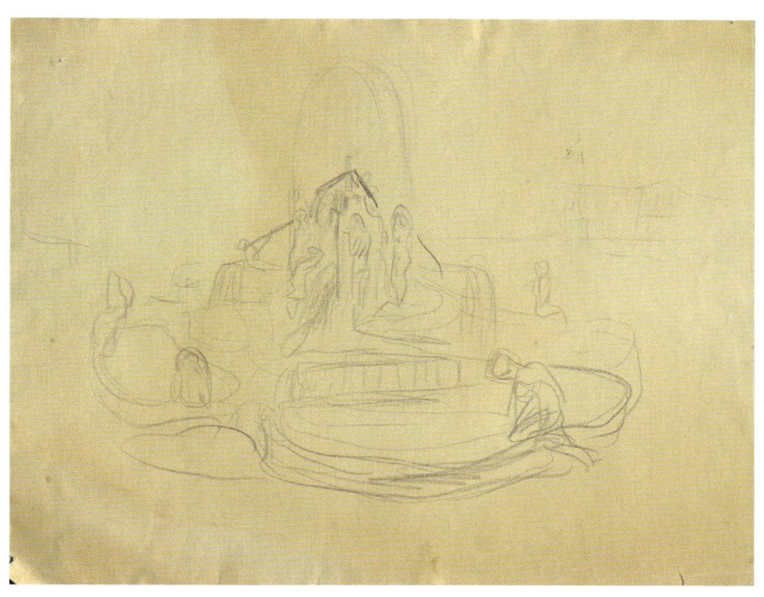

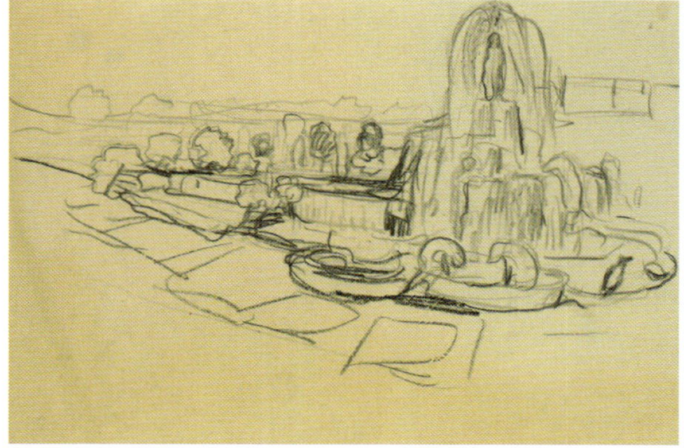

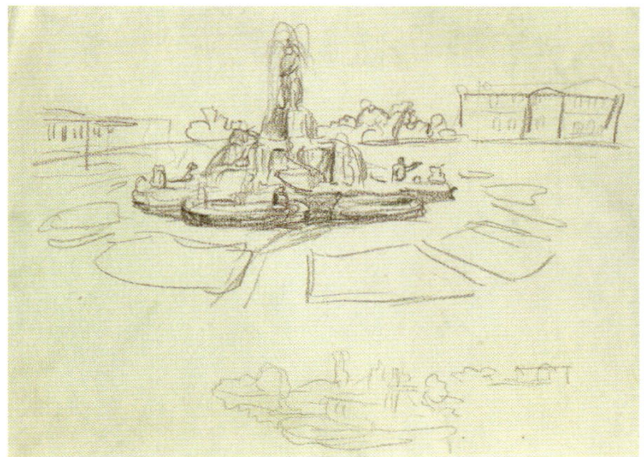

Cat. 209
Edvard Munch
*Fountain in Front of the
Royal Palace*, 1920–30

Cat. 210
Edvard Munch
*Fountain in Front of the
Royal Palace*, 1920–30

Cat. 211
Edvard Munch
*Fountain in Front of the
Royal Palace*, 1920–30

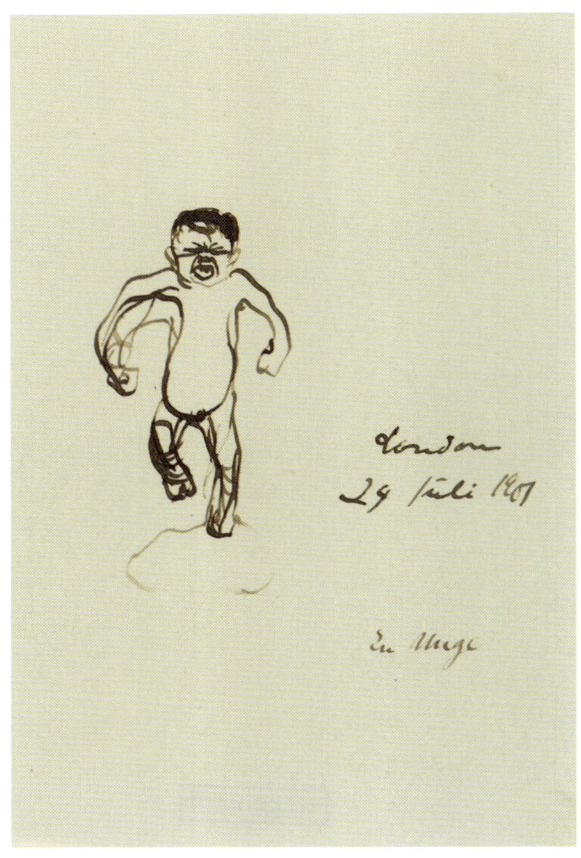

Cat. 212
Gustav Vigeland
A Child, 1901

Cat. 213
Gustav Vigeland
The Angry Boy, 1911

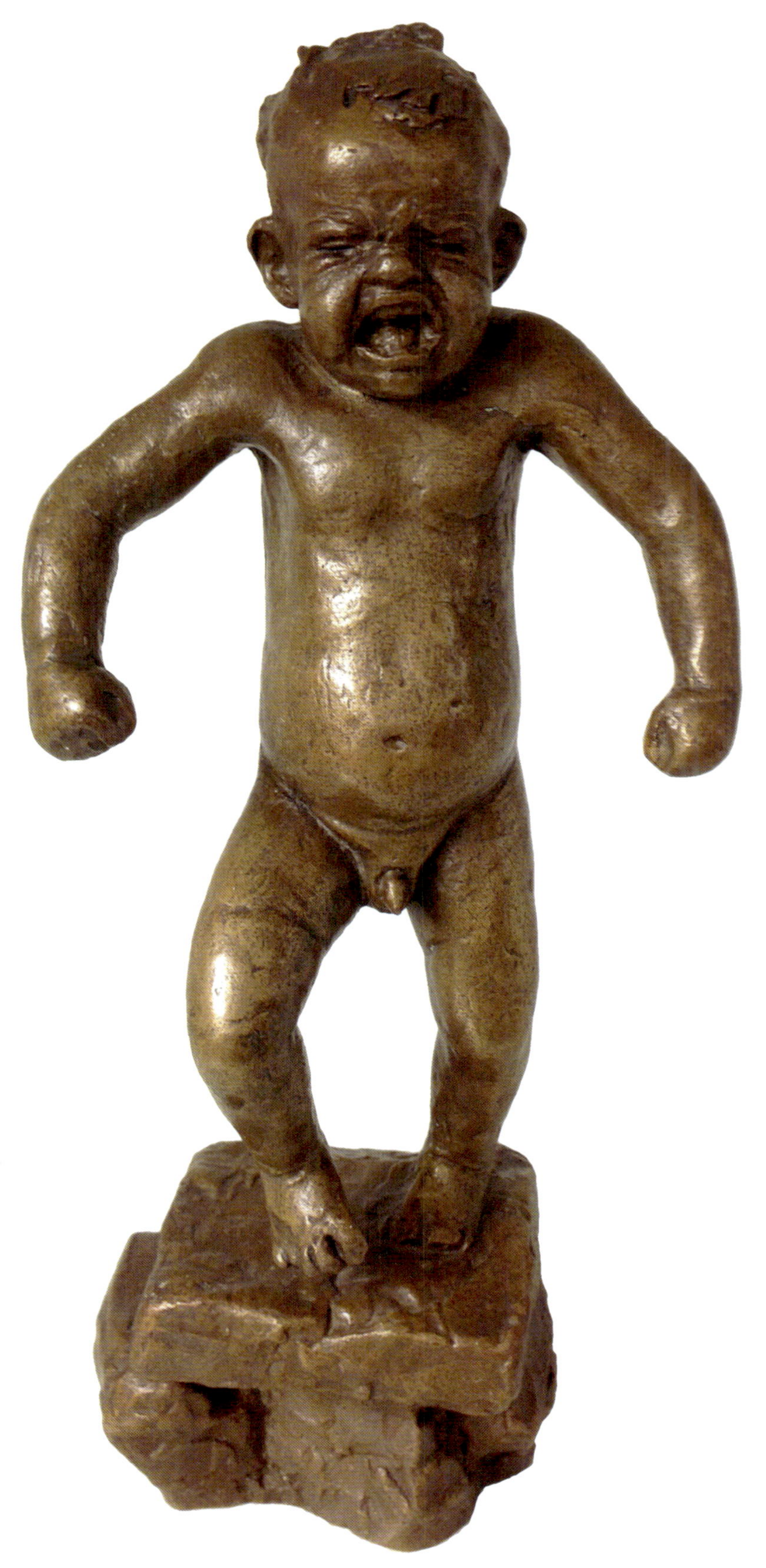

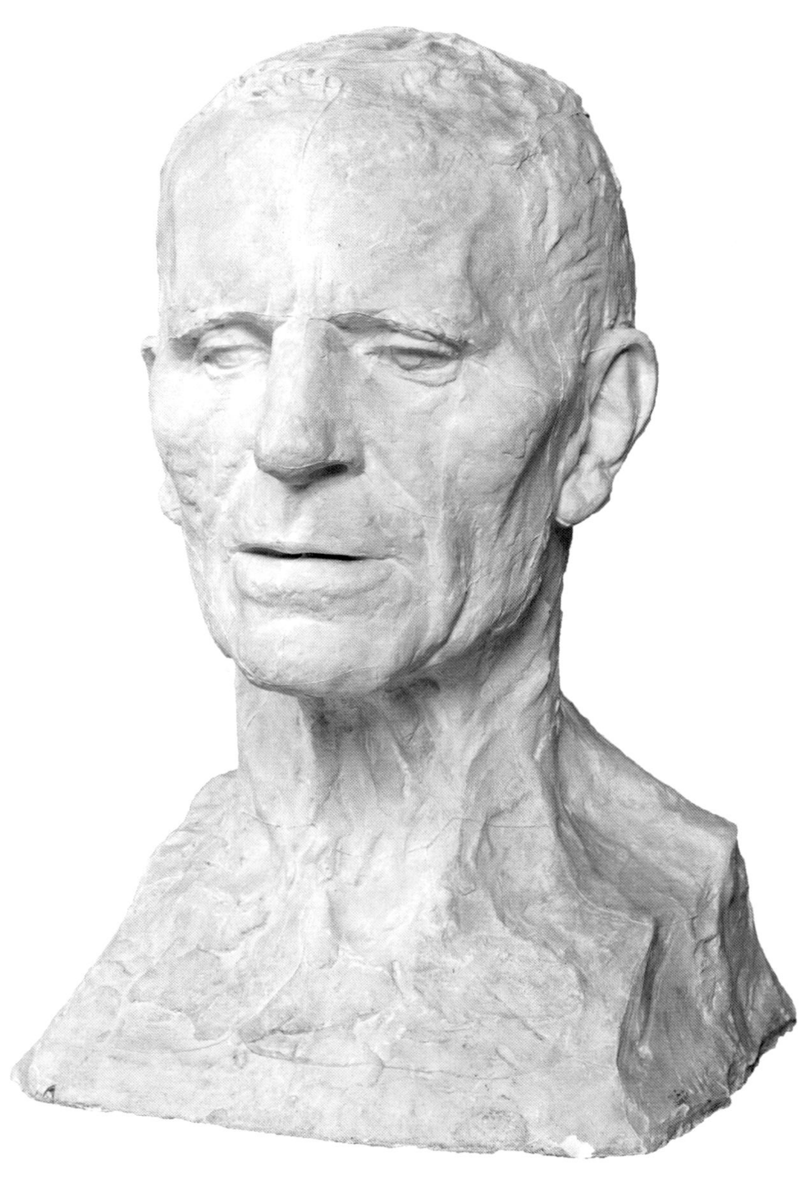

Cat. 214
Gustav Vigeland
Jonas Lie, 1904

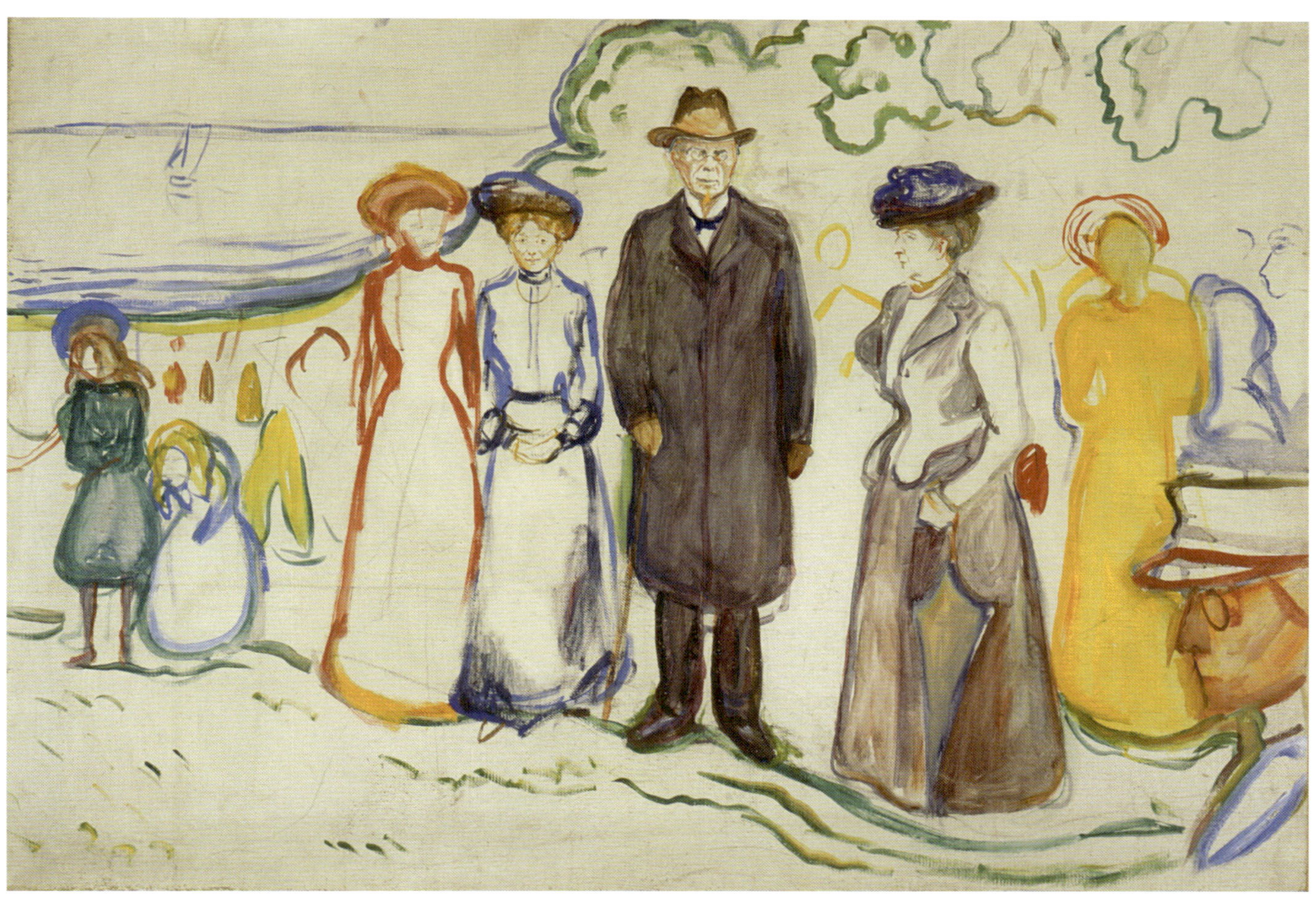

Cat. 215
Edvard Munch
Jonas Lie and His Family,
1902–03

List of Exhibited Works

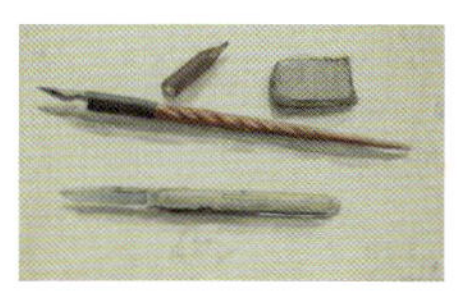

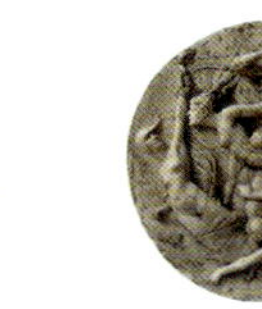

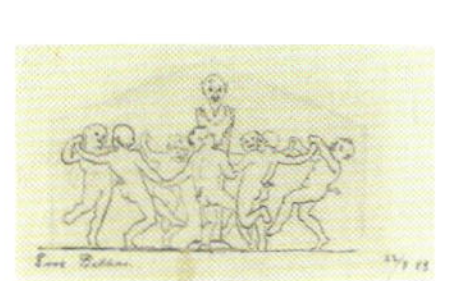

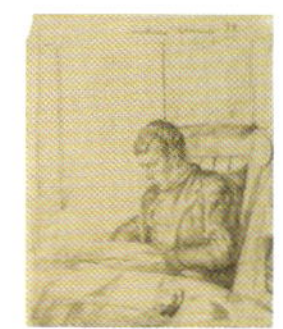

Photographs of works by Gustav Vigeland and Edvard Munch are, where not otherwise specified, © Vigeland Museum and Munch Museum respectively

Cat. 4
Edvard Munch: *Drawing Tools*, 1877
Watercolour, pencil
103 × 173 mm
Munch Museum
MM.T.00118-08

Cat. 8
Gustav Vigeland: *Tantalus is Led to the Underworld by the Eumenides*, 1890
Plaster
66 (diameter) x 8 cm
Vigeland Museum
VM.S.0911

Cat. 12
Gustav Vigeland: *Bacchus*, 1889
Ink, pencil
145 × 230 mm
Vigeland Museum
VM.T.D000.0015

Cat. 16
Edvard Munch: *Andreas Munch*, 1884
Pen
217 × 172 mm
Munch Museum
MM.T.02283-recto

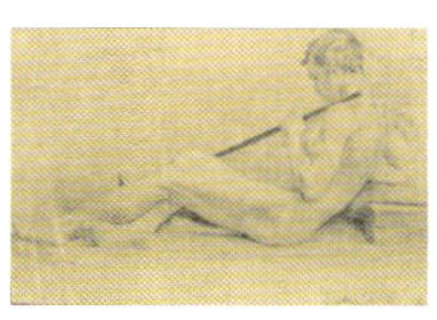

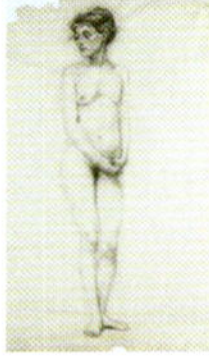

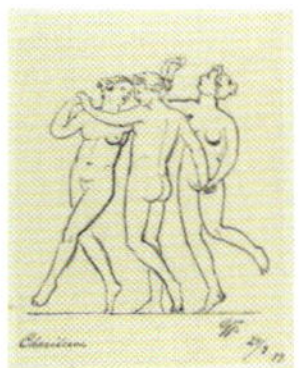

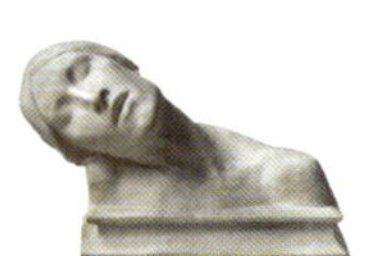

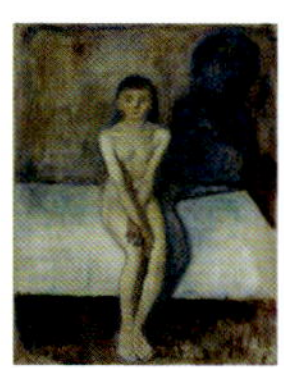

Cat. 1
Edvard Munch: *Reclining Male Nude with Stick*, 1881
Pencil
242 × 365 mm
Munch Museum
MM.T.01159

Cat. 5
Edvard Munch: *Standing Nude*, 1889
Pencil
627 × 472 mm
Munch Museum
MM.T.00858

Cat. 9
Gustav Vigeland: *The Charites*, 1889
Ink
225 × 175 mm
Vigeland Museum
VM.T.D000.0004

Cat. 13
Gustav Vigeland: *Sleeping Woman*, 1892
Plaster
28.5 × 44 × 22 cm
Vigeland Museum
VM.S.0648

Cat. 17
Edvard Munch: *Puberty*, 1894
Oil on unprimed canvas
149 × 112 cm
Munch Museum
MM.M.00281 (Woll M 346)

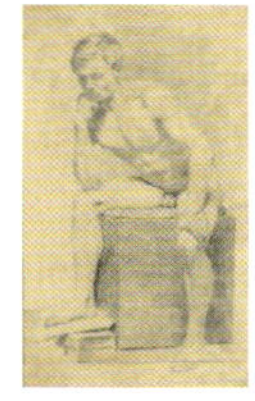

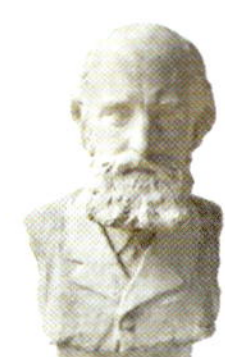

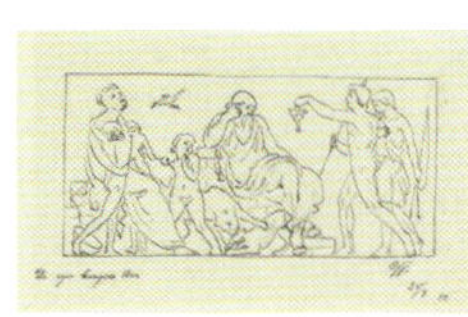

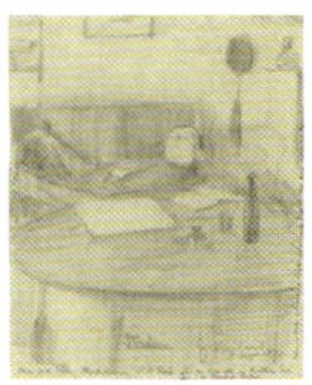

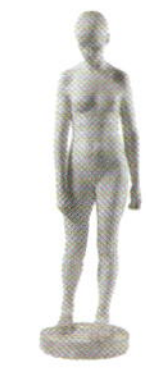

Cat. 2
Edvard Munch: *Seated Male Nude*, 1881
Pencil
420 × 256 mm
Munch Museum
MM.T.01160

Cat. 6
Gustav Vigeland: *Lorentz Dietrichson*, 1892
Plaster
48 × 30 × 28 cm
Vigeland Museum
VM.S.0650

Cat. 10
Gustav Vigeland: *The Seven Years of Hunger*, 1889
Ink
175 × 223 mm
Vigeland Museum
VM.T.D000.0005

Cat. 14
Gustav Vigeland: *O. Ström*, 1893
Pencil, ink
216 × 175 mm
Vigeland Museum
VM.T.AB00.0031

Cat. 18
Gustav Vigeland: *Young Girl*, 1892
Plaster
163 × 52 × 44 cm
National Museum of Art, Architecture and Design, Oslo. NG.S.00709. Photo © National Museum

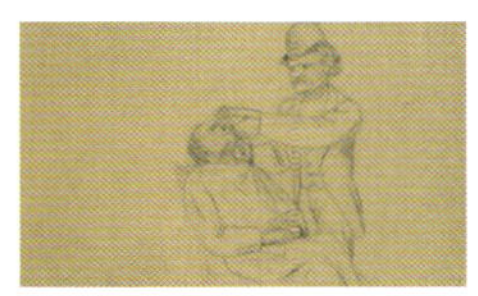

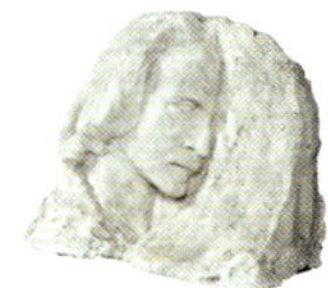

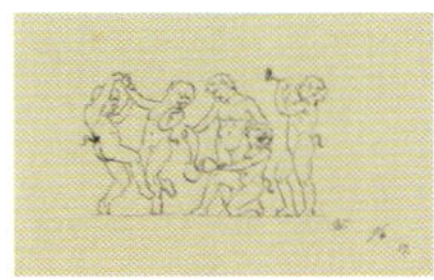

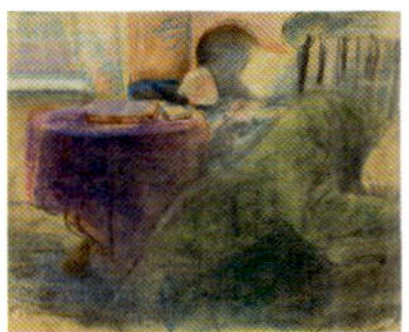

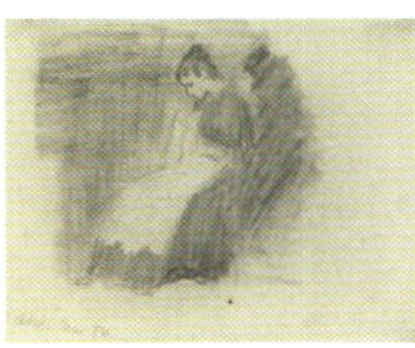

Cat. 3
Edvard Munch: *At the Barber's*, 1880
Pencil
112 × 186 mm
Munch Museum
MM.T.00120-11-recto

Cat. 7
Gustav Vigeland: *Julius Middelthun*, before 1889
Plaster
30.5 × 38 × 18 cm
Vigeland Museum
VM.S.0931

Cat. 11
Gustav Vigeland: *Little Devils Making Music*, 1889
Ink
171 × 237 mm
Vigeland Museum
VM.T.D000.0007

Cat. 15
Edvard Munch: *Interior with Sleeping People*, 1885
Pastel, pencil
291 × 360 mm
Munch Museum
MM.T.02299-recto

Cat. 19
Gustav Vigeland: *Woman Sewing*, 1894
Pencil
174 × 214 mm
Vigeland Museum
VM.T.AB00.0038

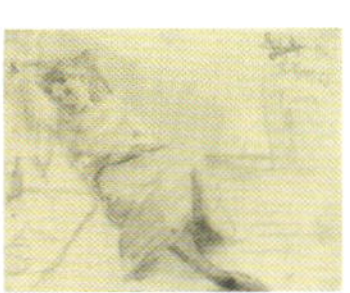

Cat. 20
Gustav Vigeland: *Sleeping Woman*, 1894
Pencil
140 × 178 mm
Vigeland Museum
VM.T.AB00.0040

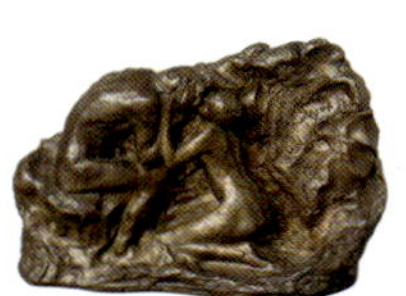

Cat. 24
Gustav Vigeland: *Consolation*, 1893
Bronze
26.5 × 36 × 19 cm
Vigeland Museum
VM.S.0928.01

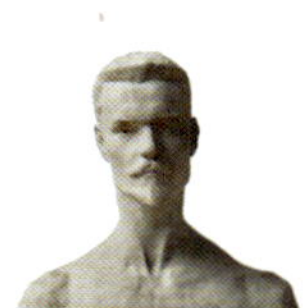

Cat. 28
Gustav Vigeland: *Jens Thiis*, 1894
Plaster
44 × 47.5 × 16 cm
Vigeland Museum
VM.S.0655

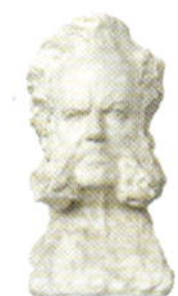

Cat. 32
Gustav Vigeland: *Henrik Ibsen*, 1903
Polyester
49 × 27.5 × 30.5 cm
Vigeland Museum
VM.S.0682

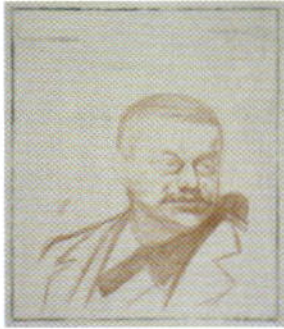

Cat. 36
Edvard Munch: *Gunnar Heiberg*, 1896
Lithograph
490 × 420 mm
Munch Museum
MM.G.00217-11 (Woll G 83)

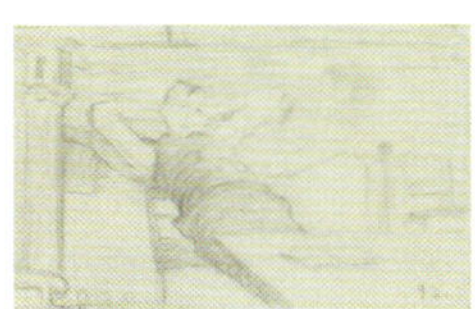

Cat. 21
Gustav Vigeland: *Young Man in Interior*, 1893
Pencil
112 × 179 mm
Vigeland Museum
VM.T.AB00.0036b

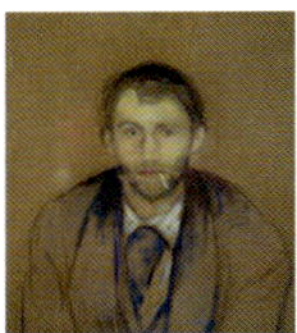

Cat. 25
Edvard Munch: *Stanisław Przybyszewski*, 1895
Mixed media on unprimed canvas
62.5 × 55.5 cm
Munch Museum
MM.M.00134 (Woll M 383)

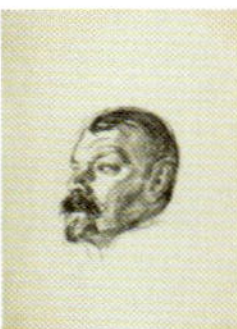

Cat. 29
Edvard Munch: *Jens Thiis*, 1913
Lithograph
292 × 237 mm
Munch Museum
MM.G.00371-06
(Woll G 447)

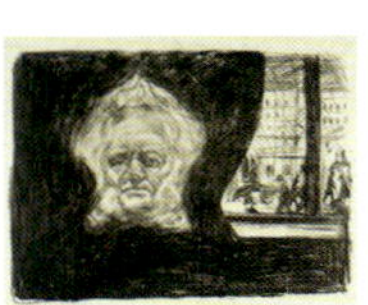

Cat. 33
Edvard Munch: *Henrik Ibsen at the Grand Café*, 1902
Lithograph
432 × 593 mm
Munch Museum
MM.G.00244-15
(Woll G 200)

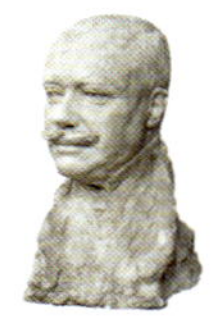

Cat. 37
Gustav Vigeland: *Gunnar Heiberg*, 1905
Plaster
41 × 23 × 30.5 cm
Vigeland Museum
VM.S.0696

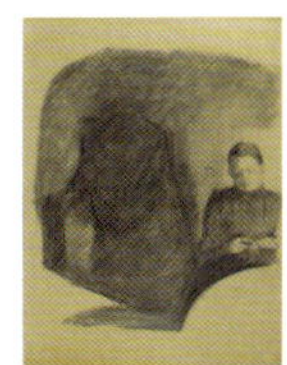

Cat. 22
Edvard Munch: *Karen Bjølstad with Shadow*, 1886–89
Pencil
485 × 355 mm
Munch Museum
MM.T.02271

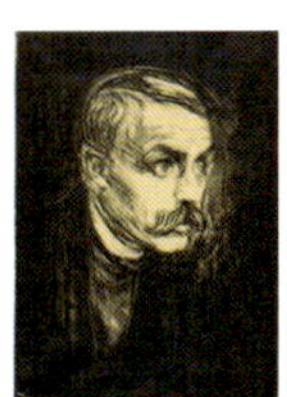

Cat. 26
Edvard Munch: *Sigbjørn Obstfelder II*, 1896
Lithograph
410 × 282 mm
Munch Museum
MM.G.00818-01
(Woll G 86)

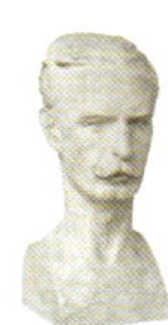

Cat. 30
Gustav Vigeland: *Vilhelm Krag*, 1903
Plaster
47 × 21 × 27 cm
Vigeland Museum
VM.S.0685

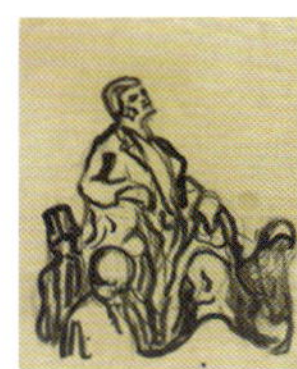

Cat. 34
Edvard Munch: *Bjørnson Speaking to the People*, 1909
Brush, charcoal
631 × 500 mm
Munch Museum
MM.T.01653-recto

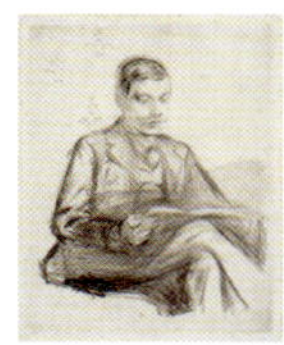

Cat. 38
Edvard Munch: *Eberhard von Bodenhausen*, 1895
Etching
243 × 194 mm
Munch Museum
MM.G.00022-01
(Woll G 24)

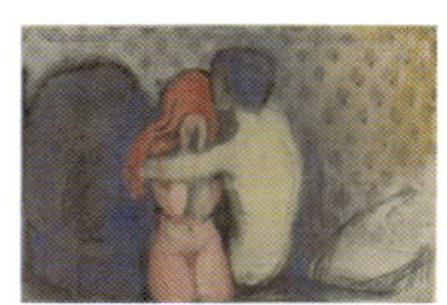

Cat. 23
Edvard Munch: *Consolation*, 1894
Hand-coloured drypoint and etching
211 × 318 mm
Munch Museum
MM.G.00006-01 (Woll G 6)

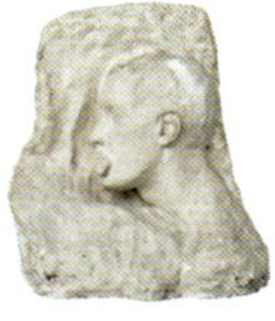

Cat. 27
Gustav Vigeland: *Sigbjørn Obstfelder*, 1895
Plaster
44 × 41 × 27 cm
Vigeland Museum
VM.S.0659

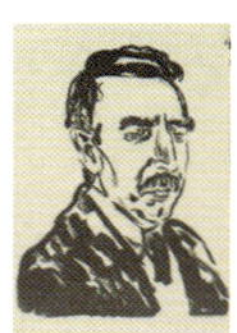

Cat. 31
Edvard Munch: *Vilhelm Krag*, 1919–20
Lithograph
430 × 350 mm
Munch Museum
MM.G.00406-09
(Woll G 634)

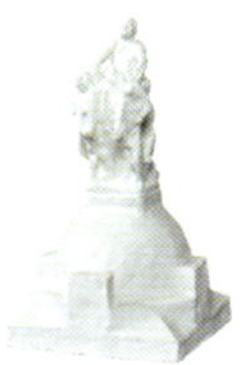

Cat. 35
Gustav Vigeland: *Bjørnstjerne Bjørnson*, prob. 1914
Plaster
31.5 × 18 × 18 cm
Vigeland Museum
VM.S.0576.01

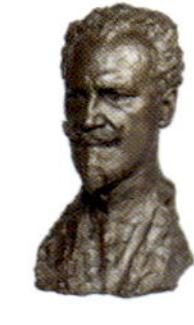

Cat. 39
Gustav Vigeland: *Ernest Thiel*, 1907
Bronze
44 × 23 × 23 cm
Vigeland Museum
VM.S.0663.01

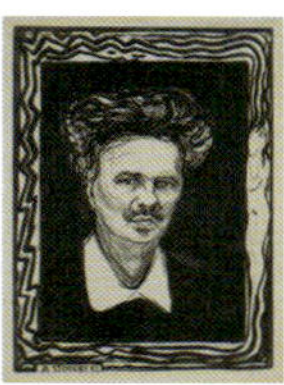

Cat. 40
Edvard Munch: *August Strindberg*, 1896
Lithograph
605 × 460 mm
Munch Museum
MM.G.00219-04
(Woll G 66)

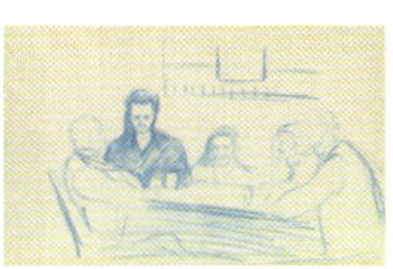

Cat. 44
Edvard Munch: *The Ferkel Circle*, 1893
Colour pencil
209 × 330 mm
Munch Museum
MM.T.02968-recto

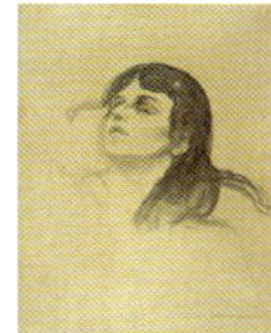

Cat. 48
Edvard Munch: *Madonna's Head*, 1894
Charcoal, gouache, crayon
615 × 470 mm
Munch Museum
MM.T.02449

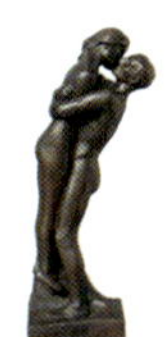

Cat. 52
Gustav Vigeland: *The Kiss*, 1898
Bronze
67 × 27 × 21 cm
Vigeland Museum
VM.S.0836.01

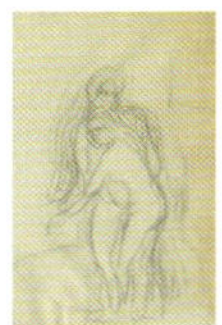

Cat. 56
Edvard Munch: *Man and Woman*, 1894–97
Pencil
467 × 280 mm
Munch Museum
MM.T.00282-recto

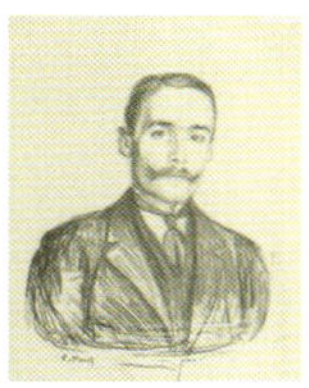

Cat. 41
Edvard Munch: *Count Harry Kessler I*, 1895
Lithograph
245 × 190 mm
Munch Museum
MM.G.00190-01
(Woll G 35)

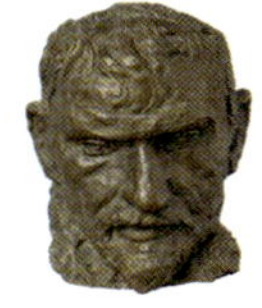

Cat. 45
Gustav Vigeland: *Stanisław Przybyszewski*, 1894
Bronze
21 × 15 × 10 cm
Vigeland Museum
VM.S.0737.01

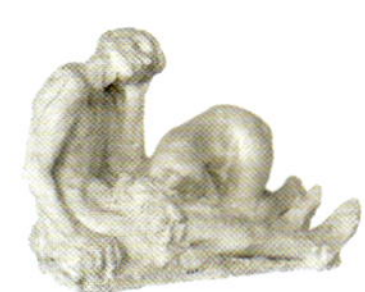

Cat. 49
Gustav Vigeland: *A Doubter*, 1894
Plaster
26.5 × 39 × 22.5 cm
Vigeland Museum
VM.S.0845

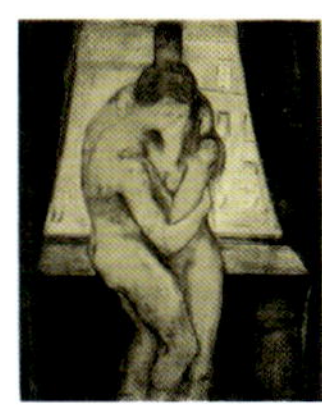

Cat. 53
Edvard Munch: *The Kiss*, 1895
Etching
345 × 276 mm
Munch Museum
MM.G.00021-04
(Woll G 23)

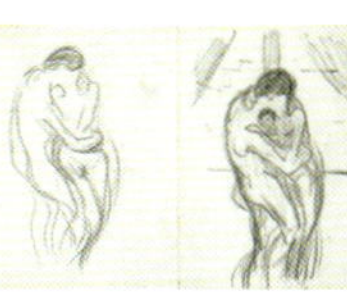

Cat. 57
Edvard Munch: *The Kiss*, c. 1895
Pencil
183 × 289 mm
Munch Museum
MM.T.00362

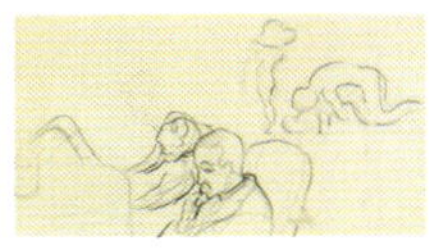

Cat. 42
Edvard Munch: *Vigeland, Obstfelder and Two Sculptures*, 1895
Pencil, pen
332 × 500 mm
Munch Museum
MM.T.00328-verso

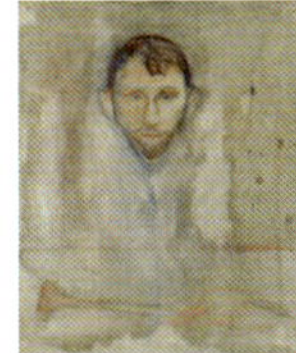

Cat. 46
Edvard Munch: *Stanisław Przybyszewski*, 1894
Casein and distemper on canvas
75 × 60 cm
Munch Museum
MM.M.00618 (Woll M 354)

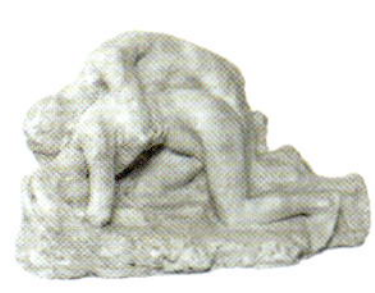

Cat. 50
Gustav Vigeland: *The Prostrated*, 1895
Plaster
29.5 × 50 × 29 cm
Vigeland Museum
VM.S.0856

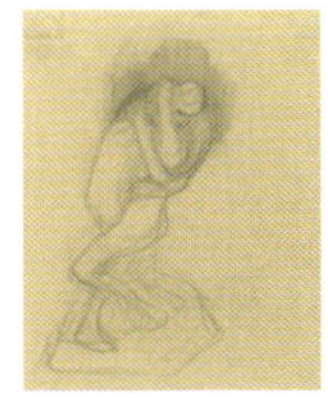

Cat. 54
Gustav Vigeland: *Embrace*, prob. 1890s
Pencil
214 × 177 mm
Vigeland Museum
VM.T.CMK0.0945

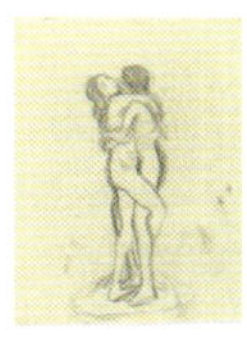

Cat. 58
Gustav Vigeland: *Kiss* (undated)
Pencil
211 × 170 mm
Vigeland Museum
VM.T.CMK0.0943

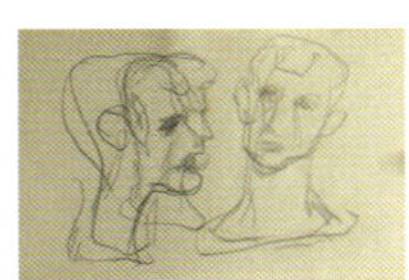

Cat. 43
Gustav Vigeland: *Double Portrait*, 1895
Pencil
111 × 193 mm
Vigeland Museum
VM.W.12-38

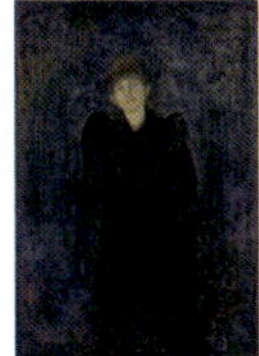

Cat. 47
Edvard Munch: *Dagny Juel Przybyszewska*, 1893
Oil on canvas
149 × 100.5 cm
Munch Museum
MM.M.00212 (Woll M 337)

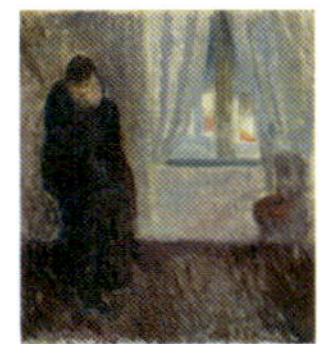

Cat. 51
Edvard Munch: *The Kiss*, 1891
Oil on canvas
72 × 64.5 cm
Munch Museum
MM.M.00622 (Woll M 257)

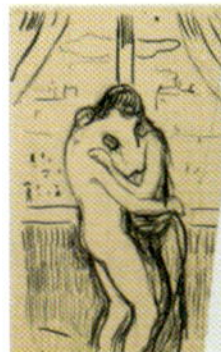

Cat. 55
Edvard Munch: *The Kiss*, c. 1895
Brush, pencil
603 × 391 mm
Munch Museum
MM.T.00421-recto

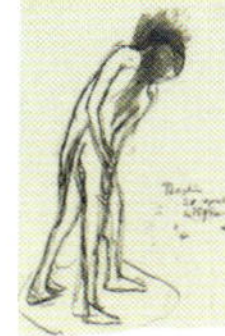

Cat. 59
Gustav Vigeland: *Man and Woman*, 1895
Ink
173 × 108 mm
Vigeland Museum
VM.T.CMK0.0051a

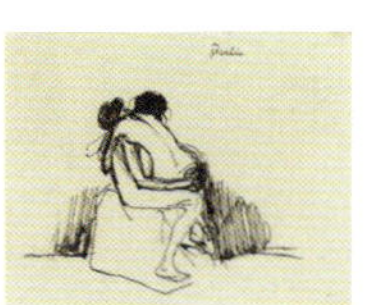

Cat. 60
Gustav Vigeland: *Man with a Woman on His Lap*, prob. 1895
Ink
166 × 210 mm
Vigeland Museum
VM.T.CMK0.0047

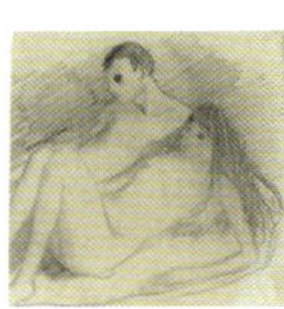

Cat. 64
Gustav Vigeland: *Reclining Man and Woman*, 1895
Pencil
209 × 214 mm
Vigeland Museum
VM.T.CMK0.0052

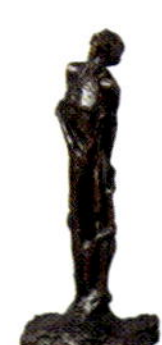

Cat. 68
Gustav Vigeland: *Man Embraced by a Tree*, 1900
Bronze
56.5 × 23 × 17.5 cm
Vigeland Museum
VM.S.0589.01

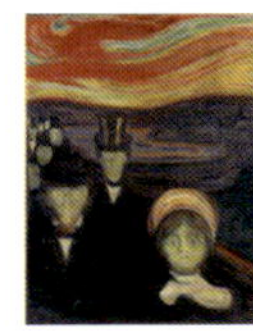

Cat. 72
Edvard Munch: *Angst*, 1894
Oil on canvas
94 × 74 cm
Munch Museum
MM.M.00515 (Woll M 363)

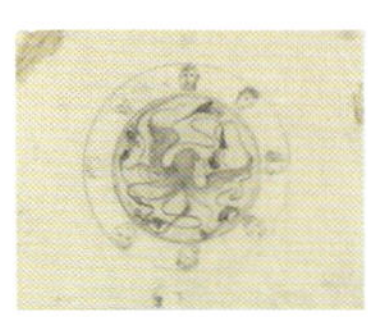

Cat. 76
Gustav Vigeland: *Medusa*, prob. 1893
Pencil
174 × 214 mm
Vigeland Museum
VM.T.OC00.0004

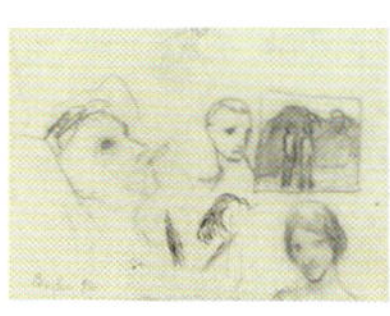

Cat. 61
Gustav Vigeland: *Man with Cigarette*, 1895
Pencil, ink
164 × 208 mm
Vigeland Museum
VM.T.AB00.0041

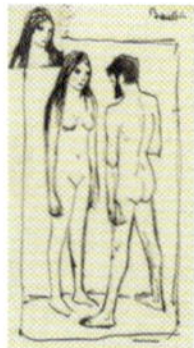

Cat. 65
Gustav Vigeland: *Man and Woman*, 1895
Ink
208 × 112 mm
Vigeland Museum
VM.T.CMK0.0044

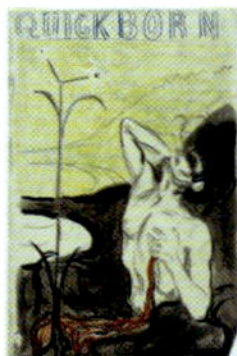

Cat. 69
Edvard Munch: *Blossom of Pain. 'Quickborn'*, 1898
Brush (wash), watercolour, crayon
500 × 330 mm
Munch Museum
MM.T.02451

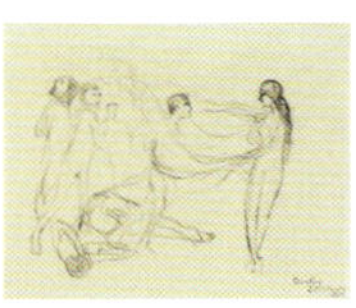

Cat. 73
Gustav Vigeland: *Attraction*, 1895
Ink
166 × 208 mm
Vigeland Museum
VM.CME0.0015

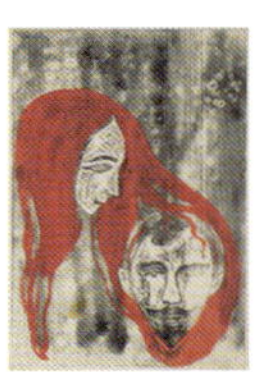

Cat. 77
Edvard Munch: *Man's Head in Woman's Hair*, 1896
Hand-coloured woodcut
547 × 380 mm
Munch Museum
MM.G.00569-05
(Woll G 89)

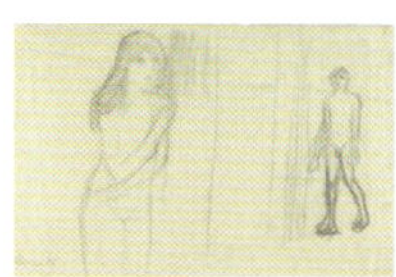

Cat. 62
Gustav Vigeland: *A Couple in the Woods*, 1895
Pencil
211 × 330 mm
Vigeland Museum
VM.T.CMK0.0032-R

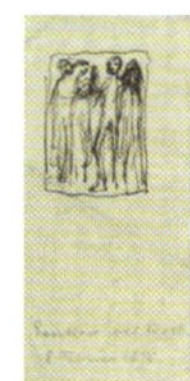

Cat. 66
Gustav Vigeland: *People Standing*, 1895
Ink, pencil
134 × 59 mm
Vigeland Museum
VM.T.CMK0.0037c

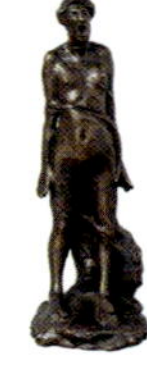

Cat. 70
Gustav Vigeland: *Fear*, 1892
Bronze
29 × 10 × 10 cm
Vigeland Museum
VM.S.2064

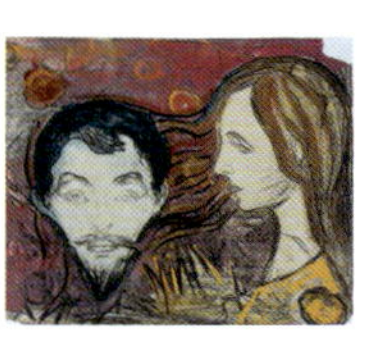

Cat. 74
Edvard Munch: *Man's Head in Woman's Hair*, 1896–97
Hand-coloured lithograph
380 × 444 mm
Munch Museum
MM.G.00544-02
(Woll G 88)

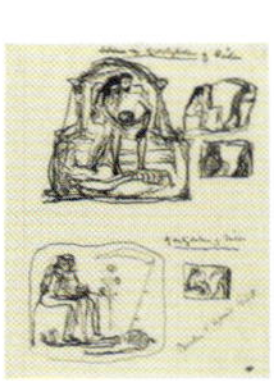

Cat. 78
Gustav Vigeland: *Love and Death*, 1895
Ink
209 × 167 mm
Vigeland Museum
VM.T.DE00.0057

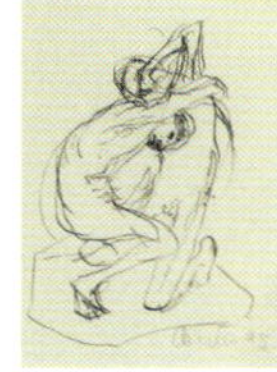

Cat. 63
Gustav Vigeland: *Fight*, 1895
Ink, pencil
167 × 126 mm
Vigeland Museum
VM.T.CMK0.0049a

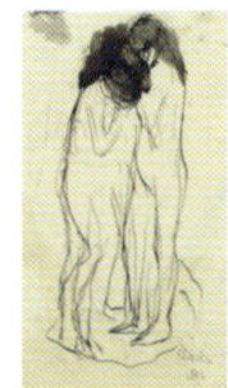

Cat. 67
Gustav Vigeland: *Man and Woman*, 1895
Ink
221 × 158 mm
Vigeland Museum
VM.T.CMK0.0048

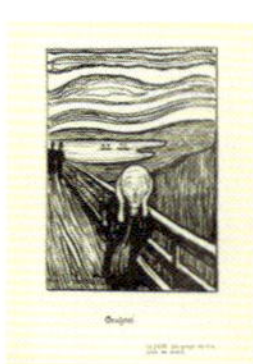

Cat. 71
Edvard Munch: *The Scream*, 1895
Lithograph
354 × 253 mm
Munch Museum
MM.G.00193-02
(Woll G 38)

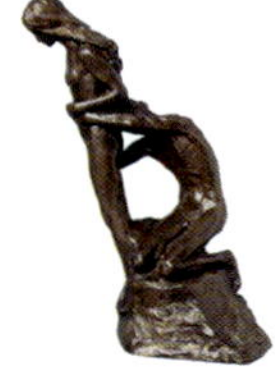

Cat. 75
Gustav Vigeland: *Orpheus and Eurydice II*, 1899
Bronze
65 × 47.5 × 31 cm
Vigeland Museum
VM.S.0861.01

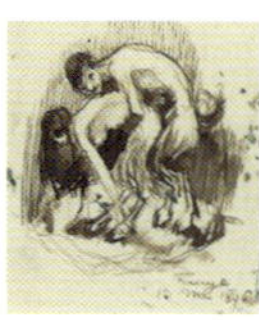

Cat. 79
Gustav Vigeland: *Copulating Fauns*, 1895
Pen, wash
208 × 165 mm
Vigeland Museum
VM.T.DB00.0020

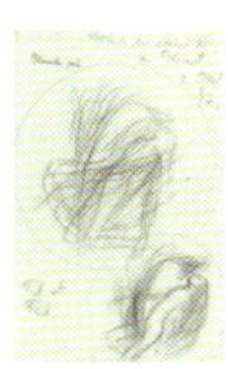

Cat. 80
Gustav Vigeland: *Woman Being Made Love to by a Flower*, 1897
Pencil
218 × 139 mm
Vigeland Museum
VM.T.OC00.0006

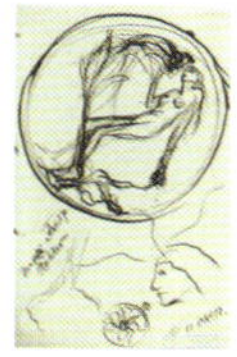

Cat. 81
Gustav Vigeland: *Woman and Flower*, 1897
Ink
219 × 139 mm
Vigeland Museum
VM.T.OC00.0007

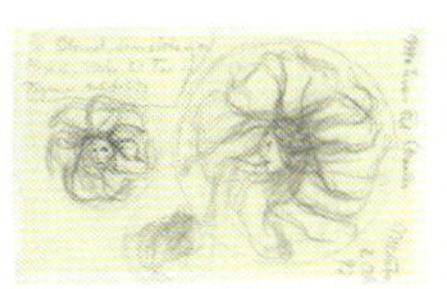

Cat. 82
Gustav Vigeland: *Medusa*, 1897
Pencil
137 × 219 mm
Vigeland Museum
VM.T.OC00.0003

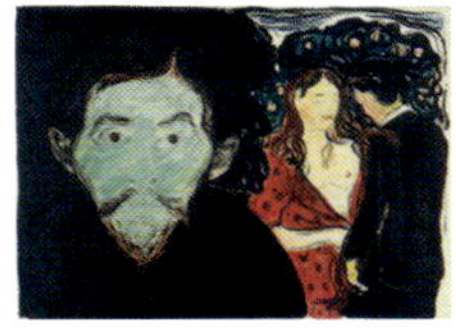

Cat. 83
Edvard Munch: *Jealousy I*, 1896
Hand-coloured lithograph
330 × 460 mm
Munch Museum
MM.T.00201-18 (Woll G 68)

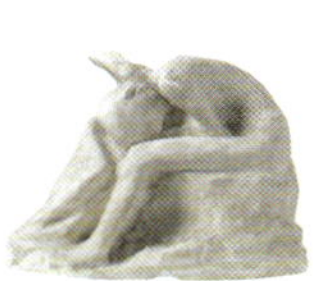

Cat. 84
Gustav Vigeland: *Leda and the Swan*, 1900
Plaster
22.5 × 24.5 × 33 cm
National Museum of Art, Architecture and Design, Oslo
NG.S.00971
Photo © National Museum

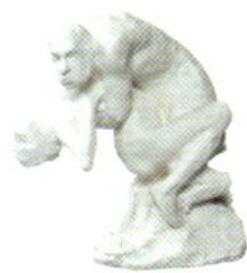

Cat. 85
Gustav Vigeland: *Woman and Faun*, prob. 1893
Plaster
17 × 16.5 × 9 cm
Vigeland Museum
VM.S.2051.02

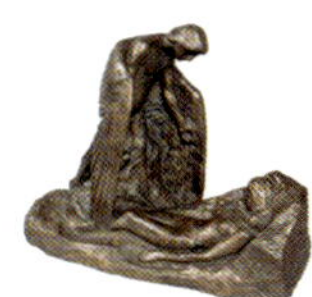

Cat. 86
Gustav Vigeland: *Cupid and Psyche*, 1898
Bronze
58 × 67.5 × 37 cm
Vigeland Museum
VM.S.0860.01

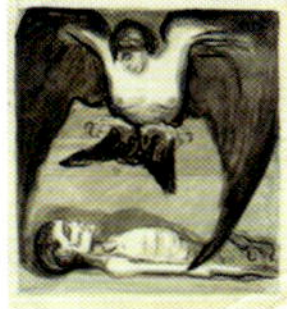

Cat. 87
Edvard Munch: *Harpy*, 1898
Pen, brush (wash), watercolour, crayon, gouache
558 × 448 mm
Munch Museum
MM.T.00433

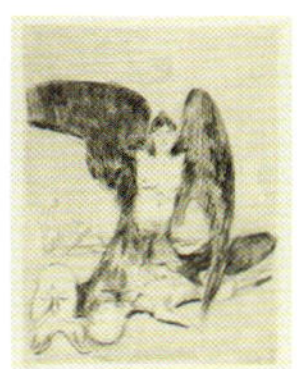

Cat. 88
Edvard Munch: *Harpy*, 1894
Drypoint
285 × 215 mm
Munch Museum
MM.G.00004-03
(Woll G 4)

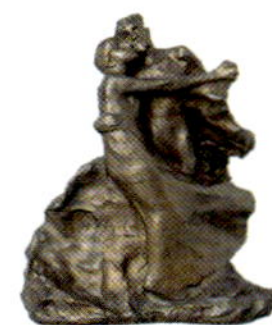

Cat. 89
Gustav Vigeland: *Dance I*, 1893
Bronze
32 × 28 × 15.5 cm
Vigeland Museum
VM.S.0862.01

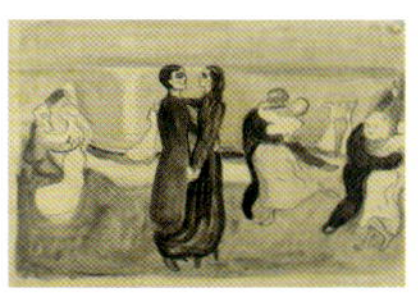

Cat. 90
Edvard Munch: *The Dance of Life*, 1899
Brush, pen, crayon
325 × 477 mm
Munch Museum
MM.T.02392

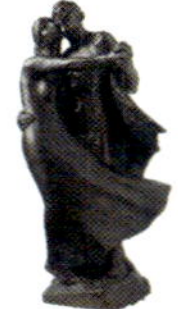

Cat. 91
Gustav Vigeland: *The Waltz*, 1896
Bronze, 76.5 × 40 × 26 cm
National Museum of Art, Architecture and Design, Oslo
NG.S.00954
Photo © National Museum

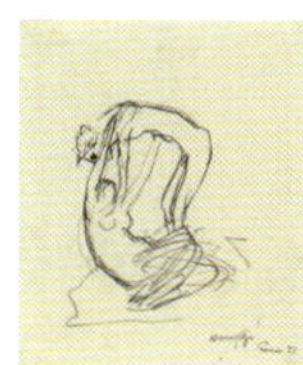

Cat. 92
Gustav Vigeland: *Vampire*, 1893
Ink
216 × 177 mm
Vigeland Museum
VM.T.CMK0.0003

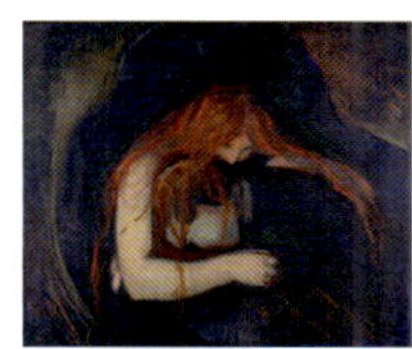

Cat. 93
Edvard Munch: *Vampire*, 1893–94
Oil on canvas
91 × 109 cm
Munch Museum
MM.M.00679 (Woll M 377)

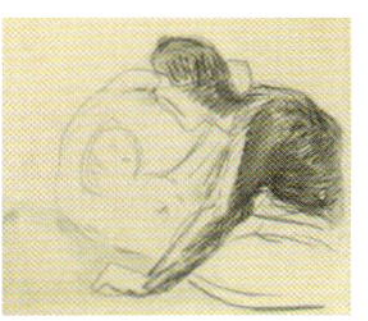

Cat. 94
Edvard Munch: *Man and Woman*, 1907
Chalk, brush
226 × 268 mm
Munch Museum
MM.T.00452

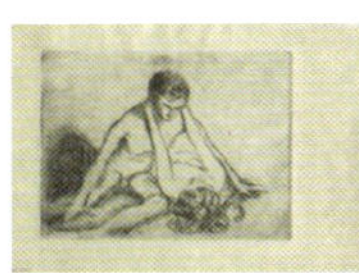

Cat. 95
Edvard Munch: *The Cat*, 1914
Etching, drypoint
237 × 318 mm
Munch Museum
MM.G.00143-05
(Woll G 470)

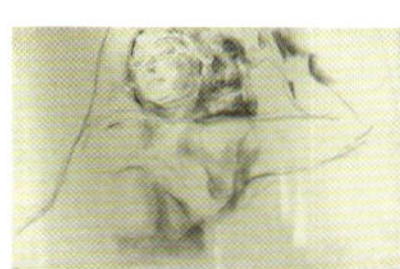

Cat. 96
Edvard Munch: *Reclining Nude with Closed Eyes*, 1911–15
Charcoal
344 × 543 mm
Munch Museum
MM.T.01129

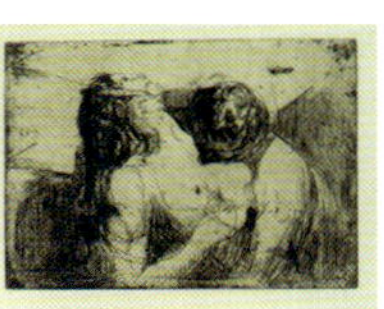

Cat. 97
Edvard Munch: *The Bite*, 1914
Etching
197 × 279 mm
Munch Museum
MM.G.00142-03
(Woll G 472)

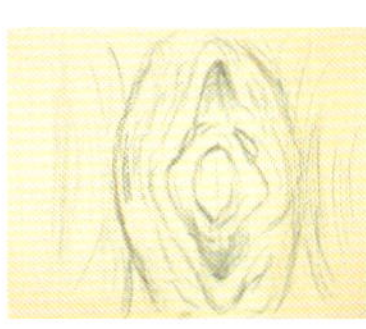

Cat. 98
Edvard Munch: *Sketch of a Vulva*, 1915–30
Pencil, charcoal
537 × 678 mm
Munch Museum
MM.T.02254

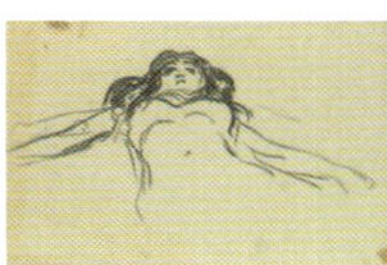

Cat. 99
Edvard Munch: *Reclining Nude*, 1912–15
Charcoal
259 × 408 mm
Munch Museum
MM.T.01017

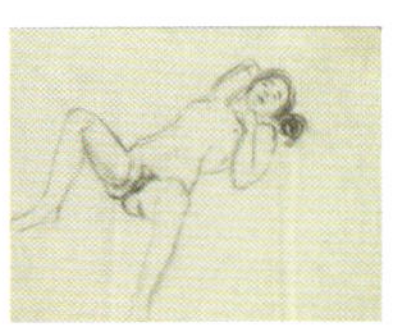

Cat. 100
Edvard Munch: *Reclining Nude*, 1911–15
Charcoal
253 × 322 mm
Munch Museum
MM.T.00935

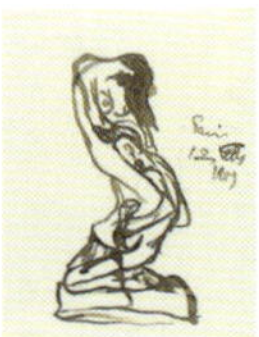

Cat. 104
Gustav Vigeland: *Man and Woman*, 1901
Ink, wash
199 × 152 mm
Vigeland Museum
VM.T.CMK0.0522

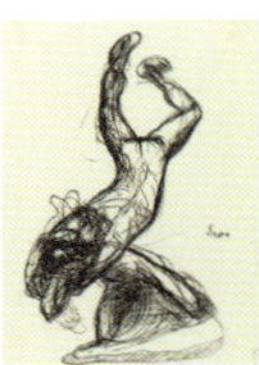

Cat. 108
Gustav Vigeland: *Eros* (undated)
Pen
185 × 142 mm
Vigeland Museum
VM.T.DB00.0248

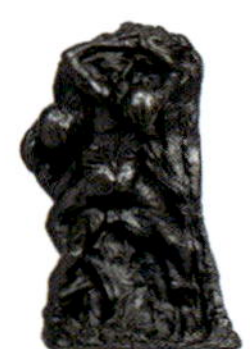

Cat. 112
Gustav Vigeland: *Man and Woman*, 1903
Bronze
70.5 × 47 × 20 cm
Vigeland Museum
VM.S.0198.01

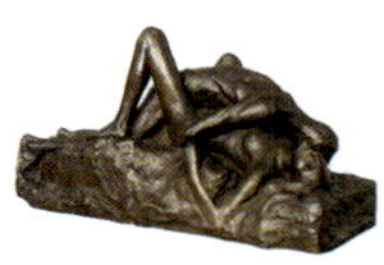

Cat. 116
Gustav Vigeland: *Coitus*, 1897–98
Bronze
28 × 59.5 × 31 cm
Vigeland Museum
VM.S.0855.01

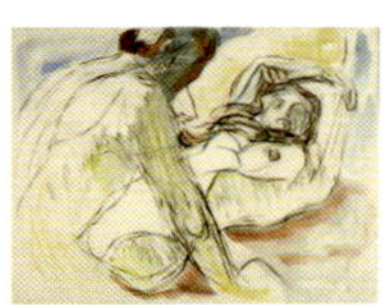

Cat. 101
Edvard Munch: *Man and Woman*, 1912–15
Charcoal, watercolour
597 × 798 mm
Munch Museum
MM.T.01362

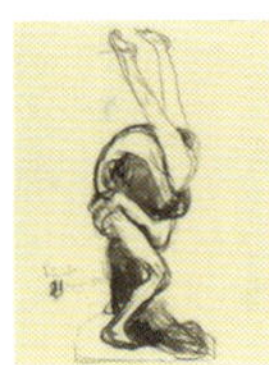

Cat. 105
Gustav Vigeland: *Man and Woman*, 1901
Ink, wash
208 × 153 mm
Vigeland Museum
VM.T.CMK0.0552

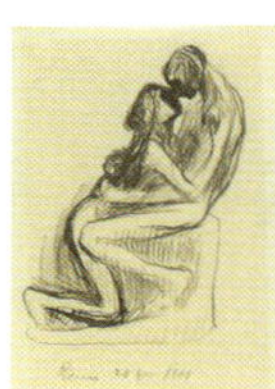

Cat. 109
Gustav Vigeland: *Man and Woman*, 1901
Ink
209 × 153 mm
Vigeland Museum
VM.T.CMK0.0610

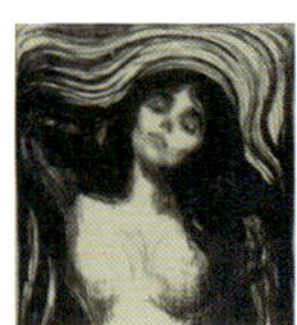

Cat. 113
Edvard Munch: *Madonna*, 1895/1902
Lithograph
358 × 330 mm
Munch Museum
MM.G.00194-14
(Woll G 39)

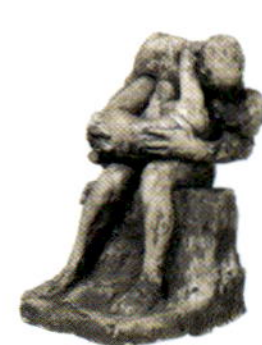

Cat. 117
Gustav Vigeland: *Man with a Woman on His Lap I*, 1895
Plaster
58 × 33.5 × 33.5 cm
National Museum of Art, Architecture and Design, Oslo
NG.S.00952
Photo © National Museum

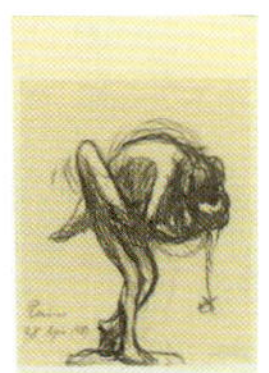

Cat. 102
Gustav Vigeland: *Man and Woman*, 1901
Ink
208 × 145 mm
Vigeland Museum
VM.T.CMK0.0608

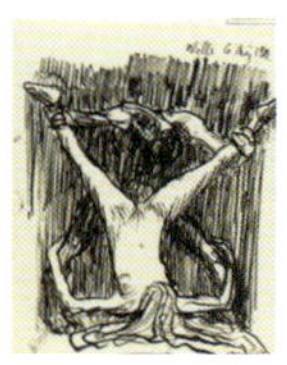

Cat. 106
Gustav Vigeland: *Man and Woman*, 1901
Ink
203 × 159 mm
Vigeland Museum
VM.T.CMK0.0839

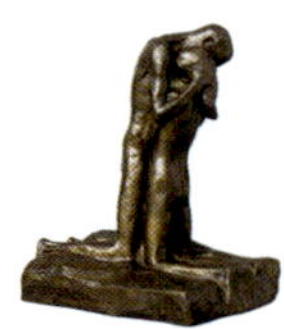

Cat. 110
Gustav Vigeland: *Man and Woman*, 1899
Bronze
48.5 × 43.5 × 31.5 cm
Vigeland Museum
VM.S.0841.01

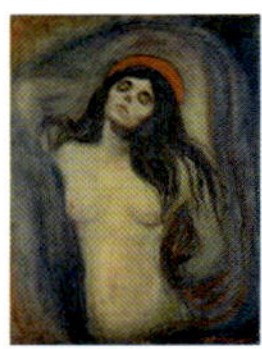

Cat. 114
Edvard Munch: *Madonna*, 1894
Oil on canvas
90 × 68.5 cm
Munch Museum
MM.M.00068 (Woll M 365)

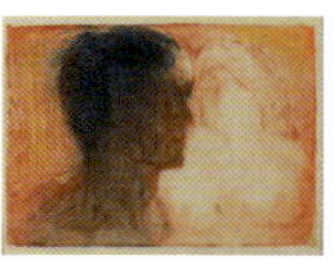

Cat. 118
Edvard Munch: *Lovers*, 1913
Etching
196 × 276 mm
Munch Museum
MM.G.00145.06
(Woll G 433)

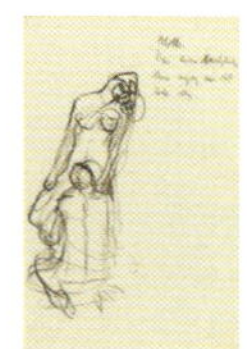

Cat. 103
Gustav Vigeland: *The Serpent of Love* (undated)
Ink
219 × 142 mm
Vigeland Museum
VM.T.CMK0.1127

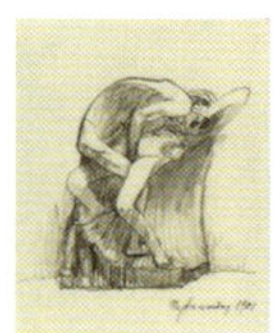

Cat. 107
Gustav Vigeland: *Man and Woman*, 1901
Ink, wash
194 × 152 mm
Vigeland Museum
VM.T.CMK0.0441

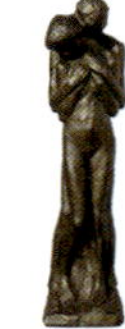

Cat. 111
Gustav Vigeland: *Man and Woman*, 1899
Bronze
66 × 17 × 16 cm
Vigeland Museum
VM.S.0839.04

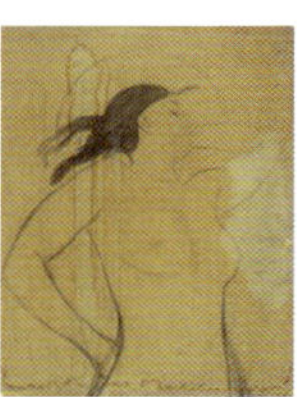

Cat. 115
Edvard Munch: *Study for Madonna*, 1893–94
Charcoal
738 × 598 mm
Munch Museum
MM.T.02430

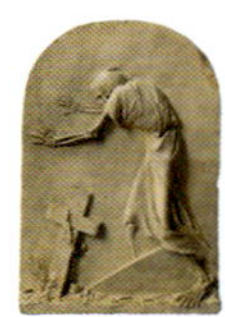

Cat. 119
Gustav Vigeland: *A Revenant*, 1889
Terracotta
48.5 × 34 × 4.5 cm
Vigeland Museum
VM.S.0910

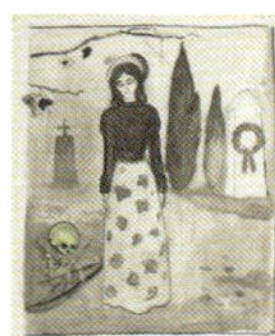

Cat. 120
Edvard Munch: *Madonna at the Cemetery*, 1896
Pen, brush (wash), crayon, gouache
560 × 448 mm
Munch Museum
MM.T.02364

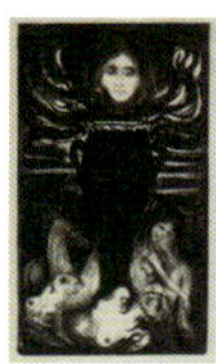

Cat. 124
Edvard Munch: *The Urn*, 1896
Lithograph
460 × 265 mm
Munch Museum
MM.G.00205-04
(Woll G 67)

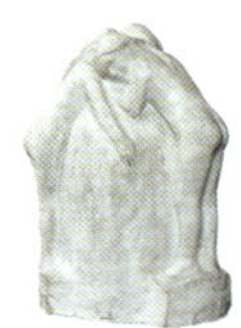

Cat. 128
Gustav Vigeland: *Ruth Syvertsen's Urn I*, 1917
Plaster
22 (diameter) x 29.5 cm
Vigeland Museum
VM.S.0300.01

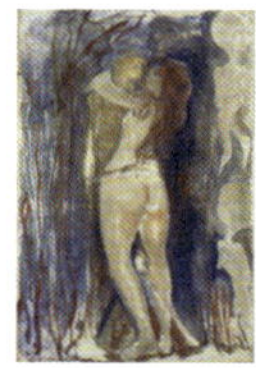

Cat. 132
Edvard Munch: *Death and Life*, 1894
Oil on canvas
128.5 × 86 cm
Munch Museum
MM.M.00049 (Woll M 345)

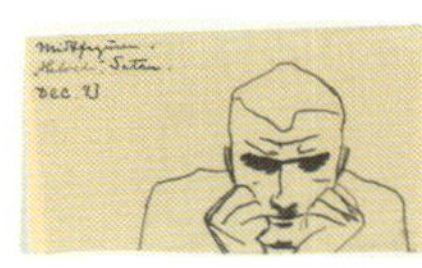

Cat. 136
Gustav Vigeland: *The Central Figure of 'Hell', Satan,* 1893
Pencil, 130 × 235 mm
National Museum of Art, Architecture and Design, Oslo
NG.K&H.B.07907
Photo © National Museum

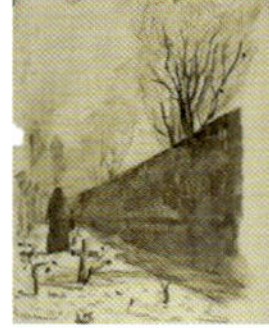

Cat. 121
Edvard Munch: *At the Cemetery*, c. 1885
Pen, brush
301 × 218 mm
Munch Museum
MM.T.00288

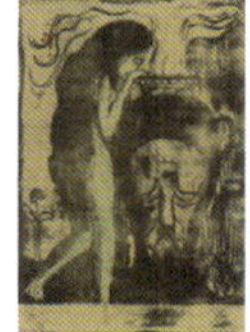

Cat. 125
Edvard Munch: *The Woman at the Urn*, 1898
Lithograph
420 × 290 mm
Munch Museum
MM.G.00230-04
(Woll G 119)

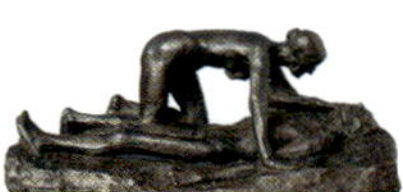

Cat. 129
Gustav Vigeland: *Old Woman Watching Her Husband Die*, 1898
Bronze
29 × 76.5 × 30.5 cm
Vigeland Museum
VM.S.0859

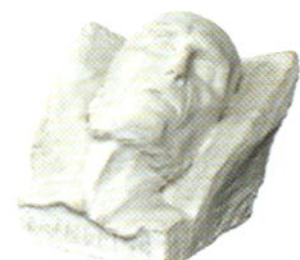

Cat. 133
Gustav Vigeland: *Remembrance*, 1892
Plaster
26 × 28 × 30 cm
Vigeland Museum
VM.S.0645

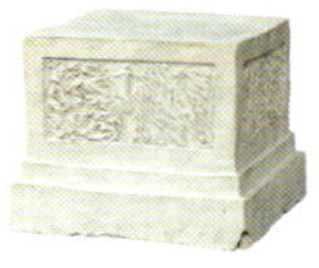

Cat. 137
Gustav Vigeland: *Altar*, 1923
Clay
12.5 × 15.5 × 15.5 cm
Vigeland Museum
VM.S.0011

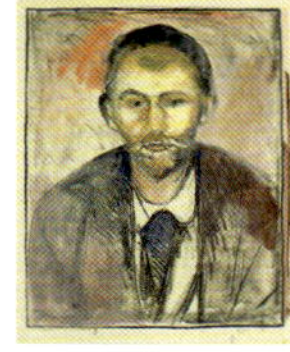

Cat. 122
Edvard Munch: *Stanisław Przybyszewski*, 1895(?)
Hand-coloured lithograph
545 × 458 mm
Munch Museum
MM.G.00231-09
(Woll G 45)

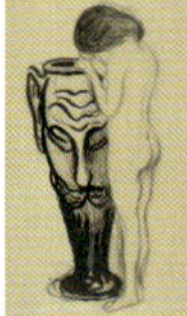

Cat. 126
Edvard Munch: *The Urn*, 1896–98
Brush, crayon
354 × 200 mm
Munch Museum
MM.T.00395

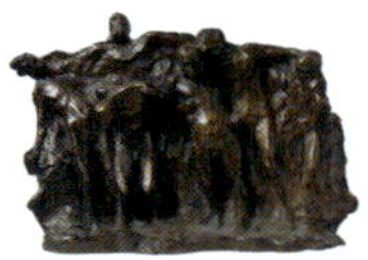

Cat. 130
Gustav Vigeland: *Woman Praying for the Drunkards*, 1893
Bronze, 24 × 38 × 16 cm
National Museum of Art, Architecture and Design, Oslo
NG.S.00937
Photo © National Museum

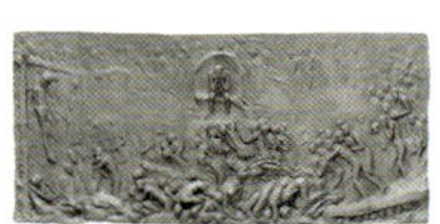

Cat. 134
Gustav Vigeland: *Hell II*, 1897
Bronze
173 × 382.5 × 30 cm
National Museum of Art, Architecture and Design, Oslo
NG.S.00658
Photo © National Museum

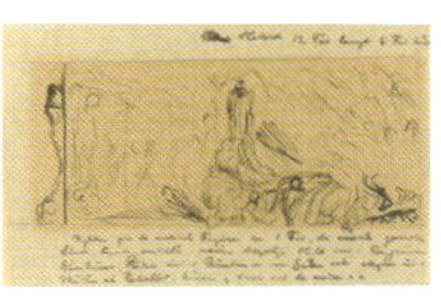

Cat. 138
Gustav Vigeland: *Hell 12 Feet Long 6 Feet High*, 1893–94
Pencil, 215 × 342 mm
National Museum of Art, Architecture and Design, Oslo
NG.K&H.B.07910
Photo © National Museum

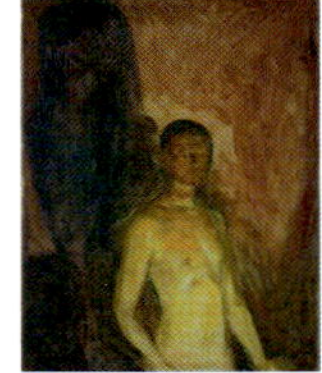

Cat. 123
Edvard Munch: *Self-portrait in Hell*, 1903
Oil on canvas
82 × 66 cm
Munch Museum
MM.M.00591 (Woll M 556)

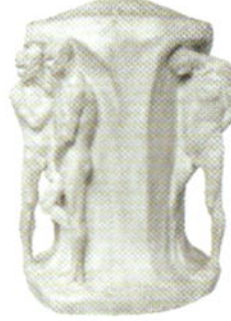

Cat. 127
Gustav Vigeland: *Urn for Jacob Lindboe*, c. 1902
Plaster
42.5 (diameter) x 56.5 cm
Vigeland Museum
VM.S.1590.01

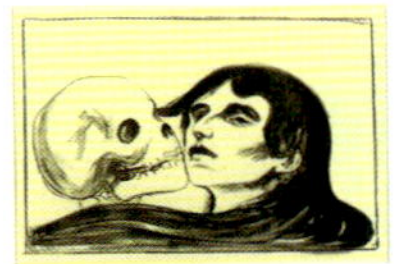

Cat. 131
Edvard Munch: *The Kiss of Death*, 1899
Lithograph
297 × 456 mm
Munch Museum
MM.G.00235-05
(Woll G 144)

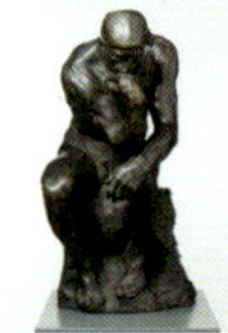

Cat. 135
Auguste Rodin: *The Thinker*, 1880
Bronze, 71 × 35.8 × 52.5 cm
National Museum of Art, Architecture and Design, Oslo
NG.S.00638
Photo © National Museum

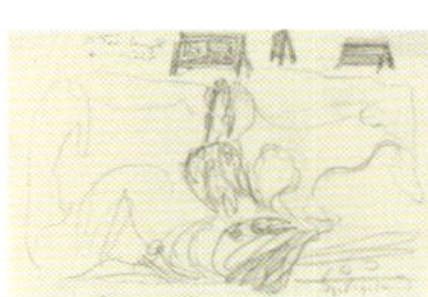

Cat. 139
Gustav Vigeland:*Ascending Human Beings*, 1893–94
Pencil, 217 × 342 mm
National Museum of Art, Architecture and Design, Oslo
NG.K&H.B.07888
Photo © National Museum

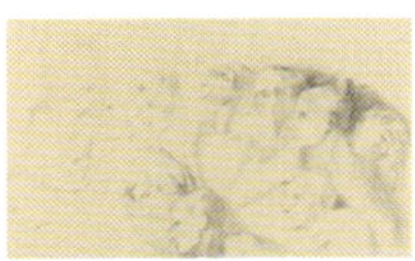

Cat. 140
Gustav Vigeland: *Fifteen Human Heads*, 1893–94
Pencil
215 × 349 mm
National Museum of Art, Architecture and Design, Oslo
NG.K&H.B.07914
Photo © National Museum

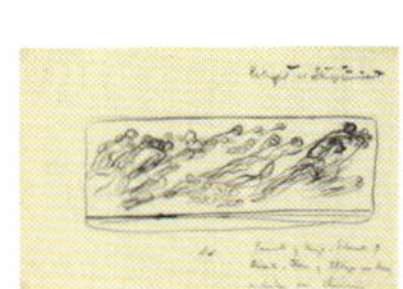

Cat. 144
Gustav Vigeland: *Relief for the Sculpture Museum*, prob. 1890s
Ink
141 × 218 mm
Vigeland Museum
VM.T.DE00.0043

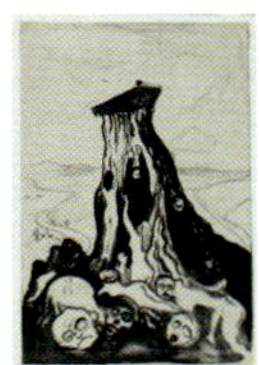

Cat. 148
Edvard Munch: *Funeral March*, 1897
Lithograph
556 × 377 mm
Munch Museum
MM.G.00226-23 (Woll G 103)

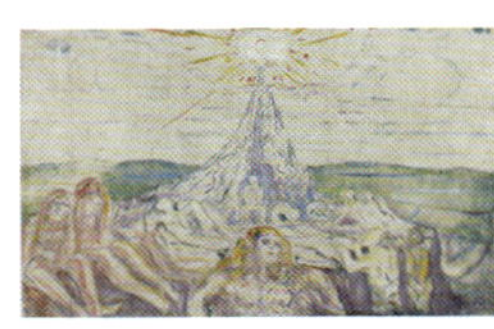

Cat. 152
Edvard Munch: *The Human Mountain*, 1909–10
Oil on canvas
96 × 158 cm
Munch Museum
MM.M.00778 (Woll M 911)

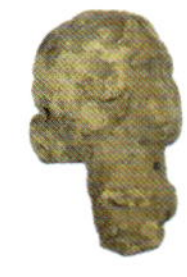

Cat. 156
Edvard Munch: *Woman's Head*, 1903–05
Plasticine
15.5 × 8.2 × 10.5 cm
Munch Museum
MM.S.00008

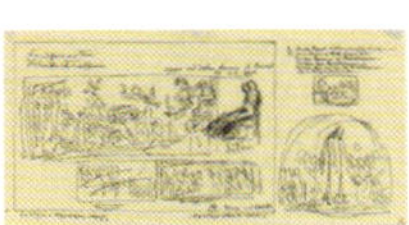

Cat. 141
Sophus Larpent: *Copy of Gustav Vigeland's Sketches for Hell*, 1893
Pencil, 174 × 350 mm
National Museum of Art, Architecture and Design, Oslo
NG.K&H.B.07880
Photo © National Museum

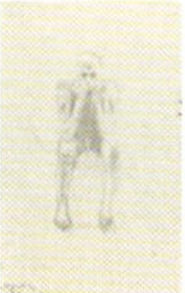

Cat. 145
Gustav Vigeland: *The Central Figure of 'Hell', Satan*, 1893–94
Pencil, 349 × 213 mm
National Museum of Art, Architecture and Design, Oslo
NG.K&H.B.07908
Photo © National Museum

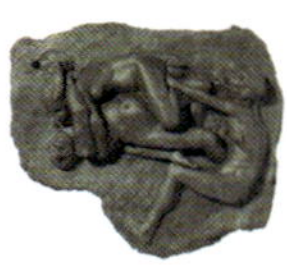

Cat. 149
Gustav Vigeland: *Sodom*, 1892
Bronze patinated plaster
40 × 45 × 9 cm
National Museum of Art, Architecture and Design, Oslo
NG.S.00915
Photo © National Museum

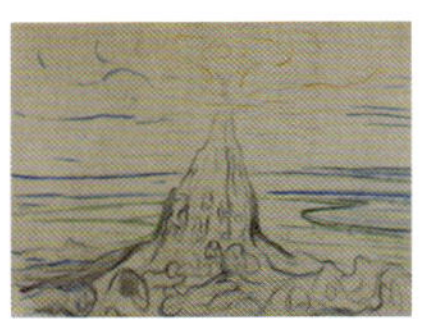

Cat. 153
Edvard Munch: *The Human Mountain*, 1909–10
Watercolour, charcoal
895 × 1225 mm
Munch Museum
MM.T.02549

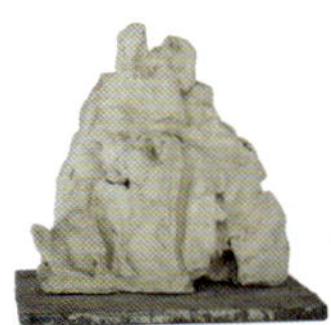

Cat. 157
Edvard Munch: *Man and Woman* (undated)
Clay
8.2 × 17.1 × 11 cm
Munch Museum
MM.S.00011

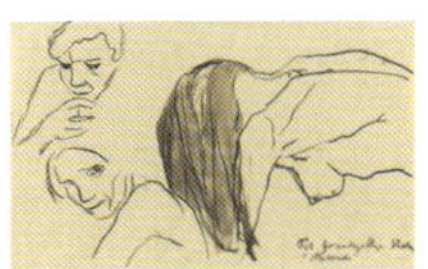

Cat. 142
Gustav Vigeland: *Sketches for 'Hell'*, 1893–94
Pencil
219 × 340 mm
National Museum of Art, Architecture and Design, Oslo
NG.K&H.B.07909
Photo © National Museum

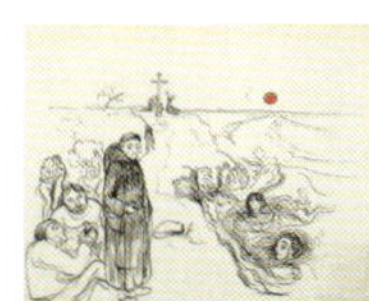

Cat. 146
Edvard Munch: *The Empty Cross*, 1899–1901
Pen, watercolour
455 × 465 mm
Munch Museum
MM.T.02547-57

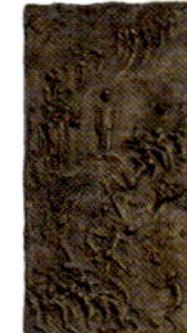

Cat. 150
Gustav Vigeland: *Judgement Day*, 1894
Bronze
122 × 53.5 × 8 cm
National Museum of Art, Architecture and Design, Oslo
NG.S.00943
Photo © National Museum

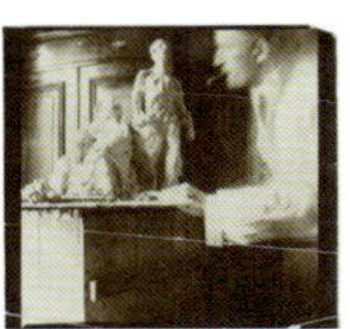

Cat. 154
Edvard Munch with *Mother Norway*, draft for a national monument, 1909–10
Photographic self-portrait
87 × 87 mm
Munch Museum
MM.F.00084-01

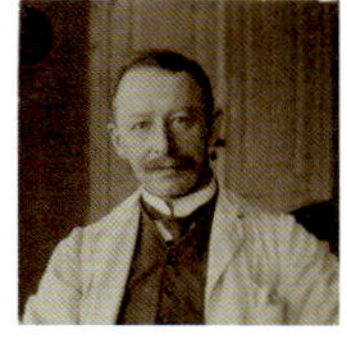

Cat. 158
Max Linde, c. 1903
Photo: Edvard Munch
55 × 56 mm
Munch Museum
MM.F.00025-01

Cat. 143
Gustav Vigeland: *Man and Woman Holding Each Other*, 1893–94
Pencil, 349 × 215 mm
National Museum
NG.K&H.B.07874
Photo © National Museum

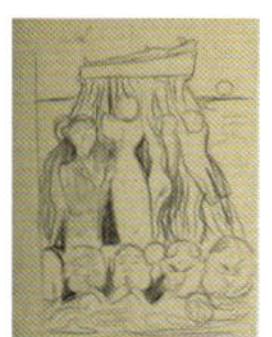

Cat. 147
Edvard Munch: *Funeral March*, 1897
Crayon
587 × 445 mm
Munch Museum
MM.T.00392

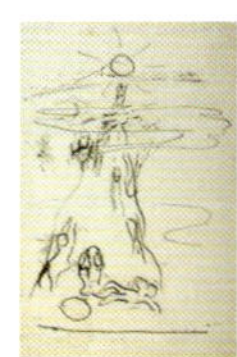

Cat. 151
Edvard Munch: *The Human Mountain*, 1897
Pen
212 × 135 mm
Munch Museum
MM.T.02414

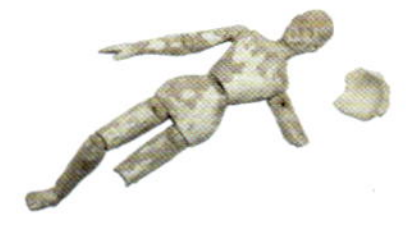

Cat. 155
Edvard Munch's jointed doll
Clay-covered wood
Length: 33 cm
Munch Museum
MM.I.01000

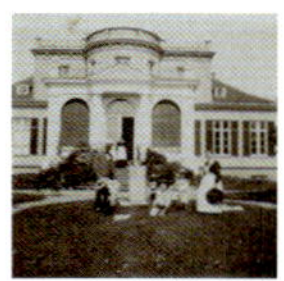

Cat. 159
Max Linde's villa in Lübeck, 1903
Photo: Edvard Munch
86 × 87 mm
Munch Museum
MM.F.00023-01

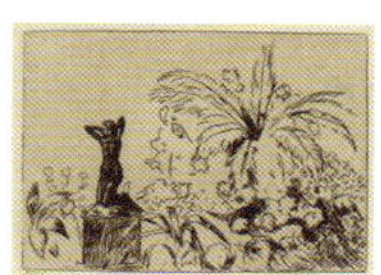

Cat. 160
Edvard Munch: *Veranda (Linde Portfolio)*, 1902
Etching
184 × 264 mm
Munch Museum
MM.G.00084-02
(Woll G 216)

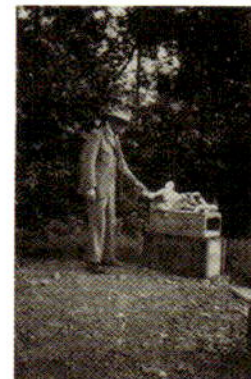

Cat. 164
Edvard Munch with the sculpture *Seated Man* in the garden at Ekely, 1932
Photographic self-portrait
141 × 90 mm
Munch Museum
MM.F.00163-01

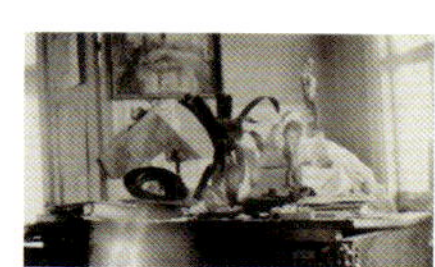

Cat. 168
Interior with sculptures, 1931–32
Photo: Edvard Munch
78 × 137 mm
Munch Museum
MM.F.00172-01

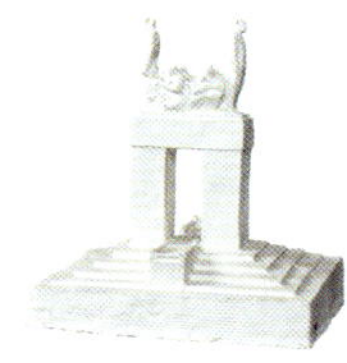

Cat. 172
Gustav Vigeland: *Draft for the Eidsvoll Monument*, prob. 1919
Plaster
27 × 25 × 19 cm
Vigeland Museum
VM.S.1579.02

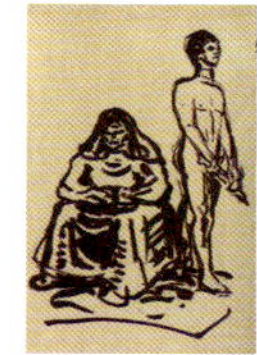

Cat. 176
Edvard Munch: *Mother Norway*, 1909–10
Brush
500 × 332 mm
Munch Museum
MM.T.01684

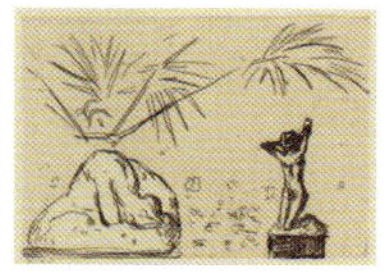

Cat. 161
Edvard Munch: *Interior with Sculptures (Linde Portfolio)*, 1902
Etching
125 × 180 mm
Munch Museum
MM.G.00085-02
(Woll G 217)

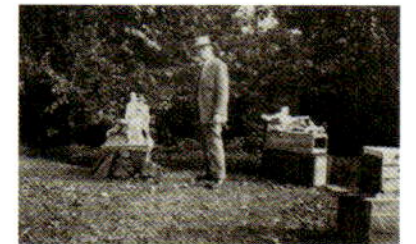

Cat. 165
Edvard Munch between the sculptures *Workers in Snow* and *Seated Man* in the garden at Ekely, 1932
Photographic self-portrait
89 × 143 mm
Munch Museum
MM.F.00164-01

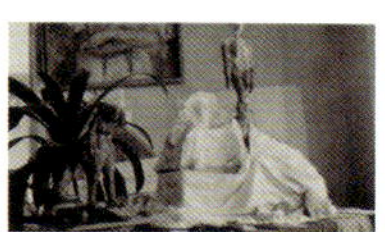

Cat. 169
Interior with sculptures, 1931–32
Photo: Edvard Munch
81 × 139 mm
Munch Museum
MM.F.00171-01

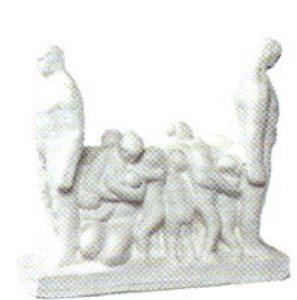

Cat. 173
Gustav Vigeland: *The Clan*, prob. 1915
Plaster
22 × 24.5 × 10 cm
Vigeland Museum
VM.S.1576.02

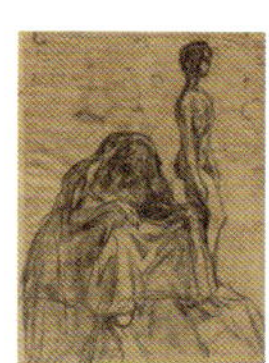

Cat. 177
Edvard Munch: *Mother Norway*, 1909–10
Crayon
385 × 306 mm
Munch Museum
MM.T.02463

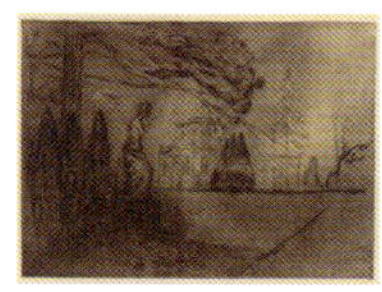

Cat. 162
Edvard Munch: *The Garden at Night (Linde Portfolio)*, 1902
Etching, drypoint
444 × 602 mm
Munch Museum
MM.G.00088-02
(Woll G 221)

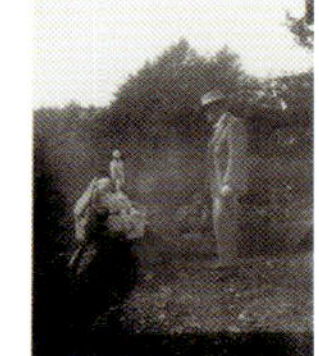

Cat. 166
Edvard Munch with the sculpture *Mother Norway*, 1932
Photographic self-portrait
106 × 78 mm
Munch Museum
MM.F.00165-02

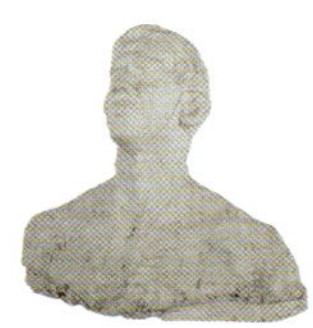

Cat. 170
Edvard Munch: *Male Bust* (undated)
Plaster
44.1 × 51.9 × 27.5 cm
Munch Museum
MM.S.00003B

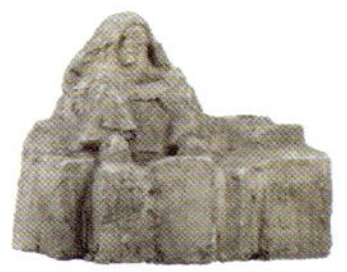

Cat. 174
Edvard Munch: *Mother Norway*, before 1932
Plaster
59.4 × 67.8 × 53.5 cm
Munch Museum
MM.S.00004A

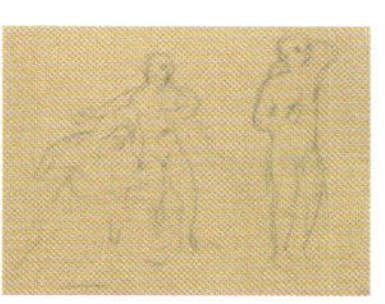

Cat. 178
Edvard Munch: *Mother Norway*, 1909–10
Pencil
273 × 363 mm
Munch Museum
MM.T.01661

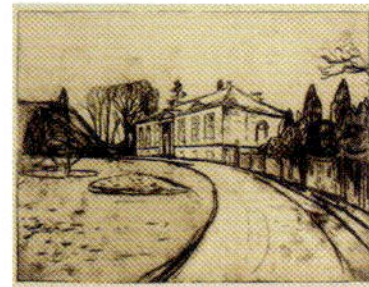

Cat. 163
Edvard Munch: *The Villa (Linde Portfolio)*, 1902
Etching
470 × 617 mm
Munch Museum
MM.G.00086-03
(Woll G 219)

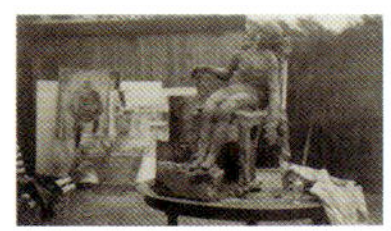

Cat. 167
Seated sculpture, 1931–32
Photo: Edvard Munch
80 × 140 mm
Munch Museum
MM.F.00168-01

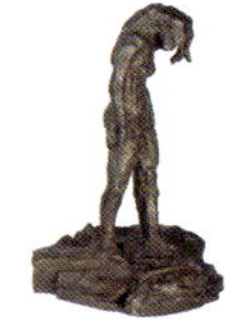

Cat. 171
Edvard Munch: *Weeping Nude*, 1914
Bronze
38.2 × 27.5 × 29.4 cm
Munch Museum
MM.S.00002

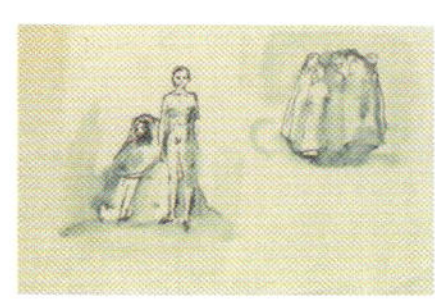

Cat. 175
Edvard Munch: *Mother Norway and Group of People*, 1920–30
Pen, brush
140 × 223 mm
Munch Museum
MM.T.01673

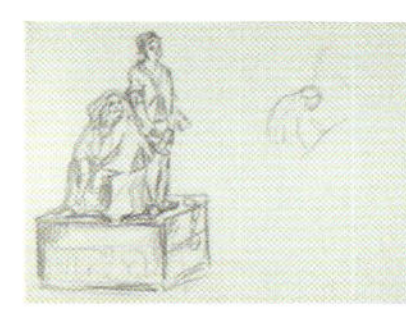

Cat. 179
Edvard Munch: *Mother Norway*, 1909–12
Pencil
257 × 357 mm
Munch Museum
MM.T.00149-22

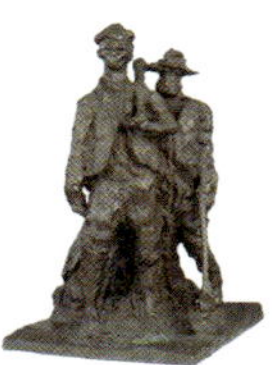

Cat. 180
Edvard Munch: *Workers in Snow*, 1910
Bronze
70 × 56.5 × 45 cm
Munch Museum
MM.S.00001

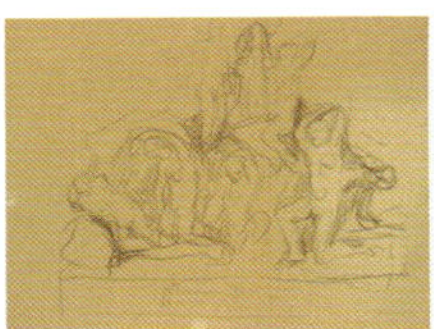

Cat. 184
Edvard Munch: *Sketch for a Monument*, 1924–25
Crayon
502 × 655 mm
Munch Museum
MM.T.01677

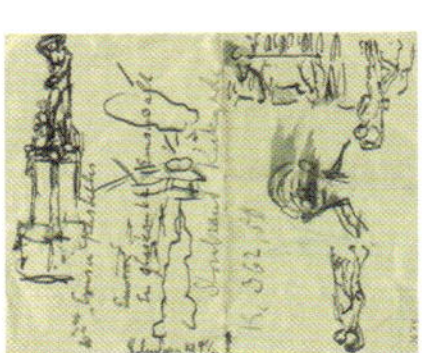

Cat. 188
Edvard Munch: *Sketch for a Monument*, 1909–10
Pen
184 × 144 mm
Munch Museum
MM.T.01674-verso

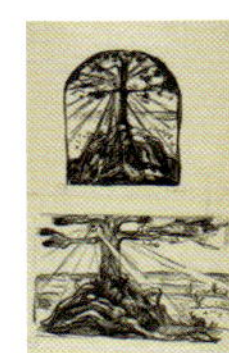

Cat. 192
Edvard Munch: *The Tree III* and *The Tree II*, 1916
Lithograph
233 × 372 mm / 248 × 220 mm
Munch Museum
MM.G.00445-03 / 00444.03 (Woll G 587/586)

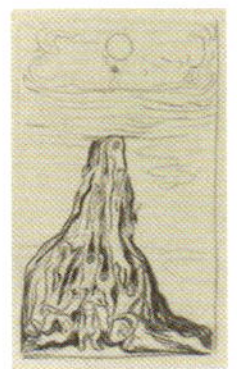

Cat. 196
Edvard Munch: *The Human Mountain*, 1897
Crayon, brush
501 × 329 mm
Munch Museum
MM.T.02888

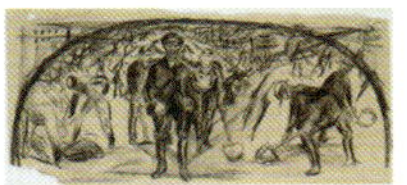

Cat. 181
Edvard Munch: *Workers at Construction Site*, 1931–33
Crayon
275 × 581 mm
Munch Museum
MM.T.02351

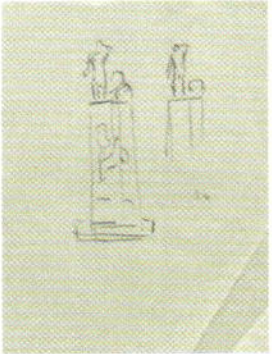

Cat. 185
Edvard Munch: *Sketch for a Monument*, 1910–19
Pen
280 × 219 mm
Munch Museum
MM.T.02935

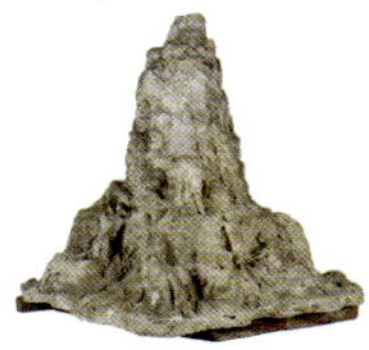

Cat. 189
Edvard Munch: *The Human Mountain*, prob. 1925–29
Plaster
88 × 100 × 100.5 cm
Munch Museum
MM.S.00005

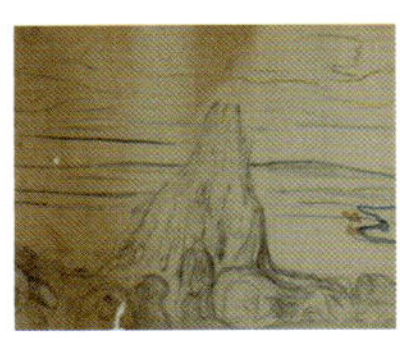

Cat. 193
Edvard Munch: *The Human Mountain*, 1909–10
Charcoal, watercolour
855 × 1105 mm
Munch Museum
MM.T.02533

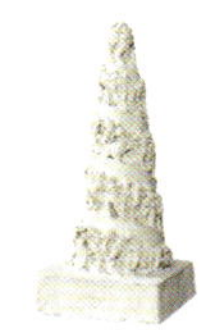

Cat. 197
Gustav Vigeland: *Cone-shaped Column*, 1923
Clay
38 × 17 × 17 cm
Vigeland Museum
VM.S.0256

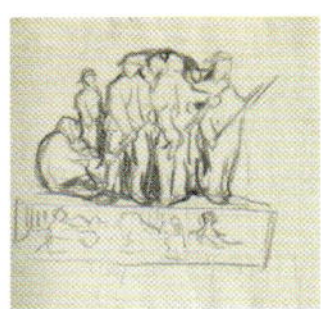

Cat. 182
Edvard Munch: *Draft for a Sculpture of Workers*, 1915–25
Charcoal
488 × 630 mm
Munch Museum
MM.T.01689

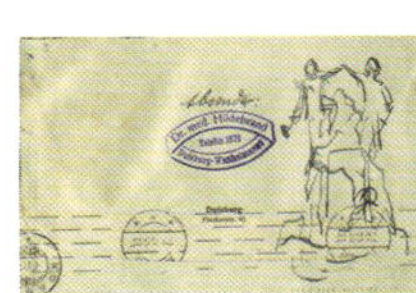

Cat. 186
Edvard Munch: *Sketch for a Monument*, 1915
Pen
104 × 159 mm
Munch Museum
MM.T.02949-recto

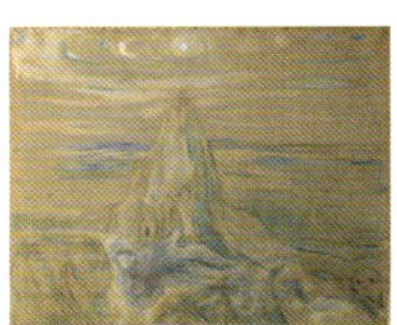

Cat. 190
Edvard Munch: *The Human Mountain*, 1909
Tempera and charcoal on unprimed canvas
129 × 160 cm
Munch Museum
MM.M.00159 (Woll M 863)

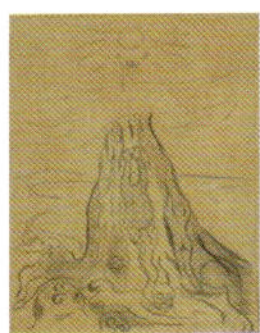

Cat. 194
Edvard Munch: *The Human Mountain*, 1897–98
Crayon
523 × 440 mm
Munch Museum
MM.T.00390

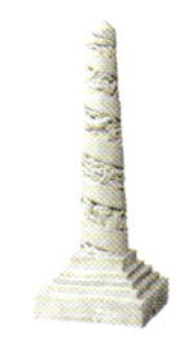

Cat. 198
Gustav Vigeland: *Column with a Spiral Frieze*, 1922
Clay
45 × 17 × 17 cm
Vigeland Museum
VM.S.0248

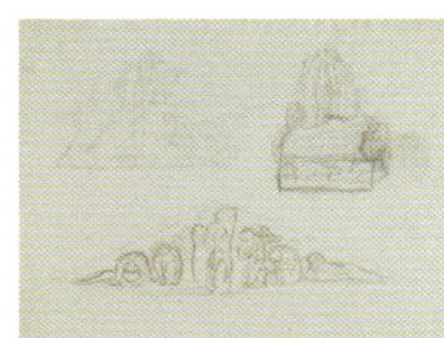

Cat. 183
Edvard Munch: *Sketches for Sculpture Drafts*, 1913–20
Charcoal, crayon
492 × 614 mm
Munch Museum
MM.T.01669

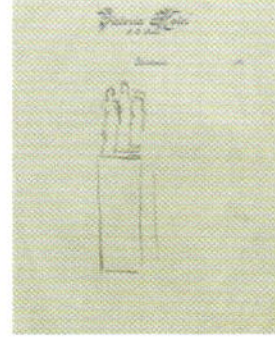

Cat. 187
Edvard Munch: *Sketch for a Monument*, 1910–19
Pen
280 × 219 mm
Munch Museum
MM.T.02936

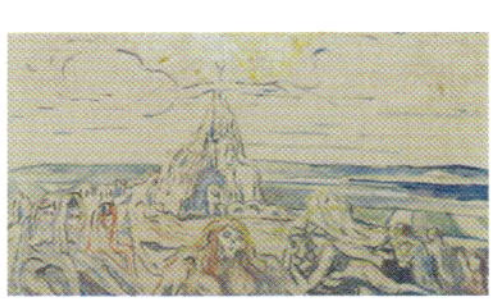

Cat. 191
Edvard Munch: *The Human Mountain*, 1909–10
Oil on canvas
70 × 125 cm
Munch Museum
MM.M.00441 (Woll M 912)

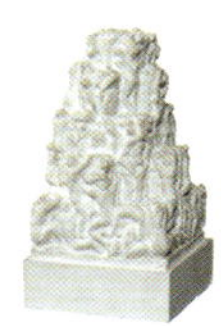

Cat. 195
Gustav Vigeland: *Human Mountain*, 1919
Plaster
25 × 13.5 × 14 cm
Vigeland Museum
VM.S.0460.02

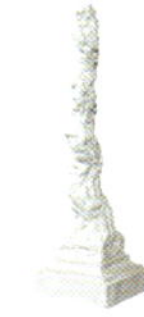

Cat. 199
Gustav Vigeland: *Column*, 1919
Plaster
54 × 17 × 16.5 cm
Vigeland Museum
VM.S.0243.02

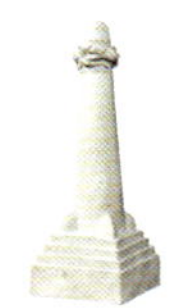

Cat. 200
Gustav Vigeland: *Column
with a Garland of Figures*,
1922
Clay
44 × 16 × 17 cm
Vigeland Museum
VM.S.0249

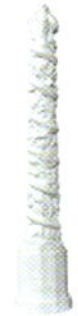

Cat. 201
Gustav Vigeland:
Column, 1919
Plaster
10.5 (diameter) x 50 cm
Vigeland Museum
VM.S.0242.03

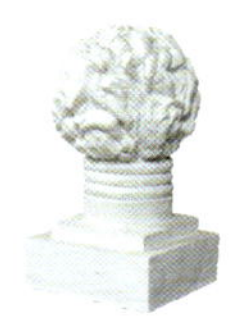

Cat. 202
Gustav Vigeland: *Human
Orb*, 1922
Plaster
28 × 16 × 15.5 cm
Vigeland Museum
VM.S.0455.02

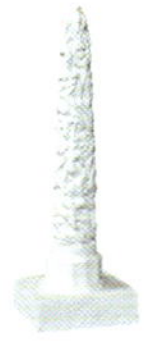

Cat. 203
Gustav Vigeland: *The
Monolith*, 1922
Plaster
45 × 15 × 15 cm
Vigeland Museum
VM.S.0251.02

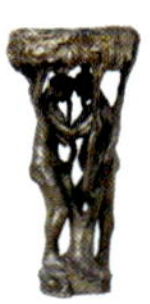

Cat. 204
Gustav Vigeland: *Boy and
Girl Touching Foreheads*,
1905
Bronze
48 × 24 × 24 cm
Vigeland Museum
VM.S.0796.02

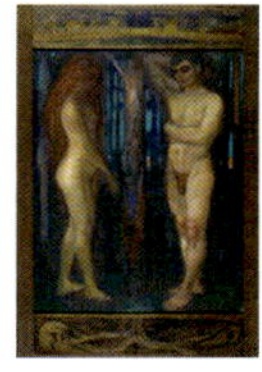

Cat. 205
Edvard Munch:
Metabolism, 1898–99
Oil on canvas
172.5 × 142 cm
Munch Museum
MM.M.00419 (Woll M 428)

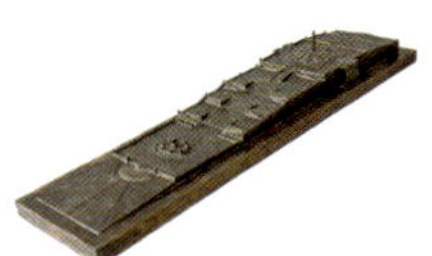

Cat. 206
Gustav Vigeland: *Model of
the Park with Monolith and
Fountain*, 1922
Bronze
14 × 100 × 24 cm
Vigeland Museum
VM.S.1880.01

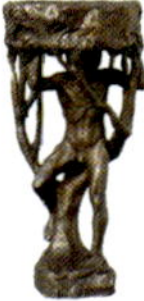

Cat. 207
Gustav Vigeland: *Man
with His Head Against the
Crown of a Tree*, 1905
Bronze
46 × 22.5 × 22.5 cm
Vigeland Museum
VM.S.0797.02

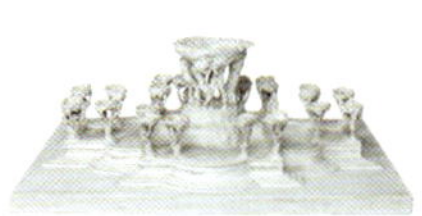

Cat. 208
Gustav Vigeland: *Model of
the Fountain*, 1905–06
Plaster
26.5 × 63.5 × 85 cm
Vigeland Museum
VM.S.1564

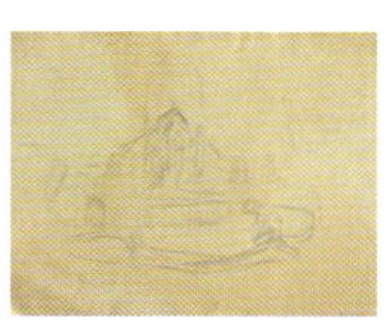

Cat. 209
Edvard Munch: *Fountain in
Front of the Royal Palace*,
1920–30
Crayon
503 × 655 mm
Munch Museum
MM.T.01667

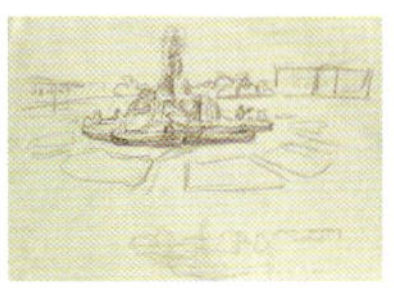

Cat. 210
Edvard Munch: *Fountain in
Front of the Royal Palace*,
1920–30
Crayon
355 × 507 mm
Munch Museum
MM.T.01680

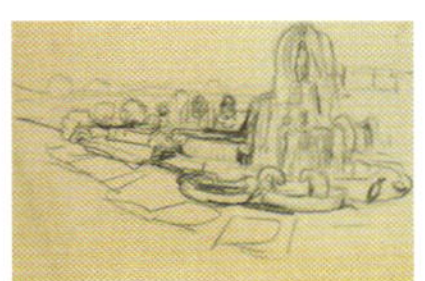

Cat. 211
Edvard Munch: *Fountain in
Front of the Royal Palace*,
1920–30
Crayon
271 × 402 mm
Munch Museum
MM.T.01676

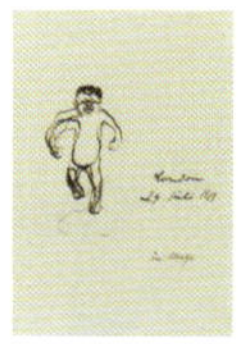

Cat. 212
Gustav Vigeland: *A Child*,
1901
Ink
203 × 158 mm
Vigeland Museum
VM.T.CB00.0018

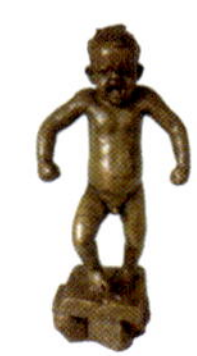

Cat. 213
Gustav Vigeland: *The
Angry Boy*, 1911
Bronze
35 × 13 × 10 cm
Vigeland Museum
VM.S.0544.02

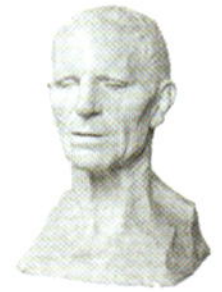

Cat. 214
Gustav Vigeland: *Jonas
Lie*, 1904
Plaster
38.5 × 27 × 27 cm
Vigeland Museum
VM.S.0694.01

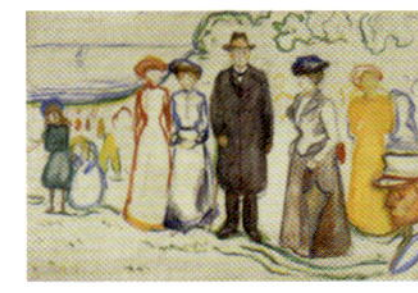

Cat. 215
Edvard Munch: *Jonas Lie
and His Family*, 1902–03
Oil on canvas
69.5 × 103 cm
Munch Museum
MM.M.00038 (Woll M 523)

List of Illustrations

Photographs of works by Gustav Vigeland and Edvard Munch are, where not otherwise specified, © Vigeland Museum and Munch Museum respectively

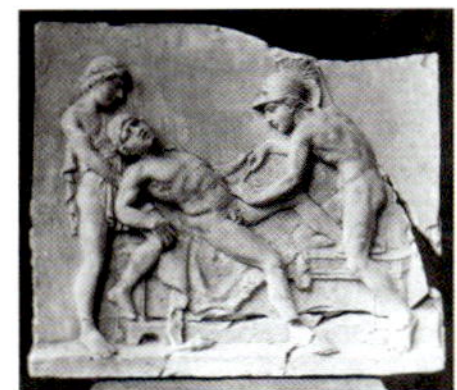

4.
Gustav Vigeland: *Patroclus Pulls the Arrow From Eurypylus's Thigh*, 1889
Plaster
Vigeland Museum

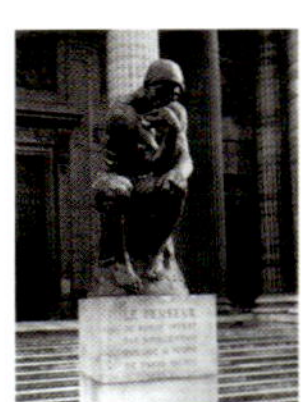

8.
Auguste Rodin: *The Thinker (Le Penseur)*, c. 1906
Bronze
Photo from Gustav Vigeland's estate
Vigeland Museum

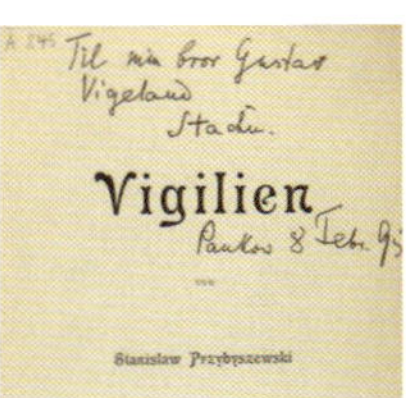

12.
Dedication in *Vigilien* from Stanisław Przybyszewski to Gustav Vigeland, Pankow, Berlin, 8.2.1895
From Gustav Vigeland's library
Vigeland Museum

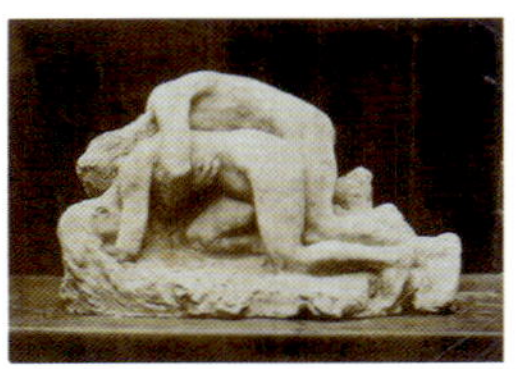

16.
Gustav Vigeland: *The Oppressed*, c. 1895
Photo from Edvard Munch's estate
Munch Museum

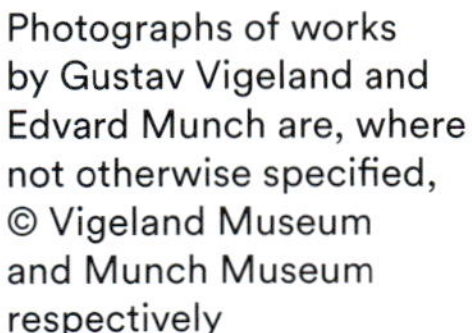

1.
The Royal School of Design on the corner of Apotekergata and Akersgata, 1897
Oslo City Museum

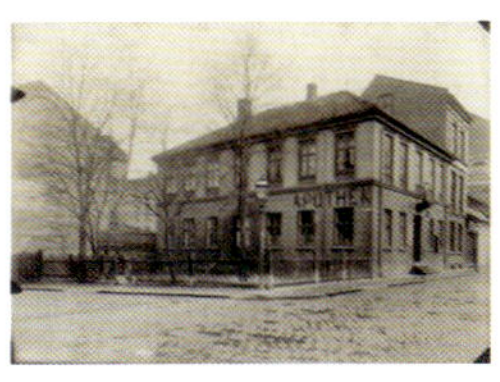

5.
Gustav Vigeland: *Hagar and Ishmael*, 1889
Plaster
Vigeland Museum

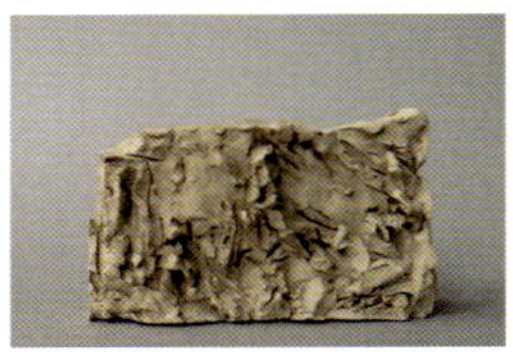

9.
Gustav Vigeland: *Hell*, 1893
Clay
National Museum of Art, Architecture and Design, Oslo
Photo © National Museum

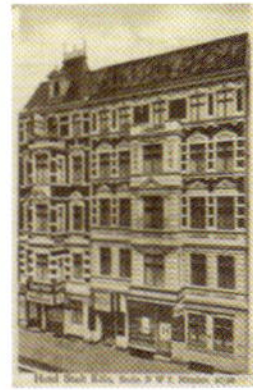

13.
Hotel Stadt Köln, 47–48 Mittelstrasse Berlin, c. 1930
Postcard

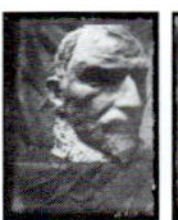
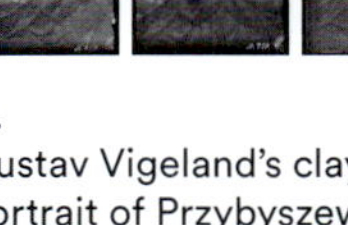

17.
Gustav Vigeland's clay portrait of Przybyszewski, c. 1900
Photo probably taken by Inga Syvertsen
Vigeland Museum

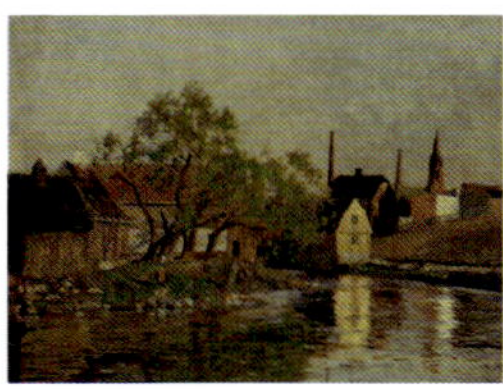

2.
Edvard Munch: *Akerselva*, 1882
Oil on unprimed cardboard
Munch Museum

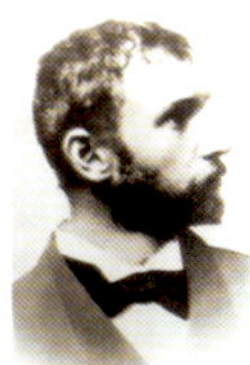

6.
Stanisław Przybyszewski, Berlin, 1892
Unknown photographer
Women's Museum, Kongsvinger

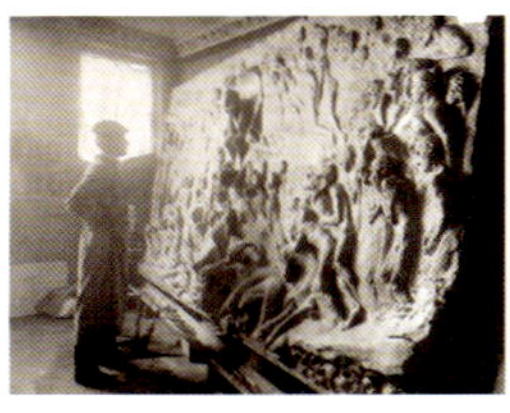

10.
Gustav Vigeland standing in front of *Hell* in his studio in 8 Pilestredet, 1894
Photo: Marie Gleditsch
Vigeland Museum

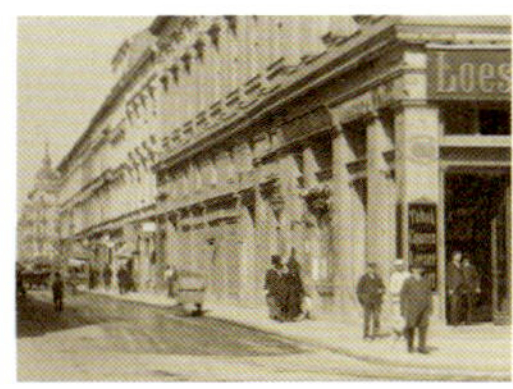

14.
View from Unter den Linden towards Neue Wilhelmstrasse, 1906
Zum Schwarzen Ferkel was situated behind the tobacconists
Photo: Hugo Rudolphy
Stiftung Stadmuseum Berlin

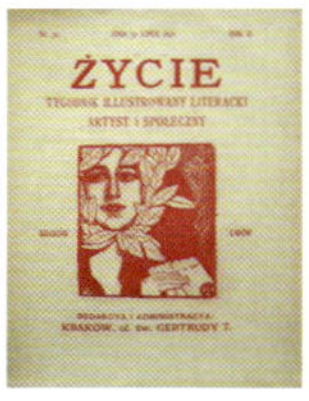

18.
Zycie (1898)
The periodical Stanisław Przybyszewski took over when he moved back to Krakow
National Museum, Krakow

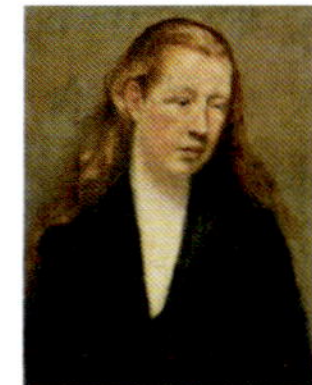

3.
Edvard Munch: *Study of a Head*, 1883
Oil on canvas
National Museum of Art, Architecture and Design, Oslo
Photo © National Museum

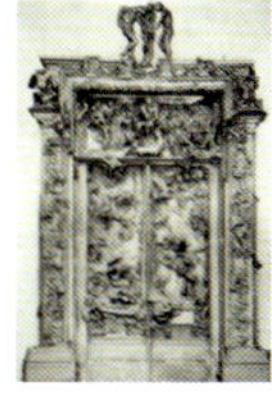

7.
Auguste Rodin: *The Gates of Hell*, 1880–1917
Bronze
Photo from Gustav Vigeland's estate
Vigeland Museum

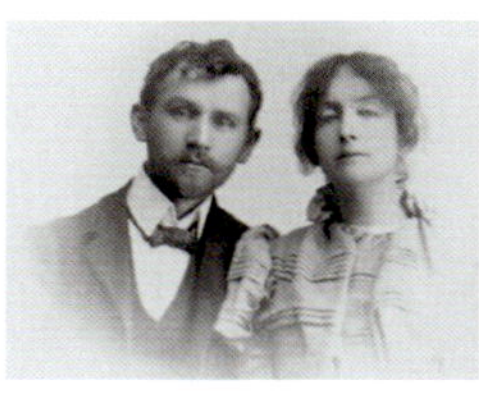

11.
Stanisław Przybyszewski and Dagny Juel Przybyszewska at Kongsvinger, 1890s
Photo: Sigrid Engebretsen
Women's Museum, Kongsvinger

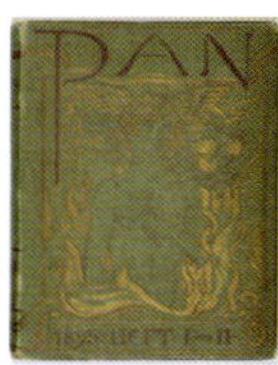

15.
Pan (1895)
Munch Museum

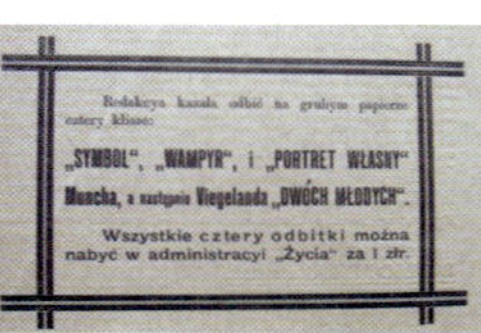

19.
Advertisement in *Zycie* (1899) urging people to buy reproductions of Edvard Munch's and Gustav Vigeland's works for one zloty each

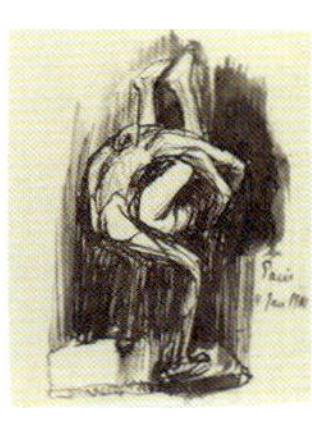

20.
Gustav Vigeland: *Erotic Drawing*, 1901
Pen
Vigeland Museum

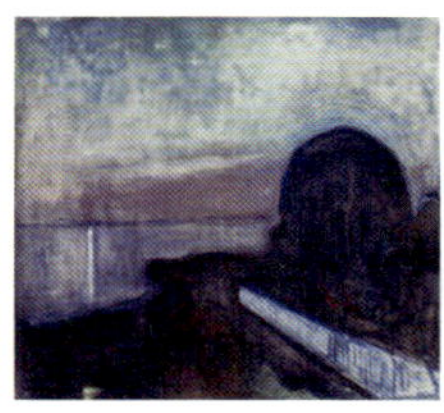

24.
Edvard Munch: *Starry Night*, 1893
Oil on canvas
Von der Heydt-Museum, Wuppertal

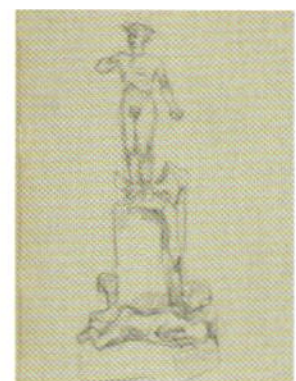

28.
Edvard Munch: *Sketch for a Monument*, 1910–20
Pencil
Munch Museum

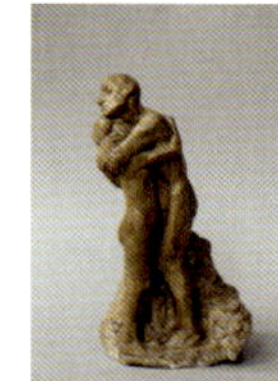

32.
Gustav Vigeland: *Man and Woman Embracing Each Other*, 1893
Clay
National Museum of Art, Architecture and Design, Oslo
Photo © National Museum

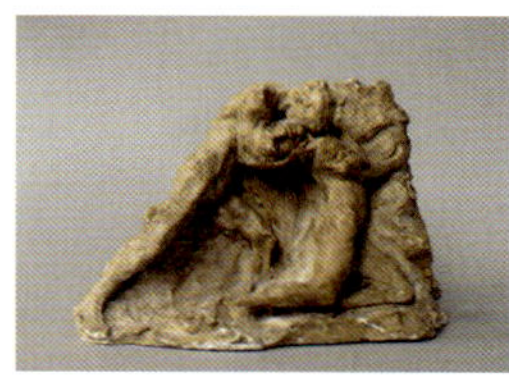

36.
Gustav Vigeland: *Woman Caught from Behind by a Man*, 1894
Clay
National Museum of Art, Architecture and Design, Oslo
Photo © National Museum

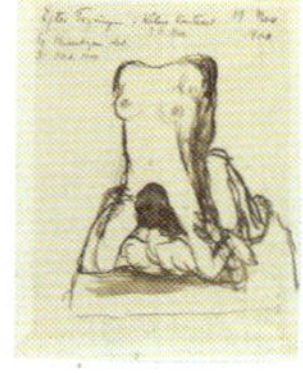

21.
Gustav Vigeland: *Erotic Drawing*, 1900
Pen
Vigeland Museum

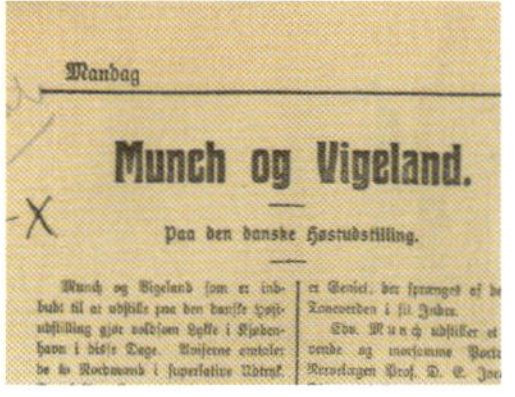

25.
'Munch and Vigeland. At the Danish Autumn Exhibition'
Dagens Nyt, 8.11.1909

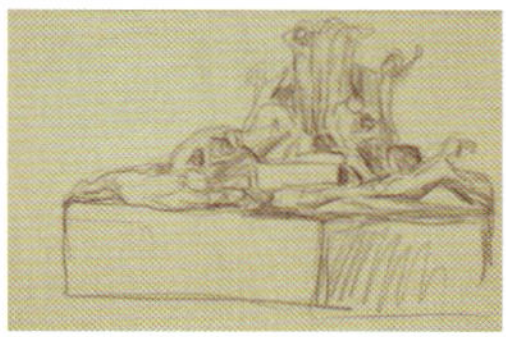

29.
Edvard Munch: *Draft for a Sculpture*, c. 1920
Crayon
Munch Museum

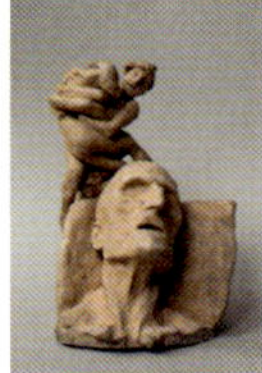

33.
Gustav Vigeland: *Death and Life*, 1893
Terracotta
National Museum of Art, Architecture and Design, Oslo
Photo © National Museum

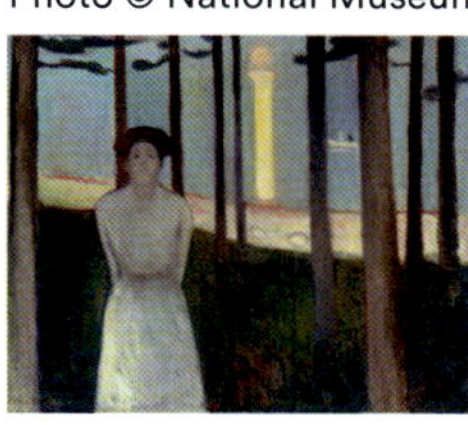

37.
Edvard Munch: *Summer Night's Dream. The Voice*, 1893
Oil on canvas
Museum of Fine Arts, Boston

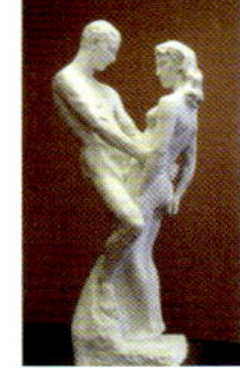

22.
Gustav Vigeland: *Young Man and Woman*, 1906
Marble
Vigeland Museum

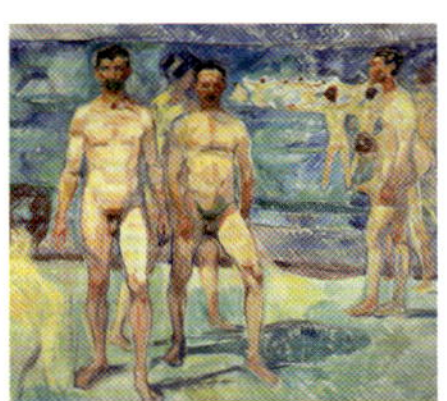

26.
Edvard Munch: *Bathing Men*, 1907
Oil on canvas
Ateneum Art Museum, Helsinki

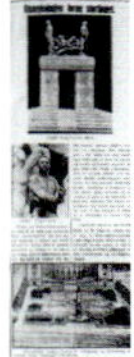

30.
'The embellishment in front of the Parliament building'
Nordre Bergenhus Amtstidende, 4.2.1924

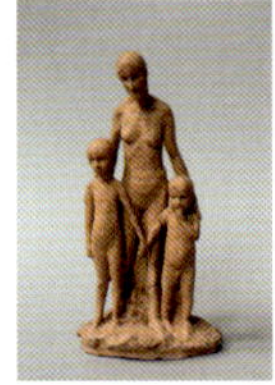

34.
Gustav Vigeland: *An Old Mother with Two Children*, 1893
Terracotta
National Museum of Art, Architecture and Design, Oslo
Photo © National Museum

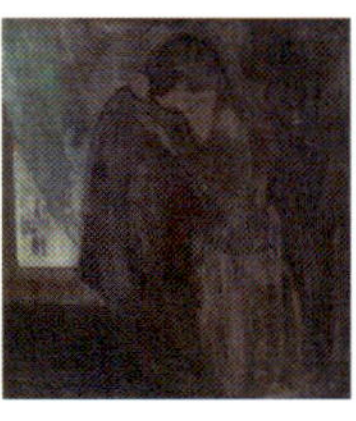

38.
Edvard Munch: *The Kiss*, 1892/97
Tempera and oil on canvas
Munch Museum

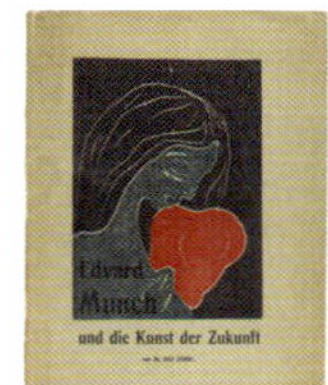

23.
Max Linde: *Edvard Munch und die Kunst der Zukunft*, 1902
From Gustav Vigeland's library
Vigeland Museum

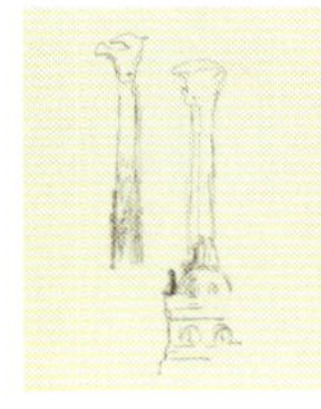

27.
Gustav Vigeland: *Draft for a Column Monument*, c. 1910
Pen
Vigeland Museum

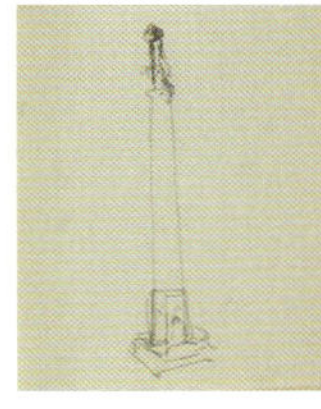

31.
Edvard Munch: *Standing Figure on a Tall Column*, 1920–30
Pen
Munch Museum

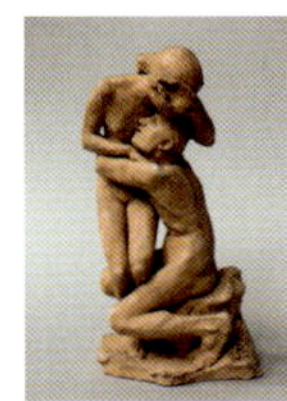

35.
Gustav Vigeland: *Man Embracing a Woman*, 1893
Terracotta
National Museum of Art, Architecture and Design, Oslo
Photo © National Museum

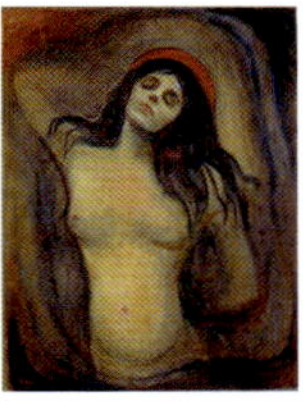

39.
Edvard Munch: *Madonna*, 1894–95
Oil on canvas
National Museum of Art, Architecture and Design
Photo © National Museum

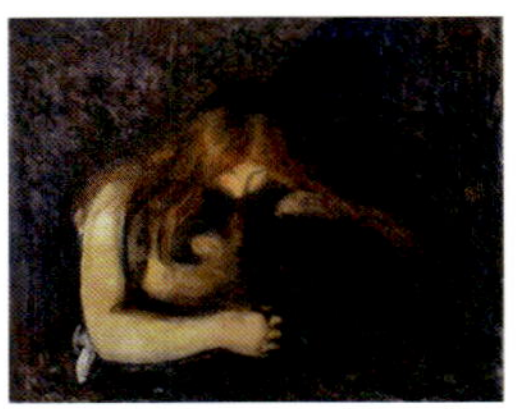

40.
Edvard Munch: *Vampire*,
1893
Oil on canvas
Gothenburg Museum of
Art

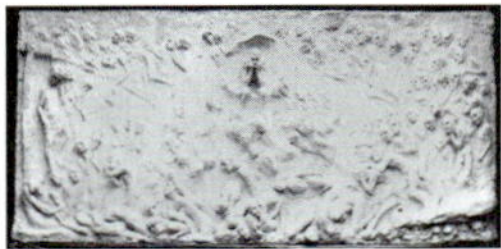

44.
Gustav Vigeland's first
version of *Hell*, 1894
Plaster
Destroyed by the artist in
1900

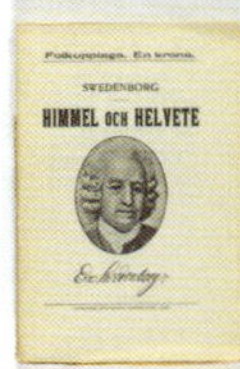

48.
Emanuel Swedenborg:
Himmel och Helvete, 1906
From Gustav Vigeland's
library
Vigeland Museum

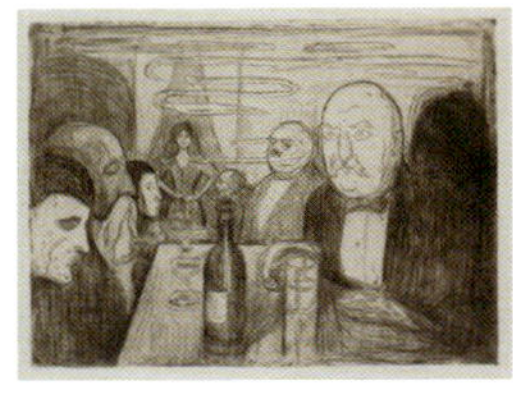

52.
Edvard Munch: *Kristiania
Bohemians II*, 1895
Etching
Munch Museum

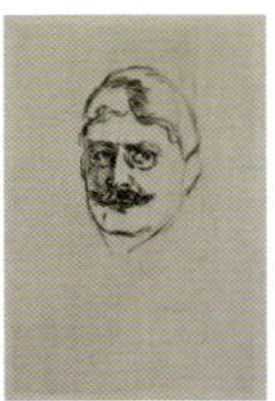

56.
Edvard Munch: *Knut
Hamsun*, 1896
Etching
Munch Museum

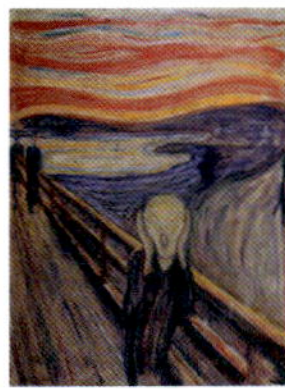

41.
Edvard Munch: *The
Scream*, 1893
Tempera and crayon on
cardboard
National Museum of Art,
Architecture and Design,
Oslo
Photo © National Museum

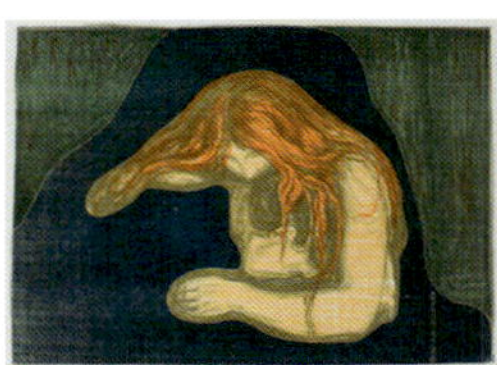

45.
Edvard Munch: *Vampire*,
1895
Lithograph
Munch Museum

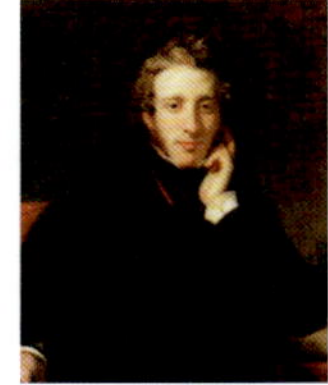

49.
Henry William Pickersgill:
Edward Bulwer-Lytton,
c. 1831
Oil on canvas
National Portrait Gallery,
London

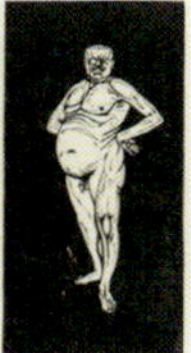

53.
Gustav Vigeland: *Gunnar
Heiberg*, 1918
Woodcut
Vigeland Museum

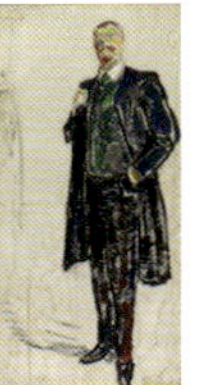

57.
Edvard Munch: *Jens Thiis*,
1909
Oil on canvas
Munch Museum

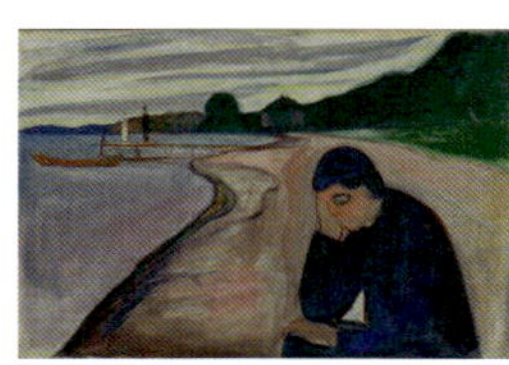

42.
Edvard Munch:
Melancholy, 1893
Oil on canvas
Munch Museum

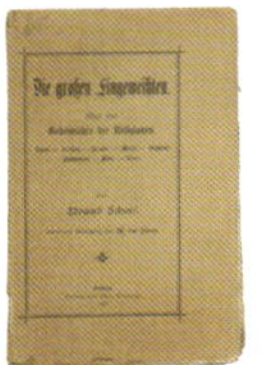

46.
Edouard Schuré: *Die
grossen Eingeweihten.
Skizze einer Geheimlehre
der Religionen*, 1907
German translation of
Schuré's esoteric bestseller
From Edvard Munch's
library, Munch Museum

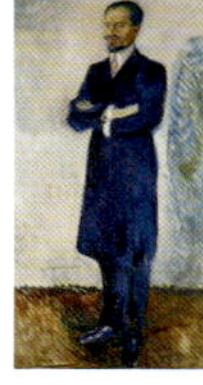

50.
Edvard Munch: *Ernest
Thiel*, 1907
Oil on canvas
Thiel Gallery, Stockholm

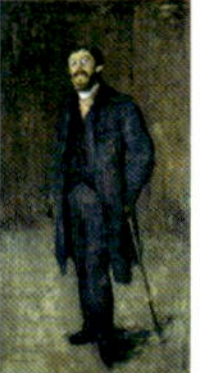

54.
Edvard Munch: *Karl
Jensen-Hjell*, 1885
Oil on canvas
Private collection

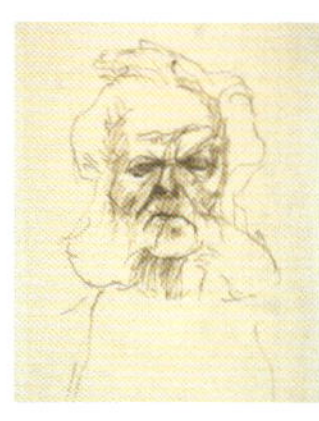

58.
Gustav Vigeland: *Henrik
Ibsen*, c. 1902
Ink
Munch Museum

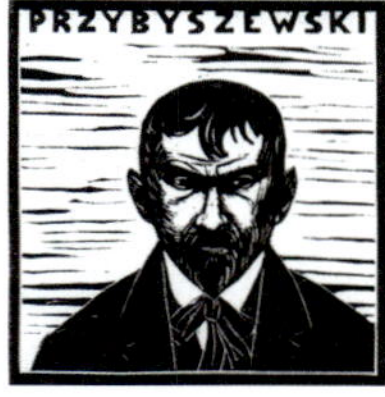

43.
Gustav Vigeland: *Stanisław
Przybyszewski*, c. 1929
Woodcut
Vigeland Museum

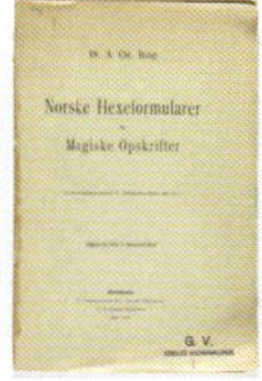

47.
Anton Christian Bang:
*Norske Hexeformularer og
magiske Opskrifter*,
1901–02
From Gustav Vigeland's
library. Vigeland Museum

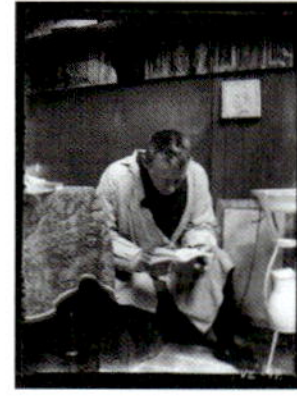

51.
Gustav Vigeland reading
Hans Jæger, February 1903
Photo: Inga Syvertsen
Vigeland Museum

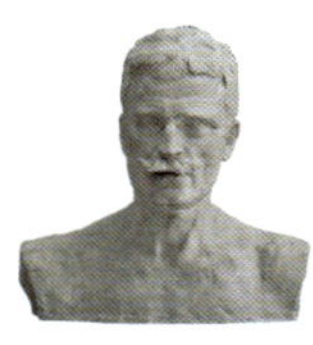

55.
Gustav Vigeland: *Knut
Hamsun*, 1903
Plaster
Vigeland Museum

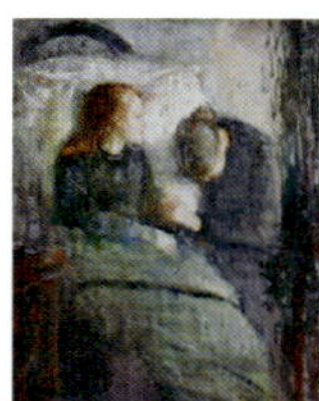

59.
Edvard Munch: *The Sick
Child*, 1885–86
Oil on canvas
National Museum of Art,
Architecture and Design,
Oslo
Photo © National Museum

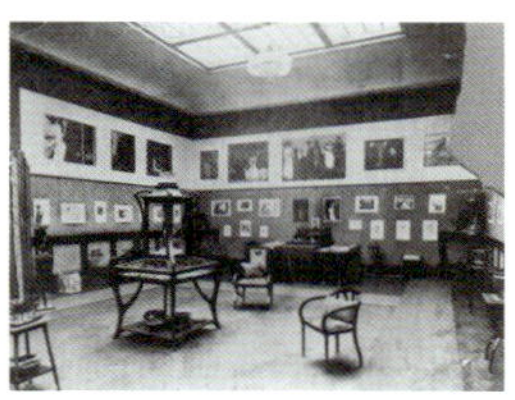

60.
Edvard Munch's exhibition of *The Frieze of Life* at P.H. Beyer & Sohn in Leipzig, 1903
Unknown photographer
Munch Museum

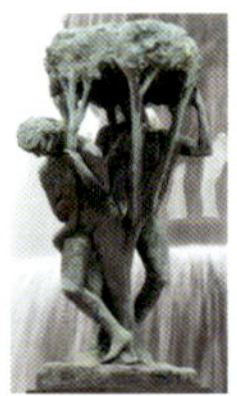

64.
Gustav Vigeland: *Man Standing Behind a Woman*
One of the tree groups around *The Fountain*, 1906–14
Bronze
Vigeland Park

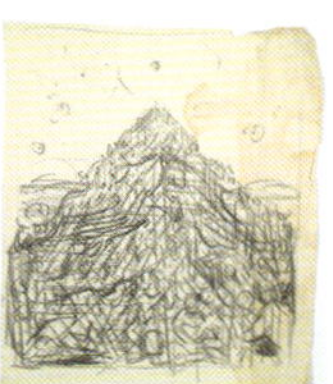

68.
Edvard Munch: *The Human Mountain*, 1916–17
Charcoal
Munch Museum

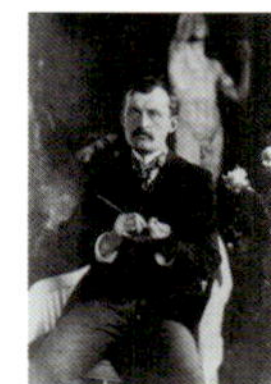

72.
Edvard Munch in front of Rodin's *Age of Bronze* in Max Linde's garden in Lübeck, 1902
Unknown photographer
Munch Museum

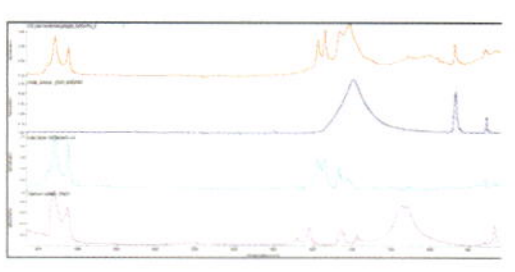

76.
FTIR spectrograph of the sample taken from Edvard Munch's *Woman's Head*.
Munch Museum

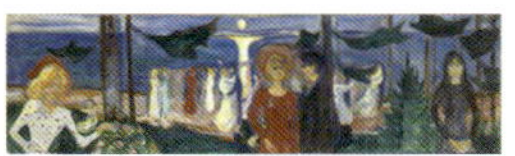

61.
Edvard Munch: *Dance on the Beach*, 1904
Oil on canvas
Munch Museum

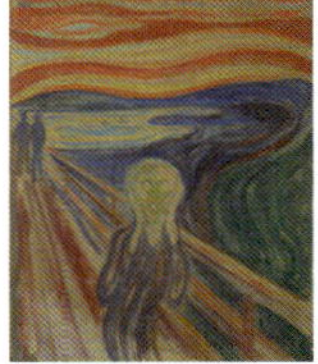

65.
Edvard Munch: *The Scream*, 1910?
Tempera and oil on cardboard
Munch Museum

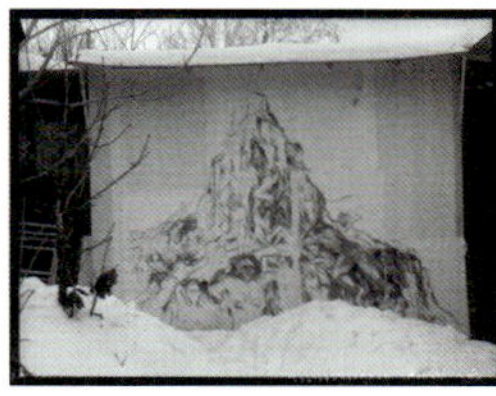

69.
Edvard Munch's *Human Mountain* composition in his outdoor studio at Ekely, 1926
Photo © O. Væring Eftf.
Munch Museum

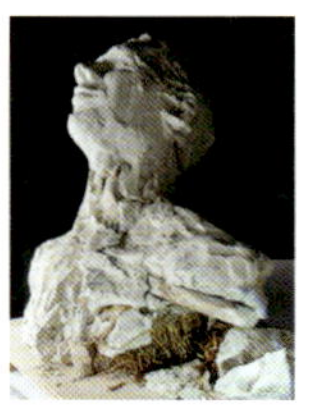

73.
Reinforcement materials exposed at the lower right of Edvard Munch's clay sculpture *Man's Head*
Munch Museum

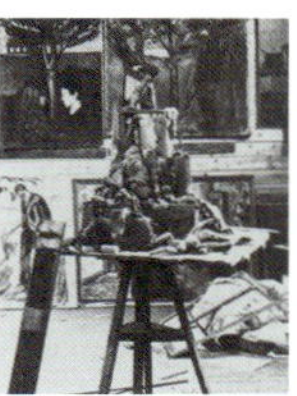

77.
Draft for Edvard Munch's *Human Mountain* at Ekely, 1929, detail
Photo © O. Væring Eftf.
Munch Museum

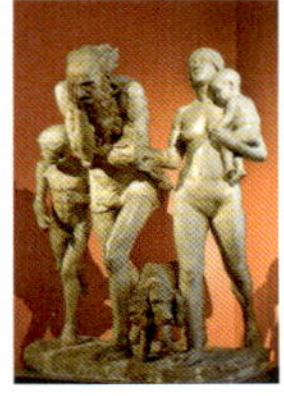

62.
Gustav Vigeland: *The Accursed*, 1891
Plaster
Vigeland Museum

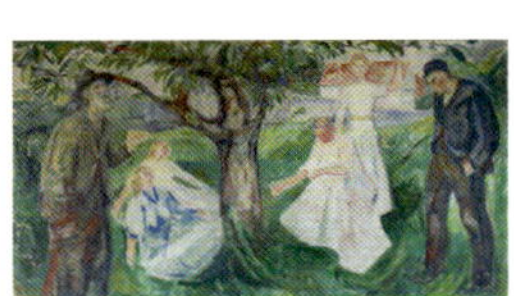

66.
Edvard Munch: *Life*, 1910
Oil on canvas
Oslo City Hall

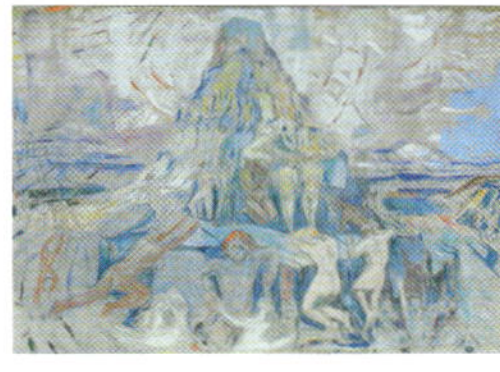

70.
Edvard Munch: *The Human Mountain/Towards the Light*, 1927–29
Oil on canvas
Munch Museum

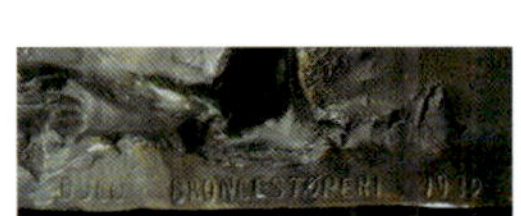

74.
Detail of Edvard Munch's *Weeping Nude*
Munch Museum

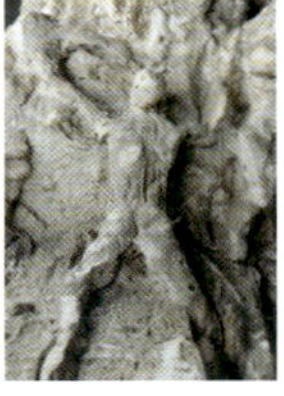

78.
Detail of Edvard Munch's *Human Mountain*
Munch Museum

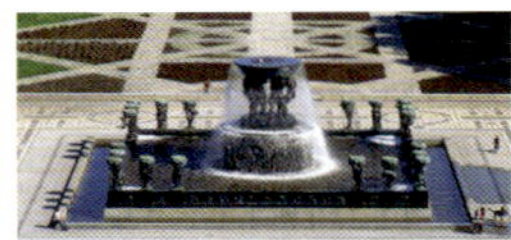

63.
Gustav Vigeland: *The Fountain*, 1909
Bronze
Vigeland Park

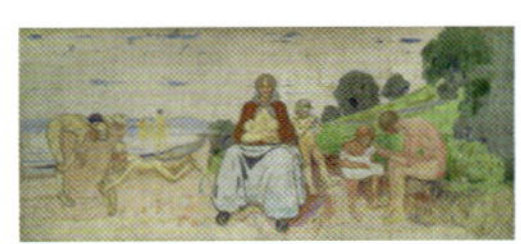

67.
Edvard Munch: *The Researchers*, 1910–11
Mixed media on canvas
Munch Museum

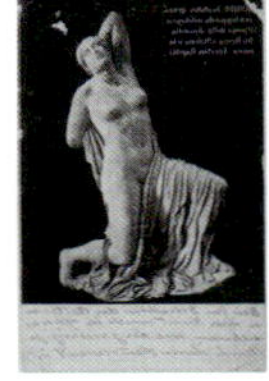

71.
Dying Niobid (450–440 BC)
Postcard from Albert Kollmann to Edvard Munch, 1910
Munch Museum

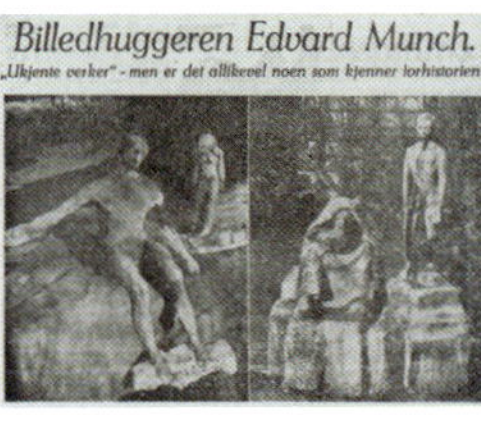

75.
Edvard Munch's *Seated Man, Weeping Nude* and *Mother Norway* outdoors at Ekely
Aftenposten, 4.4.1944

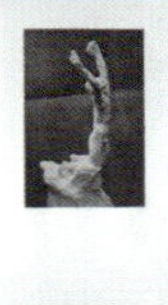

79.
Auguste Rodin: *The Prodigal Son*, 1886–89
Catalogue from the Rodin exhibition at the Manes Artists' Association, Prague, 1902. From Edvard Munch's library. Munch Museum

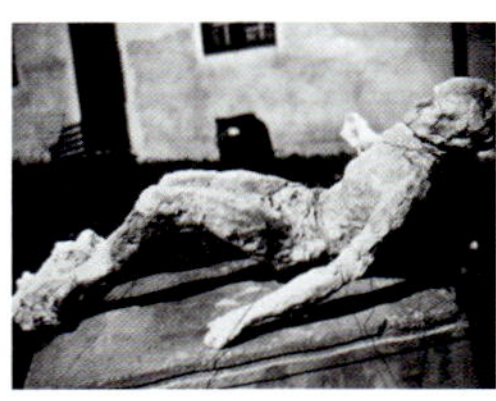

80.
Edvard Munch: *Seated Man*, c. 1930–32
Photo © O. Væring Eftf.
Munch Museum

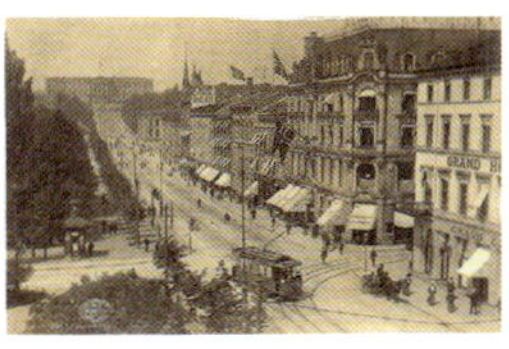

84.
Karl Johan Street, Kristiania (Oslo), 1900
Photo: H. Abel
Oslo City Museum

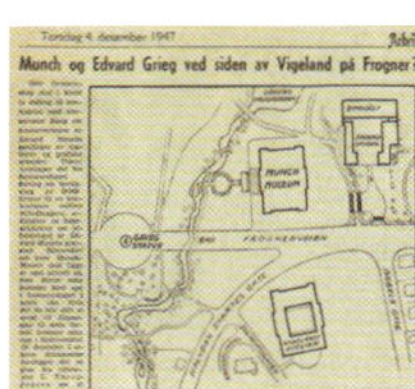

88.
Captain L. Thrap-Jensen's design for a proposed location of the Munch Museum in Frogner
Arbeiderbladet, 4.12.1947

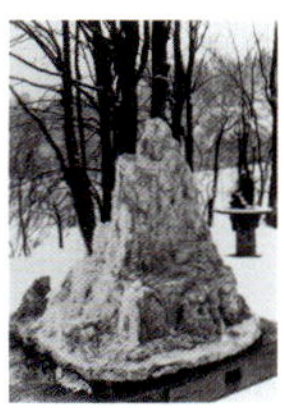

81.
Edvard Munch's *Human Mountain* in the garden at Ekely, after 1932
Photo © O. Væring Eftf.
Munch Museum

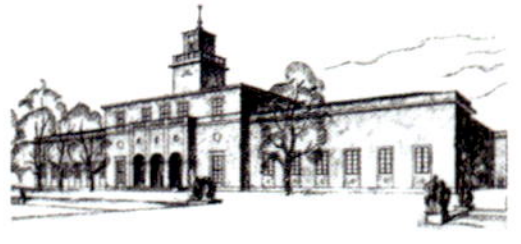

85.
Drawing from the early 1920s by architect Lorentz Harboe Ree, who was commissioned to design a new studio building for Gustav Vigeland in Frogner
Vigeland Museum

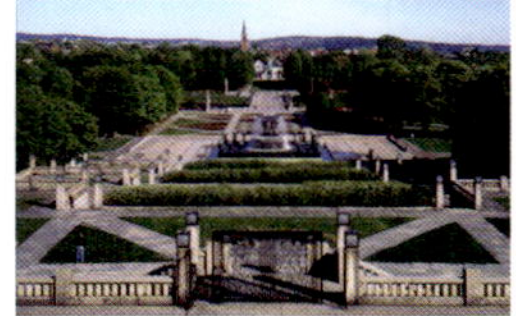

89.
Vigeland Park seen from the *Monolith* plateau
Unknown photographer
Vigeland Museum

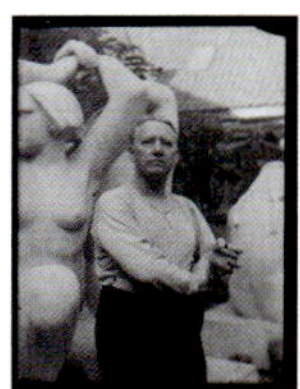

82.
Gustav Vigeland in his garden studio in Hammersborg, 28.5.1917
Unknown photographer
Vigeland Museum

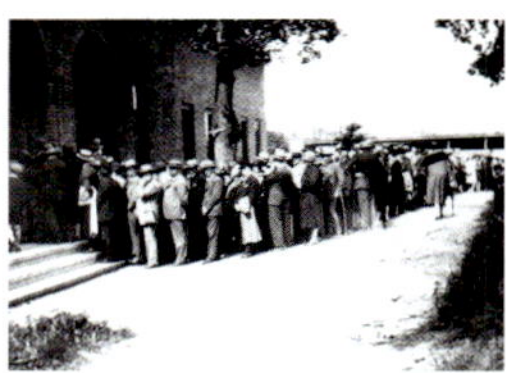

86.
People queuing outside Gustav Vigeland's studio in Frogner for an exhibition, 12.6.1930
Unknown photographer
Vigeland Museum

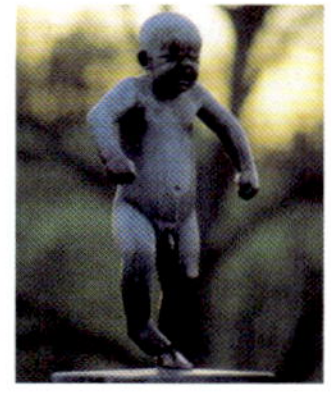

90.
Gustav Vigeland: *The Angry Boy*, c. 1928
Bronze
Vigeland Park

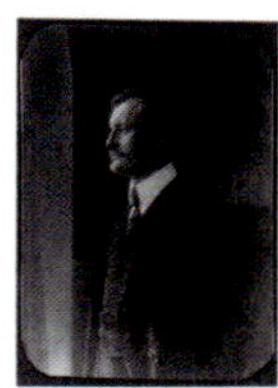

83.
Edvard Munch in Chemnitz, 1905
Unknown photographer
Munch Museum

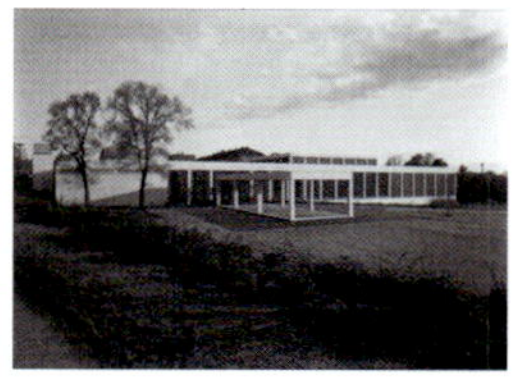

87.
Munch Museum, 1963
Photo: Teigens Fotoatelier
Oslo City Museum

About the Authors

Per Faxneld (b. 1978) obtained his PhD in the History of Religions at Stockholm University, with a thesis (2014) about 'satanic feminism' in nineteenth-century esotericism, art and literature. He has published extensively on heterodox religiosity in a variety of academic journals and with publishers including Brill, Routledge, Palgrave Macmillan and Oxford University Press. Faxneld is currently working on a monograph on the reception among gentiles of Lilith, a figure from Jewish folklore and mysticism.

Trine Otte Bak Nielsen (b. 1978) is a curator at the Munch Museum with an MA in art history from the University of Oslo (2006). The subject of her thesis was Edvard Munch's 'bathing pictures'. She was previously a curator at the Vigeland Museum, where she was responsible for the exhibitions *Michael Johansson. Familiar Abstractions* (2013) and *On the Paths of the Soul. Gustav Vigeland and Polish Sculpture around 1900* (2010) and co-curator of the exhibitions *No Base* (2010) and *The Sculptor Gustav Vigeland's One-Man Exhibition 1894* (2008). As a freelancer Nielsen has undertaken research into Louis Moe's dark symbolism (No Comprendo Press, 2013) and she is co-editor of the art journal *Kunstforum*.

Petra Pettersen (b. 1965) is a curator at the Munch Museum with an MA in art history from the University of Oslo (1995). The subject of her thesis was Edvard Munch's exhibition in Prague in 1905, and its influence on the Czech avant-garde. Between 2004 and 2007 she collaborated on the project *Edvard Munch. Complete Paintings*, vols. I–IV, where her article 'Munch's Aula Decorations' was published. In 2011 she curated the Munch Museum's exhibition *Munch's Laboratory. The Path to the Aula*, which presented several of the decoration drafts she wrote about in the exhibition catalogue. Pettersen has published numerous articles on various aspects of Munch's art.

Stanisław Przybyszewski (1868–1927) was a legendary Polish literary figure, known for his eccentric behaviour in the artist circles of Berlin during the 1890s. After August Strindberg left the city Przybyszewski became a leader figure for the infamous 'Ferkel group'. It was he who published the first articles on Vigeland and Munch for an international audience, and who introduced their work to Central Europe. His enthusiasm for the two artists lasted for many years. His marriage to the Norwegian pianist and writer Dagny Juel Przybyszewska (1867–1901) led to his acquiring a large following among Norwegian artist circles. After returning to Krakow in 1898 he became the editor of the periodical *Zycie*, which would become very important for the generation of artists known as 'Young Poland' (Młoda Polska).

Erika Gohde Sandbakken (b. 1969) is a painting conservator at the Munch Museum. She holds an MA from the University of Oslo (2014) and a four-year BSc (*cum laude*) from the Helsinki Metropolia University of Applied Sciences (2004). She has co-authored several research papers on issues relating to the material condition of Munch's paintings, in particular on the use of efflorescence in examining some of his cotton canvases as well as paint layers.

Guri Skuggen (b. 1973) is a curator at the Vigeland Museum. She has an MA in art history from University College London (1999). Skuggen has published numerous articles on Gustav Vigeland's artistic career and has curated exhibitions focusing on various aspects of his art, including *Gustav Vigeland and Photography* (2012), *In the Melting Pot* (2012), *Vigeland and Hamsun* (2009) and, as co-curator, *The Sculptor Gustav Vigeland's One-Man Exhibition 1894* (2008).

Jarle Strømodden (b. 1965) has been director of the Vigeland Museum since 2005. He has an MA in art history from the University of Oslo (1995). His thesis was a discussion of three different approaches to Lucian Freud's paintings. Strømodden has previously worked at the Museum of Contemporary Art in Oslo, the Tromsø Art Association and the Kistefos Museum. He is particularly interested in sculpture and three-dimensional art, and how these are experienced by the public, both in public spaces and in art institutions. Since 2010 he has been a member of the Artistic Committee for the Ekeberg Sculpture Park, and Head of the Committee for the placement of the HM King Olav V monument (unveiled June 2015).

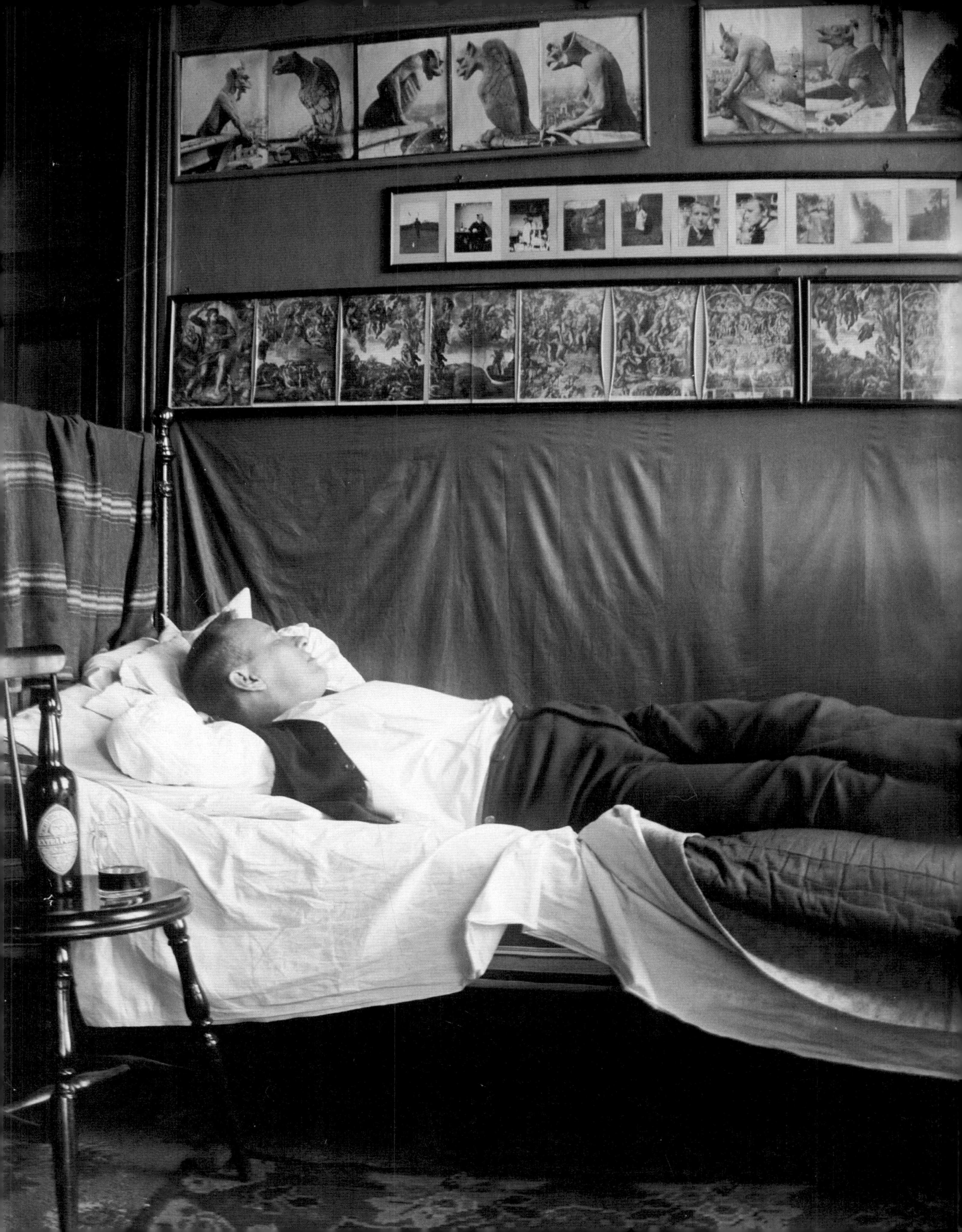

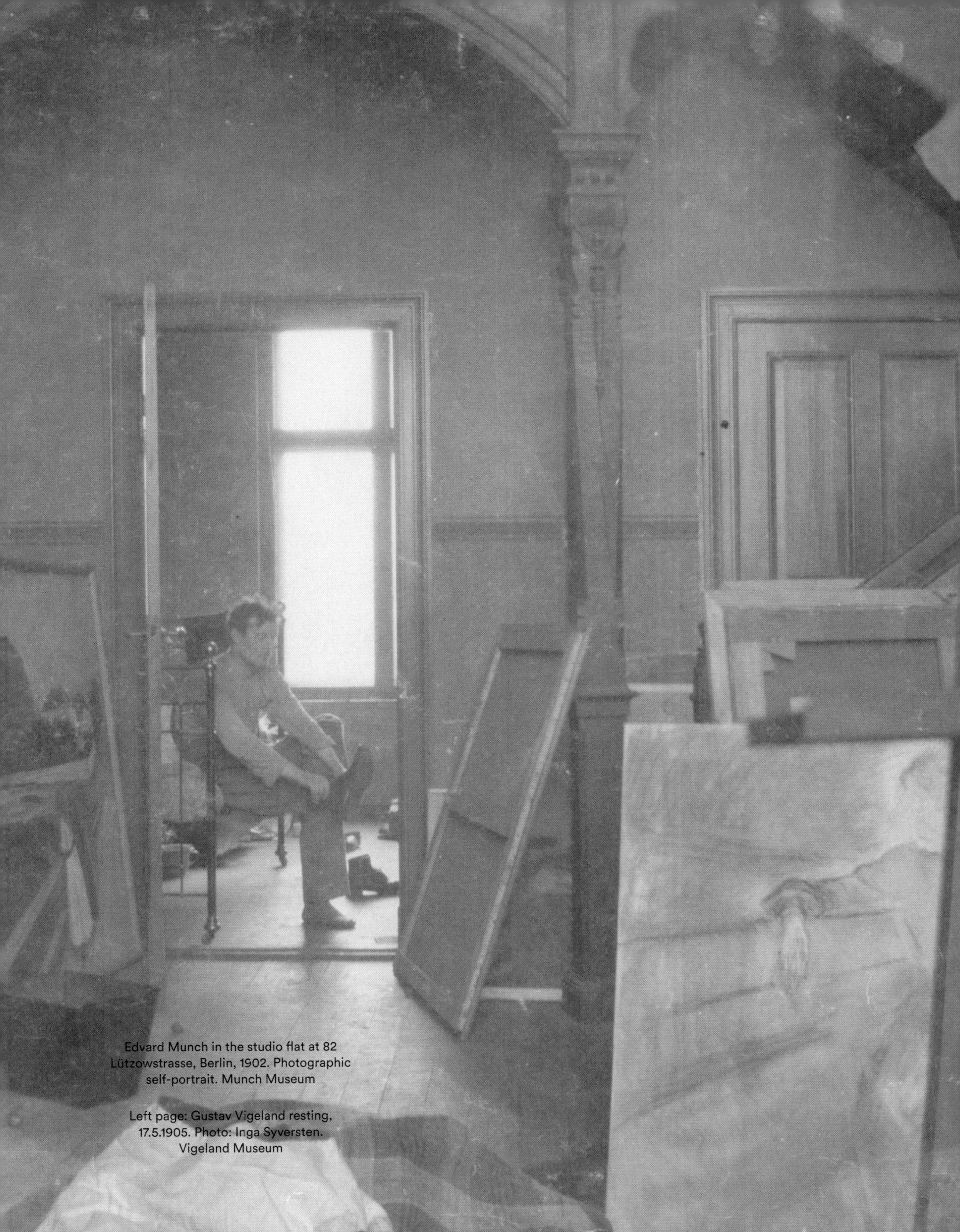

Edvard Munch in the studio flat at 82
Lützowstrasse, Berlin, 1902. Photographic
self-portrait. Munch Museum

Left page: Gustav Vigeland resting,
17.5.1905. Photo: Inga Syversten.
Vigeland Museum

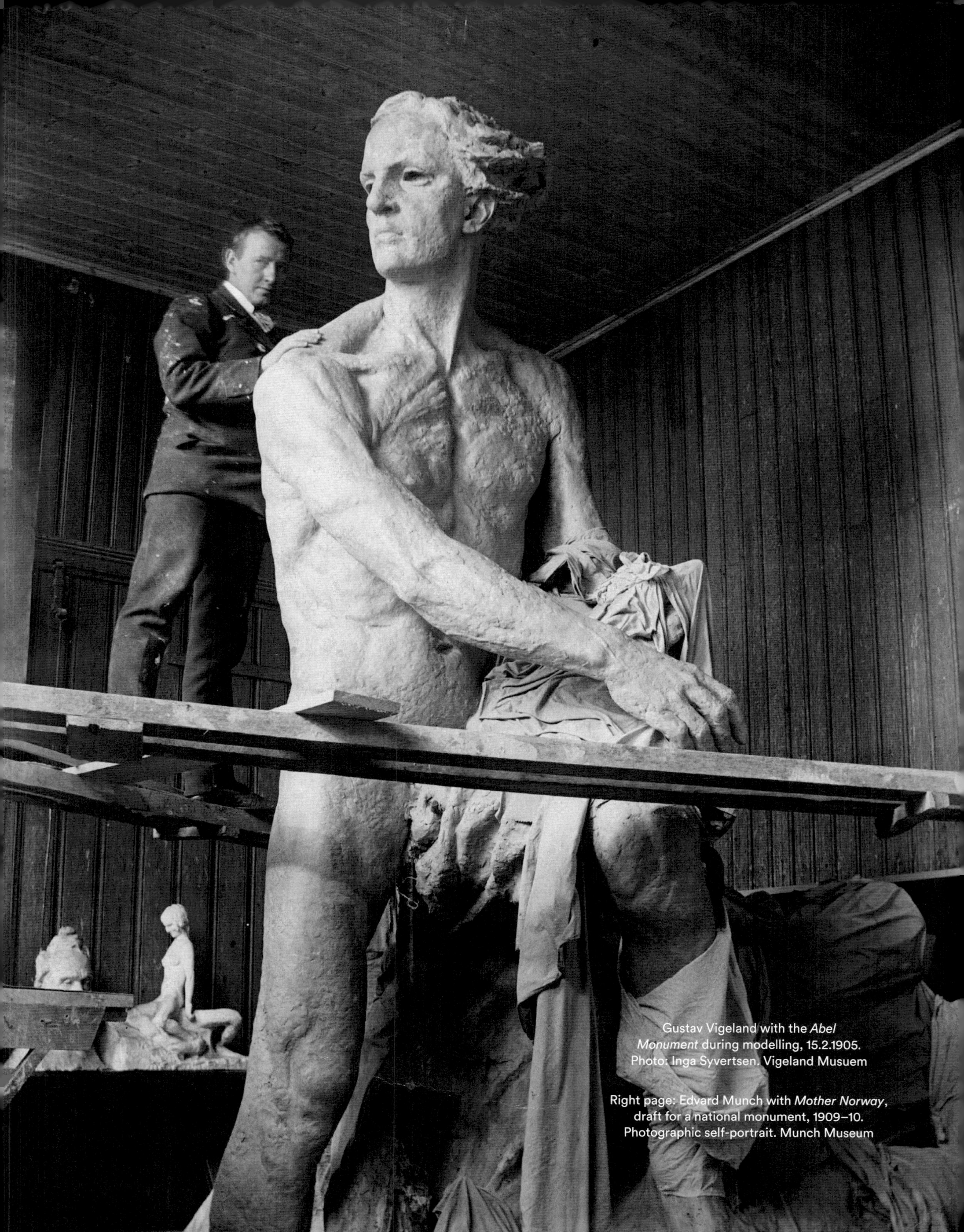

Gustav Vigeland with the *Abel Monument* during modelling, 15.2.1905. Photo: Inga Syvertsen. Vigeland Musuem

Right page: Edvard Munch with *Mother Norway*, draft for a national monument, 1909–10. Photographic self-portrait. Munch Museum

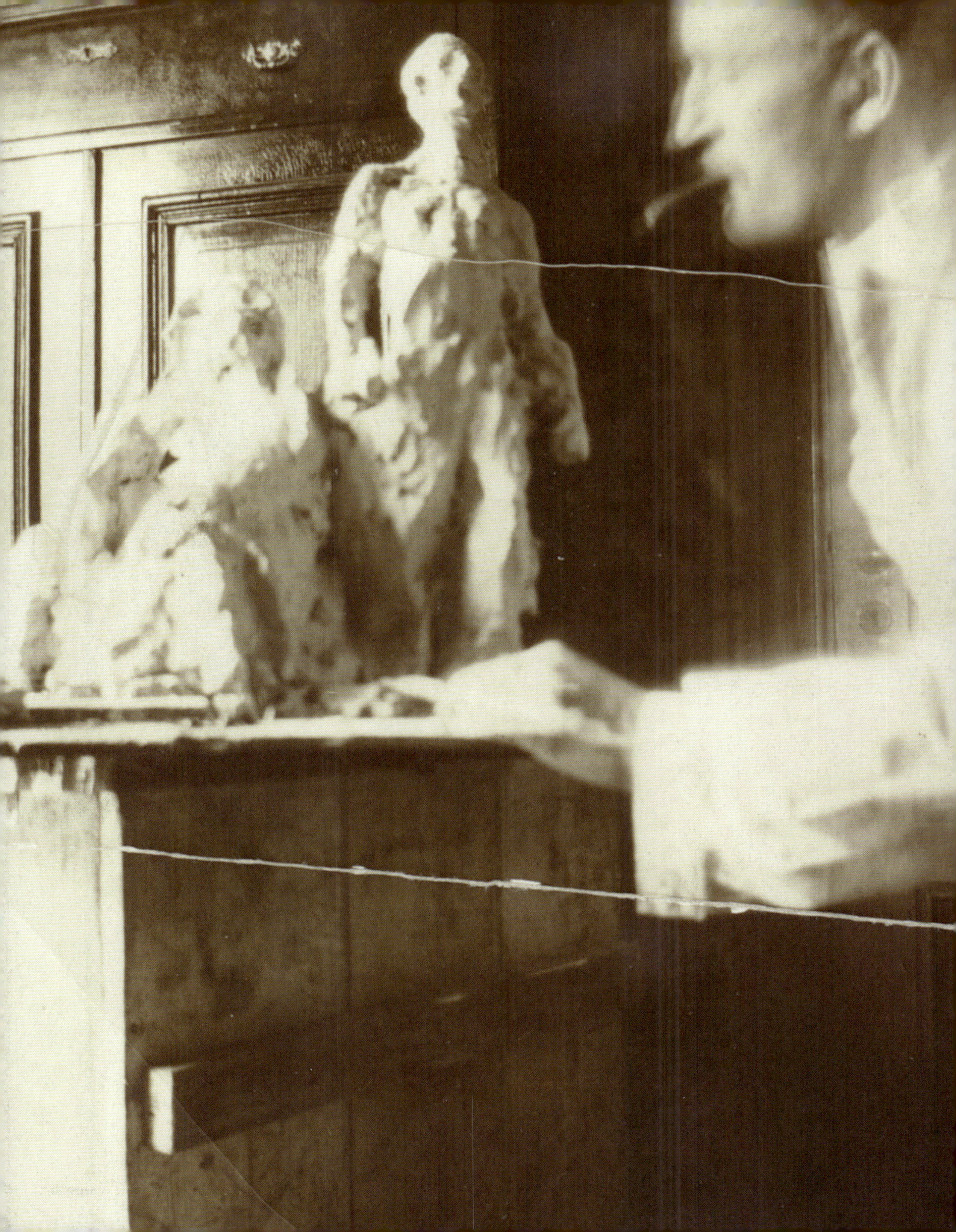

Index

A

Abel, Niels Henrik (1802–1829): 110, 118, 151, 152, 301
Aksakow, Alexander (1832–1903): 100
The Angry Boy: 11, 152, 155, 276
Aubert, Andreas (1851–1913): 45
Aula Decorations: 7, 11, 18, 45, 47, 114, 118, 124, 127, 128, 130, 132, 155

B

Backer, Harriet (1845–1932): 23
Bang, Anton Christian (1840–1913): 101, 102
Bergslien, Brynjulf (1830–1898): 15, 24, 146
Bissen, Vilhelm (1836–1913): 15, 27
Bjølstad, Karen (1839–1931): 14, 22, 166
Bjørnson, Bjørnstjerne (1832–1910): 114, 117, 118, 176
Bødtker, Sigurd (1866–1928): 26, 42, 111, 113
Bonnat, Léon (1833–1922): 15, 26
Brenna, Arne (1917–2005): 113, 118
The Bridge: 126, 150, 155
Bulwer-Lytton, Edward (1803–1873): 93, 102

C

Campbell, Colin (1940–): 96
Cézanne, Paul (1839–1906): 18
Chavannes, Pierre-Cécile Puvis de (1865–1918): 97

D

Dedekam, Hans (1872–1928): 42, 45
Dee, John (1527–1609): 62, 79, 100
Dehmel, Richard (1863–1920): 16, 35, 85
Delville, Jean (1867–1953): 87, 97
Dietrichson, Lorentz (1834–1917): 107, 146, 159
Dons, Ebba (1843–1908): 15, 26

E

Eggum, Arne (1936–): 143
Elias, Julius (1861–1927): 117

F

Fåhraeus, Klas (1863–1944): 106
Faivre, Antoine (1934–): 95, 96
Finne, Gabriel (1866–1899): 26, 29, 113
Fladmoe, Torsten Kristensen (1831–1886): 14, 24, 146
The Fountain: 18, 19, 44, 45, 47, 48, 49, 110, 124, 126–128, 130–132, 147, 150, 272, 274
The Frieze of Life: 10, 16, 17, 28, 40, 48, 49, 51, 120, 122–124, 126–128, 130–132, 150

G

Gallén, Axel, from 1907 Gallen-Kallela, Akseli (1865–1931): 16, 35, 92, 97, 101, 102, 123
The Gates of Hell: 15, 28, 127
Gauguin, Paul (1848–1903): 18
Gogh, Vincent van (1853–1890): 7, 18
Goya, Francisco de (1746–1828): 61

H

Hamsun, Knut (1859–1952): 36, 112–114, 122
Hanegraaff, Wouter (1961–): 92, 93, 95, 96, 100
Hedlund, Torsten (1855–1935): 102
Heiberg, Gunnar (1857–1929): 36, 42, 45, 108, 110, 111, 114, 118, 177
Hell: 15, 16, 17, 28, 29, 30, 33, 35, 75–76, 97, 100–101, 114, 127, 235, 236, 238, 239
Hille, Peter (1854–1904): 35, 90
Holst, Johan Throne (1868–1946): 49, 155
The Human Mountain: 7, 9, 19, 28, 128, 130–132, 138–141, 143, 145, 242, 243, 261–266

I

Ibsen, Henrik (1828–1906): 43, 108, 114, 117, 122, 175

J

Jacobson, Daniel (1861–1939): 18, 45, 113
Jæger, Hans (1854–1910): 14, 24, 68, 108, 122
Jensen-Hjell, Karl (1862–1888): 111
Juell, Dagny *see* Przybyszewska, Dagny Juel
Juell, Ragnhild (1871–1908): 26

K

Kandinsky, Wassily (1866–1944): 93
Kessler, Count Harry (1868–1937): 16, 33, 106, 179
Kielland, Gabriel (1871–1960): 110, 113, 114
Kiss: 33, 35, 85, 86, 123, 126, 127, 134, 186, 188, 190
The Kiss: 35, 36, 127, 187, 190
Kjær, Nils (1870–1924): 26
Klee, Paul (1879–1940): 93
Klinger, Max (1857–1920): 33
Klint, Hilma af (1862–1944): 93
Kloumann, Henning (1860–1941): 45, 47
Kokkinen, Nina (1978–): 95, 96, 102
Kollmann, Albert (1837–1915): 42, 134
Krag, Vilhelm (1871–1933): 15, 26, 27, 112, 113, 174
Krohg, Christian (1852–1925): 14, 23, 45, 107, 110
Krohg, Per (1889–1965): 131

L

Larpent, Sophus (1838–1911): 37, 107, 108, 112, 114, 238
Larsen, Tulla (1869–1942): 40, 111
Leistikow, Walter (1865–1908): 123
Leonardo da Vinci (1452–1519): 96, 100, 155
Lévi, Eliphas (1810–1875): 93, 95, 100
Lie, Jonas (1833–1908): 40, 43, 114, 118, 278, 279
Liebermann, Max (1847–1935): 58, 60, 90
Linde, Max (1862–1940): 17, 40, 124, 137, 139, 246
Lødrup, Hans P. (1885–1955): 33, 36

M

Madonna: 11, 39, 85, 86, 123, 183, 218–220
Maillol, Aristide (1861–1944): 152
Meier-Graefe, Julius (1867–1935): 16, 82, 106
Middelthun, Julius (1820–1886): 14, 23, 139, 159
Mondrian, Piet (1872–1944): 93
The Monolith: 7, 9, 11, 19, 45, 48, 126, 128, 130–132, 141, 147, 150, 151, 268, 272
Moreau, Gustave (1826–1898): 97
Mother Norway: 18, 47, 48, 138, 140, 141, 145, 244, 248, 254, 255, 301
Munch, Inger (1868–1952): 14, 24, 140

N

Nærup, Carl (1864–1931): 113
Næss, Atle (1949–): 51
Nerdrum, Odd (1944–): 147
Nietzsche, Friedrich (1844–1900): 73, 74, 76, 91, 101
Nilssen, Jappe (1870–1931): 49
Nordraak, Rikard (1842–1866): 110, 152, 155
Normann, Adelsteen (1848–1918): 151

O

Obstfelder, Sigbjørn (1866–1900): 15, 16, 26, 29, 30, 33, 35, 36, 37, 112–114, 170, 171, 180

P

Paracelsus (1493–1541): 62, 67, 79, 100
Partridge, Christopher (1961–): 95, 96
Pater, Walter (1839–1894): 96, 100
Paulsen, Olav Herman (1862–1948): 45
Péladan, Joséphin (1858–1918): 96, 97, 102
Picasso, Pablo (1881–1973): 18

The Prostrated: 10, 35, 36, 185
Przybyszewska, Dagny Juel (1867–1901): 16, 17, 26–30, 33, 36–37, 40, 183
Przybyszewski, Stanisław (1868–1927): 7, 10, 16, 17, 22, 27–30, 33, 35–37, 39, 57, 80, 92, 93, 95–97, 100–102, 170, 182, 226

R

Ransve, Bjørn (1944–): 147
Rasmussen, Wilhelm (1879–1965): 48
Ravensberg, Ludvig (1871–1958): 45, 113, 114, 140
Reinhardt, Max (1873–1943): 117, 124
Revold, Axel (1887–1962): 131
Riffard, Pierre A. (1946–): 102
Rodin, Auguste (1840–1917): 11 15, 17, 28, 110, 124, 127, 134, 137, 138, 141, 152, 236
Rolfsen, Alf (1895–1979): 131, 132
Rops, Félicien (1833–1898): 57, 61, 68, 70, 74, 75, 84, 85

S

Schiefler, Gustav (1857–1935): 47, 140
Schulte, Eduard (1891–1966): 151
Schuré, Edouard (1841–1929): 101
The Scream: 11, 28, 85, 89, 122, 123, 127, 152, 155, 197
Skeibrok, Mathias (1851–1896): 15, 23, 26
Sørensen, Henrik (1882–1962): 131
Stenersen, Rolf (1899–1978): 9, 33
Strindberg, August (1849–1912): 27, 61, 92, 93, 96, 97, 100, 102, 122, 179
Stuckrad, Kocku von (1966–): 96
Swedenborg, Emanuel (1688–1772): 101, 102
Syvertsen, Inga (1883–1968); 39, 40, 111, 112, 118, 299, 301

T

Thaulow, Frits (1847–1906): 23, 83
Thiel, Ernest (1859–1947): 45, 106, 107, 151, 178
Thiis, Jens (1870–1942): 15, 16, 18, 19, 23, 26, 29, 30, 33, 35, 43, 44, 51, 106, 112–114, 128, 148, 150, 172, 173
The Thinker: 28, 127, 134, 137, 236
Thorvaldsen, Bertel (1770–1844): 24, 27
Thrap-Jensen, Lauritz (1878–1964): 148, 151

U

Utsond, Gunnar (1864–1950): 45

V

Vampire: 85–87, 100, 123, 210, 211
Verlaine, Paul (1844–1896): 97
Vigeland, Emanuel (1875–1948): 132
Vigeland Park: 7, 10, 11, 18, 19, 45, 48, 49, 119, 120, 126, 130, 132, 133, 151, 152, 272
Vogt, Nils Collett (1864–1937): 113

W

Wagner, Richard (1813–1883): 97
Werenskiold, Erik (1855–1938): 44
Wexelsen, Vilhelm Andreas (1849–1909): 106
Widerberg, Frans (1934–): 147
Woll, Gerd (1939–): 47

Y

Yeats, William Butler (1865–1939): 93

Z

Zola, Emile (1840–1902): 60, 78, 97, 102

This publication accompanies the exhibition
Vigeland+Munch. Behind the Myths
Munch Museum, Oslo, 3 October 2015 – 17 January 2016

Editor and Curator
Trine Otte Bak Nielsen, Munch Museum

Editorial Assistant
Karen E. Lerheim, Munch Museum

Publisher
Mercatorfonds, Brussels
Managing Director: Bernard Steyaert

Production
Pièce Montée, Ghent
Managing Directors: Ronny Gobyn and
Rik Jacques

Coordination
Barbara Costermans and Bregje Provo,
Pièce Montée;
Ann Mestdag, Mercatorfonds

Copy-editing
Kate Bell

Translations
From Norwegian to English: Francesca M.
Nichols (texts by Trine Otte Bak Nielsen,
Guri Skuggen, Petra Pettersen, Erika Gohde
Sandbakken and Jarle Strømodden; foreword,
introduction, timeline, about the authors)
From German to English: Margaret
Clarke (text by Stanisław Przybyszewski,
The Work of Edvard Munch)
From Polish to English: Elżbieta
Chrzanowska-Kluczewska (text by
Stanisław Przybyszewski, *On the Paths of
the Soul*).

Design
Henrik Haugan, Snøhetta, Oslo

Colour separations, printing and binding
Die Keure, Bruges

Typeset in Circular Std. and Typ1451 (Lineto)

Paper
Luxo Samt Art 150g

Museum edition
ISBN 978-82-90128-87-1 (English edition)

Trade edition
Distributed in Belgium, the Netherlands and Luxembourg by Mercatorfonds, Brussels
ISBN 978-94-6230-098-9
D/2015/703/28

Distributed outside Belgium, the Netherlands and Luxembourg by Yale University Press,
New Haven and London
www.yalebooks.com/art – www.yalebooks.co.uk
ISBN 978-0-300-22003-2
Library of Congress Control Number: 2015948594

Special thanks to:
Kate Bell, Halvor Bjørngård, Arne Borgan, Elzbieta Chrzanowska-Kluczewska, Margaret
Clarke, Barbara Costermans, Aleksandra Danielak, DHL Quality Cargo EXEL Fine Art,
Per Faxneld, Filippo Gazzola, Magdalena Godzimirska, Henrik Haugan, Beth Heald,
Frank Høifødt, Lasse Jacobsen, Tiril J. Krabbesund, Ove Kvavik, Gry Landro, Karen E.
Lerheim, Siri Lindberg, Ann Mestdag, Ingebjørg Mogstad, Oliver Møystad, Francesca
M. Nichols, Petra Pettersen, Bregje Provo, Siri Refsum, Erika G. Sandbakken, Anja
Sandtrø, Guri Skuggen, Bernard Steyaert, Jarle Strømodden, Iris Otte Thomsen,
Sivert Thue, Samson Valland.

The exhibition and the catalogue have received generous support from

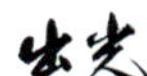

Illustrations
Cover: Edvard Munch's drawing of Gustav Vigeland's sculpture *The Prostrated* (1895)
placed over Munch's photograph of the sculpture
Page 4: Interior of Gustav Vigeland's studio at 8 Pilestredet, c. 1900. Unknown
photographer. Vigeland Museum
Page 6: Interior with sculptures at Ekely, 1931–32. Photo: Edvard Munch. Munch Museum